Premiere Pro 1.5

HANDS-ON TRAINING

Includes Exercise Files & Demo Movies

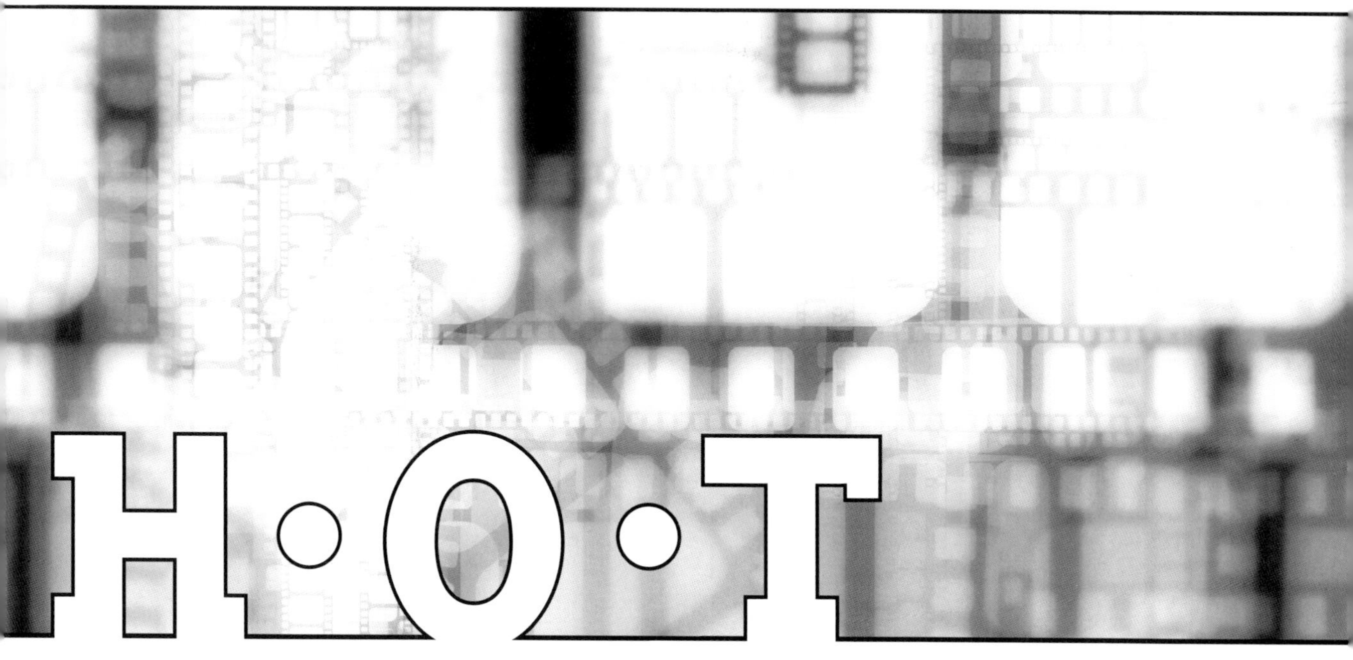

H•O•T

Jeff Schell

Premiere Pro 1.5 | H•O•T
Hands-On Training

By Jeff Schell

lynda.com/books | Peachpit Press
1249 Eighth Street • Berkeley, CA • 94710
800.283.9444 • 510.524.2178 •
510.524.2221(fax)
http://www.lynda.com/books
http://www.peachpit.com

lynda.com/books is published
in association with Peachpit Press,
a division of Pearson Education

ISBN: 0-321-29398-3

0 9 8 7 6 5 4 3 2 1

Printed and bound in the
United States of America

H•O•T | Credits

Original Design: Ali Karp, Alink Newmedia (alink@earthlink.net)

Editor: Karyn Johnson

Copyeditor: Darren Meiss

Production Coordinator: Myrna Vladic

Compositors: Rick Gordon, David Van Ness

Beta testers: Adam Fischer, Steven Gotz

Proofreader: Emilia Thiuri

Cover Illustration: Bruce Heavin (bruce@stink.com)

Indexer: Julie Bess, JBIndexing Inc.

H•O•T | Colophon

The original design for *Premiere Pro 1.5 H•O•T* was sketched on paper. The layout was heavily influenced by online communication–merging a traditional book format with a modern Web aesthetic.

The text in *Premiere Pro 1.5 H•O•T* was set in Akzidenz Grotesk from Adobe and Triplex from Emigre. The cover illustration was painted in Adobe Photoshop and Adobe Illustrator.

This book was created using QuarkXPress and Microsoft Office on an Apple Macintosh using Mac OS X. It was printed on 60 lb. Influence Matte at Courier.

Premiere Pro 1.5 | H•O•T — **Table of Contents**

Bonus Chapters on Premiere Pro HOT DVD

An Introduction to Adobe Premiere Pro

This Introduction provides an overview of video editing, Adobe Premiere Pro, its workflow, and concepts involved with editing video on a computer. It concludes with instructions for using the sample files located on the DVD-ROM included with the book.

H•O•T

Premiere Pro HOT DVD

What Is Video Editing?

Video editing is the act of taking a long video recording—like that four-minute panorama from your tropical vacation that puts friends to sleep—and whittling it down to a much shorter length of time that tells a more concise and clear story. Video editing is also used as a catch-all phrase that includes assembling many video recordings, combining them to create a new recording, complete with titles, pictures, and special effects. In other words, video editing means both editing a single recording, as well as the entire process of creating new video.

What Is Adobe Premiere Pro?

Adobe Premiere Pro is video editing software that aids you in the editing of recordings, and the creation of video for playback on television, CD-ROMs, DVDs, the Web and more. With Premiere Pro, you can produce television commercials, make training tapes, create wedding videos, or just delete that embarrassing scene where you're applying sunblock on vacation. Both television professionals and home enthusiasts use Premiere Pro.

A popular question asked about Premiere Pro is: *is it professional*? The short answer is yes. The longer answer goes like this... Premiere Pro will not make your video professional, nor make your video unprofessional. It's professionally ambiguous. It's no different than any other editing software on the market in this respect. If you give it professional video, it will give you professional video in return. If you give it lousy video, it'll give you lousy video in return. In other words, Premiere Pro has very little to do with the question of professionalism. It is as professional as you need it to be.

What Is Non-Linear Editing?

A major advantage of Premiere Pro is that it allows for non-linear editing. Non-linear is an unfamiliar term that might sound scary but truly isn't. *Non-linear* literally means not in a straight line. In video editing terms, it means you can assemble your project in any order that you want.

In the dinosaur days of video editing (circa 1990), video editors were forced to build their projects in order of time. They started at zero seconds, added a video clip, moved to the end of that clip, added a second clip, and so on. If they wanted to make a change to the beginning, they had to go back and start all over.

With the advent of video editing software, an editor can start assembling video at any point in a project. Clips can be shuffled around backwards and forwards like three-card monte, with multiple levels of undo! (The Undo key is an editor's best friend.)

Premiere Pro's non-linear editing provides you the ability to build your video in any order, make changes at any point in time, and do it all without having to start over.

How Do I Get Video into Premiere Pro?

With Premiere Pro, you can choose to use video that is already saved in your computer, or you can choose to capture video from your DV camera. *Capturing* is another word for copying the video recorded on a tape and saving it to a file on your computer. Of course, it's much quicker just to say "capturing."

Premiere Pro has built-in support for DV cameras. This means that you can connect a DV camera to your computer and capture video from it, without the use of any other software or hardware. Furthermore, Premiere Pro talks with your camera! It tells the camera when to start and stop playing. It automatically rewinds and fast forwards your camera for you. And when it's all done, it saves the video as a file on your computer.

In order to take advantage of Premiere Pro's built-in DV support, you need a computer with an IEEE-1394 interface. IEEE-1394 is technical jargon for the protocol that allows your computer and camera to talk to each other. But because the word IEEE-1394 can put people to sleep, Apple calls it **FireWire**, and Sony calls it **iLink**. (If you own a Sony DV camera, you will see the word "iLink" above the IEEE-1394 port.)

There are other times when you may want to capture analog video. Analog refers to any camera that is nondigital. The most popular analog formats for home use are VHS, VHS-c, Hi-8, 8mm, and Betamax (yes, Betamax, Mr. Disco). Capturing video from analog cameras is a bit more tricky because the camera cannot communicate directly with Premiere Pro. In order to capture analog video, you need a separate piece of hardware, such as a capture card or analog converter.

Both capture cards and analog converters have special ports that allow you to connect an analog camera or VCR. The device converts the analog video to a digital file on your hard drive, ready for use in Premiere Pro.

Tip: Many users who were migrating from the popular Hi-8 and 8mm analog formats found themselves in the frustrating position of needing to purchase extra hardware if they wanted to convert their analog video to digital. Sony came up with a fine solution: its Digital8 line of cameras. Digital8 cameras are modified Hi8 cameras that record digitally onto a 8mm or Hi8 tape. But wait, there's more! Digital8 cameras also send *your old Hi8 and 8mm tapes* out via IEEE-1394 (FireWire/iLink). In essence, the Digital8 camera can act as your analog converter. Plop your decade-old tape into a Digital8 camera and plug it straight into Premiere Pro as if it was a DV camera. Many people use Digital8 cameras solely as a VCR for tape playback. In addition, the cost difference is nominal (in fact Digital8 cameras are cheaper than some capture cards), plus you've got yourself a new camera as well.

NOTE | About DV Video

So what's the big deal about digital video (DV)? Here's what:

- *Digital video is transferred digitally from camera to computer. This means that there is no generation loss from copy to copy. The finished product looks just as pristine as the original version in your camera, no matter how many times you copy it.*
- *DV cameras record the video in digital format on tape. Because the video is already in digital format, you do not need a costly capture card or converter box. Instead, you just copy the video directly using Premiere Pro.*
- *Premiere Pro uses the digital connection to store information about your video. This allows it to remember where on the tape the video is, which saves you the trouble of rewinding and fast forwarding to find it.*
- *Digital video is extremely efficient. Because the video signal is really just a binary series of 1s and 0s, the files sizes are smaller than comparable analog formats.*
- *Digital video has more clarity, better color accuracy, and less static than comparable analog formats.*

Here's the bad news: DV video is *technically* NOT broadcast quality. (Broadcast means the quality is suitable for playback on television.) But then again, VHS, VHS-c, Hi8, and 8mm are not broadcast quality either. However, DV is darn close! Although it falls short in some of the technical requirements, many people cannot tell a difference, even with side-by-side comparison.

Because of the relatively small size and reasonable price of cameras, DV video is being used all over broadcast television, and in feature Hollywood movies as well even though it is technically not "broadcast" quality. Icons like Spike Lee have made movies shot in DV. More and more Independent movies and documentaries are shot in DV. Recently, a movie shot in DV won the Dramatic Grand Jury Prize at the Sundance Film Festival. Most news stations use DV cameras, alongside their larger and more expensive traditional cameras, for news gathering. The list goes on.

Is DV technically broadcast? Maybe. Is it worthy of broadcast? Definitely!

How Do I Use Premiere Pro?

Before you can begin step one in Premiere Pro, you must first create a project file. Every task you perform in Premiere Pro is done within a project file. In fact, Premiere Pro will not allow you to do any work unless you make a new project, or open an existing one. Every program that you make must be part of a project.

Video-geek vocabulary note: The word *program* refers to your creation. Like a television program, it is the final piece of video that you are producing. A program can be a slide show, a wedding video, a commercial, a movie… anything!

Creating a project is similar to writing an email; to write an email, you must first create a blank email letter and then fill it in with words. In Premiere Pro, you create a blank project and fill it in with video.

Once you have created a blank project, the work of making a program in Premiere Pro can be broken down into three steps:

1. Import the video.
2. Edit the video.
3. Export the video.

Importing video sounds complex, but it's really just a fancy way of saying "collecting the video you want to use in one folder." As described earlier, you can import video already saved as a file, or connect to your DV camera and choose what video you want saved to your computer. Once the video is saved as a file on your hard drive, you can import it into Premiere Pro. Of course, you can also import much more than just video, such as

- Music from CDs
- MP3 files
- Audio from a microphone
- Photographs
- Internet graphics
- Titles
- Logos
- Adobe Photoshop and Illustrator files

After you import the files you want to use, it is time to edit the video. This step consists of building your new creation one piece of video at a time. You can rearrange your video clips in any order, you can shorten their lengths, play them in slow-motion, change their size, rotate them, and more.

Once you've created your award winning masterpiece, the third and final step is to export the video to your choice of many different formats. The most common formats are

- Camera or VCR tape
- CD-ROM for computer playback
- DVD movie
- Internet video (email or Web site)

The purpose of this book is to explain each of these steps and demonstrate how each task fits into the overall goal of creating video with Premiere Pro.

Computer Considerations

The secret to digital video editing is the IEEE-1394 interface mentioned earlier. If you are considering a computer purchase, a built-in OHCI-compliant IEEE-1394 port is absolutely essential. But what else might you want in a robust video editing workstation?

Processor: Video is actually a series of 30 images played in 1 second. To our human eye, this creates the illusion of motion. Playing 30 images a second requires a lot of computing power under the hood. A Pentium 4 3.0 GHz (or higher) or equivalent processor should be enough. One nice thing about Premiere Pro is that it will intelligently lower the quality of your preview if your computer is not fast enough.

Memory: How much memory? Can you ever have too much? Well, yes and no. Many people purchase overkill on their memory, simply because memory is cheap and the perception is "the more the merrier." If you're trying to build a low-cost system, then a good amount for today's computer systems seems to be 512 MB. 256 MB would be a minimum, but it is hard to find less than 512 MB with today's newer computers. 1 GB of memory gives your system some "breathing room," and you can certainly upgrade beyond that if your computer supports more memory.

Capture card: This is optional, and only necessary if you need to capture video from non-DV sources. For example, if you plan to have clients who may provide video on analog formats, then a capture card would be essential. Some capture cards provide additional bells and whistles for DV video as well, and for that reason they may be worth a look. But the frugal DV-only editor can do without and spend that money elsewhere–like on more hard drive space.

Operating system: Premiere Pro requires Windows XP or later to run. The biggest pitfall is having too many background applications running on your Desktop. Playing all that video is hard work, and your system will be begging for power. Background applications (like all of those little icons in your system tray) take away power from Premiere Pro. The moral is, be very cautious about what you allow to run in your system tray, be vigilant about ending unnecessary background applications, and try not to run too many other tasks while editing video. (Like oil and water, Web surfing and video editing do not mix!)

Computer monitor: As you will learn in future chapters, screen real estate is very tight in Adobe Premiere Pro. There are many windows–Project, Monitor, Timeline, Effects palette–and sometimes it requires a lot of shuffling to be able to see everything at once. Many professionals have workstations that can display the software across two monitors. This definitely provides some elbow room to work, but this also carries a price tag. Many users do just fine with one monitor, but make sure the computer monitor is capable of a 1280 x 1024 resolution.

NTSC monitor (TV): You do not need to spend a lot of money on a computer monitor. After all, the image is a preview of what your video will look like. To see the real deal, it's a good idea to invest in a separate NTSC (television) monitor. Computer monitors can display millions of more colors than TV monitors, so a color that looks gorgeous on a computer monitor may reproduce horribly on a TV. Make sure that your DV camera or VCR has the capability to send a signal to your TV, unless you have an analog capture card with this capability.

Hard drive: Although too much memory is overkill, too much hard drive is a thrill. There are two factors that determine a hard drive's worth: rpm speed (rotations per minute), and capacity (size). Hard drives tend to come in one of three speeds: 5400 rpm, 7200 rpm, or 10,000 rpm. The faster the drive, the more expensive the hard drive. 5400 rpm drives are inexpensive and can get the job done but definitely will "feel the burn" during intensive editing workouts. 7200 rpm drives are a nice mix of speed and cost and should experience fewer problems than a 5400 rpm drive. 10,000 rpm drives are the top performers and come with the highest price tag.

The capacity of the hard drive is equally as important. Standard DV video eats up nearly 13 GB of hard drive space for every hour of video that you save. Keep in mind that you *always* end up capturing more video on your hard drive than you eventually use per project. In other words, a one-hour movie will need much more than one hour of storage. You might end up capturing 3 or 4 (or 12) different takes of the same shot. Each take requires more hard drive space.

Planning to add titles and effects? Premiere Pro creates a temporary copy of each file that has been modified. For example, if you add a title on a 5-second clip, Premiere Pro creates a temporary 5-second clip that blends the title and the original video. Now you have the original 5-second clip and the copy with the title for a total of 10 seconds. This doubles your requirements to 26 GB of storage for one hour. Granted, this is a worst-case doom scenario of hard drive requirements, but better safe than sorry, right?

Before Getting Started

This book comes with sample exercises, video, audio, and still images. These files are stored on the DVD that came with this book. Before moving on to the next chapter, you should copy the samples files from the DVD to your computer's hard drive.

1. Double-click the **My Computer** icon on your desktop.

Note: If the icon name has been changed, it will not say My Computer.

---

2. Double-click the **DVD Drive** that has the **Premiere Pro HOT** DVD.

---

3. Click once on the **Premiere Pro HOT** folder to select it, and from the top menu select **Edit > Copy to Folder**. This will open the **Copy Items** window.

4. In the Copy Items window, select **Local Disk (C:)** and click **Copy**. A dialog should pop up, displaying the progress of the copy.

*Note: If you have a second hard drive exclusively dedicated for video storage, you can copy the **Premiere Pro HOT** folder to that drive instead of the **C:** drive. If you choose to copy to a separate drive, please navigate to that drive whenever you see references to the **C:** drive throughout this book.*

NOTE | Copying to the C: Drive

This book asks you to copy the class exercises and supporting files to the **C:** directory, only for purposes of instruction, to ensure compatibility with all users. However, when you are using Premiere Pro in a real-world situation, you should *definitely avoid* capturing to or editing from the C:\ directory. If you only have one hard drive in your system, then you should use a subfolder of your **My Documents** folder, such as "My Documents\Project Name." This will help keep your files manageable and organized.

If you have a separate storage drive, then you should definitely use that drive for all of your future Premiere Pro projects for increased performance. You'll learn more about the reasons for this in Chapter 15, "Capturing Digital Video." For now, just remember–using the C:\ directory is normally bad, except for instructional purposes of this book.

Making Exercise Files Editable

By default, all content that is copied to your hard drive from DVD-ROM is "read-only" (meaning, you can't modify it). In order to follow the exercises in this chapter, you should remove the read-only formatting. To do this:

1. Double-click the **My Computer** icon on your desktop.

---

2. Double-click **Local Disk (C:)** to view its contents.

Note: If you copied the exercise files to a separate drive, then you should navigate to that drive.

---

3. Right-click on the **Premiere Pro HOT** directory and choose **Properties**. This will open up the Properties Window.

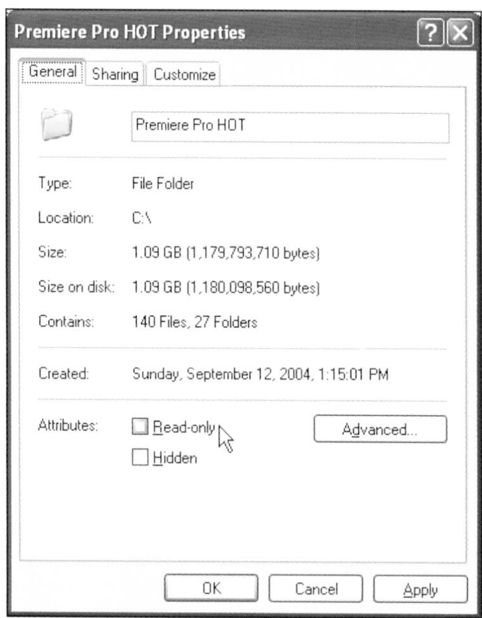

4. Make sure the **Read-only** Attributes box is not selected. You may have to click this box several times until there is no checkmark and no color fill inside the box. Click **OK**.

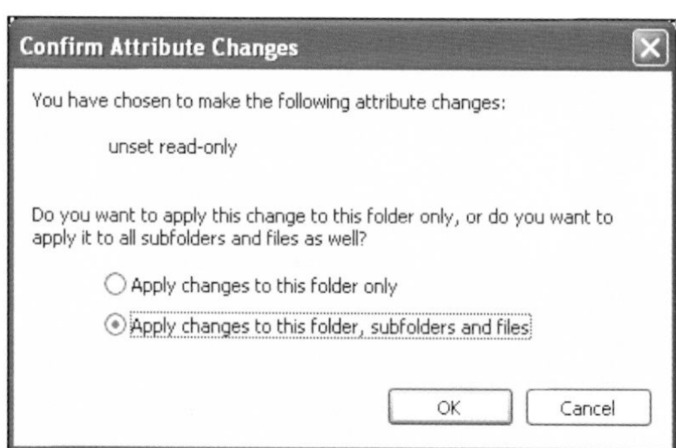

5. As soon as you click OK, the Confirm Attribute Changes dialog will appear. Make sure to select **Apply changes to this folder, subfolders and files**. Click **OK**. This will ensure that all files within this directory are usable for the exercises in this book.

Making File Extensions Visible

Because this book deals with files of many different types (videos, music files, graphics, titles, etc.), it will be helpful for you to view the extensions of your files in order to tell them apart. In Windows XP, all extensions are hidden by default. To make them visible:

1. Double-click the **My Computer** icon on your desktop.

2. Select **Tools > Folder Options.** This opens the **Folder Options** dialog box.

3. Click on the **View** tab at the top. This opens the **View** options screen so that you can change the view settings for Windows XP.

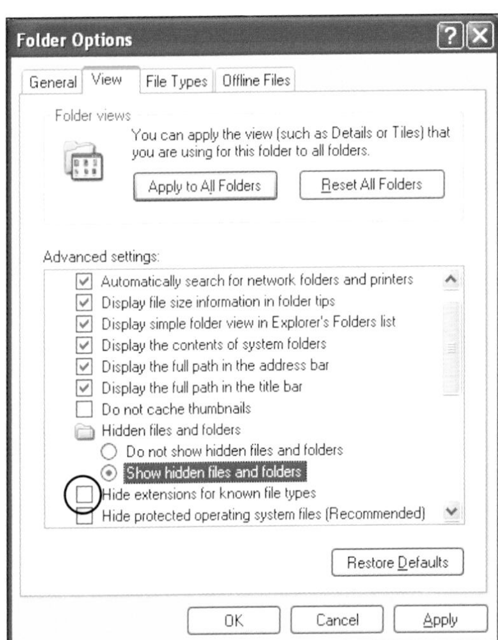

4. Make sure that the **Hide extensions for known file types** option is not selected.

The Premiere Pro HOT DVD-ROM

In addition to the exercise files, the **Premiere Pro HOT** DVD contains tutorial movies of some of the exercises throughout this book. It's my hope that by watching me perform the exercises myself, these movies will help you understand some of the more difficult concepts in this book. If you like these movies, then you should definitely check out **www.lynda.com** for additional ones on Premiere Pro.

And if that's not enough, the DVD also contains two bonus chapters–Chapters 16, "Project Management," and Chapter 17, "The Next Step."

Acknowledgments

This book would not have been possible without a strong team of dedicated, enthusiastic, and talented individuals. Most notably:

The love of my life and my best friend, Jennifer. You keep me grounded and laughing. And thanks for doing my share of the chores while I wrote the book.

Our families and friends. Mom and Dad, I owe everything to you. Maria, you are the best Oma. Jack, thanks for watching over us.

Peachpit Press. Karyn, thanks for putting up with me. Darren, thanks for cleaning up my mess.

Everyone at Lynda.com. Garo and Lynda, thanks for taking a chance! Brian, thanks for your booth coaching.

Kendall, for letting me use your photo in this book. Also, thanks to the folks at Standard Films (www.standardfilms.com) and CNN Image Source (www.cnnimagesource.com) for the terrific footage used in the book.

Outstanding work by the beta testers, Steven Gotz and Adam Fischer. Thank you for your thoroughness, your feedback, and your support.

My students, without whom, there'd be no book to write.

Special thanks to each and every one of you.

I

The Project

| What Is a Project? | Project Presets |

| Creating a New Project |

| The Premiere Pro Workspace |

H•O•T

Premiere Pro HOT DVD

All of the editing work you do in Premiere Pro will be done in a project file. In fact, you cannot even launch Premiere Pro without opening a project or creating a new one. The first step in making a program is to create a new project.

This chapter takes you through the steps of creating a project and choosing the proper settings. You will also learn the core components that make up a project and how they interact to help you create new video.

What Is a Project?

The Adobe Premiere Pro project is a single file that contains all of your work. It holds all of the audio, video, and graphics you plan to use. It remembers which files were captured from your camera. Most importantly, it contains the blank canvas you will use to create your program.

Every clip you import will be imported into a project. Every edit will be made inside of a project. When you export your video, you export from inside of a project. Notice a pattern? In short: without a project, you can't work.

When you create a project file to begin working, you are asked to choose the type of project. For example, do you want your project to be shaped like a television screen or a wide movie screen? Are you using video from a special camera? What audio format did you record on tape? In the next exercise, you will learn how to answer each of these questions to choose the optimum settings for your project.

Project Presets

Before you can create a new project in Premiere Pro, you must first specify your project settings. These settings include pixel aspect ratio, editing mode, frame size, color depth, field priority, and more! Whew. Don't worry. This daunting task is made much easier by the use of project presets.

A **preset** is a preconfigured template that automatically chooses the optimal settings for your project. When you choose a preset, Premiere Pro specifies and locks each setting so you don't accidentally choose incompatible options.

Ninety-nine times out of 100 you will select a preset when you begin your project. Of course, you can customize the project settings if you wish, however this is usually unnecessary–and can be downright risky! With so many settings that must perfectly match your video, choosing a preset is not only the easiest thing to do, it's the safest.

Choosing the proper preset must be done with care, because once the project settings are chosen, you cannot change them. (Insert ominous clap of thunder to underscore this point.) This may cause little concern when you're five minutes into a project, but it may be harder to start over when you're five days into a project. For this reason, choose wisely! (Of course, if you do choose incorrectly, there is a workaround to salvage your project, which will be discussed in a later chapter.)

Tip: When editing, you want the project settings to match the format of the source video as closely as possible. For example, if you shot footage on a DV camera, choose the DV preset.

Standard or Widescreen?

When you start a new Premiere Pro project, you are asked to choose a video format: standard or widescreen. Which to choose? Most often you will choose the format the video was shot in.

Here is a brief primer on standard video versus widescreen video.

NTSC television (the standard for North America) uses a 4:3 aspect ratio. This means the picture is four units wide for every three units tall. Have you ever noticed that your TV screen is slightly wider than it is tall? That's because the ratio of its width to height is 4:3.

With the increased popularity of independent moviemaking, shot on video, a widescreen 16:9 aspect ratio was introduced for DV video. For every 16 units of width, there are 9 units of height. Many videographers feel this gives their video a more theatrical look, since this is closer to the ratio of movie screens.

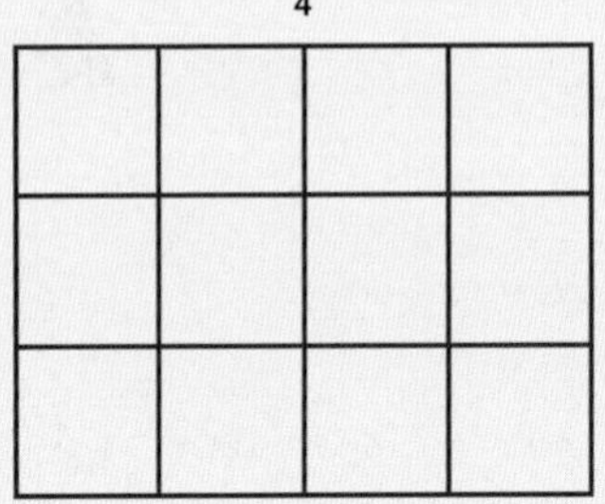

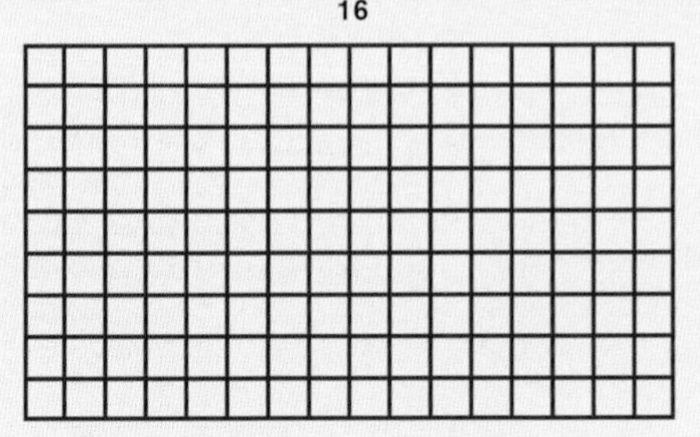

Nearly all NTSC DV cameras can shoot 4:3, since that is the standard. Some NTSC DV cameras can switch to 16:9 as well. Which format to shoot in? Premiere Pro can handle either, so ultimately the decision should be based on what you are shooting. A commercial for television should probably be shot 4:3, since most televisions are 4:3. A movie should be shot 16:9, since that is what moviegoers have come to expect.

Pick your ratio before shooting and stick with it. It is not a good idea to mix and match 4:3 and 16:9 ratios in your Premiere Pro project. When production (shooting) has wrapped and post-production (editing the video) begins, the rule of thumb is to choose the format that matches the video. If you shot a 4:3 video, choose a 4:3 project in Premiere Pro. If the video was shot 16:9, then create a 16:9 project in Premiere Pro.

I. Creating a New Project

In this exercise, you are going to walk through the steps of creating a new project and learn how to choose the best preset for your project.

1. Launch Premiere Pro.

2. At the **Welcome Screen**, you are given the choice to start a new project or open an existing project. Click the **New Project** button.

Tip: If you have existing projects, the most recent ones will be listed below the ***Recent Projects*** *heading. This is a quick way to open an existing project without having to navigate through the* ***Open Project*** *folder.*

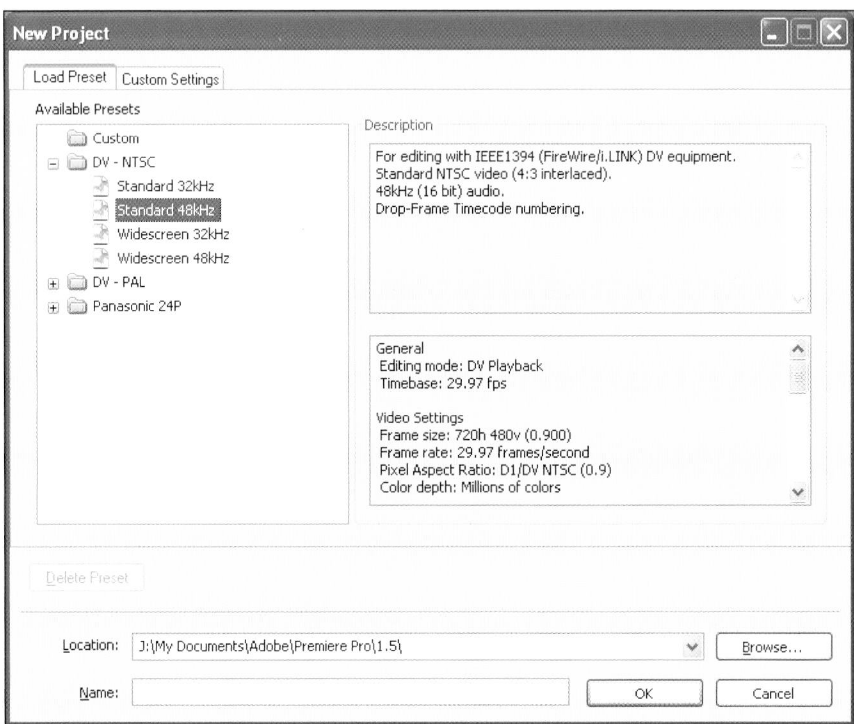

3. In the **New Project** dialog box, you are presented with a list of **Available Presets**. Premiere Pro automatically comes installed with three groups of presets, each represented by a folder that you can expand or minimize by clicking on the plus or minus sign next to the folder icon. Expand the **DV – NTSC** preset folder and select the **Standard 48kHz** preset.

Note: *If you own a video capture card that came bundled with Premiere Pro, you may see additional presets in the Available Presets list.*

To the right of the Available Presets, you will see a ***Description*** *of each preset. In the window pane below that, you will see a list of the preset settings. If you scroll through the settings, you will see why choosing a preset is so helpful.*

4. Click **Browse** to specify where to save the project file. Navigate to your **c:\Premiere Pro HOT\ Chapter01** directory, and click **OK**.

Ideally you should specify a location that you won't have to change later. By default, Adobe Premiere Pro saves video from your camera, as well as temporary files, in the same directory as your project file. This means that all of the work you do will be saved in the directory you choose. Decide now where you want your project and associated files to reside on your hard drive. Moving these files later on is very difficult.

5. Click in the **Name** text box and name your project **Exercise01**. Click **OK**.

This will create a new project file with the chosen settings and automatically open up your project. Now your project is ready for use. You have specified the proper settings and location, and you have named your file. Next you will become familiar with the templates and windows of the workspace.

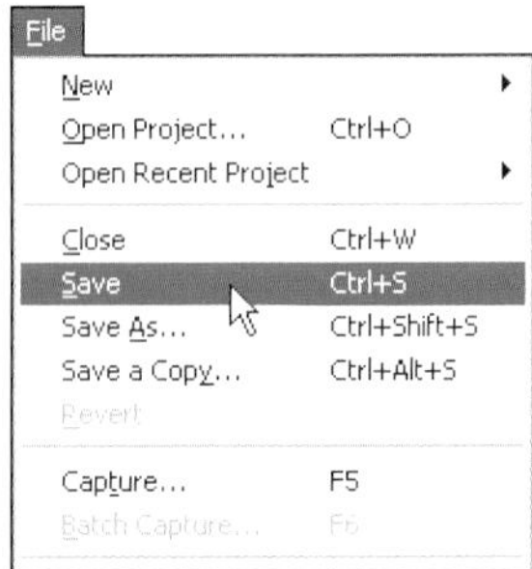

6. From the top menu, choose **File > Save.**

This is how you save a project. At the end of each exercise, you will be asked to save your project. It's also a good idea to save frequently because you can never predict when a dreaded "crash" will occur. (Hopefully not that often, but better safe than sorry.)

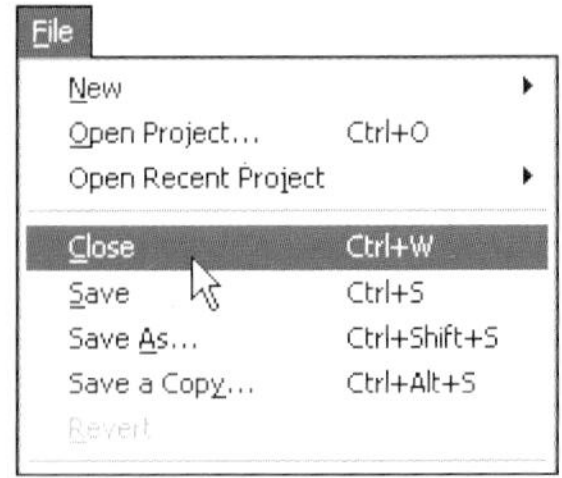

7. From the top menu, choose **File > Close.**

This is how you close a project. At the end of each exercise, you will either be asked to close your project, or leave it open before moving onto the next exercise. If you are asked to leave a project open, it usually means that the following exercise builds upon the same project. (Of course, you don't have to leave it open. You can always close a project and open it later, when you are ready to move onto the next exercise.)

DV? NTSC? PAL? 48 kHz? What's it all mean? The following table gives a breakdown of each option and when to choose it.

Making Sense of Presets	
Preset Group	**Description**
DV – NTSC	**DV** stands for digital video. **NTSC** is the standard for broadcast television in the United States. Select an NTSC preset when your source video is shot with a DV NTSC camera.
DV – PAL	**PAL** is the television standard in most of Europe, Asia, and Africa. Select a PAL preset when your video is shot with a DV PAL camera.
Panasonic 24p	Some DV NTSC cameras have the capability to shoot in **24p** mode (roughly 24 frames of video per second instead of the usual 30 with most DV NTSC cameras). Some videographers believe this gives the video a more filmic look. Panasonic was the first manufacturer to create 24p DV cameras, hence the preset is labeled **Panasonic 24p** (although more manufacturers are creating 24p cameras). Choose this preset only if your video is shot with an NTSC DV camera in 24p mode.
Standard 32kHz	As described earlier in this chapter, the DV format comes in two flavors: standard 4:3 (like a television screen) and widescreen 16:9 (like a movie screen). The DV format also has two flavors of audio: 32 kHz and 48 kHz. The higher the number, the better the audio quality. To give you some perspective, audio CDs are always 44.1 kHz. Most DV cameras provide the capability to switch between 32 kHz and 48 kHz. Choose this preset if your source video is shot 4:3 standard with 32 kHz audio.
Standard 48kHz	Choose this preset if your source video is shot 4:3 standard with 48 kHz audio, or if you are unsure of the audio source.
Widescreen 32kHz	Choose this preset if your source video is shot 16:9 widescreen with 32 kHz audio.
Widescreen 48kHz	Choose this preset if your source video is shot 16:9 widescreen with 48 kHz audio, or if you are unsure of the audio source.

The Premiere Pro Workspace

The Premiere Pro workspace refers to the layout and arrangement of the windows, palettes, and toolboxes in your project. You can move and resize the windows and palettes to create the workspace environment that best suits your editing style.

Note: Premiere Pro remembers the previous workspace that you had open. By default, Premiere Pro uses the Editing workspace. However, if you have been playing with Premiere Pro already, you may have made changes to your workspace. Choose **Window > Workspace > Editing** to ensure that your workspace matches the tutorial.

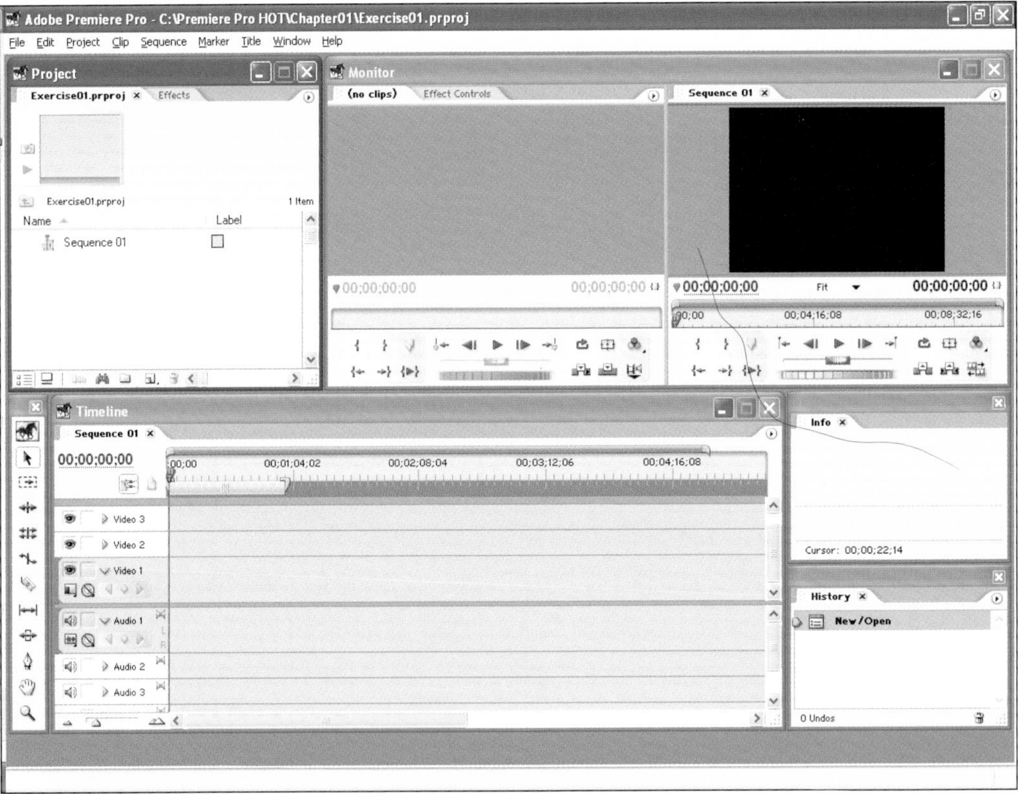

The three primary windows of the Editing workspace are the Project window, Monitor, and Timeline. In the coming chapters, each of these windows will be discussed in detail. Right now it is important to get an overview of these windows and understand how they fit into the big picture.

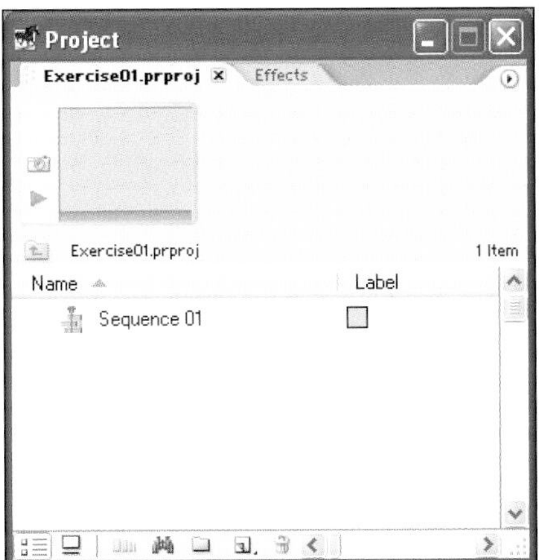

The **Project** window is the holding area for all of your clips. Every audio, video, and graphic clip that you plan to use in your project must first be imported into the Project window. When you capture video from your camera, the files are stored on your hard drive and imported into the Project window.

All Premiere Pro projects come with one clip, named Sequence 01. Sequences are the blank canvases where you will do your editing. Sequences will be discussed in Chapter 4, "*The Timeline Window*."

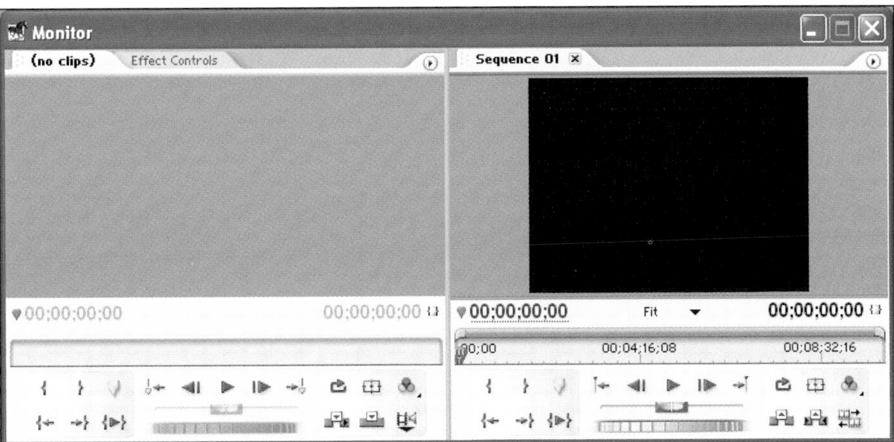

The **Monitor** window is your television screen. All audio, video, and graphics are played in the Monitor window. When you make changes in your project, the changes are reflected in the Monitor window.

In the Editing workspace, the Monitor window is divided into two sides: source and program. Source clips (the original files) are played in the left side. The program (your video creation) is played in the right side.

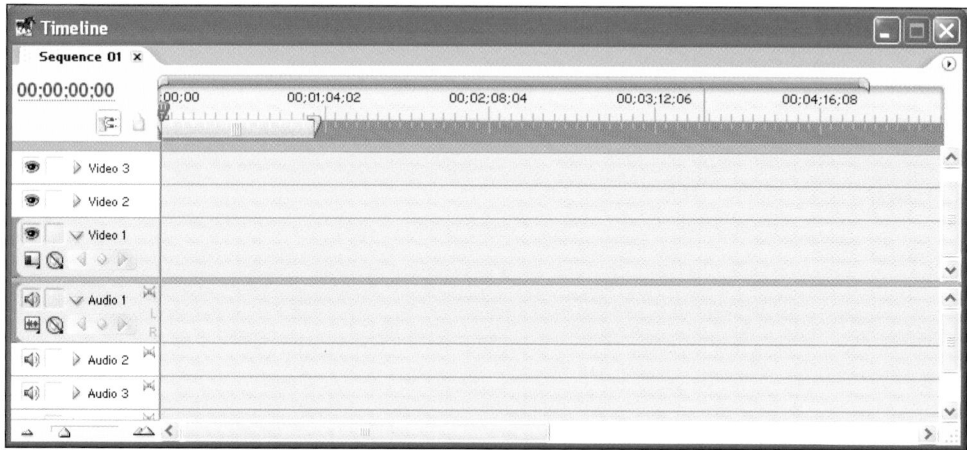

If the Monitor window is the visual representation of your project, the **Timeline** window is the temporal (time) representation of your project. This window is where you will do 99 percent of your work in Premiere Pro. It is where you'll make edits, rearrange clips, and add transitions. The Timeline starts at zero seconds on the far left, and increases to infinity. (Actually, the Timeline stops at 24 hours in length, but a movie that is 24 hours long will *feel like infinity.*)

The presets described in this chapter contain detailed information for over 20 possible settings. At this point you do not need to worry about any of those settings, so the following table is extra credit. Refer to it if you need to, but this table is not required in order to successfully complete the exercises in this book.

Note: Do not operate heavy machinery after reading this table.

Extra Credit: What About Those Other Settings?

Setting	Description
Editing Mode	Tells Premiere Pro what type of source files you will be using and how to play them.
Timebase	Specifies the time divisions of your video. NTSC is divided into 30 frames per second of video. (Actually 29.97 frames per second, but 30 is easier to remember.) PAL is divided into 25.0 frames per second.
Frame Size	Specifies the width and height of your video. The frame is the container that holds the video. Frames at a movie theater are measured in feet. Frames on a big screen TV are measured in inches. Frames of video displayed on a computer monitor are measured in *pixels.* A frame of NTSC DV video is 720 pixels wide by 480 pixels tall.
Pixel Aspect Ratio	The aspect ratio describes the shape of the video frame. There are three common aspect ratios you deal with in video editing: **1.0 aspect ratio pixel (computer monitor)** A pixel in a computer monitor is perfectly square, so the ratio of its width to height, or *aspect ratio,* is 1:1, the same as 1÷1, which equals 1.0. **0.9 aspect ratio pixel (NTSC DV standard 4:3)** A pixel of DV video is not square, but slightly skinny. Here's why: NTSC DV video is always 720 pixels by 480 pixels, which is a ratio of 720 ÷ 480 = 1.5. But standard televisions have a ratio of 4:3 = 1.333. This means that 1.5 ratio DV video is too wide to fit on a 1.333 ratio TV screen. To fix this problem, each pixel of DV video is a bit thinner, by 0.9 to be exact, which helps it squeeze into a standard 4:3 TV screen. Hence 0.9 "pixel aspect" ratio. **1.2 aspect ratio pixel (NTSC DV widescreen 16:9)** A pixel of widescreen DV video, on the other hand, is *wider* than a square pixel. Since NTSC DV video is always 720 x 480—yes, even widescreen NTSC DV video—this poses a unique problem. How do you get the same number of pixels to fill a 16:9 ratio screen? Answer: make the pixel *wider*! This is how 720 x 480 pixels expand to fit a 16:9 ratio TV screen. For you mathaholics: (16:9) ÷ (720:480) = 1.2.

continues on next page

Extra Credit: What About Those Other Settings? *(continued)*

Setting	Description
Color Depth	Specifies how many possible colors can be used in your video. DV video is always "millions of colors," and it cannot be changed.
Quality	A value of 0–100, 100 is the maximum. DV can only be set to 100%.
Compressor	Compresses and decompresses the video stream so it plays smoothly on your computer. Uncompressed video is very large (25 MB/sec), and the average computer would choke trying to play such a massive file size. Compression is a method of efficiently condensing the video into a smaller size so that your computer can handle playing it smoothly. DV video always uses DV compression and cannot be changed. DVDs always use MPEG-2 compression, and that cannot be changed. There are other compressors, and you will learn which ones are best for exporting your program to the web, CD-ROM, DVD, and more.
Fields	**Upper field + Lower field = Full frame** + = A full DV frame is divided into two fields. Every odd numbered line is stored in the upper field, and even numbered lines are stored in the lower field. This is called *interlacing fields* (picture the teeth of a zipper). DV video is interlaced with its *lower field first*. If you could slow down an interlaced TV screen when playing DV video, you would see the lower field drawn and then the upper field. DV video is sometimes called "60i," short for *60 frames interlaced* (30 frames per second × 2 fields per frame). Computer monitors are not separated into fields, so each horizontal line of the frame is drawn progressively in numeric order (1,2,3,4,5...). This is called *progressive scan.*

continues on next page

Extra Credit:
What About Those Other Settings? *(continued)*

Setting	Description
	Why does this matter? When you watch interlaced video on an interlaced TV screen, you don't see the interlacing; things play smoothly. But, when youwatch interlaced video on a progressive scan computer screen, the interlacing effect becomes apparent. Later in this book you will learn how to convert interlaced video to progressive video for playback on the Internet or CD-ROMs.
Audio Sample Rate	Defines how frequently the audio is sampled and how much is sampled each time. DV video comes in two audio flavors: 48 kHz 16-bit and 32 kHz 12-bit. When a camera records 48 kHz 16-bit audio, the microphone samples 48,000 times per second and collects 16 bits of data each time. **Tip:** Many DV cameras default to 32 kHz 12-bit audio, and many DV camera owners never change it. Refer to your camera's manual for help selecting 48 kHz 16-bit audio.

Creating a new project file is always the first step in any Premiere Pro project. And now that you are familiar with the primary windows of a project file, it is time to move to the next step: importing and playing your clips.

2

The Project Window

| What Is Importing? | Importing vs. Capturing | Importing Clips |

| Previewing Clips | Setting a Poster Frame | Changing Views |

| Creating Bins | Organizing Clips in Bins |

| Rearranging and Sorting

H•O•T

Premiere Pro HOT DVD

The Project window is the base of operations from where you store and organize all of your footage. All clips you plan to use in your program must be imported through the Project window. The Project window provides many options for displaying, sorting, organizing, and previewing your clips. In this chapter, you will import, sort, and preview clips in the Project window and grow comfortable with your knowledge through hands-on experience.

What Is Importing?

Premiere Pro can import three types of files: audio, video, and still images. If you plan to use a file in your program, you must first import it into a project first. When these files are imported, they are called **clips**, and they are organized in the Project window.

So what exactly *is* importing? It's the act of bringing a file from your hard drive into your Premiere Pro project. However, keep in mind that the original file stays on your hard drive, and you are not copying the real file. For example, when you **copy** a 3 MB file from a CD-ROM to your hard drive, you are copying the entire 3 MB file to a specific location on your hard drive. There are now two instances of that file: the 3 MB file on the CD-ROM, and the 3 MB file on your hard drive. The file on the hard drive is an exact replica.

However, when you **import** a file into Premiere Pro, a link is made to the original file, but a copy is never made. Every time you play the file in Premiere Pro, you are actually playing the original file on the hard drive, not a copy of it.

This has advantages and disadvantages. The advantage is twofold: no additional hard drive spaced is used up since a copy is not made, *and* any updates you make to the file on the hard drive will be automatically reflected in Premiere Pro (as long as the file name is the same). The disadvantage is that if you move the file to a different directory, Premiere Pro will need help locating the file because the path is no longer valid.

Importing vs. Capturing

The words *importing* and *capturing* are often confused. **Capturing** is the act of transferring video from tape and saving it to a file on your hard drive. **Importing** is the act of bringing a file from your hard drive into your project.

It may help to think of it in these terms: Capturing is getting video from camera to computer. Importing is getting video (and audio and still images) from computer to Premiere Pro. In Chapter 15, "Capturing Digital Video," you will learn how Premiere Pro helps you capture video from a DV tape. In this chapter, you will import files that are already on your hard drive.

NOTE | What File Types Can Be Imported?

Beyond video, Premiere Pro can import graphics and audio files. This allows you to add company logos, text, music, and much more to your project. Here are some of the most common graphic and audio types that Premiere Pro can import:

Common Graphic Types	***Common Formats***
Photos from digital camera	*JPG, BMP, TIF, PNG*
Images from Internet	*JPG, GIF, BMP, TIF, PNG*
Macintosh graphics	*PICT*
Photoshop layers	*PSD*
Logos, titles, text	*Any format with alpha channel (more on this later in the book)*
Common Audio Types	***Common Audio Formats***
CD audio	*MP3, WAV, AIF, WMV, WMA. (Premiere Pro cannot copy directly from CD. Instead, use a CD copying program, such as Windows Media Player, to capture the audio in one of the compatible formats.)*
Audio from a microphone	*Can be recorded directly into Premiere Pro project*
Audio from the Internet	*MP3, WAV, AIF, WMV, WMA*
Macintosh audio file	*AIF*

NOTE | Title Bar Focus

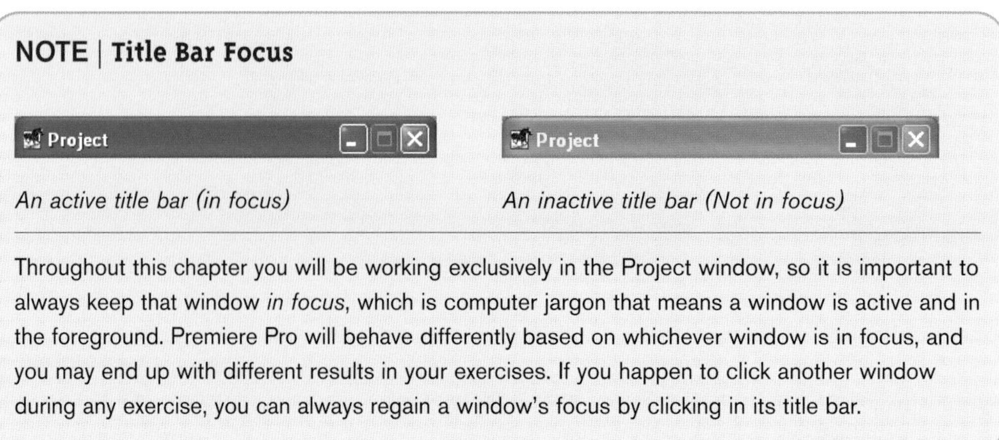

An active title bar (in focus) *An inactive title bar (Not in focus)*

Throughout this chapter you will be working exclusively in the Project window, so it is important to always keep that window *in focus*, which is computer jargon that means a window is active and in the foreground. Premiere Pro will behave differently based on whichever window is in focus, and you may end up with different results in your exercises. If you happen to click another window during any exercise, you can always regain a window's focus by clicking in its title bar.

I. Importing Clips

In this exercise, you will import different types of clips from your hard drive into a Premiere Pro project.

1. If you have the previous exercise open from Chapter 1, skip directly to Step 2. If Premiere Pro is not running, launch it and click **Open Project** at the **Welcome Screen**. Navigate to the **c:\Premiere Pro HOT\Chapter02** folder, select **Exercise01.prproj**, and click **Open**.

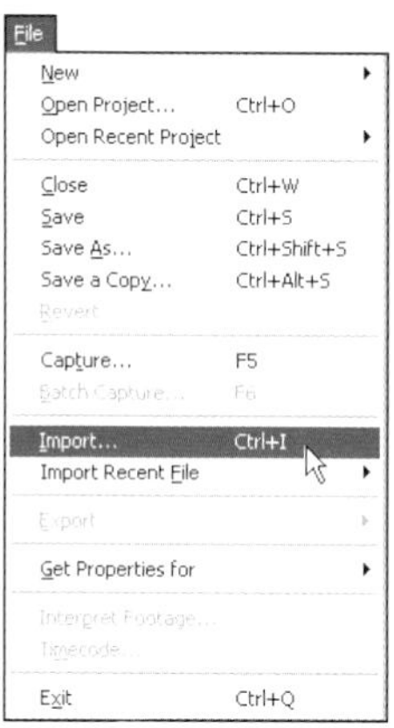

2. Choose **File > Import**.

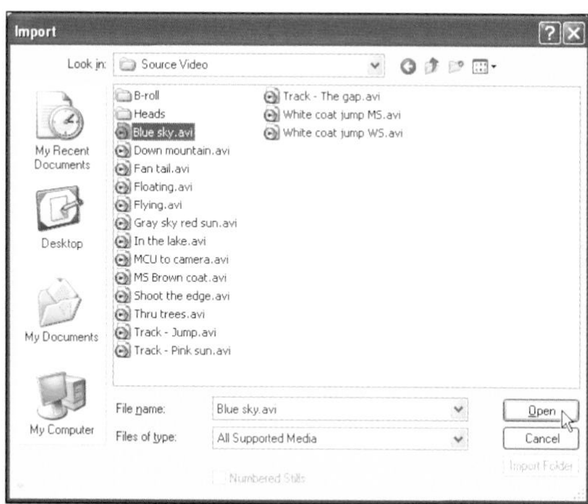

3. Navigate to the **c:\Premiere Pro HOT\Source Video** directory, select **Blue sky.avi**, and click **Open**.

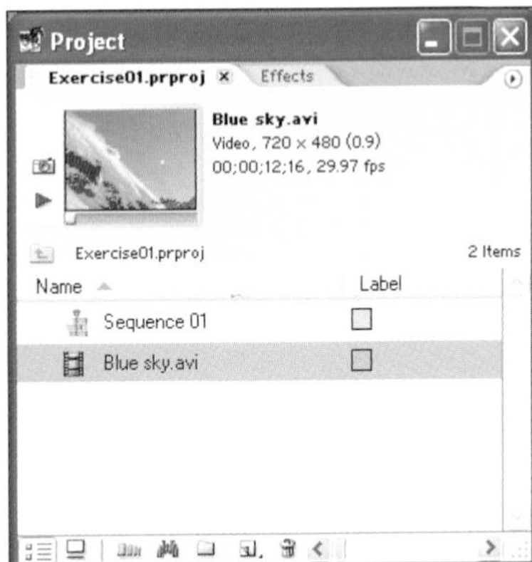

The Blue sky.avi clip is now displayed in the Project window with a film-strip icon, indicating that it is a movie clip. It also has a dark gray border around it, meaning that it is selected.

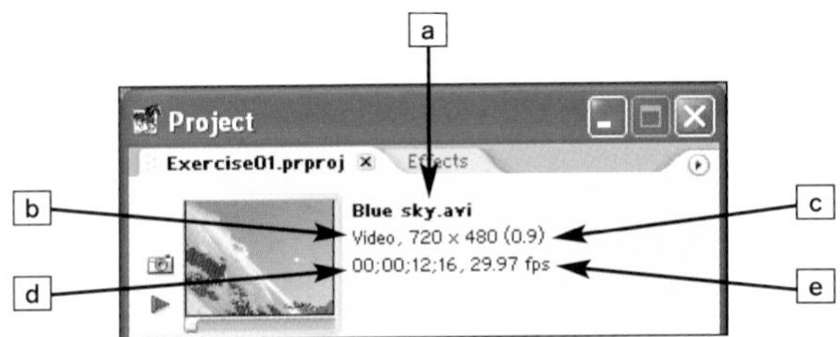

Tip: The Project window displays vital information about the currently selected clip:

(a) Name of the selected clip
(b) Type of clip
(c) Frame size and aspect ratio
(d) Duration in hours;minutes;seconds;frames
(e) Frames per second

Remember, DV NTSC video is always 720 × 480 (0.9) 29.97 fps.

---

4. Next, import a graphic clip. As you did in Step 2, choose **File > Import**.

---

5. Navigate to the **c:\Premiere Pro HOT\Source Graphics** directory, select **baseball.jpg**, and click **Open**.

*The **baseball.jpg** clip is displayed in the Project window. Notice that its icon is different than the movie clip, indicating that **baseball.jpg** is a still image.*

***Note:** The vital information reflects the currently selected clip. In this case, **baseball.jpg** is a still image that contains 720 x 666 pixels, has a 1.0 pixel aspect ratio, and has a duration of 00 hours ; 00 minutes ; 05 seconds; 00 frames (although still images don't really have a duration–more on that later in this book).*

---

6. Import an audio clip. Choose **File > Import**.

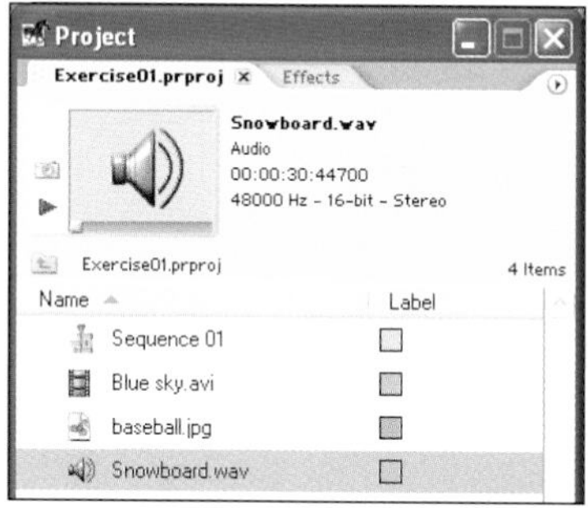

7. Navigate to **c:\Premiere Pro HOT\Source Audio**, select **Snowboard.wav**, and click **Open**.

*The **Snowboard**.wav clip is displayed in the Project window with the audio clip icon. Once again, the vital information shows that this is an audio clip, with a duration of slightly more than 30 seconds, and a quality of 48000 Hz, 16-bit, Stereo. (For now, ignore the 30:44700 duration display, which represents the audio sampling units, a phrase that may sound like complete gibberish at this point in your Premiere Pro education.)*

You have just imported one of every type of clip–video, still image, and audio. In addition, you can sort, preview, and organize all clips the same way. When you think about it–you now know how to import every type of file.

---

8. Save and keep this project open before moving on to the next exercise.

2. Previewing Clips

In the upper-left area of the Project window is a small preview monitor that displays the currently selected clip. In this exercise, you will learn how to preview your clips.

1. If you have the previous exercise open, skip directly to Step 2. If Premiere Pro is not running, launch it and click **Open Project** at the **Welcome Screen**. Navigate to the **c:\Premiere Pro HOT\Chapter02** folder, select **Exercise02.prproj** and click **Open**.

2. In the **Project** window, click the icon next to **Blue sky.avi** to select it.

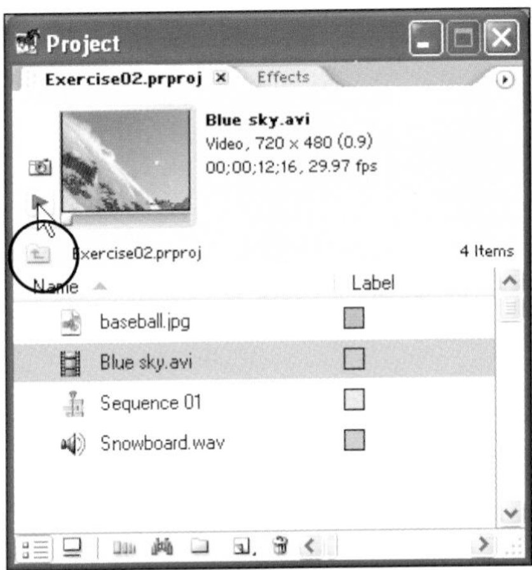

3. Click the **Play** button to the left of the preview monitor to preview your clip. As your video plays, a cursor moves from left to right along the bottom of the preview, to indicate the relative position of the playback. The left side indicates the beginning of the clip, and the right side indicates the end of the clip. When the cursor is in the middle, you are halfway through the video clip.

*Tip: You can directly click and drag the cursor right or left to fast forward or reverse the preview. This is called **scrubbing.***

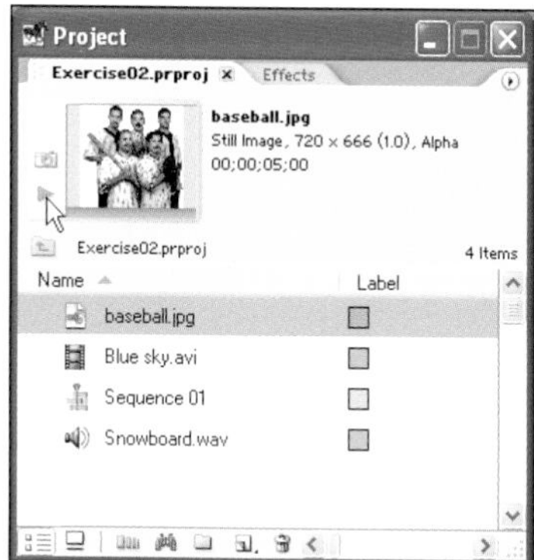

4. To preview the graphic clip, click the icon next to **baseball.jpg** to select it. Notice that the **Play** button to the left of the preview monitor is grayed out, preventing you from clicking it. This is because **baseball.jpg** is a still image and cannot be played like a video.

Note: *The clips in your Project window may be sorted in a different order. Premiere Pro automatically sorts your clips alphabetically when you open a project that contains imported clips. Don't worry if your sort order looks different than the image above–it does not affect your project.*

5. Finally, you will preview the audio clip. In the **Project** window, click the icon next to **Snowboard.wav** to select it.

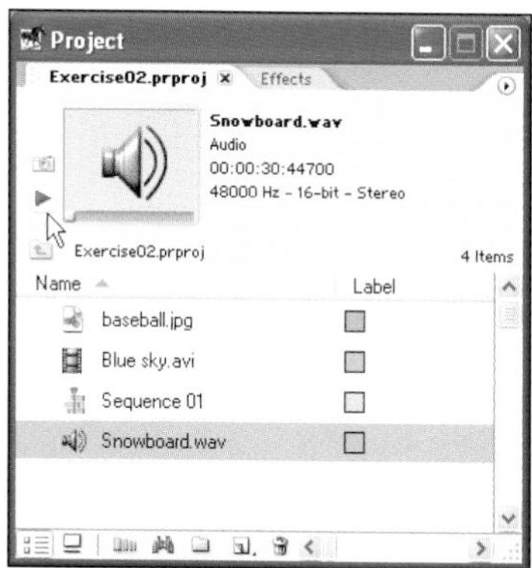

6. Click the **Play** button to the left of the preview monitor. This time, there is no picture in the preview monitor since it is an audio file, but the audio will play through your computer speakers.

Using the preview area of the Project window is a great way to get information about a clip, as well as watch or listen to a preview of the entire clip.

7. Save this project and keep it open before moving on to the next exercise.

3. Setting a Poster Frame

A **poster frame** is a single frame of a video clip that represents the entire clip. You can decide which frame of video is most representative of the clip, and then set it as the poster frame. When you select a clip in the Project window, the preview monitor displays the poster frame, so you can quickly surmise the content of the clip without having to preview the entire clip. In this exercise you will practice setting poster frames.

1. If you have the previous exercise still open, skip directly to Step 2. If Premiere Pro is not running, launch it and click **Open Project** at the **Welcome Screen**. Navigate to the **c:\Premiere Pro HOT\Chapter02** folder, select **Exercise03.prproj**, and click **Open**.

2. In the **Project** window, choose **File > Import**.

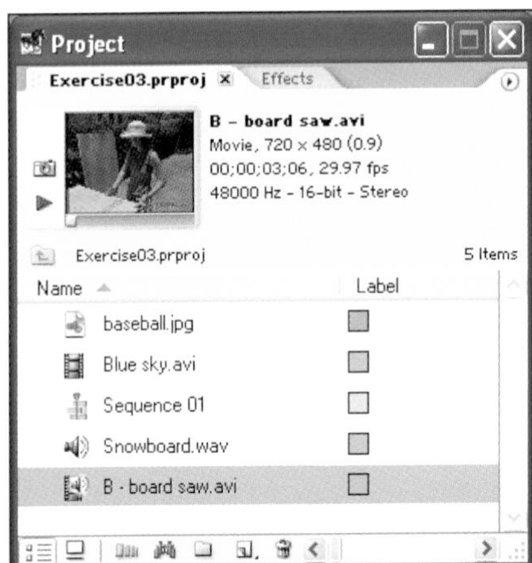

3. Navigate to the **c:\Premiere Pro HOT\Source Video\B-roll** directory, select **B – board saw.avi**, and click **Open**.

Notice that the first frame is displayed in the preview monitor. In this case, the first frame is a woman holding plywood.

4. Click the **Play** button to the left of the preview monitor to play the video.

As it plays, notice that the camera pans from the woman holding the plywood to a man sawing the plywood. The purpose of this clip is to show wood being cut with a saw. However, the first frame of the video does not illustrate that very well. This is a perfect example of when you would want to set a custom poster frame.

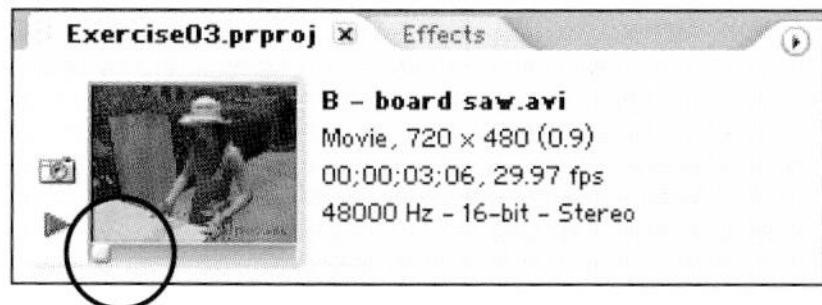

5. To change the poster frame, click and drag the preview cursor to the right to scrub through the video, until you see the man sawing wood.

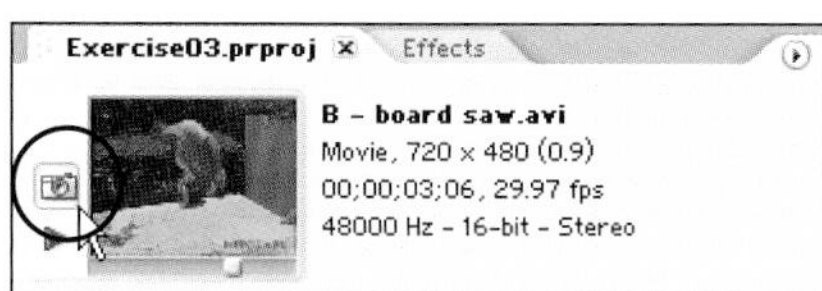

6. Click the **Set Poster Frame** icon to specify a custom poster frame.

This frame will now show in the preview monitor each time you select B – board saw.avi.

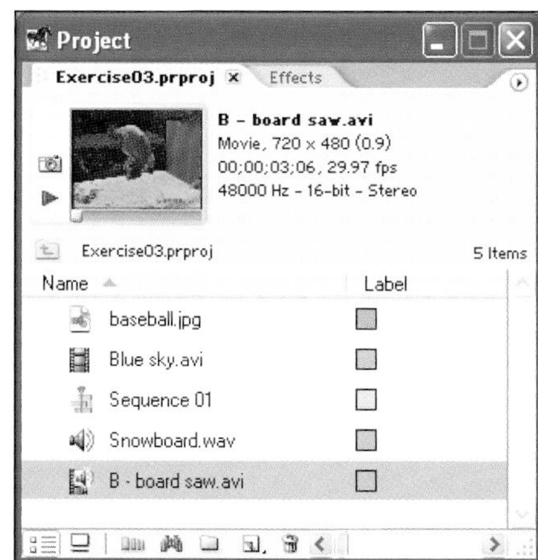

7. To illustrate this point, in the **Project** window click the icon next to **Sequence 01**. Now click the icon next to **B – board saw.mov** again. The preview monitor automatically displays the frame of the man sawing wood. You should see the poster frame displayed in the preview area, even though it is not the first frame of the clip.

Setting poster frames is a simple method to help keep your clips organized and quickly determine the content of a clip without previewing.

---

8. Save and keep this project open before moving on to the next exercise.

4. Changing Views

The Project window provides many different methods of viewing your clips, similar to the many ways you can view the contents of a folder in Windows XP.

1. If you have the previous exercise open, skip directly to Step 2. If Premiere Pro is not running, launch it and click **Open Project** at the **Welcome Screen**. Navigate to the **c:\Premiere Pro HOT\Chapter02** folder, select **Exercise04.prproj**, and click **Open**.

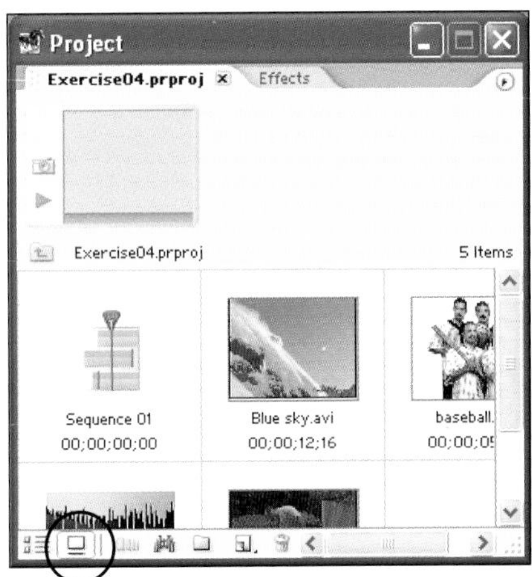

2. In the **Project** window, click the **Icon View** button. This view displays a grid of your clips, as well as the icons. Use the scroll bar to the right of the **Project** window to scroll through your clips. Also notice that the **B – board saw.avi** displays the poster frame set in the previous exercise.

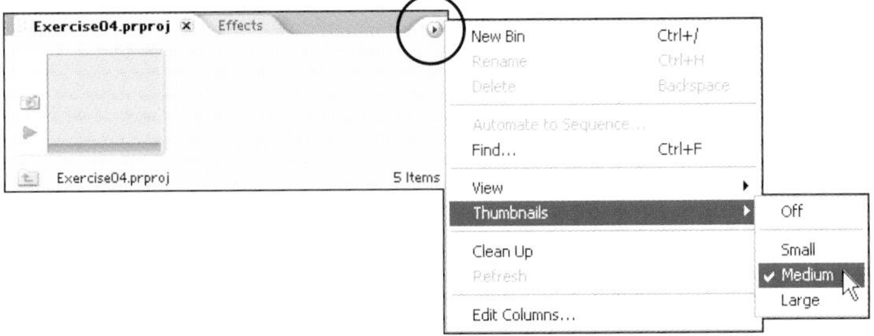

Note: *If your Project window looks slightly different than the one shown in Step 1, click the wing menu (the little circle arrow in the upper-right corner of the* ***Project*** *window) and make sure that* ***Thumbnails*** *are set to* ***Medium.***

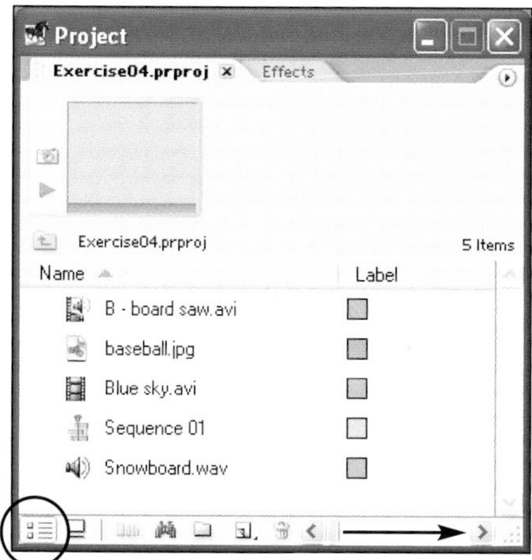

3. In the **Project** window, click the **List View** to change the view back to list mode. Now click the scroll bar at the bottom of the **Project** window to scroll to the right and see the many columns of information the List view includes.

Choose the view that is most comfortable for you. The List view can show more clips, but you have to scroll to see the other detailed information to the right. The Icon view shows you poster frames of each clip, but you may not be able to see as many in the Project window without scrolling up or down.

---

4. Save and keep this project open before moving on to the next exercise.

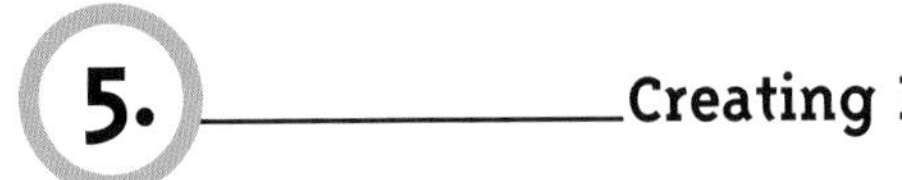

5. Creating Bins

Another great feature of the Project window is that you can use it to create folders to organize and group your clips. In Premiere Pro, the folders are called **bins**. The bins act just like the file folders in Windows XP.

1. If you have the previous exercise still open, skip directly to Step 2. If Premiere Pro is not running, launch it and click **Open Project** at the **Welcome Screen**. Navigate to the **c:\Premiere Pro HOT\Chapter02** folder, select **Exercise05.prproj**, and click **Open**.

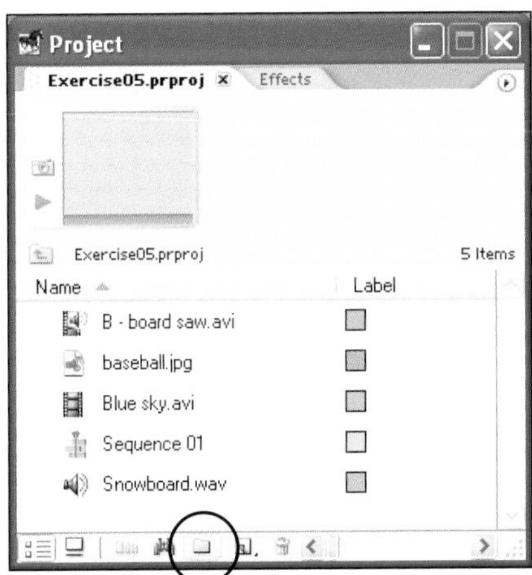

2. In the **Project** window, click the **New Bin** icon to create a new bin.

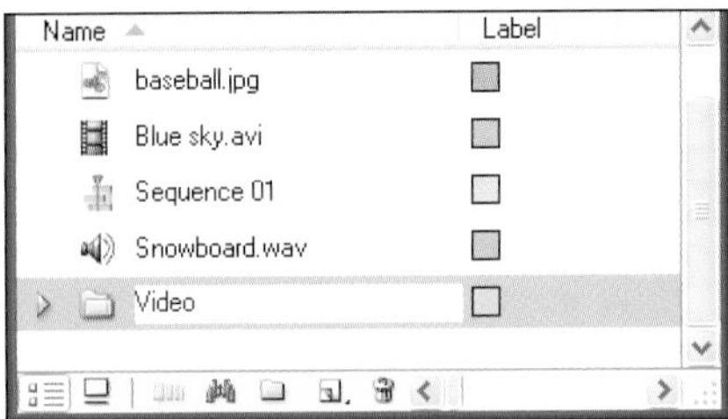

3. Name the new bin **Video** and press **Enter**.

***Note:** If you click somewhere else, or wait too long, Premiere Pro will automatically name the new bin **Bin 01** (or **02** or **03** and so on depending on how many bins you've created). To rename a bin, click the folder icon next to the bin's name, and then click the bin name. This brings up a text box where you can rename the bin. Make sure you press **Enter** when you're done naming it.*

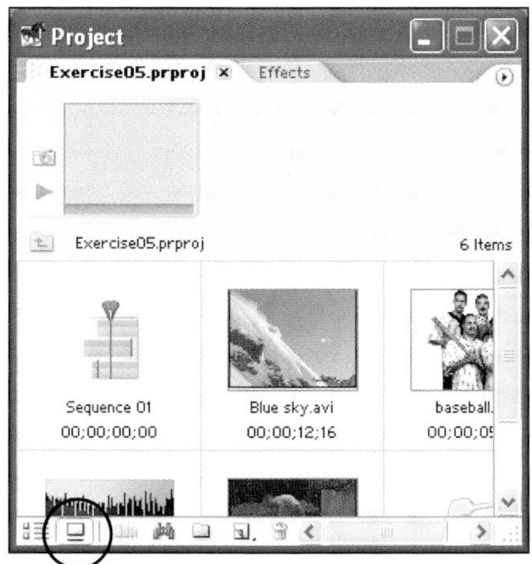

4. Next, you'll create a bin for your graphics and audio clips. But first, switch to **Icon** view by clicking the **Icon View** button.

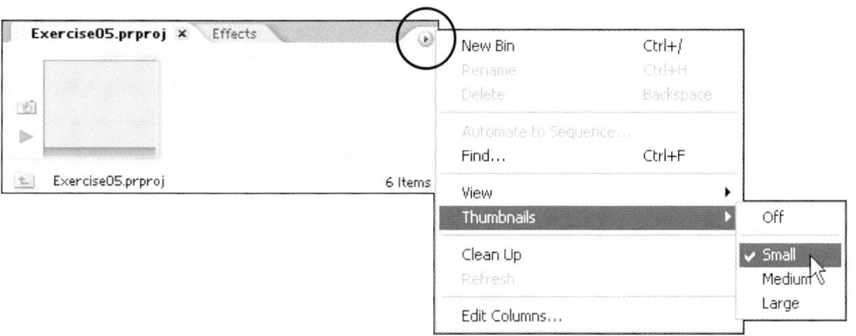

5. To see more clips in the **Project** window without having to scroll, change the thumbnail size. Click the wing menu in the **Project** window and choose **Thumbnails > Small**.

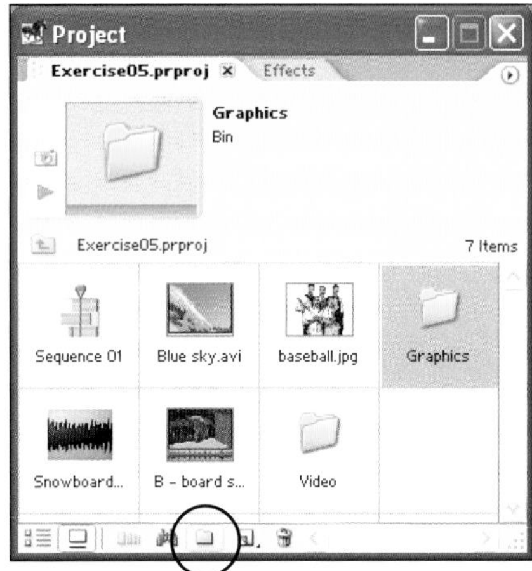

6. Click the **New Bin** icon, and name the bin **Graphics**. Then press **Enter**.

Note: *Don't worry if your clips are arranged in a different order than shown in this exercise.*

---

7. Click the **New Bin** icon, and name the bin **Audio**, then press **Enter**.

You have created three bins, one in the List view, and two in the Icon view. No matter what view you are in, the bins behave the same. Keep in mind that the bins are not created anywhere on your hard drive. They exist only in Premiere Pro as an internal tool to help organize your clips.

---

8. Save this project and keep it open before moving on to the next exercise.

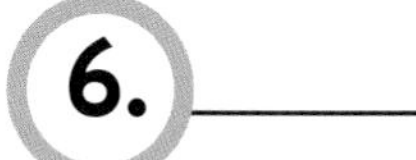

6. Organizing Clips in Bins

What's the fun of having a bin if you don't know how to place clips into a bin? In this exercise, you will organize your clips by dragging them into their bins.

1. If you have the previous exercise still open, skip directly to Step 2. If Premiere Pro is not running, launch it and click **Open Project** at the **Welcome Screen**. Navigate to the **c:\Premiere Pro HOT\Chapter02** folder, select **Exercise06.prproj**, and click **Open**.

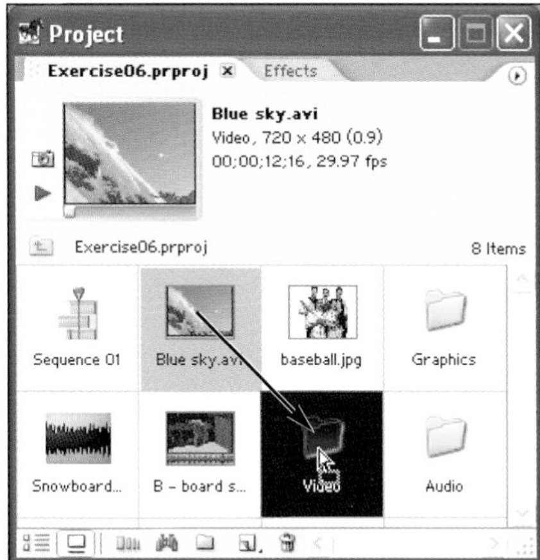

2. Click the **Blue sky.avi** clip to select it, and drag and drop it into the **Video** bin.

Note: *Your clips may be arranged in a different order than the grid shown in this exercise. The order of the clips in the grid has no effect on your project. A key advantage of the Icon view is that you can drag and drop the clips onto a new grid square to rearrange them in any order.*

3. Click the **Snowboard.wav** clip to select it, and drag and drop it into the **Audio** bin.

4. Click the **B – board saw.avi** clip to select it, and drag and drop it into the **Video** bin.

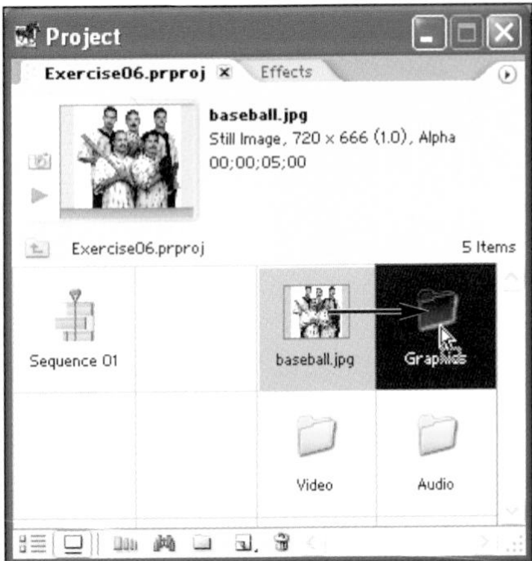

5. Click the **baseball.jpg** clip to select it, and drag and drop it into the **Graphics** bin.

*The **Project** window should now display only **Sequence 01** and the three bins.*

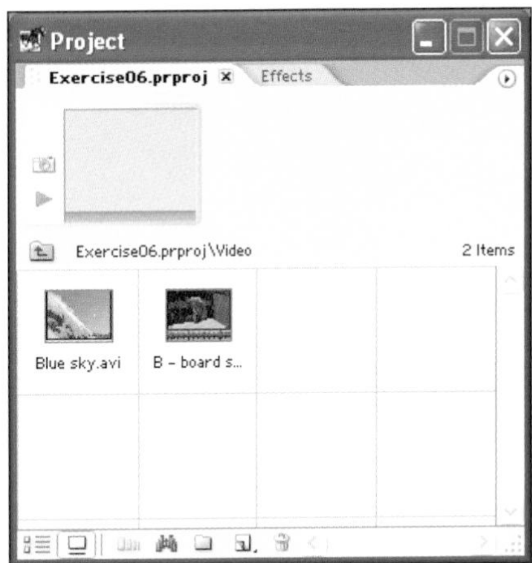

6. Double-click the **Video** bin to display its contents. Notice that all of the other clips and bins are not displayed in the **Project** window. Currently, you are looking "inside" the **Video** bin.

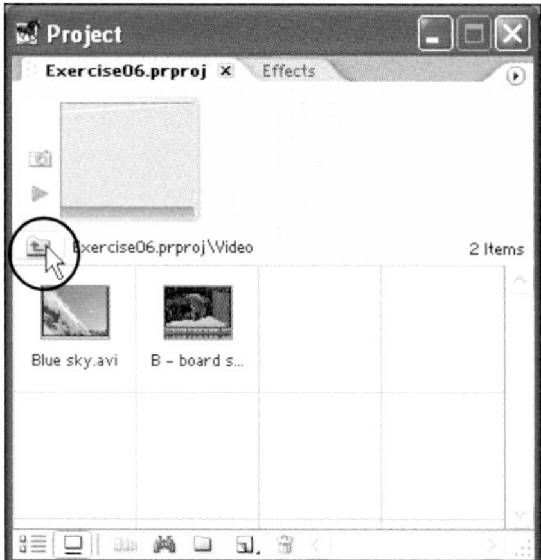

7. To return to the **root** level (computer jargon for the top-most directory), click the **Up-Folder** button.

You have just placed clips inside of bins. If you double-click a bin to view its contents, remember to return to the root level, or all of the clips outside of the bin will not be visible.

---

8. Save this project and keep it open before moving on to the next exercise.

7. Rearranging and Sorting

Earlier in this chapter, you learned that Premiere Pro provides two methods of viewing the Project window: List view and Icon view. The Icon view allows you to rearrange clips and bins in any pattern of the grid; the List view sorts based on the column headings.

1. If you have the previous exercise still open, skip directly to Step 2. If Premiere Pro is not running, launch it and click **Open Project** at the **Welcome Screen**. Navigate to the **c:\Premiere Pro HOT\Chapter02** folder, select **Exercise07.prproj**, and click **Open**.

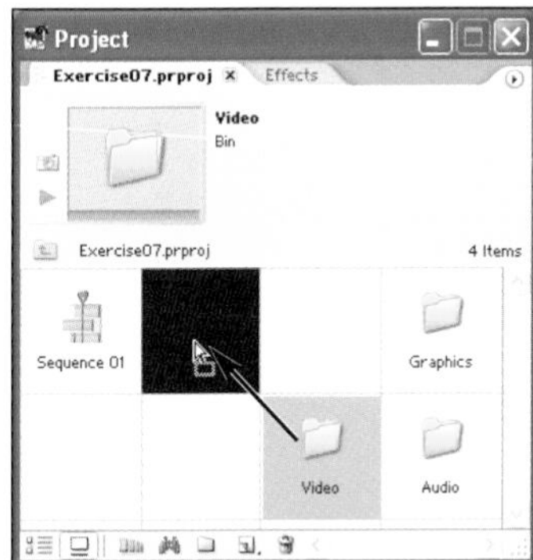

2. You should still be in **Icon** view from the previous exercise. Drag and drop the **Video** bin to the square indicated in the figure.

Note: *Don't worry if your folders are initially in a different square. Remember that Premiere Pro re-sorts your files and folders anytime it opens a project that already contains bins and clips.*

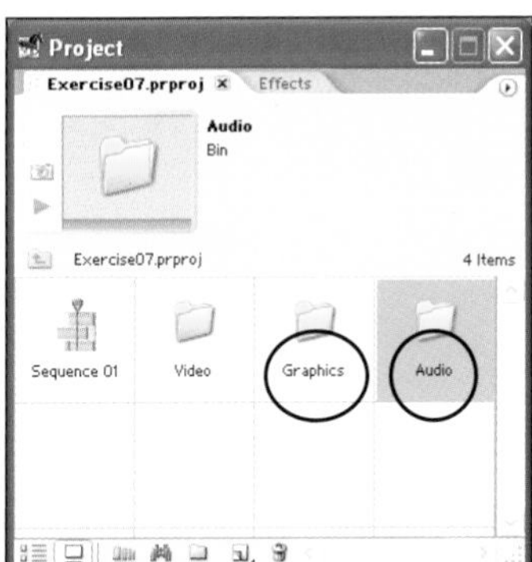

3. Next, drag and drop the **Graphics** bin and **Audio** bin to the squares indicated in the figure.

4. In the **Project** window, click the **List View** button to change the view.

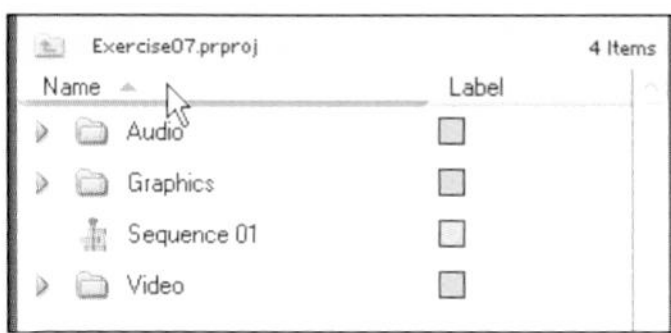

5. In the **Project** window, click inside of the **Name** column heading. This will toggle between A–Z sorting and Z–A sorting.

Tip: *You can sort clips/bins based on any column of the* ***List*** *view. There are more than 20 different columns available to sort. (However, you rarely will use more than a few of the most useful columns.)*

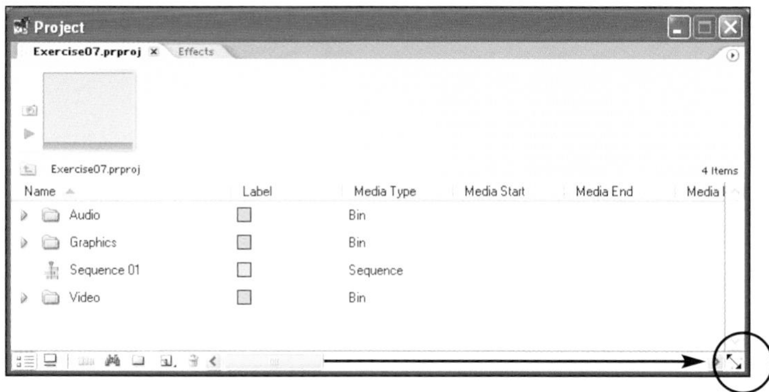

6. To see more columns at once, resize the window by dragging the handle in the lower-right corner of the **Project** window. (This feature is available to many windows in Premiere Pro.) This allows you to see more information in the **Project** window's **List** view, but other important windows may be obstructed.

You have just learned the ease of sorting clips in the Project window.

7. Save this project and close it before moving on to the next exercise.

In this chapter, you have learned the primary functions and capabilities of the Project window. A few buttons and tools in the Project window were not covered in this chapter. Fear not! They will be in due time, Grasshopper. For now, it is time to move on to the next piece of the Premiere Pro puzzle: the Monitor window.

3
The Monitor Window

| Source vs. Program | Playing Source Video |
| In and Out Points | Setting In and Out Points |
| Clearing In and Out Points |

H•O•T

Premiere Pro HOT DVD

The Monitor window is the built-in television within Premiere Pro. You can watch your source video, as well as watch changes that are made to the program video. Beyond playing your video, the Monitor window also allows you to make initial edits to your source video. Before you add video to the Timeline, most of the time you will want to take it to the Monitor window and *trim off the fat*, so to speak. Any edits you make in the Monitor window are temporary, and you can always undo or fine-tune them later on.

In this chapter, you will learn the function of the Monitor window, as well as how to perform these functions inside the Monitor window: play source video, preview edit points, and add clip markers.

Source vs. Program

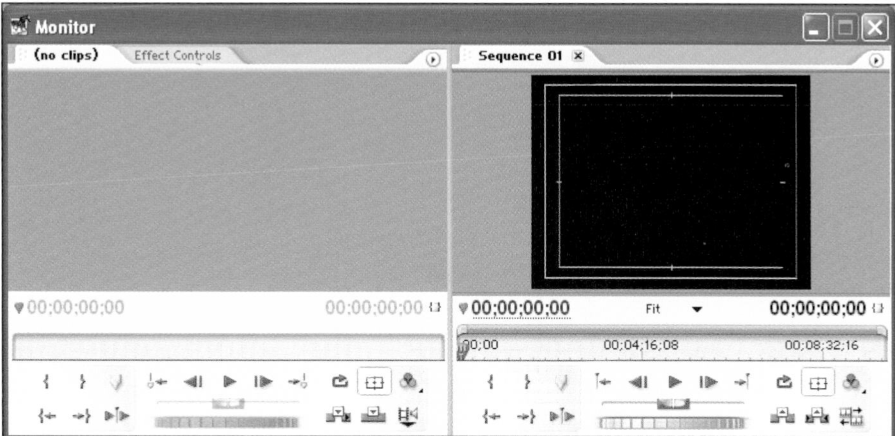

The Monitor window comes in a couple of different flavors, depending on which workspace you are in. Thus far you have been working with the Editing workspace, which arranges the Premiere Pro desktop so the most useful windows and palettes for editing are available. In the Editing workspace, the Monitor window has two sides: the left side is the **Source view**, and the right is the **Program view**.

The source is the original video; all of the clips sitting in your computer, waiting to be used, are the source materials. The program refers to the video you are creating, as if you were creating a television *program* (get it?). If this book was a tutorial on oil painting, the **source** would be your paint, and the **program** would be the canvas. (And your mouse would be the paintbrush?)

This chapter will cover the Source view of the Monitor window exclusively.

I. Playing Source Video

The first step to editing video in Premiere Pro is to play the video in the **Source view** (the left side of the Monitor window). This exercise will walk you through the steps of playing source video, shuttling backward and forward, and stepping frame-by-frame.

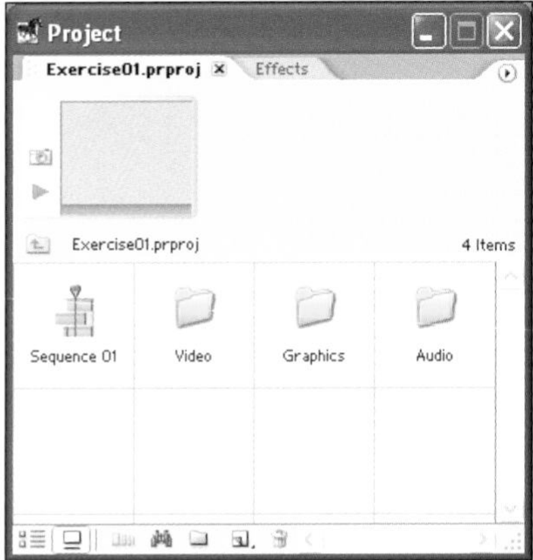

1. If Premiere Pro is not running, launch it and click **Open Project** at the **Welcome Screen**. If Premiere Pro is already open, choose **File > Open Project**. Navigate to the **c:\Premiere Pro HOT \Chapter03** folder, select **Exercise01.prproj**, and click **Open**.

Tip: A nice feature about Premiere Pro is that it remembers the workspace and Project window view when a project is saved. Exercise 01 uses the Editing workspace, and the Project window is in the Icon view–the same view used in Chapter 2.

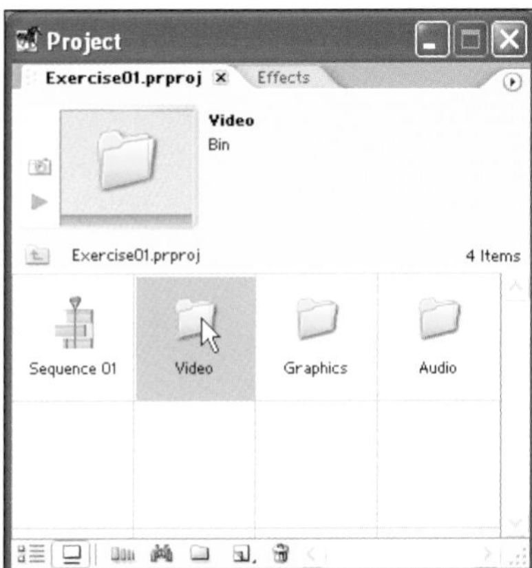

2. In the **Project** window, double-click the **Video** bin to view its contents.

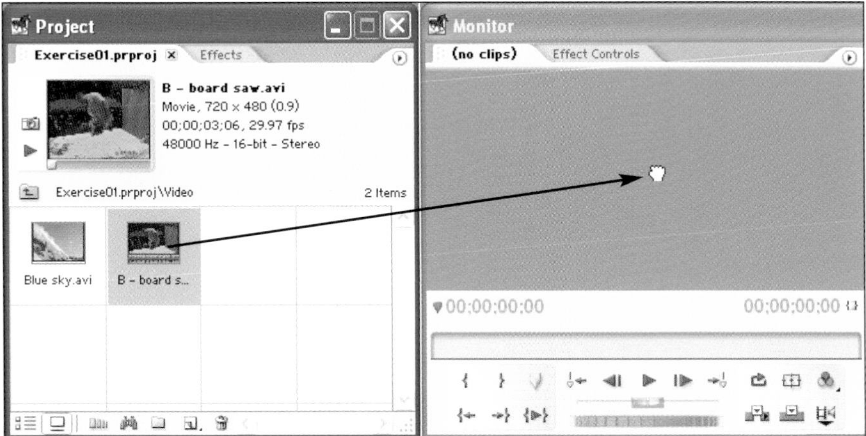

3. In the **Project** window, click the icon for **B – board saw.avi** and drag and drop it in the **Source** view.

Tip: Notice that the **Source** view displays the first frame of the source video, but not the poster frame that you set in Chapter 2, "*The Project Window.*" The poster frame is only used in the **Project** window, and it does not have an effect on your editing or other windows.

4. In the **Source** view, click the **Play** button. Your video will play in the monitor above. Click the button once more to stop.

Note: *If you have the* ***Title Safe/Action Safe*** *guides activated, you may see two thin boxes around the perimeter of the* ***Source*** *view. (These are used for creating titles, which is covered in Chapter 6, "Title Designer.") You can temporarily hide these guides by toggling the* ***Title Safe/Action Safe*** *button. Click the button until the guides disappear.*

5. Click the **Play** button again, and you will see a few interesting things happening in the **Source** view: the current time indicator (a) moves across the time ruler (c), and the current time display (b) increases to reflect the current running time. [See the following Note.] Also note the play button (e) switches to a stop button during playback.

NOTE | Displaying Current Time

The **current time indicator** (a) shows you the exact frame you are viewing in the Source view. As the video plays, the current time indicator travels from left to right across the time ruler. The far left is the beginning of the clip, and the far right is the end of the clip. When the current time indicator reaches the end of the clip, playback automatically stops.

The **current time display** (b) shows the frame number that is being viewed. When the current time indicator is at the beginning of a clip, the time display is always 00h;00m;00s;00f.

The **time ruler** (c) displays the divisions of time in your clip. The far left is always 00;00;00;00 and the far right is always the end of the clip. Even if the clip was 1 hour long, the far right is always the end, but the divisions of time would be *much* larger.

The **clip duration** (d) displays the total number of frames in the clip. Curiously, when playback stops in the current exercise, the current time display reads 00;00;03;05 (3 seconds 5 frames). However, the clip duration reads 00;00;03;06 (3 seconds 6 frames). Why the 1 frame difference? This is because Frame 1 was displayed as 00;00;00;00, which means that Frame 2 was displayed as 00;00;00;01, and Frame 3 was displayed as 00;00;00;02, and so on.

As an added bonus, when you play DV video that was captured via IEEE-1394 (FireWire), the current time display shows the original timecode on the tape. More on that in Chapter 15, *"Capturing Digital Video,"* which talks about capturing video.

6. Another way to change the current time is to drag the current time indicator left and right in the time ruler. In the **Source** view, click and hold your mouse button on the current time indicator (the blue tab) as you drag the indicator all the way to the left in the time ruler. Now drag the indicator all the way to the right. This is a very quick way to jump to any point in the time ruler.

7. In the **Source** view, drag the current time indicator until the current time display shows **00;00;01;00**. If you have trouble dragging the current time indicator to that exact time, you can advance the current time indicator one frame at a time with the **Step Back** and **Step Forward** buttons.

Tip: The left and right arrow keys on your keyboard are shortcuts for the Step Back and Step Forward buttons. Some users can edit quicker with keyboard shortcuts. Do what is most comfortable for you.

8. As if you didn't have enough ways to change the current time, Premiere Pro provides two more convenient methods. Click and drag the **shuttle slider** slowly to the left and then the right. This is a helpful way to watch the **Source** view in slow motion. The center is pause, and playback accelerates the farther away from center you drag the shuttle slider.

---

9. Directly below the shuttle slider is the **jog disk**, which has a similar effect as the shuttle slider. Click and drag your mouse to the left and right to rewind or forward the **Source** view.

Tip: *These are just a few ways of accomplishing the same task: moving the current time indicator. There is no single correct method to follow. With so many ways to complete the same task, it becomes a matter of comfort.*

You have just learned the basic functions of the ***Monitor*** *window* ***Source*** *view, and how it interacts with the* ***Project*** *window. You've also practiced the different methods of moving the current time indicator.*

---

10. Save this project and keep it open before moving on to the next exercise.

Premiere Pro provides no less than nine different methods to change the current time. (There's actually more that you have yet to learn!) Here is a summary of each method and its keyboard equivalent, if applicable.

The Many Ways to Change Current Time	
Button or Method	**What It Does**
Play/Stop toggle button	Plays and stops Source view (spacebar).
Drag the current time indicator	Changes current time to mouse position.
Click mouse in time ruler	Snaps current time indicator to mouse.
Step Back button	Reverses current time by one frame (left arrow).
Step Forward button	Advances current time by one frame (right arrow).
Shuttle slider	Accelerates playback based on distance from center position.
Jog disk	Rewinds or forwards Source view.
Click in current time display	Allows you to manually enter in the frame number to view. You can enter in an absolute number, like 03;00 (3 seconds 0 frames), or a relative number (+5), which moves you 5 frames forward from the existing current time.
Go to In Point button	Jumps to the Source view's In point (Q).
Go to Out Point button	Jumps to the Source view's Out point (W).
Go to Previous Marker	Jumps to the previous marker set in the Source view.
Go to Next Marker	Jumps to the next marker set in the Source view.
Play In to Out	Plays from Source view In point to Source view Out point.

In and Out Points

In and **Out** points are the bookends of your source clip. When you import a clip into the Project window, you don't have to use the entire clip. You can trim a little fat from the beginning and end of the clip, or you can use just a small segment of the source clip. This process of whittling down your video to the most essential part is the heart and soul of video editing.

The most common workflow in Premiere Pro is to set In and Out points in the Monitor window. The idea is to watch your original clip, and then choose which portions of that clip you want to use. Keep in mind that changing In and Out points does not permanently delete any video from the clip. The In and Out points affect only the copy of the clip in the Project window, never the original file on your hard drive. In and Out points can be changed as often as you'd like, and they can also be removed. In other words, you are doing no damage to any of your clips, so don't worry about practicing with your own video.

Once you are satisfied with the In and Out points you have specified, the next step is to bring the clip into the Timeline window and begin building your program. The next chapter covers this process and the Timeline window.

2. Setting In and Out Points

Now that you know your way around the Source view of the Monitor window, it is time to set In and Out points. In this exercise, you are given a clip of a snowboarder jumping off of a cliff (don't try this at home). Your goal is to whittle the source clip down to the essential portion of the clip and to trim off the excess at the beginning and the end.

1. If Premiere Pro is not running, launch it and click **Open Project** at the **Welcome Screen**. If Premiere Pro is already open, choose **File > Open Project**. Navigate to the **c:\Premiere Pro HOT\Chapter03** folder, select **Exercise02.prproj**, and click **Open**.

2. Double-click the **Video** bin to view its contents.

3. Choose **File > Import**.

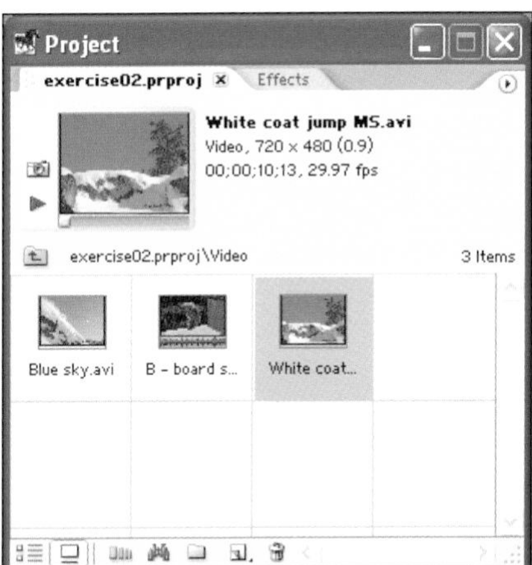

4. Navigate to the **c:\Premiere Pro HOT\Source Video** directory, select **White coat jump MS.avi**, and click **Open**.

Note: The file will be imported into the currently displayed bin. In this case, the clip was placed into the **Video** bin since you were viewing the **Video** bin. If you were viewing the root directory (top-most level), the clip would have been placed in the root directory.

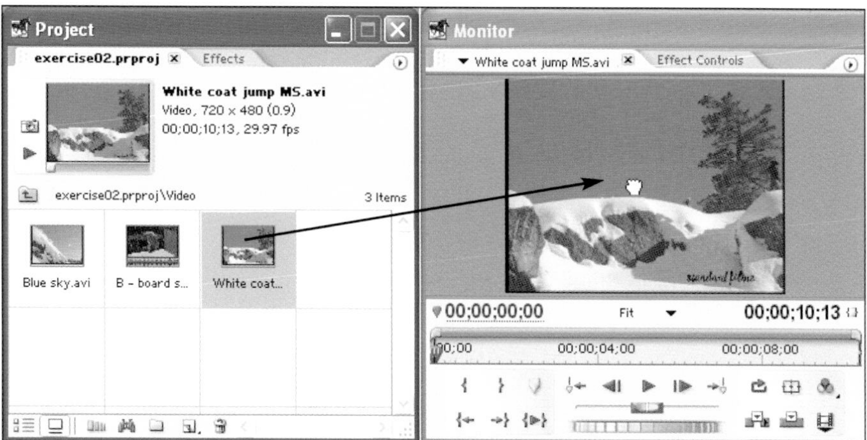

5. In the **Project** window, click the icon for **White coat jump MS.avi** and drag it to the **Source** view of the **Monitor** window. Right away, you will see the first frame displayed in the **Source** view, and the clip duration of **00;00;10;13** (10 seconds 13 frames).

Pop Quiz: If this clip had 17 more frames, what would be the clip's duration? Answer: 10 seconds 13 frames + 17 frames = 11 seconds 0 frames. Remember, there are 30 frames per second in DV NTSC video.

6. In the **Source** view, click the **Play** button to play the video. Watch the entire video.

7. Move the current time indicator to the point just before you see the snowboarder at the cliff, about **00;00;02;12**. Click the **Set In Point** button. This sets an **In** point at **00;00;02;12**, and tells Premiere Pro that you want to start using the video at this point.

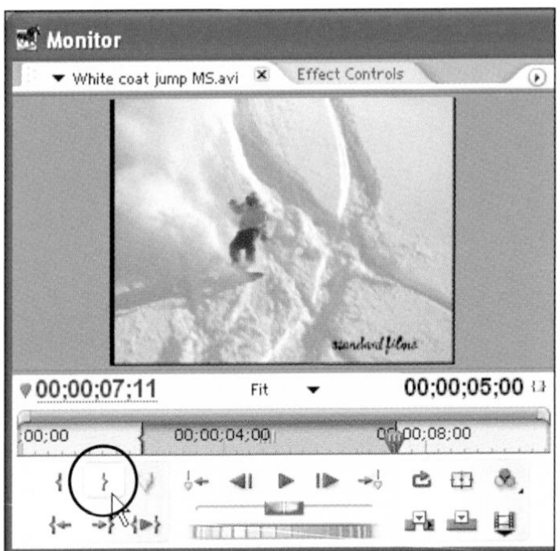

8. Move the current time indicator to the point just after the snowboarder lands, about **00;00;07;11**. Click the **Set Out Point** button. This sets an **Out** point at **00;00;07;11**. The **Out** point tells Premiere Pro that you want to stop using the video at this point.

Note: The dark gray area in the time ruler represents the **In to Out.**

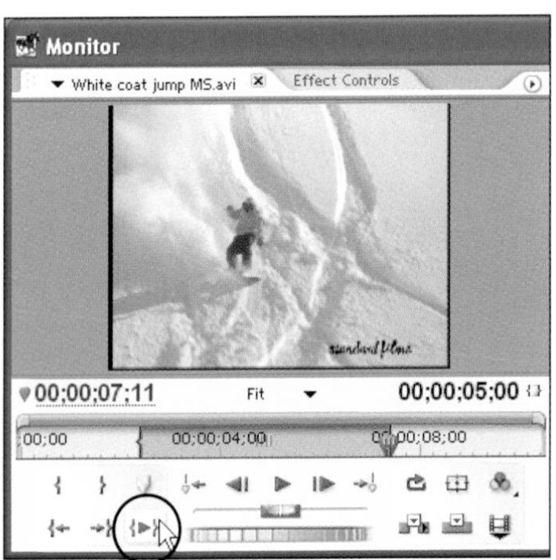

9. Click the **Play In to Out** button. This plays the **Source** view starting at the **In** point and stopping at the **Out** point.

Note: Notice that the clip duration now shows the total duration of the **In to Out** point, instead of the clip's total duration. In this case, you have chosen exactly 5 seconds of source video to use.

10. To quickly move the current time indicator to the **In** point, click the **Go to In Point** button. This changes the current time to the **In** point, in this case **00;00;02;12**.

11. Premiere Pro provides the flexibility to change the **In** point as many times as you'd like. In this case, you want to change the **In** point to a little later, maybe right as the snowboarder leaves the cliff. To change the **In** point, advance the current time indicator to **00;00;02;27** with the **Step Forward** button (1), and click the **Set In Point** button (2).

12. An even quicker method to change the **In** or **Out** point is to click and drag the point directly. In this case, you will want to change the **Out** point to a little earlier, maybe when the snowboarder first makes contact. To change the **Out** point in this method, hover your mouse over the **Out** point bracket **]** until the **Trim Out** cursor appears, and drag the mouse to the left, to roughly **00;00;05;21**.

Tip: Don't worry if you can't get to exactly 00;00;05;21. The advantage of the **Trim** cursor is that it saves a step, and it can be a quicker way to approximate a new **In** or **Out** point. The disadvantage is that it is not as precise as advancing frame-by-frame with the **Step Back** or **Step Forward** buttons.

---

13. Click the **Play In to Out** button to preview your new **In** and **Out** points.

You have successfully performed your first edit. The good news is that all source clips are edited this way—music, video, graphics, everything. There is still much more in-depth editing to learn, but you now understand the basics and are well on your way to efficient editing.

---

14. Save and keep this project open before moving on to the next exercise.

3. Clearing In and Out Points

An editor never makes mistakes, right? Even so, now that you know how to set and modify In and Out points, this quick exercise will walk you through the steps of clearing them, should you make a... well, you know.

1. If Premiere Pro is not running, launch it and click **Open Project** at the **Welcome Screen**. If Premiere Pro is already open, choose **File > Open Project**. Navigate to the **c:\Premiere Pro HOT\Chapter03** folder, select **Exercise03.prproj**, and click **Open**.

2. Double-click the **Video** bin to view its contents.

3. Choose **File > Import**.

4. Navigate to the **c:\Premiere Pro HOT\Source Video** directory, select **MS Brown coat.avi**, and click **Open**.

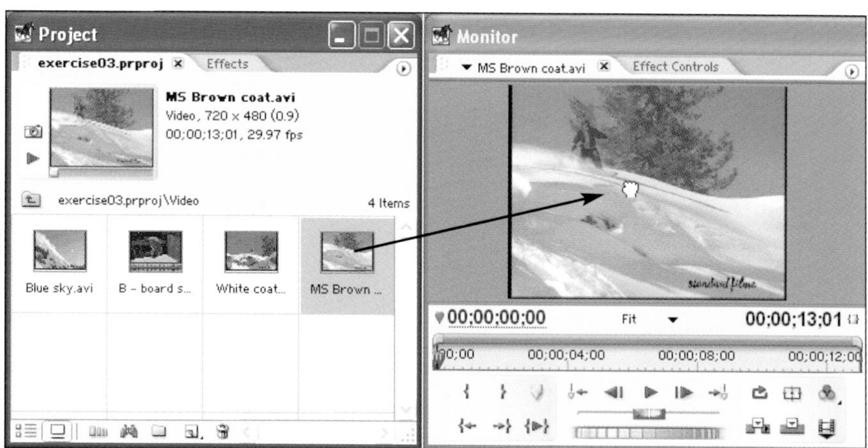

5. In the **Project** window, click the icon for **MS Brown coat.avi** and drag it to the **Source** view of the **Monitor** window.

Pop quiz: What is the total duration of the clip? 00;00;13;01. Extra credit: If it had two less frames, what would the duration be? 00;00;12;29.

6. In the **Source** view, click the **Play** button to preview the clip.

7. Move the current time indicator to **00;00;09;20**. Use the **Step Back** and **Step Forward** buttons if needed. Click the **Set In Point** ({) button.

8. Oops. Perhaps that was an accident. In order to clear your **In** point, right-click anywhere in the time ruler, and choose **Clear Clip Marker > In** from the shortcut menu. The **In** point marker disappears.

Tip: Follow the exact same steps when you want to clear an **Out** point–except choose **Clear Clip Marker > Out**, of course. Or, you can clear them together by choosing **Clear Clip Marker > In and Out.** This option will only be available to you if you have both **In** and **Out** points specified.

*There's no mystery to setting **In** and **Out** points. Plus, the same steps we just outlined apply equally to both audio clips and still images.*

---

9. Save this project and close it before moving on to the next exercise.

*Now that you know how to play your source clip and select the portion of the clip that you'd like to use–what do you do with it? It all comes together in the next chapter, as you learn the ins and outs (get it?) of the **Timeline** window.*

4

The Timeline Window

The Timeline Window	Adding Clips to the Timeline
Snapping Clips	Rearranging Clips	Moving Multiple Clips
The Ripple Delete	Trimming Clips in the Timeline
The Ripple Trim Pointer

H•O•T

Premiere Pro HOT DVD

Remember timelines from your grade school history books? The far left of the timeline represented many years ago, and the right of the timeline represented present day. The Timeline in Premiere Pro behaves in a similar manner–the far left of the Timeline is the beginning of your program (zero seconds) and time increases as you scroll to the right.

The Timeline is the construction site for your program. In the Timeline window, you can arrange, rearrange, edit, move, copy, transition, and add special effects to clips (to name just a few features). The Timeline window is the window where you'll do most of your work.

So far, you've learned that the Project window is the collection site for all of the clips you want to use, and the Monitor window is the television screen that allows you to view all of your source clips. Now it is time to explore the Timeline window and discover how all three windows work together to help you create your program.

In this chapter, you will learn the primary functions and editing capabilities of the Timeline window. You will build your first program and discover how the Timeline window fits into the big Premiere Pro picture.

The Timeline Window

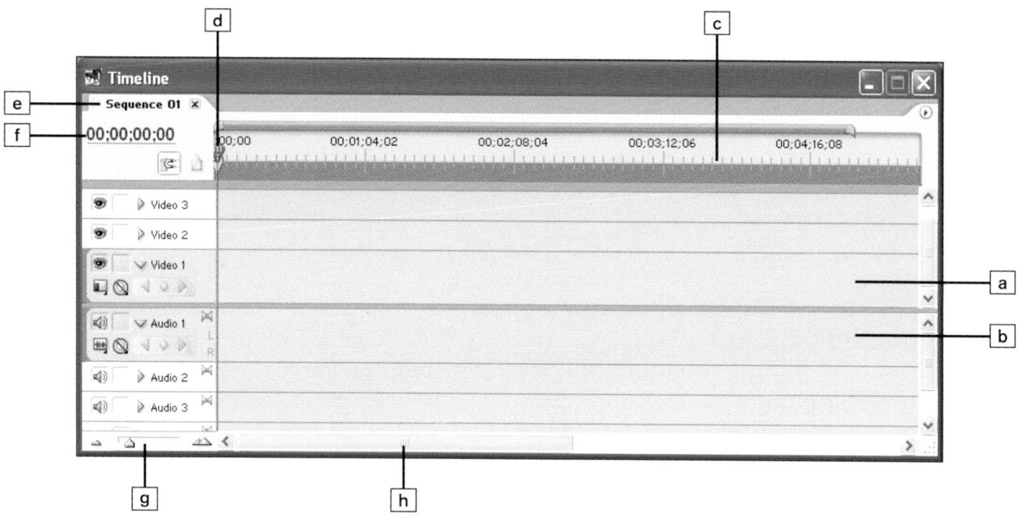

The Timeline window is the blank canvas of your program. Each program you create is assembled in the Timeline window, one clip at a time. Here, you can assemble the clips in any order and rearrange them as many times as you'd like. Once you've imported a clip into the Project window, then modified In and Out points in the Monitor window, the third step is to place the clip into the Timeline window.

Before jumping into the Timeline window, take a minute to familiarize yourself with the major features:

(a) The Timeline window is divided into tracks. The default Timeline has three **video tracks** (labeled Video 1, Video 2, Video 3) and three audio tracks (Audio 1, Audio 2, Audio 3). At the far left of the tracks are the track names. Video tracks can accept any clip that has video to display–such as clips from a DV camera, titles, photographs, and so on.

(b) Audio tracks can accept any clip that has audio–such as clips from a DV camera and sound files (MP3, WAV, AIF, and so on). So far, many of the clips you have been practicing with have been video-only. However, when you have a clip that contains audio *and* video, a clip representing the video is placed in the video track, and a clip representing the audio is placed into the corresponding audio track.

(c) The **Timeline ruler** is similar to the time ruler in the Monitor window. It represents the time divisions of your program and acts as a guide to show you "when in time" you are viewing. In the screen shot shown here, you are viewing from 00;00;00;00 at the far left, and past 00;04;16;08 at the right side of the Timeline.

(d) The **current time indicator** represents the frame that you are viewing in the Timeline. This corresponds to the current time indicator in the program side of the Monitor window. More on that later.

(e) The **active sequence** shows as a tab in the Timeline window. Each Timeline is a sequence. You can have multiple sequences, thus multiple Timelines. Sequences and Timelines go hand-in-hand, and sometimes the distinction can be very blurry. The Timeline window is a container that holds sequences.

(f) The Timeline **time display** shows the position of the current time indicator. In the screen shot, the current time indicator is all the way to the left, which represents 00;00;00;00.

(g) The **zoom slider** changes the zoom level of the Timeline.

(h) The **horizontal scroll bar** allows you to view a later point in time. Like scrolling to the end of a web page, the horizontal scroll bar lets you scroll to the end of the Timeline.

NOTE | Audio and Video Tracks

The Timeline is divided into tracks, like a highway is divided into lanes. When you place a clip in the Timeline, you place it into one of the predefined tracks. When you drive your car on the interstate, you can only drive in one of the predefined lanes. (Hopefully you do!)

Video and graphic clips can only be placed into video tracks. Audio clips can only be placed into audio tracks. Some Timelines have four video tracks and one audio track, others can have four audio tracks, and only one video track. You can add and subtract tracks from any Timeline, based on the needs of your program.

On the far left of the track is the beginning of the Timeline (0 seconds). To the right, the track stretches into infinity (well, almost infinity–24 hours to be exact).

I. Adding Clips to the Timeline

It is time to begin building your Timeline, one clip at a time. In this chapter, you will use footage and interviews from a hurricane to build a news story.

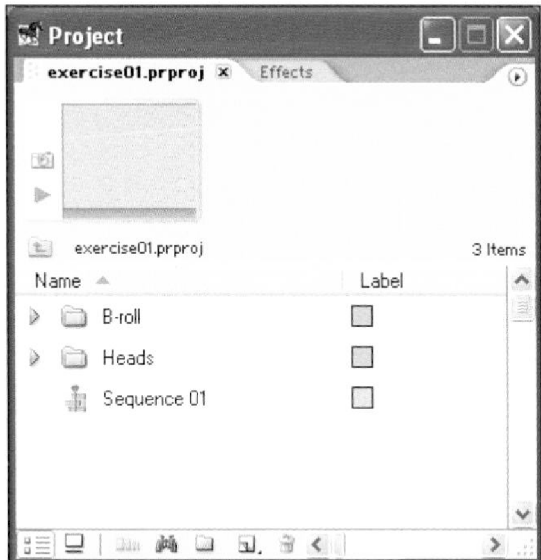

1. If Premiere Pro is not running, launch it and click **Open Project** at the **Welcome Screen**. Navigate to the **c:\Premiere Pro HOT\Chapter04** folder, select **Exercise01.prproj**, and click **Open**.

The Project window contains three items: two bins and a default sequence.

Note: *This project already has two bins labeled **B-roll** and **Heads.** Video clips have already been imported into each bin. The **Project** window is in **List** display mode.*

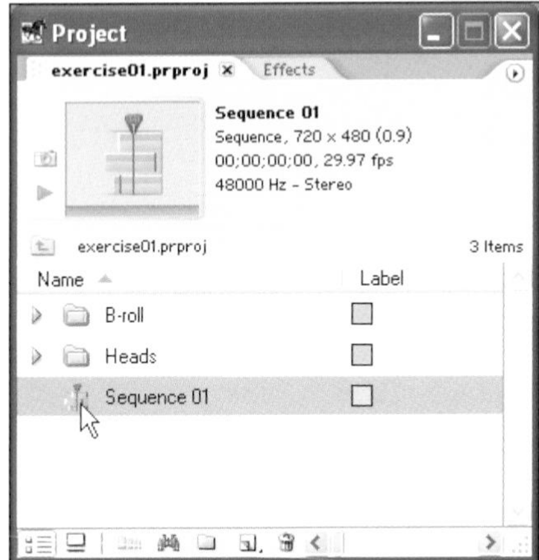

2. You may notice that this project has no **Timeline** window. To view the **Timeline** window, you must open up a sequence. In this case, double-click the icon next to **Sequence 01** to view it in the **Timeline** window.

*This will open **Sequence 01** in the **Timeline** window. **Sequence 01** has three video tracks and three audio tracks. The current time indicator is positioned at **00;00;00;00**.*

***Tip:** If you accidentally close the **Timeline** window, you can quickly open it up by double-clicking a sequence in the **Project** window.*

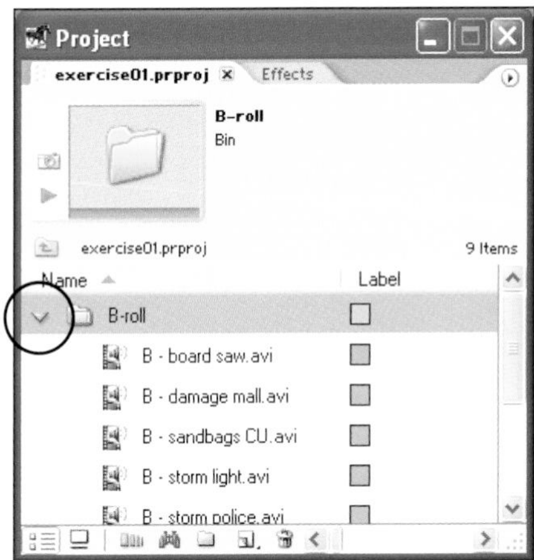

3. In the **Project** window, click the **B-roll** "twirl-down" (triangle to the left of the bin) to expand the bin and view its contents.

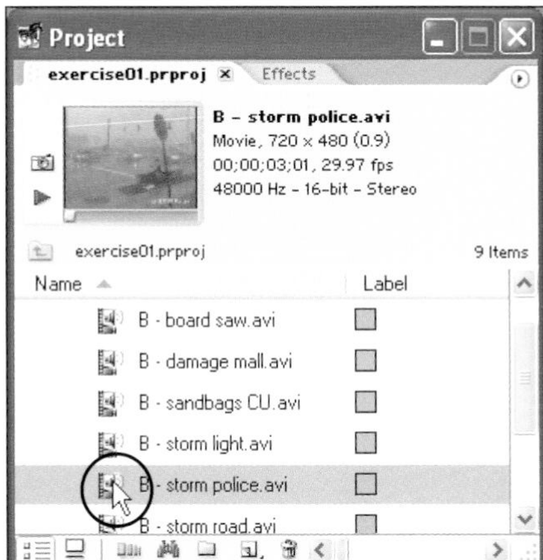

4. Next you will set **In** and **Out** points for your source clips in the **Monitor** window. In the **Project** window **Heads** bin, scroll down and double-click the icon next to **B – storm police.avi** to open it in the **Monitor** window.

5. In the **Source** view of the **Monitor** window, click the **Play** button to preview the clip.

6. In the same window, move the current time indicator to **00;00;00;07** and then click the **Set In Point** button to set an **In** point.

Tip: A nice feature of Premiere Pro is that you don't have to set an ***Out*** *point. Unless you make your own* ***Out*** *point, Premiere Pro assumes you want to use the entire remainder of the clip in the* ***Timeline.***

7. The next step is to drag the clip into the **Timeline** window. Make sure that the current time indicator in the **Timeline** window is positioned all the way to the left, at **00;00;00;00**. Click and drag the **Source** view display into track **Video 1** in the **Timeline** window. Don't let go of your mouse until you see the clip icons in **Video 1** and **Audio 1**.

*Note: The clips will be placed into the **Timeline** at the point when you let go of your mouse. If your mouse is not all the way to the left (at **00;00;00;00**) or if it is not in **Video 1**, the clips will be placed in the wrong spot. You can always undo by choosing **Edit > Undo.** (The keyboard shortcut is **Ctrl+Z**)*

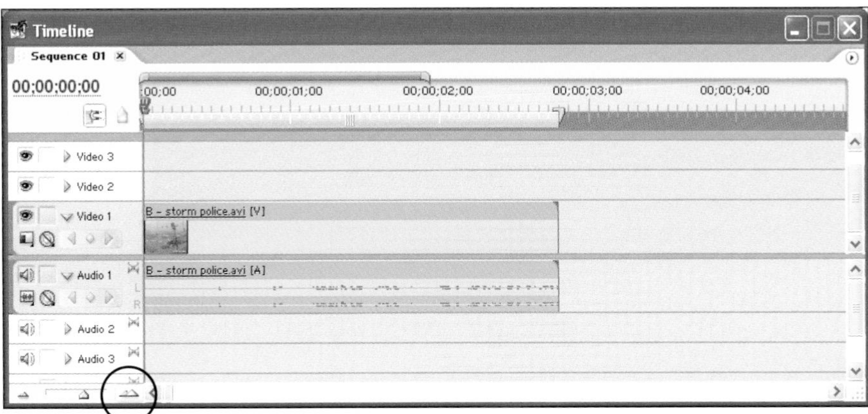

8. Right now the **Timeline** window is zoomed out very far, making the clips in the tracks look very small (like viewing the Earth from a satellite high above). To zoom in on the **Timeline** window, click the **Zoom In** button until the clip takes up most of the **Timeline**. Notice that the original source clip is now represented by two clips in the **Timeline**: one clip in the **Video 1** track and one clip in the **Audio 1** track.

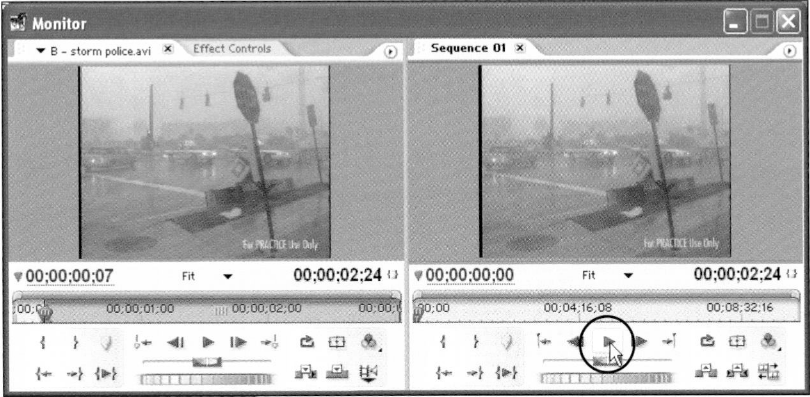

9. Click the **Play** button in the **Monitor** window program view (the right side) to play the **Timeline**.

*In the previous chapter, you learned that the left side of the **Monitor** window is called the **Source** view, and it is used for playback of your source clips. The right side of the **Monitor** window is called the **Program** view, and it is used for playback of the **Timeline** window.*

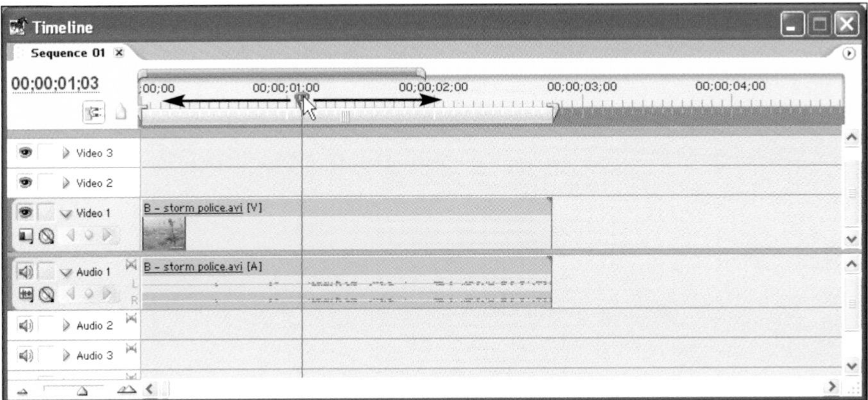

10. In the **Timeline** window, click and drag the blue tab of the current time indicator left and right, across the clip. This is called **scrubbing**. Notice that as you scrub, the program view of the **Monitor** window always displays the exact frame of video where the current time indicator is positioned.

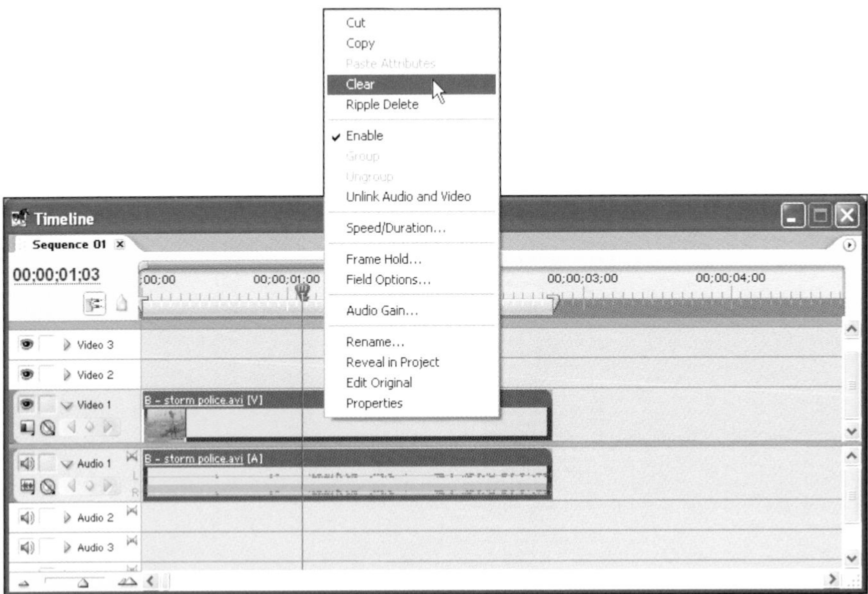

11. What would be the fun in adding clips if you don't know how to remove clips? Right-click in the middle of the clip you want to remove–in this case right-click **B – storm police.avi** in either the video portion of the clip in track **Video 1** or the audio portion of the clip in track **Audio 1**. From the pop-up menu that appears, choose **Clear**. POOF! It's gone.

***Tip:** Some editors are more comfortable using keyboard shortcuts instead of using the mouse. The keyboard shortcut to clear a clip from the Timeline is the **Delete** key. Simply select the clip in the **Timeline** and press the **Delete** key.*

*In this exercise, you learned to add and remove clips from the **Timeline** window. You have also learned the ease of zooming in to view your clips. These steps may seem simple, but they will become the base of everything you do in the **Timeline**. You'll perform them dozens of times with each project you create.*

---

12. Save and close this project before moving on to the next exercise.

NOTE | What Is a Sequence?

So what exactly *is* a sequence, and how does it relate to the Timeline window?

A sequence is a Timeline. When you add clips to the Timeline window, you are actually adding clips to a sequence. Premiere Pro allows you to create multiple sequences, thus you can have *multiple* Timelines, all independent of each other.

The Timeline window is a container for sequences. Remember that source clips open up in the Monitor window? Well, sequences open up in the Timeline window. In this respect, the Timeline window is merely a viewer for displaying whichever sequence you are currently editing in.

Why is this helpful? Pretend you are the lead editor on a motion picture. The movie has 20 scenes that need to be edited. (Scene 01: The cat burglar prepares for the heist; Scene 02: The night guard at the museum falls asleep, and so on.) In order to stay on schedule and under budget, you want to start editing right away but there's a problem; the movie is being shot out of order. Scene 05 was shot yesterday, and Scene 18 will be shot tomorrow.

Being the expert Premiere Pro user that you are, you decide to create 20 different sequences, which means you have 20 Timelines to choose from. You can start building Scene 05 in its own Timeline window, instead of waiting to start at Scene 01, then Scene 02, and so on. Tomorrow you will build Scene 18 in its own Timeline window.

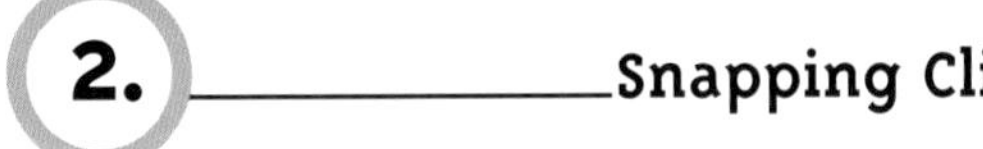

2. Snapping Clips

Snapping is a behavior in Premiere Pro that causes edges of clips to get "sticky." Sounds weird, but it is extremely useful. Imagine a magnet at the beginning and end of every clip you add to your Timeline. When the clip edges get near each other, they will "snap" together. If you move the clip far enough away, they will not be attracted to each other.

Snapping prevents small gaps between clips, which otherwise could result in blank video when played. The following exercise will demonstrate the art of snapping.

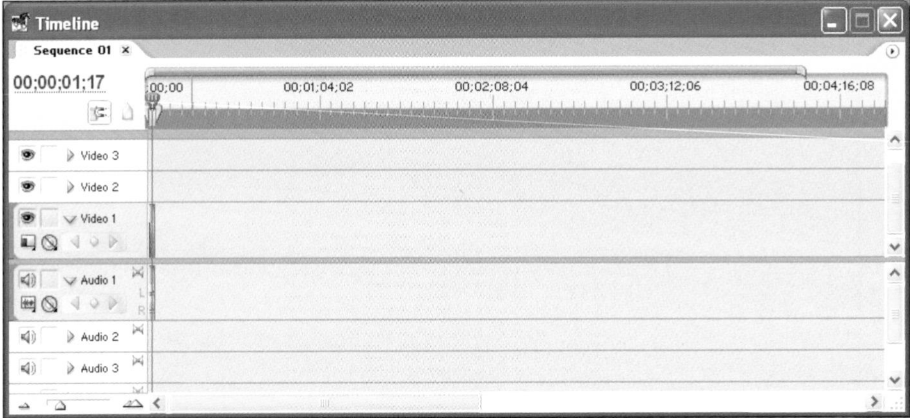

1. If Premiere Pro is not running, launch it and click **Open Project** at the **Welcome Screen**. Navigate to the **c:\Premiere Pro HOT\Chapter04** folder, select **Exercise02.prproj**, and click **Open**.

Right now, you can see only a tiny sliver of a clip in the **Timeline** *window. The clip is actually of normal size, but the* **Timeline** *window is zoomed out very far.*

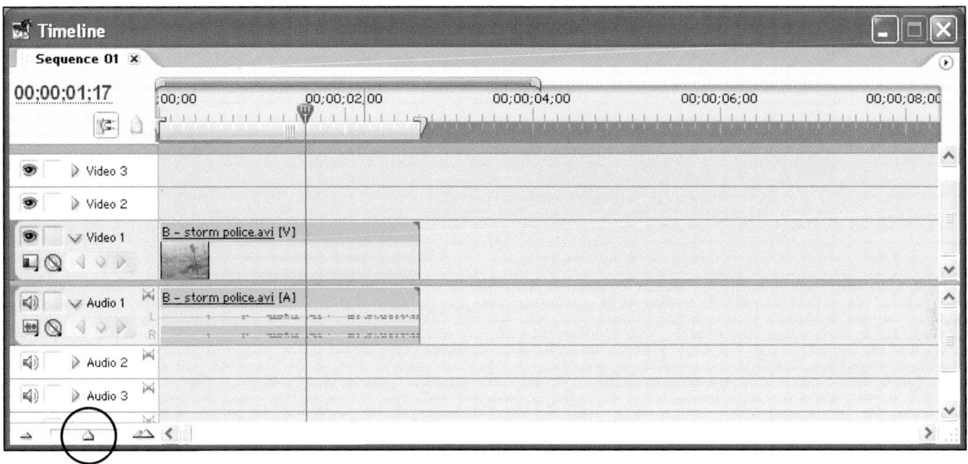

2. In the lower right of the **Timeline** window, drag the **Zoom** slide bar to the left to zoom out. Drag until the clip takes up about a third of the **Timeline** window.

---

3. In the **Project** window **Heads** bin, double-click the icon next to **Bush – Emergency.avi** to open it in the **Monitor** window **Source** view.

4. In the **Monitor** window **Source** view, set an **In** point at **00;00;00;22** and an **Out** point at **00;00;09;21**.

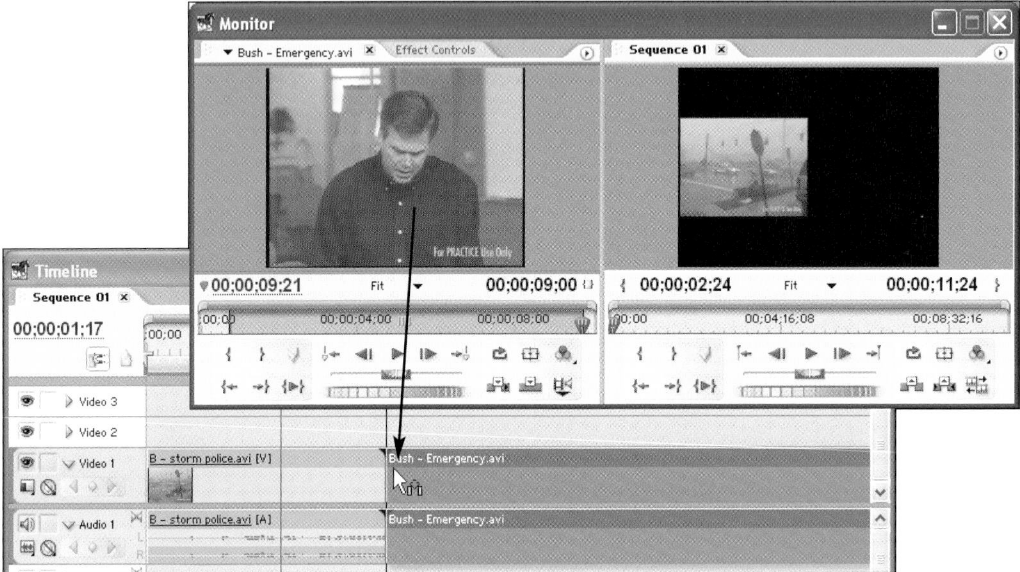

5. In the **Monitor** window **Source** view, drag the preview to track **Video 1** immediately after the first clip in the **Timeline**. Don't let go of the mouse until you see the black line at the edit point of the two clips, indicating that the clips have butted together and will not contain any small, blank gaps between them.

*Did you notice the snapping feature? If not, choose **Edit > Undo** and repeat the step. Drag the clip very slowly and you should see the beginning of the new clip appear to jump and latch on to the end of the first clip.*

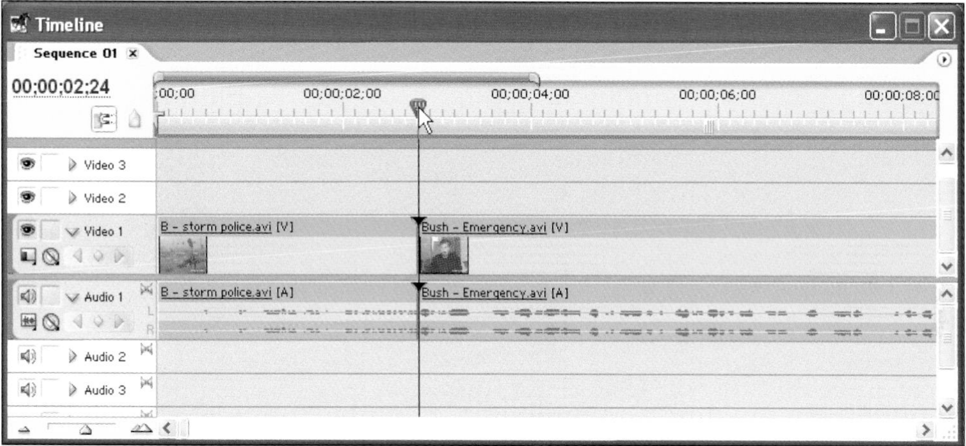

6. You can also snap the current time indicator to any **edit point**. An edit point is where two clips meet. To snap the current time indicator, hold down the **Shift** key on your keyboard, then click and drag the blue tab of the current time indicator near the edit point of Clip 1 and Clip 2. As you get near the edit point, you should feel the indicator snap, and you will see a horizontal black line indicating that you are at the edit point. You can then let go of the **Shift** key and the mouse.

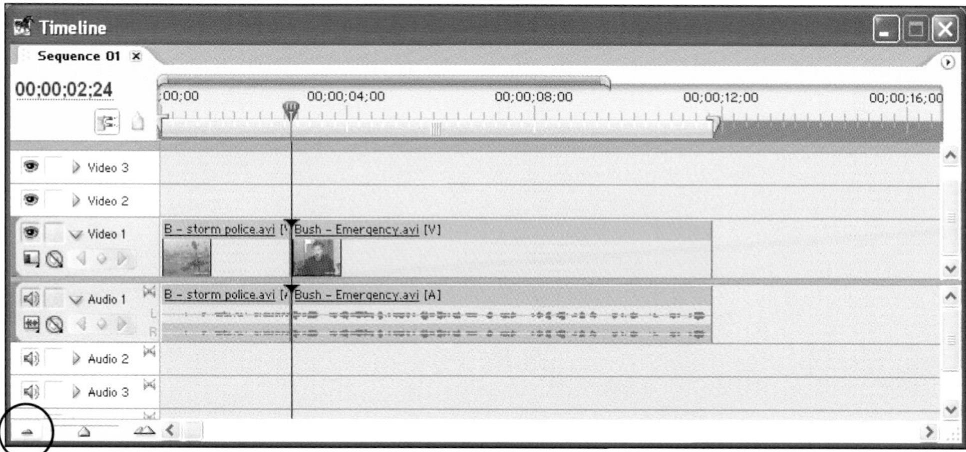

7. Click the **Zoom Out** button until you can see both clips in the **Timeline** window.

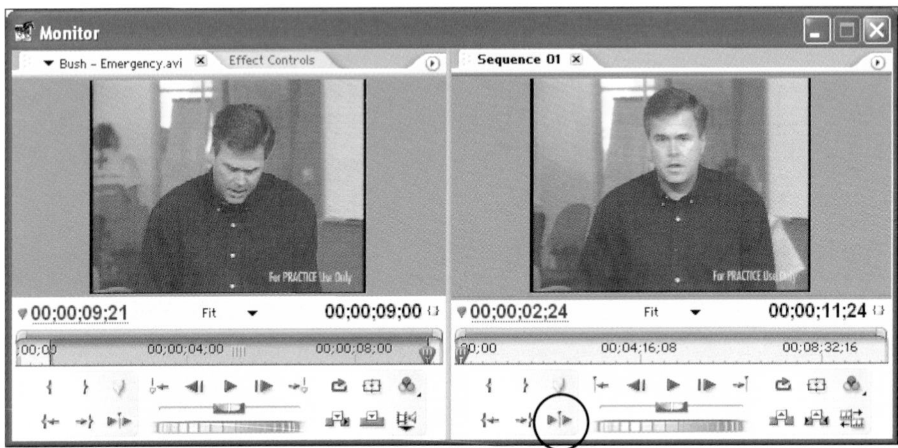

8. In order to preview your edit point, hold down the **Alt** key on your keyboard and click the **Play Edit** button. (Make sure you are holding down the **Alt** key, or you will not see the **Play Edit** button.) The **Play Edit** button begins playback 2 seconds before the current time indicator and automatically stops playback 2 seconds after the current time indicator.

*You have now created your first edit point, as well as experienced the feature of snapping in the **Timeline** window. Next you will learn how to rearrange clips in the **Timeline** window.*

---

9. Save and keep this project open before moving on to the next exercise.

NOTE | Snap On Snap Off

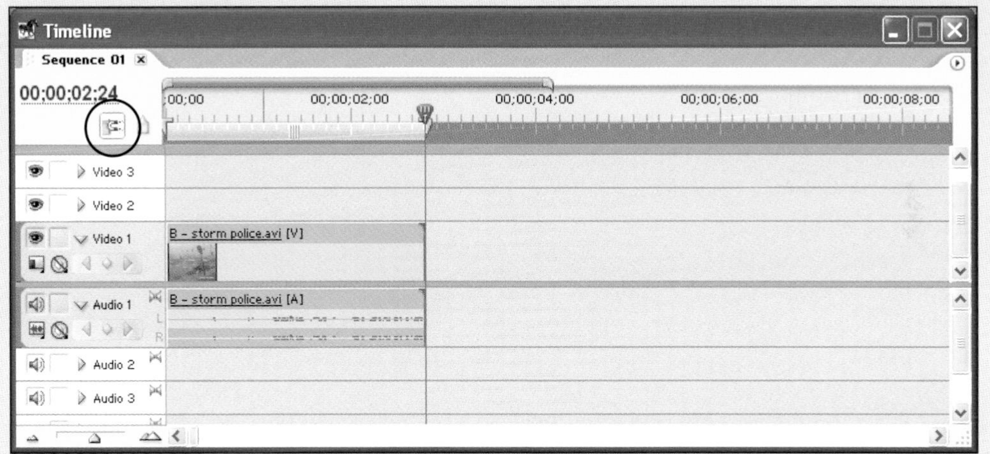

Premiere Pro allows you to toggle snapping on and off. (But, why would you want to do a crazy thing like turn snapping off?) The Snap toggle, which disables or enables the snapping feature, is found in the upper-left corner of the Timeline window. When the Snap icon is highlighted, snapping is enabled, as shown in the above figure.

Unfortunately, the Premiere Pro designers decided to place the Snap toggle in the one spot where you will be guaranteed to accidentally click it. Thanks to less-than-ideal placement in the Timeline window, it is extremely common to inadvertently disable snapping. If you are having trouble getting a clip to snap, make sure that the Snap toggle is highlighted.

3. Rearranging Clips

The advantage of non-linear editing is the capability to add, subtract, and rearrange clips without having to start from scratch each time. So far you have added clips, and now it is time to remove and rearrange them. Rearranging clips is a breeze–the following exercise will walk you through the simple steps.

1. If Premiere Pro is not running, launch it and click **Open Project** at the **Welcome Screen**. Navigate to the **c:\Premiere Pro HOT\Chapter04** folder, select **Exercise03.prproj**, and click **Open**. This exercise starts where the previous exercise finished.

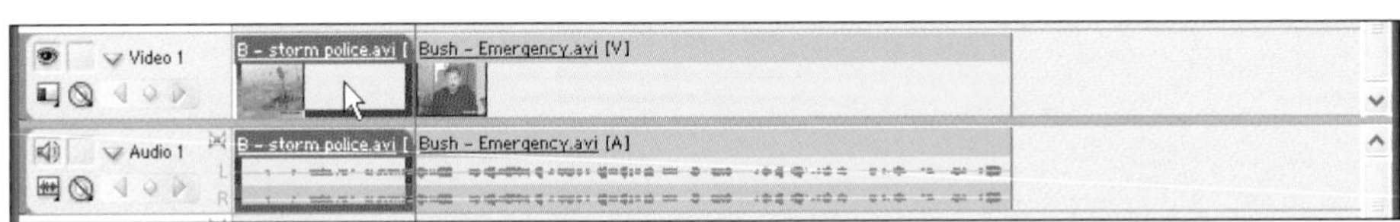

2. In the **Timeline** window, click in the middle of the first clip. The color of the box representing the clip will change to represent that it is selected.

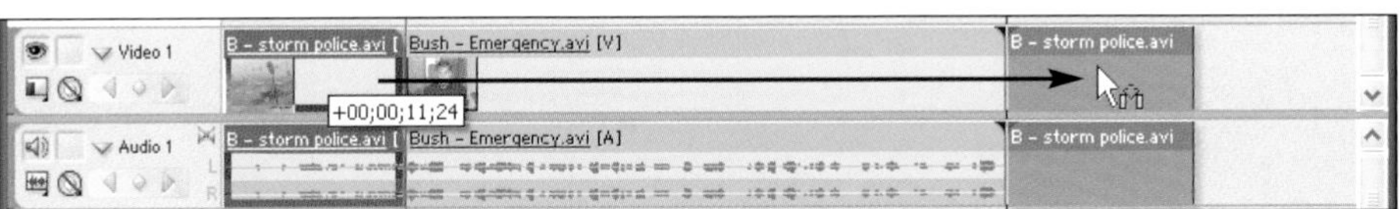

3. Click in the middle of the clip and drag it to the right, snapping it to the **Out** point of Clip 2. Make sure you keep your mouse in track **Video 1**. Let go of the mouse when you feel it snap to the **Out** point. You should see a thin black horizontal line at the new edit point, indicating that you have successfully snapped.

Tip: *When you move a clip in the* ***Timeline*** *window, Premiere Pro displays a yellow box displaying how far (in terms of duration) you are moving the clip. In this example, the clip is being moved +11 seconds 24 frames. Moving it to the left would display a negative number.*

Note: *Be careful when moving clips by dragging. If you move your mouse too far up or down, you may end up dragging a clip to a different track. If this happens, don't panic. You can easily move a clip up or down to the track you intended it to be on.*

4. Now click in the middle of the first clip (the left-most clip) to select it, and drag it as far left as it will go.

Tip: Did you notice that both the video and audio clips moved as one? Premiere Pro locks the audio and video clips together so the sound doesn't get out of sync with the movement of the lips (like a bad Kung Fu movie). The audio and video can also be unlocked (see Chapter 5, "Audio").

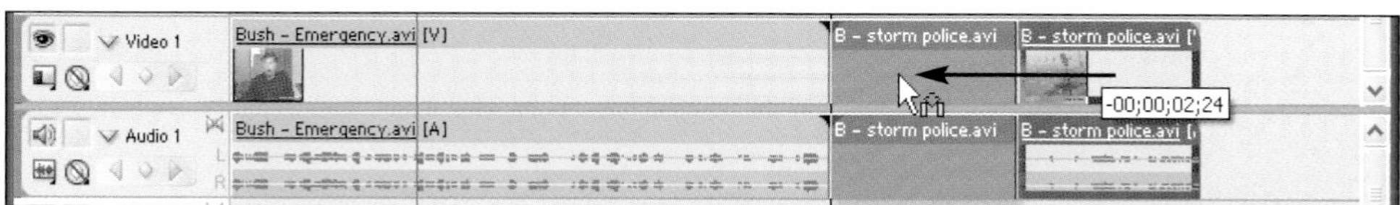

5. Now click in the middle of the second clip (the right-most clip) and drag it to the **Out** point of Clip 1.

Again you should feel the snapping effect as well as see the black horizontal line indicating a successful edit point with no blank gaps.

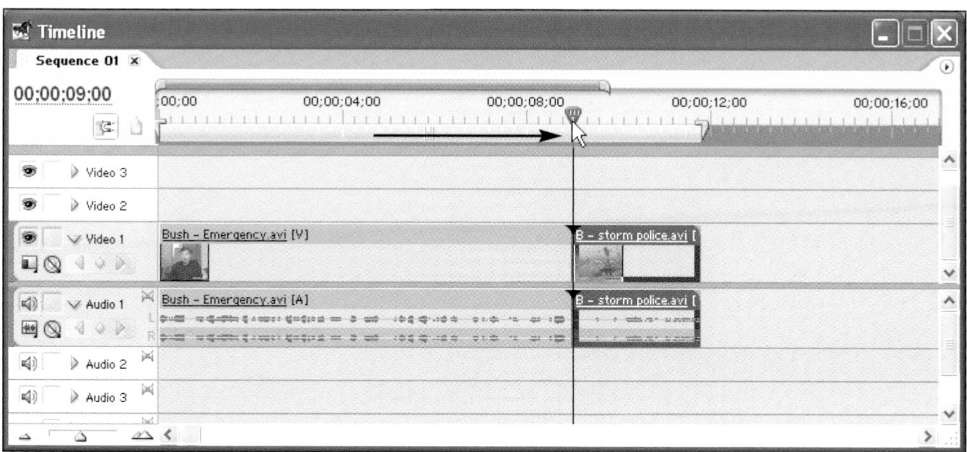

6. Hold down the **Shift** key as you click and drag the current time indicator to the edit point. Make sure you hold the **Shift** key until the indicator snaps to the edit point.

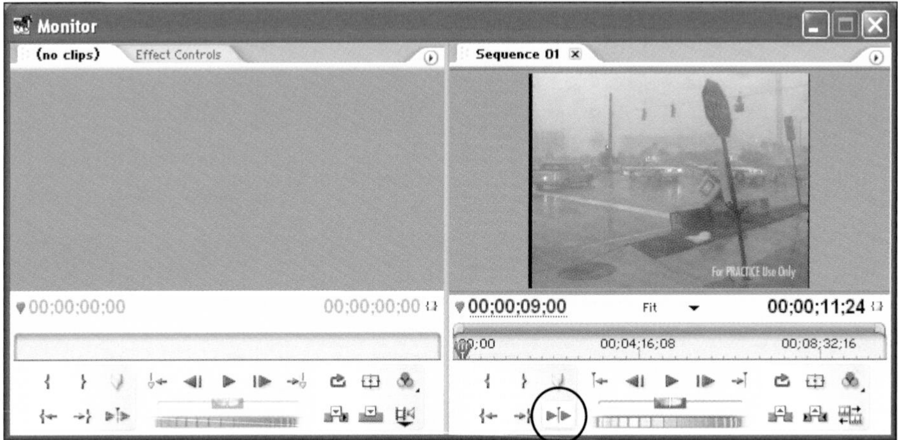

7. Hold down the **Alt** key and click the **Play Edit** button in the **Monitor** window **Program** view to preview the edit point closest to the current time indicator.

Even though you have been practicing with video clips containing audio, a nice feature of Premiere Pro is that all clips are treated equally. In other words, these same exercises would apply to images, titles, music files, and any other type of clip you can import.

---

8. Save this project and keep it open before moving on to the next exercise.

4. Moving Multiple Clips

Earlier you learned how to select and move one clip at a time. Premiere Pro also provides the capability to select multiple clips in the Timeline and move them as one group, or to remove them all at one time. To accomplish this, you will use the Track Select tool.

1. If Premiere Pro is not running, launch it and click **Open Project** at the **Welcome Screen**. Navigate to the **c:\Premiere Pro HOT\Chapter04** folder, select **Exercise04.prproj**, and click **Open**. This exercise starts where the previous exercise finished.

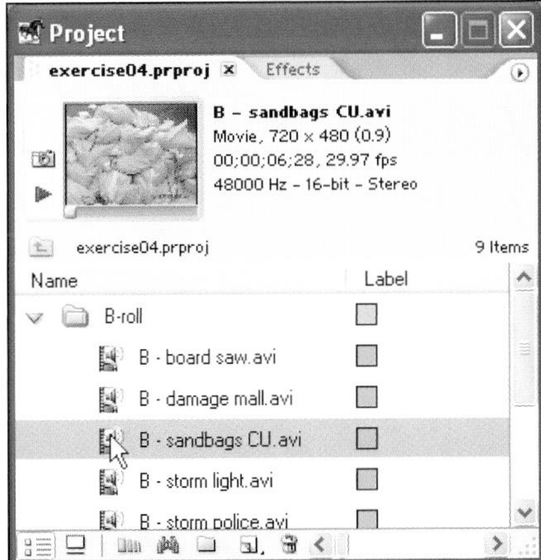

2. In the **Project** window **B-roll** bin, double-click **B – sandbags CU.avi** to open it in the **Monitor** window **Source** view.

3. This clip has too much b-roll off the top, so you are going to use only the second half of the clip. In the **Monitor** window **Source** view, set an **In** point at **00;00;03;20**. Do not set an **Out** point, so you can use the entire remainder of the clip.

*Tip: Keep in mind that a clip's **In** and **Out** points can always be changed later. Most editors prefer to make approximate **In** and **Out** points in the **Monitor** window, and then fine-tune the edit points in the **Timeline.***

4. Drag the **Source** view preview to the **Timeline** window track **Video 1**. You should feel the snap.

5. In the **Toolbox**, to the left of the **Timeline** window, click the **Track Select** tool. This tool is used to select and move multiple clips at one time and drag them to a new location and/or track.

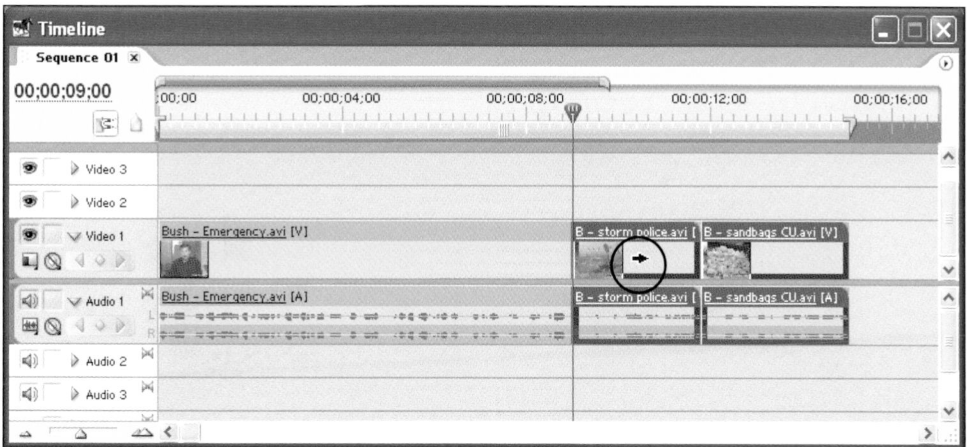

6. In the **Timeline** window, click in the middle of the second clip in track **Video 1**. This will select the second clip and all clips to the right. (In this case, only the second and third clips since there are no more clips to the right.) Notice that Clip 1 was not selected, because it is to the left of your mouse position.

Note: *Since the* ***Track Select*** *tool is active, the cursor has changed from the default white arrow to a black arrow pointing right.*

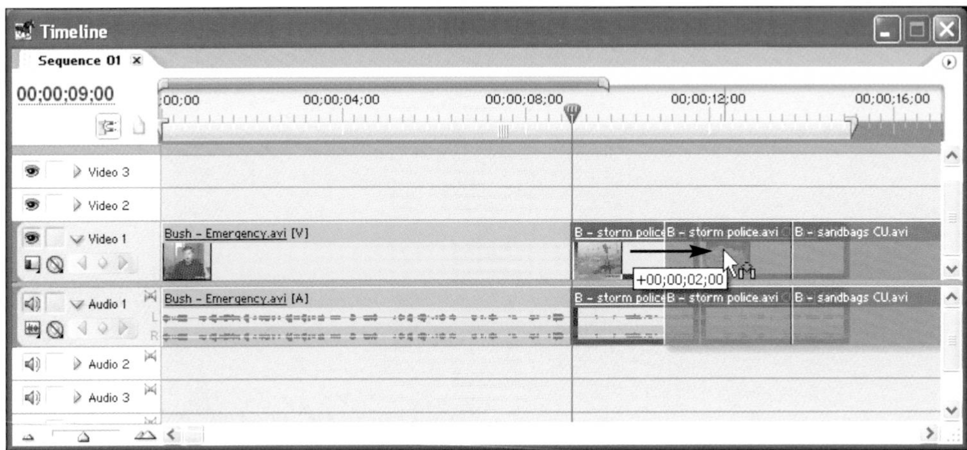

7. In the **Timeline** window, click Clip 2 and drag it **+00;00;02;00** to the right (doesn't have to be exact). All of the clips to the right of the mouse should move together at the same time. In addition, you should be able to use the yellow duration box as a guide to know when you have moved +2 seconds.

Tip: *Notice that Premiere Pro provides a "ghost" image representing the "proposed" new location of the clips. The change doesn't actually take place until you release the mouse button.*

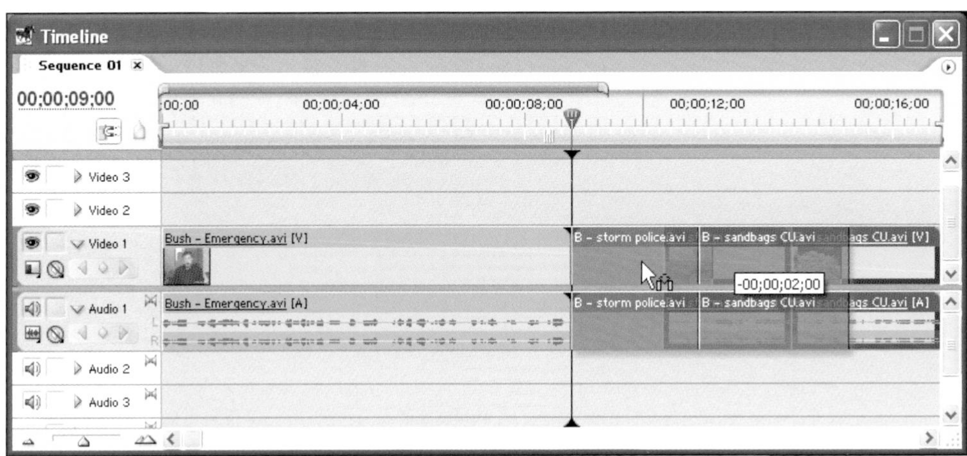

8. To move the clips back, repeat the procedure: click and drag the middle of the second clip to the left until it snaps to the end of Clip 1.

Tip: *You could also choose* ***Edit > Undo****, but there's no fun in that!*

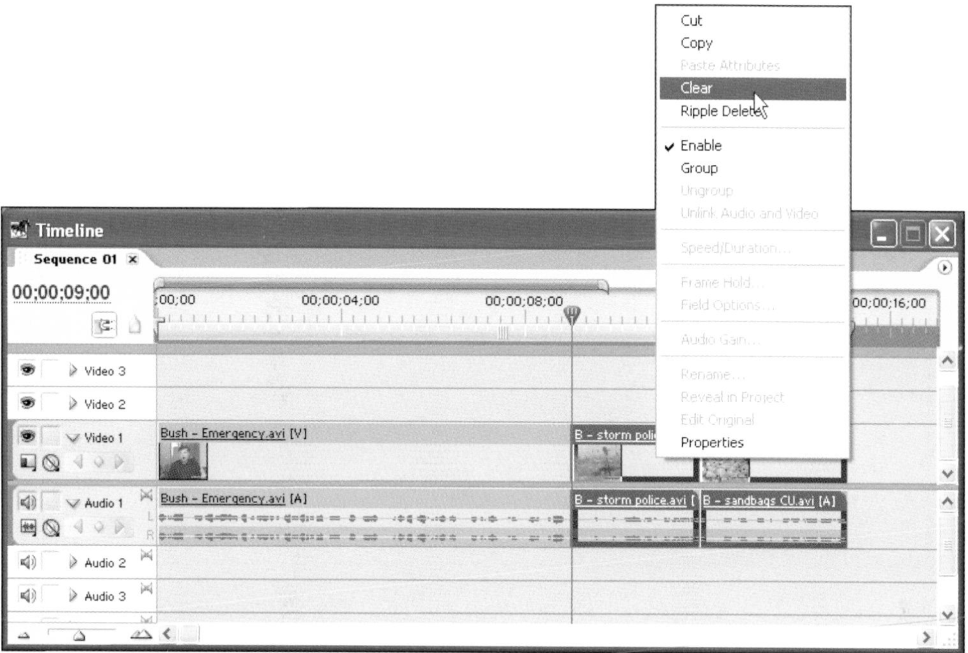

9. Hopefully the idea behind selecting multiple clips is clear: You can do everything with multiple selected clips that you can do with a single selected clip. This also applies to removing clips from the **Timeline**. With the **Track Select** tool still chosen, right-click in the middle of **B – storm police.avi**. From the pop-up menu that appears, choose **Clear**.

---

10. When you are done, click the default **Selection** tool in the **Toolbox**.

Note: *It is very important to get in the habit of always clicking the default* ***Selection*** *tool after using another tool. This is because Premiere Pro will behave differently depending on which tool is chosen in the* ***Toolbox.*** *Forgetting which tool is chosen can lead to many accidents down the road.*

That is the ease and simplicity of moving multiple clips. Granted, you moved only two clips in this exercise, but the action would have been the same even if it was 200 clips.

---

11. Save and close this project before moving on to the next exercise.

5. The Ripple Delete

A **Ripple Delete** is similar to the Clear function that you just practiced, except that after you remove a clip from the Timeline, it "scoots" all of the other clips over to close the gap that was left behind. In this exercise, you will practice the art of Ripple Delete.

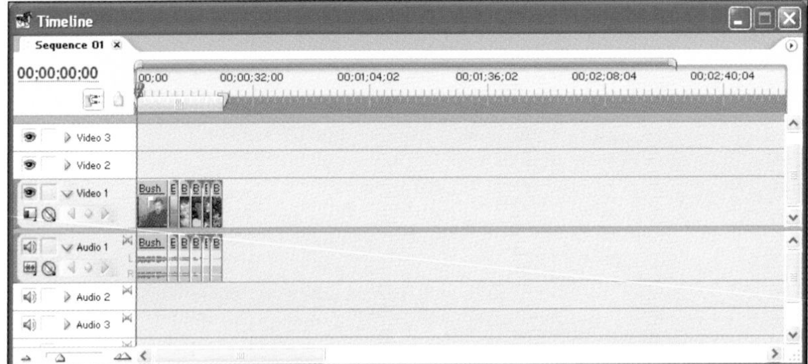

1. If Premiere Pro is not running, launch it and click **Open Project** at the **Welcome Screen**. Navigate to the **c:\Premiere Pro HOT\Chapter04** folder, select **Exercise05.prproj**, and click **Open**.

*You should see a **Timeline** that has six clips, although the **Timeline** window is zoomed out very far, and the clips appear very tiny.*

2. If it's not already selected, click the default **Selection** tool in the **Toolbox**.

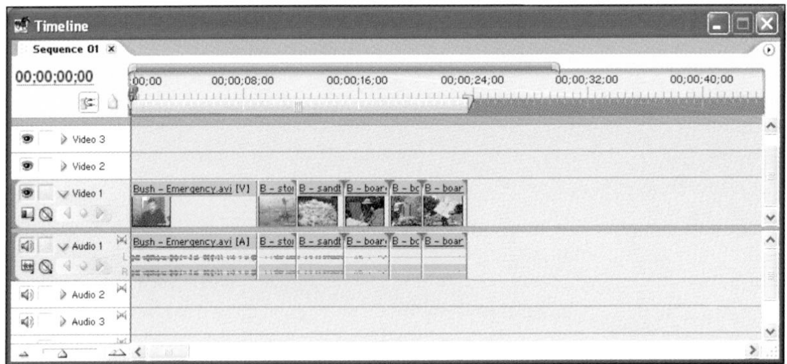

3. Currently, the **Timeline** window is zoomed out, making it hard to see the clips. In the lower-left corner of the **Timeline** window, click the **Zoom In** button until the six clips take up at least half of the **Timeline**.

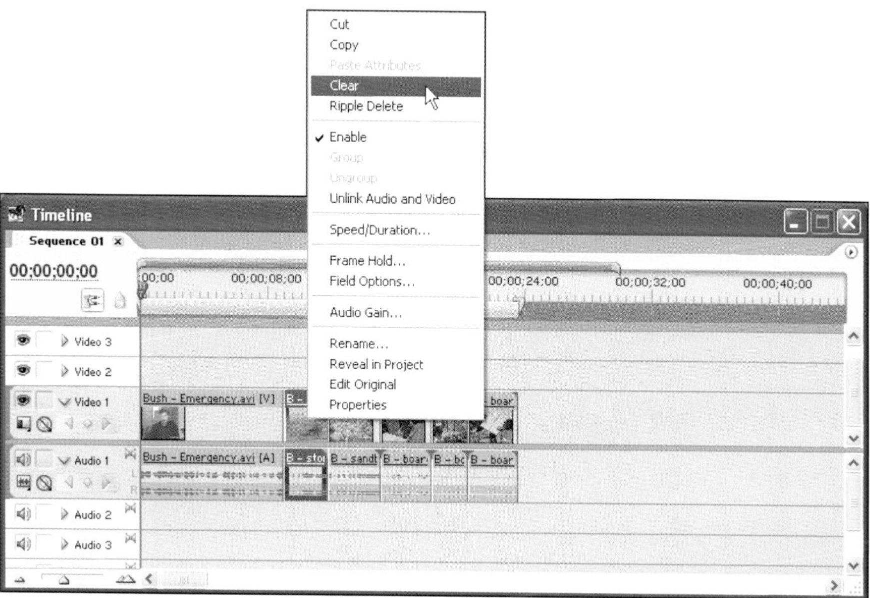

4. First, take a look at what happens when you clear a clip. Right-click in the middle of the second clip on the **Timeline**. From the pop-up menu that appears, choose **Clear**.

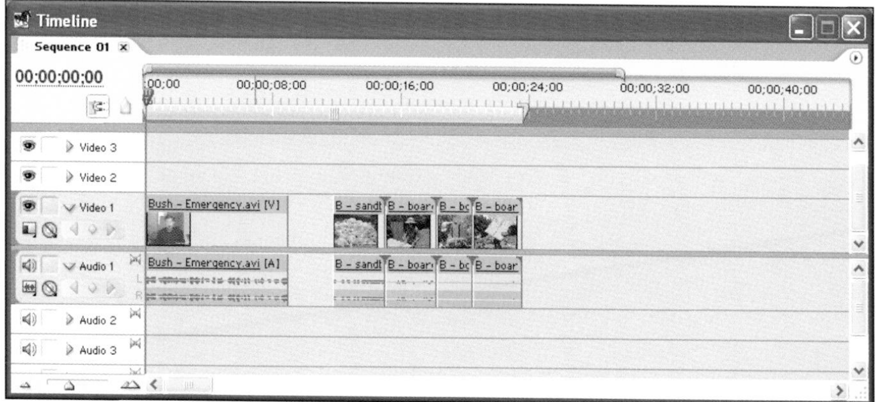

*Notice that a gap, approximately 3 seconds long, was left where the clip had previously been. If you were to play the **Timeline**, you would see 3 seconds of black video where the gap is—that's not good!*

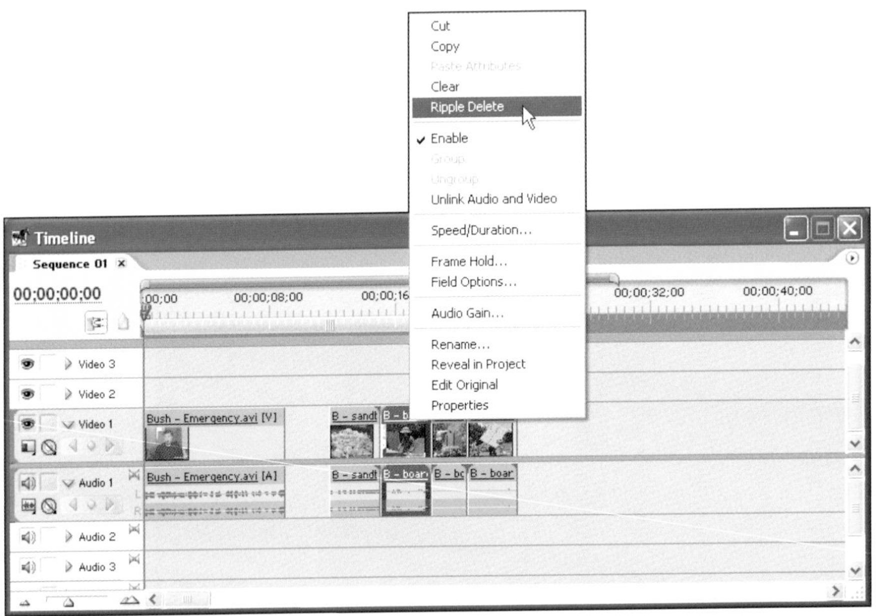

5. This time, use the **Ripple Delete** function and watch what happens. Select the third clip on the **Timeline**. From the pop-up menu that appears, choose **Ripple Delete**.

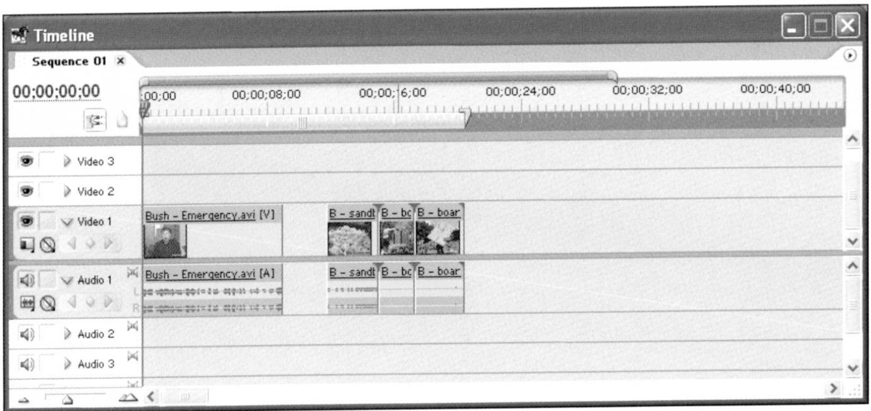

*Notice that all of the remaining clips on the **Timeline** (the clips to the right of the one you deleted) were all shifted to the left, closing the gap that would have been created. This prevents any black video between your clips.*

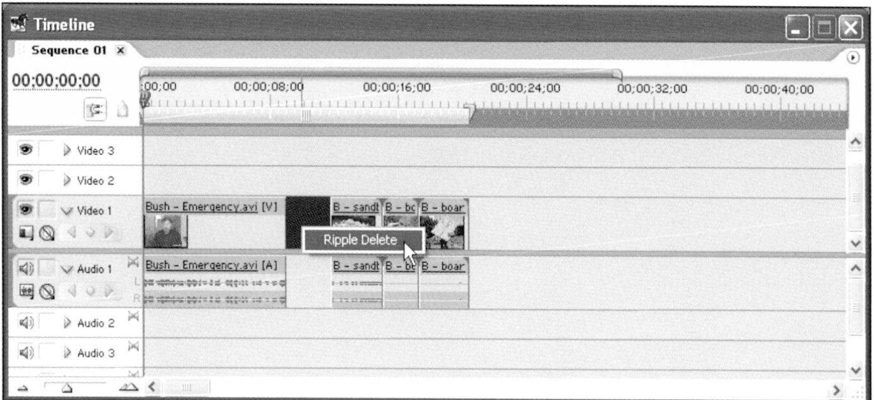

6. The only problem you have left is that you still have the 3-second gap from Step 4. A nice feature of Premiere Pro is that you can right-click in gaps to **Ripple Delete** them. In this case, right-click your mouse in the 3-second gap. From the pop-up menu that appears, choose **Ripple Delete**. This will shift all remaining clips on the **Timeline** to the left in order to close the gap.

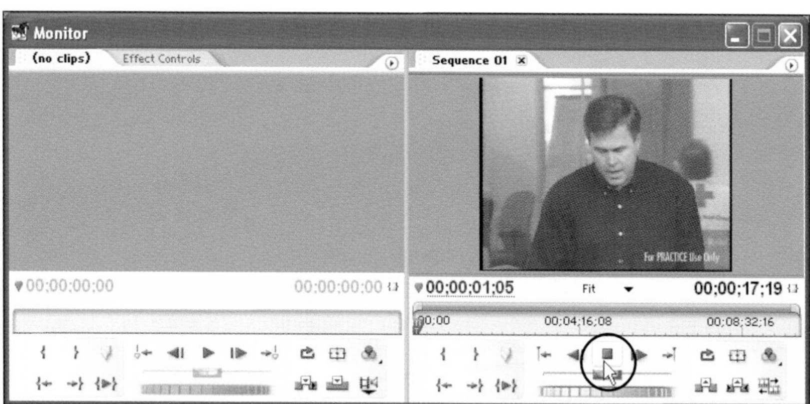

7. In the **Program** view of the **Monitor** window, click the **Play** button to watch the sequence in the **Timeline**.

*The **Ripple Delete** function is an editor's best friend. Remember, you can **Ripple Delete** clips in order to prevent gaps, and you can also **Ripple Delete** any existing gaps in your **Timeline**.*

8. Save and close this project before moving on to the next exercise.

6. Trimming Clips in the Timeline

In the previous chapter, you set In and Out points for clips in the Monitor window. Now that the clips are in the Timeline, you can fine-tune them by trimming their In and Out points even further. In this exercise, you will learn how to change the In and Out points of a clip in the Timeline window by using the Trim pointers.

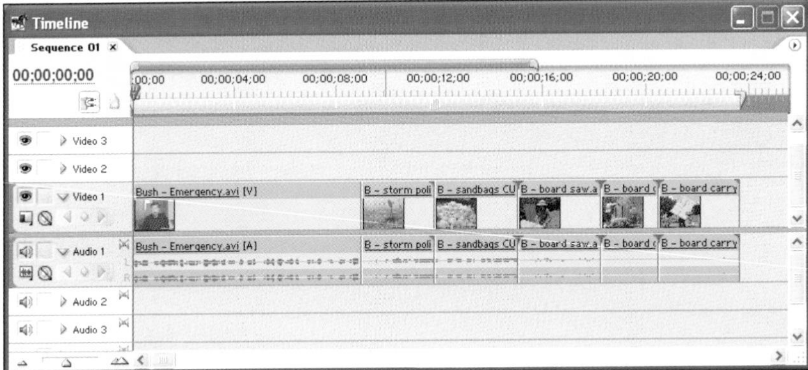

1. If Premiere Pro is not running, launch it and click **Open Project** at the **Welcome Screen**. Navigate to the **c:\Premiere Pro HOT\Chapter04** folder, **select Exercise06.prproj**, and click **Open**. You should see a **Timeline** that has six clips.

---

2. If it's not already selected, click the default **Selection** tool in the **Toolbox**.

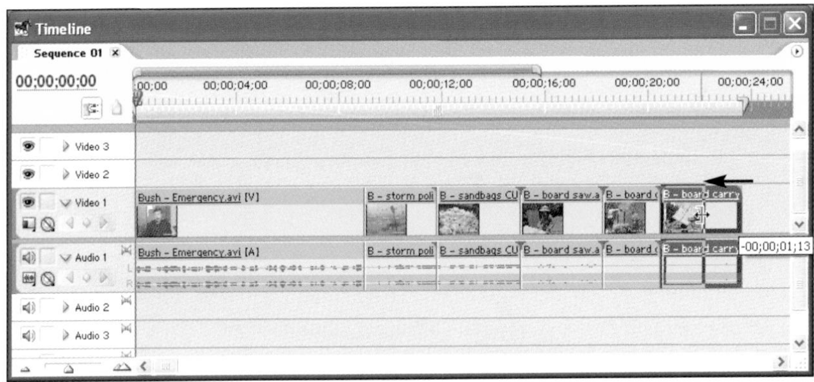

3. Perhaps you want to shorten the duration of the last clip in the **Timeline**. In this case, you are going to trim excess video off the end of the clip. Hover your mouse over the end of the last clip in the **Timeline**. Your mouse pointer changes to the **Trim Out** pointer. Slowly drag the end of the clip to the left, until you shorten the clip by about half.

*As you drag, you will see a yellow box pop up that tells you how much video you are trimming off. In the above picture, **00;00;01;13** seconds of video was removed.*

***Tip:** As you drag the **Trim Out** pointer to the left, notice that the **Program** view of the **Monitor** window shows you the current position of the **Trim Out** pointer.*

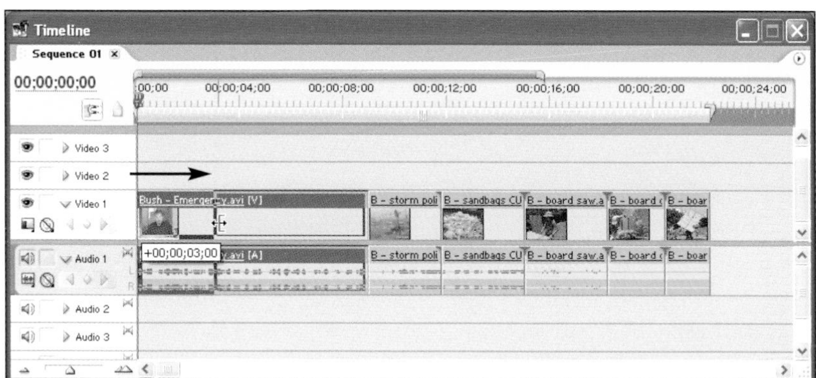

4. You can also do the same with the **In** point of any clip. In this case, you want to trim some of the video off the **In** point of the first clip. Hover your mouse over the **In** point of the first clip on the **Timeline**. Your mouse pointer changes to the **Trim In** pointer. Slowly drag the beginning of the clip to the right, until you've trimmed off about 3 seconds.

***Tip:** Remember to watch the yellow pop-up box to see how much you are trimming off. Don't worry if you are having trouble trimming exactly 3 seconds, just get as close as you can.*

5. In the **Program** view of the **Monitor** window, click the **Play** button to watch the sequence in the **Timeline**.

***Tip:** Notice the 3-second gap at the beginning? Remember how to get rid of that? **Hint:** see Step 6 of Exercise 5.*

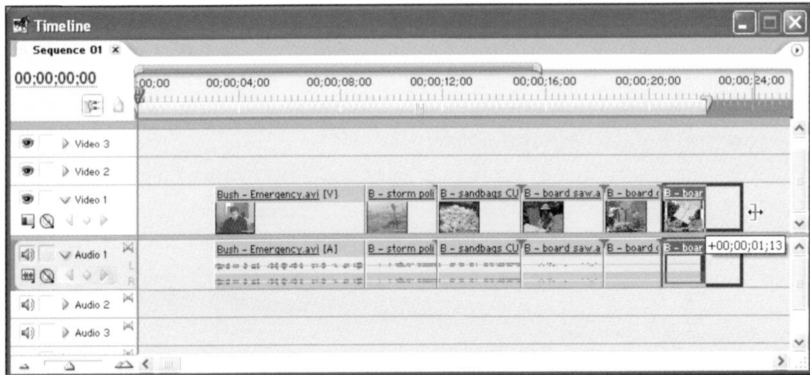

6. So far we have used the **Trim** pointers to *shorten* the duration of clips. You can also do the opposite and make clips *longer*. In this case, perhaps you changed your mind and want the last clip to play for a longer duration. Hover your mouse over the **Out** point of the last clip on the **Timeline** until the mouse pointer changes to the **Trim Out** pointer, and then drag the **Out** point as far right as you can.

Note: *You will notice that the clip can only be dragged to a certain point, and it will go no further. This means you have reached the end of the clip.*

That is the ease of trimming clips. Keep in mind that you can trim any type of clip this way: video, audio, titles, graphics, and so on.

---

7. Save and close this project before you move on to the next exercise.

NOTE | Making Clips Shorter and Longer

So what exactly is going on when you shorten or lengthen a clip's duration in the Timeline window? Hopefully this will help clear things up.

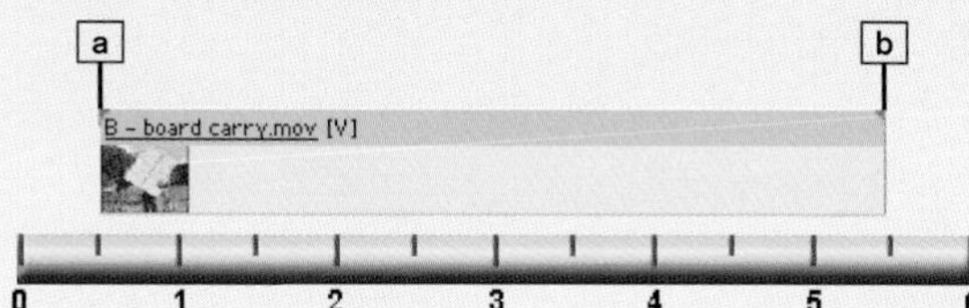

The above image depicts a source clip on the **Timeline**. The clip's **In** point (a) is at 0.5 seconds, which means the clip starts playing at 0.5 seconds in the **Timeline**. The clip's **Out** point (b) is at 5.5 seconds, which means the clip stops playing at 5.5 seconds.

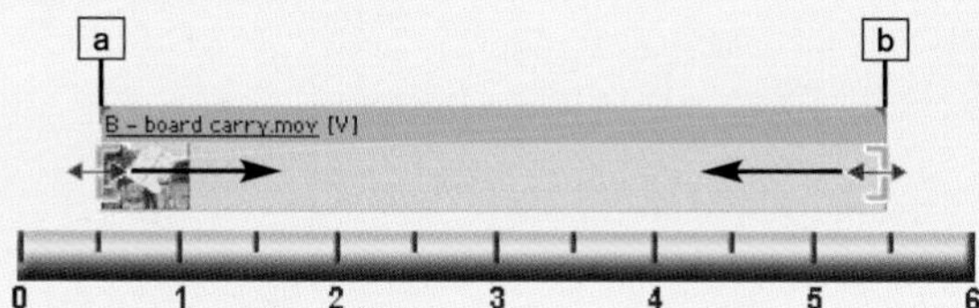

Using the **Trim In** pointer, you drag the clip's **In** point (a) to the right. With the **Trim Out** pointer, you drag the clip's **Out** point (b) to the left.

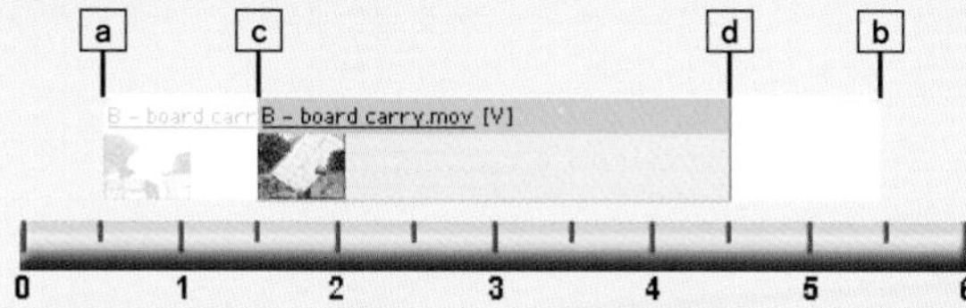

The clip on the **Timeline** now starts playing at the new **In** point (c) and stops playing at the new **Out** point (d). Points (a) and (b) have not moved and remain at the same place on the **Timeline**.

This is important and worth repeating: the clip has not moved to a new point in time. You've only changed when the clip starts and stops on the **Timeline**. But the clip still remains at the same spot on the **Timeline**.

7. The Ripple Trim Pointer

As you experienced in the previous exercise, the Trim In and Trim Out pointers allow you to change the In and Out points of a clip on the Timeline; however, this leaves a gap behind. Fortunately, Premiere Pro has another type of Trim pointer called the **Ripple Trim** pointer that automatically closes the gap, just like the Ripple Delete command that you learned earlier.

1. If Premiere Pro is not running, launch it and click **Open Project** at the **Welcome Screen**. Navigate to the **c:\Premiere Pro HOT\Chapter04** folder, select **Exercise07.prproj**, and click **Open**.

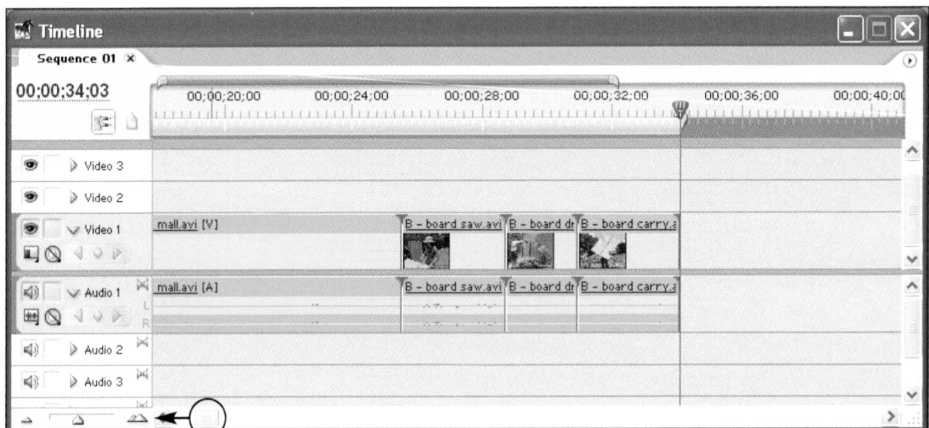

2. The first thing you may notice is that this **Timeline** is zoomed in, which means there are clips to the left of the **Timeline** window that you cannot see. Drag the **Timeline** window scroll bar all the way to the left to view the beginning of the **Timeline**.

Note: *When the* ***Timeline*** *is zoomed in too far to see all of the clips in the* ***Timeline*** *window (which will happen as your programs get longer), you can drag the scroll bar left and right to view other portions of the* ***Timeline.*** *Notice that the current time indicator does not move. The scroll changes only what is viewed in the* ***Timeline*** *window, but it does not change the placement of the current time indicator.*

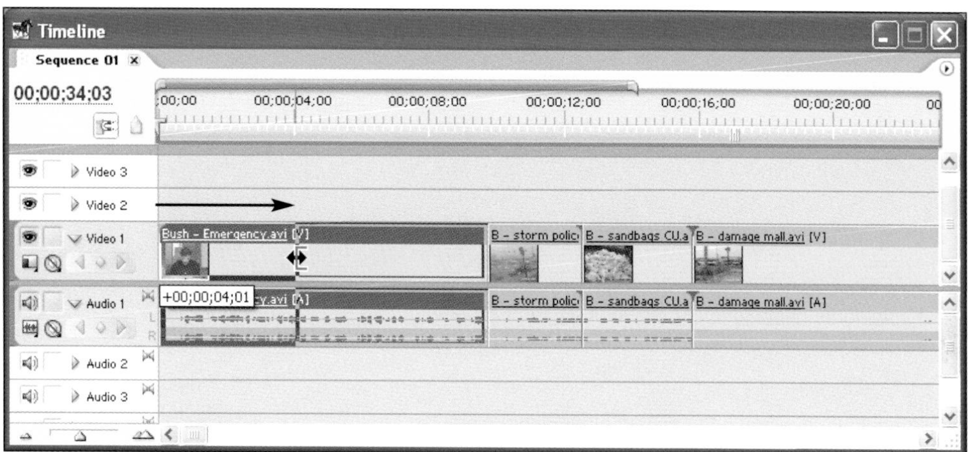

3. Perhaps the first clip on the **Timeline** is too long. In order to **Ripple Trim** the **In** point, hover your mouse over the **In** point of the first clip on the **Timeline**, until you see the **Trim In** pointer. Then, hold down the **Ctrl** key, and the **Trim In** pointer will change to the **Ripple Trim In** pointer. Continue to hold down the **Ctrl** key, and drag the **In** point of the clip approximately 4 seconds to the right.

When you let go of your mouse, the clip should appear shorter, and all of the clips should shift to the left in order to close the gap.

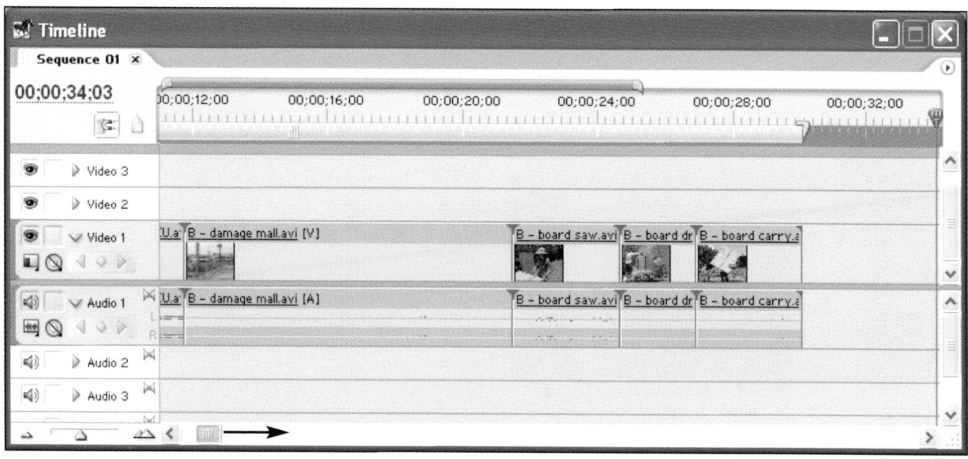

4. Scroll the **Timeline** window to the right until you can see the last four clips in the **Timeline** window.

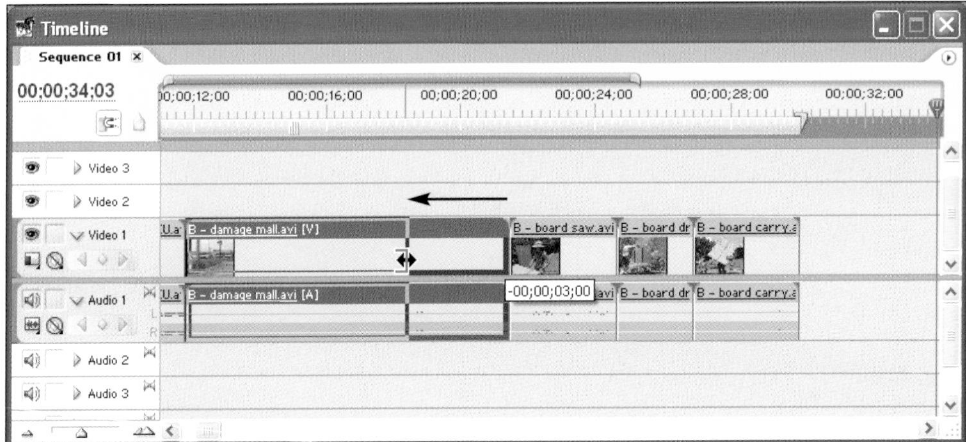

5. Hover your mouse over the **Out** point of **B – damage mall.avi**. When you see the **Trim Out** pointer, hold down the **Ctrl** key on your keyboard to change it to the **Ripple Trim Out** pointer. With the **Ctrl** key still held down, drag the **Out** point approximately 3 seconds to the left.

*Just like before, the **Out** point was modified, and the remaining clips on the **Timeline** were shifted to the left in order to close the gap.*

*In both of these examples, you used the **Ripple Trim** pointer to shorten a clip. In addition, you can lengthen a clip with the **Ripple Trim** pointer. Just like the other tools you have learned in the **Timeline** window, the **Ripple Trim** pointer applies to every type of clip.*

---

6. Save and close this project before moving on to the next exercise.

Congratulations. You have reached a milestone! You now know the basics of editing video in Adobe Premiere Pro. You can add and subtract clips in the Timeline, reshuffle clips in any order, Ripple Delete gaps, and trim their Ins and Outs. Even more exciting is that every exercise in this chapter applies for both audio clips and still images. This means that not only do you know how to assemble video, you also know how to assemble audio and images in a sequence, and you're only at Chapter 4! Of course, there's still plenty left to learn about editing audio, which you will discover in Chapter 5.

NOTE | The Big Picture

How exactly do projects, sequences, tracks, and clips all fit together? Just in case you're feeling overwhelmed at this point, take a minute to review the components that make up a Premiere Pro project. It may help you to see the big picture if you consider this book in your hands.

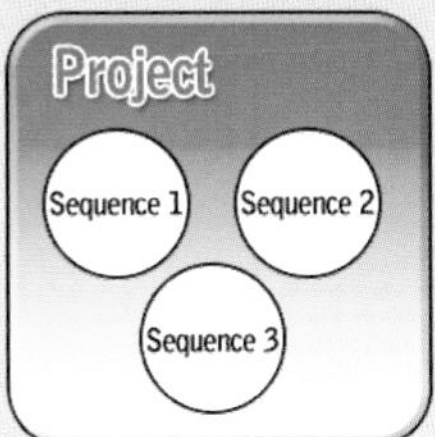

This book is like the Premiere Pro project. A book has multiple chapters. A project has multiple sequences (Timelines). Each chapter is written independently of other chapters. Each sequence is edited independently of other sequences.

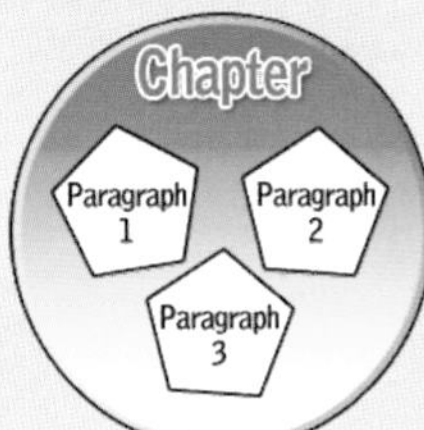

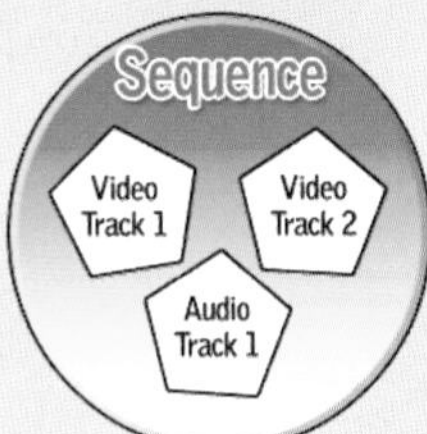

Within the pages of each chapter are multiple paragraphs. Within the Timeline of each sequence are multiple tracks.

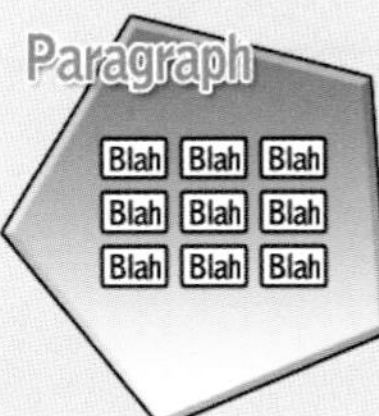

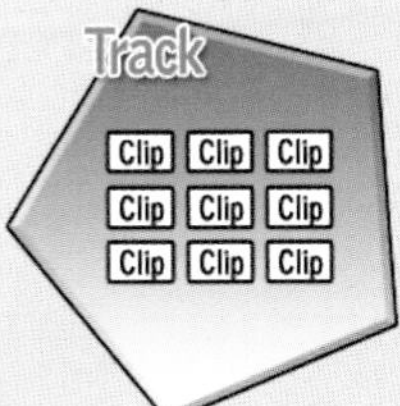

Each paragraph is filled with words that are strung together, one after another, to tell a story. Each track is filled with clips that are strung together, one after another, to tell a story.

Hopefully keeping the book analogy in mind will help you to see the big picture, and understand the relationship between projects, sequences, tracks, and clips.

5 Audio

There's nothing like adding a little music to spice up your program. Even the simple act of overlapping two pieces of video on top of the same audio clip can really increase the interest and pacing of your creation. In this chapter, you will learn the ins and outs (pun!) of adding and using audio in your Premiere Pro project.

H•O•T

Premiere Pro HOT DVD

Audio Clips vs. Video Clips

What's the difference between audio and video clips in Premiere Pro? Except for the fact that one has sound and the other has moving graphics, the two types of clips are virtually identical in Premiere Pro. Everything you've done to video clips in the previous chapters also applies equally to audio clips: importing, adding In and Out points, dragging to the Timeline, previewing–everything!

Like all good rules, there are a few exceptions. The major difference between editing audio and editing video is the *measurement of time*. Sounds fancy, but it's not.

Video is measured in terms of frames and frames per second. (Your commute to work is measured in terms of miles and miles per hour.) NTSC video has a timebase of 30 frames per second. A frame of video is the smallest segment of time into which your video can be divided.

Audio, on the other hand, doesn't play by the same rules. Each audio file can be divided into its *sampling rate*. Audio is sampled much more frequently than video's 30 times per second, and here's where it gets tricky. NTSC DV audio can be recorded at a sampling rate of 48,000 Hertz (Hertz = cycles per second). That means that for every second of audio, there are 48,000 divisions that can have an In or Out point. Remember that for every second of video, there are only 30 divisions, so that's quite a difference.

Why does Premiere Pro allow you to set In and Out points based on the audio sample rate instead of the frame rate? Because some audio edits require greater precision. For example, you may want to place an In point between two words in a sentence, but the tiny division between words doesn't conveniently fall between frames. However, since the audio samples occur much more frequently than the video frames, you can set much more precise audio In and Out points.

NOTE | Understanding Audio Sample Rate

The audio sample rate of an audio file defines how frequently the audio is sampled and how much is sampled each time. DV video comes in two audio flavors: 48 kHz 16-bit and 32 kHz 12-bit. (Almost all Premiere Pro users use 48 kHz 16-bit in their projects, for reasons that are far too boring to describe.)

Tip: Many DV cameras default to 32 kHz 12-bit audio, and many DV camera owners never change it. Refer to your camera's manual for help selecting 48 kHz 16-bit audio. Unless you are in the 1 percent of users who know when to use the 32 kHz 12-bit audio, you should definitely change your camera's audio recording properties to 48 kHz.

Here's what's going on inside your camera when you record 48 kHz 16-bit audio:

Remember from kindergarten (or maybe it was high school physics) that 1 Hertz = 1 cycle per second. DV camera microphones sample the audio 48,000 times per second, or 48 kHz. The more frequently your microphone samples, the smoother the audio file will be. If your microphone sampled only one time per second, you would hear a brief sound once a second, and you would miss a lot of what is being said.

Each time your microphone takes a sample, it samples 16 bits of audio. The larger the bit rate, the more accurate the audio file will be. Imagine that you are painting a picture of a gorgeous sunset. If you use only one paint color, you won't be able to reproduce the sunset very realistically. However, if you use 16 colors, you can mix and match to create many different color combinations, and your picture will be much more accurate.

And now you know all there is to know about audio sample rates. Next time you are at a party you can impress (or put to sleep) your friends and family.

I. In and Out Points with Audio Units

In this exercise, you will import an audio file and set In and Out points based on the audio samples in the Monitor window.

1. If Premiere Pro is not running, launch it and click **Open Project** at the **Welcome Screen**. Navigate to the **c:\Premiere Pro HOT\Chapter05** folder, select **exercise01.prproj**, and click **Open**.

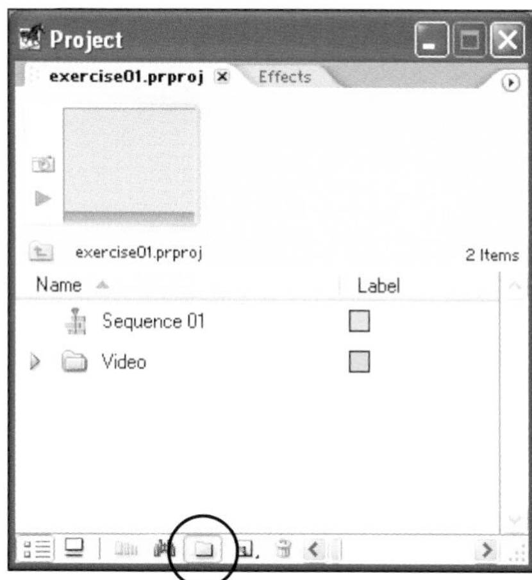

2. In the **Project** window, click the **New Bin** button to create a new bin. Title the new bin **Audio** and then press **Enter**.

Note: *As soon as you create your new bin, you can start typing the name. If you missed your chance, you can always rename the bin by right-clicking the bin and choosing* ***Rename*** *from the shortcut menu.*

3. Choose **File > Import**. Navigate to the **c:\Premiere Pro Hot\Source Audio** directory and select **Snowboard.wav**. Click **Open** to import it into your project.

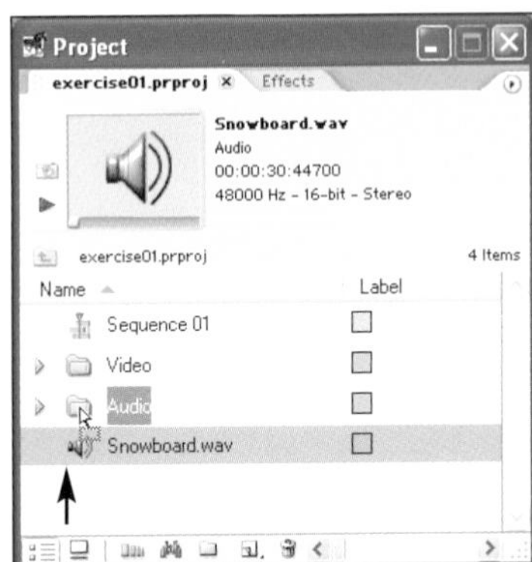

4. To place the audio file into the **Audio** bin, drag and drop the icon of **Snowboard.wav** onto the icon for the **Audio** bin.

Note: *Notice that the duration of the audio clip shown in the preview area of the* ***Project*** *window is shown in audio samples, instead of frames. The duration of the audio clip is* ***00:00:30:44700.*** *Since there are 48,000 samples per second (48kHz), the duration could also be written as* ***30 seconds + 44700ths/48000ths*** *of a second, which is nearly 31 seconds.*

---

5. In the **Project** window, double-click the icon of **Snowboard.wav** to open it in the **Monitor** window.

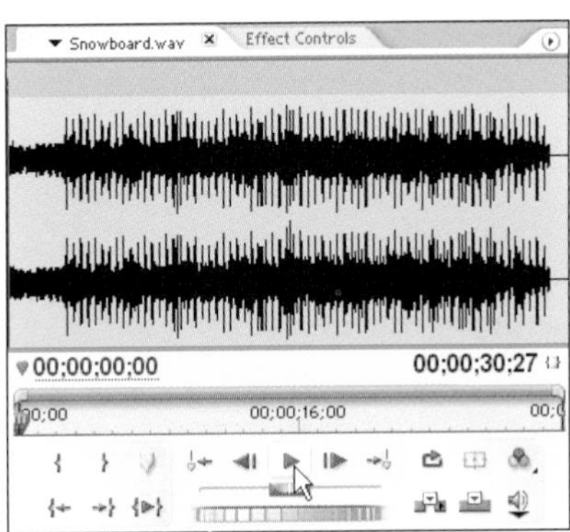

6. Notice that the **Monitor** window **Source** view shows the waveform of the audio file. The waveform represents the loudness at each point in the audio file. The louder the sound, the taller the line on the waveform. In the **Monitor** window, click the **Play** button to listen to your audio file.

Note: *At this point you should hear audio through your computer speakers. If you do not hear any sound, make sure that your speakers are plugged in, turned on, and properly connected to your PC. If you still do not hear any sound, make sure that the volume control of your operating system is properly configured and set at an appropriate level.*

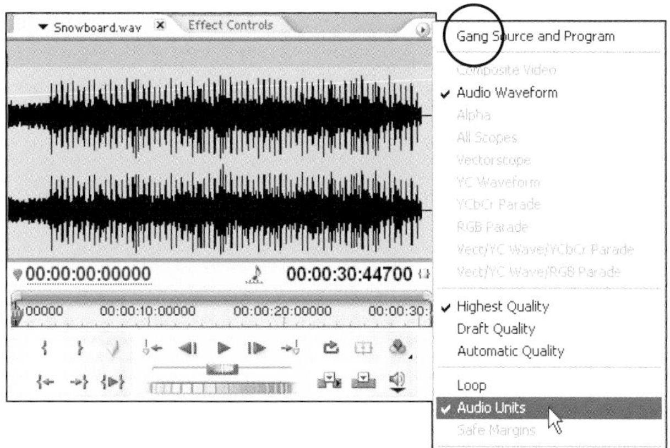

7. Currently, the **Monitor** window **Source** view is showing the duration of the clip as **00;00;30;27**, which you may recognize as a frame rate. In order to display the audio sampling rate, you must change the time display from frames of video to audio samples. To do this, click the **Monitor** window wing menu (the little triangle-circle icon in the upper right of the window), and choose **Audio Units** from the pop-up menu.

*The **Monitor** window **Source** view displays a music note icon, which indicates that you are viewing the audio units. Also note that the duration of the audio clip now shows **00:00:30:44700**.*

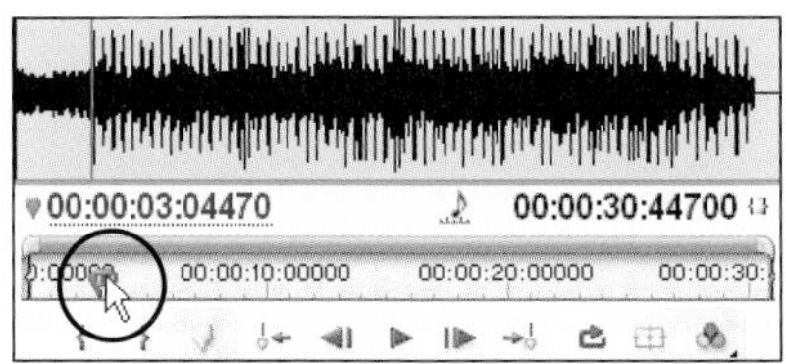

8. Next you will set an **In** point in the **Monitor** window **Source** view using the sample rate as a guide. In the case of this song, you are going to set an **In** point *after* the 3-second introduction. The goal is to set an **In** point on the beat of the music, so nobody notices your edit. Drag the current time indicator in the **Monitor** window **Source** view to approximately **3** seconds. Use the waveform as your guide. You can easily see where the music *kicks in*, as the waveform gets taller.

***Note:** Audio files are represented by waveforms in the **Monitor** window. The taller the waveform, the louder the sound. Right now the waveform looks more like vertical lines than a wave. This is because you are zoomed out very far.*

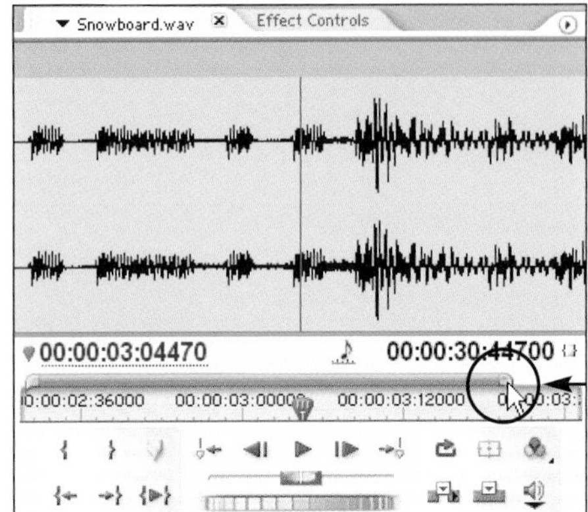

9. Because you want a very precise **In** point, you need to zoom in on the **Monitor** window. Above the time ruler is a dark gray bar, with curved handles on each side. This is the viewing area bar, and it represents how much of the original clip is viewed in the **Monitor** window. When the viewing area bar is at its maximum width, the entire clip is visible. When the viewing area bar is contracted, the **Monitor** window zooms in for a more detailed view of the clip. Drag the right handle of the viewing area bar slowly to the left, in order to zoom in the **Monitor** window.

Tip: *As you zoom in, notice that the waveform actually starts to look like a wave. If you condensed the viewing area bar to its minimum, you would see one continual wave, like a string.*

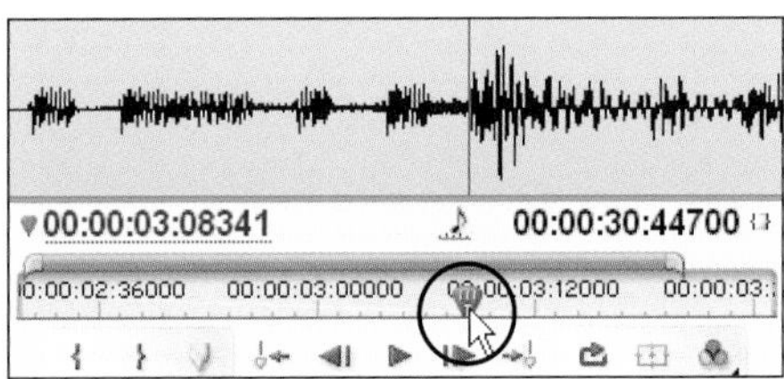

10. Unless you have rock-solid mouse dragging skills, you probably noticed as you zoomed in that your current time indicator was not exactly at the start of the beat. Drag the current time indicator up to the very start of the beat.

Tip: *The beat is represented by an increase in the amplitude of the waveform. Remember, as the amplitude increases (waveform grows taller), the music gets louder. Music beats tend to have a drum rhythm or other percussion effect that causes the amplitude to quickly "spike." These amplitude increases can be used to gauge the start of any beat. In the above example, the waveform is very thin between beats, but you can clearly see where the volume rapidly increases at the beat.*

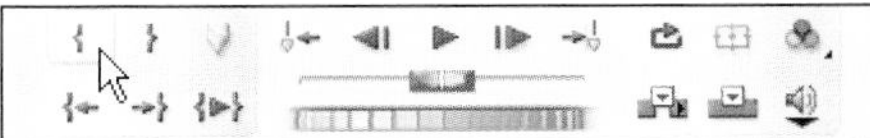

11. Once you are satisfied with the placement of your current time indicator, click the **Set In** point button to set an **In** point.

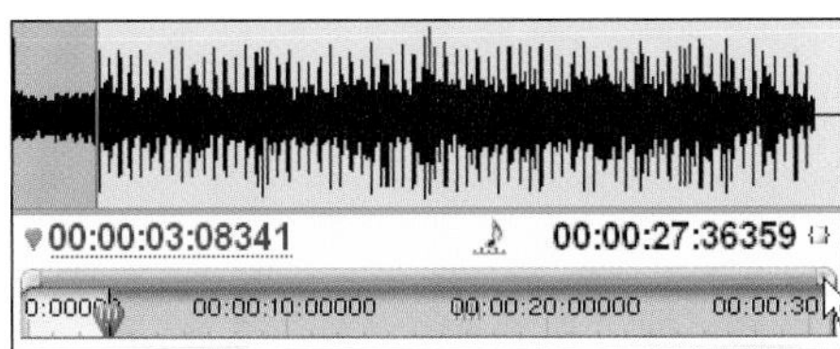

12. Don't forget to zoom back out! Drag the handle of the viewing area bar all the way to the right to maximize the viewing area.

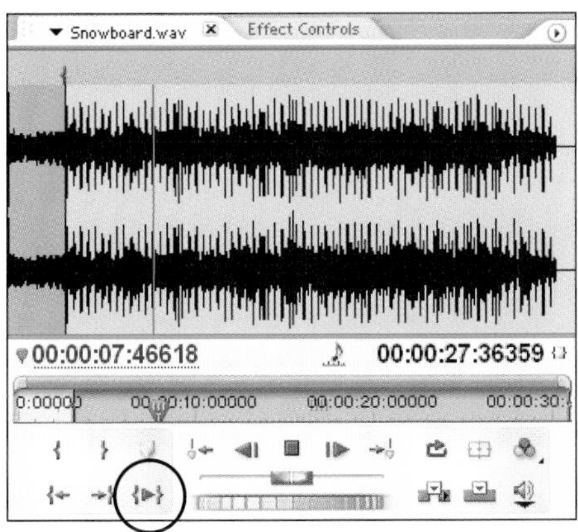

13. Click the **Play In to Out** button to listen to your music starting at the **In** point you just set.

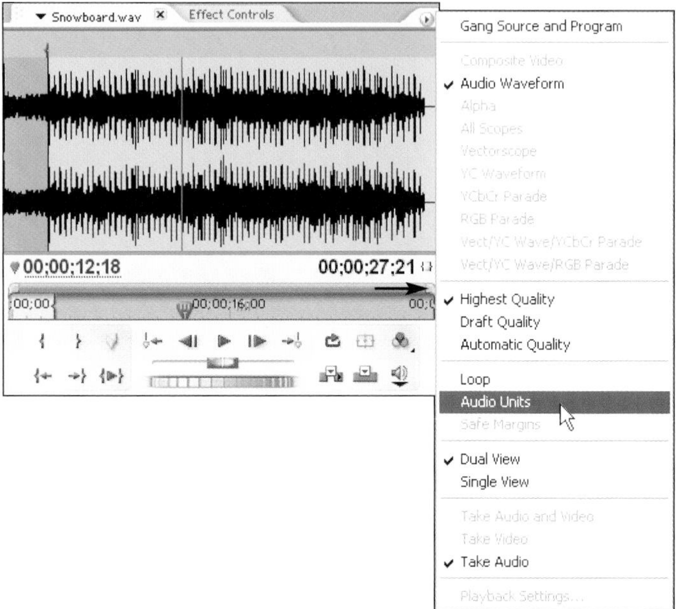

14. The **Monitor** window will display audio units for every future clip until you turn off **Audio Units**. So it's always a good idea to turn them off when you are done setting audio **In** and **Out** points. To do this, click the **Monitor** window wing menu and choose **Audio Units** from the pop-up menu, which toggles them off. Your **Monitor** window should no longer show the music note icon above the viewing area bar.

*Whew! That was by far one of the most difficult types of edits you can make in Premiere Pro. Congratulations. The next step is to place the clip in the **Timeline**.*

---

15. Save this project and close it before moving on to the next exercise.

NOTE | Audio Scrubbing

Remember from earlier chapters that dragging the current time indicator in the Monitor or Timeline windows is called *scrubbing*. A nice feature of Premiere Pro is that you can choose to hear the audio as you scrub across a clip, or you can mute the audio as you scrub. When you are fine-tuning the audio, hearing each frame of audio as you scrub can be helpful.

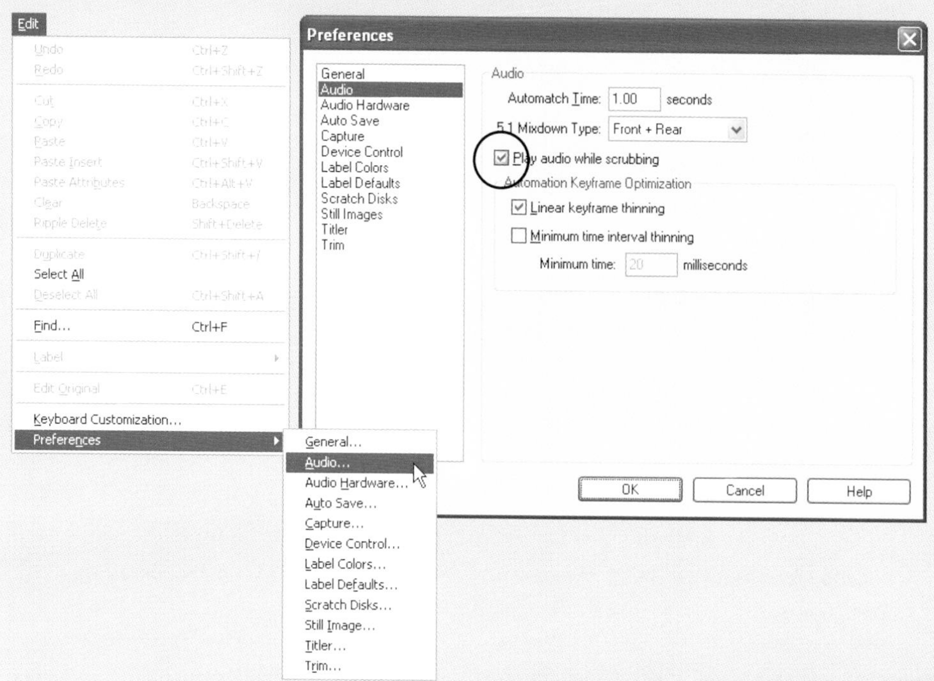

You can turn audio scrubbing on or off through the **Preferences** menu. (Of course, you can't get to the **Preferences** menu unless you have a project open.) To access this feature when you have a project open, choose **Edit > Preferences > Audio**. In the **Preferences** dialog box, check or uncheck **Play audio while scrubbing**. Click **OK** when you're done.

2. Snap Edit to Sequence Marker

In this exercise, you will place an audio clip into the Timeline, set a sequence marker in the Timeline window, and snap your Trim Out pointer using the marker as an edit point.

1. If Premiere Pro is not running, launch it and click **Open Project** at the **Welcome Screen**. Navigate to the **c:\Premiere Pro HOT\Chapter05** folder, select **exercise02.prproj**, and click **Open**.

2. Notice that the **Timeline** window already has some clips placed in **Sequence 01**. Click the **Play** button in the **Monitor** window **Program** view (the *right* side) to watch **Sequence 01**. Exciting video, but a tad boring without any audio.

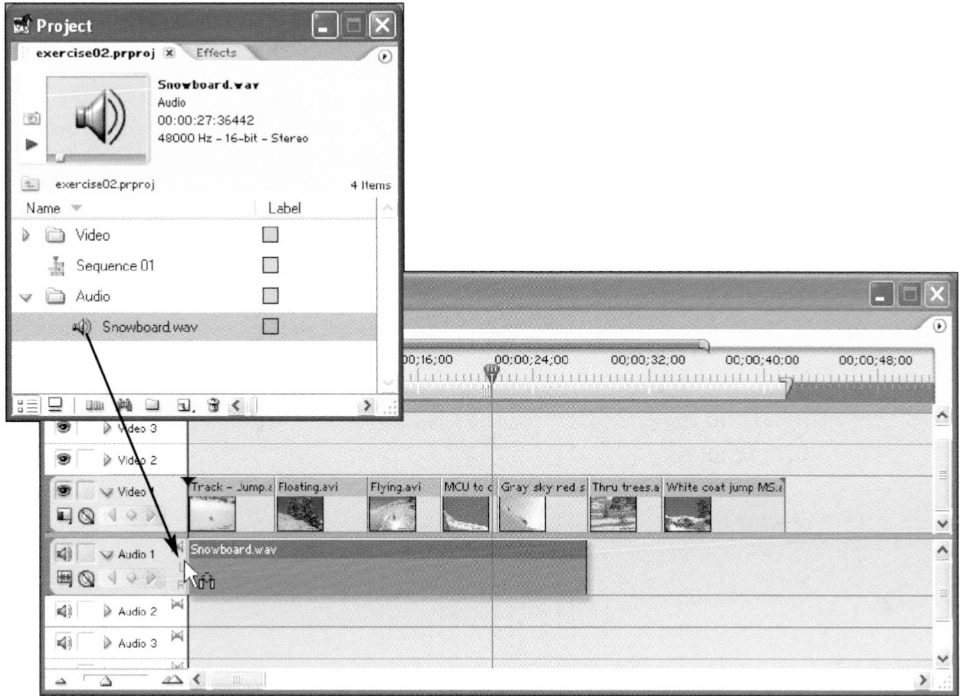

3. From the **Audio** bin of the **Project** window, drag **Snowboard.wav** to the far left of track **Audio 1** in the **Timeline** window. If you have it as far left as possible, you will see a vertical black line that shows you where the clip will be placed.

4. To watch **Sequence 01** from the beginning, click the **Play In to Out** button in the **Monitor** window **Program** view. Much more exciting with music!

*Tip: The regular **Play** button begins playback at the position of the current time indicator. The **Play In to Out** button begins playback at the beginning of the sequence/clip, or at the **In** point if one has been set.*

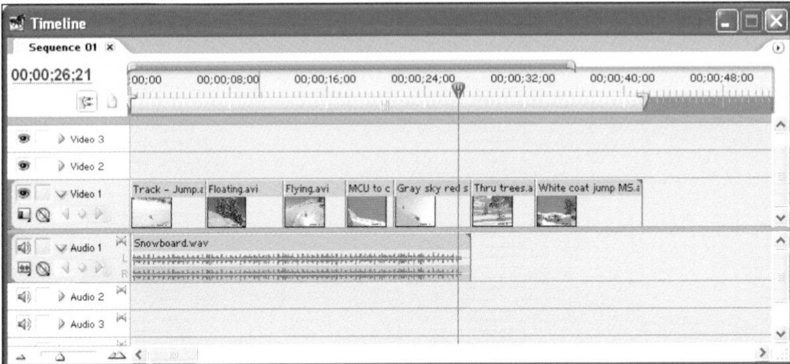

5. A slight problem: the music runs out before the video does. It's always eye-catching (ear-catching?) when the music and video end at the same time. It's a clean end, and even better–it's easy to do! To accomplish this task, you are going to create a **Timeline** marker to remember where the audio ends. In the **Timeline** window, drag the current time indicator to the frame when you last hear the music. In the example above, the current time indicator is positioned at **00;00;26;21**.

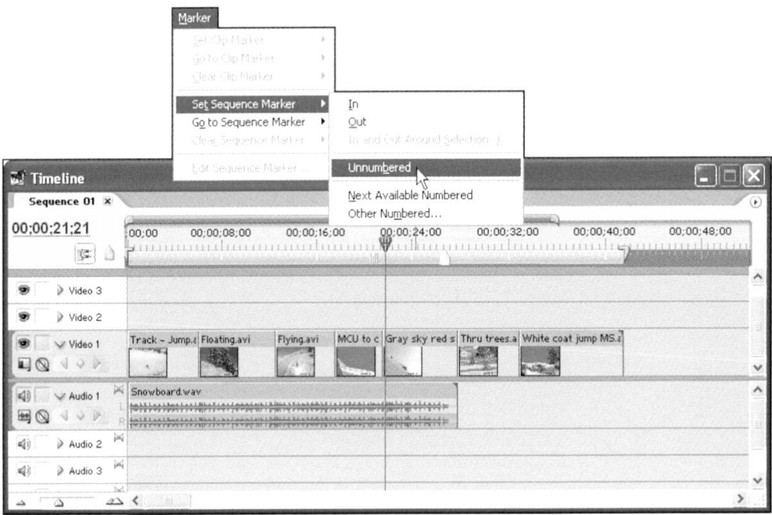

6. To set a marker in the sequence at the position of the current time indicator, choose **Marker > Set Sequence Marker > Unnumbered**. Notice that a sequence marker was placed in the **Timeline** ruler at the current time indicator. Drag the current time indicator to the left so you can clearly see the sequence marker.

Tip: *Markers are a great way to bookmark when certain events happen. You can use markers to remember when a certain action takes place in a video clip, or as you are doing in this case, to remember when an audio event happens, like the music ending.*

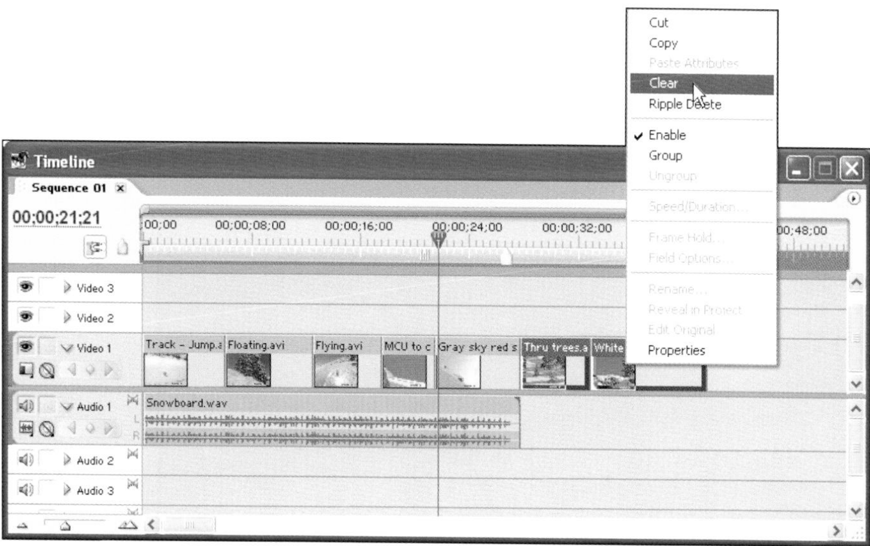

7. You won't need the final two clips on the **Timeline**, since they play long after the music stopped. To select the last two clips on track **Video 1**, hold down the **Shift** key and click once on each clip. (The **Shift** key allows you to select multiple clips.) Right-click either clip and choose **Clear** from the shortcut menu.

Note: *You could also choose* ***Ripple Delete****; however, in this case* ***Clear*** *and* ***Ripple Delete*** *do the exact same thing because there are no trailing clips to shift to the left.*

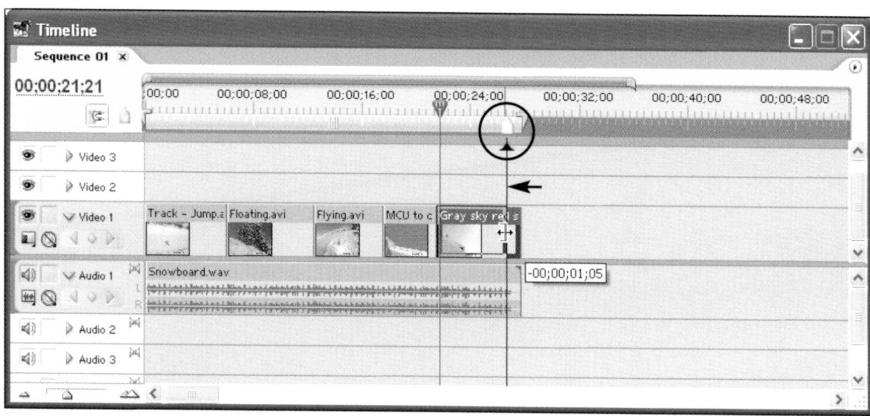

8. Hover your mouse over the **Out** point of the last clip on the **Timeline**, until you see the **Trim Out** pointer. Slowly drag the **Out** point of the clip to the left, until it snaps to the sequence marker.

Tip: *Yes folks, that's right! You can also snap to sequence markers. Life is good.*

9. Now play back your sequence to watch the music and video end at the same time. You have two options: in the **Monitor** window **Program** view, you can click the **Play In to Out** button (if you want to watch the entire sequence), or you can click the **Play** button to begin playback at the current time indicator.

*Tip: To save time, press the **spacebar** on your keyboard, which is the same as clicking the **Play** button. Press it again to stop playback.*

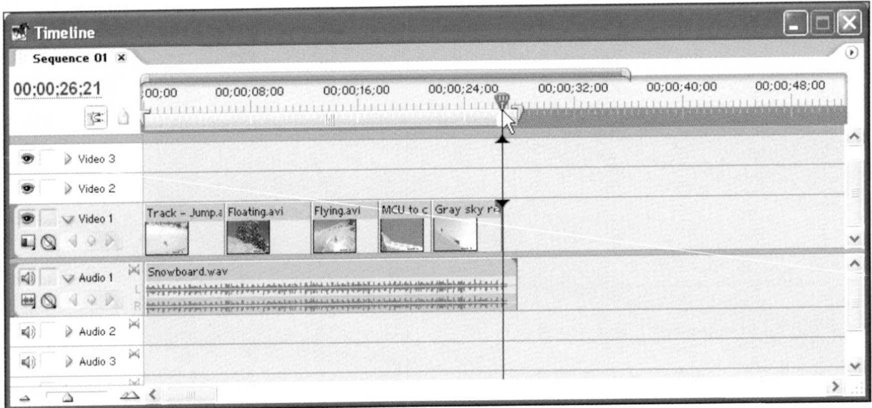

10. Just in case you want to clear the sequence marker, it'd be a good idea to know how. The first step is to move your current time indicator to the sequence marker. To do this, hold down the **Shift** key and slowly drag the current time indicator until it snaps to the sequence marker. Look for the vertical black line indicating that the current time indicator is snapping to the correct spot.

11. To clear the marker at the current time indicator, choose **Marker > Clear Sequence Marker > Current Marker**. If the current time indicator is not positioned exactly at the marker, you will not be able to choose this option from the menu. (That's why it's so important to snap the current time indicator in Step 10.)

*Tip: You could also choose **Marker > Clear Sequence Marker > All Markers** to get rid of all of them, no matter the location of your current time indicator.*

*You have just learned to add audio to the **Timeline**, navigate the current time indicator to an audio event, and add sequence markers.*

12. Save and close this project before moving on to the next exercise.

Linked Audio and Video

In the previous exercise, you used video clips that had no audio, and audio clips that had no video. But when you import clips captured from your camera, they almost always have both video and audio. Premiere Pro describes these types of clips as "linked."

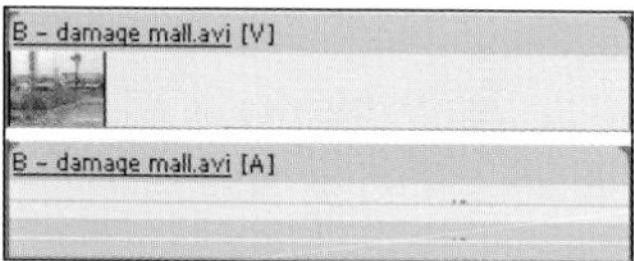

When you place linked clips into a sequence, they are represented as two clips on the Timeline: a video clip and an audio clip. Because they are linked, when you move one of the clips on the Timeline, the other one follows. It is important to remember that these are two separate clips on the Timeline, but they act as one.

Thankfully, they are not permanently attached. Premiere Pro allows you to unlink clips, as well as link unrelated clips together. For example, perhaps the audio of Take 3 was better than Take 1, but the video of Take 2 was the best shot. You can choose to separate the audio and video of the linked clip, and combine the audio of Take 3 with the video of Take 2, and so on. You can mix and match to your heart's content.

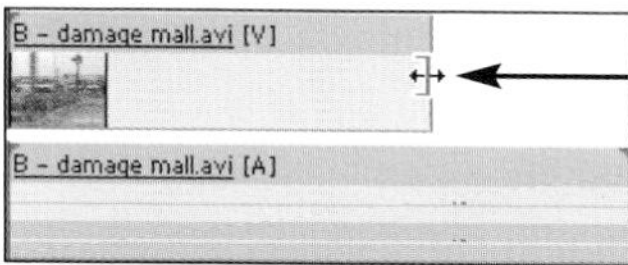

Remember the Trim In and Trim Out pointers from the previous chapter? When you edit the In point or Out point of linked video, the audio is also affected. And vice versa. However, if you hold down the **Alt** key, Premiere Pro edits only the selected portion of the clip. This allows you to have the audio from the first clip continue to play underneath the video of the next clip on the Timeline. This is a great way to create continuity between different shots, and it can prevent the audience from noticing an abrupt edit.

In the next exercise, you'll learn how to unlink audio and video, and how to edit linked clips independently.

3. Separating Linked Audio and Video

There are three methods to editing audio and video separately. You can unlink two clips, you can use the Trim pointers to edit only one portion of a linked clip, and you can choose to take only the video or audio portion of a clip in the Monitor window. In this exercise, you will practice unlinking audio and video.

1. If Premiere Pro is not running, launch it and click **Open Project** at the **Welcome Screen**. Navigate to the **c:\Premiere Pro HOT\Chapter05** folder, select **exercise03.prproj**, and click **Open**.

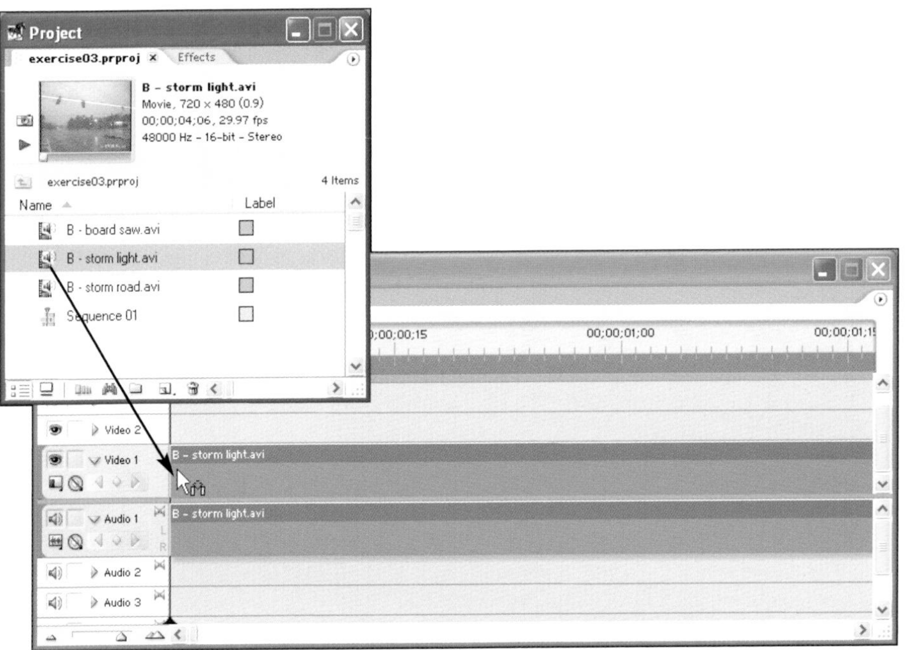

2. Next, you will place clip **B – storm light.avi** into the **Timeline** window. In the previous chapters, you opened a clip in the **Monitor** window and set **In** and **Out** points before dragging the clip to the **Timeline** window. Here's a shortcut: if you don't need to set any **In** or **Out** points, you can drag the clip directly from the **Project** window to the **Timeline** window. To do this, click and drag **B – storm light.avi** from the **Project** window to the **Timeline** window. Make sure to drag the clip to the far left (the beginning) of track **Video 1**.

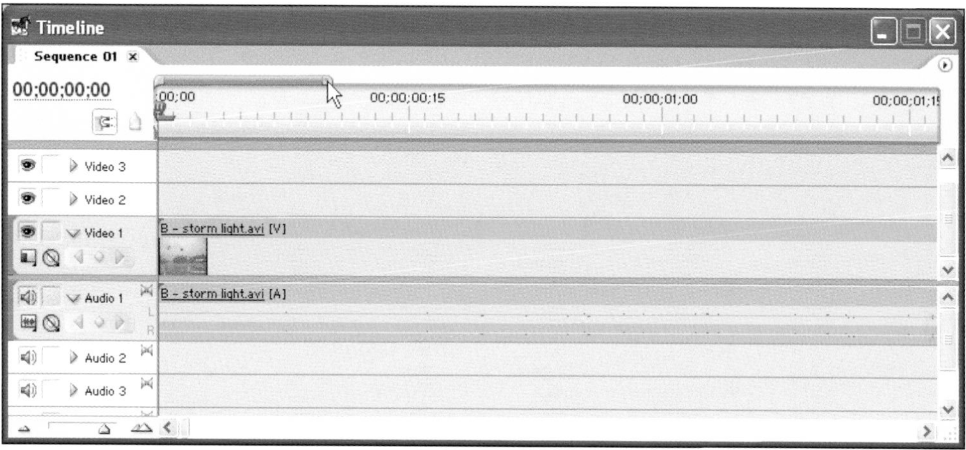

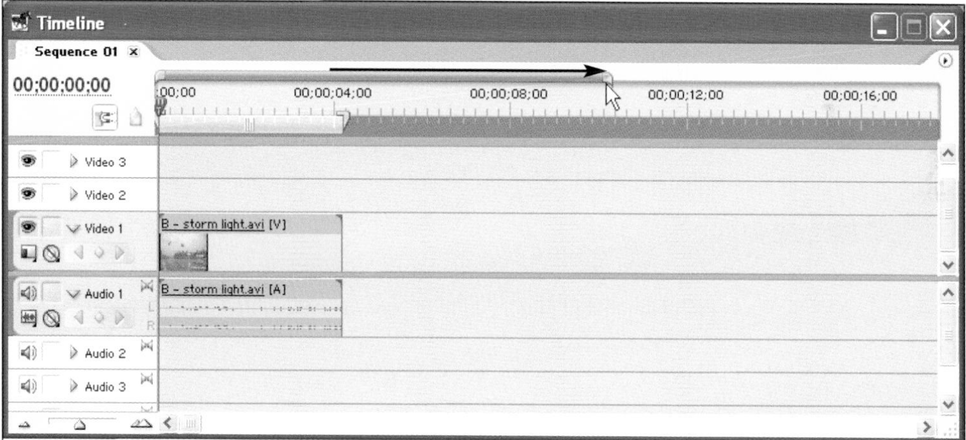

*Because the **Timeline** window is zoomed in, the clip you just placed does not fit entirely in the **Timeline** window. In the previous chapter, you learned how to zoom in or out of the **Timeline** with the **Zoom** slider bar in the lower-left corner of the **Timeline** window. Another way to change the zoom is to drag the **Timeline** window viewing area bar. (This behaves exactly like the **Monitor** window viewing area bar in Exercise 1.)*

---

3. To increase the viewing area of the **Timeline** window, drag the right handle of the viewing area bar slowly to the right. As you drag, the window zooms out, allowing you to fit the entire clip in the window.

4. Preview the sequence to watch and listen to the clip you've added to the **Timeline**. To do this, press the **spacebar** on your keyboard, or click the **Play** button in the **Monitor** window **Program** view.

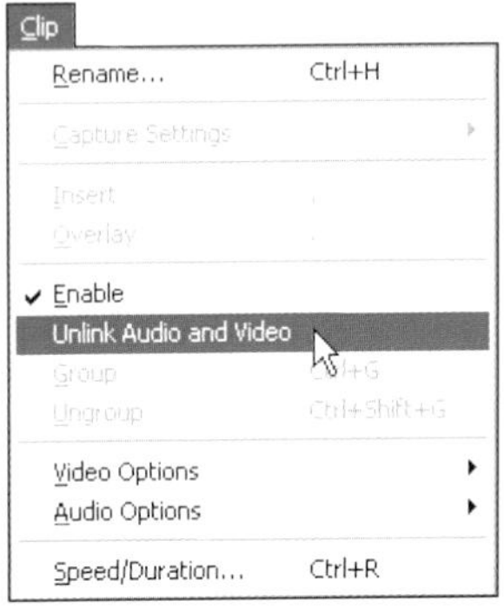

5. Did you notice that the audio was not very clean due to raindrops hitting the microphone? In this instance, you are going to keep the video, but you are going to unlink the audio so you can remove it. In the **Timeline** window, click the clip to select it, and choose **Clip > Unlink Audio and Video**. They are now two separate clips.

*Tip: All of the options in the **Clip** menu are available when you have a clip selected. If you ever have trouble remembering where a certain menu item is, just ask yourself "what am I trying to modify?" If you're trying to modify a clip, chances are you'll find what you want in the **Clip** menu. If you're trying to modify a marker, check the **Marker** menu, and so on. This is a nice organizational feature of Premiere Pro.*

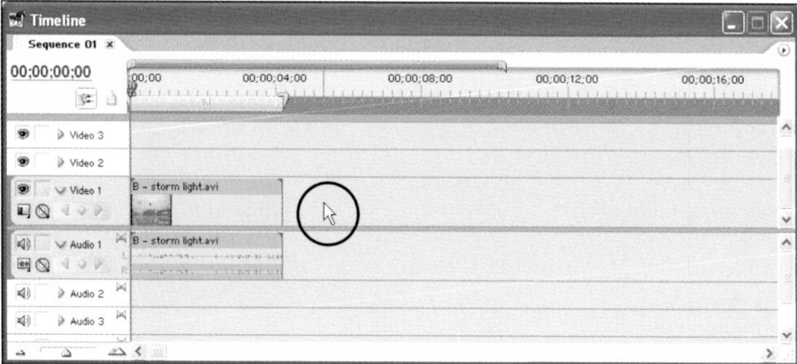

6. Now there are two independent clips on the **Timeline**. However, both clips are still shaded dark, indicating that they are still selected. (It would be nice if Premiere Pro automatically *unselected* the clips after you unlink them.) The easiest method to unselect the clips is to click in any empty track of the **Timeline** window. Click your mouse in the empty area in track **Video 1**, to the right of the clip. The clip coloring returns to cyan, indicating that they are no longer selected.

***Tip:** When a change is made to a clip, Premiere Pro affects all clips that are selected. In this case, you want to clear the audio. However, if the video portion would have been still selected, it too would have been cleared, which is why it is equally important to know how to unselect clips.*

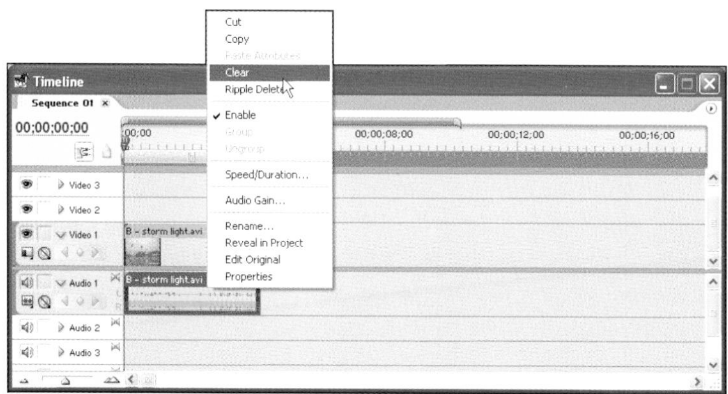

7. Now you can remove just the audio clip. As you did in previous chapters, right-click the audio clip and choose **Clear** from the shortcut menu. If you did this properly, the audio should be gone, but the video clip should remain.

That is the first method to separating a clip's audio from its video. The next method is equally as simple, and you will learn it in the next exercise.

8. Save this project, and keep it open before moving on to the next exercise, which builds on this exercise.

4. Taking Audio and Video

The next method of separating audio and video is called taking audio and video, and it is done in the Monitor window. In this exercise, you will learn how to take audio and video from the Monitor window to the Timeline window.

1. If you have the project from the previous exercise still open, skip to Step 2. If Premiere Pro is not running, launch it and click **Open Project** at the **Welcome Screen**. Navigate to the **c:\Premiere Pro HOT\Chapter05** folder, select **exercise04.prproj**, and click **Open**.

2. The next method to remove the audio or video is to *take* only the portion you want from the **Monitor** window to the **Timeline**. In the **Project** window, double-click **B – storm road.avi** to open it for editing in the **Monitor** window **Source** view. Preview the source clip by clicking **Play** in the **Source** view, or press the **spacebar**.

Note: *This is another case in which Premiere Pro will behave differently depending on which window is "active," as described in Chapter 2,* "The Project Window." *If the* ***Source*** *view of the* ***Monitor*** *window is active, pressing the* ***spacebar*** *will play the source video. If the* ***Program*** *view of the* ***Monitor*** *window is active, or the* ***Timeline*** *window is active, pressing the* ***spacebar*** *will play the sequence in the program side.*

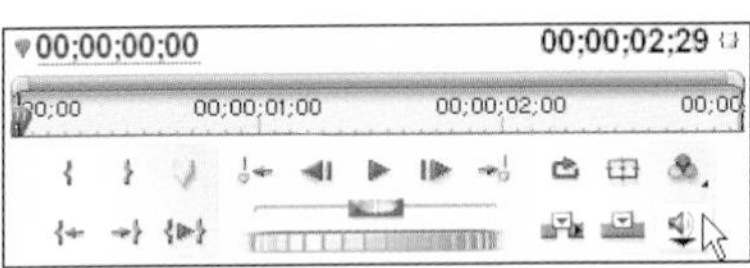

3. Normally when you drag a clip from the **Monitor** window **Source** view to the **Timeline** window, Premiere Pro takes both audio and video. However, you have the option to take only the video portion or only the audio portion. To do this, click the **Take Audio and Video** toggle button in the lower-right corner of the **Monitor** window **Source** view. Click the button until you have chosen only the audio, represented by the speaker icon.

Tip: If you want just the video, click the toggle button until you see the filmstrip icon. Or, you could take both audio and video by toggling the button until you see the filmstrip + speaker icon.

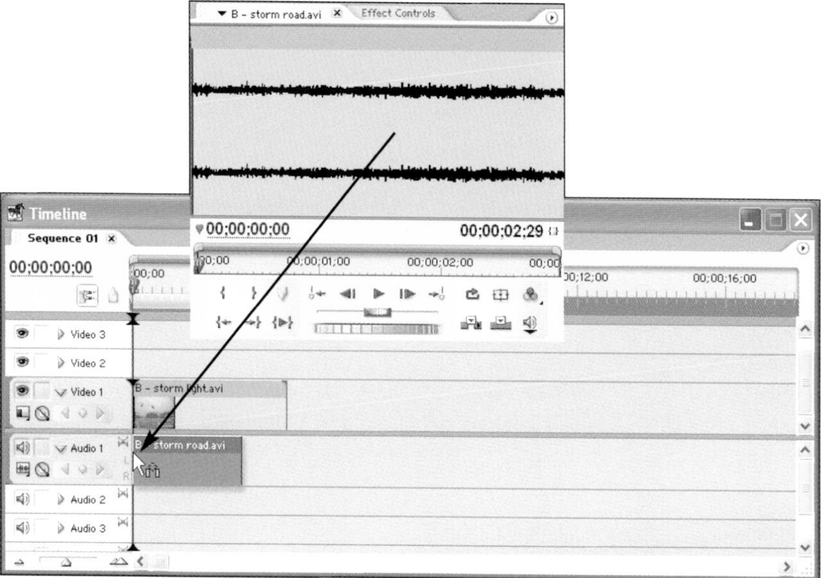

4. To place the audio from the **Source** view into the sequence, drag the **Source** view clip from the **Monitor** window to track **Audio 1** of the **Timeline** window. Make sure you align the clip to the far left. A vertical black line represents that you are snapping to the beginning of the sequence.

5. Preview the sequence by clicking the **Play** button in the **Monitor** window **Program** view. The audio and video are from two different clips, but nobody will be able to tell.

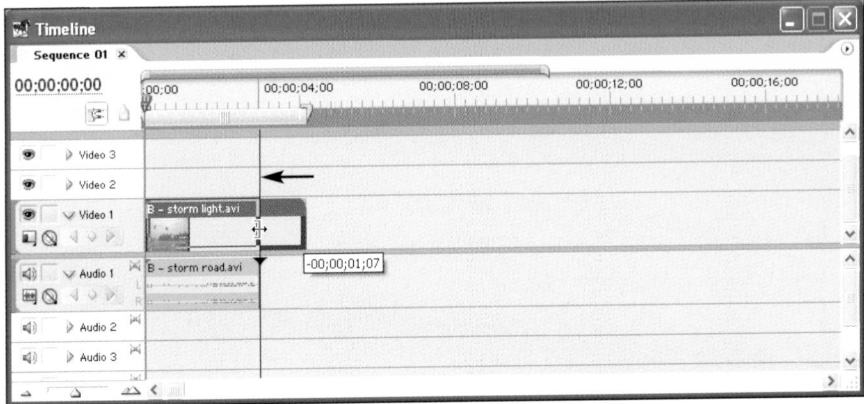

6. One slight problem: The video plays longer than the audio. Since you're now a **Trim Out** pointer expert, hover your mouse over the **Out** point of the video clip and drag the **Out** point to the left until it snaps with the **Out** point of the audio clip.

7. Perhaps you want to link the two clips together? Simple enough: hold down the **Shift** key, and click once on each clip to select them both. Choose **Clip > Link Audio and Video**. Now they will move and be edited as one.

That is the ease of taking audio and video. (See, this editing stuff is not so hard!)

8. Save and keep this project open before moving on to the next exercise, which builds on this exercise.

5. Trimming Audio and Video

The last method of separating audio and video that you will learn is to trim the audio and video in the Timeline. In the past, you have used the Trim pointer to change the In or Out point of a clip. You can also choose to only trim the audio or video portion of a clip. You will practice trimming in this exercise.

1. If you have the project from the previous exercise still open, skip to Step 2. If Premiere Pro is not running, launch it and click **Open Project** at the **Welcome Screen**. Navigate to the **c:\Premiere Pro HOT\Chapter05** folder, select **Exercise05.prproj**, and click **Open**.

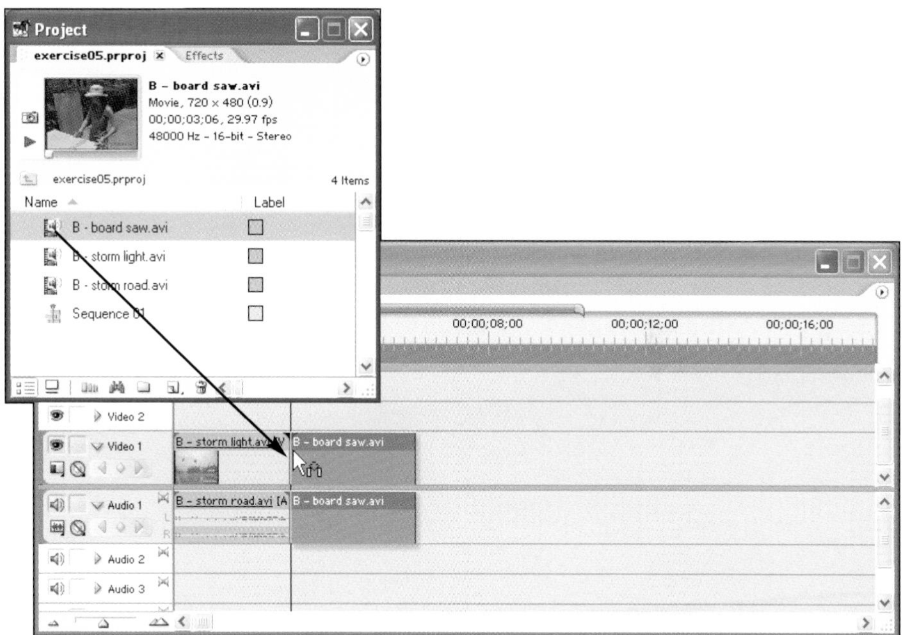

2. In the **Project** window, drag **B – board saw.avi** to the **Timeline** window. Make sure to snap it to the end of the existing clip in the sequence.

3. Preview the entire sequence by clicking the **Play In to Out** button in the **Monitor** window **Program** view.

Right now the edit (or "cut") is very abrupt. A trick to help smooth out this problem is to have the audio of the next clip begin playing before the audience sees the video of the second clip.

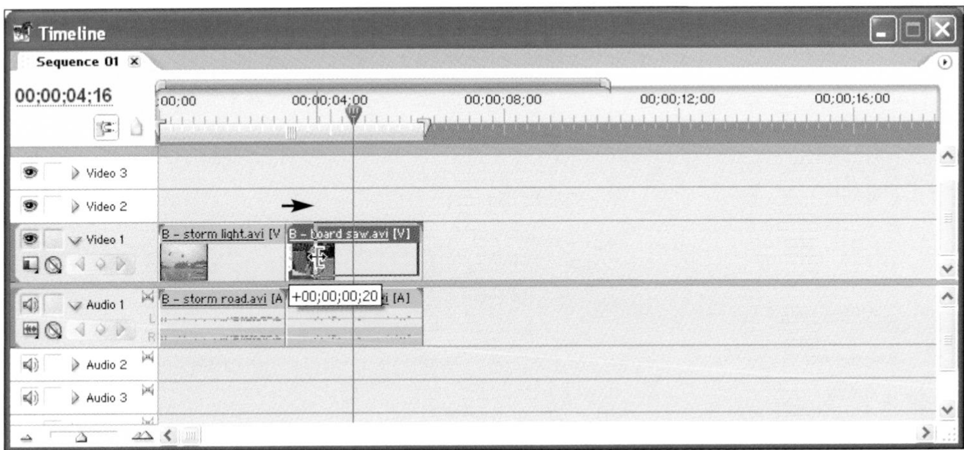

4. Hover your mouse (don't click yet!) over the **In** point of the second clip, until you see the **Trim In** pointer. Hold down the **Alt** key, and then drag the **In** point of the second clip about 20 frames to the right.

*Remember, holding down the **Alt** key selects only one part of the clip (either the video **or** audio). If both the audio and video portions of the clip are shaded, then you should click in an empty part of the Timeline, and try reselecting just the video portion of the clip. The goal is to have only the video portion shaded.*

5. Preview the entire sequence by clicking the **Play In to Out** button in the **Monitor** window **Program** view. Notice the gap in the video where you trimmed the **In** point.

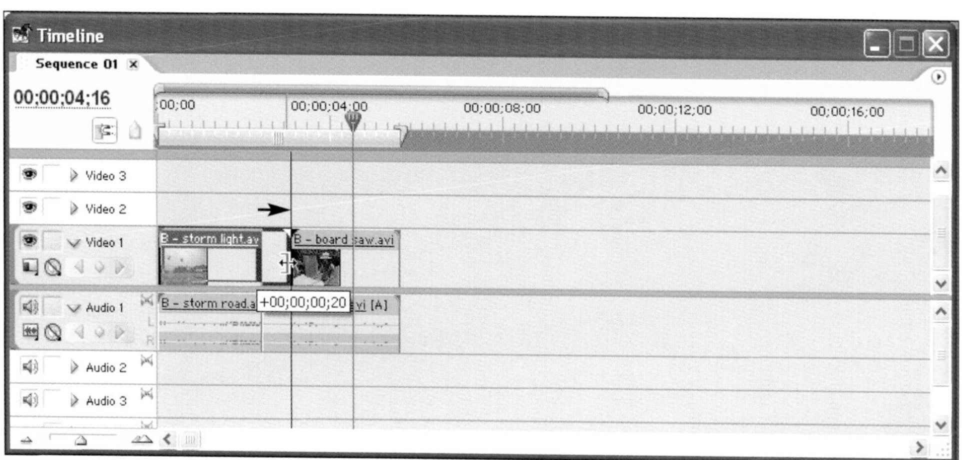

6. Now you are going to fill that gap with the excess video of the first clip. Hover your mouse over the **Out** point of the first clip, until you see the **Trim Out** pointer. Hold down the **Alt** key, and then drag the **Out** point of the first clip about 20 frames to the right.

7. Preview the entire sequence by clicking the **Play In to Out** button in the **Monitor** window **Program** view. Notice that the saw audio starts while the first video is still playing. This helps to minimize the abruptness of such an edit, and it can help make your final product look more polished.

*You now know how to perform the most common edits in the **Timeline** window.*

8. Save and close this project before moving on to the next exercise.

Hopefully this chapter helped to dispel any mystery about adding audio to your Premiere Pro projects. The idea to keep in mind is that Premiere Pro treats all clips equally, and these same techniques even hold true for graphics, titles, and any other type of clip you can import.

Now that you have a firm grasp on the concepts of building your sequence in the Timeline window, it's time to add some visual spice with titles.

6

Title Designer

Adobe Title Designer	A Basic Title
A World of Style	Editing Title Clips in the Timeline
Font Properties	Fills, Strokes, and Shadows
Title Templates	Rolling and Crawling Titles

H•O•T

Premiere Pro HOT DVD

The next frontier to conquer is the art of adding titles to your program. At its most basic, a title is text on a screen. A title can be one simple line, like the subtitle of a foreign movie. Or a title can a full screen of text, like a PowerPoint presentation. Titles can roll up and down like the end credits of movies, or they can scroll left and right to add visual interest.

So far you've learned to add audio and video to your projects. Titles are another type of clip that you can add to your project. In the Timeline window, titles are treated just like audio and video clips. They can be shortened, lengthened, moved in time, and so on. Many of the exercises that you have practiced in this book apply equally well to title clips.

Those are the similarities between titles and audio/video clips. However, titles differ from these other types of clips because titles are created by and within Premiere Pro. For example, all of the audio and video clips you have worked with so far were created outside of Premiere Pro; they already existed, and you just imported them into a Premiere Pro project. Titles, on the other hand, are created entirely from scratch by Premiere Pro. In fact, Premiere Pro comes with a special title-making software aptly named Adobe Title Designer. And it does just that.

Adobe Title Designer

The Adobe Title Designer is built into Premiere Pro, so if you own Premiere Pro, you own the Adobe Title Designer. The Designer is very powerful, and it allows you to create and customize your titles with great precision. However, because it is so powerful, the user is presented with a lot of buttons and menu options. At first glance, it can seem quite intimidating. But the goal of this chapter is to help you learn the Title Designer in small, digestible bites. In the end, you'll see that it's not that tough at all.

This is the interface for the Adobe Title Designer. There are eight components to the Designer that you will become familiar with:

(a) **Title type menu:** The available choices are **Still** (doesn't move), **Roll** (rolls up or down), and **Crawl** (scrolls left to right or right to left).

(b) **Title Designer toolbox:** You will always first select a tool before performing any action.

(c) **Align and Distribute buttons:** This chapter doesn't spend too much time on this menu, since it primarily affects titles with multiple text boxes and objects. This menu is used to align multiple items together, so they look much neater.

(d) **Style library:** A library of premade styles, so you don't have to spend a lot of time changing fonts, adding shadows, and so on. First click a style, and then type your text.

(e) **Font and paragraph buttons:** This is very similar to the options available in a Microsoft Word document. You can browse different fonts installed on your system, and you can change the alignment of text in a paragraph (left, center, or right).

(f) **Object styles:** Each time you type text into your title, you create a text object. The text object has many different properties that can be customized. In addition, you can add gradient fills, strokes, and drop shadows.

(g) **Composition window:** This is where you will do all of your work. It's like the drawing board for your title.

(h) **Transform properties:** You can rotate your text object, change its X and Y coordinates, increase or decrease size, and lower or raise opacity. (Opacity = opaqueness, or how "solid" an object is. For example, a ghost has a very low opacity, and a brick wall has a high opacity.)

NOTE | Title Safe Area

Inside of the Title Designer's composition window, you will see two very thin rectangles. These rectangles represent the **action safe** and **title safe** margins of your screen. These guides represent the boundaries you should adhere to, in order to have your titles seen by all television sets.

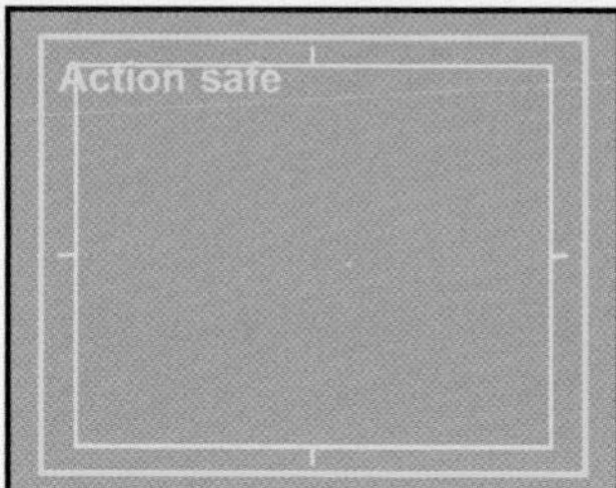

The problem is this: most consumer television sets do not show the entire video screen. Everything outside of the action safe area may be hidden. If you are creating your project for playback on a television set, make sure that all vital action takes place inside of the action safe area (especially any action that *must be seen*).

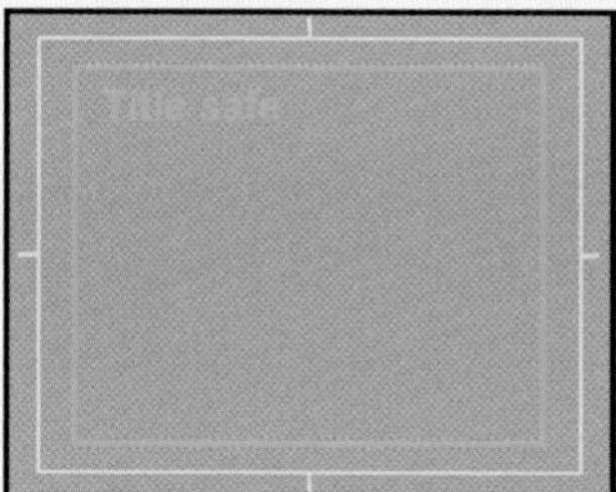

But, you're still not out of the clear. The inside boundary is called the title safe area, and it represents the margins that all titles should fall within. This ensures that all television sets will be able to clearly display any text that you have incorporated into your program. Any portion of a title that falls outside of the title safe area may be unreadable on some television sets.

Keep in mind that these guides apply only to projects that will be played back on television monitors. Computer monitors, on the other hand, do not exhibit this problem. If you are creating a project that will only be shown on the Web, you can turn off the title safe and action safe margins. To turn them off inside the Title Designer, choose **Title > View > Safe Title Margin** or **Title > View > Safe Action Margin**. The margin is on if a checkmark appears beside its name.

By the way, you may recognize these rectangles from the Monitor window Source and Program views in previous chapters. They've been there all along, and now you know their purpose in life!

I. A Basic Title

In this exercise, you will create a basic title in the Title Designer and place it in a sequence.

1. If Premiere Pro is not running, launch it and click **Open Project** at the **Welcome Screen**. Navigate to the **c:\Premiere Pro HOT\Chapter 06** folder, select **Exercise01.prproj**, and click **Open**.

2. You will notice that **Sequence 01** already has some video clips and an audio clip. Click the **Play In to Out** button in the **Monitor** window **Program** view to become familiar with the sequence.

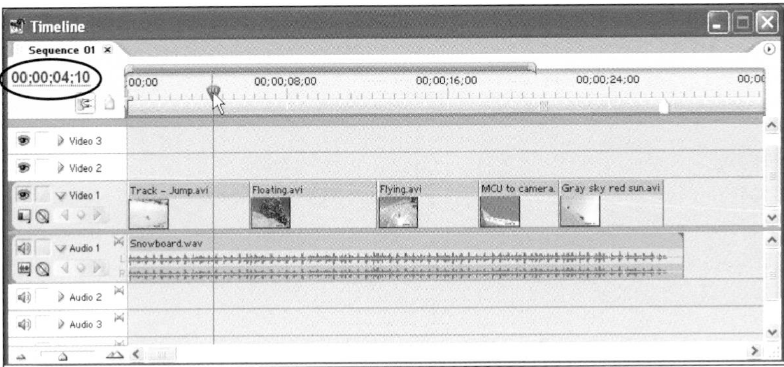

3. In the **Timeline** window, position the current time indicator at **00;00;04;10**. You can achieve this by dragging the indicator to the desired time, or by clicking in the **Timeline** window time display and typing in **00;00;04;10**.

Tip: You can also abbreviate this by typing **0410**.

4. Choose **File > New > Title** to open a new title in the **Title Designer**.

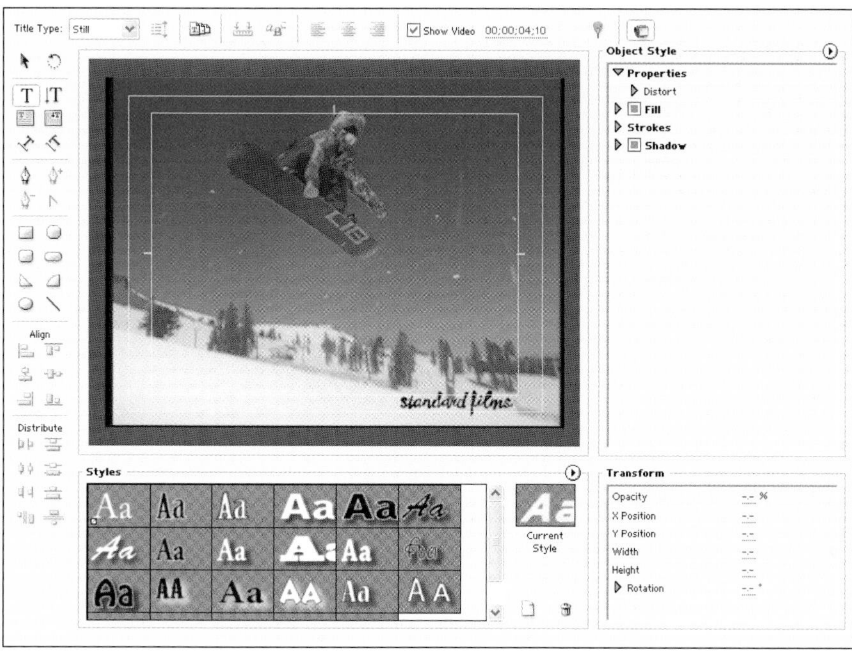

*Tip: Notice that the **Title Designer** composition window displays a frame of video from your sequence. The exact frame shown correlates to the position of the current time indicator in the **Timeline** window. (This is why you moved the current time indicator in Step 3.)*

5. Now you will create a title that says **Boost!** The first step in creating any title is to select the proper tool. Since you are about to type text in your title, select the **Text** tool in the **Title Designer** toolbox.

***Note:** Just in case you were wondering, "boost" is snowboard-lingo that means to catch air off a jump or halfpipe. (And you thought you'd only be learning Premiere Pro.)*

6. Next, position your cursor where you'd like the lower-left corner of the title to be. In this case, hover your mouse in the lower-left corner, just inside of the **title safe** area.

Note: Depending on your monitor's resolution, it may be hard to see the lower-left corner of the ***title safe*** *area since the white guides blend into the video frame's white snow.*

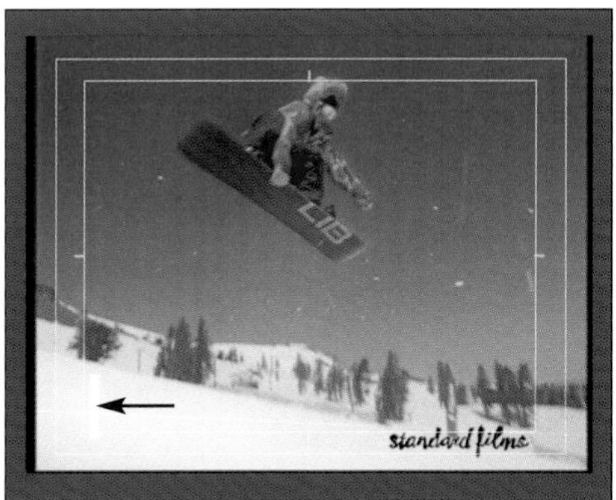

7. After you've hovered your mouse in the correct position, click once to create a text object. This will create an empty text box and a blinking cursor.

8. Type **Boost!** and then select the **Selection** tool in the **Title Designer**. Clicking the **Selection** tool once you are finished tells the **Title Designer** that you are done typing in the text box. As soon as you select the **Selection** tool, the **Title Designer** places a bounding box and handles around the text object, indicating that you are ready to modify the text object.

Note: *Keep in mind there is a difference between modifying the text itself (retyping a word, changing letters, and so on) and modifying the text object–such as changing the font, the color, the size, and so on.*

9. Currently, the text has the default style applied to it. Next, you will select a style from the **Title Designer's** style library. With the **Selection** tool, click the object you wish to modify (in this case the text object **Boost!**), and then click the style you'd like to apply. The text object now has the format of the selected style.

Tip: *If you want to experiment, you can click each style to see how it affects your text object. You can choose and rechoose any style as many times as you want. Knock yourself out!*

10. A slight problem presents itself: the style you choose may increase the size of your text object. This means that part of the text may fall outside of the **title safe** area. To remedy this, use the **Selection** tool to drag the title slowly up until it is completely within the **title safe** guides.

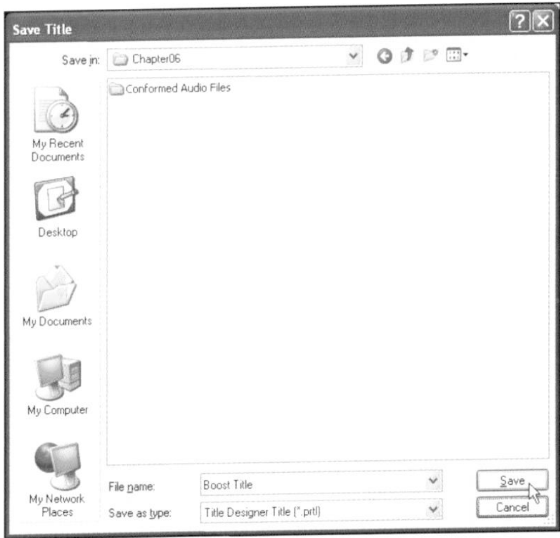

11. Now it is time to save the title and place it in your sequence. Choose **File > Save**. Navigate to the **c:\Premiere Pro HOT\Chapter 06** directory and name your title **Boost Title**. Click **Save**.

12. Close the **Title Designer** by choosing **File > Close**, or click the **Close** button in the upper-right corner of the window.

*Note: The **File > Close** option can be dangerous because it will close the active window. If the **Title Designer** is not the active window, you might end up closing something else by accident–like your project! If you accidentally close your Project, Premiere Pro will prompt you to save any changes.*

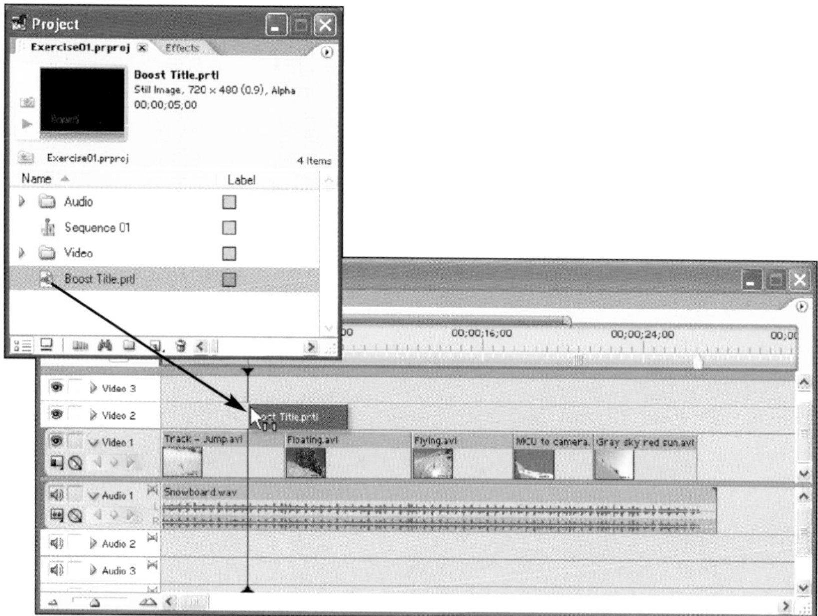

13. Premiere Pro automatically imports your newly created title into the **Project** window. To place the title into your sequence, drag the **Boost Title.prtl** title clip from the **Project** window to track **Video 2**, snapping it to the current time indicator. (Your current time indicator should still be at **00;00;04;10** from Step 3.) Look for the vertical black snapping line to ensure proper "snappage."

Tip: *You can place a title into any video track. But, if you want the title to play* on top *of existing video, then you need to place it in a track* above *the video.*

14. Preview the entire sequence by clicking the **Play In to Out** button in the **Monitor** window **Program** view. You can tap the **spacebar** to stop playback if you do not wish to watch the entire sequence.

You have just learned the Title Design 3-Step. *Remember: 1) Select the* ***Text*** *tool, 2) Type your text, 3) Select a style. You will become very familiar with this process as you repeat it for every title you create.*

15. Save this project and keep it open for the next exercise.

A World of Style

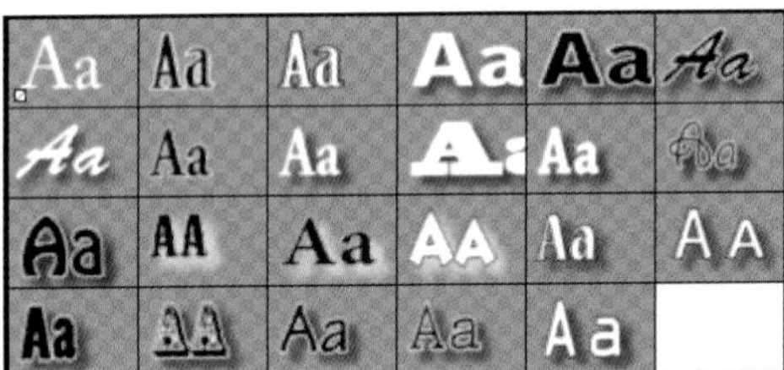

Premiere Pro's default style library

Here's a tip that is sure to knock your socks off. The Premiere Pro style library comes installed with 23 styles in the Adobe Title Designer. However, Premiere Pro ships with another *116* styles–and most Premiere Pro users don't even know about them!

A *style library* is a collection of styles, grouped by themes. The 23 styles that come preloaded in the Title Designer are all part of a single library called the **default style library**. In addition to the default library, there are eight more libraries you can load into the same window. However, for reasons known only to the Premiere Pro software designers, the other eight libraries are hidden.

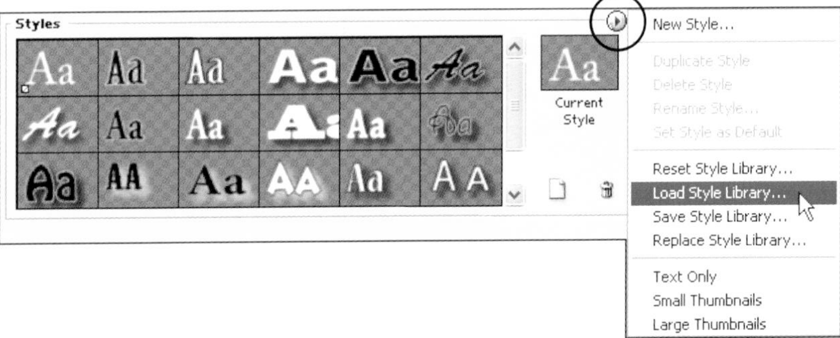

To load the hidden style libraries, click the styles library wing menu (the circle button with a triangle, to the right of the **Styles** window), and choose **Load Style Library** from the pop-up menu.

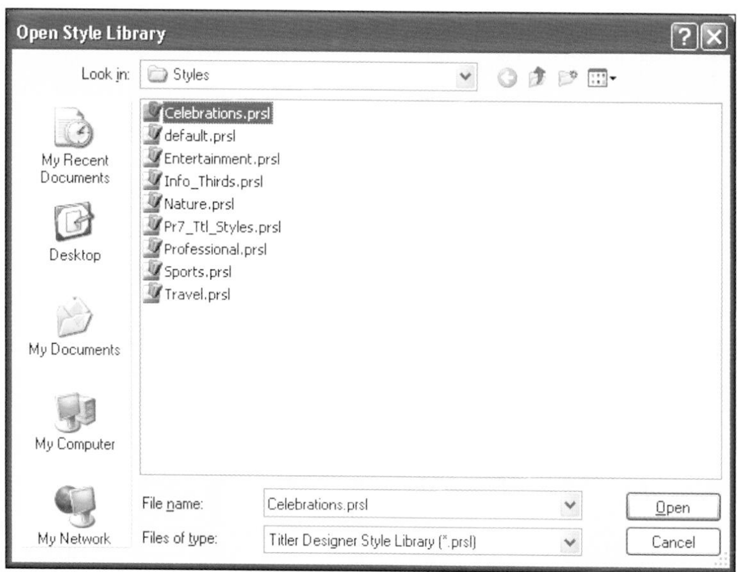

When the **Open Style Library** window appears, you are presented with eight new library files that you can load into the **Title Designer**. (There are a total of nine; **default.prsl** is the default library that comes preloaded.) To load a style library into the **Title Designer**, select the file and click **Open**. In this example, **Celebrations.prsl** was opened.

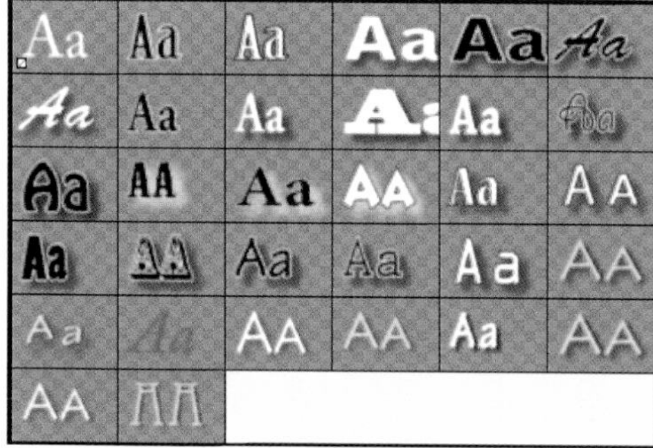

The new styles are appended to the end of the original default library. Now, instead of 23, there are a total of 32, which means that 9 new styles were added.

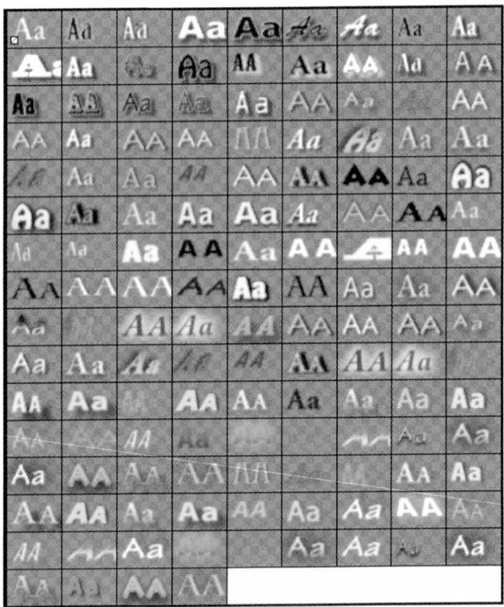

Repeat this process for each of the remaining style libraries you would like to open in the **Title Designer**. And before you know it, you have 139 styles to choose from.

The only downside is that it gets tough to scroll through all 139 styles. In order to view many styles at one time, you can reduce the size of the style *thumbnails* (the icons), so that more fit in the window. To do this, simply click the **Styles Library** wing menu and choose **Small Thumbnails**.

2. Editing Title Clips in the Timeline

This may not come as a shock to you anymore, but you can edit a title clip in the Timeline just like an audio or video clip. Which means this should be a very short lesson!

1. If you have the project open from the previous exercise, skip to Step 2. If Premiere Pro is not running, launch it and click **Open Project** at the **Welcome Screen**. Navigate to the **c:\Premiere Pro HOT\Chapter 06** folder, select **Exercise02.prproj**, and click **Open**.

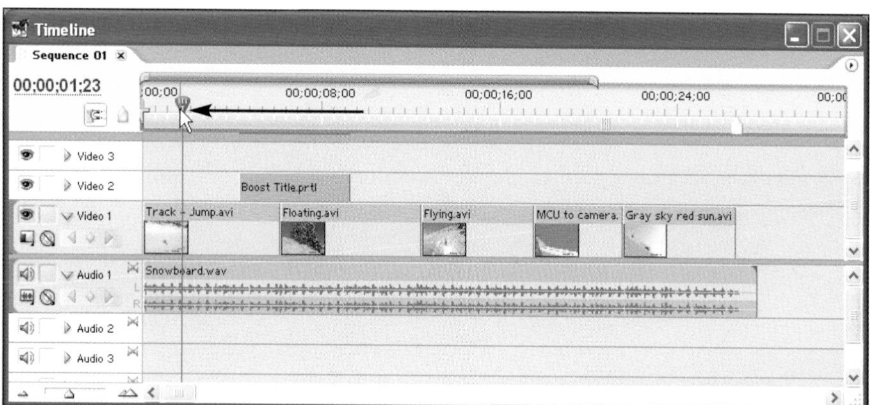

2. Perhaps you want the title clip to start a little earlier in the sequence, such as right when the snowboarder "boosts." This requires finding the appropriate spot before moving the title clip. To find the correct frame of video, slowly drag the **Timeline** window current time indicator to the left, to approximately **00;00;01;23**. (Use the time display in the upper-left corner of the **Timeline** window as your guide.)

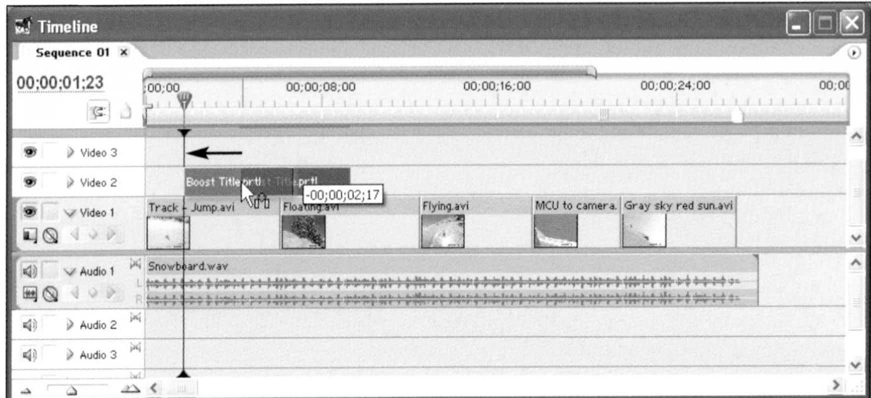

3. Next, drag the title clip to the left, until it snaps to the current time indicator.

4. Click the **Play In to Out button** in the **Monitor** window **Program** view to preview the sequence. You can press the **spacebar** after the title plays if you do not wish to watch the entire sequence.

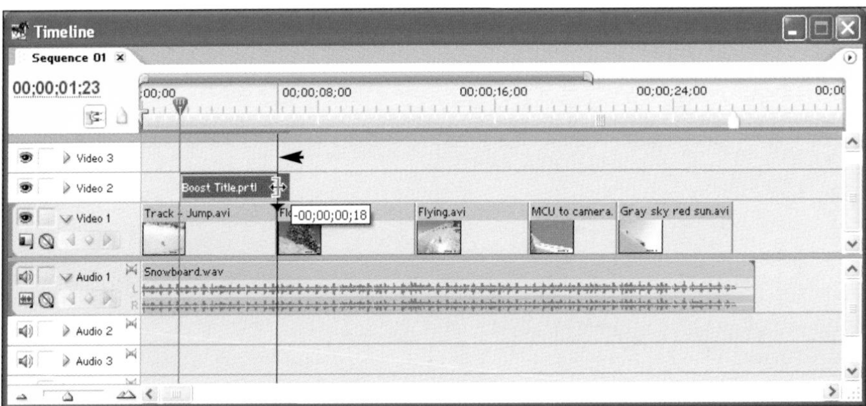

5. The sequence is looking better, but it would be nice if the title clip ended at the same time as the clip it is combined with. As you have done in previous chapters, use the **Trim Out** pointer to snap the **Out** point of the title clip to the **Out** point of the first clip on the **Timeline**.

6. Click the **Play In to Out** button in the **Monitor** window **Program** view to preview the sequence.

7. By now, you should be really comfortable moving and trimming clips in the **Timeline**. Then again, can you ever have enough practice at snapping? Save this project and keep it open for the next exercise.

In the next exercise you will modify your title by tweaking the object properties. Title objects include words, letters, polygon shapes, and custom paths. The following table lists the available properties and how they affect your objects.

Object Properties

Property	Description
Font	The font face (such as Arial, Times New Roman, Helvetica). You can choose one font at a time, or browse all of the fonts available to your computer. Thick or bold fonts display better on television monitors and in heavily-compressed Web formats. In general, a sans-serif font (no feet, like Arial) tend to work better than serif fonts (like Times New Roman).
Font Size	Changes how big or small your text is. For television, font sizes smaller than 20 can be difficult to read.
Aspect	The width (%) of your font, relative to the font's inherent width. Values below 100% narrow the text; above 100% widen the text.
Leading	The amount of space between lines of text. This will only affect text objects that have more than one line.
Tracking	The amount of space between letters. Tracking expands or condenses spacing uniformly between all letters.
Kerning	The amount of space between certain letters. Kerning does not adjust uniformly like tracking; rather it is meant to remedy uneven spacing between certain letter pairs. The example below shows unkerned pairs and kerned pairs. Ke To Ve Wo r, y, 115 Ke To Ve Wo r, y, 115
Baseline Shift	The distance a character is raised or lowered from its normal position (like x^2 or H_2O).
Slant	The *slant* of an object, in degrees.
Small Caps	When selected, makes lowercase text APPEAR IN SMALL UPPERCASE.
Small Caps Size	The size of the small cap (%) relative to regular height.
Underline	Underlined text.

continued on next page

Object Properties *continued*	
Property	**Description**
Distort	Changes the shape of an object along its x axis or y axis. This one isn't as easy to describe, so the best method is to create a title and simply change the values to discover its effects.
Fill	Provides different options for filling in each object. You can do a solid fill (one color), a gradient fill (a subtle blend from one color to another), or a texture fill (using a separate image to fill in the body of each shape). **Tip:** Avoid bright reds on titles meant for playback on television monitors. Pure reds tend to smear and can make the text more difficult to read.
Strokes	A line along the edge of an object. Outer stroke draws a line around the perimeter of a shape, and Inner stroke draws a line inside the shape.
Shadow	Provides options for a shadow behind an object. You can control the color, size, depth, and angle of the shadow.

3. Font Properties

So far you have created a simple text object in a title and applied a style. In this exercise, you will create another text object and learn to tweak some of the most common font properties, and add the title over the second clip on the Timeline.

1. If you have the project open from the previous exercise, skip to Step 2. If Premiere Pro is not running, launch it and click **Open Project** at the **Welcome Screen**. Navigate to the **c:\Premiere Pro HOT\Chapter 06** folder, select **Exercise03.prproj**, and click **Open**.

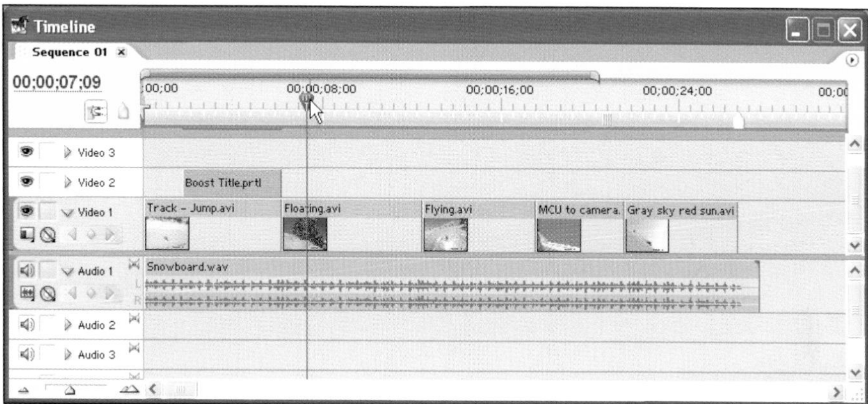

2. Drag the current time indicator in the **Timeline** window to the position where you would like the next title to start. For purposes of this exercise, move the current time indicator to **00;00;07;09**.

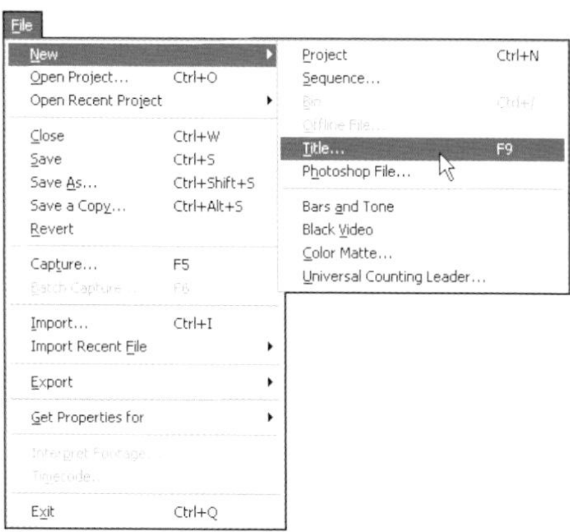

3. Next, create a blank title by choosing **File > New > Title**.

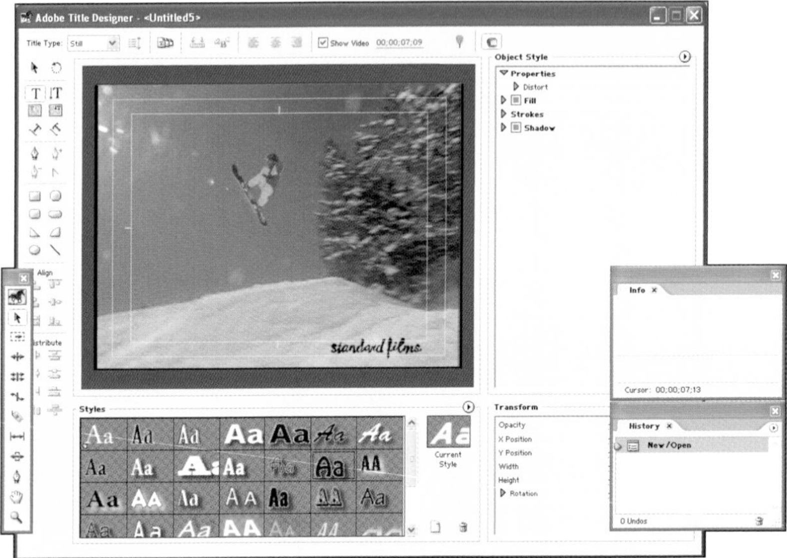

Press the Tab key and...

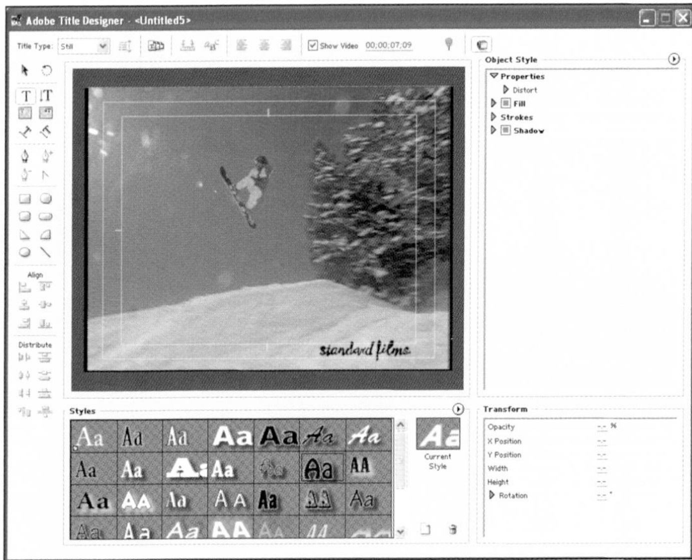

POOF! Those pesky windows and palettes are gone.

4. It's a tad annoying that Premiere Pro opens the **Title Designer** window behind the project's toolboxes and palettes. On your screen, the **Info** and **History** palettes, as well as the **Timeline** window toolbox, may obscure access to parts of the **Title Designer**. In order to hide these palettes and windows, press the **Tab** key. Pressing the **Tab** key again toggles them back on, if you want to get them back. However, in this exercise, keep them hidden.

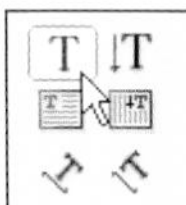

5. Select the **Text** tool in the **Title Designer**.

6. With the **Text** tool selected, click in the composition window in the area where you would like the text object to be placed. In this case, click in the upper third and right third of the composition window. (See picture).

7. When you see the blinking cursor, your text object is in "type" mode, ready for you to begin typing. Type **Method**, press **Enter**, and type **Air**.

Note: *The* ***Enter*** *key moves the word "Air" to a new line, but keeps it as part of the same text object.*

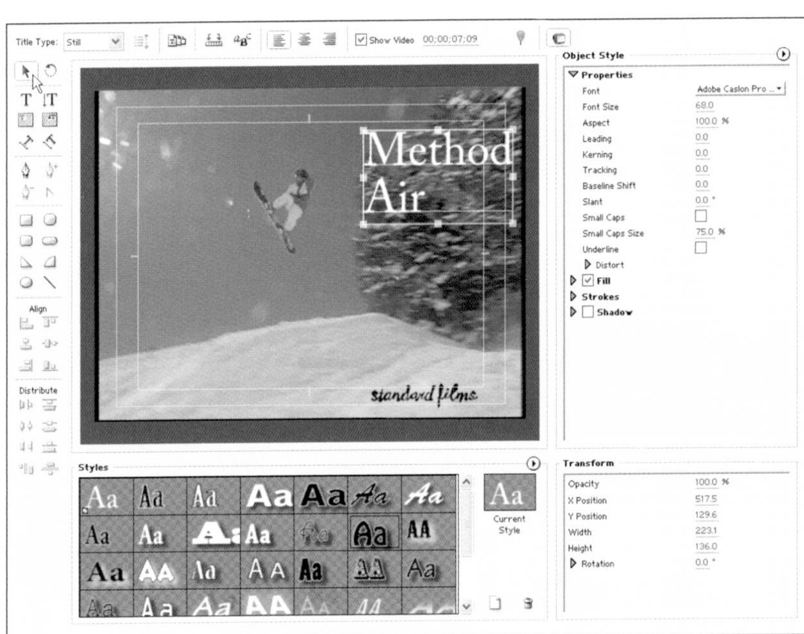

8. When done typing, promptly click the **Selection** tool in the **Title Designer**. This tells the software that you are finished typing, and it also takes the text object out of "type" mode and puts it in "modify" mode.

Tip: *When you see the handles and a bounding box around your object (represented by eight tiny white squares), your object is ready to be modified. Any changes you make will now affect the entire object. You can drag, rotate, resize, and change the properties of an object in modify mode. The bounding box and handles do not show up when you play your project in the Timeline.*

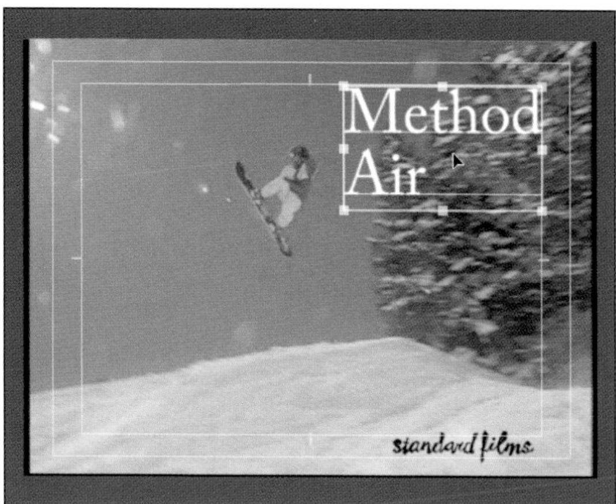

9. Depending on where you clicked your mouse to begin the text object, your text may not be in the correct spot. Click in the middle of the object and drag it so that the top and right edges of the text object align just inside the top and right guides of the **title safe** area.

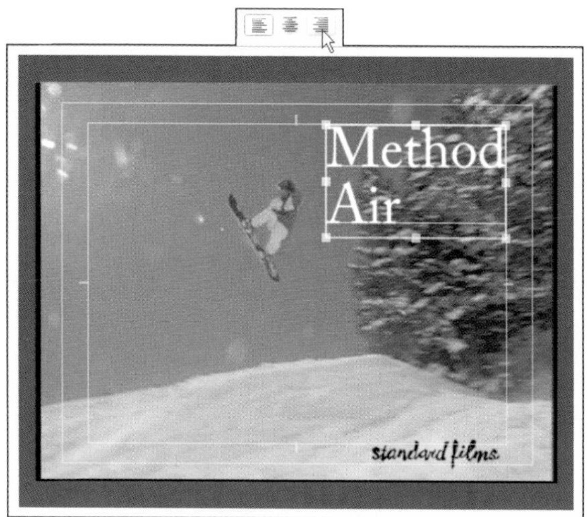

10. Just like in a word processing program, you can change the alignment of your text–left, centered, or right. In this case, click the **Align Right** button to align your text along the right edge of the text object.

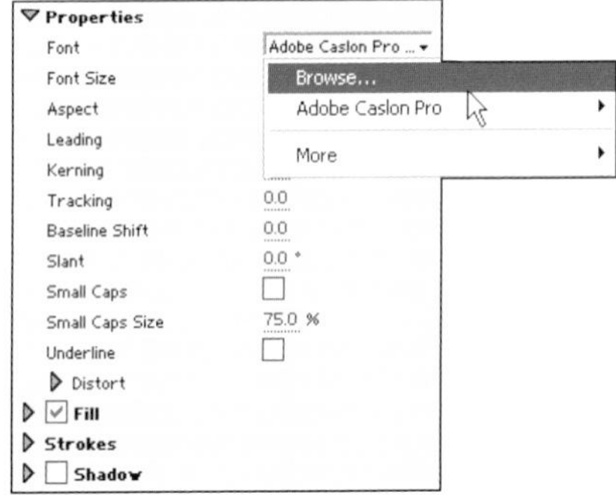

11. Now you are going to modify the formatting of the text object without using a style. The first property to change is the **Font**. Click the **Font** button to the right of the **Font** property. In the pop-up menu, click **Browse**.

Note: *The fonts listed are based on the fonts installed on your computer. You may have different fonts installed, and therefore the fonts listed on your computer will differ from those shown in the examples throughout this exercise.*

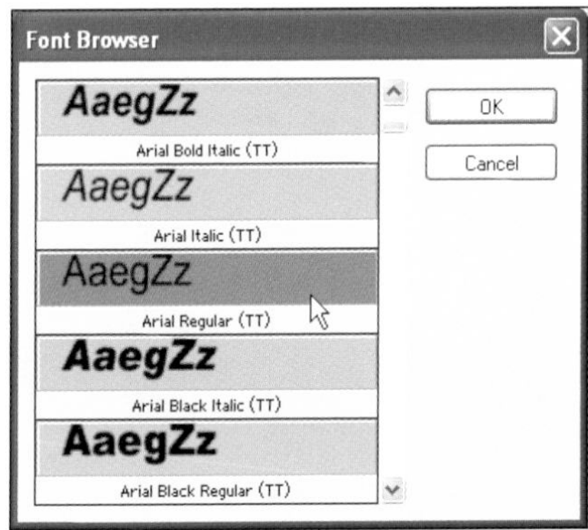

12. In the **Font Browser** window, scroll down to **Arial Regular (TT)** and select it, then click **OK**. This will change the font face of the selected text object to **Arial Regular (TT)**.

Tip: *Arial Regular or Arial Bold are good choice when you require a small font size. Not just the Arial family of fonts, but any font face of a similar style, sans-serif (no feet), with easy-to-read lettering and thick lines.*

13. The next property to change is the **Font Size**. Hover your mouse over the **Font Size** value, click your mouse and slowly drag it to the right. As you drag (don't let go of the mouse button!), the font size will steadily increase. Drag until the font size is approximately **80.0**. (It doesn't have to be perfect.)

Note: *You can decrease or increase all font properties' values by dragging left or right. If you have a specific value in mind, you can click once on the value, type in the new number at the blinking cursor, and then press* ***Enter.***

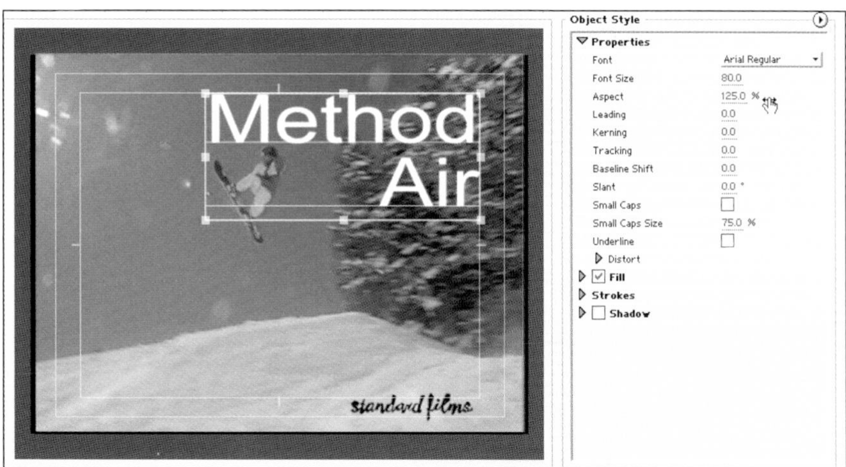

14. The next property to change is the **Aspect** (width of the font). You can either drag the value to the right to **125.0%**, or you can click once on the value, type in **125.0**, and press **Enter**. Both methods achieve the same result.

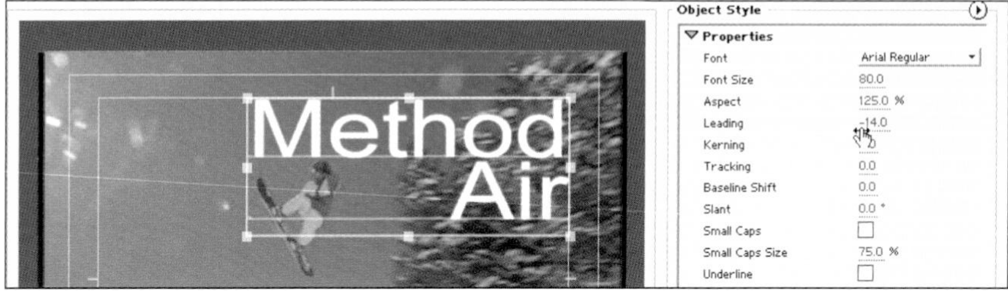

15. Next click the **Leading** value, type in a new value of **–14.0**, then press **Enter**. (Or drag the value to **–14.0**). Negative leading values reduce the spacing between lines. As you reduce the value, the word **Air** should scoot up closer to the word **Method**.

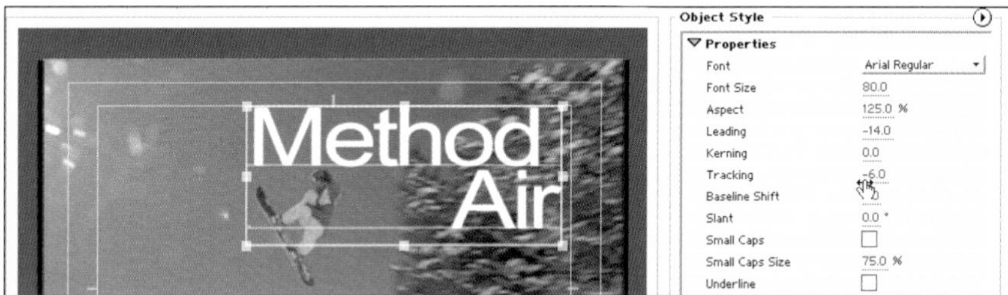

16. In this exercise, you are not going to adjust the **Kerning**, but you will adjust the **Tracking**. (See the table on page 131 for descriptions of each.) Change the tracking value to **–6.0**. Negative tracking values reduce the spacing between letters.

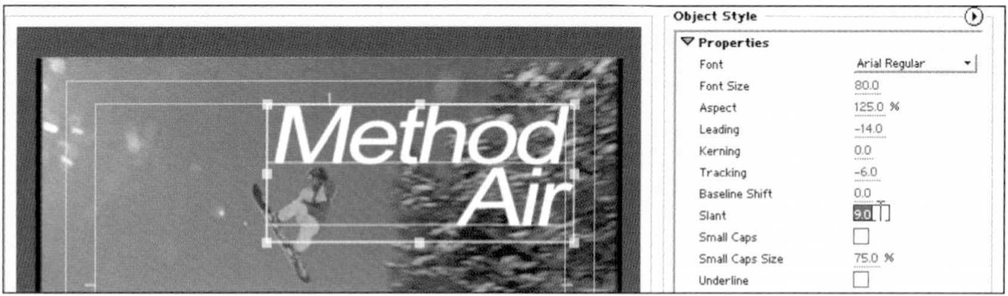

17. Next, adjust the **Slant** value to **9.0°**. This property "slants" your words (like a politician!).

18. Now save your title by choosing **File > Save**. Navigate to the **Chapter 06** folder, and name the file **Method Air title** and click **Save**. Close the **Title Designer** by choosing **File > Close**, or by clicking the **Close** button in the upper-right corner of the **Title Designer**.

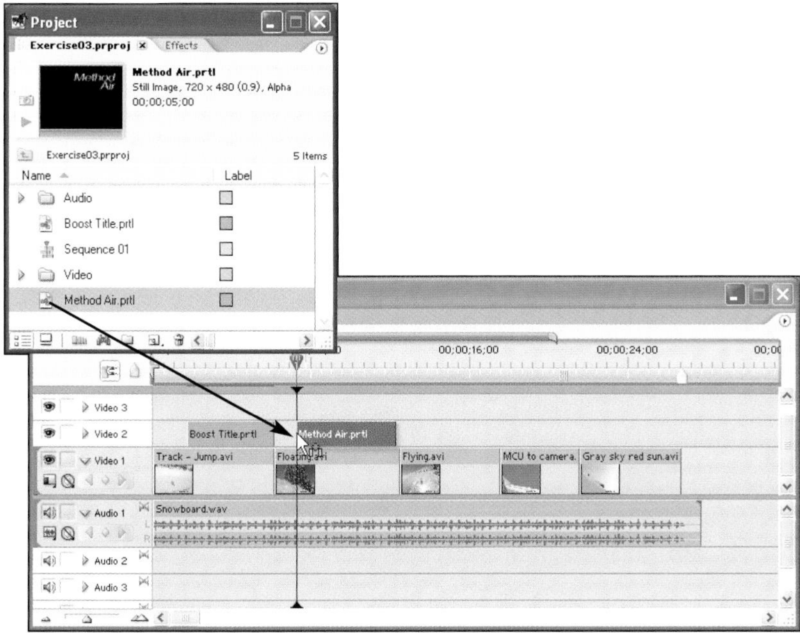

19. This automatically places the title clip in your **Project** window. Drag the clip from the **Project** window to track **Video 2** in the **Timeline** window, snapping the **In** point to the current time indicator.

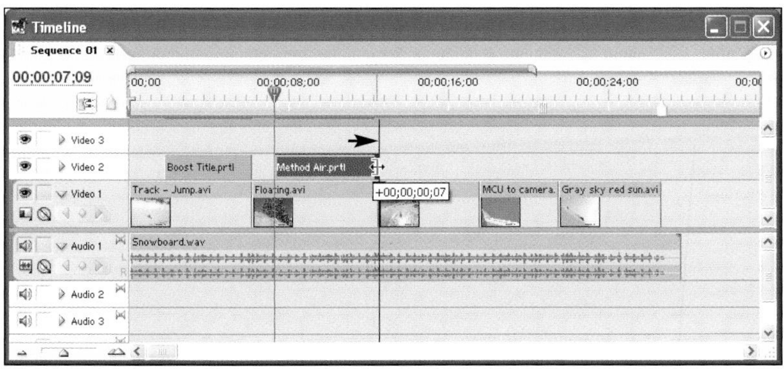

20. Last, align the **Out** point of the title clip with the **Out** point of the **Floating.avi** clip. Using the **Trim Out** pointer, drag the title clip **Out** point and snap it to the **Floating.avi Out** point.

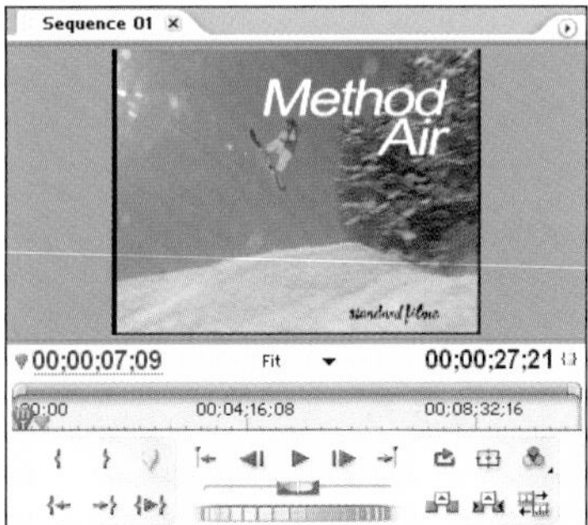

21. In the **Monitor** window **Program** view, click the **Play In to Out** button to preview the sequence.

22. Save this project and keep it open before moving on to the next exercise.

Whew, that was a long exercise–good job. Now you can see how much time you can save with the premade style library. Even though this exercise focused on the most common properties, you can always venture out and dabble with the others. Don't worry–the Undo feature is always a click away!

4. Fills, Strokes, and Shadows

In the previous exercise, you modified a text object's font properties. Keep in mind that those properties apply only to *text* objects and not to polygon shapes or paths. In this exercise, you will modify the other types of properties–fills, strokes, and shadows–which can be applied to any type of object.

1. If you have the project open from the previous exercise, skip to Step 2. If Premiere Pro is not running, launch it and click **Open Project** at the **Welcome Screen**. Navigate to the **c:\Premiere Pro HOT\Chapter 06** folder, select **Exercise04.prproj**, and click **Open**.

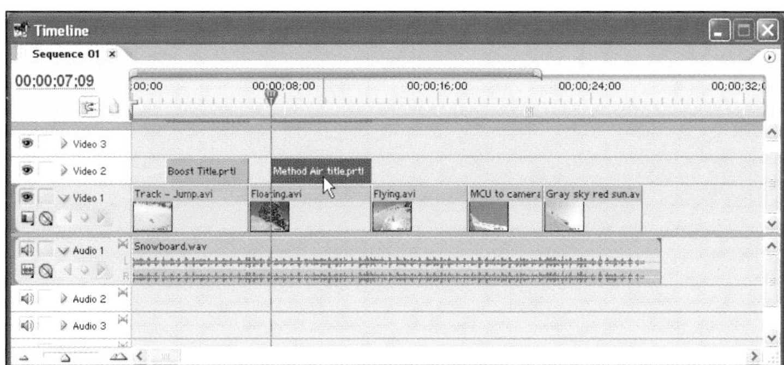

2. No need to reinvent the wheel, since you spent all that time in the last exercise. In this exercise, you will continue where you left off. To modify a title that has already been created, double-click it in the **Project** or **Timeline** window. In this case, you can double-click **Method Air title.prtl** in the **Timeline** window. This will open the title in the **Title Designer**.

3. Since you do not need to create a new text object–you will be modifying the existing one–choose the **Selection** tool from the **Title Designer** toolbox. When you click this tool, it will put handles around the text object, indicating that is ready to be modified.

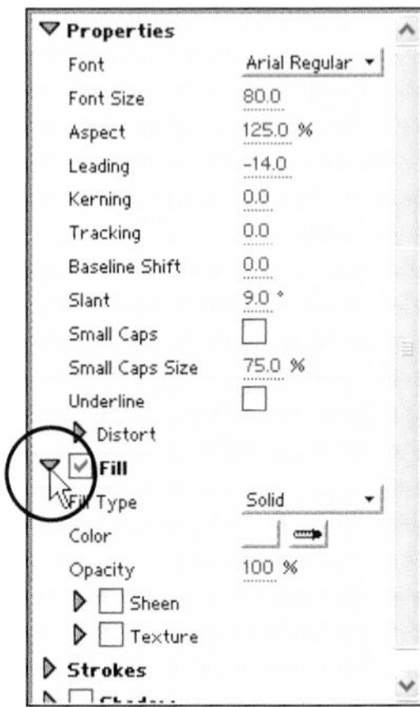

4. Right now this title is boring white. In order to add some interest, you are going to change the **Fill** color. First, expand the **Fill** property by clicking its twirl-down. This will expand the **Fill** property and display available options.

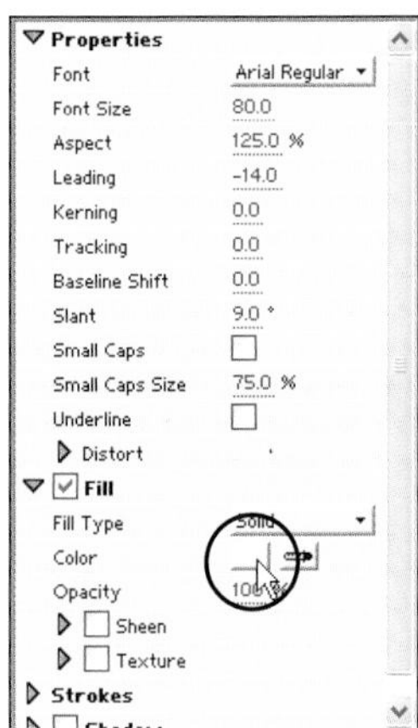

5. Click the white box next to the **Color** property. This opens up the **Color Picker** and allows you to select a new color.

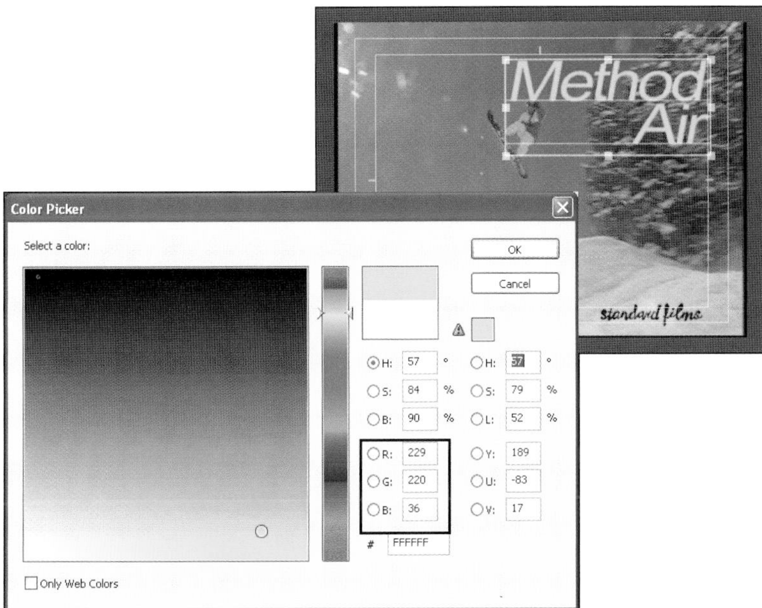

6. In the **Color Picker** window, type in a **R**ed **G**reen **B**lue (**RGB**) value of **229**, **220**, **36**. Click **OK**, and your text object should now be filled in with the yellow color you specified.

Note: *For ease of this exercise, the RGB value was supplied for you. However, you will usually eyeball the color you want, instead of knowing the exact RGB value. See the Note following this exercise to learn more about choosing a color with the* ***Color Picker.***

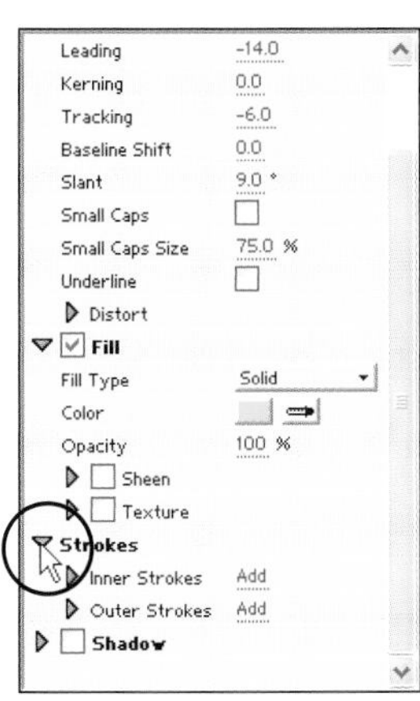

7. Scroll to the bottom of the **Object Style** menu, and twirl down the **Strokes** property to expand its options.

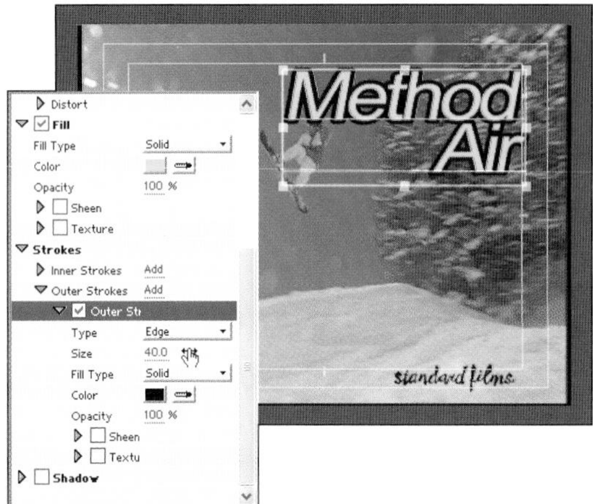

8. Add an outer stroke by clicking the **Add** link next to **Outer Strokes**. This will add an outline around the outside of your letters. To increase the size (thickness) of the stroke, drag the **Size** value to the right, to approximately **40.0**. You will see a thick black stroke around your text.

Tip: *An inner stroke behaves similarly, but it places the stroke inside the perimeter of each letter.*

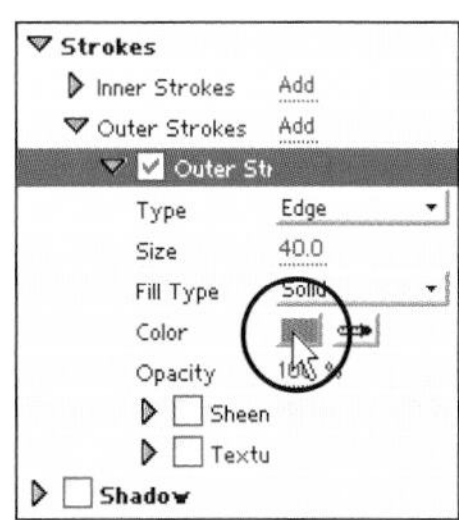

9. To change the color of the stroke, click in the box next to the **Color** property.

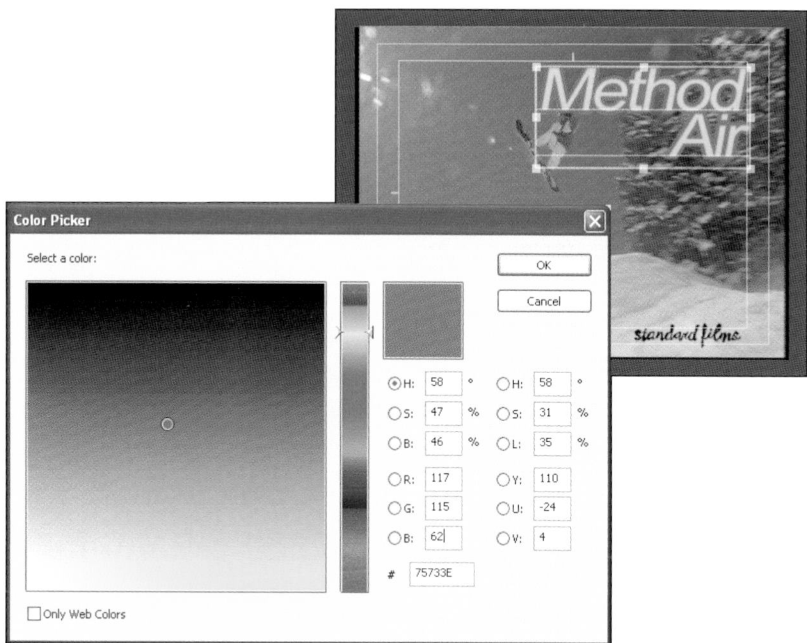

10. Type in a **R**ed, **G**reen, **B**lue value of **117**, **115**, **62**. Click **OK**. The stroke color around your text should be a dirty yellow.

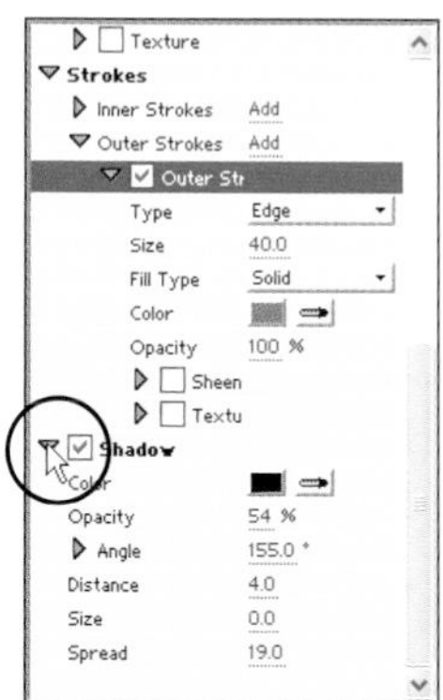

11. Now you are going to add a drop shadow to give your title some depth, as if it's hovering above the screen. Click the check box next to the **Shadow** property, and then twirl down the **Shadow** property in order to expand its options. Scroll to the bottom to see all of the available options.

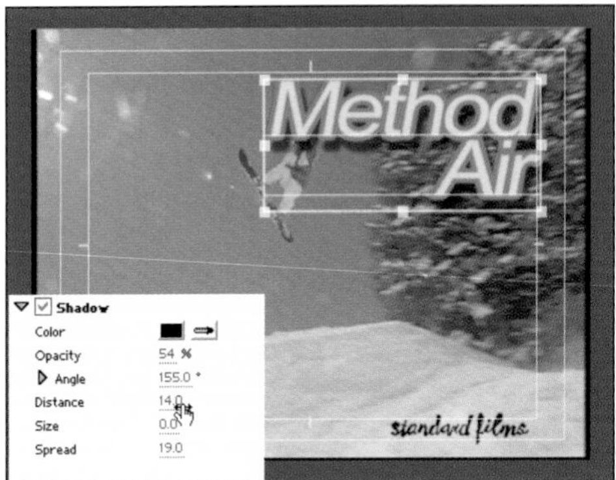

12. Drag the **Distance** value to the right to approximately **14.0** to increase the distance of the shadow from the original text. The larger the distance number, the farther away the shadow appears.

13. Save and close the **Title Designer**. Click the **Play In to Out** button in the **Monitor** window **Program** view. You will see that Premiere Pro has automatically updated your title.

14. Save and keep this project open before moving on to the next exercise.

*Although this exercise did not cover every available option of the **Fill**, **Stroke**, and **Shadow** properties–that would make this a very long chapter–the goal is to arm you with the knowledge to venture out on your own. You have learned the different methods of changing property values, selecting colors, and expanding twirl-down menus. Hopefully, when this book is closed (as if you could put it down!), you will be able to discover and understand the purpose and effect of each object property.*

NOTE | Picking Colors

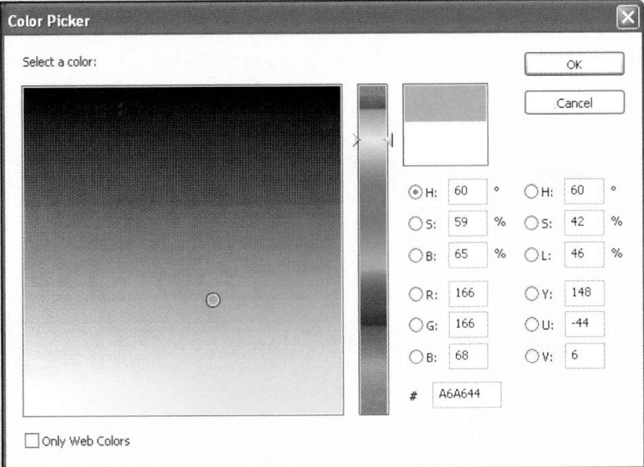

The Color Picker is the standard window that pops up any time a color needs to be selected. You will use this Color Picker when changing colors in the Title Designer, and also with many video effects and transitions.

In the previous exercise, you typed in RGB (Red-Green-Blue) values to select a new color. This is one of many ways to choose a color, including HSB, HSL, YUV, and Hexadecimal #. There's no need for you to understand what any of these acronyms stand for, so don't worry. Just remember that each one is a different method of describing the exact same thing: a color.

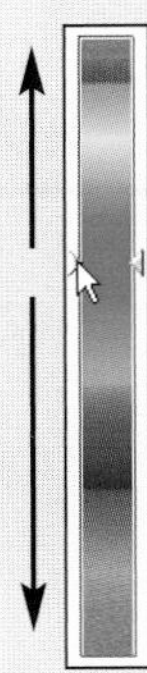

continues on next page

NOTE | Picking Colors *continued*

The first step to picking a color is to choose the hue. To pick a hue, drag the hue bar to the desired hue range.

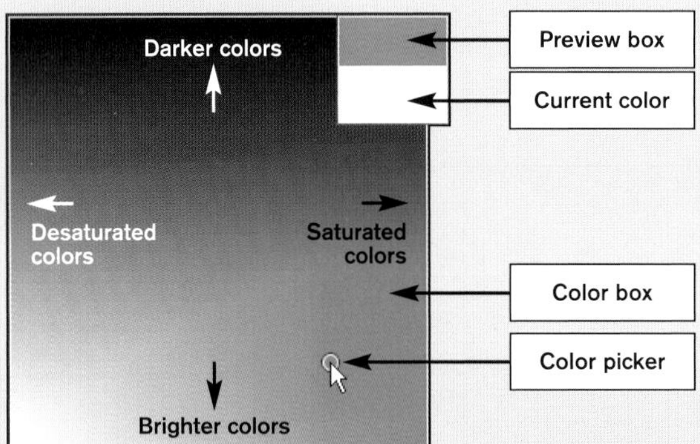

After you have chosen a hue, you can click in the **color box** to fine-tune your choice. As you click in the color box, your selected color will be shown in the **preview box** to the upper right. The **color picker** (round circle in the color box) represents the newly selected color. The top half of the preview box shows your newly selected color, and the bottom half represents the **current color** of the object.

In the color box, colors to the top are darker, and colors to the bottom are brighter. Colors to the left are desaturated (they lose their color intensity), and colors to the right are more saturated (intense).

A word of caution: computer monitors have a much larger color range than television monitors. This means that a subtle gray color on your computer screen may end up as just white on a television screen. Always preview your program on a television screen before sending it to tape–or worse–a client!

Another video faux-pas when picking colors is selecting bright reds. Reds tend to smear when played on a television set and some Web formats. (This holds true for all very bright colors, but reds especially.) Avoid picking very bright colors, which are those towards the bottom of the color box.

Here's an easy rule of thumb: stay at least one mouse-pointer away from the bottom of the color box when selecting colors.

5. Title Templates

Now that you've learned how to manually change your text objects, it's time to let you in on a little secret: templates. Premiere Pro comes built-in with dozens of premade templates, which allow you to quickly and easily create a title. In this exercise, you will create a new title based on an existing template, and then place it over the third clip in the sequence.

1. If you have the project open from the previous exercise, skip to Step 2. If Premiere Pro is not running, launch it and click **Open Project** at the **Welcome Screen**. Navigate to the **c:\Premiere Pro HOT\Chapter 06** folder, select **Exercise05.prproj**, and click **Open**.

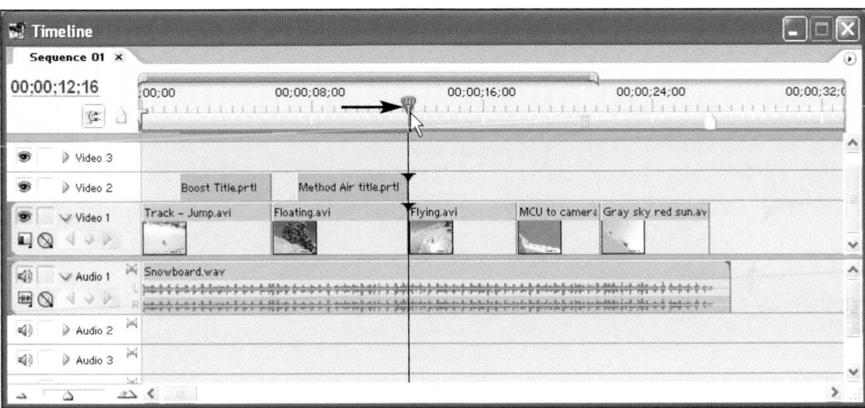

2. You are going to add a new title over the third clip in the **Timeline**. Move the **Timeline** marker to the position where the new title will be placed. Hold down the **Shift** key, and then drag the current time indicator until it snaps to the **Out** point of the second clip (which also happens to be the **Out** point of the second title, since they end at the same point in time).

***Tip:** The **In** point of the third clip is the same as the **Out** point of the second clip, since the two clips meet at the same point in time.*

3. Choose **File > New > Title** to create a new title.

4. At the top of the **Title Designer**, click the **Templates** button to open up the **Template Browser**.

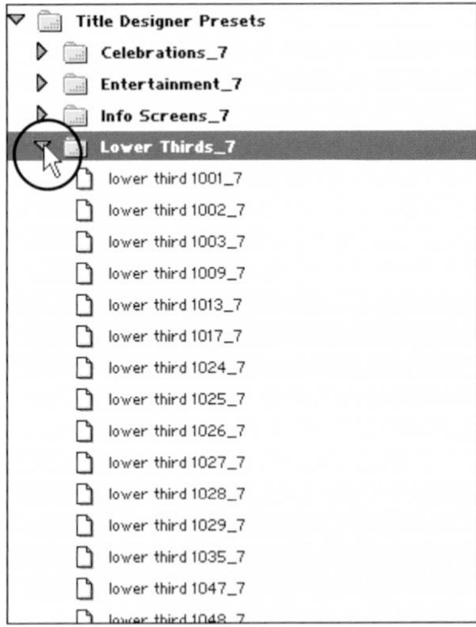

5. Twirl down the **Title Designer Presets** folder to view all available subfolders. Twirl down the **Lower Thirds_7** subfolder to view all available templates.

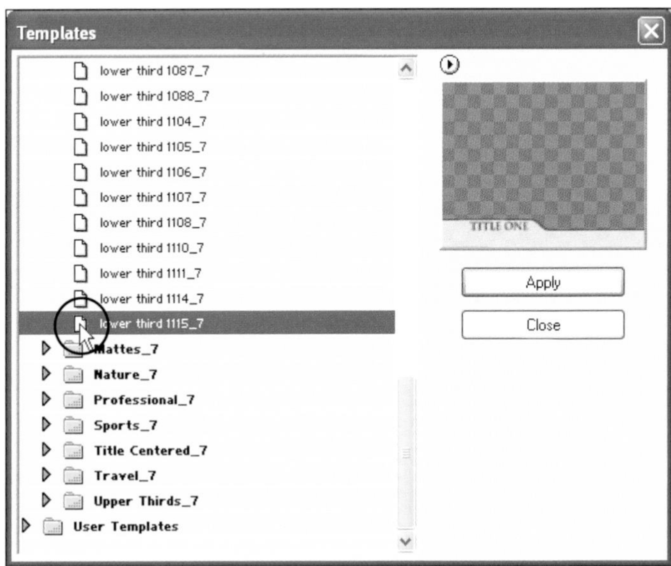

6. Scroll to the end of the **Lower Thirds_7** folder and select template **lower third 1115_7**. You will see a preview of the template in the upper-right preview window. Click **Apply**.

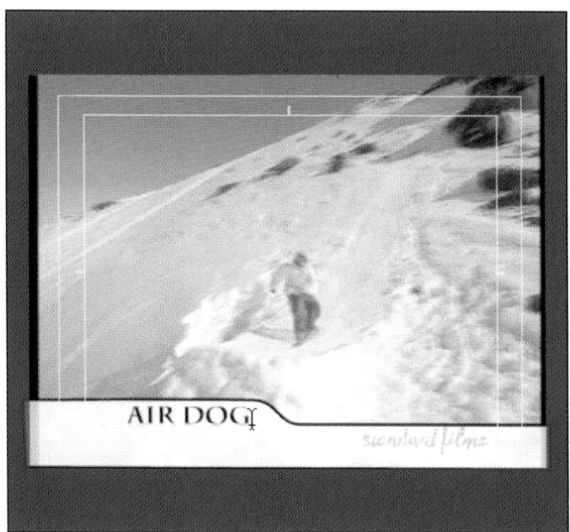

7. You will now see the template applied in the composition window. Select the **Type** tool and then click in the middle of the text **TITLE ONE**. Replace the text with **AIR DOG**.

8. When done, be sure to choose the **Selection** tool to signify that you are done typing, as well as prevent any accidental changes to the text you just typed. Since this is a template, you don't need to modify the text or polygon objects.

Note: *All elements of the template were created within* ***Title Designer.*** *Oh sure, you could create these exact objects and titles on your own–but then again, why reinvent the wheel?*

9. Save the title to the **Chapter 06** folder on your hard drive, and call it **Air Dog Title**. Click **Save**. Close your title after saving.

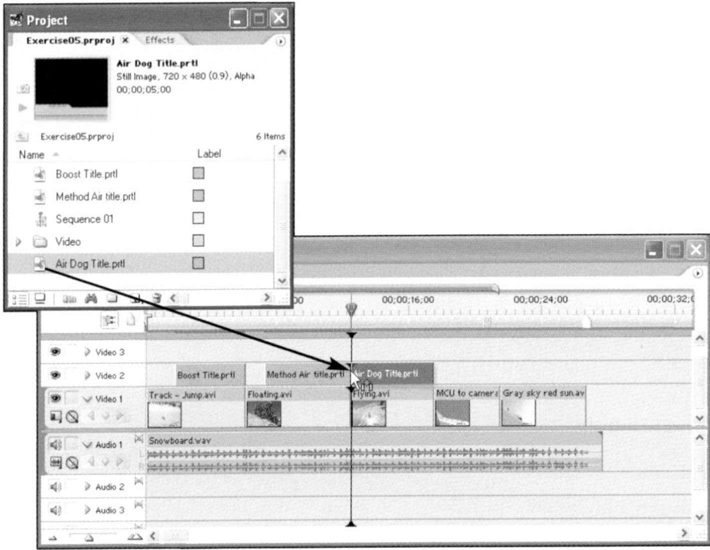

10. Drag the **Air Dog Title.prtl** clip from the **Project** window to the **Timeline** window. Snap it to the current time indicator.

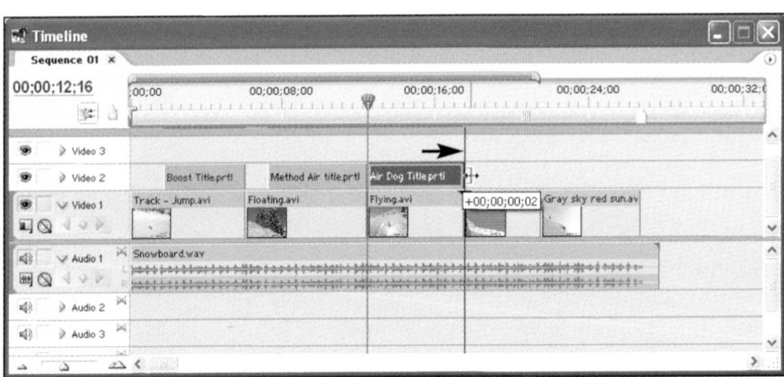

11. The length of the title is close to, but not precisely, the same length of the **Flying.avi** clip that it is above. In order to fix this, use the **Trim Out** pointer and drag the **Out** point of the **Air Dog Title.prtl** clip in the sequence and snap it to the **Out** point of the **Flying.avi** clip. (As you can see, it is only two frames off, but the trained eye will notice the difference during playback.)

12. Play the **Timeline** window to preview your sequence.

13. Save and keep this project open before moving on to the next exercise.

By now you're a pro at creating new titles, using styles, modifying properties, and building upon existing templates.

6. Rolling and Crawling Titles

Rolling titles scroll vertically, like the end credits of a movie. Crawling titles scroll horizontally, like the news ticker along the bottom of a news channel. Premiere Pro automates the task of creating rolling or crawling titles with a click (or two) of the mouse. In this exercise, you will create a rolling title over the fourth clip in the sequence.

1. If you have the project open from the previous exercise, skip to Step 2. If Premiere Pro is not running, launch it and click **Open Project** at the **Welcome Screen**. Navigate to the **c:\Premiere Pro HOT\Chapter 06** folder, select **Exercise06.prproj**, and click **Open**.

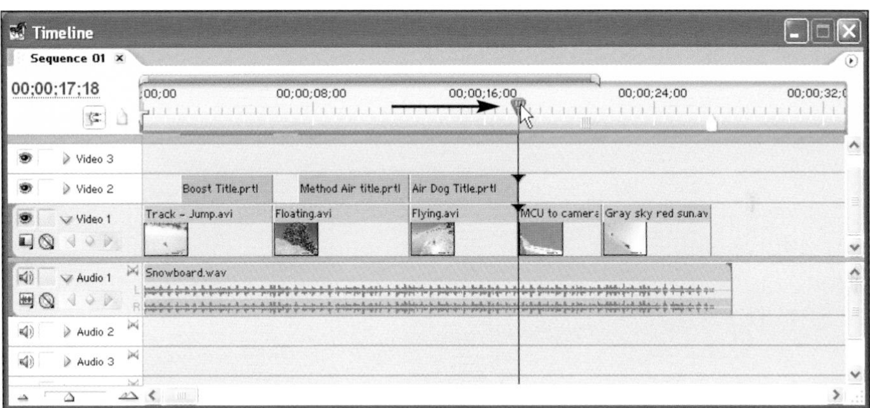

2. Before creating a title, move the current time indicator to the location where the title will start. Hold down **Shift** on the keyboard and drag the current time indicator to the **In** point of the fourth clip. Make sure to keep the **Shift** key held down, otherwise the current time indicator will not snap to the **In** point of the clip.

3. Choose **File > New > Title**.

4. In the **Title Designer** toolbar, select the **Type** tool.

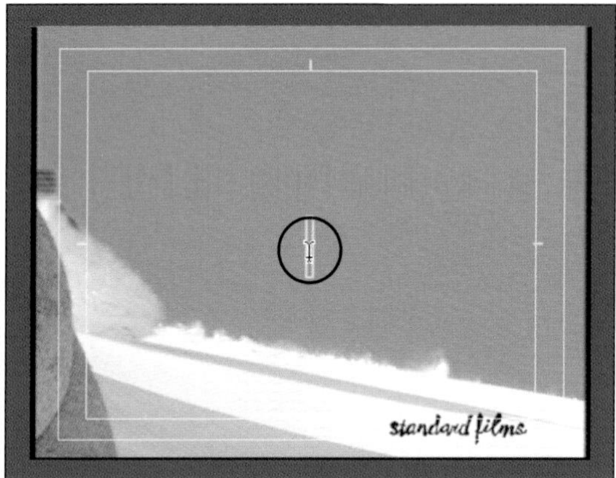

5. Click the mouse in the center (approximately) of the composition window.

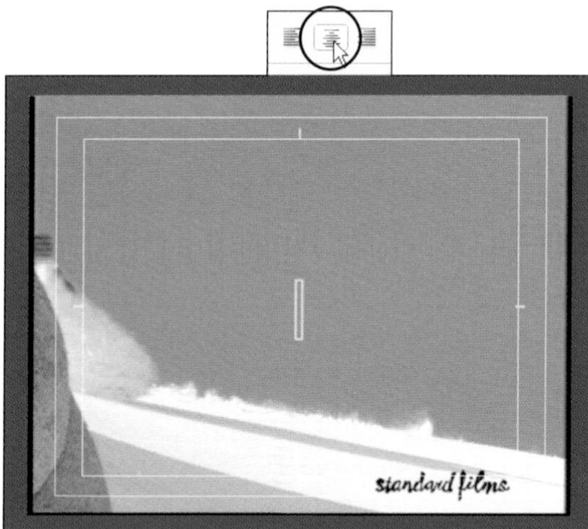

6. Before typing in text, click the **Center** button to set the paragraph alignment to center.

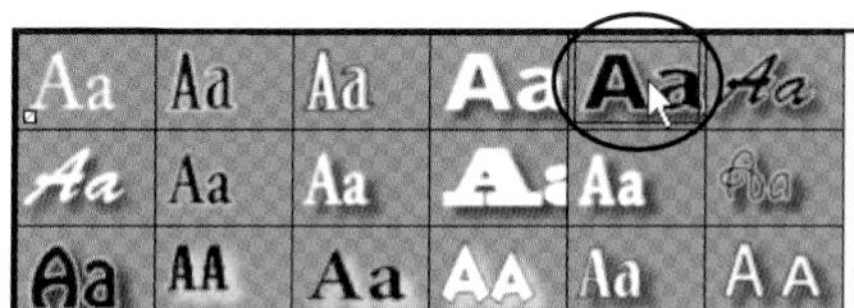

7. Before typing any text, you can also choose a style formatting. Click the fourth style from the left, in the top row.

8. Now that you have chosen a paragraph alignment and text style, you can (finally!) type your title. Type **Work hard**. Press **Enter**. Then type **Play harder**.

9. The only problem is that the second row, because it is longer, falls outside of the **title safe** area. To remedy this, you can reduce the font size of the second row only. With the **Text** tool still selected, click and drag your mouse over the second row of text to highlight it.

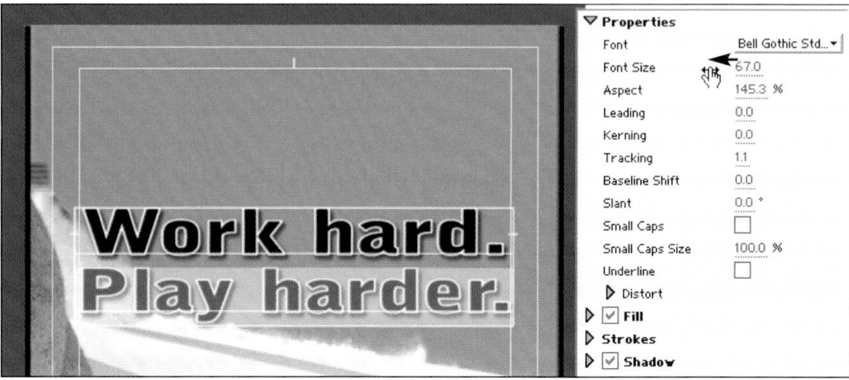

10. Hover your mouse over the **Font Size** property, then click and drag your mouse to the left, until the value is roughly **67.0**.

Tip: *Notice that only the highlighted text is affected. In an earlier exercise, you first chose the* ***Selection*** *tool to modify the entire text object. However, the* ***Text*** *tool allows you to highlight some of the text so you can modify just a portion of the letters.*

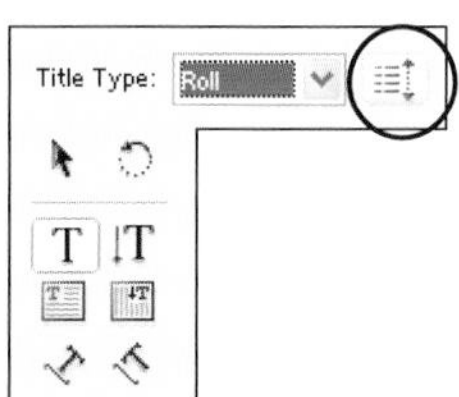

11. Now that you've created the text object, you can specify the type of title movement: **Still** (not-moving), **Roll**, or **Crawl**. From the **Title Type** drop-down menu, choose **Roll**. Then click the **Roll/Crawl Options** button to the right of the drop-down menu.

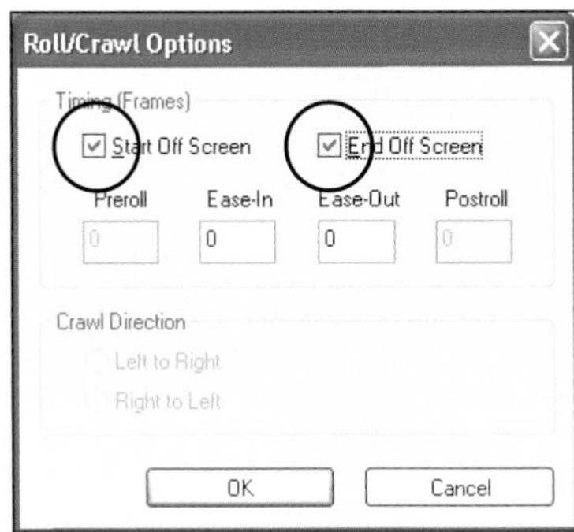

12. The **Roll/Crawl Options** window appears. You can choose to have your title start offscreen and end offscreen. Check the **Start Off Screen** check box, and then the **End Off Screen** check box. Click **OK**.

Note: *You can also mix and match by selecting just one of the boxes. Perhaps you want your title to start onscreen but to then move offscreen; or, you want the title to start offscreen but finish onscreen.*

13. Choose **File > Save** to save the title. Navigate to the **Chapter 06** directory and name it **Play Hard**. Click **Save**. Choose **File > Close** to close the title.

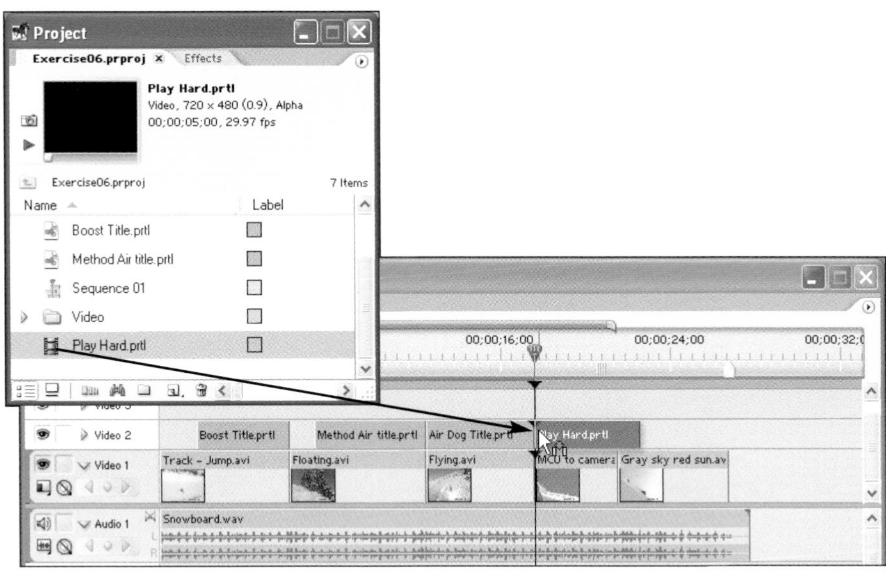

14. After you close the title, it is automatically imported into the **Project** window. Drag the title from the **Project** window to the **Timeline** window. Snap it to the **In** point of the fourth clip. (As always, look for the *snappy* black line. Get it? Snappy?)

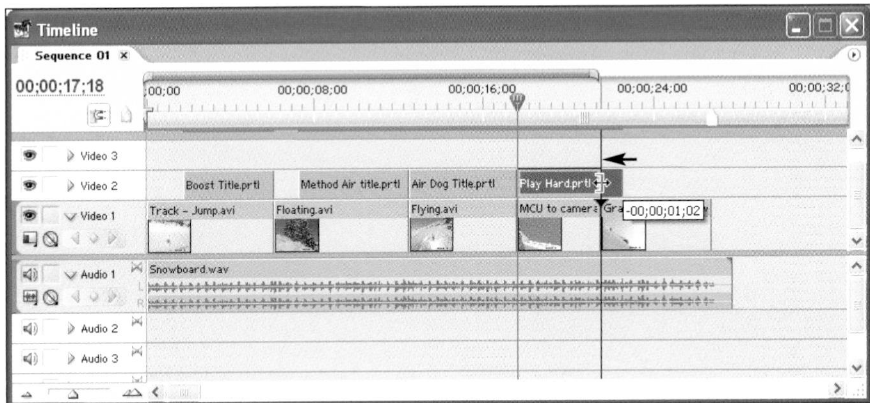

15. The last problem to fix is that the title extends beyond the clip it is playing over. Using the **Trim Out** pointer, snap the **Out** point of the title to the **Out** point of the fourth clip.

Tip: The best feature of a rolling/crawling title is that it automatically changes the speed of the roll/crawl to match the duration of the title. If you made the title one second long, the roll would scroll very fast, in order to finish in one second. Likewise, if the title was 10 seconds long, the roll would take exactly 10 seconds to finish.

---

16. Preview the sequence by clicking play in the **Monitor** window **Program** view. If all goes well, your new title should start offscreen, from the bottom, then scroll up, and eventually finish off the top part of the screen.

---

17. Save and close this project.

*In this exercise, you created a rolling title. You didn't practice a crawling title, but the steps are almost identical. Choose **Crawling** instead of **Rolling**, and everything else is the same.*

Congratulations. You've just made it through the entire chapter. You may have noticed that creating titles themselves is not so tough–but changing all of the styles and font properties can be overwhelming. In this chapter, you learned all of the types of titles you can create, as well as the luxury of using the style and template libraries.

Titles are one type of graphic file that Premiere Pro can import. However, there are many times when you'll import graphics like photographs or company logos. Of course, now that you've mastered the arduous tasks of creating and modifying titles, importing graphics will be a piece of cake.

---

7 Still Images and Fixed Effects

Converting Still Images to Video	Still Images Sizes
The Fixed Effects	Image Scale and Position
Alpha Channels and Rendering	Alpha Channel Vignette
Artificial Widescreen

H•O•T

Premiere Pro HOT DVD

So far you've imported, edited, and trimmed video and audio clips. Plus you've created a title or two. Now it's time to venture into the world of still images. The good news is that still images are treated like any other type of clip, so you already know the ease of importing and trimming still images. In this chapter, you will review importing and trimming still images, uncover additional features that apply only to still images, and also learn to avoid the common pitfalls of using still images in your projects.

Converting Still Images to Video

In the real world, everyone knows how a movie differs from a photograph. However, in the world of video editing, there is hardly any difference. Huh? It sounds crazy, but think of it like this...

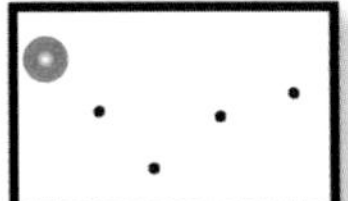 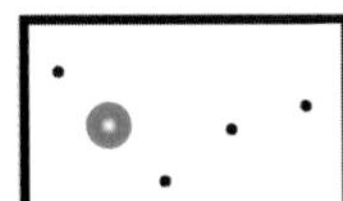 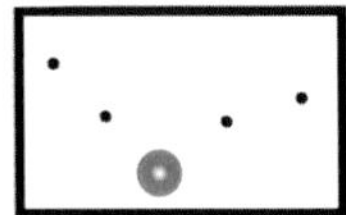 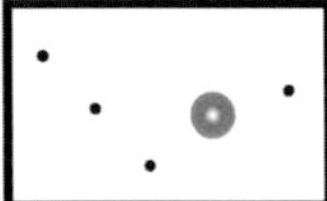 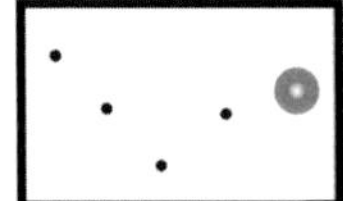

A video clip is a series of still images (or *frames)* being played before your eyes–like a flipbook–at 30 frames per second (30 frames per second in the Americas, Japan, and South Korea; 25 just about everywhere else).

Unlike a video clip, a still image has only one *frame*. Simple so far, right? In order to import the still image into your project, Premiere Pro converts the still to video, so it must play at video's rate of 30 frames per second. Since a still image has only one frame, the same image is repeated 30 times per second.

Both video and still images flip through 30 frames per second, the subtle difference is that each frame of video is different than the previous, creating the illusion of movement, whereas a still image appears still because all 30 frames are the same.

This leads to another difference between video clips and still images: video clips have a finite duration. When a video clip is captured to your hard drive from tape, you specify a time to start capturing and a time to stop capturing. The total number of frames you capture determines the length of the clip. You don't have to use all of the frames you capture, but you definitely can't use more than you captured.

On the other hand, a still image has no beginning and no end (how Zen!), and thus can play for an infinite duration. Since Premiere Pro plays the same image over and over 30 times per second, it can repeat the image for as long as you need it to play.

Premiere Pro can import the most commonly used types of still images (and in some cases, some rarely used types as well). No matter how your image starts out–as a scanned photograph, a logo on a business card, or a Web graphic–the end goal is to make sure the final format is one shown in the following table. The table lists the file types (such as JPG) and the most common use of that format.

If your format is not listed, you may need to convert your image to a common format with software such as Photoshop before Premiere Pro can import the file.

Types of Still Images	
Format Supported	**Common Uses of the Format**
AI	Adobe Illustrator
EPS	Adobe Illustrator, Adobe Photoshop, Macromedia Freehand
BMP	Windows bitmap (used by Microsoft Paint, some Desktop backgrounds)
FLM	Filmstrip (animations that can be rotoscoped in Photoshop)
GIF	Web image
JPG	Web image
PNG	Lesser-known Web format, superior to (and soon to replace) GIF format
ICO	Icon file (Windows Desktop or Start menu icons)
PCX	A rarely-used format
PSD	Adobe Photoshop
PIC, PCT, PICT	Macintosh Pict format (Apple QuickDraw)
TGA	Targa (used by high-end graphic applications and CAD design software)
TIF, TIFF	Tiff image (used often by graphic designers and print professionals)
PRTL	Adobe Title Designer
PTL	Adobe Premiere 6 Title (from earlier version)

Still Image Sizes

Still images is a broad category that includes pictures, logos, photographs, Web graphics, scanned documents, digital camera stills, and files from programs such as Photoshop and Illustrator. There's really no mystery to using stills in Premiere Pro. Once the image has been imported into a project, Premiere Pro treats the image like any other clip. Nearly everything you've learned about importing and trimming video clips applies equally to still images. In fact, you could go back to previous chapters, scratch out the phrase *video clip*, replace it with *still image*, and most of the exercises would still hold true (not recommended if you checked this book out from the library).

So, you've already learned how to import still images into the Project window and trim images in the Timeline window with the Trim In and Trim Out pointers. However, still images do have a few differences and features that do not hold true for video clips. The primary difference between video and still images is the *size*.

Video clips usually come from a camera, and clips that come from DV cameras (in North America) are exactly 720 pixels wide by 480 pixels tall—*always*. This works out well because that happens to be the size you chose for your project back in Chapter 1, "*The Project*," when you selected a project preset.

Still images, on the other hand, have no size restrictions because they come from many different sources. Some graphics can be twice the size of a Premiere Pro project, and others can be half. Some have the same rectangular shape as your project; others are square shaped. This presents a unique set of problems (and also opportunities) that apply to still images

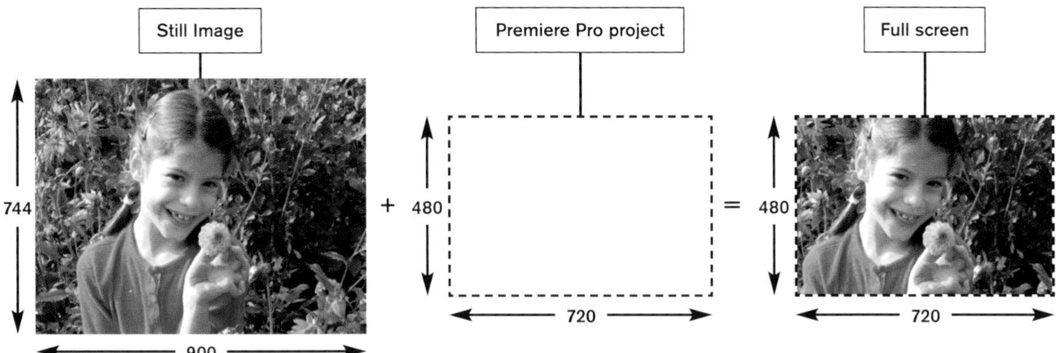

Images that are equal to or larger than your Premiere Pro project can be played **full-screen**, meaning they take up the entire display, just like video does. An example of a full-screen image is a slideshow of photos from your vacation. If an image is larger than your project, the part of the image that falls outside of the project screen will be cropped.

Images that are smaller than your project can be **overlayed**, meaning they play in a small section of the screen on top of an existing video clip. This allows the underlying video clip to be seen in the area behind the still image.

The Fixed Effects

Remember everything you just read about full-screen and overlayed image sizes? Well throw it out. It's all a lie.

Okay, not really. However, as with all good rules, there are exceptions. The good news is that you are not stuck with the size of your still image. Premiere Pro gives you the ability to resize still images; you can take a full-screen image and shrink it to an overlayed image, or take an overlayed image and enlarge it to full-screen. You can also move images left, right, up, or down.

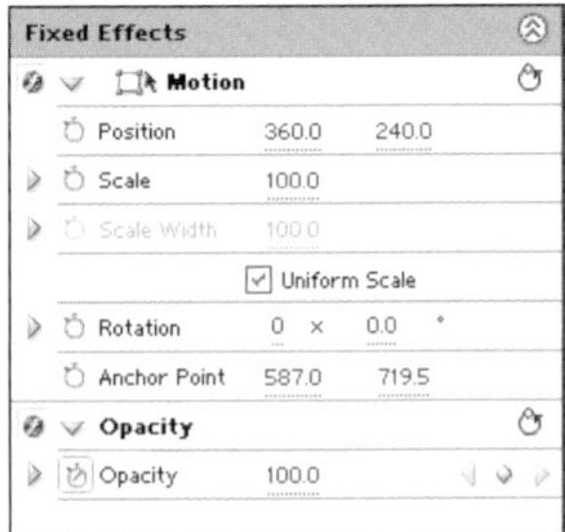

The secret to resizing and moving images lies within the **fixed effects**. Fixed effects are attributes of a clip that cannot be removed–they are *fixed*. In other words, they are properties that are built-in to every clip; you can modify these properties, but you can never delete them. Even the clips you've been using in this book have fixed effects. (You just didn't know how to find them, until now.)

Image and video clips have five fixed effects: Position, Scale, Rotation, Anchor Point, and Opacity. These five properties define the look of the clip during playback.

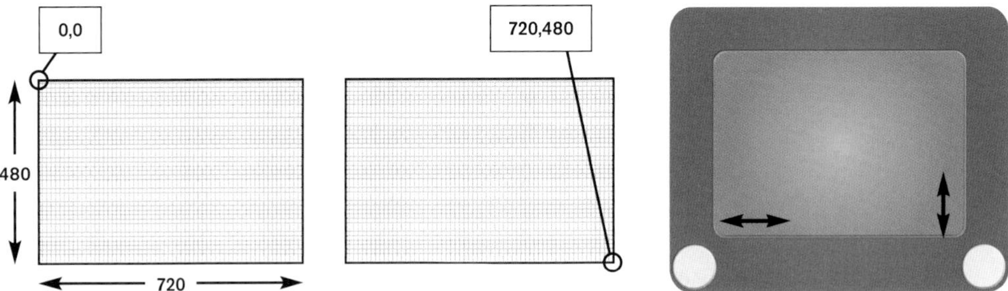

The **Position** property defines the location of the clip within the Monitor window. You can move a clip to the left or right by changing the horizontal value, or you can move a clip up and down by changing the vertical value. Think of the Monitor window like a big grid. For DV NTSC projects, the upper-left corner is (0,0); the lower-right corner is (720,480). That's because there are 720 pixels across and 480 pixels down. The horizontal and vertical values of the position property behave just like an Etch-a-Sketch–the first knob moves the image left and right, and the second knob moves it up and down. (Please do not turn your monitor upside down and shake it to undo your work!)

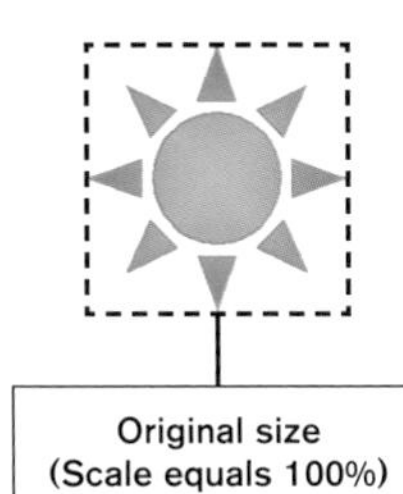

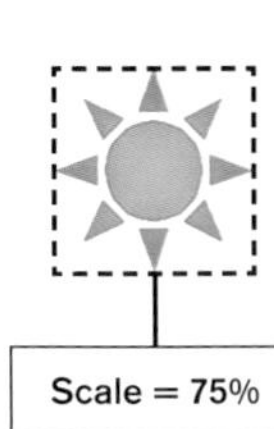

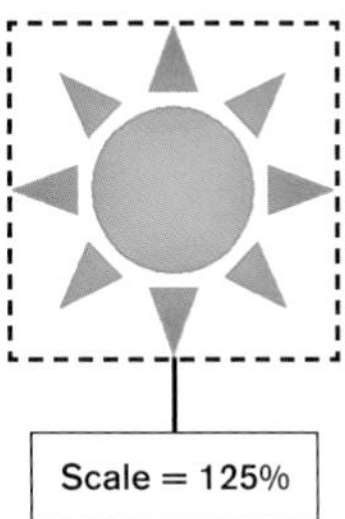

The **Scale** property defines the size of the clip. All clips are imported at their original sizes, which is 100% Scale. Any Scale value less than 100% reduces the size of the clip, and any value over 100% increases the size of the clip. If an image is too big to fit inside the Monitor window, you can scale it down so that the entire picture is visible.

The **Rotation** property changes the angle of the clip, in degrees. 90 degrees is sideways, 180 degrees is upside-down, and 360 degrees is one full revolution, back to where you started.

The **Anchor Point** is the pivot point of the image. When you rotate a clip, it rotates around the anchor point. When you scale an image, it zooms out from the anchor point. There will rarely be a time, at this level in your Premiere Pro education, when you will need to modify the Anchor Point, so you can pretty much ignore it.

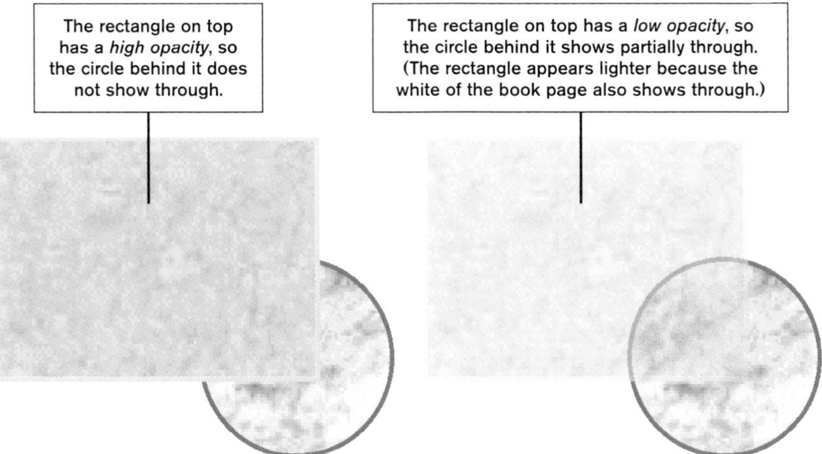

The rectangle on top has a *high opacity*, so the circle behind it does not show through.
The rectangle on top has a *low opacity*, so the circle behind it shows partially through. (The rectangle appears lighter because the white of the book page also shows through.)

The **Opacity** property changes the overall transparency of the clip. In other words, it defines how much the object allows other objects to "show through" from behind. For example, if you stand behind a brick wall, which has a high opacity, you can not be seen by an observer on the other side of the wall. However, if you stand behind a shower curtain, which has a low opacity value, the people on the other side can see you (and think you're a little creepy).

NOTE | Scaling Clips Over 100%

Warning: Scaling a clip over 100% causes the image to blur and pixilate. (There's a technical reason behind this truth, but it's not a very interesting read.)

Long story short, the further beyond 100% you scale, the more noticeable the blurriness and pixilation. It may not be noticeable at 105%, but at 150%, your image may be downright ugly.

When in doubt, always start with a bigger image than you'll need and reduce the scale to fit your project. For example, perhaps you want to create a video montage of photographs from a vacation. Before you take any photos, make sure you set your digital camera to take pictures larger than 720 × 480, if possible. This will allow you to play the images full-screen or choose to scale them down or move them around so you can focus on certain areas.

Rule of thumb with still images: larger equals better. It's always better to start at 100% of the image size and scale down to fit the image into the Monitor window. (FYI: Premiere Pro does have a 4000 × 4000 pixel limit, so bigger is better, up to a point.)

I. Image Scale and Position

In this exercise, you will change the scale and position fixed effects of an image clip.

1. If Premiere Pro is not running, launch it and click **Open Project** at the **Welcome Screen**. Navigate to the **c:\Premiere Pro HOT\Chapter 07** folder, select **Exercise01.prproj**, and click **Open**.

2. Choose **File > Import**.

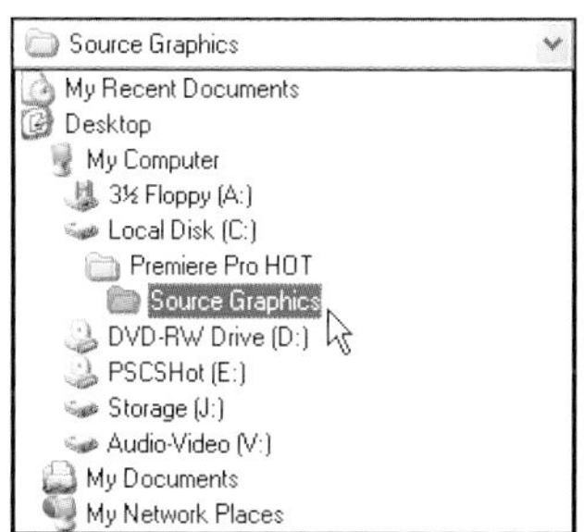

3. Navigate to the **c:\Premiere Pro HOT\Source Graphics** directory.

4. Select **flowergirl.tif** and click **Open**.

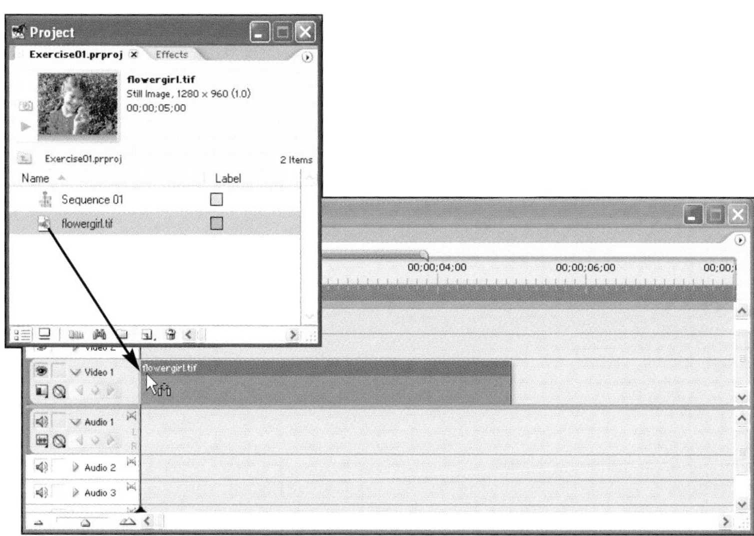

5. Drag **flowergirl.tif** from the **Project** window to track **Video 1** of the **Timeline** window. Make sure you drag the clip to the far left of the track, so it starts at **00;00;00;00**.

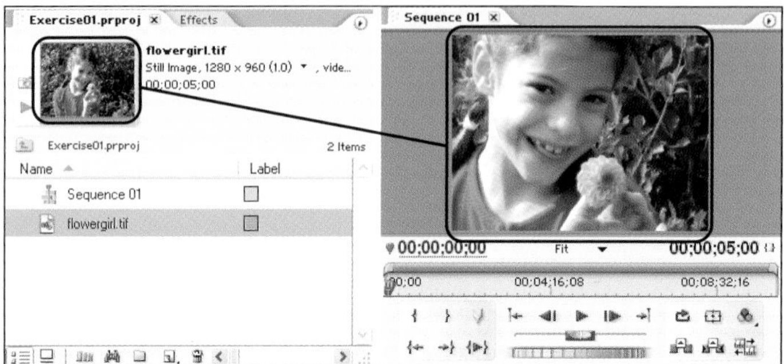

*The **Monitor** window **Program** view (right side) displays how the image currently looks in the sequence. Notice the difference between the original image, shown in the preview area of the **Project** window, and the final version in your sequence. The image, which is 1280×960 pixels, is much bigger than the 720×480 size of the project, so you can only see part of the image in the Monitor window.*

***Note:** Make sure the current time indicator in the **Timeline** is still at the beginning of the sequence, or over the still image on the **Timeline**, otherwise you won't be able to see the still image in the **Program** view.*

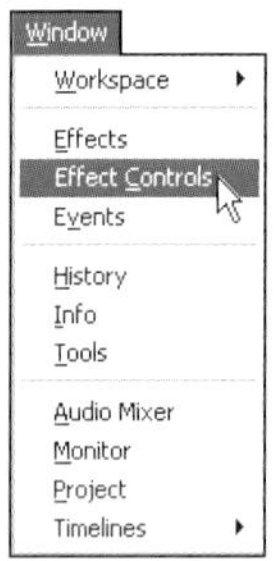

6. Now you are going to scale down the image so you can see more of it in the **Monitor** window. Choose **Window > Effect Controls**. This opens up the **Effect Controls** palette, in what was previously the left side of the **Monitor** window.

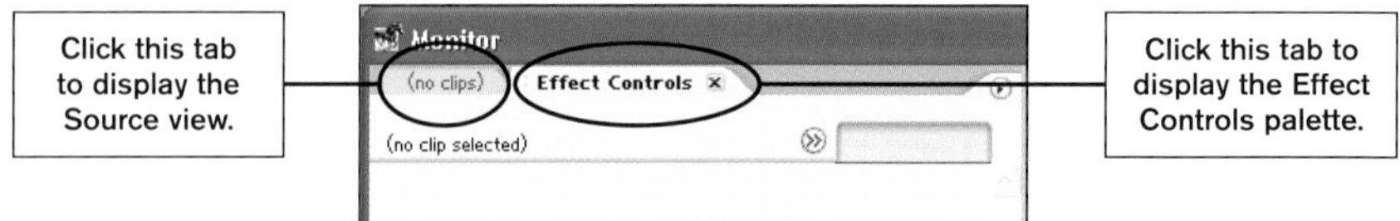

Note:** Because space is at a premium in Premiere Pro, the **Monitor** window **Source** view and **Effect Controls** palette share the same window. Each palette in a window has its own tab. You can display the **Source** view again by clicking its tab to bring it to the foreground. You can then view the **Effect Controls** by clicking its tab. This is the same as choosing **Window > Effect Controls.

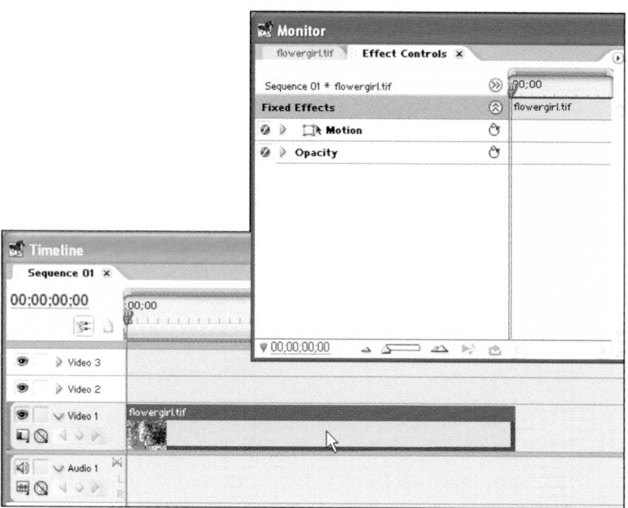

7. The **Effect Controls** palette displays the fixed effects for the currently selected clip. If you have no clip selected in the **Timeline** window, the **Effect Controls** palette will be empty. Click the **flowergirl.tif** clip in the **Timeline** window to select it, and the **Effect Controls** palette displays the **Motion** and **Opacity** fixed effects for that clip.

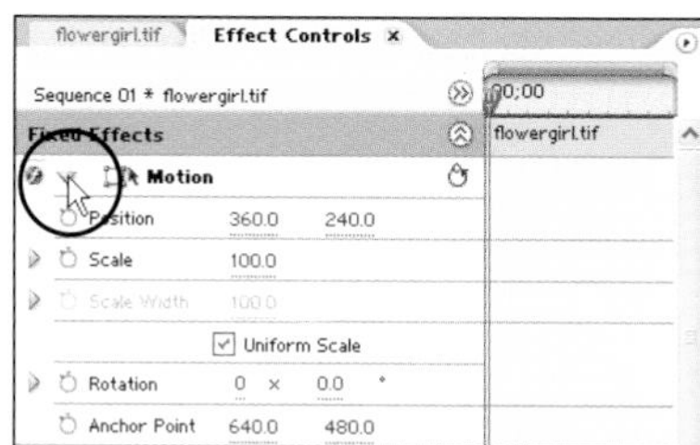

8. Click the twirl-down arrow for **Motion** to expand its properties. You should recognize the five properties discussed earlier: **Position**, **Scale**, **Rotation**, **Anchor Point**, and **Opacity**. (Opacity gets its own twirl-down menu, for reasons that are known only to the Adobe software developers.)

Note: *If you accidentally* deselect *the clip in the* **Timeline** *window, you will not be able to see any fixed effects. The* **Effect Controls** *palette shows only the fixed effects for the selected clip.*

9. Hover your mouse over the **Scale** property in the **Fixed Effects** palette. When the mouse cursor changes from an arrow to a finger with a dual arrow, hold down your mouse button (don't let go) and drag it slowly to the left, until the value is approximately **60.0**. As you drag to the left, you will see the still image slowly get smaller.

Tip: You can also single click the value itself and type in ***60.0.***

10. The top part of the image is cut off, so the next step is to "scoot" it down just a smidge. To move the image down, hover your mouse over the vertical position value (the second number) until the arrow changes to a finger, hold down the mouse button and drag to the right (the image will slowly move down). Drag until the vertical position value is **260.0**. (That's not very far from its original distance.)

11. Click the **Play** button in the **Monitor** window **Program** view to preview the clip in the **Timeline**. (The **Monitor** won't appear to do much, because it's showing a still image.)

*You have just changed the **Scale** and **Position** fixed effects of a still image, which are the two most common modifications you will make to still images. (In fact, nearly every still image you import will need to be scaled and/or repositioned.) The steps are the exact same for the lesser-used **Rotation** and **Opacity** properties. Just remember the basics: first open the **Effect Controls**, and then select a clip on the **Timeline**.*

---

12. Save and keep this project open before moving on to the next exercise.

Alpha Channels and Rendering

Here is another difference between video clips and image clips: **alpha channels**. Although the phrase sounds like either a military code or a cable network, an alpha channel is actually a method of defining transparent regions in a still image.

(Most) video clips do not have alpha channels. They are completely opaque, so that any clips underneath do not show through. However, some still images have alpha channels, which allow any clips underneath to show through the transparent portions of the image. If an image does not have an alpha channel, it will be completely opaque like a video clip–meaning that nothing underneath will show through.

Image without alpha channel.

Image without alpha channel on top of video. No video shows through the image.

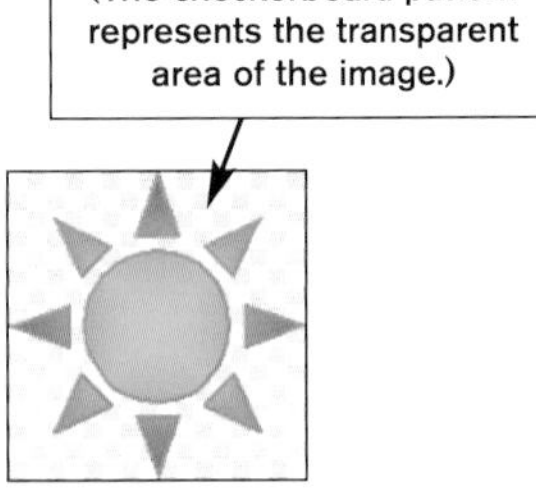

(The checkerboard pattern represents the transparent area of the image.)

Image with an alpha channel.

Image with alpha channel on top of video. Video shows through the transparent region.

Here's how an alpha channel works: When an image is saved with an alpha channel from a program such as Photoshop, the alpha channel information is embedded into the image. When the image is imported as a clip into a project, Premiere Pro automatically reads the alpha channel and creates a transparent area. When the clip is placed on a track above a video clip, the video underneath shows through.

You don't have to do anything to "turn on" alpha channels–Premiere Pro automatically does it for you. Unfortunately, Premiere Pro cannot create an alpha channel where none exists. It can only read in existing alpha channels. The original image must be saved with an alpha channel by the software that created it.

Earlier in this chapter you learned how opacity works. About now you may be wondering, how does an alpha channel differ from opacity? Opacity defines the transparency for the *entire image*, so it can only make the entire image more or less opaque. An alpha channel defines the transparency for just *a portion of the image*, so it can make any region of the image more or less opaque.

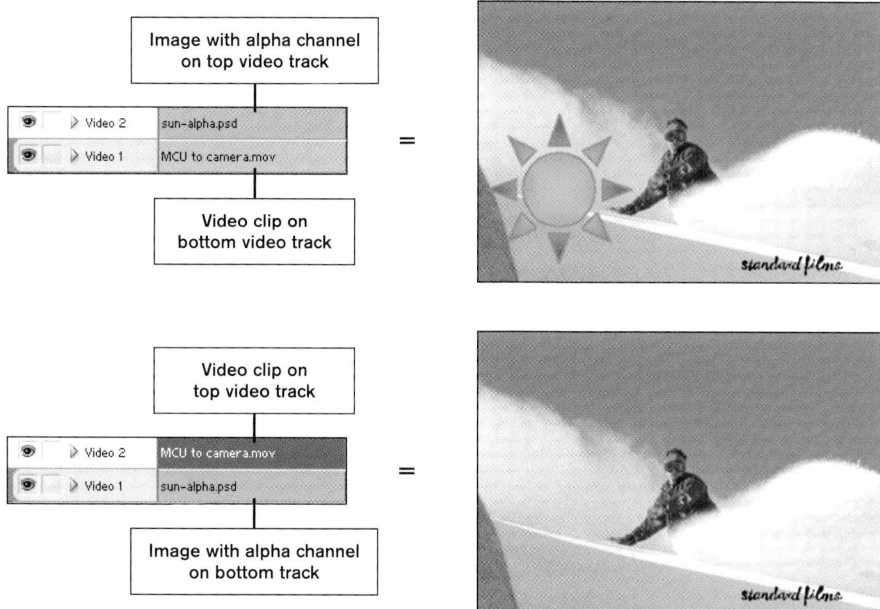

So how exactly do you place an alpha channel image on top of a video clip? In reality, you're not placing it on top of the image. Instead, you are placing it in the video track above the image. Premiere Pro renders from the top down. This means that whichever clip is in the top-most video track will display on top in the Monitor window Program view. If you place the alpha channel image on the top track, it will show on top of the video.

If you placed a video clip on the top track and an alpha channel image below it, you would see only the video, because video clips are (usually) completely opaque. The alpha channel image is still there, it's just being obstructed by the video clip, which is on top.

You can add more video tracks and place more images on top of each other. You can also place a title on top of an image, or an image on an image. And, yes, even though you will rarely come across this, some video clips generated by computer will have an alpha channel. (This is rare, since most clips are "generated" by your video camera, which *never ever* creates an alpha channel.)

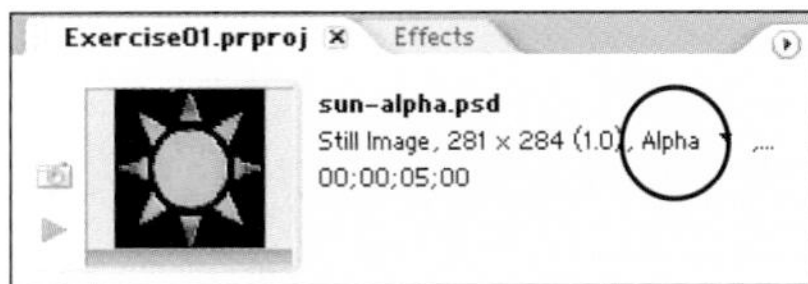

If you're not sure whether a clip has an alpha channel, select the clip in the Project window to view its information in the Project window preview area; look for the word *Alpha* next to the clip's pixel information.

In the next exercise, you will get to experience for yourself the fun of overlaying alpha channels on other clips.

2. Alpha Channel Vignette

Importing still images with alpha channels and dragging them to the top-most video track is a piece of cake. Instead, this exercise will show you one of the best tricks of overlaying still images with alpha channels: creating a **vignette**. In this exercise, you will overlay a vignette on top of a video clip and another still image.

1. If you have the project open from the previous exercise, skip to Step 2. If Premiere Pro is not running, launch it and click **Open Project** at the **Welcome Screen**. Navigate to the **c:\Premiere Pro HOT\Chapter 07** folder, select **Exercise02.prproj**, and click **Open**.

---

2. First you need to import a video clip. Choose **File > Import**.

---

3. Navigate to the **c:\Premiere Pro HOT\Source Video** directory, and import **MCU to camera.avi**. Click **Open**.

---

4. Navigate to the **c:\Premiere Pro HOT\Source Graphics** directory, and import **vignette.png**. Click **Open**.

The vignette image has an alpha channel. The edges are black, but there is a soft "hole" right in the middle of the image. Any clip that is behind the vignette clip in the ***Timeline*** *window will show through the hole.*

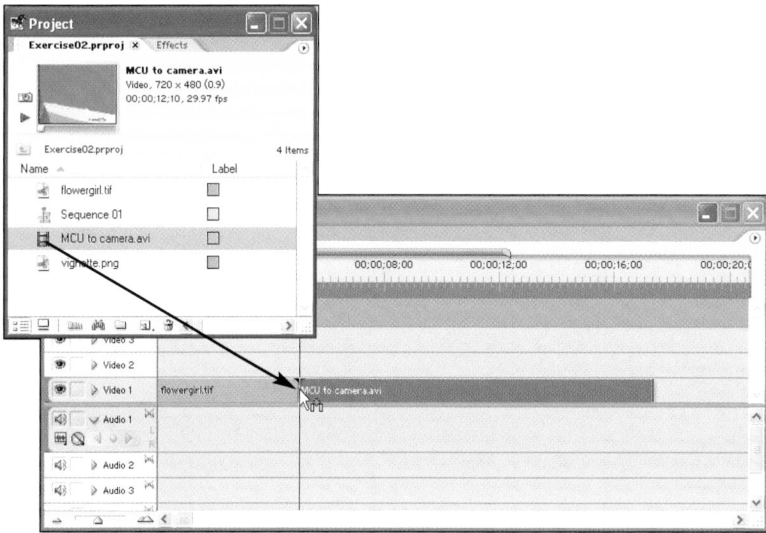

5. First, drag the **MCU to camera.avi** video clip from the **Project** window to track **Video 1** in the **Timeline** window, snapping it to the end of **flowergirl.tif**.

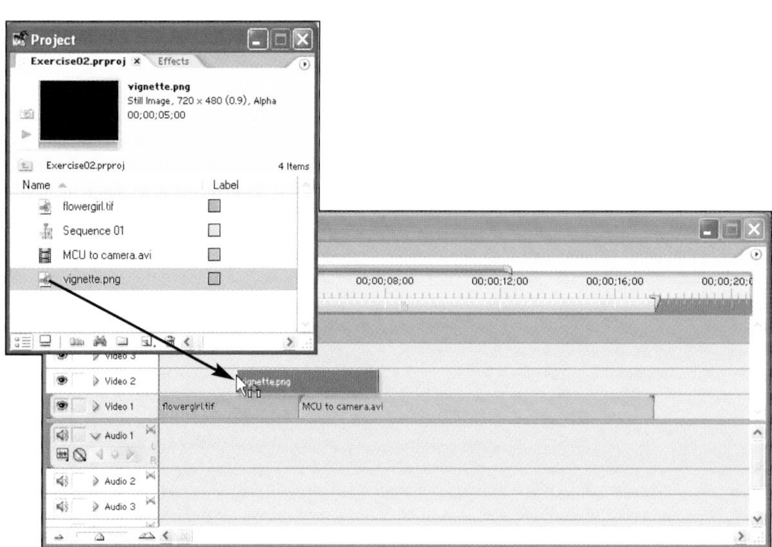

6. Next, drag **vignette.png** from the **Project** window to track **Video 2**. Instead of snapping it, try to place it so it is centered above the edit point where the clips in track **Video 1** meet. It doesn't have to be perfect, and if you are unhappy with your clip placement in track **Video 2**, you can always click the clip and move it in the **Timeline** window.

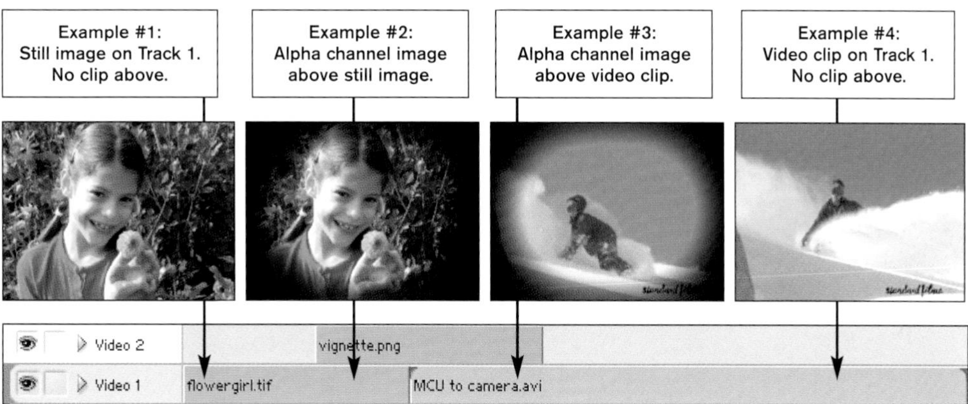

7. The sequence you've just built contains three clips, but it has four different examples to observe. In the **Monitor** window **Program** view, click the **Play** button to preview the entire sequence.

Did you notice how the vignette alpha channel allowed the image or video below to show through the hole? The vignette clip is a great way to add an "olde-time" look to your projects. You've probably seen similar effects created on television, with binoculars, hunting scopes, periscopes, night-vision goggles, and so on. These are all examples of images with alpha channels placed over video clips.

---

8. Save and keep this project open before moving on to the next exercise.

NOTE | Changing Default Duration

You learned earlier that your still image is converted into video when it is imported into Premiere Pro. But you also learned that image clips have no duration and can be stretched to infinity. So why do all of the image clips you've used so far seem to be about 5 seconds long? This is because Premiere Pro assigns the clips a duration of 5 seconds at the time they are imported into the project. This is an arbitrary number chosen by the Premiere Pro software development team, and you can easily change it to your liking.

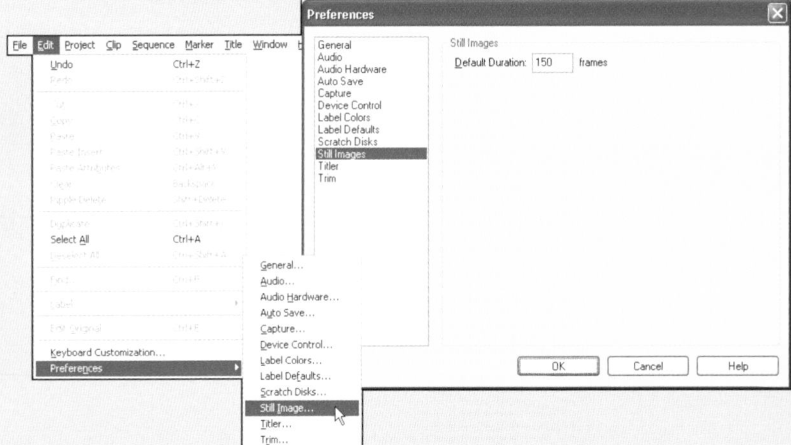

To change the default image duration, choose **Edit > Preferences > Still Image**. In the **Preferences** window, you will see all of the **Still Images** options. (Well, there's only one option!) This is where you can change the **Default Duration**. Keep in mind that the number is in frames, so 150 frames ÷ 30 frames per second = 5 seconds.

Also be aware that this will not affect any clips that you have already imported into your project. This will only affect future clips. (No, future clips are not clips with time machines or jet packs.)

3. Artificial Widescreen

While we're on the subject of overlays with alpha channels, there's another great type of image that you will want to know how to create: an **artificial widescreen** (also called **letterbox**). This gives your 4:3 footage the look of 16:9 with a black bar along the top and bottom. In this exercise, you will create an artificial widescreen with the use of a title template.

1. If you have the project open from the previous exercise, skip to Step 2. If Premiere Pro is not running, launch it and click **Open Project** at the **Welcome Screen**. Navigate to the **c:\Premiere Pro HOT\Chapter 07** folder, select **Exercise03.prproj**, and click **Open**.

---

2. To create a new title, choose **File > New > Title**.

3. In the upper-left corner of the **Title Designer**, click the **Template** button to open the list of available templates.

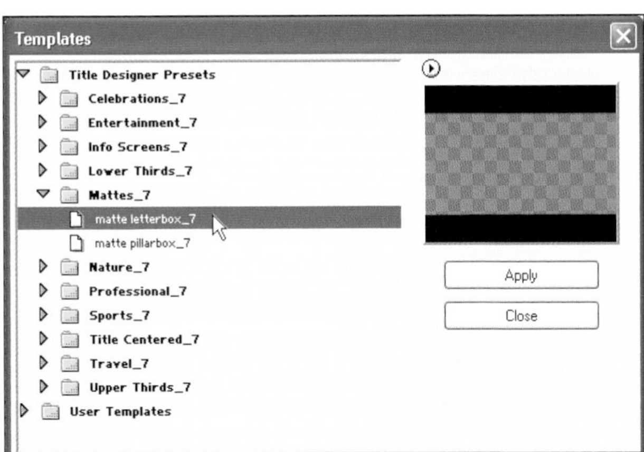

4. In the **Templates** window, twirl down the arrow next to **Title Designer Presets** to expand the folder and view its contents. Next twirl down the arrow next to **Mattes_7** to expand and view its contents. Select **matte letterbox_7** and click **Apply**.

---

5. Your title now has rectangular objects on the top and on the bottom of the **Title Designer** composition window. Choose **File > Save** to save the title. Navigate to the **c:\Premiere Pro HOT\Chapter 07** directory and save it with the name **letterbox title**. After you save the title, close the **Title Designer**.

Tip: *You can change the fill, stroke, and shadow properties of these polygon objects just like you did to text objects in the previous chapter. But for this example, that's not necessary.*

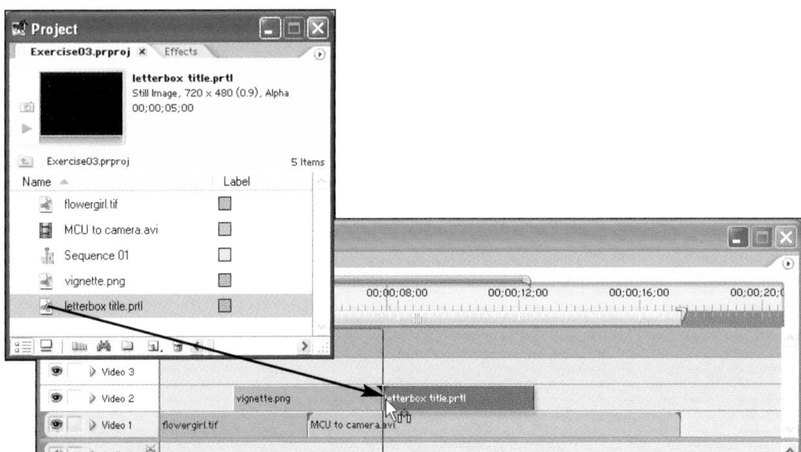

6. The title has automatically been placed in your **Project** window. Drag the title from the **Project** window to the **Timeline** window, onto track **Video 2**, snapping it to the end of **vignette.png**.

7. Click the **Play** button in the **Monitor** window **Program** view to preview the sequence. Notice that the letterbox title lets the video underneath show through.

8. Save and close this project before moving on to the next exercise.

The lesson of this exercise was twofold: 1) titles have alpha channels, and that's what allows them to play on top of other clips and let the video show through; 2) you can create much more than just text with the ***Title Designer****.*

This chapter contained a lot of useful information describing how graphics, fixed effects, and alpha channels work. One of the exciting features of fixed effects is that you can change their values over time. (For example, a still image can start on the left side of the screen and slowly pan across to the right.) You'll learn how to do that in Chapter 11, "Video Effects."

To sum up this chapter, remember that all video and graphic clips have five fixed effects (attributes) that define how they look during playback. Also remember that not all clips have alpha channels.

Now you've added video, audio, titles, and still images (with and without alpha channels) to your Premiere Pro project. Next you will learn how to add transitions, which create smooth fades between your clips.

8

Transition Effects

What Is a Transition Effect?	Adding Video Transitions
How Transitions Works	The Effect Controls Window
Modifying Transitions	Adding Transitions to Titles
Single-Sided Transitions	Adding Single-Sided Transitions
Clips Without Heads or Tails	Creating Head or Tail Materials

H•O•T

Premiere Pro HOT DVD

So far in this book you have built sequences with straight cuts, where one clip butts up against the next clip. The last frame of a clip is followed by the first frame of the next clip. Transition effects, on the other hand, blend two clips together at the edit point, and create continuity from Clip A to Clip B. In other words, a transition effect is "edit point spackle"; it smoothes out the scene change where two clips meet. In this chapter, you will learn how to apply, modify, and remove transitions effects.

What Is a Transition Effect?

A transition is a video effect that changes the look of a scene change. That's the short and simple explanation, but if that didn't quite resonate with you, it might be helpful to first understand how **edit points** work.

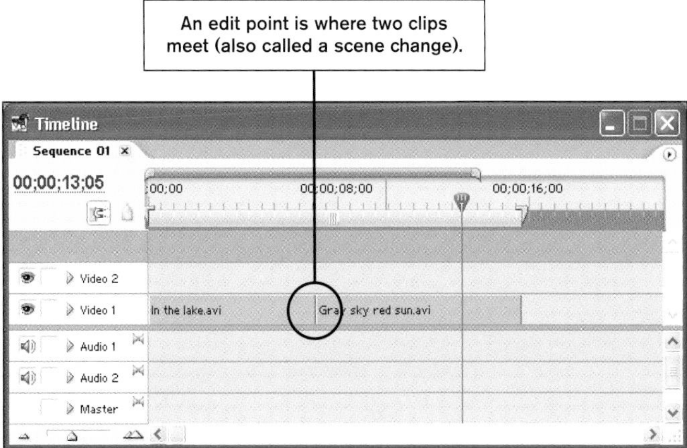

An edit point is the spot on the Timeline where two clips meet. This is also called a **scene change**, because the scene changes from the first clip to the second clip.

The scene can change in many different ways. The most common type of scene change is called a **straight cut**, which means that the last frame of a clip is followed by the first frame of the next clip. This is the only type of scene change you have created in the previous exercises.

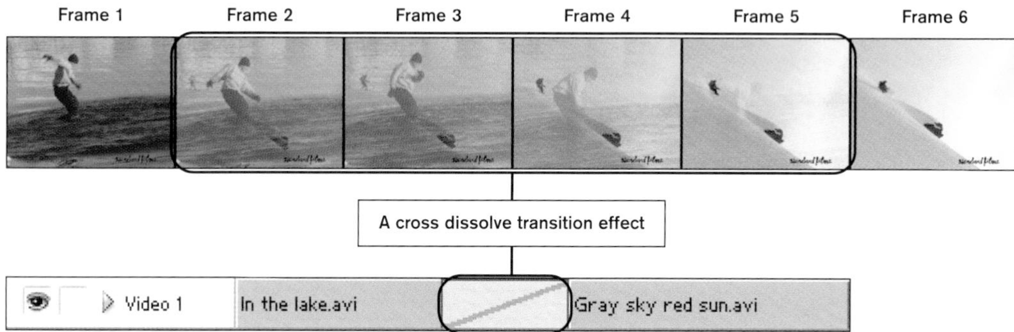

When a transition effect is added to the scene change, the two clips are combined in a variety of ways. Instead of a straight cut, you can change scenes with cross dissolves, zooms, wipes, 3D motion, pushes, and dozens more transitions. For example, a cross dissolve transition effect slowly fades out the first clip while fading in the second clip. You can specify the length of the transition, so that longer transitions take longer to blend the two clips together. The transition effect is represented by a purple clip on the Timeline, applied over the edit point where the two clips meet.

I. Adding Video Transitions

Video transitions are located in the Effects window. To apply a transition to a scene change, first view the transitions in the Effects window and then drag the desired transition to the edit point. In this exercise, you will open the Effects window and apply a basic cross dissolve transition over an edit point.

1. If Premiere Pro is not running, launch it and click **Open Project** at the **Welcome Screen**. Navigate to the **c:\Premiere Pro HOT\Chapter 08** folder, select **Exercise01.prproj**, and click **Open**.

*The sequence in the **Timeline** window has five clips, which have already been trimmed and placed in track **Video 1**.*

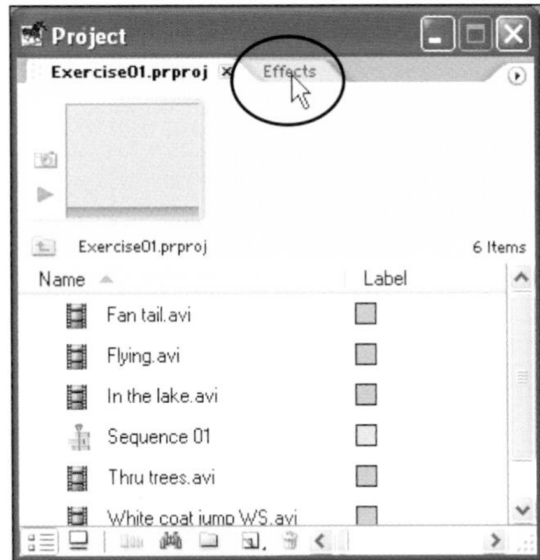

The Effects Window in the background.

The Effects Window in the foreground.

2. The **Effects** window lists all of the available video and audio effects, as well as audio and video transitions. Because there are so many windows in Premiere Pro, some windows share space with others. The **Effects** window shares space with the **Project** window. To bring the **Effects** window to the foreground, click the **Effects** tab in the **Project** window.

3. The **Effects** window lists five folders: **Presets**, **Audio Effects**, **Audio Transitions**, **Video Effects**, and **Video Transitions**. Twirl down the arrow next to **Video Transitions** to expand the folder and view the available video transitions.

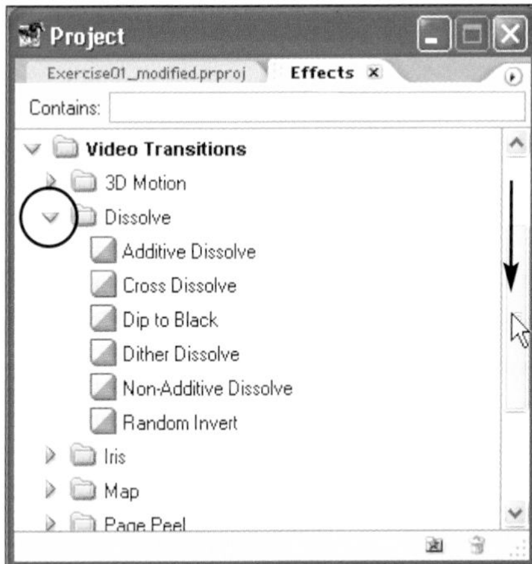

4. Within the **Video Transitions** folder are many subfolders, each containing more transitions. The transitions are grouped by the subfolders: dissolves are all grouped in the **Dissolve** subfolder, the page peels are all grouped in the **Page Peel** subfolder, and so on. Twirl down the arrow next to the **Dissolve** subfolder to view the available dissolve transitions. If you cannot see all six dissolve transitions, scroll down until they're all displayed in the **Effects** window.

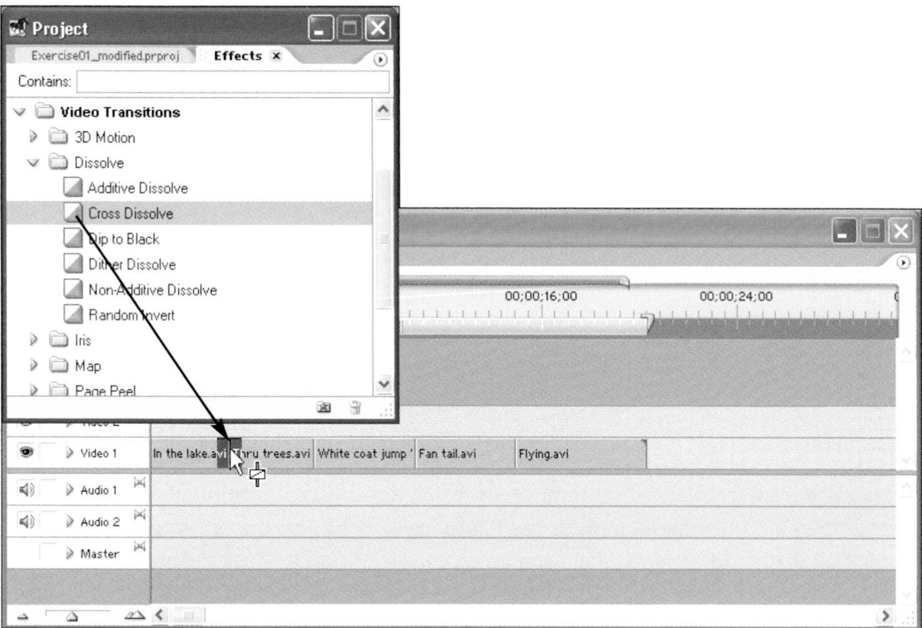

5. You can apply a transition to a scene change by dragging a transition from the **Effects** window and dropping it on top of an edit point. To do this, select the **Cross Dissolve** transition in the **Dissolve** subfolder, then drag it to the edit point between **Clip 1** and **Clip 2** in the **Timeline** window. Be sure to drag to the exact middle of the edit point, then let go of the mouse.

Note: *You can drag a transition to three different positions around an edit point. See the Note following this exercise for a description of each.*

6. In the **Monitor** window **Program** view, click the **Play** button to preview the sequence. You should see **Clip 1** slowly dissolve into **Clip 2**.

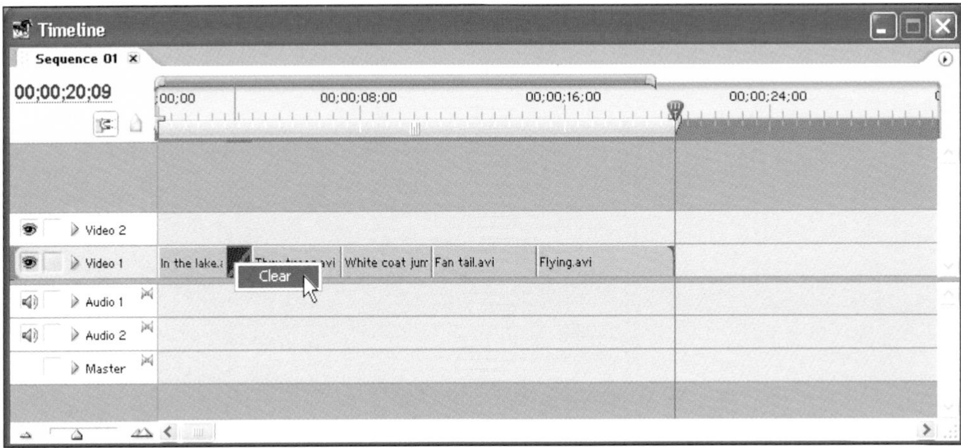

7. You can remove a transition from the **Timeline** window with equal ease. Select the transition in the **Timeline** window, right-click the mouse, and choose **Clear** from the shortcut menu. Poof! The transition is gone, and you are left with a straight cut between **Clip 1** and **Clip 2**.

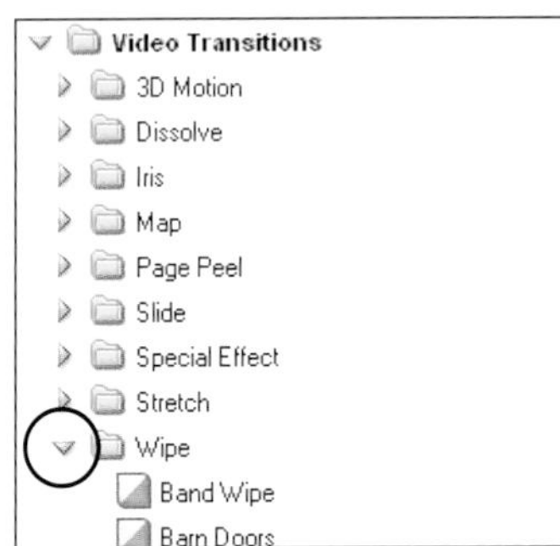

8. Now you are going to apply a different transition to the same edit point. Scroll down to the **Wipe** subfolder and twirl its arrow down to expand its contents.

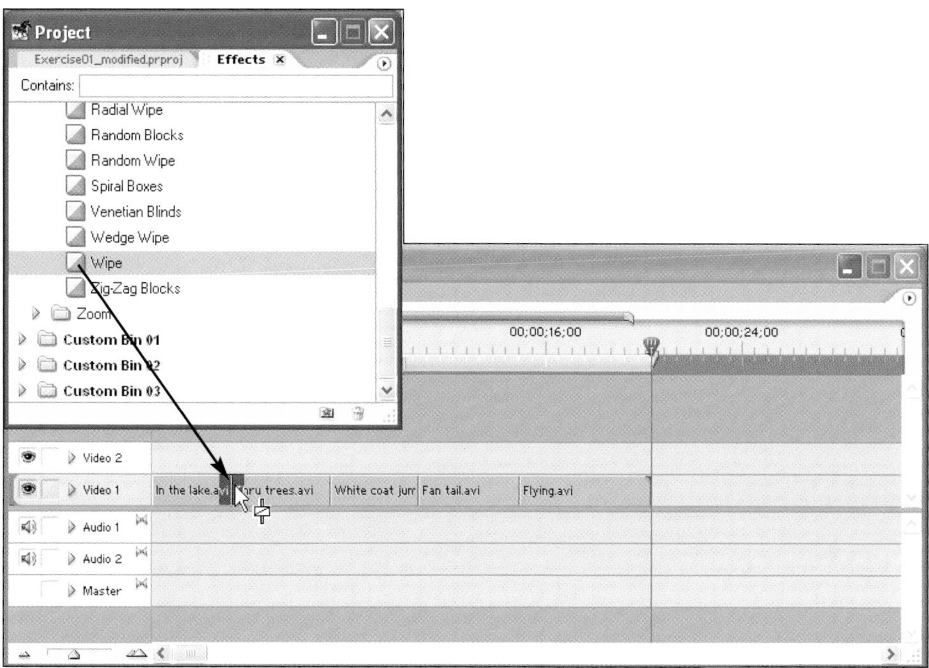

9. Scroll to the bottom of the **Wipe** subfolder and drag the **Wipe** transition from the **Effects** window to the edit point between **Clip 1** and **Clip 2** on the **Timeline**. Do not let go of the mouse until you have aligned the transition over the center of the cut. The mouse cursor should display the **Center at Cut** icon.

10. Click the **Play** button in the **Monitor** window to preview the sequence. Notice that the **Wipe** transition appears to "wipe away" the first clip. (Or wipe on the second clip, depending on how you look at it.)

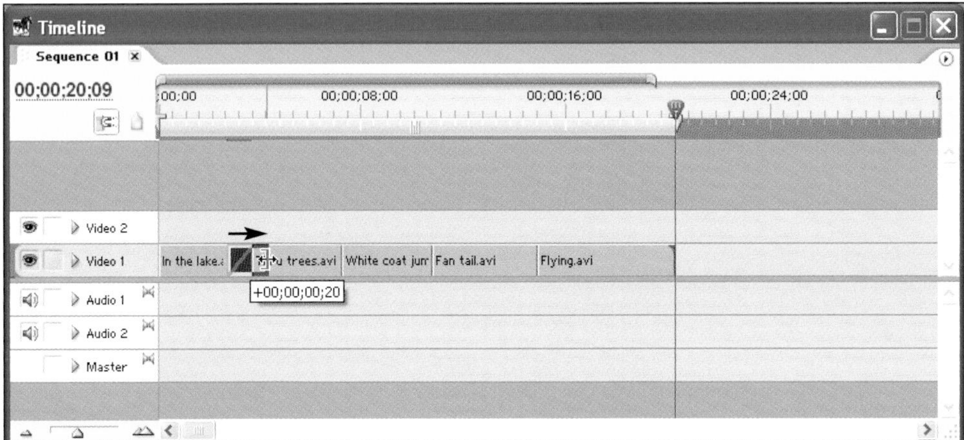

11. Transitions are given a default duration of 30 frames (1 second). You can quickly change the duration of a transition by dragging the start or end of the transition with the **Trim** pointers. This should be very familiar, since you've used the **Trim** pointers on video clips, audio clips, and still images. Hover your mouse over the end of the transition, until you see the **Trim Out** pointer, and drag the transition **20** frames to the right.

Tip: Use the yellow pop-up box as a guide to know when you reach approximately 20 frames. Drag until it displays ***+00;00;00;20.***

12. Click the **Play** button in the **Monitor** window to preview the sequence again. This time, the transition should take a little longer to complete.

You have just learned how to apply, remove, and change the duration of transitions. There are dozens of available transitions, and the steps you followed in this exercise apply equally to all transitions.

13. Save this project and keep it open before moving on to the next exercise.

NOTE | The Three Transition Locations

When you drag a transition on top of an edit point, there are three different ways you can align the transition over the scene change. In each of the following examples, the transition is 30 frames (1 second) long.

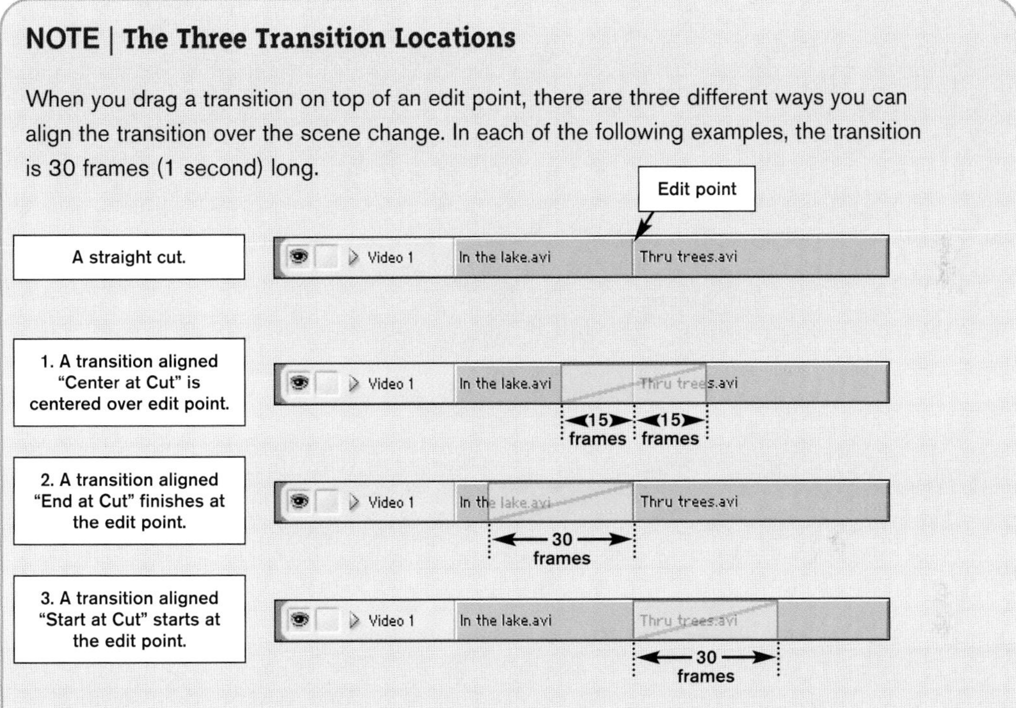

The first, and most common, alignment is the **Center at Cut**, which centers the transition over the edit point. In this case, the transition begins 15 frames before the edit point, and finishes 15 frames after the edit point. A Center at Cut alignment requires 15 additional frames of media for each clip.

The second choice of alignments is the **End At Cut**, which finishes transitioning at the edit point. 30 frames prior to the edit point, the first clip begins to transition into the second clip. At the edit point the transition has finished completely, and you can only see the second clip.

The third alignment is the **Start at Cut**, which starts transitioning at the edit point. At the edit point the first clip begins to transition into the second clip. 30 frames later the transition has finished, and you can only see the second clip.

How Transitions Works

A transition requires heads or tails. No, it's not the flip of a coin. The head material of a clip is the unused video before the In point. The tail material is the unused video after the Out point. If a clip on the Timeline does not have sufficient material at its head or tail, then a transition is not possible. Hopefully the following example will clear up any confusion about how a transition works.

You learned in previous chapters that when you set In and Out points for a source clip in the Monitor window, you are trimming the clip to the portion that you want to place in a sequence. The extra video to the left of the In point, that you have chosen to trim off, is called the **head material**. The extra video that you are not using, to the right of the Out point, is called the **tail material**.

As you practiced earlier in this book, when you drag a clip from the Monitor window to the Timeline window, you are bringing the video between the In and Out points; the head and tail materials are not included. This part is review, and it should support what you already know about trimming source clips. But what you may not know is *why* head and tail materials are vital to a transition effect. Read on...

Figure 1. Picture these two video clips on the Timeline, Clip A and Clip B.

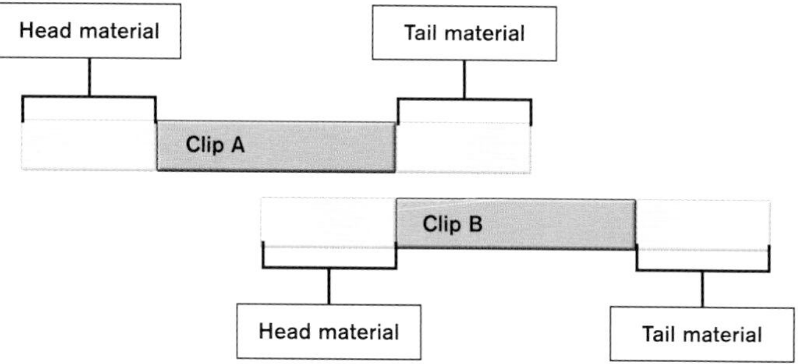

Figure 2. Both clips have unused head and tail material that was trimmed off before the clips were added to the Timeline.

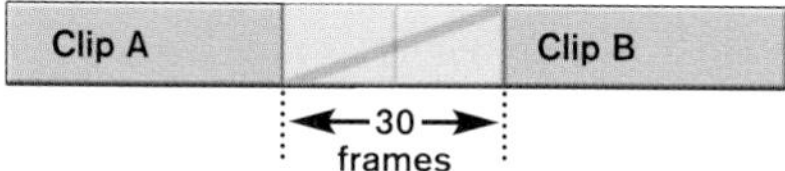

Figure 3. A 30-frame Cross Dissolve transition is placed at the edit point between Clip A and Clip B. The transition is aligned **Center at Cut**, so the transition is centered over the edit point. There are 15 frames of transition to the left of the edit point and 15 frames of transition to the right.

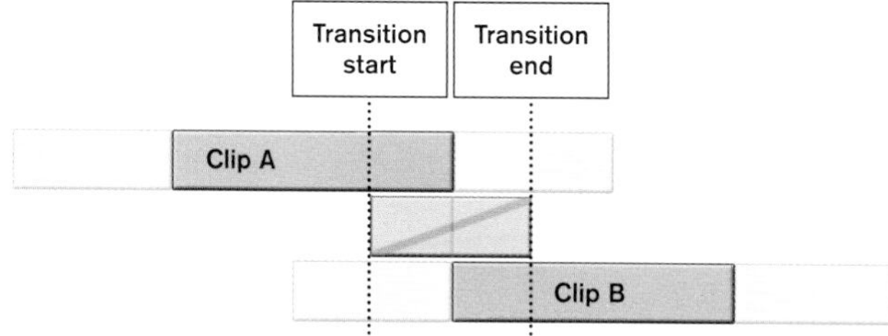

Note: In order to demonstrate how a transition works, Figure 4 shows Clip A above clip B, with the transition placed between them. Keep in mind that both clips are still on the same video track, as shown in Figure 3.

Figure 4. At the transition start, Clip B slowly fades in while Clip A fades out. In order to have Clip B start to fade in 15 frames before the edit point, the transition uses **15 frames of head material from Clip B**. After the edit point, the transition uses **15 frames of tail material from Clip A**.

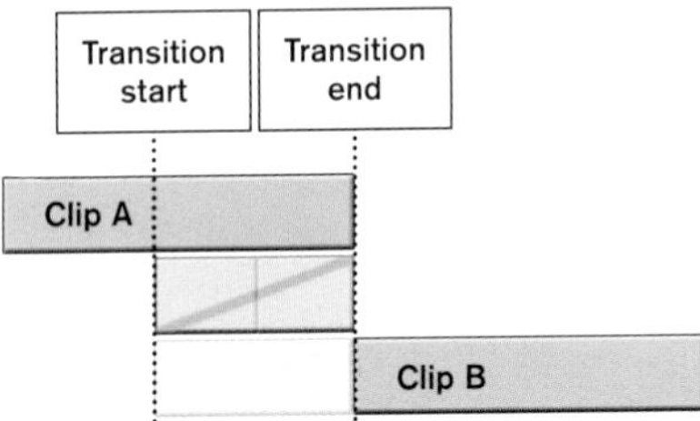

Figure 5. Take a look at a transition aligned **End at Cut**. The transition–still 30 frames long–needs 30 frames of head material from Clip B in order to slowly fade in Clip B. Once the transition reaches the edit point, is has ended (hence the name End at Cut).

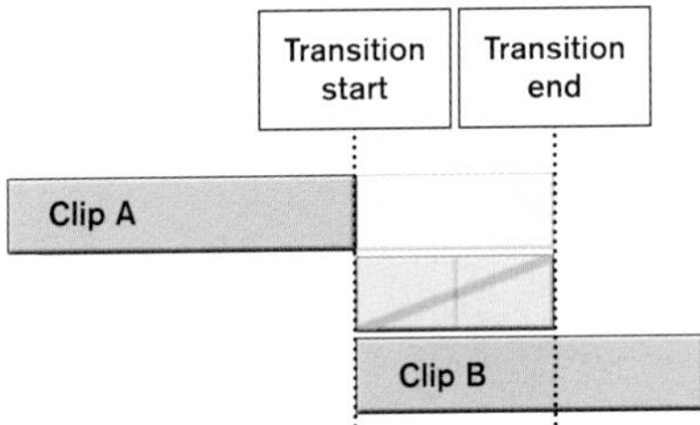

Figure 6. This illustrates a **Start at Cut** transition. The transition starts at the edit point, and finishes 30 frames later. The transition uses 30 frames of tail material from Clip A to slowly fade out clip A.

These examples underscore the importance of having plenty of head and tail material around your source clips. When we discuss capturing video from a DV camera in Chapter 15, "*Capturing Digital Video*," you will learn how to capture extra head and tail material.

The Effect Controls Window

Remember the Effect Controls window from Chapter 7, "*Still Images and Fixed Effects*"? You used it to alter the fixed properties of still images, by moving its position and changing its scale. The Effect Controls window is also used to change transitions as well. However, when you have a transition selected, you are presented with a slightly different set of options. Well, not quite. Rather, you are presented with a *completely new* set of options.

The Effect Controls window may appear intimidating at first, but the options are all very intuitive. Take a moment and get to know the most frequently used features of the Effect Controls window.

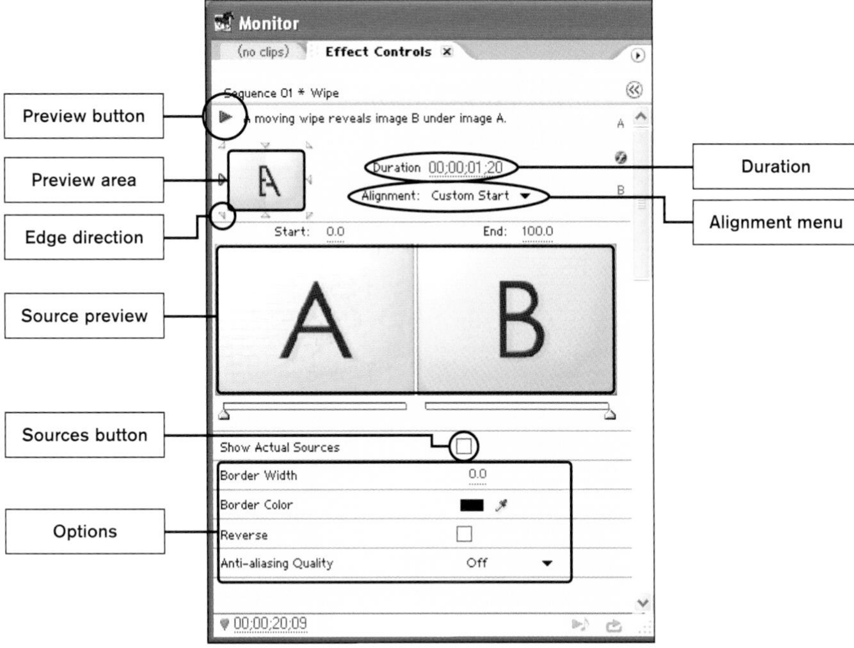

Preview button: This is like the Preview button in the Project window. It plays the transition so you can see what it will look like.

Preview area: This is the monitor where the preview plays back. Any option that you change will be instantly updated in the preview area for you to see.

Edge direction: This is a very fun option; it allows you to change which edge the transition begins from. You can click any of the triangles along the perimeter of the preview area, and the transition will begin from that edge. This applies only to transitions that have directions, like a wipe.

Source preview: If you click the **Sources** button, the actual sources will be shown in the preview. Instead of a big letter A, you will see the first clip in the transition. The second clip in the transition will replace the letter B.

Options: Each transition has different options that you can modify. For example, the Wipe transition allows you to change the border color and width. The anti-aliasing quality will soften the edge of the transition.

Duration: This is a very handy feature; instead of using the Trim pointers to change the duration in the Timeline window, you can manually change the duration in the Effect Controls window. The duration changes based on the alignment.

Alignment. Remember the three alignment "positions?" If you want to change the alignment, you can use this option to choose among Center at Cut, End at Cut, and Start at Cut.

See, that wasn't so bad. Now, there's one more part of the Effect Controls window to learn: the **Timeline view**.

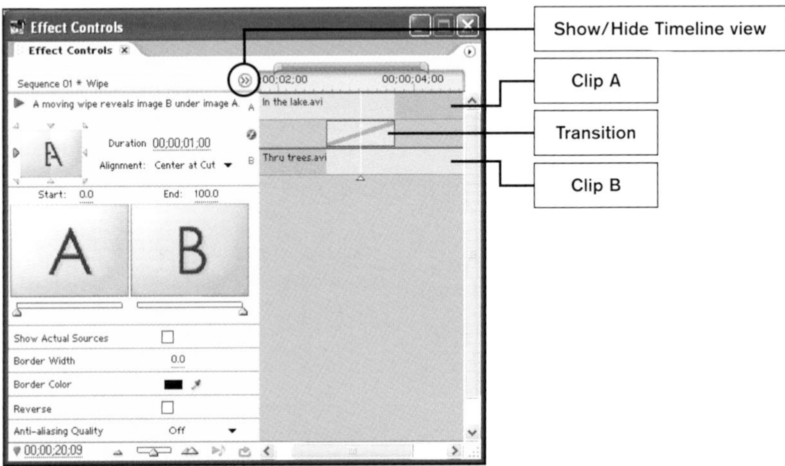

Does the Timeline view look familiar? It should! This is the same view from Figure 4 a couple of pages back. Clip A represents the first clip in the transition, and Clip B represents the second clip. (Of course, on the actual Timeline the clips are side by side, and the transition overlaps them both.) The thin white line represents the edit point.

The Effect Controls Timeline view provides yet another method to change the duration or location of your transition. Some editors like this because they feel it gives them more precise control over the transition. Other editors never use it. It's all a matter of taste.

If you happen to fall into the latter category and don't want to be bothered by the Timeline view, you can always hide it by toggling the **Show/Hide Timeline View** button. Click it again and the Timeline view reappears.

Note: This does not hide the original Timeline window at the bottom of the Premiere Pro screen. The Show/Hide Timeline View button only applies to the miniature Timeline representation in the Effect Controls window.

2. Modifying Transitions

Now that you are well acquainted with the Effect Controls window, it is time to put that knowledge to the test. In this exercise, you will modify a transition's options in the Effect Controls window.

1. This exercise begins where Exercise 1 left off. If the project from Exercise 1 is still open, skip to Step 2. If Premiere Pro is not running, launch it and click **Open Project** at the **Welcome Screen**. Navigate to the **c:\Premiere Pro HOT\Chapter 08** folder, select **Exercise02.prproj**, and click **Open**.

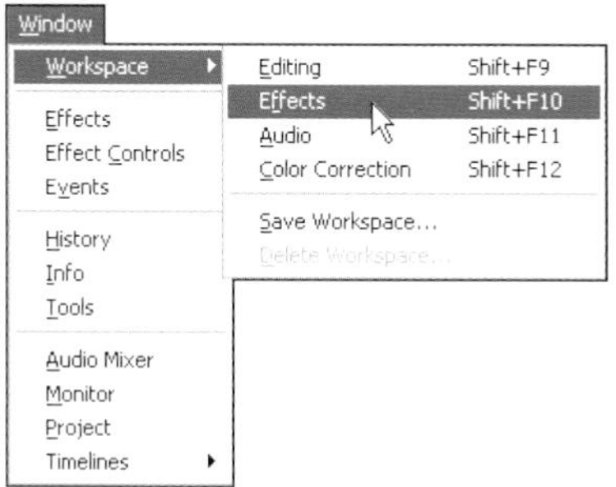

2. In previous exercises, you used the **Editing** workspace, which displays and organizes the windows that are used most frequently when editing. There is also a workspace for doing effects work, such as adding transitions. To select the **Effects** workspace, choose **Window > Workspace > Effects**.

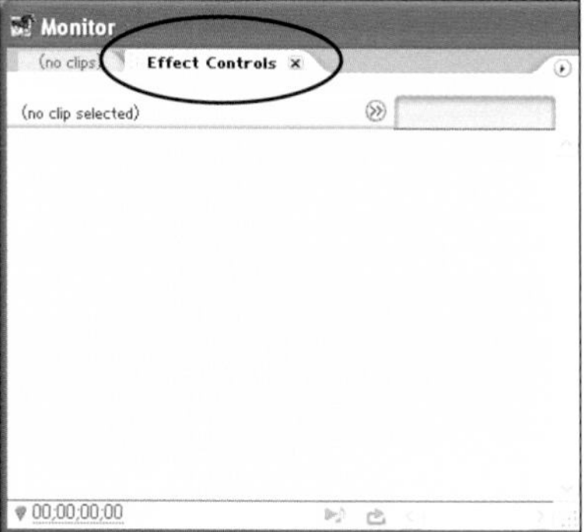

Note: *The **Effects** workspace brings to the foreground the windows most frequently used when adding effects. In the **Project** window, the **Effects** window is brought to the foreground. In the **Monitor** window, the **Effect Controls** window is brought to the foreground, and the **Source** view is sent to the background.*

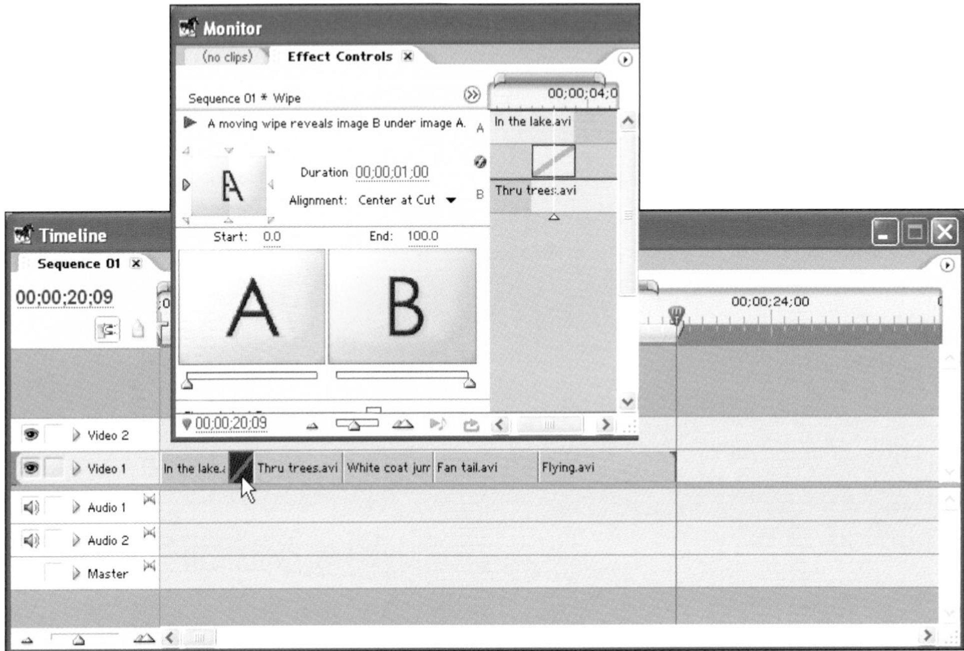

3. In the **Timeline** window, click the **Wipe** transition between **Clip 1** and **Clip 2**. This will open the transition's options in the **Effect Controls** window.

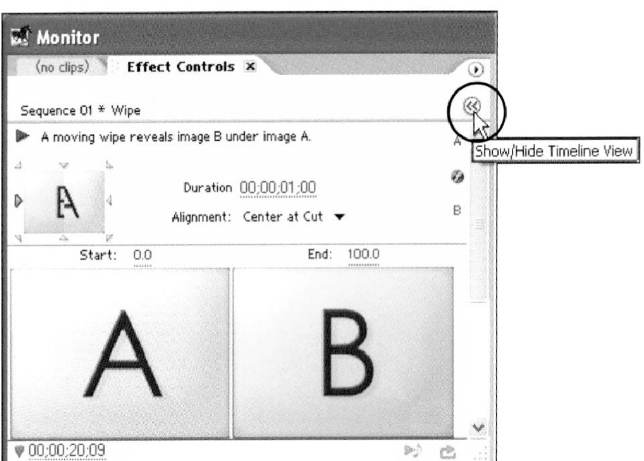

4. Because you will not need the **Effect Controls Timeline** view, click the **Show/Hide Timeline View** button to collapse the **Timeline** view.

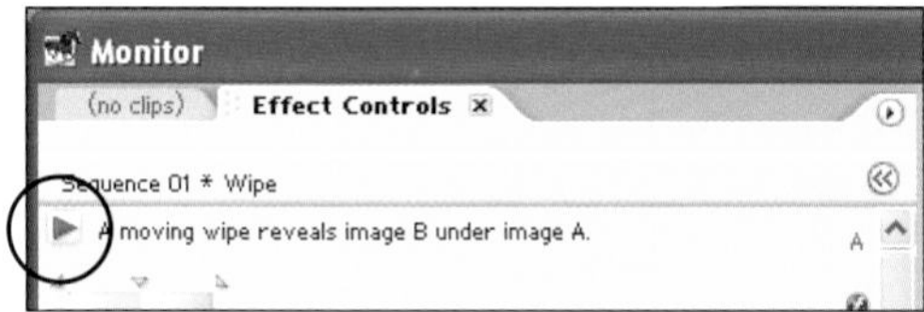

5. Before making any changes, preview the transition by clicking the **Preview** button. The A/B preview will play back in the preview area. Watch the wipe move from left to right. Click the **Preview** button again to stop playback.

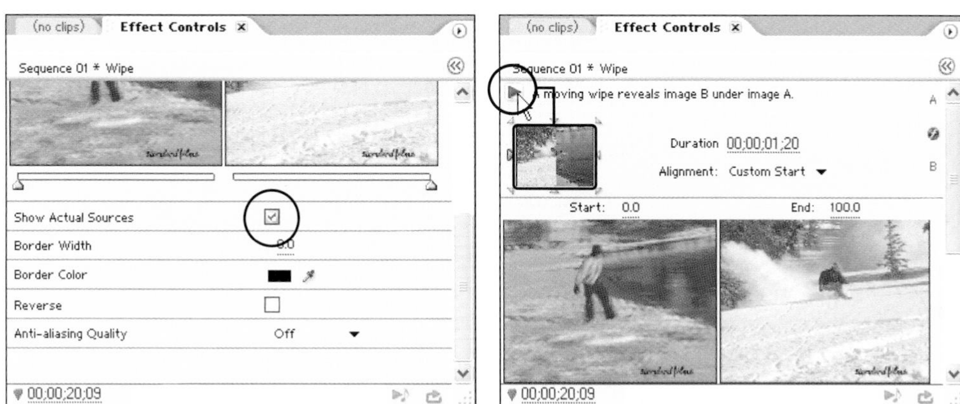

6. At the bottom of the **Effect Controls** window, check the **Show Actual Sources** check box, which replaces the big letters A and B with the actual video. **Click** the **Preview** button again, and you should see the video in the preview area. Click the **Preview** button to stop playback.

7. The **edge direction** option lets you change the direction of the transition. Click the upper-left triangle angle around the preview area. The wipe will now travel from upper-left to lower-right. Click the **Preview** button to play back the transition in the preview area to watch this. Click the **Preview** button to stop playback.

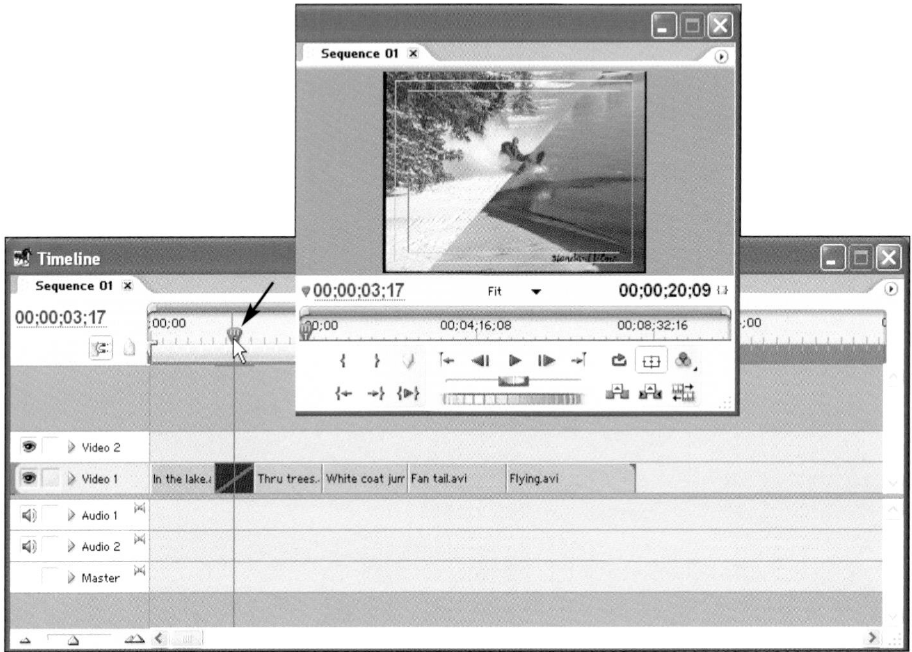

8. The preview area is handy, but it's a little too small to accurately display some of the transition options. To fix this problem, drag the current time indicator in the **Timeline** window to the middle of the transition between **Clip 1** and **Clip 2**. This will display the finished transition effect in the **Monitor** window **Program** view.

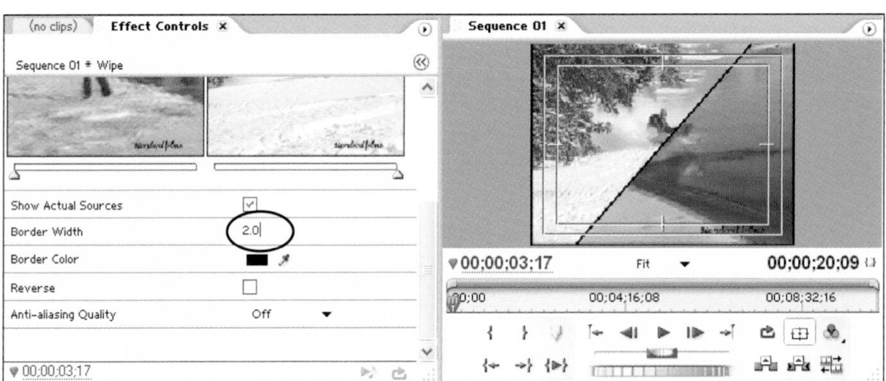

9. Scroll to the bottom of the **Effect Controls** window, and click the **Border Width** value to change it. Type in a value of **2.0** and press **Enter**. The **Monitor** window **Program** view shows a much larger version of the transition. You can clearly see the thin border you have applied to the wipe.

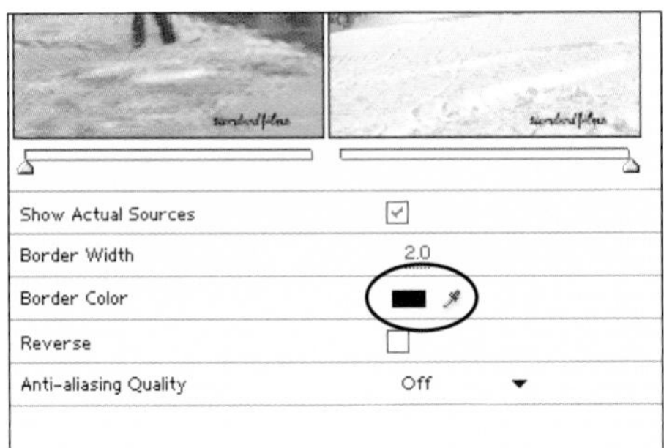

10. Another option you can change is the border color. This is similar to changing the color of title text objects, which you did in Chapter 6, "*Title Designer*." Click the color box to open the **Color Picker**.

11. Perhaps you'd like a light-green color for the wipe border. In the **Color Picker**, first drag the **Hue** slider to the middle of the greens. Second, click in the lower-left corner of the color display to pick a color. (It doesn't have to be precise, any color will do.) Click **OK** to close the **Color Picker**. The wipe now has a light green border, which you can see in the **Monitor** window.

Note: *Colors to the left are less saturated, and colors to the bottom are brighter. For a refresher course on how the* ***Color Picker*** *works, refer to Chapter 6,* "Title Designer."

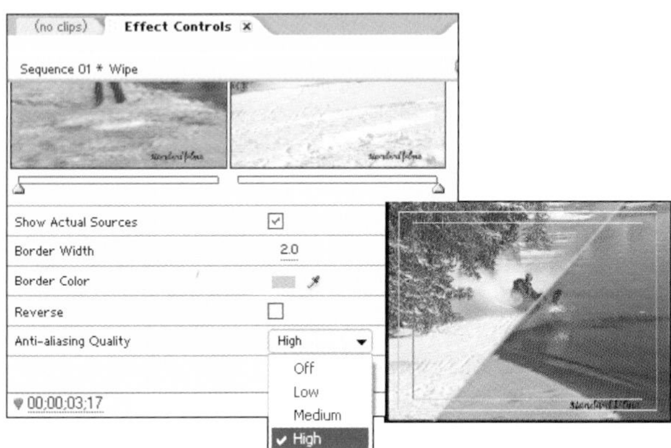

12. The **Anti-aliasing Quality** changes the softness of the transition edge. When set to **Off**, the edge is very crisp. A **High** setting softens the edge considerably. Click the **Anti-aliasing Quality** menu and choose **High**. The transition edge in the **Monitor** window appears softer.

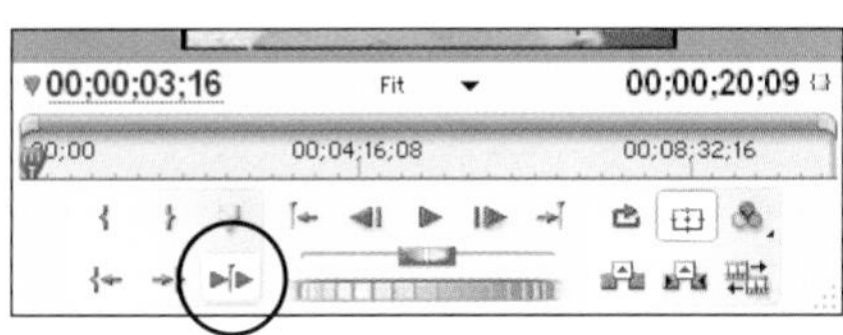

13. Time to preview the transition. Here's an easy method from earlier in the book: hold down the **Alt** key and click the **Play Edit** button.

*Tip: Normally this is the **Play In to Out** button, which you have used many times, but when the **Alt** key is held down, the current time indicator rewinds a few seconds and begins playback. But that's not all...the sequence plays for 4 seconds, and then the current time indicator is returned to the starting point. How convenient!*

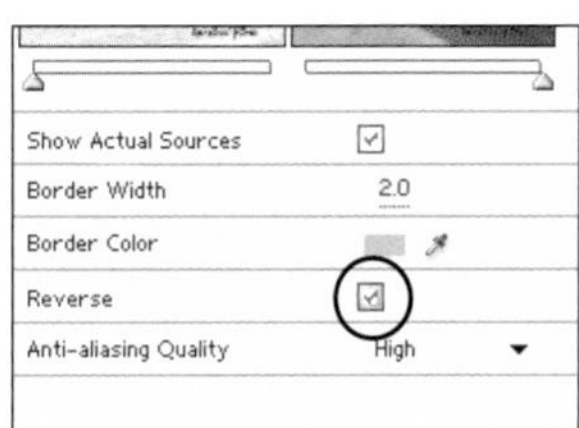

14. The wipe played back from upper left to lower right, correct? Good. The last option to change for this transition is the **Reverse** option. In the **Effect Controls** window, check the **Reverse** check box. The wipe will switch directions, and now play lower right to upper left.

15. Hold down the **Alt** key and click the **Play Edit** button again. Now the wipe is reversed.

Note: *If you didn't hold down the* ***Alt*** *key this time, or in Step 13, the current time indicator may not be returned to its previous position. If this is the case, drag the current time indicator in the* ***Timeline*** *window to the midpoint of the transition and repeat Step 15.*

---

16. Save this project and keep it open before moving on to the next exercise.

Way to go! You have finished this exercise. Not only have you learned to modify the options for this wipe transition, but you've just learned 98 percent of the options for all transitions. However, a few quirky transitions have additional options; when you bump into one, don't be afraid to explore on your own. Remember, the ***Undo*** *command is your friend.*

So far you've only touched the tip of the ice berg with the transitions. There's dozens more to choose from. On the bright side, you know how to apply all of the transitions, and you can venture out on your own to discover your personal favorites. Here is a quick guide to the transition groups:

All Those Transitions	
Transition Group	**What It Does**
3D Motion	Includes many spinning and swinging door transitions that appear to have depth (instead of the 2D transitions you've used so far).
Dissolve	The classiest of the bunch. Dissolves are basic fades from one clip to the next. You can never go wrong with a cross dissolve.
Iris	Includes many shapes opening or closing from the center of the screen.
Map	Advanced options that are rarely used. Not worth describing.
Page Peel	A computer-animated effect of the video being peeled off like a book page.
Slide	Slides the next video in. Also has pushes that push the existing video off.
Special Effect	Not as exciting as the name implies. Like Map, contains advanced options not useful to the beginner.
Stretch	Stretches the video in, like a sheet of rubber being pulled.
Wipe	Includes many wipe shapes and wipe rotations for wiping video on or off.
Zoom	The clip can zoom in or out to reveal the next clip.

NOTE | Less is More

Premiere Pro and many other editing programs use their zillions of transitions as a selling point. There are even companies who sell nothing but extra transitions you can load into Premiere Pro. Are they worth it? Or is this just marketing hype?

The next time you watch a movie, count how many *different* transitions you see. Odds are there will be just one: a cross dissolve. Some action-adventure movies may use a wipe (with the requisite "woosh" sound effect). You will rarely see more than a dissolve or wipe, unless there is a darn good reason. (Even then, the transition is being used to serve a purpose, and not just for the sake of using a transition.) Watch the evening news, and you will rarely see any transitions beyond dissolves, wipes, and slides. Why? Because the video should speak for itself, and the transition should not draw attention away from the content.

The moral here? Less is more. Be consistent with your transitions. Never mix and match just for the sake of variety. Any transition you use should be a conscious decision based upon the theme of your project, and it should support—not detract from—the story you are creating.

3. Adding Transitions to Titles

Transitions wouldn't be nearly as fun if you couldn't apply them to other types of clips such as titles and still images. Transitions are great ways to fade in and fade out titles, as well as wipe on an image with a little flare (as long as it supports the overall look and feel of the project, of course). In this exercise, you will add transitions to two titles.

1. This exercise begins where Exercise 2 left off. If the project from Exercise 2 is still open, skip to Step 2. If Premiere Pro is not running, launch it and click **Open Project** at the **Welcome Screen**. Navigate to the **c:\Premiere Pro HOT\Chapter 08** folder, select **Exercise03.prproj**, and click **Open**.

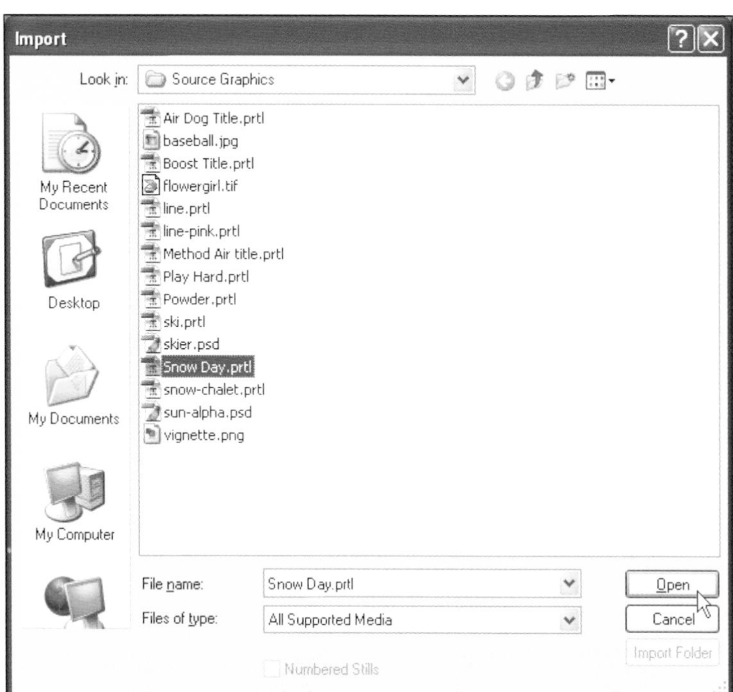

2. The first thing you need to do is import a title into your project. Choose **File > Import**. Navigate to the **c:\Premiere Pro HOT\Source Graphics** directory, select **Snow Day.prtl**, and click **Open**.

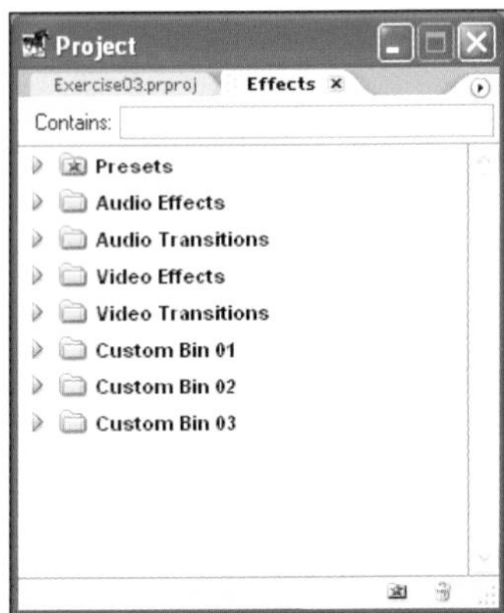

The Effects window in the foreground.

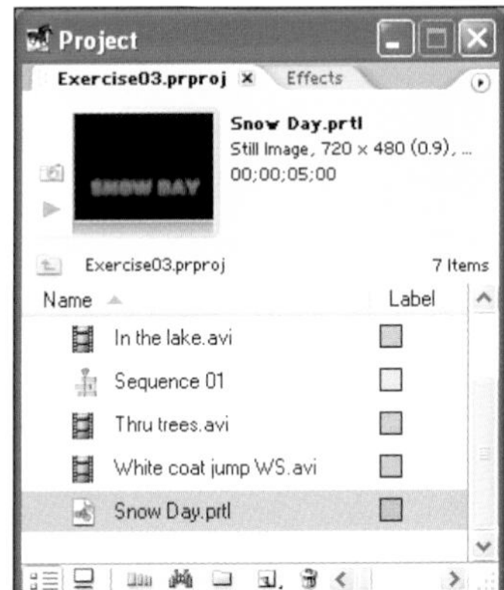

The Project window in the foreground.

3. Tiny problem: the imported clip is not visible because the **Effects** window is in the foreground. To bring the **Project** window to the foreground, click the **Project** tab (displays the name of the project). You can now see the list of imported clips.

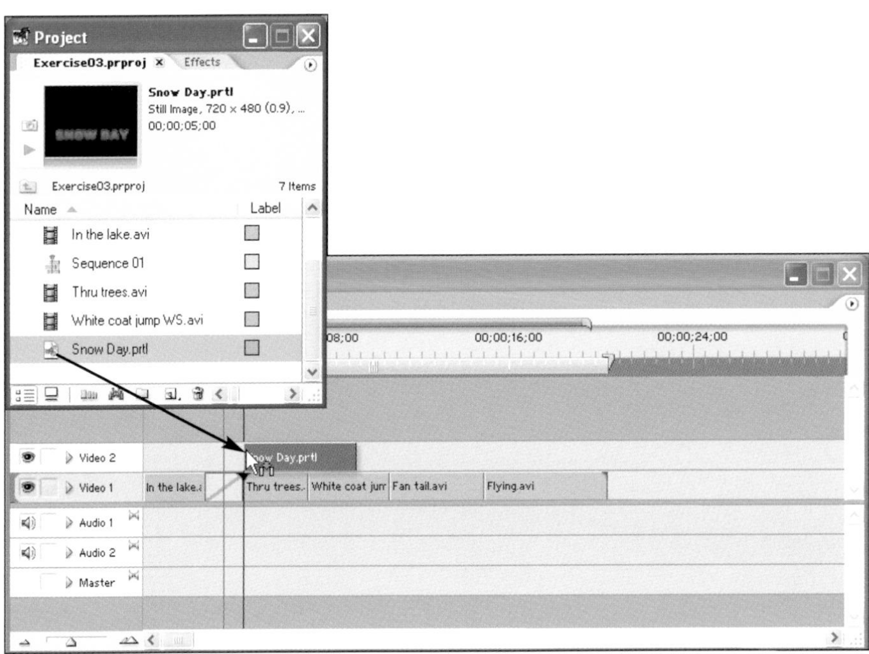

4. Drag **Show Day.prtl** from the **Project** window to track **Video 2** of the **Timeline** window. Snap it to the end of the transition already on the **Timeline**. (Look for the friendly black snap indicator!)

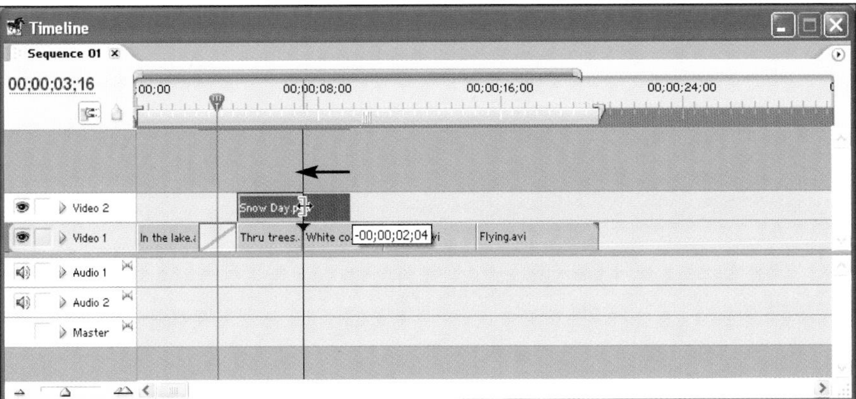

5. Trim the **Out** point of the title clip so that it snaps to the end point of **Clip 2**.

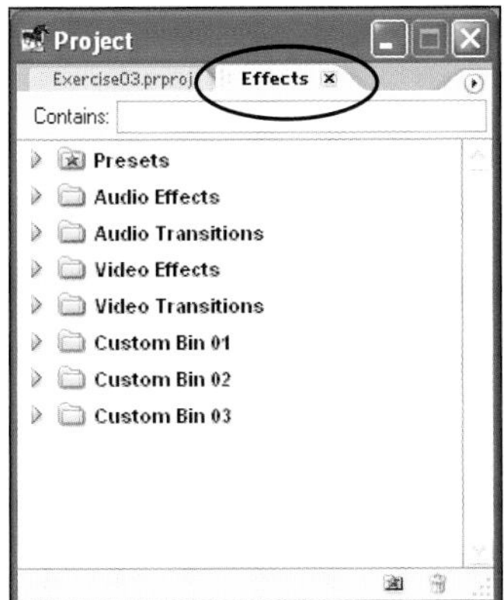

6. To see the **Effects** window again, click the **Effects** tab in the **Project** window.

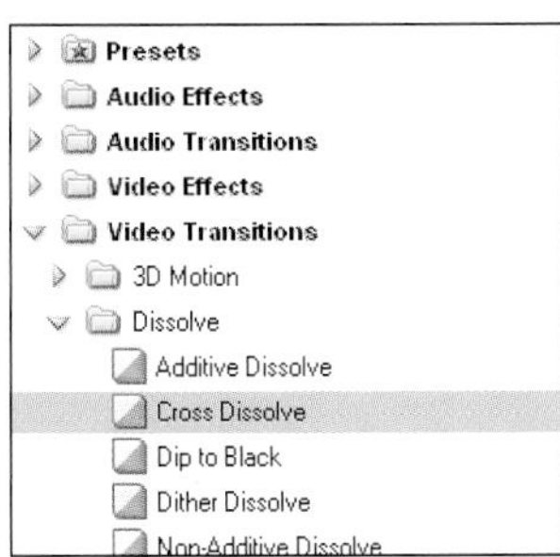

7. In the **Effects** window, twirl down the **Video Transitions** folder and then twirl down the **Dissolve** subfolder to view the list of dissolve transitions.

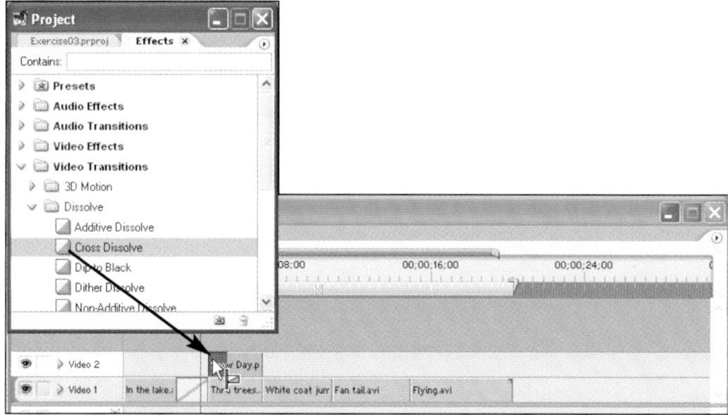

8. Drag the **Cross Dissolve** transition from the **Effects** window to the **In** point of the title. Make sure your mouse is slightly *inside* of the **In** point (to the right) so the transition correctly aligns with the start of the title.

9. Click the **Play** button in the **Monitor** window to preview the transition. The title slowly fades in.

Tip: *This type of effect is possible on any title or still image with an alpha channel (transparency).*

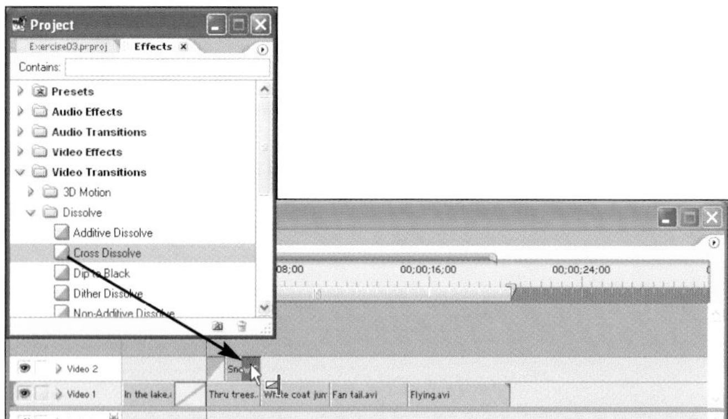

10. Drag the **Cross Dissolve** transition from the **Effects** window to the **Out** point of the title. Make sure your mouse is slightly *inside* of the **Out** point (to the left) so the transition correctly aligns with the end of the title. You have just created a fade-out.

11. Click the **Play** button in the **Monitor** window to preview the transition. The title slowly fades in and then out.

Tip: *You can also use this effect to fade video clips in and out. More on that later in this chapter.*

12. Now, you are going to import another title, and add a slide and zoom transition to its **In** and **Out** points. Choose **File > Import**. Navigate to the **c:\Premiere Pro HOT\Source Graphics** directory, select **Powder.prtl** and click **Open**.

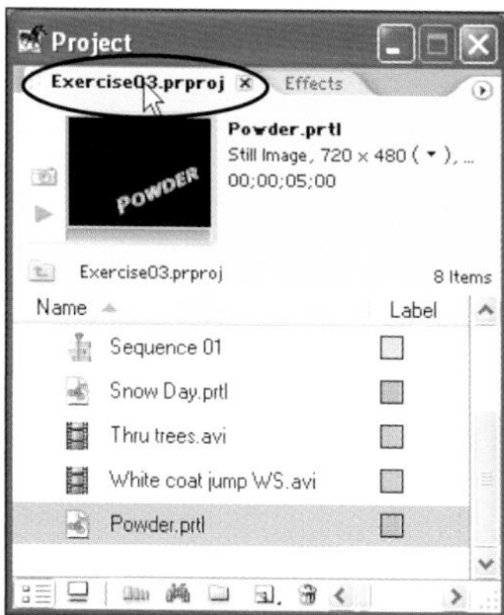

13. Click the **Project** window tab to bring it to the foreground.

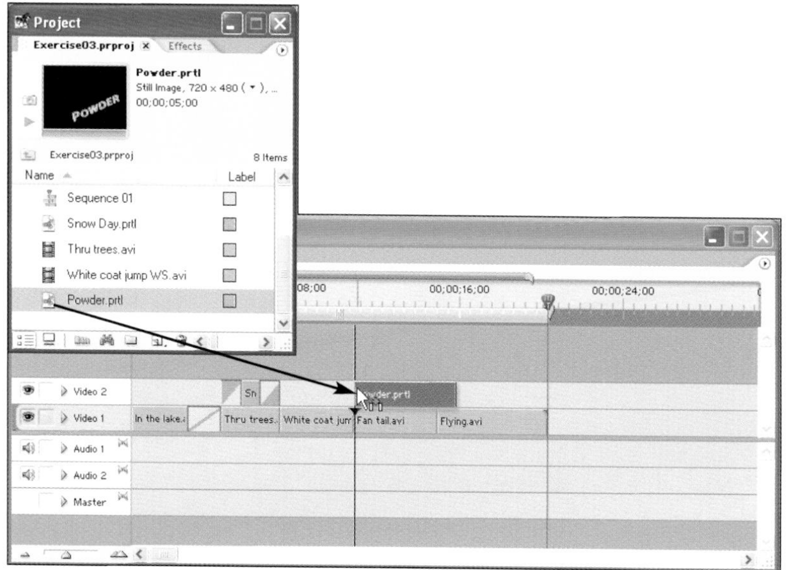

14. Drag **Powder.prtl** from the **Project** window to track **Video 2** of the **Timeline** window. Snap it to the **In** point of **Fan tail.avi** (the fourth clip on the **Timeline**).

15. To bring the **Effects** window back to the foreground, click the **Effects** tab in the **Project** window.

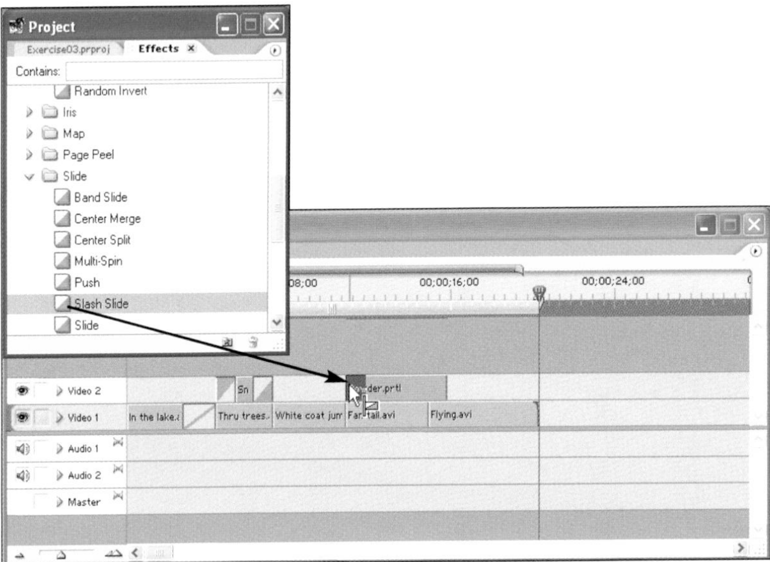

16. Scroll to the bottom of the **Effects** window and twirl down the **Slide** subfolder to view its contents. Drag the **Slash Slide** transition from the **Effects** window to the **In** point of **Powder.prtl** in the **Timeline** window.

17. To preview the transition effect, click the **Play** button in the **Monitor** window. The **Slash Slide** transition slides on pieces of the title in strips.

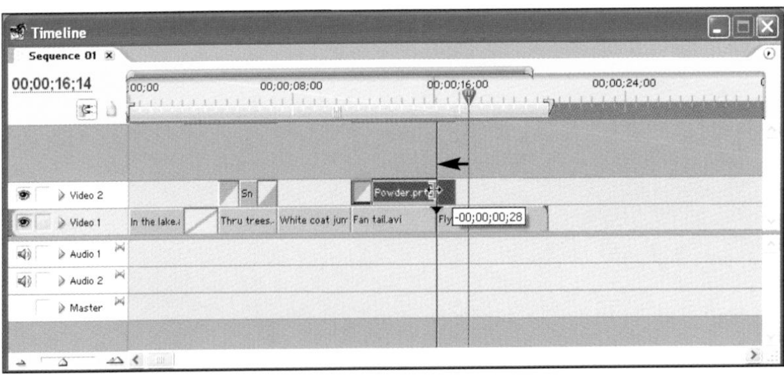

18. The title plays a little too long, so...you know the drill! Use the **Trim Out** pointer and snap the **Out** point of **Powder.prtl** to the **Out** point of **Fan tail.avi**. As usual, look for the snap indicator.

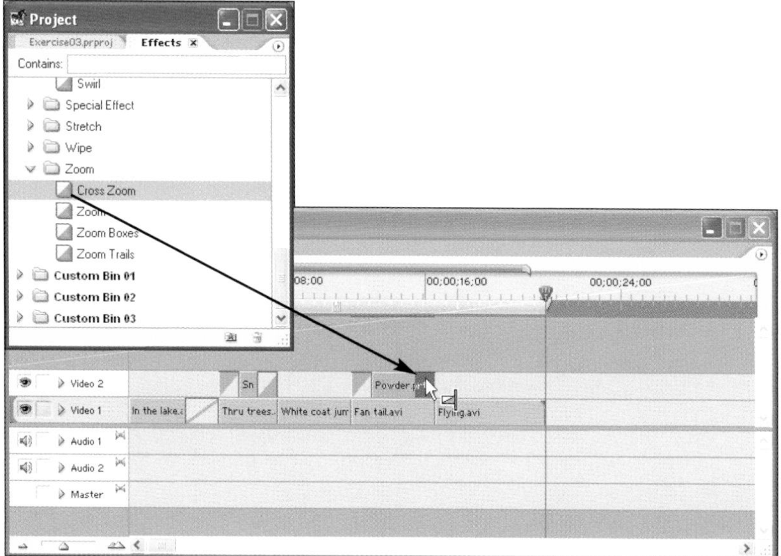

19. Now, add the **Cross Zoom** transition to the title's **Out** point. Scroll to the bottom of the **Effects** window and twirl down the **Zoom** subfolder. Drag the **Cross Zoom** transition from the **Effects** window to the **Out** point of **Powder.prtl** in track **Video 2** of the **Timeline** window.

20. To preview the transition effect, click the **Play** button in the **Monitor** window. The **Cross Zoom** transition zooms the title out.

You have just applied three different types of transitions to titles. There are many different transition effects you can create from titles and still images with alpha channels, but the steps to applying them are always the same.

21. Save this project and keep it open before moving on to the next exercise.

NOTE | Transition Default Duration

Transitions, like still images and titles, have no finite length. They can stretch to infinity if need be (well, almost). By default, Premiere Pro makes transitions exactly 30 frames long (1 second for NTSC video, which plays back at 30 frames per second). To change the length of transitions, use the **Transition Default Duration** setting.

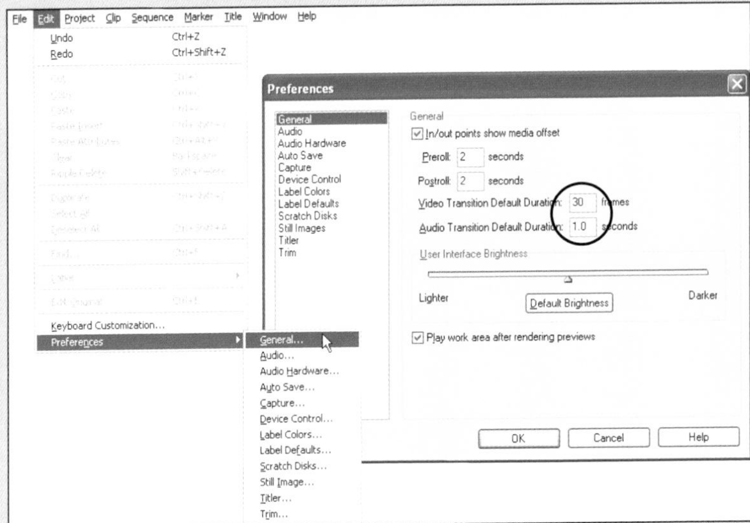

To access the **Default Transition Duration**, choose **Edit > Preferences > General**. This opens up the **General** section of the **Preferences** window. There are options to change both the **Video Transition Default Duration** and the **Audio Transition Default Duration**.

You are not bound to the durations by any means. You are still able to change the duration of each individual transition you apply to the Timeline, just as you have in this chapter. The default duration affects only the *initial length* of the transition when it is first applied.

When would you use this? You may have a project that requires many transitions, and perhaps you just want to slap on the transition and go, without fussing. If you know that every transition will be 20 frames long, you can change the default duration, and all transitions applied thereafter will be exactly 20 frames long. You do not have to fiddle with the duration of each transition.

The Transition Default Duration setting is remembered at the Premiere Pro system level. This means it will apply not only to the existing project, but to all future projects you create in Premiere Pro, until you change it again. In fact, any changes made in the Preferences window apply to all Premiere Pro projects, not just the currently open one.

Single-Sided Transitions

You may not realize it, but you have applied two distinctly different types of transitions: **double-sided** and **single-sided**.

Double-sided transitions are those that transition a scene change, from one clip of video to the next. Double-sided transitions blend two clips–the first clip on the Timeline and the clip that follows it. Hence the name, double-sided.

Single-sided transitions are attached to the In or Out point of a single clip. Instead of transitioning to the next clip, single-sided transitions affect only one clip. The transitions you applied to titles in Exercise 3 were all single-sided, because they affected only the title.

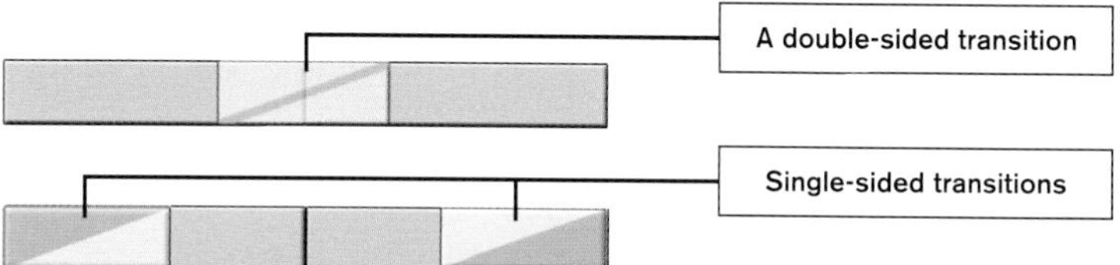

Premiere Pro shades half of the transition icon to signify that it is single-sided.

When you apply a transition in the Timeline window, Premiere Pro selects a single- or double-sided transition for you. If a transition is applied at an edit point, where two clips butt together, then a double-sided transition is chosen. If a transition is applied to the In point or Out point of a single clip, that is not butted up against another clip, then a single-sided transition is chosen.

This begs an awfully important question (and the reason for this section): what if you want to apply a single-sided transition at an edit point? After all, Premiere Pro discreetly chooses on your behalf, but at edit points it always chooses double-sided.

Clip A Clip B

Picture this scenario: you have two clips, A and B, that meet at an edit point. You want to apply a cross dissolve to Clip A, and have it fade out before the edit point. But you want Clip A to fade out completely to black, instead of cross fading to reveal Clip B. This is a situation when you want to apply a single-sided transition to the end of Clip A. In order to do this, when you drag the transition to the Timeline window, hold down the **Ctrl** key. The Ctrl key is the proverbial transition bully, and it forces Premiere Pro to apply a single-sided transition. (Say uncle!)

In the next exercise, you will re-create this scenario.

4. Adding Single-Sided Transitions

In the previous exercise, you applied single-sided transitions to titles. Premiere Pro automatically chose to make the transition single-sided, because the titles were by themselves, and there were no other clips to transition from or to. In this exercise, you will learn how to apply singled-sided transitions to video, and you'll also learn the secret to forcing a single-sided transition.

1. This exercise begins where Exercise 3 left off. If the project from Exercise 3 is still open, skip to Step 2. If Premiere Pro is not running, launch it and click **Open Project** at the **Welcome Screen**. Navigate to the **c:\Premiere Pro HOT\Chapter 08** folder, select **Exercise04.prproj**, and click **Open**.

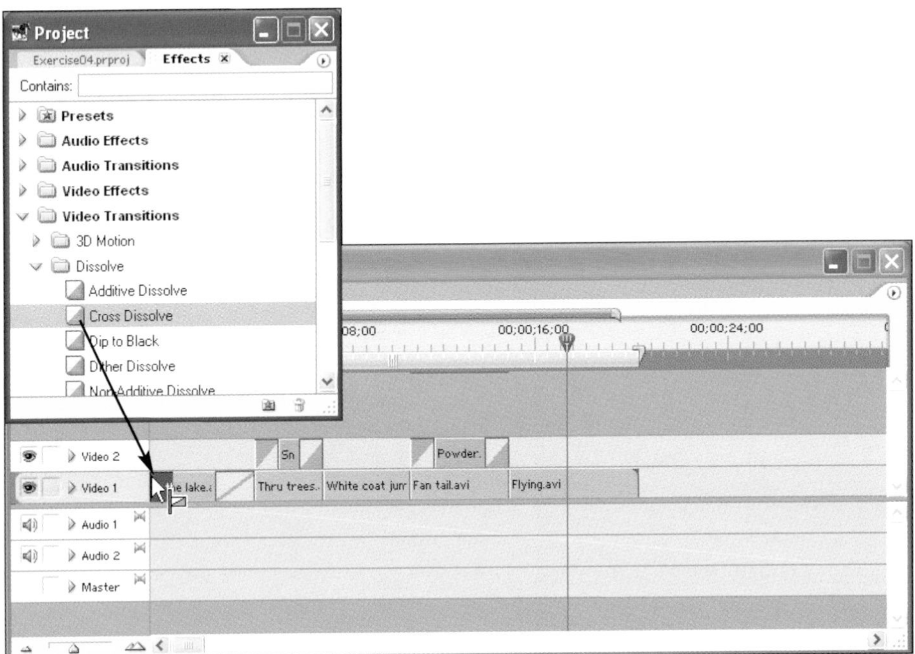

2. Twirl down the **Video Transitions** folder, and then twirl down the **Dissolve** subfolder. Drag the **Cross Dissolve** transition from the **Effects** window to the **In** point of **Clip 1** in track **Video 1** of the **Timeline** window. To confirm that you are correctly applying a single-sided transition, look for the mouse pointer.

3. In the **Monitor** window, click the **Play** button to preview the transition.

The clip should fade in from black. This is a single-sided transition, similar to the ones you applied to the titles in the previous exercise. Because there was no clip before this clip, it was easy for Premiere Pro to choose a single-sided transition.

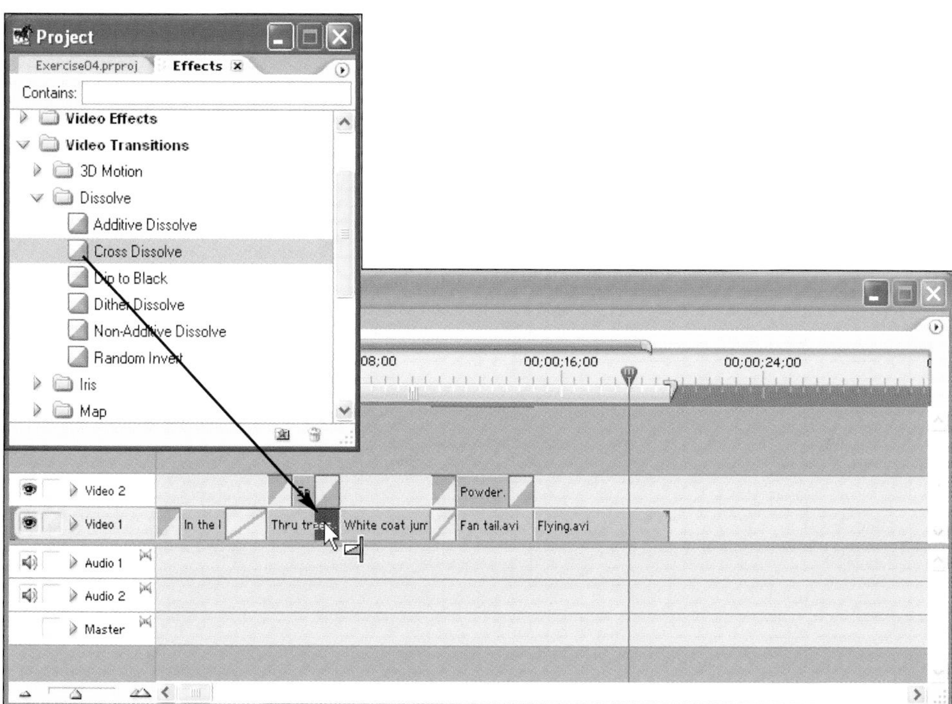

4. Now you will force a single-sided transition to the **Out** point of the second clip on the **Timeline**. Because the end of this clip is part of an edit point, Premiere Pro will want to choose a double-sided transition. However, when you hold down the **Ctrl** key, you can force a single-sided transition. To do this, drag the **Cross Dissolve** transition from the **Effects** window to the **Out** point of the second clip in track **Video 1** on the **Timeline.** When the mouse gets near the **Out** point of **Clip 2**, hold down the **Ctrl** key until you see the single-sided transition pointer.

Note: *If the **Ctrl** key is properly held down, the pointer should appear. Otherwise, you may see the pointer, which indicates a double-sided transition, which you do not want.*

5. In the **Monitor** window, click the **Play** button to preview the transition. At the end of the second clip, the screen should fade out completely to black.

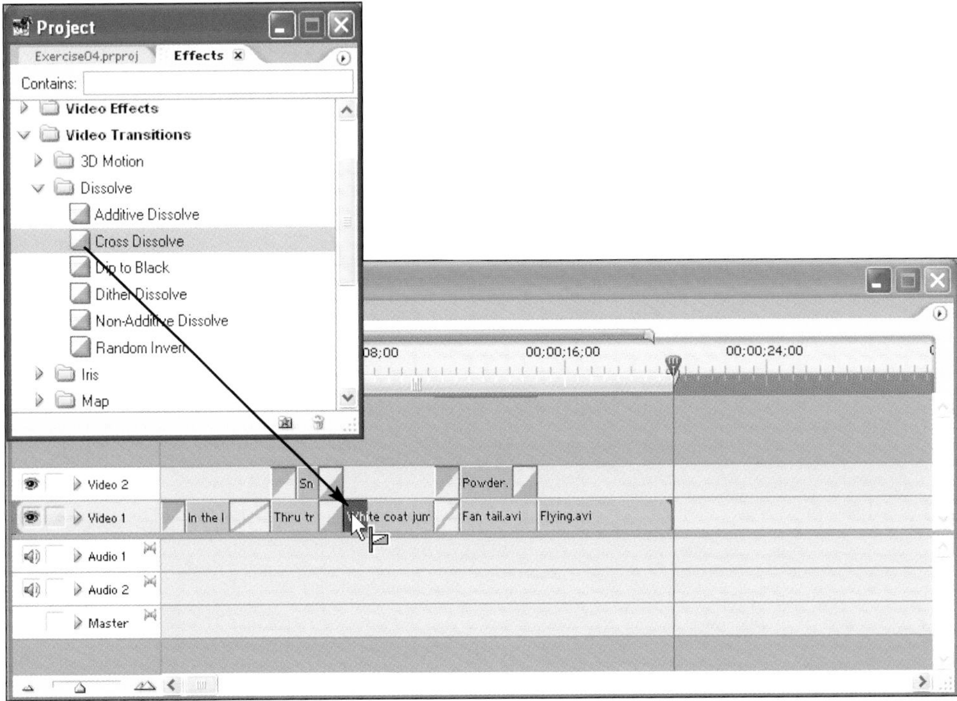

6. Now, add the same single-sided transition to the **In** point of the third clip on the **Timeline**. To do this, drag the **Cross Dissolve** transition from the **Effects** window to the **Out** point of the second clip in track **Video 1** on the **Timeline**. When the mouse gets near the **Out** point of **Clip 2**, hold down the **Ctrl** key until you see the single-sided transition pointer.

---

7. In the **Monitor** window, click the **Play** button to preview the transition. The second clip should still fade out to black, and the third clip should now fade in from black. This creates a **Dip to Black** effect at the edit point.

*Tip: You may notice that there already is a **Dip to Black** transition in the **Dissolve** subfolder. You could achieve this same look by using the **Dip to Black** transition as a double-sided transition across the edit point. (There is a subtle difference, but at this point in your Premiere Pro journey, it's not that important.)*

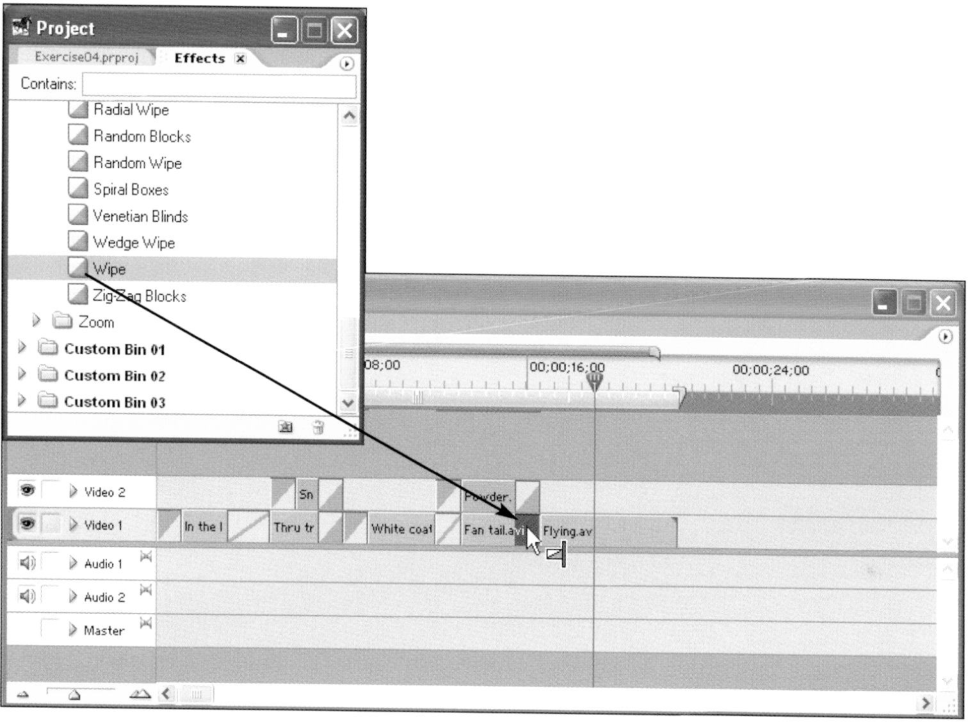

8. You can also force other types of transitions to be single-sided as well. In the next part of this exercise, you are going to add a single-sided wipe. To do this, scroll down the **Effects** window and twirl down the **Wipe** subfolder. Scroll to the bottom of the subfolder and drag the **Wipe** transition from the **Effects** window to the **Out** point of the fourth clip **(Fan tail.avi)** in track **Video 1** on the **Timeline**. When the mouse gets near the **Out** point, hold down the **Ctrl** key until you see the single-sided transition pointer.

9. In the **Monitor** window, click the **Play** button to preview the transition. The **Fan tail.avi** video clip should wipe off, leaving a blank (black) screen.

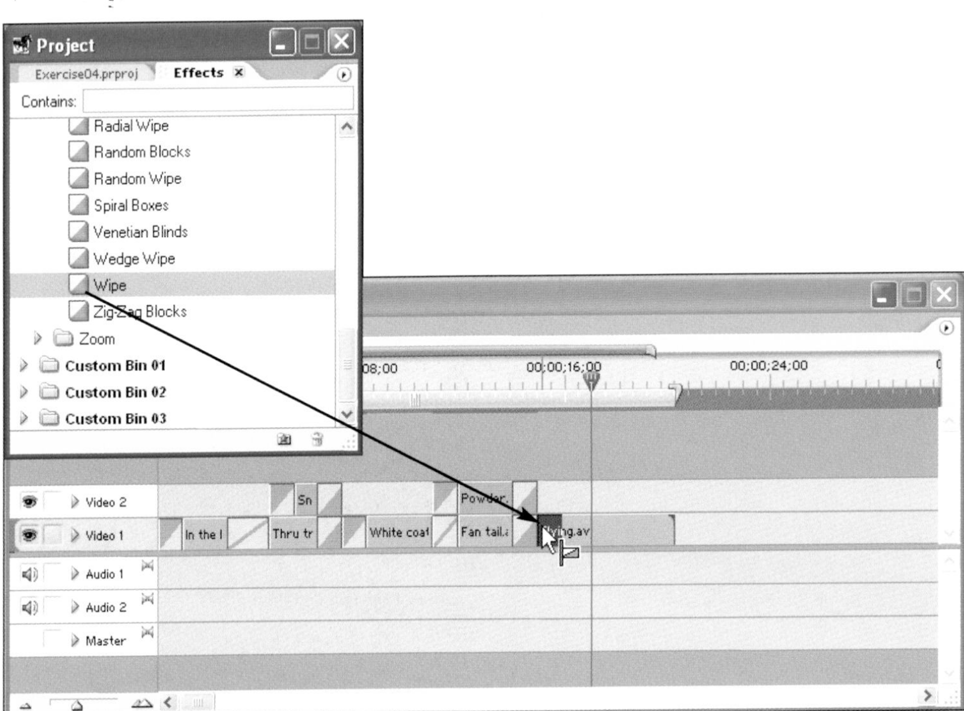

10. Right now, the final clip (**Flying.avi**) pops on, immediately after a black screen. Since the previous clip wipes off, it would be nice if this clip *wiped on* so it doesn't look so jarring. Once again, drag the **Wipe** transition from the **Effects** window to the **In** point of **Flying.avi**. When the mouse gets close to the **In** point, hold down the **Ctrl** key until you see the single-sided transition pointer.

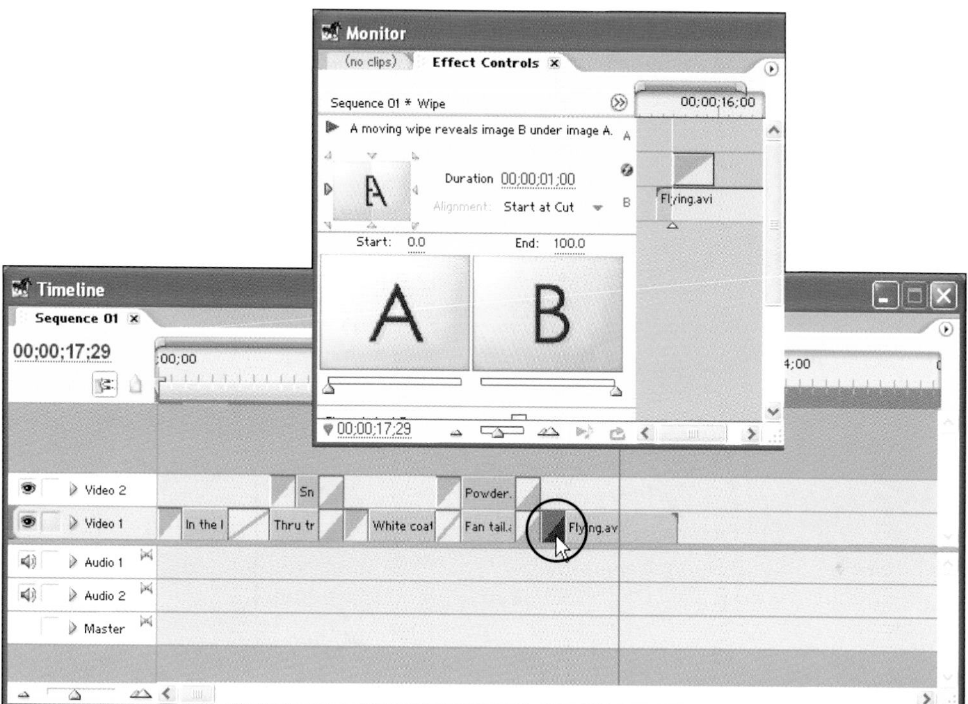

11. You probably aren't surprised to learn that you can also modify the options of single-sided transitions just like you did for double-sided transitions earlier in this chapter. In this case, you are going to have the final transition wipe on from top to bottom. To do this, double-click the last transition in the **Timeline** to open its options in the **Effect Controls** window.

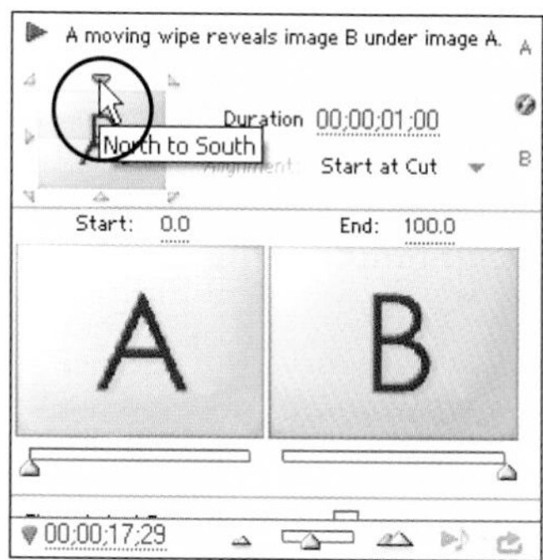

12. This wipe transition lets you choose the edge where the wipe will start. In this case, we want the wipe to move **North to South**. To do this, click the edge selector's top triangle in the **Effect Controls** window.

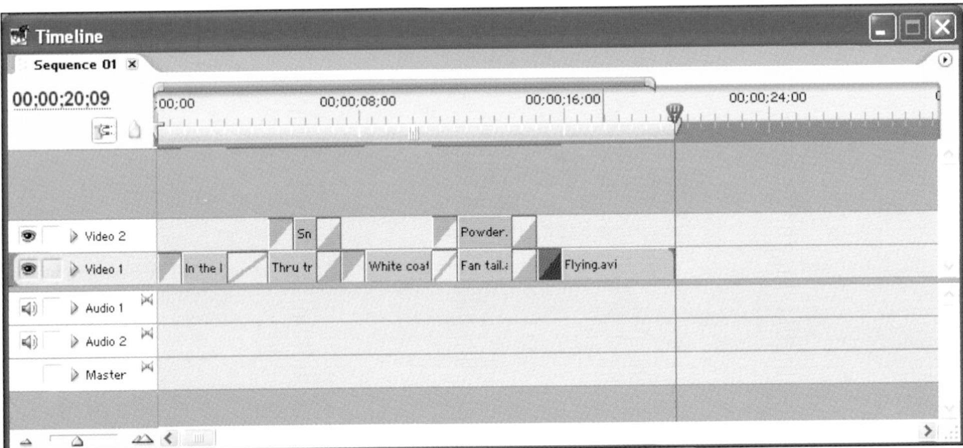

13. In the **Monitor** window, click the **Play** button to preview the transition. The **Fan tail.avi** video clip should still wipe off **West to East**, and **Flying.avi** should now wipe on **North to South**.

14. Save this project and keep it open before moving on to the next exercise.

In this exercise, you have forced single-sided transitions to the start and end of clips at edit points. Keep in mind that in the real world, you probably won't want to use as many transitions, nor so many types of transitions. For purposes of this exercise, it was fun to do, but when you're out there editing on your own, remember the golden rule of transitions: less is more.

Clips Without Heads or Tails

Single-sided transitions are nice because they don't require any head or tail material, as the previous exercise demonstrated. Singled-sided transitions are only attached to one clip. Either they start when that clip starts or they end when the clip ends–but there's no additional head or tail material needed.

Earlier in this chapter, you learned that double-sided transitions, those that transition from Clip A to Clip B, definitely require head and/or tail material. These are the types of transitions you applied back in Exercise 1 (at that time you didn't know they were secretly called double-sided transitions.)

Although having plenty of head and tail material is helpful, in the real world this doesn't always happen. You don't always have unused, trimmed material at the beginning or the end of a clip; sometimes the entire, original clip is on the Timeline. Since double-sided transitions require head or tail material, what do you do in these situations? And how do you even know if there's head/tail material available?

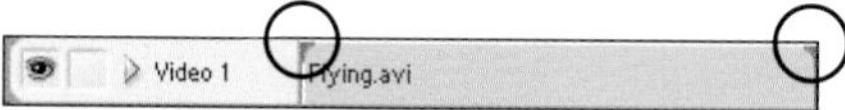

When there is no additional head material before the In point of a clip, Premiere Pro displays a tiny notch in the upper-*left* corner of the clip on the Timeline. When there is no additional tail material after the Out point of a clip, Premiere Pro displays a tiny notch in the upper-*right* corner. These notches alert you that any transition placed at an edit point with a notch will not have any head or tail material to use, because you are using the *whole* clip.

There are two different ways to remedy this problem. The easiest solution is to trim the clip in the **Timeline** with the **Trim In** or **Trim Out** pointer. This creates unused head and tail material for the clip, which gives your transition something to work with.

The downside to this solution is that you are trimming off video you may need. Otherwise, if you did not need that video, why was the whole clip on the Timeline in the first place? Sometimes very important action occurs right at the beginning or end of a clip, and trimming the video is just not an option.

The second solution is to apply the transition as normal, and let Premiere Pro "duplicate" the first or last frame in order to simulate head/tail material. In other words, the first or last frame is turned into a still image, and that image is repeated for every frame of the transition. The downside to this solution is that your video will "freeze" and then suddenly move again when the transition completes.

The next exercise lets you practice both of these solutions.

5. Creating Head or Tail Materials

In this exercise, you will practice creating head or tail material, in order to apply a transition between two clips.

1. This exercise begins where Exercise 4 left off. If the project from Exercise 4 is still open, skip to Step 2. If Premiere Pro is not running, launch it and click **Open Project** at the **Welcome Screen**. Navigate to the **c:\Premiere Pro HOT\Chapter 08** folder, select **Exercise05.prproj**, and click **Open**.

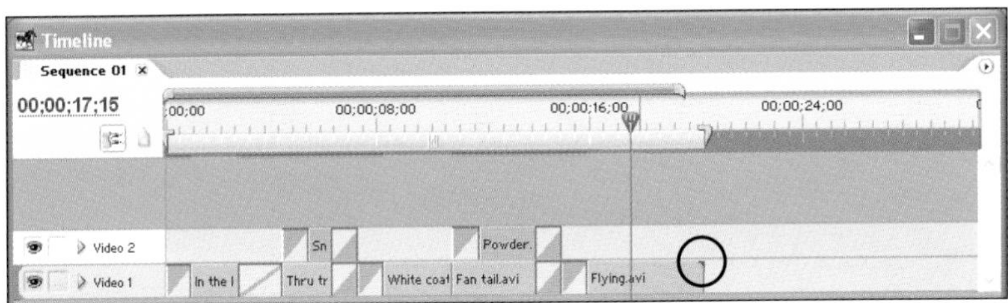

*The **Out** point of the last clip on the **Timeline (Flying.avi)** has a tiny notch in the corner, indicating that the clip has no additional tail material available.*

---

2. Now you are going to import and add a clip to the **Timeline**, immediately after **Flying.avi**. To do this, choose **File > Import**. Navigate to the **c:\Premiere Pro HOT\Source Video** folder, select **Shoot the edge.avi** and then click **Open**.

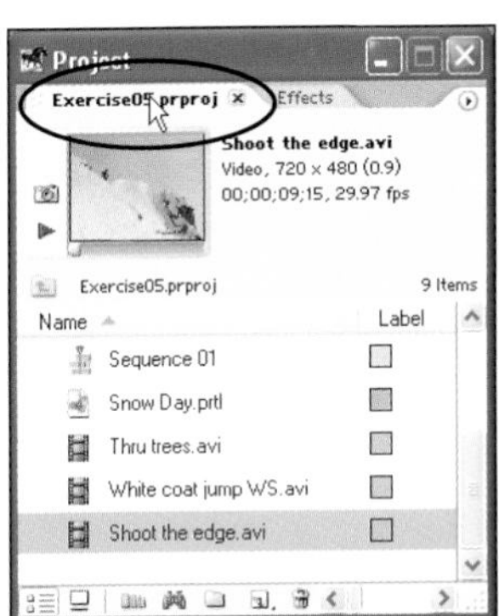

3. If the **Effects** window is still in the foreground, click the **Project** tab to bring it to the foreground. Scroll to the bottom of the **Project** window until you see the imported clip, **Shoot the edge.avi**.

Note: *Your screen may vary slightly from the above image. Premiere Pro re-sorts the* ***Project*** *window whenever a project is closed and then reopened. If you still have the previous exercise open, the imported clips in your* ***Project*** *window may be sorted differently.*

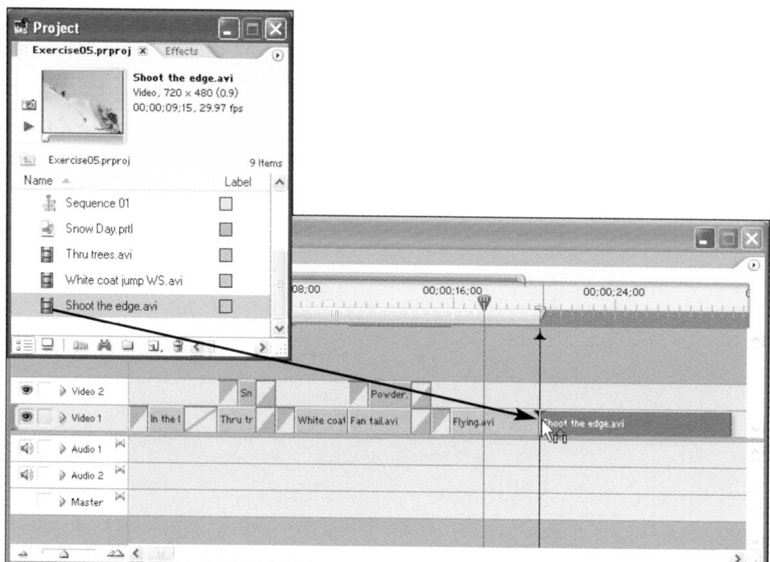

4. You are going to drag the clip straight from the **Project** window to the **Timeline** window, without setting any **In** or **Out** points. (This means there will be no head or tail material for this clip, because you are placing the entire clip in the **Timeline**.) To do this, drag **Shoot the edge.avi** from the **Project** window to the **Out** point of **Flying.avi** in the **Timeline** window. Look for the vertical, black snap indicator to ensure there is no gap between the two clips.

Note: *Notice that a notch appears at the* ***In*** *point of* ***Shoot the edge.avi.*** *Since you did not trim off any material, there is no extra head material to use.*

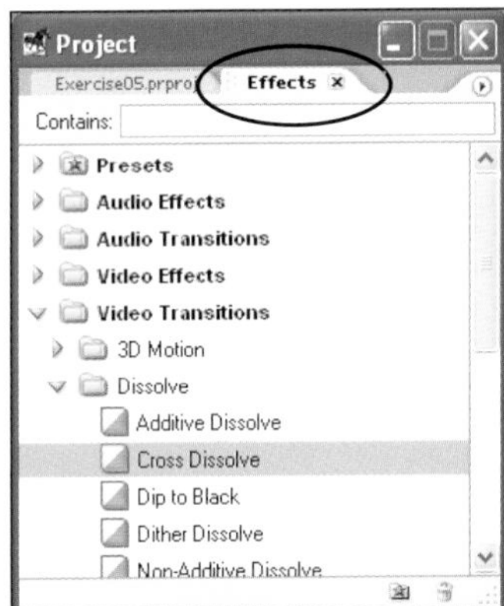

5. Now you are going to apply a transition to edit point between **Flying.avi** and **Shoot the edge.avi**. To do this, first click the **Effects** tab to bring it to the foreground. Twirl down the **Video Transitions** folder, and then twirl down the **Dissolve** subfolder to view its contents.

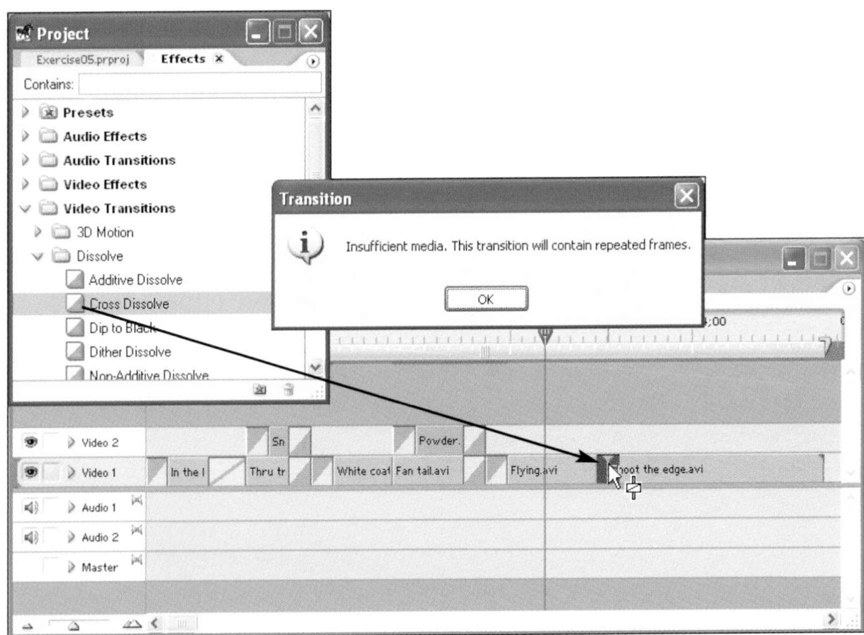

6. Select the **Cross Dissolve** transition from the **Effects** window, and drag it to the edit point between **Flying.avi** and **Shoot the edge.avi**. As soon as you drop the transition, an error message will appear, telling you that there is "Insufficient media." This is Premiere Pro's way of explaining that you have no head or tail material available. Click **OK**.

*Notice that the transition that was applied looks very different from the other transitions. There are many diagonal lines across the transition clip, which is Premiere Pro's way of telling you that frames were repeated. This means that the last frame of **Flying.avi** was duplicated over and over, like a still image, until the transition was complete. Likewise, the first frame of **Shoot the edge.avi** was repeated from the transition start until the edit point. This makes both clips appear "frozen" during the transition.*

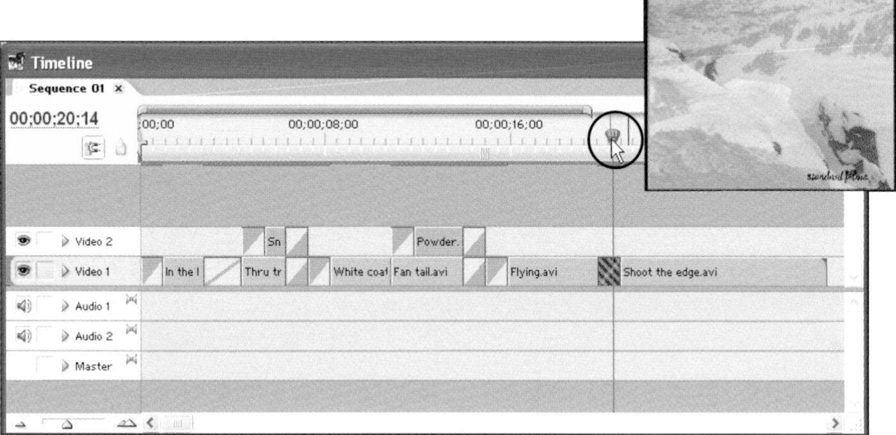

7. To help understand this better, click **Play** in the **Monitor** window **Program** view to watch this transition. You will see that the skier at the top of the mountain in **Shoot the edge.avi**, appears to hold still until the edit point. You can also slowly drag the current time indicator back and forth, above the transition in the **Timeline** window. This will let you watch the transition frame-by-frame, to see how the frames are repeated.

8. There may be a better solution than using repeated frames, since the clips are noticeably "frozen" during the transition. (There will be other times when the repeated frames are not as noticeable, and therefore a good solution.) In this case, however, you are going to undo the transition. Choose **Edit > Undo**, which will remove the transition you just added.

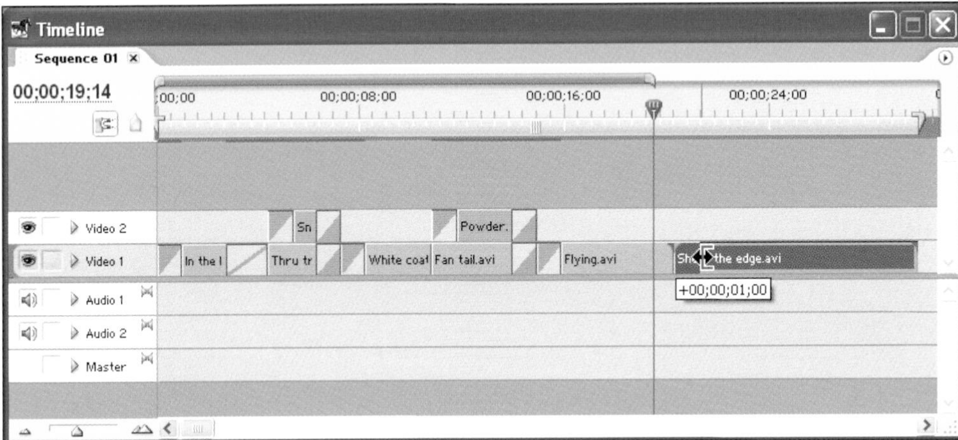

9. The second solution to try is to trim off some of the beginning of **Shoot the edge.avi** to create some head material that a transition can use. To do this, hover your mouse over the **In** point of **Shoot the edge.avi**, wait until you see the **Trim In** pointer, hold down the **Ctrl** key to turn the pointer into the **Ripple Trim** pointer, and then drag the **In** point approximately 1 second to the right.

Tip: In previous chapters, you learned to use the ***Ripple Trim*** *tool from the toolbar. However, a shortcut to this tool is to hold down the* ***Ctrl*** *key when you see the* ***Trim In*** *pointer. Using the* ***Ripple Trim*** *pointer closes the gap created by trimming.*

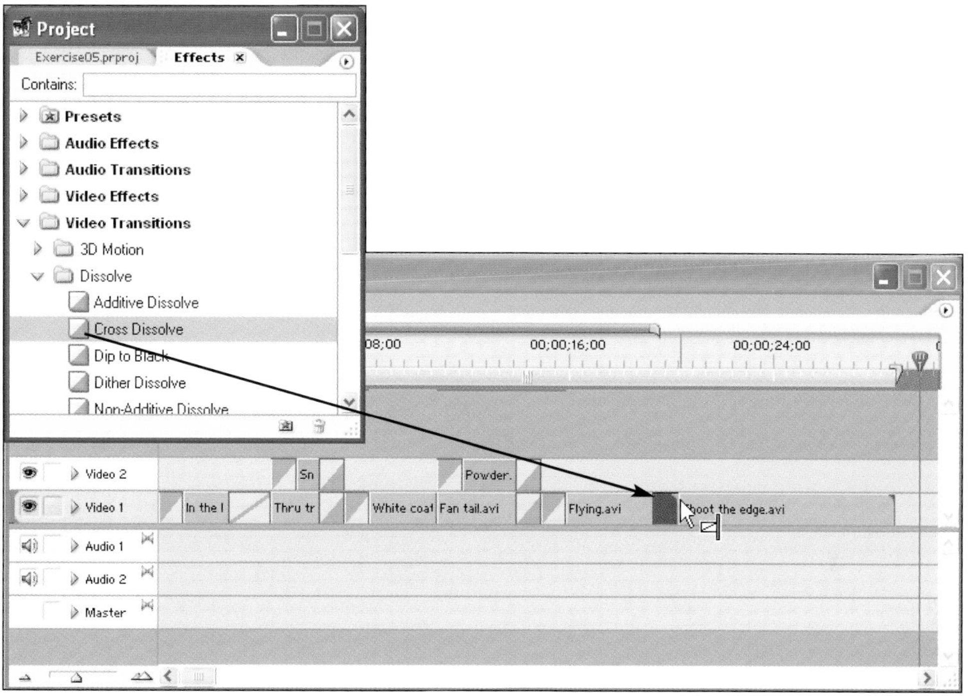

10. Drag the **Cross Dissolve** transition from the **Effects** window to the edit point between **Flying.avi** and **Shoot the edge.avi**. Notice that Premiere Pro only allows you to drop the transition aligned **End at Cut**. Premiere Pro recognizes that the only material available for the transition is the head material of **Shoot the edge.avi**, and thus prevents you from aligning the transition any other way.

11. Preview the sequence by clicking **Play** in the **Monitor** window **Program** view. This time, the transition looks more smooth because no frames are repeated. This solution worked because there was enough material at the beginning of **Shoot the edge.avi** before any vital action took place.

12. Save and close this project before moving on to the next exercise.

In this exercise, you experimented with both solutions to the "no head or tail" material problem. Of course, you could always head *(pun!) this problem off before it becomes a problem by always trimming a little video at the beginning and end of your clips.*

You have reached the end of yet another chapter. You can now add video transitions to still images, titles, and video clips. But what about audio transitions? Good question. They're covered in the next chapter.

9 Audio Transitions

| About Audio Transitions | Fading In and Out |
| A Seamless Crossfade | Crossfading Speech |
| Single-Sided Transition |

H•O•T

Premiere Pro HOT DVD

Audio transitions are just like the video transitions of Chapter 8, "*Transition Effects*." But they're even easier. Much easier. After all, they don't have any options in the Effect Controls window like video transitions, and believe it or not, there are only *two* audio transitions–and there's only one that you'll actually use. So you might think this is going to be a fluff chapter that you can breeze through. Actually, to make up for the ease of audio transitions, this chapter has been packed chock full of advanced audio editing tips and tricks!

About Audio Transitions

Now that you already understand the concept and theory behind transitions, there is little more to show. Audio transitions are exactly the same as video transitions. (Okay, almost the same ... one deals with video and the other deals with audio, but you get the idea, right?)

In the previous chapter, you learned how to apply, modify, and remove transitions. The steps will be the same for audio. You will notice one major difference between audio transitions and video transitions: there are only *two* audio transitions. And they're almost identical!

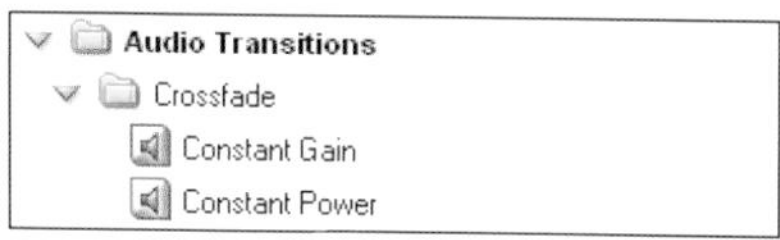

Premiere Pro's audio transitions are found in the aptly-named **Audio Transitions** folder. Within this folder, you'll find one subfolder–**Crossfade**. A crossfade transition slowly fades out the first clip while fading in the second clip. (Think of a crossfade like a cross dissolve but for audio.)

Within the **Crossfade** subfolder are two transitions: **Constant Gain** and **Constant Power**. The Constant Gain transition creates a fade that is mathematically linear. The Constant Power, although not a true linear fade, is perceived as linear by the human ear (weird, but true).

Audio transitions are held to the same requirements of video transitions: if you want to crossfade two clips, you need ample head and/or tail material. If you want to add a single-sided transition to fade-in or fade-out just one clip, no head or tail material is required.

But what's the fun in reading about it when you can try it for yourself? The next exercise will demonstrate the simple act of adding an audio crossfade.

I. Fading In and Out

Instead of showing you how to merely add an audio transition–you already know how to add transitions from the previous chapter–you're going to learn the best ways to *use* an audio transition. The first exercise teaches you how to fade out audio, especially when your audio clip is too long for your video.

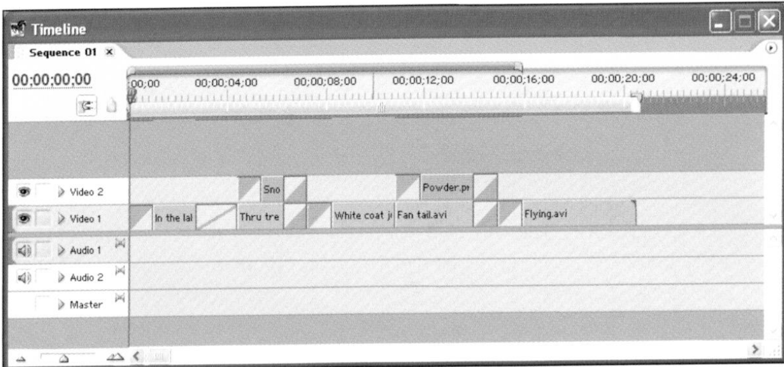

1. If Premiere Pro is not running, launch it and click **Open Project** at the **Welcome Screen**. Navigate to the **c:\Premiere Pro HOT\Chapter09** folder, select **Exercise01.prproj**, and click **Open**. The sequence in the **Timeline** window is similar to the sequence you were building in the previous chapter (although not identical).

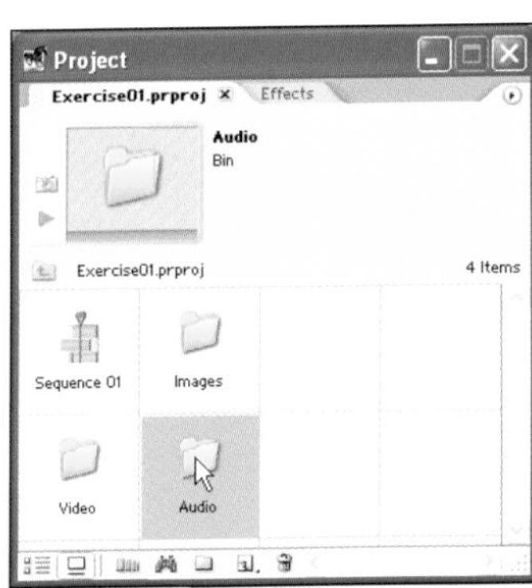

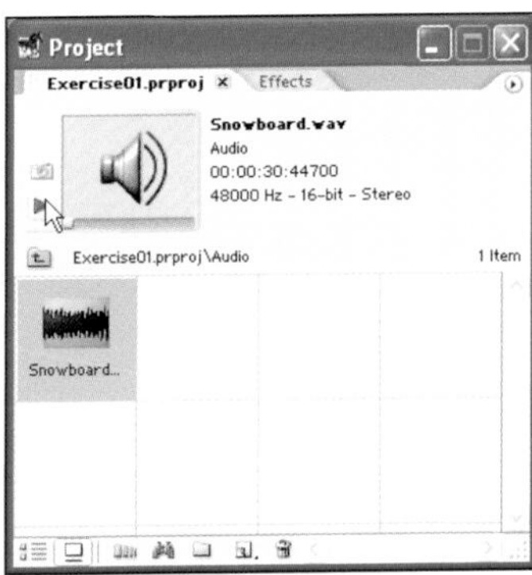

2. Double-click the **Audio** bin in the **Project** window to view its contents. Click once on the audio clip **Snowboard.wav** to select it, and then click the **Play Preview** button in the preview area of the **Project** window. Notice that the preview area shows the clip as roughly 30 seconds long.

Note: *Depending on the resolution of your computer monitor, the* ***Snowboard.wav*** *clip may display with a truncated name, such as* ***Snowboard....***

3. Click the **Play** button in the **Monitor** window **Program** view to preview the sequence. The sequence should look vaguely familiar. It is similar, but not identical to, the exercise you created in the previous chapter.

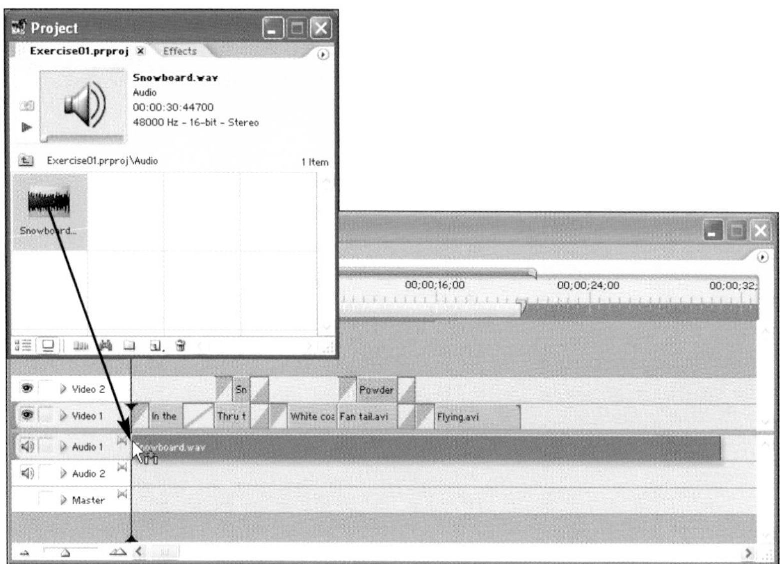

4. This sequence is in some desperate need of audio–STAT! (It's always fun to edit like you're a doctor.) Drag **Snowboard.wav** from the **Project** window to track **Audio 1** of the **Timeline** window. Make sure you drag it to the far left, and look for the black, vertical snap indicator, signifying snappage to the start of the sequence. Click the **Play** button in the **Monitor** window **Program** view to preview the sequence.

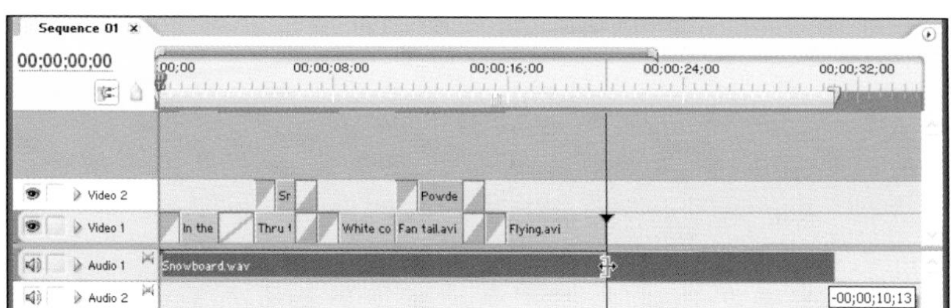

5. A problem presents itself: the video stops playing at approximately 20 seconds, but the audio plays until 30 seconds. This is a perfect time to use an audio transition to create a fade-out. The first step is to trim the audio so it ends at approximately the same time. To do this, hover your mouse over the **Out** point of **Snowboard.wav** in track **Audio 1**, until you see the **Trim Out** pointer, and drag it to the left until you snap it to the **Out** point of **Flying.avi**, the last clip in the sequence.

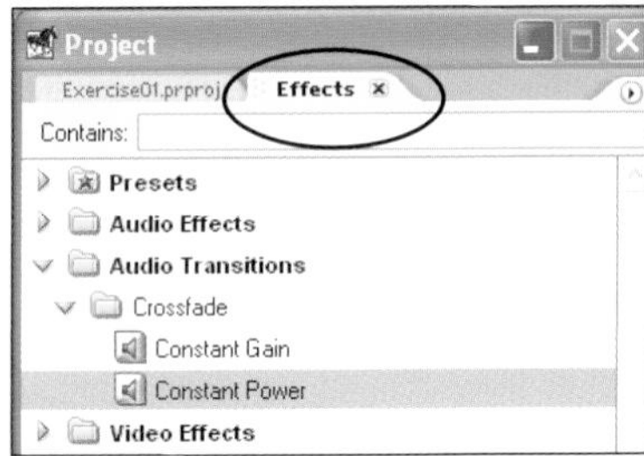

6. To add an audio transition, click the **Effects** tab in the **Project** window to bring it to the foreground. Twirl down the **Audio Transitions** folder and twirl down the **Crossfade** subfolder to view its contents.

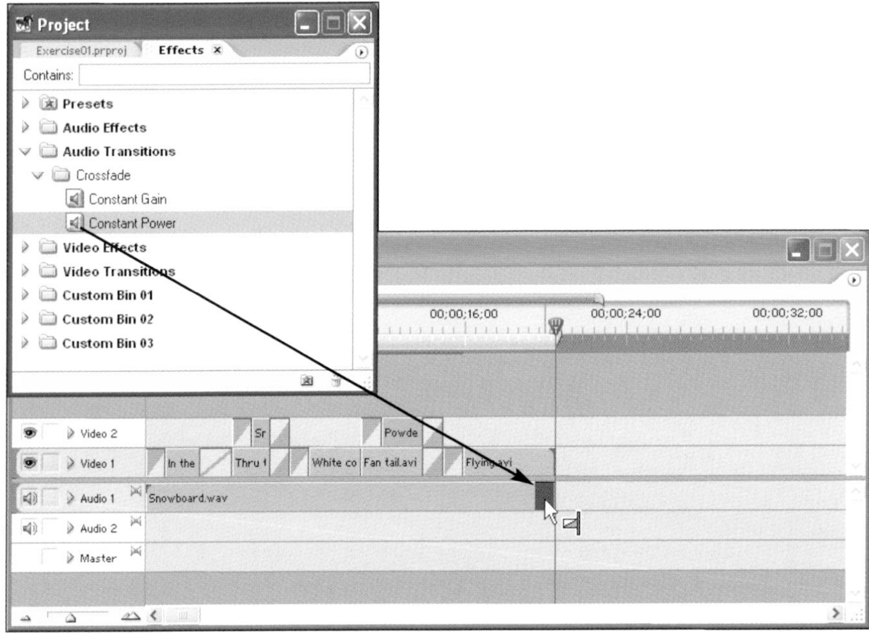

7. To create an audio fade-out, drag the **Constant Power** audio transition from the **Effects** window to the **Out** point of **Snowboard.wav** in track **Audio 1** of the sequence. Click the **Play** button in the **Monitor** window Program view to preview the fade-out.

There are two ways to sneak out *audio with an audio transition; you can make the audio transition very long, which slowly fades out over time, hopefully without drawing attention to itself. Or, you can make it very short, so it sounds quick but hopefully clean.*

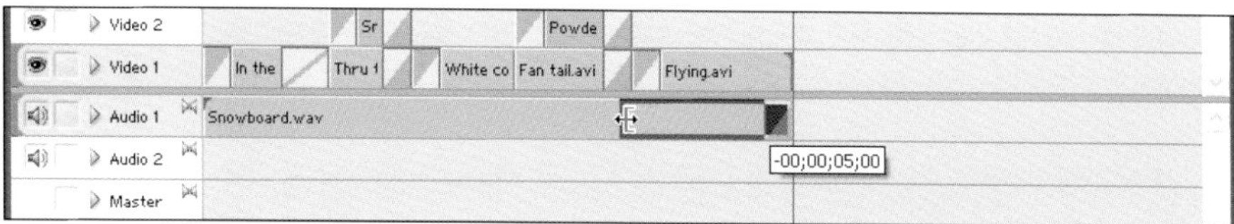

8. First, try making the transition very long. To lengthen the transition, hover your mouse over the start of the transition, and drag it approximately 5 seconds to the left. Be sure to use the yellow pop-up box to guide you to **-00;00;05;00**.

Tip: Lengthening the audio crossfade creates a very gradual audio fade-out. The longer the crossfade, the less noticeable it will be to your audience.

---

9. Click the **Play** button in the **Monitor** window **Program** view to preview the transition.

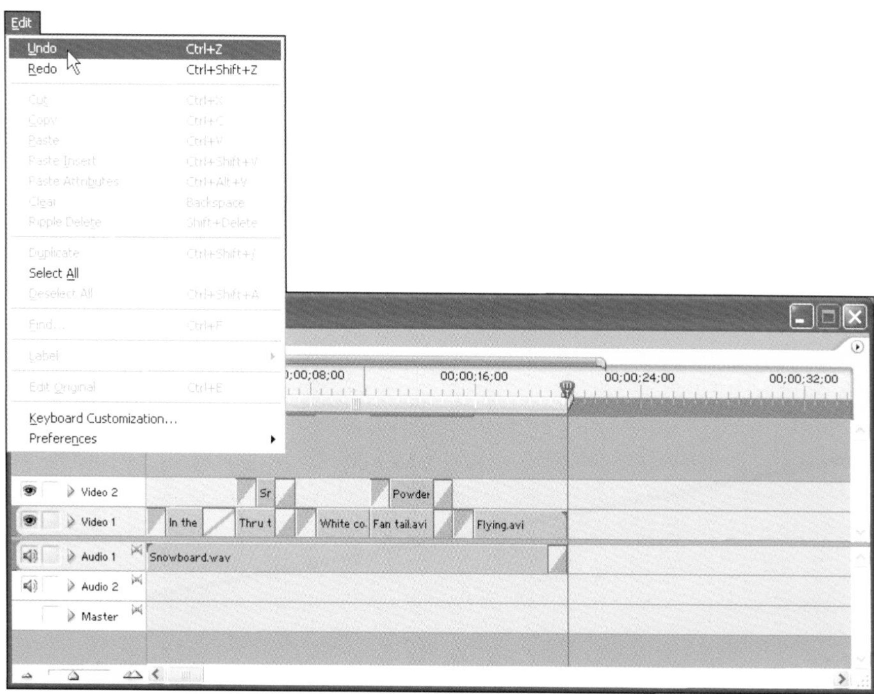

10. Lengthening the transition does a good job to mask the fact that you trimmed off 10 seconds of the song, however, it doesn't quite work in this fast-paced winter sports video. Instead, try shortening it. First, undo the last step by choosing **Edit > Undo**. The audio transition should return to its original length at the end of **Snowboard.wav**.

---

11. Zoom in the **Timeline** window to get a closer look at the transition in the sequence. To make this easier, it's time to learn another tool in the **Toolbox**. Select the **Zoom** tool from the **Toolbox**.

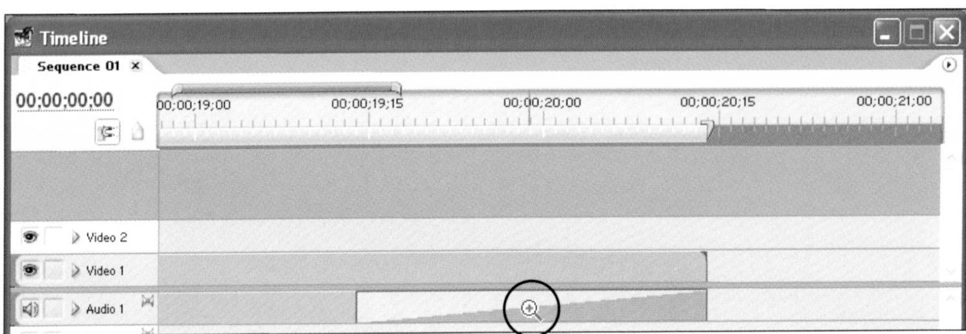

12. With the **Zoom** tool selected, click the area you would like to enlarge. With each click, the area zooms in one level. In this case, click on top of the audio transition in the sequence several times until the transition takes up about one-third of the **Timeline** window. If you zoom too far, hold down the **Alt** key and click the **Zoom** tool to zoom out one level.

*Tip: If you are familiar with other Adobe products, the **Zoom** tool should be familiar. As with other Adobe products, you can also drag the Zoom tool over the entire area you want to enlarge to make a custom zoom.*

13. Before doing anything else, make sure you choose the default **Selection** tool in the **Toolbox**, or use the shortcut **V** on the keyboard.

*Tip: This can't be stressed enough! Get in the habit of always choosing the default **Selection** tool as soon as you finish any task with another tool. Having the wrong tool selected can cause the wrong action to be performed, and you can accidentally do some major damage to your project (nothing that can't be undone with the **Edit > Undo** command, of course).*

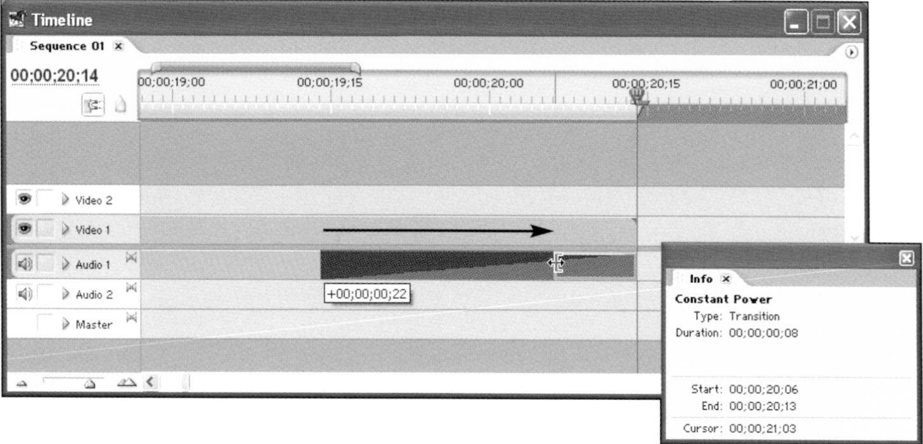

14. Back to the exercise! The whole purpose of zooming was so you could shorten the audio transition with greater precision. In this case, you are going to try to fade out the audio with a very short audio transition. To do this, hover your mouse over the start of the audio transition, and with the **Trim In** pointer, drag the transition about 22 frames to the right. Use the yellow pop-up box to guide you to **+00;00;00;22**.

*Tip: You have just created an eight-frame transition. How can you tell? The **Info** window, to the right of the **Timeline** window, shows you useful information on the currently selected clip or transition. In this case, the **Constant Power** transition is selected, and the **Info** window displays the duration of **00;00;00;08.***

---

15. Click the **Play** button in the **Monitor** window **Program** view to preview the sequence. The eight-frame audio transition fades out the audio just enough so it does not seem so abrupt.

You have just learned two different ways you can mask the abrupt ending of an audio clip with a single-sided audio transition. Some projects will be better suited to a gradual, lengthy fade out, and others will appear cleaner with a short fade out. In this exercise, you also learned a new tool, as well as a new window. Three lessons in one!

---

16. Save and close this project before moving on to the next exercise.

MOVIE | zooming_transitions.mov

To learn more about zooming in to create audio fade-outs of different lengths, check out **zooming_transitions.mov** from the **movies** folder on the **Premiere Pro HOT** DVD.

2. A Seamless Crossfade

Exercise 1 taught you one way to shorten an audio clip with a crossfade. This exercise teaches you another method, which uses a crossfade to create a *seamless* audio clip. For example, the audio clip is 30 seconds, but the video is 20 seconds. If you edit with precision, you can "lift out" 10 seconds from the middle of the clip, blending the beginning and the end of the song, while preserving the tempo. Make sense? Hopefully it will after this exercise.

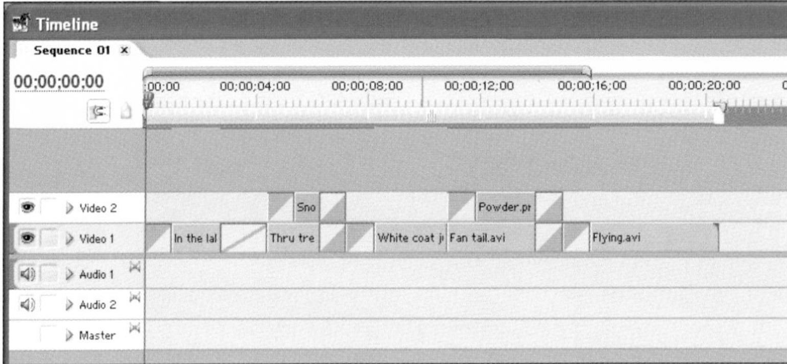

1. If Premiere Pro is not running, launch it and click **Open Project** at the **Welcome Screen**. Navigate to the **c:\Premiere Pro HOT\Chapter09** folder, select **Exercise02.prproj**, and click **Open**. This exercise starts the same way as Exercise 1, in order to show you the alternate method you could have chosen.

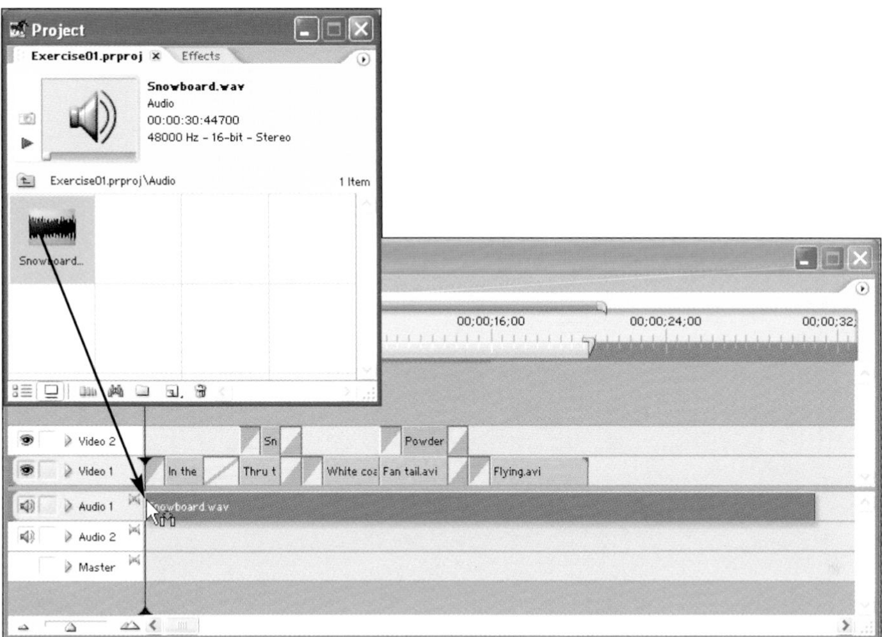

2. Double-click the **Audio** bin in the **Project** window to view its contents. Drag **Snowboard.wav** from the **Project** window to track **Audio 1** in the **Timeline** window. As always, look for the snapping indicator and snap to the beginning of the sequence.

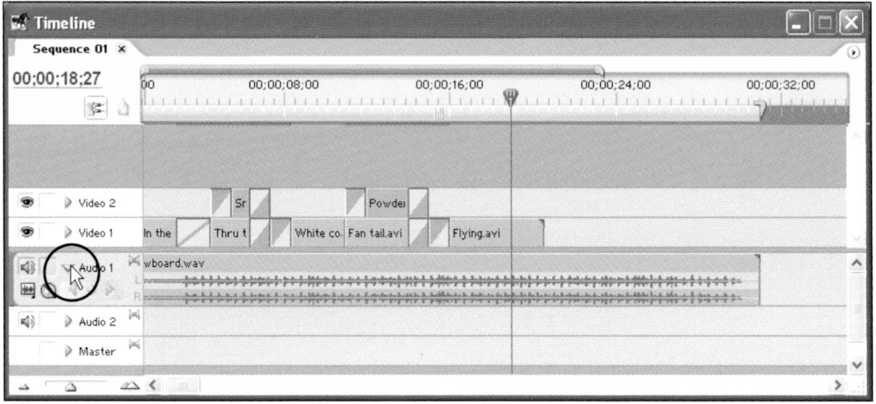

Here's where it gets tricky and involves some brain power. You want to remove roughly 10 seconds of audio from the audio clip in the ***Timeline****. To do this, you are going to set sequence* ***In*** *and* ***Out*** *points around the section to remove. (Yes, this is a little counterintuitive, since all of the edits you have made until now have been defining the section you want to* keep*. Now, you are defining the section you want to* remove.*)*

3. First, you need to view the waveform properties in the **Timeline** window, so you can clearly view where each beat starts and stops. To do this, twirl down track **Audio 1** by clicking the arrow to the left of the track name. This expands the waveform properties below the audio clip.

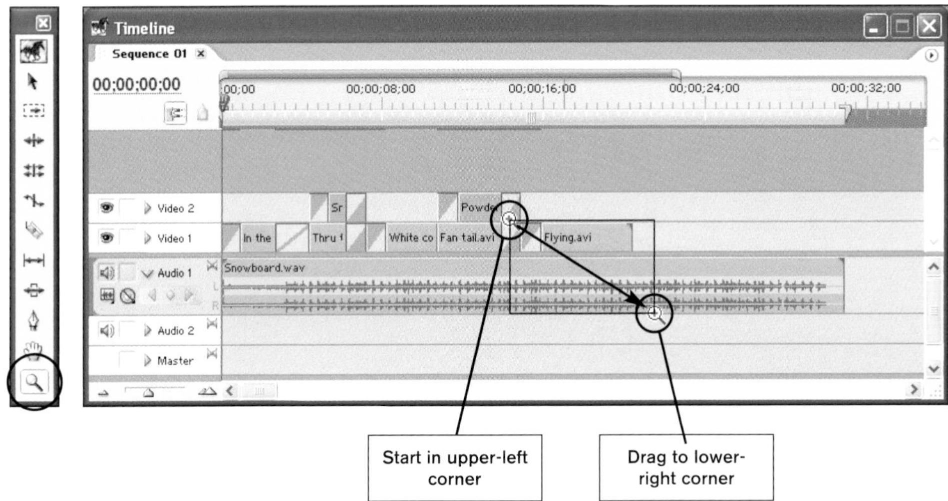

Start in upper-left corner

Drag to lower-right corner

4. Next you are going to zoom in on the **Timeline** window, so you can better see the divisions of the beats. To do this, select the **Zoom** tool from the **Toolbox**, and instead of single-clicking in the **Timeline** window like you did in the previous exercise, you are going to practice *dragging* the **Zoom** tool over the area you want to zoom in on. In this case, you want to zoom in on **Flying.avi** and the audio below it. It's always good to start a little before and finish a little after, so click and drag your mouse from the left of the **In** point of **Flying.avi**, to the right, slightly after the **Out** point of **Flying.avi**, as shown in the diagram.

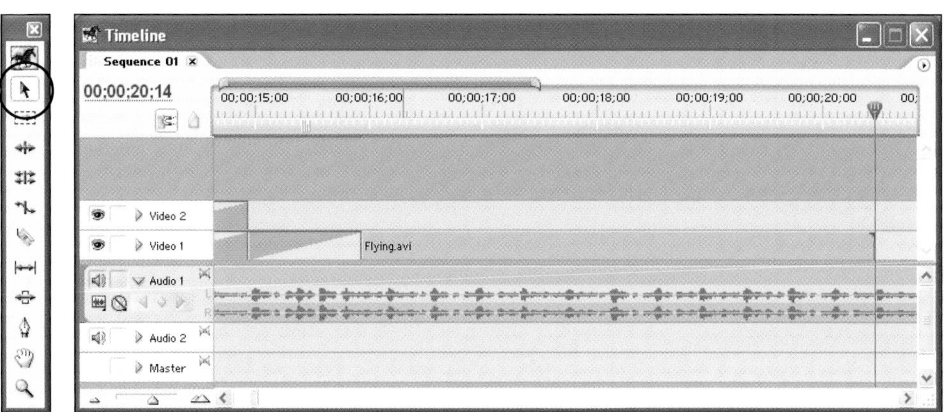

5. As soon as you finish dragging the **Zoom** tool, the **Timeline** window will zoom in the area you specified. In this case, the **Timeline** view starts a little before the **In** point of **Flying.avi** and finishes slightly after the **Out** point of **Flying.avi**. Before doing anything else, make sure you choose the default **Selection** tool in the **Toolbox**, or use the shortcut **V** on the keyboard.

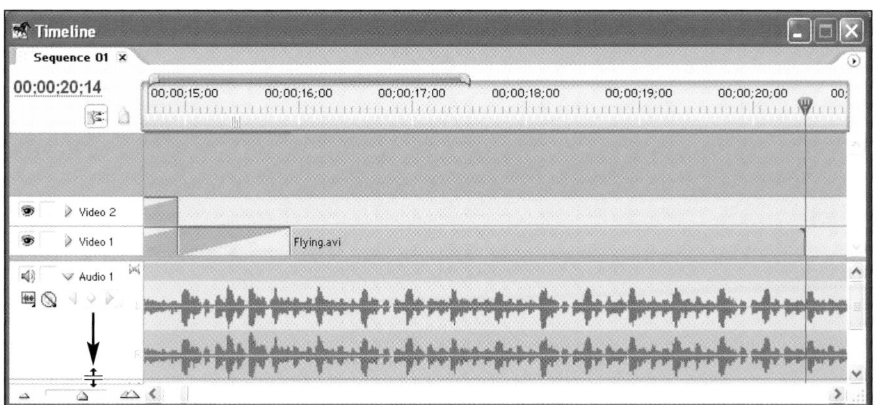

6. Even though you zoomed in to the width you want, it still is a tad difficult to see the waveform of the audio clip, because the audio track is not tall enough. To remedy this, hover your mouse over the bottom edge of track **Audio 1**, below the track name, until the mouse pointer changes to the **Track Resize** pointer (‡).Then drag the track edge to the bottom of the **Timeline** window. This will increase the display height of the track.

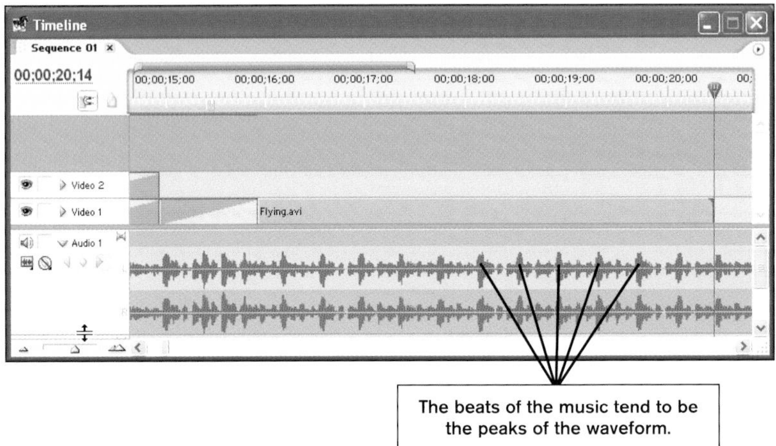

The beats of the music tend to be the peaks of the waveform.

Now it is much easier to see the waveform of the audio clip. The track beats, as described previously in this book, tend to be the tall parts of the waveform, because they are usually accompanied by a loud bass drum or percussion effect. In this clip, it is easy to see the beats, because the waveform spikes with a uniform tempo across the clip.

Note: *The waveforms will display bigger, but keep in mind this does not change the sound or volume of the clips in the audio track. The* ***Track Resize*** *pointer changes only how tall or short a track displays in the* ***Timeline*** *window.*

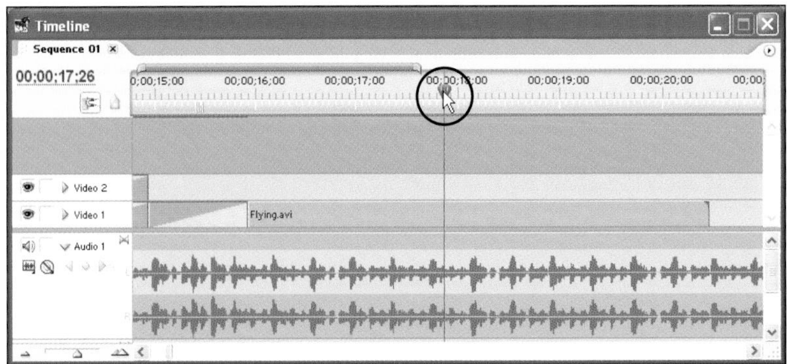

7. The next step is to determine which section you'd like to remove, and more importantly, when you want to start removing it. For music, the section to remove *should start on a beat and end on a beat.* (This will allow you much more flexibility, and you'll see why shortly.) To do this, you need to see the current time indicator. However, since you zoomed in, your current time indicator may not be visible in the **Timeline** window. Click your mouse anywhere in the **Timeline** ruler to make the current time indicator appear in the **Timeline** window.

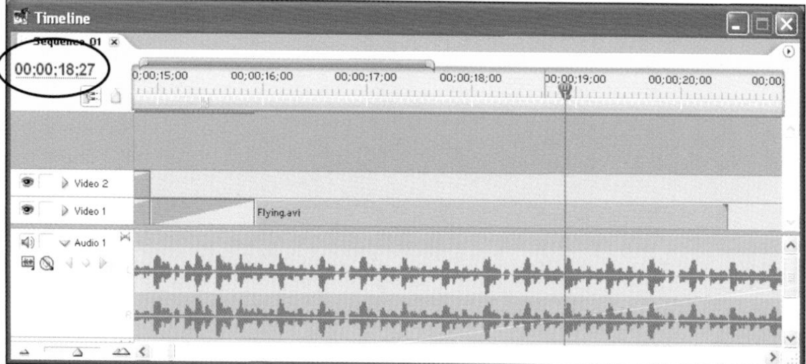

8. Now you are going to drag the current time indicator to the first frame of the section to remove. Remember that you want to start removing on the first frame of a beat. In this case, count four beats (a full measure) from the end of **Flying.avi**, and drag the current time indicator to the beginning of that beat. In the above figure, the current time indicator was taken to **00;00;18;27**. Use the time display in the upper-left corner of the **Timeline** indicator as a guide.

9. Next you are going to set a sequence **In** point. Up until now, you've only set **Source Ins** and **Outs** in the **Monitor** window **Source** view. To set a sequence **In** point, click the **Set In Point** button in the **Monitor** window ***Program*** view (not the **Source** view, but the **Program** view on the right side).

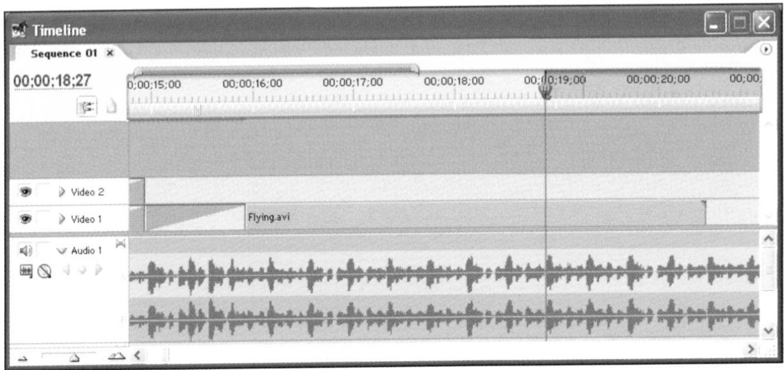

*As soon as you click the **Set In Point** button, an **In** point is displayed in the **Timeline** ruler at the exact frame of the current time indicator. Just like setting **In** and **Out** points in the **Source** view, a dark gray area represents the currently selected area.*

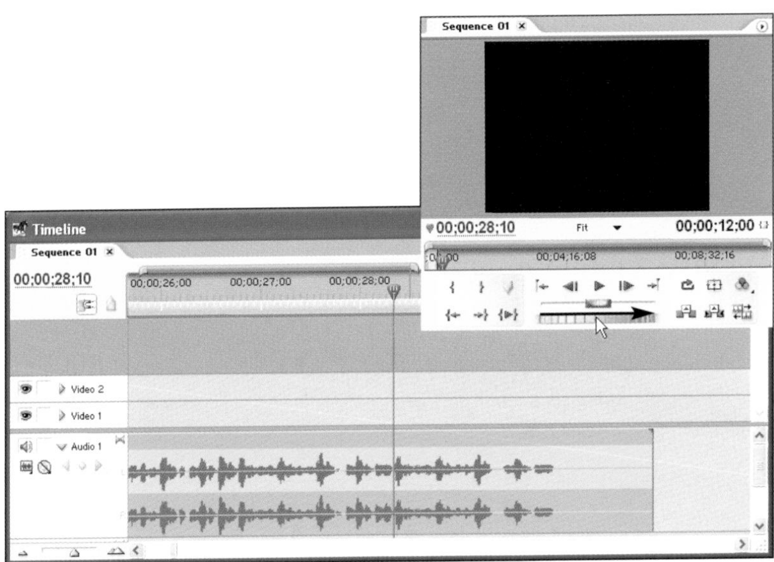

10. The next step is to move the current time indicator to the end of the section you want to remove. In this case, you want to remove everything but the last measure (four beats) of the song. Another handy tool that moves the current time indicator is the jog wheel in the **Monitor** window **Program** view. Drag the jog wheel in the **Monitor** window **Program** view until the current time indicator in the **Timeline** window is placed four beats from the end of the song. In the figure above, the current time indicator was taken to **00;00;28;10**.

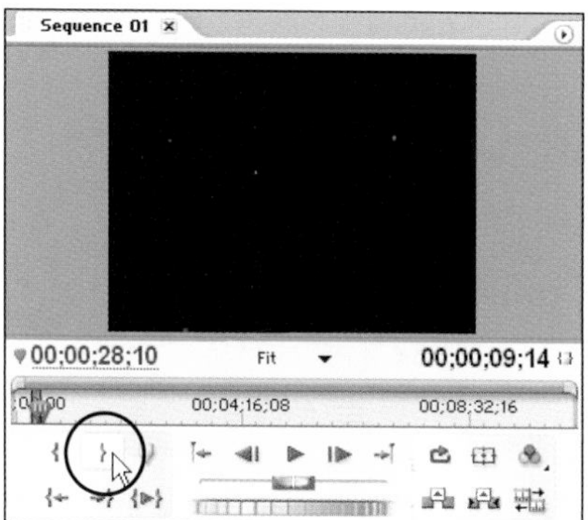

11. Set a sequence **Out** point to "bookend" the section you want to remove. To do this, click the **Set Out Point** button in the **Monitor** window **Program** view. The **Timeline** ruler in the **Timeline** window displays an **Out** point at the current time indicator.

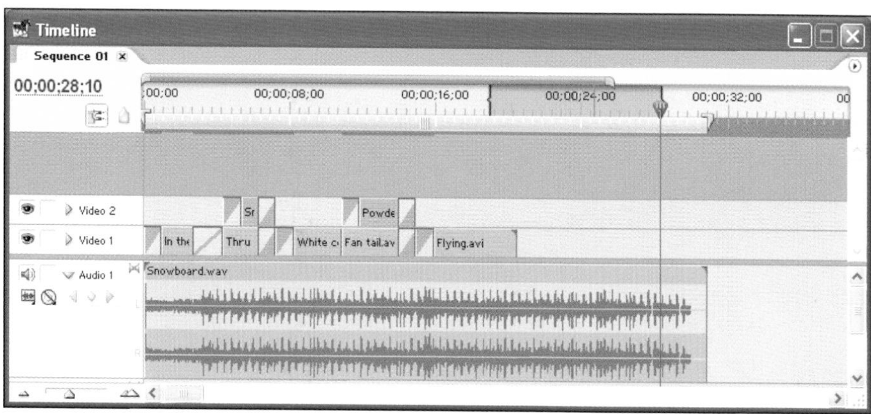

12. Now that you have set sequence **In** and **Out** points, you do not need to be zoomed in as far. Premiere Pro provides a great way to quickly zoom out to the duration of your sequence. On your keyboard, press the \ key, and the **Timeline** window will automatically zoom out *just far enough* to allow viewing of every clip in the sequence. With the **Timeline** window zoomed out, you can easily see the **In** and **Out** points displayed in the **Timeline** ruler.

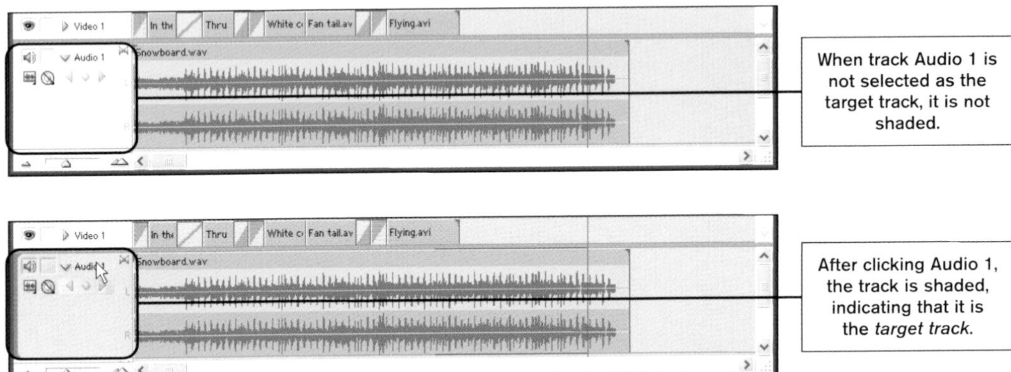
Video 1
In the
Thru
White c
Fan tail.av
Flying.avi
Audio 1
Snowboard.wav
When track Audio 1 is not selected as the target track, it is not shaded.
After clicking Audio 1, the track is shaded, indicating that it is the *target track*.

13. The **Lift** button in the **Monitor** window **Program** view is a very convenient way to remove the section of the sequence between the **In** and **Out** points. The **Lift** button works in a two-step process: first, select the track to lift from–which is called the target track–and then click the **Lift** button. In this case, your target track is track **Audio 1**, because you want to remove the clip from that track. To select **Audio 1** as the **target track**, click the track name, which will shade the track a darker color, indicating it is selected.

***Note:** Make sure that track **Audio 1** is the only track name that is shaded dark. If any of your video tracks are shaded dark, click their names to unselect them.*

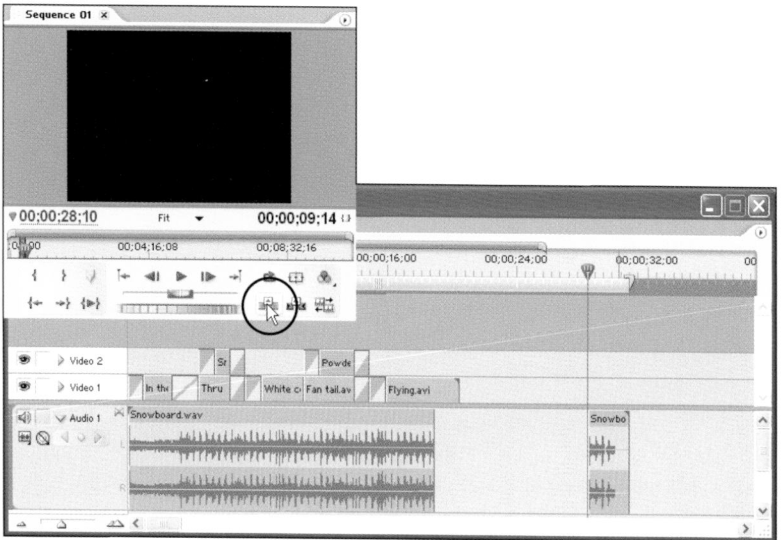

14. Once you have selected a target track, you can click the **Lift** button to remove the desired section from the target track. To do this, click the **Lift** button in the **Monitor** window **Program** view. This will "lift out" the section of the clip between the sequence **In** and **Out** points. Furthermore, it will lift out the audio of the target track. The **Lift** command also clears the sequence **In** and **Out** points you set.

***Note:** The **Lift** command affects only the target track(s). But, if you have no target track chosen, Premiere Pro will "lift out"* any *clip on* any *track that falls between the sequence **In** and **Out** points.*

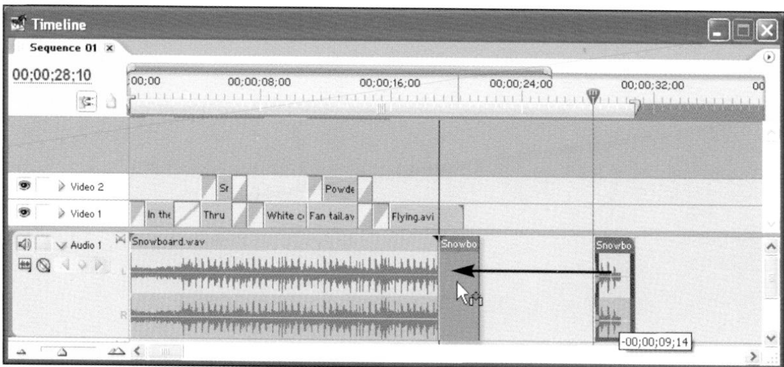

15. Just as you have done in the past when a gap is created, click in the middle of the audio clip at the end of the **Timeline**, and drag it to the left until it snaps to the **Out** point of the first audio clip on the **Timeline**.

***Tip:** Just to the right of the **Lift** button is the **Extract** button. Both buttons do the same thing, except the **Extract** button automatically closes the gap for you, like a ripple delete.*

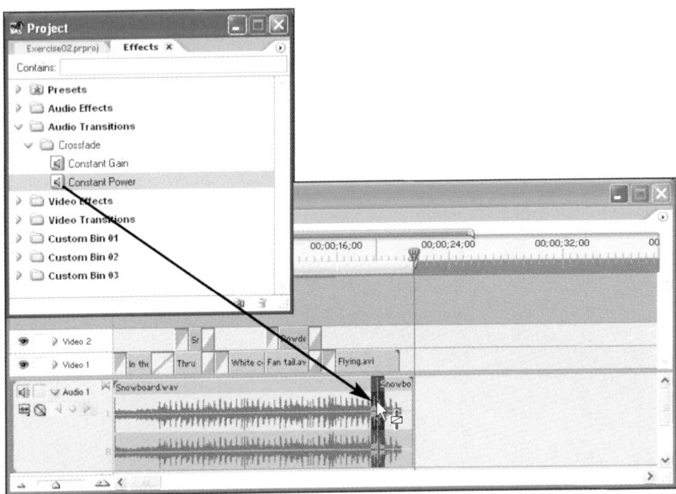

16. Click the **Play** button in the **Monitor** window **Program** view to listen to the audio edit. You'll notice that the tempo was preserved because of the precise edit points set at the music beats. However, there is a noticeable difference in the music at the edit point. This sounds (pun!) like a job for an audio crossfade. To do this, drag the **Constant Power** transition from the **Audio Transitions > Crossfade** subfolder to the center of the edit point in track **Audio 1** in the **Timeline** window.

Note: *You may first have to click the **Effects** tab to bring it to the foreground and then twirl down the **Audio Transitions** and **Crossfade** folders. However, that phrase has been repeated ad nauseam since the previous chapter, so you probably don't need to be shown again.*

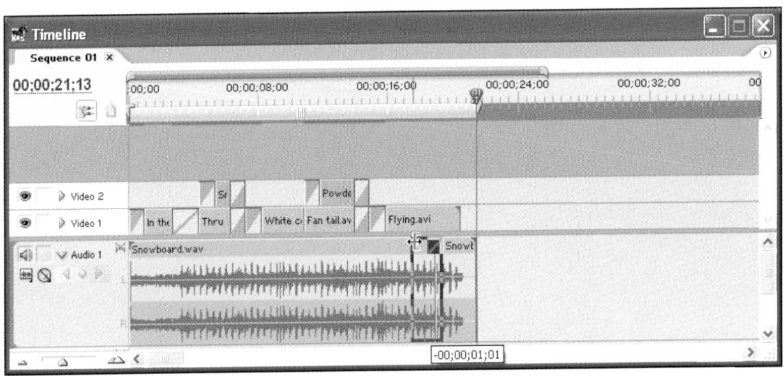

17. Click the **Play** button in the **Monitor** window **Program** view to listen to the audio transition you just applied. You'll hear that it definitely sounds better, but it's not up to par just yet. To smooth out the transition even more, you can drag the transition length to make it transition longer. To do this, hover your mouse over the start of the transition, and drag the **Trim In** pointer to the left about 1 second.

18. Click the **Play** button in the **Monitor** window **Program** view again. This time, the transition takes longer to fade in, which sounds much more smooth.

The primary motive of this exercise was to show you how to make a crossfade to shorten an audio clip—which took all of one step. The ulterior motive was to demonstrate one of the most complex but rewarding audio edits you can make in Premiere Pro. (Adding a crossfade is pretty straightforward, so the real fun is teaching you new editing techniques along the way!)

*This was also a perfect time to highlight some of the other advanced features of the **Timeline** window, such as drag-zooming, resizing tracks, and setting sequence **In** and **Out** points. Keep in mind, the key to editing audio this way is to set your edit points right before the beats. This is so that the two clips can be butted together and still keep the tempo.*

---

19. Save and close this project before moving on to the next exercise.

NOTE | Clearing In and Out Points in a Sequence

With the awesome power of sequence In and Out points, like those you have just set in the previous exercise, comes awesome responsibility. Okay, not really. But, In and Out points in a sequence can definitely cause some unexpected behaviors in Premiere Pro, so it is important to know how to manually remove them.

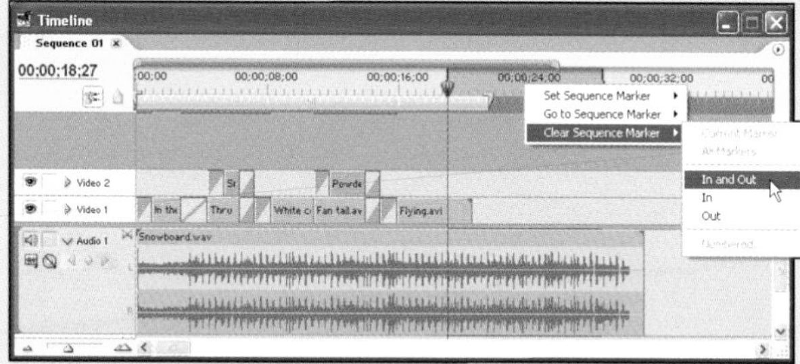

Clearing In and Out points in the sequence is simple; it is also similar to the way you clear them in the Monitor window Source view. Right-click in the **Timeline** ruler and choose **Clear Sequence Marker > In and Out** from the shortcut menu.

3. Crossfading Speech

In the previous exercise, you set edit points based on the beats of music to allow a seamless crossfade between two audio clips. In this exercise, you will perform a similar type of edit and crossfade, except you will set edit points based on words being spoken. This is a handy trick to use when you need to edit out parts of a sound bite.

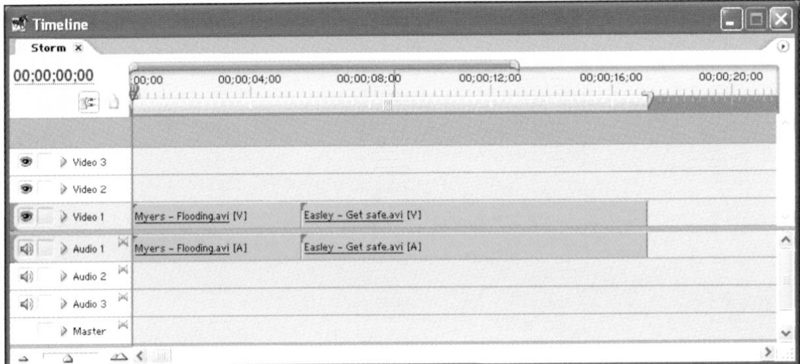

1. If Premiere Pro is not running, launch it and click **Open Project** at the **Welcome Screen**. Navigate to the **c:\Premiere Pro HOT\Chapter09** folder, select **Exercise03.prproj**, and click **Open**. Click the **Play** button in the **Monitor** window **Program** view to preview the sequence. There are two movie clips that each have video and audio.

The goal for this exercise is to remove part of the speech from ***Myers – Flooding.avi****. Being the savvy editor that you are, your aim is to whittle this sound bite to the bare essentials. (Otherwise, the News Producer will have a tantrum.) Here is the edit you will make to the sound bite:*

"I think the big thing that we'll be focused on here obviously ~~is the tornadoes, but the big thing~~ will be the flooding."

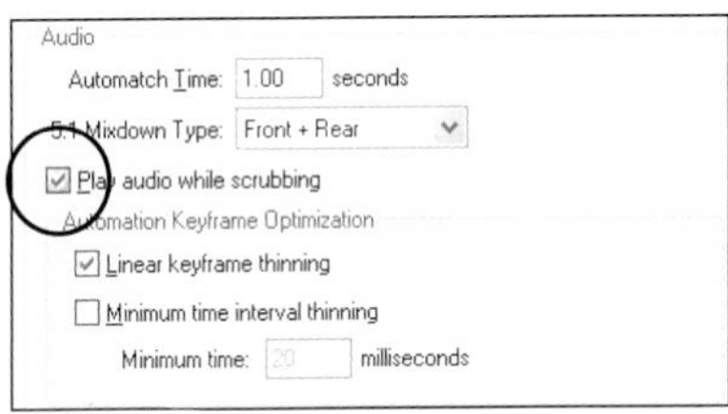

2. For this exercise, make sure that you have audio scrubbing turned on, so you can listen to the sound bite one frame at a time. To turn on audio scrubbing, choose **Edit > Preferences > Audio**. In the **Preferences** window, make sure **Play audio while scrubbing** is checked. Click **OK**.

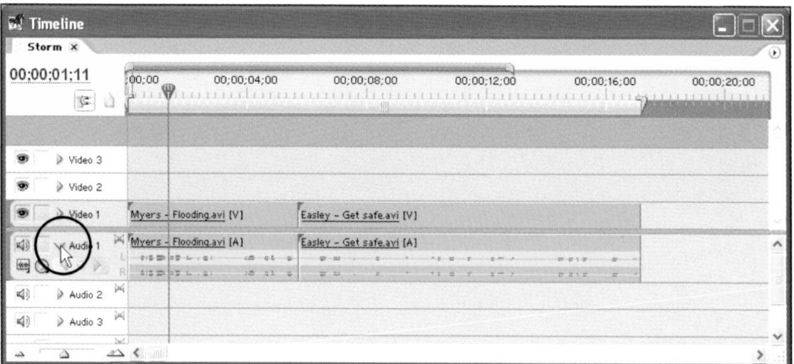

3. Expand track **Audio 1** by twirling down the arrow to the left of the track name. Now you can see the audio waveform for the movie clip. Because this clip is in stereo, the top waveform represents the left audio, and the bottom represents the right audio.

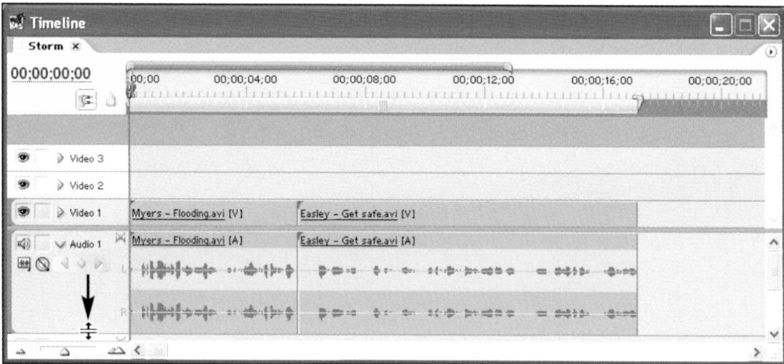

4. To see the waveform properties easier, expand the track height by dragging the bottom of the track (below the track name) down to the bottom of the **Timeline** window. As you drag, the height of the track will increase.

Note: *Remember, this doesn't increase the volume. This increases only the waveform display.*

5. When editing speech, the goal is to set edit points in the "waveform valley"; that is, find a spot between waveform peaks. This is a good indication that you are between words, and there is little noise. The less noise, the less noticeable the edit will be. Click **Play** in the **Monitor** window to play back the sequence, and then click **Stop** immediately after the word "obviously." In this case, playback was stopped at **00;00;03;02**.

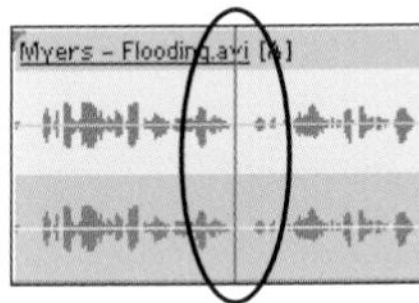

Tip: In the ***Timeline*** *window, notice that you stopped playback between waveform peaks. The flat line of the waveform correlates with the speaker's pause after he says "obviously". The waveform appears flat because there is very little sound. This is a great location to start your edit.*

---

6. This will be the start of the section you will remove. In the previous exercise, you set sequence **In** and **Out** points in the **Monitor** window and then lifted the section out. However, in this exercise you are going to learn a new tool. In the **Toolbox**, select the **Razor** tool.

Tip: The ***Razor*** *tool splices your clip wherever you click in the* ***Timeline*** *window. If you have one long clip, you can splice the clip into two shorter clips. You can splice again and again to create as many segments of a clip as you need.*

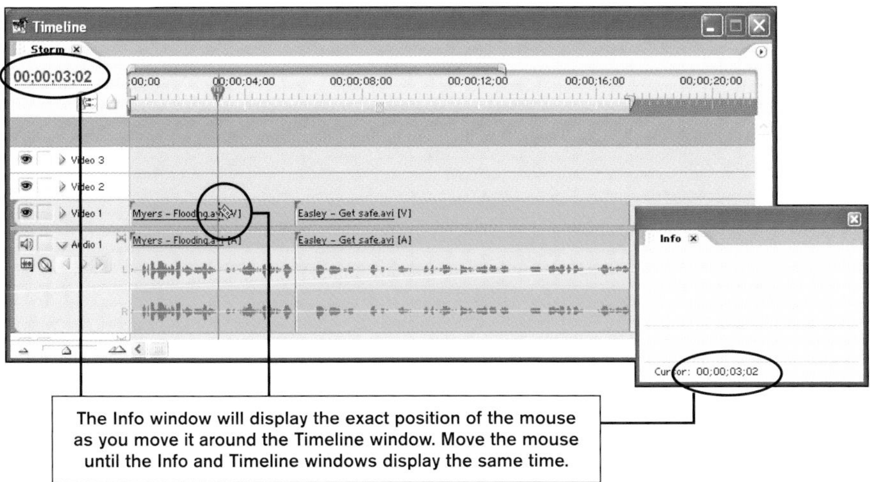

7. In the **Timeline** window, the current time indicator should still be at **00;00;03;02**, after the word "obviously." Using the **Info** window as a guide, hover the **Razor** near the current time indicator in the movie clip, until the **Razor** tool is also hovering at **00;00;03;02**. The **Info** window will show you the current location of your mouse pointer. Carefully click the mouse to split the clip in two.

Note: *The* ***Razor*** *tool, more than any other tool, requires deft mouse handling. If you accidentally move the mouse when clicking, you will create a split at the wrong point in time.*

8. Now there are three clips in the sequence. The first clip was divided in two, and the third clip remains the same. Next you will split the clip again after the phrase "but the big thing...." First, you need to decide where you will create the split. In the **Monitor** window, click **Play** and then **Stop** right after the word "thing." In this case, playback was stopped at **00;00;04;27**. (But listen to the clip and try for yourself!)

Tip: *This may prove more difficult than it sounds (pun!), because the speaker doesn't put a break between the words "...thing will be...." You may have to use the* ***Step Back*** *and* ***Step Forward*** *buttons (same as left and right arrows on the keyboard) to scrub the sequence one frame at a time, until you find the exact frame between the words "thing" and "will."*

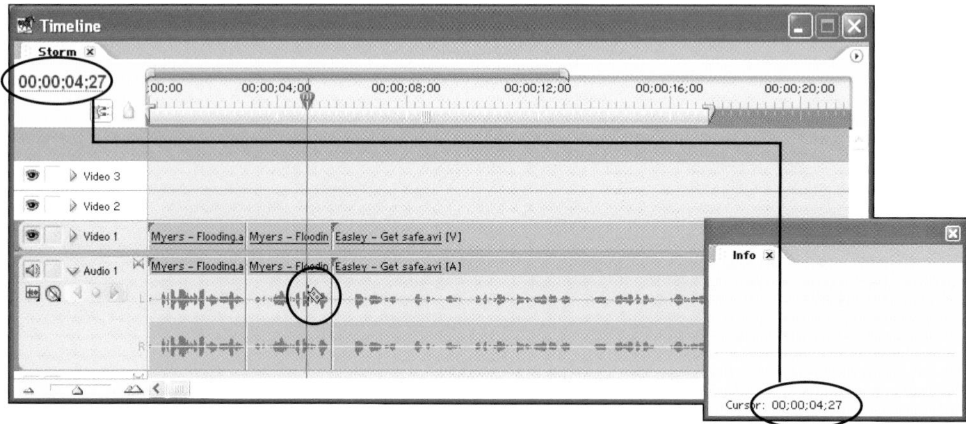

9. With the **Razor** tool still selected, hover the mouse near **00;00;04;27**. Again, use the **Info** window as a guide. When the mouse is at the correct spot, click the mouse button to create a split in the clip.

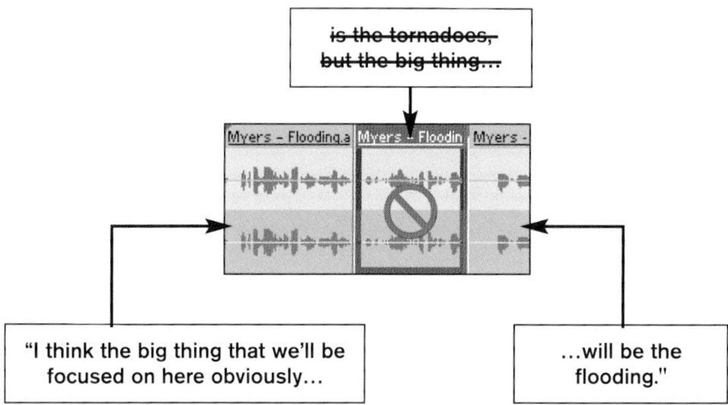

*You have turned the original sound bite into three separate clips by using the **Razor** tool. With two clicks of the **Razor** tool, you spliced the clip before the edit point and spliced the clip after the edit point.*

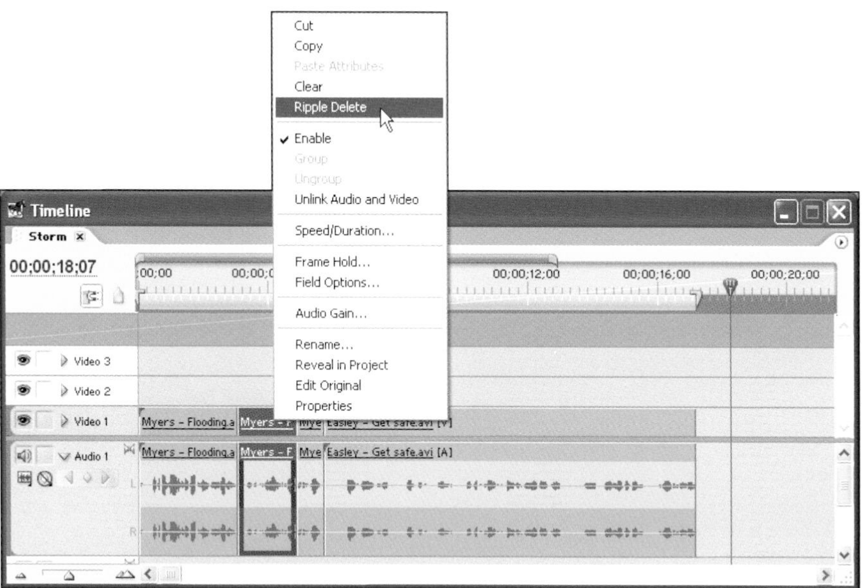

10. Now you can delete the second clip like you would any other clip. Do you remember the **Ripple Delete** command from earlier in this book? Here's another chance to brush up on it: Right-click the second clip in the **Timeline** window, and choose **Ripple Delete** from the shortcut menu. This deletes the clip and also "ripples" the remaining clips to the left, to close the gap.

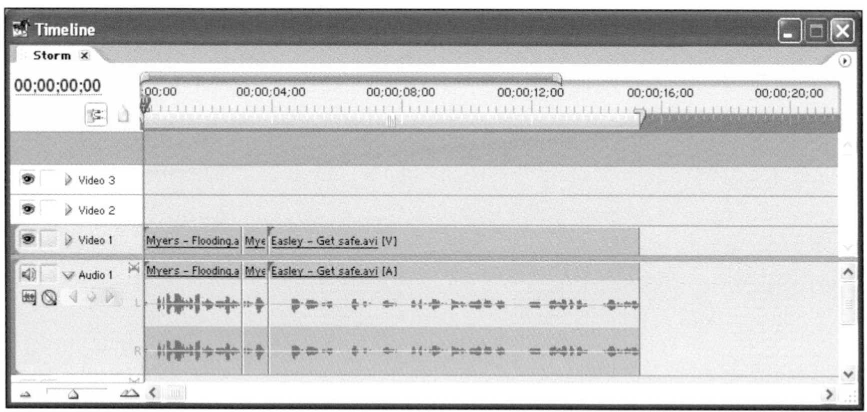

11. Play the sequence to listen to the edit you've just made. Pretty smooth. Even so, it's a good idea to add an audio transition any time you create this type of edit to smooth it out even more. Right now the start of the word "will" is cut off a bit (because the speaker didn't enunciate the word) and may be noticeable to a trained ear. A very short audio crossfade will fix this.

12. Before doing anything else, make sure you choose the default **Selection** tool in the **Toolbox**.

Tip: Imagine what would happen if you left the Razor ***tool*** *selected. You click a clip to move it to a new location... but oops! You just spliced the clip in two. At the risk of sounding like a broken record (or your mother), please remember to choose the default* ***Selection*** *tool as soon as you finish using any other tool.*

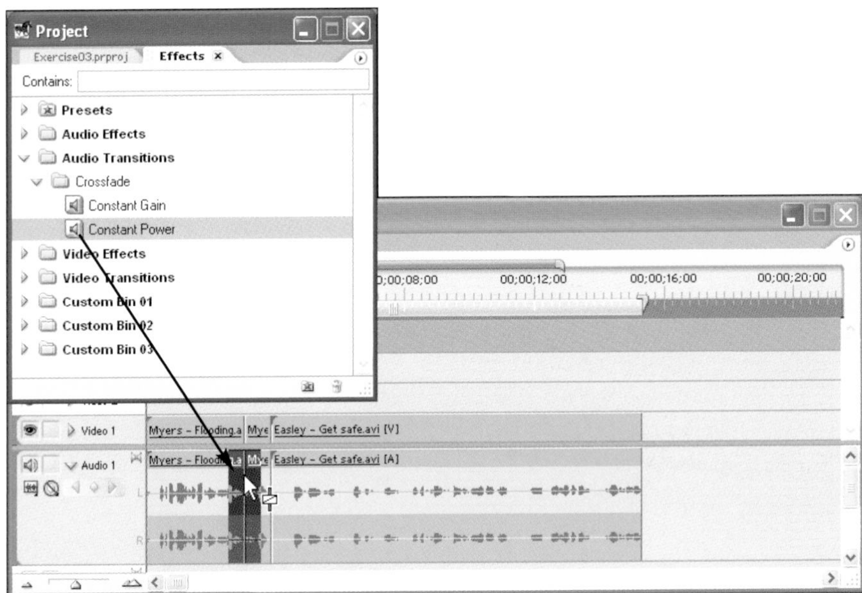

13. Click the **Effects** tab to bring it to the foreground. Twirl down the **Audio Transitions** folder and then twirl down the **Crossfade** subfolder. Apply an audio crossfade by dragging the **Constant Power** transition to the center of the edit point between audio Clip 1 and audio Clip 2.

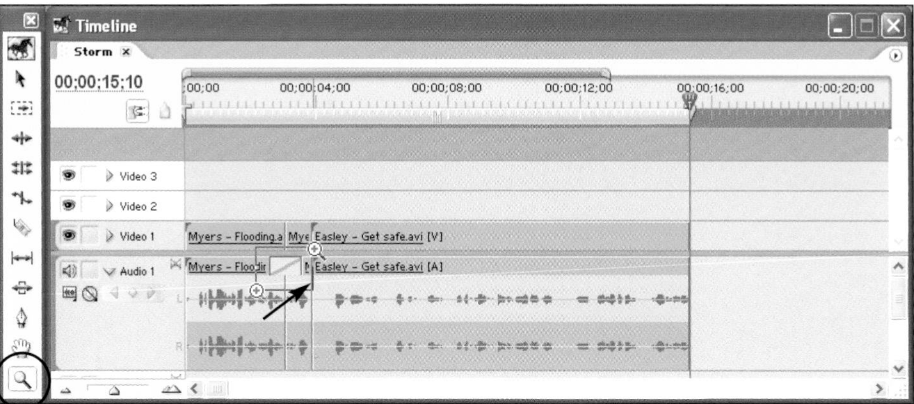

14. Play the sequence to preview it. The transition has a default duration of 30 frames (1 second), which is a bit too long for this type of edit, because you can hear the speaker overlapping on himself. In this case, you need to shorten the transition. To do this, select the **Zoom** tool in the **Toolbox**, and then drag a box from the lower left of the transition to the upper right of the transition to zoom in on that area. Don't forget, after zooming, choose the default **Selection** tool in the **Toolbox**. (Nag, nag, nag.)

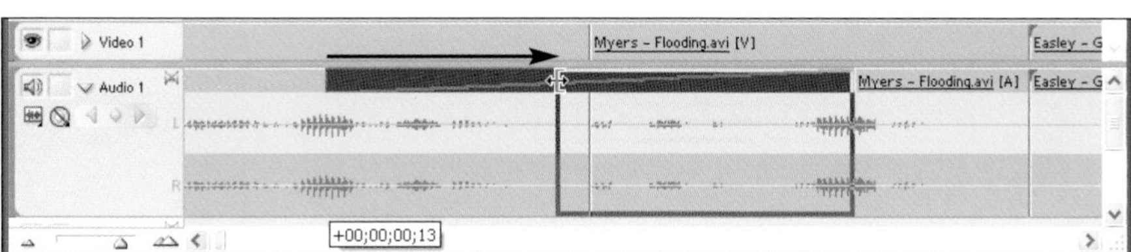

15. To shorten the transition, use the **Trim In** pointer and drag the start of the transition 13 frames to the right. Use the yellow pop-up box as a guide.

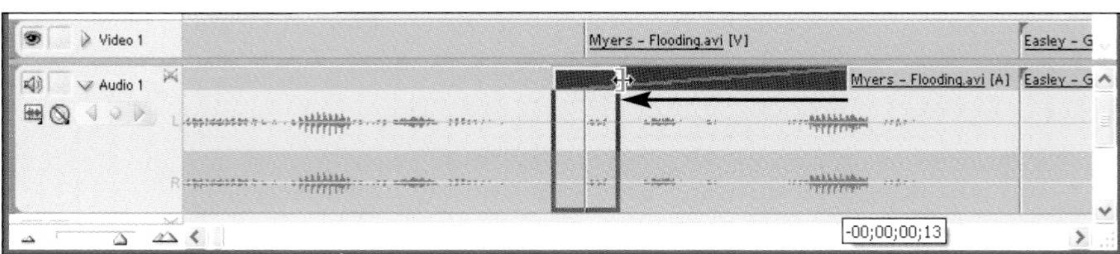

16. Drag the end of the transition 13 frames to the left with the **Trim Out** pointer.

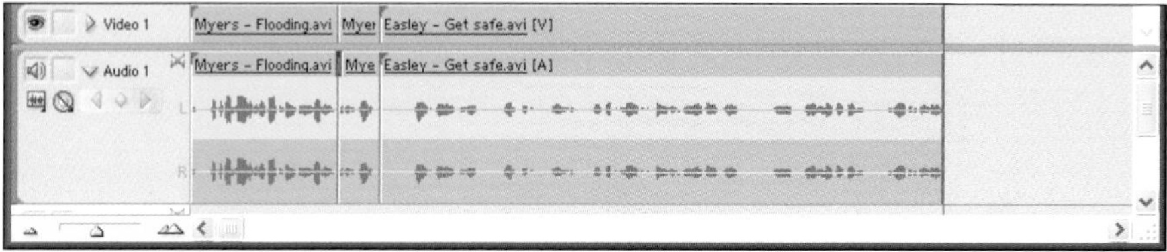

17. To quickly zoom out to view the entire sequence, press the \ key on the keyboard.

Tip: To zoom in or out one level, you can use the + and – keys on the keyboard. However, the \ key will automatically find the best zoom level to fit all of the clips in the sequence in the ***Timeline*** *window.*

18. Play the sequence to preview the transition. The video jumps suddenly at the cut, which can make the audio seem less smooth. Here's a trick: close your eyes and play back the sequence again. When your eyes are closed, the audio jump won't be as noticeable because you can't see it! (Weird, but true.)

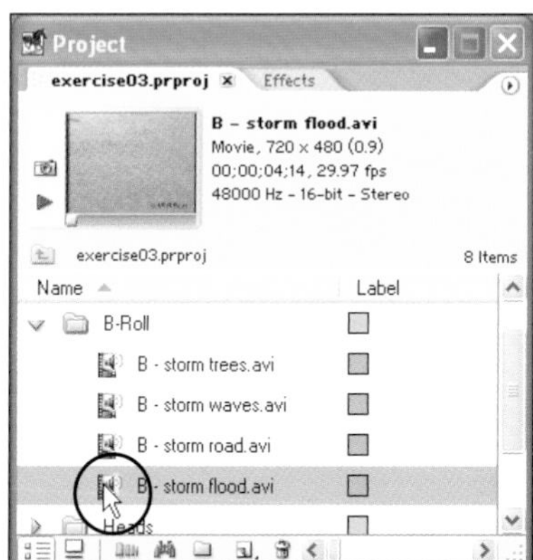

19. Since the audio edit is less noticeable when it can't be seen, the last task is to cover the video edit with some extra footage, called B-roll. This is a very common practice, and no editor should ever be without extra B-roll to cover this type of edit. To do this, click the **Project** tab to bring it to the foreground, twirl down the **B-Roll** bin, and then double-click **B – storm flood.avi** to open it in the **Monitor** window **Source** view.

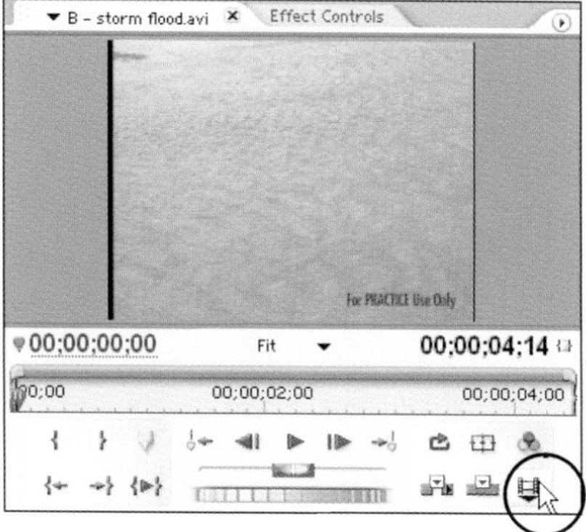

20. In the **Monitor** window **Source** view, click the **Toggle Take Audio and Video** button until it is represented by the film strip icon (no speaker icon). This means that you only want to use the video from the source clip.

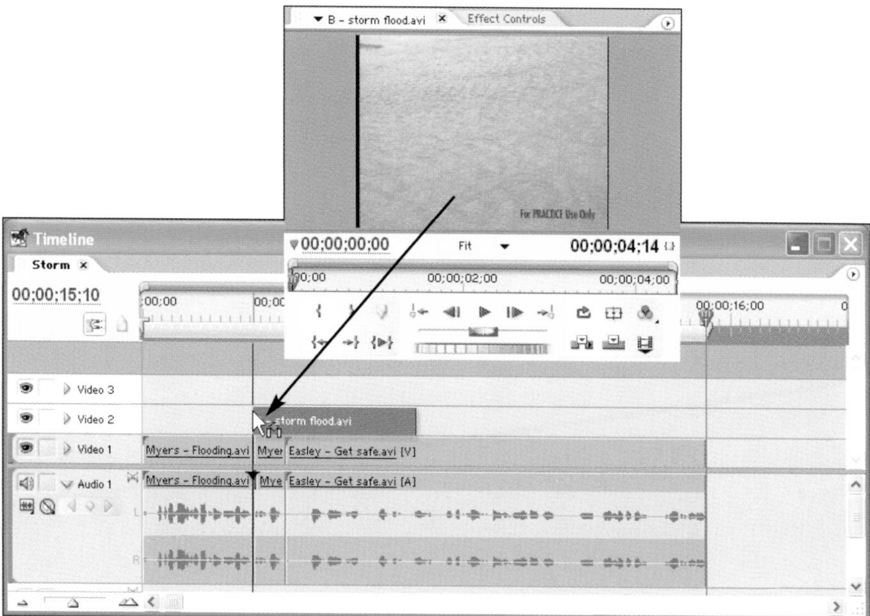

21. Drag the **Monitor** window **Source** view to track **Video 2** of the **Timeline** window. Snap the clip to the start of the audio transition.

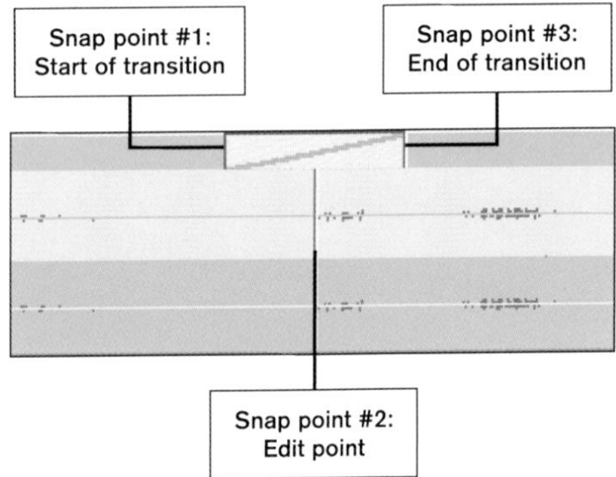

***Note:** There are three possible "snapping points" that are all very close to each other, near the edit point of clip 1 and clip 2. Try to snap to the farthest left snapping point of the three. It may prove helpful to drag a little too far to the left, and then slowly move the mouse back to the right until it snaps to point #1.*

22. Play the sequence to preview the changes you've made. Since the B-roll is covering the video jump, the audio edit and transition are much less noticeable.

The keys to making this type of edit are finding the gaps between words and having B-roll to cover the jump in video. When the video is covered, the viewer should not be able to discern that an audio edit was made.

23. Save this project and keep it open before moving on to the next exercise.

4. Single-Sided Transition

If you recall from Chapter 8, "*Transition Effects*," when applying transitions to edit points, Premiere Pro defaults to double-sided transitions to transition from Clip A to Clip B. However, as you also learned in Chapter 8, you can force Premiere Pro to apply a single-sided transition to the beginning or end of a clip. In this exercise, you will again get to apply a single-sided transition, but this time using an audio transition.

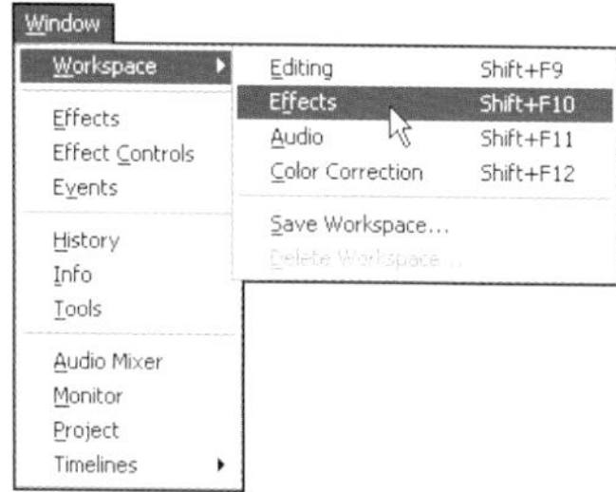

1. If you have the project open from the previous exercise, choose **Window > Workspace > Effects** (to make sure that your screen matches the examples in this exercise), and then skip to Step 2. If Premiere Pro is not running, launch it and click **Open Project** at the **Welcome Screen**. Navigate to the **c:\Premiere Pro HOT\Chapter09** folder, select **Exercise04.prproj**, and click **Open**. This exercise continues where the previous exercise left off.

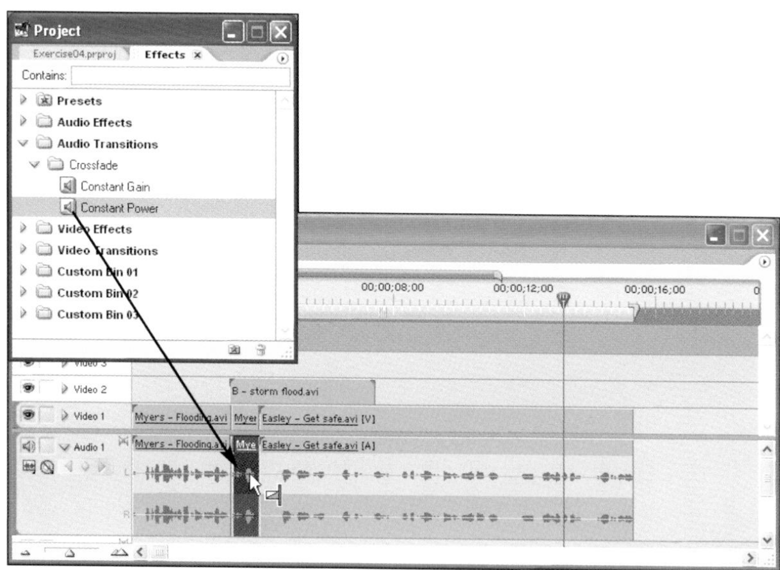

2. In this exercise, you are going to apply a single-sided crossfade to the end of the second clip in the sequence. In the **Effects** window, twirl down the **Audio Transitions** folder and then twirl down the **Crossfade** subfolder. Drag the **Constant Power** crossfade to the **Out** point of the second audio clip in track **Audio 1**. While dragging, hold down the **Ctrl** key on the keyboard to force a single-sided transition. (First let go of the mouse, then the **Ctrl** key.)

Note: *If you do not hold down the* ***Ctrl*** *key, Premiere Pro will assume you are trying to apply a double-sided transition to the edit point. When the* ***Ctrl*** *key is held down, the mouse pointer will look like this ⊠ instead of this ⊠.*

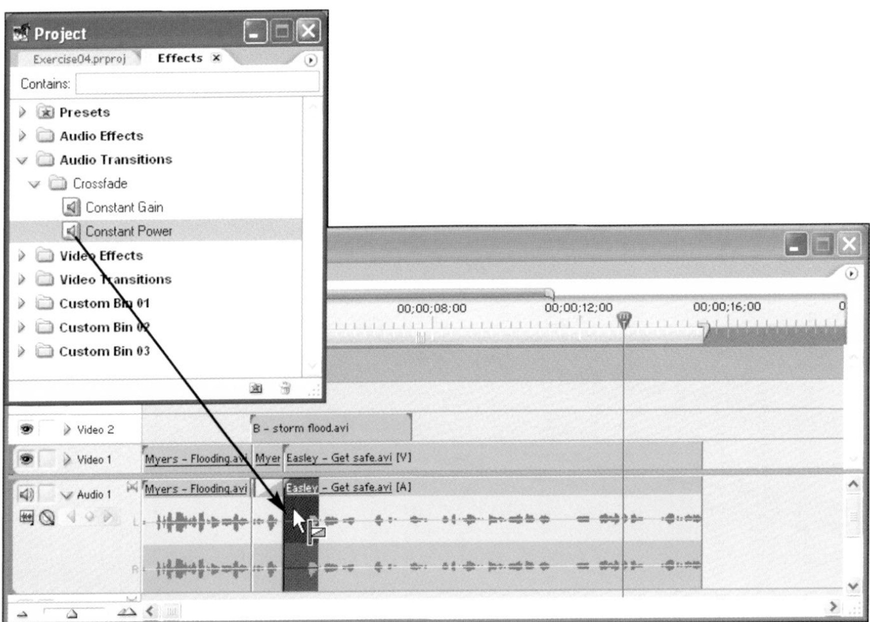

3. Next, drag the **Constant Power** crossfade to the **In** point of the third audio clip in track **Audio 1**. Make sure to hold down the **Ctrl** key to force a single-sided transition.

Tip: *The transition pointer should be facing a different direction than the pointer in Step 2, since you are applying it to the* ***In*** *point instead of the* ***Out*** *point.*

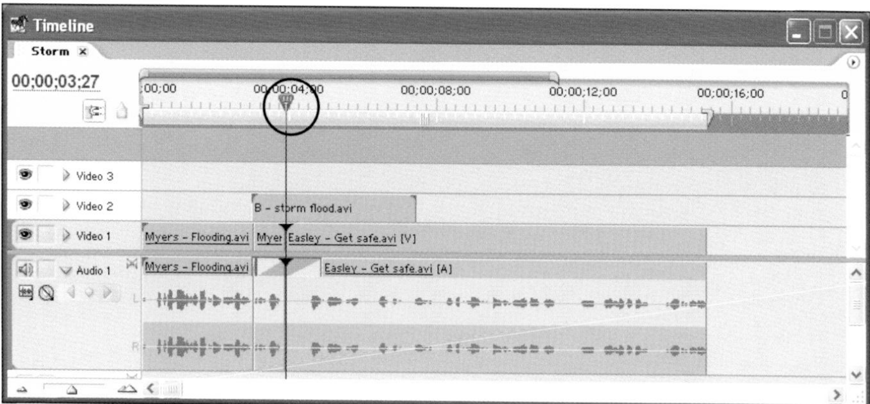

4. We now have back-to-back single-sided transitions. The transitions are given a default duration of 30 frames, which is a little long in this case. Ideally, the audio crossfade should start right after the last word is spoken, or it should finish right before the first word is spoken (so you don't start fading out or in any vital words that must be heard). Before changing the transition duration, it will help to zoom in on both of them. With the **Shift** key held down, drag the current time indicator to the edit point between movie clips 2 and 3. Look for the black vertical line at the snapping point.

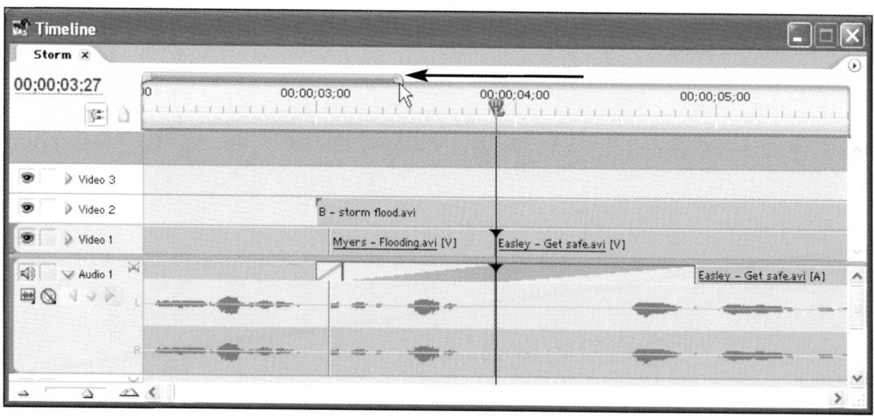

5. To zoom in on the **Timeline** window, instead of using the **Zoom** tool, drag the end handle of the viewing area bar slowly to the left (as shown above) until both transitions take up about half of the **Timeline** window display.

*Tip: The viewing area zooms centered around the current time indicator. (In other words, when zooming, it puts the current time indicator in the center of the **Timeline** window.)*

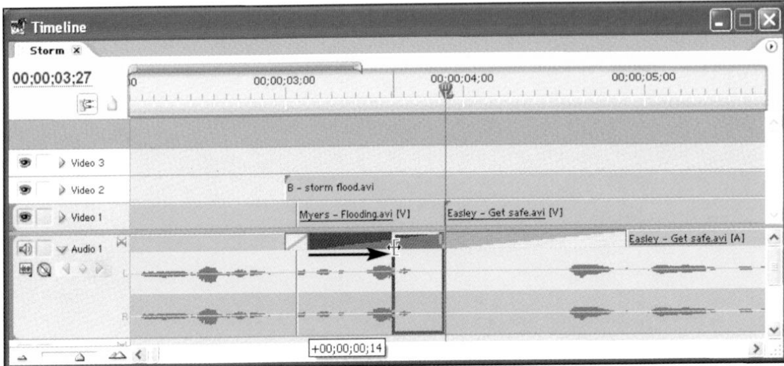

6. Using the **Trim In** pointer, drag the start of the first single-sided transition to the right, just after the speaker finishes talking (about 14 frames to the right).

Tip: Use the audio waveform as a guide–the last big "peak" of the waveform represents the final word of the sound bite.

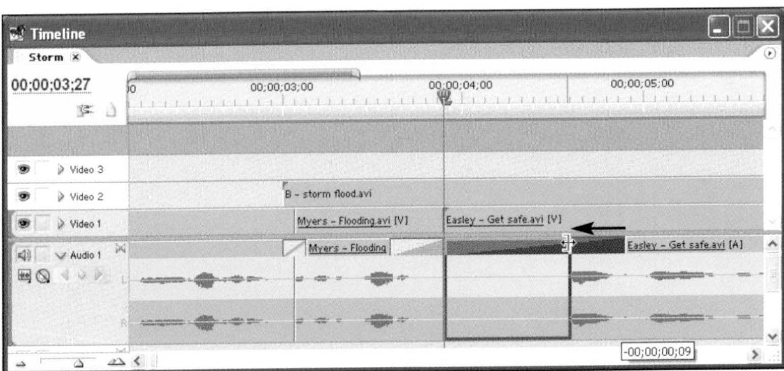

7. Using the **Trim Out** pointer, drag the end of the second single-sided transition to the left, just before the speaker starts talking (about 9 frames to the left).

8. Zoom out the **Timeline** by pressing the \ key on the keyboard.

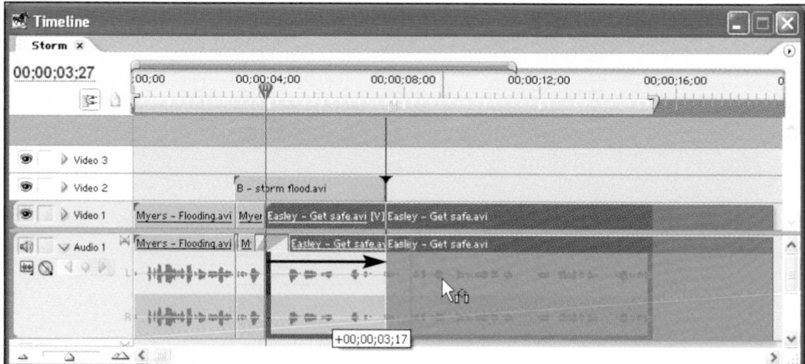

9. A strength of the single-sided transitions is that they are attached to clips–not to edit points. The regular double-sided transitions are attached to edit points; when the edit point changes, the transition goes away. However, a single-sided transition *moves with the clip it is applied to.* To experience this, click in the middle of the third movie clip, and drag it so that its **In** point snaps to the **Out** point of the clip on track **Video 2**.

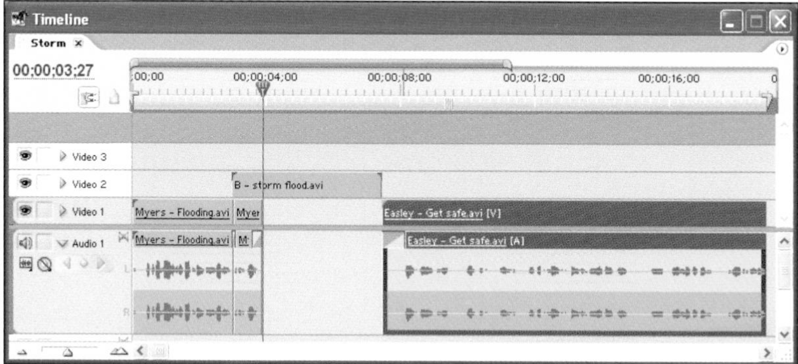

10. Play the sequence to preview the changes. Notice that even though the edit point between Clips 2 and 3 was changed, the single-sided transitions remained attached to their respective clips.

11. Save and close this project open before moving on to the next exercise.

Applying audio transitions may be the easiest task you can perform in Premiere Pro. However, knowing why to apply them in certain situations is equally as important to understand. Hopefully, throughout this chapter you learned both the steps to applying good audio transitions and the reasons behind those steps. Now that you have mastered audio transitions, it is time to move on to the wonderful world of audio effects.

10

Audio Effects

| What Is an Audio Effect? | Clip Volume |
| Changing Volume Keyframes | Volume and the Effect Controls |
| Displaying Keyframes in the Effect Controls |
| Creating Keyframes in the Effect Controls |
| Changing Volume with Effect Controls | Volume vs. Gain |
| Normalizing Gain | Applying Standard Effects |

H•O•T

Premiere Pro HOT DVD

Audio effects allow you to alter a clip's sound, such as audio files like MP3s, as well as movie clips that have both audio and video. You can change the volume, add an echo, and even make someone sound as if she's talking through a telephone. This is just the surface of what audio effects can do. In this chapter, you will learn the many ways you can alter the sound of an audio clip.

What Is an Audio Effect?

An audio effect can change the sound of a clip. Audio effects are divided into three categories:

- Transitions
- Fixed effects
- Standard effects

You've already learned how to apply, remove, and modify audio transitions. Fixed effects, you may remember from Chapter 7, "*Still Images and Fixed Effects*," are properties of a clip that can be modified but cannot be removed. Standard effects are those effects that can be added to and removed from a clip. This chapter will focus on the fixed and standard audio effects.

Clip Volume

In Chapter 7, you modified fixed effects of still images, including position, scale, and rotation. Audio clips have one fixed effect: **volume**. You can modify a clip's volume, but you can never remove the volume property. (You can certainly mute the volume, but the volume property remains.)

Volume is an effect that changes the sound level of a clip. All sound is measured in decibels (dB); a jet engine 100 feet away measures about 150 dB, someone whispering 5 feet away measures 20 dB. The volume fixed effect increases or decreases a clip's decibel level.

You can change the volume fixed effect in two ways: manually in the Timeline window, or automatically in the Effect controls window. In this chapter, you will learn both methods. Users migrating from previous versions of Premiere may find the Timeline method more familiar. Other users may find the Effect Controls method easier.

Before going any further, it's important that you understand how the clip volume is displayed and modified in the Timeline window.

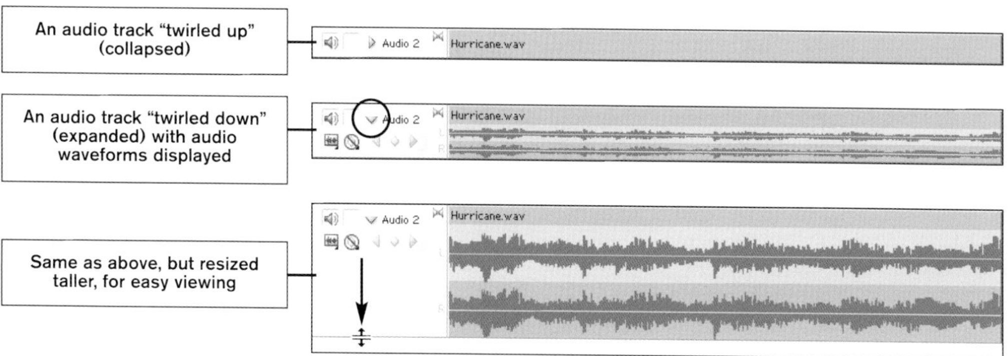

Here's a review of what you've already learned: To view a clip's waveform in the Timeline window, you twirl down the audio track. To increase the height of the track, to view the waveform easier, you drag the bottom edge of the track down. (Conversely, drag it up if you want to decrease the height.)

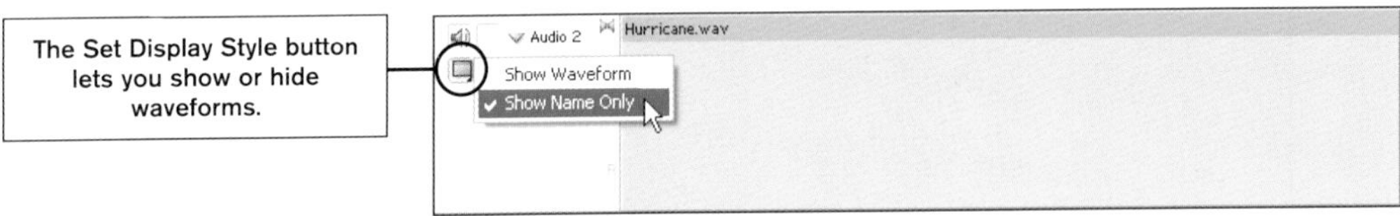

Twirling down the audio track not only displays the clip's waveform, it also displays some additional buttons. The first button on the left is the **Set Display Style** button. This button will show or hide the waveforms. When **Show Name Only** is checked, the waveform is hidden, and only the clip name is displayed.

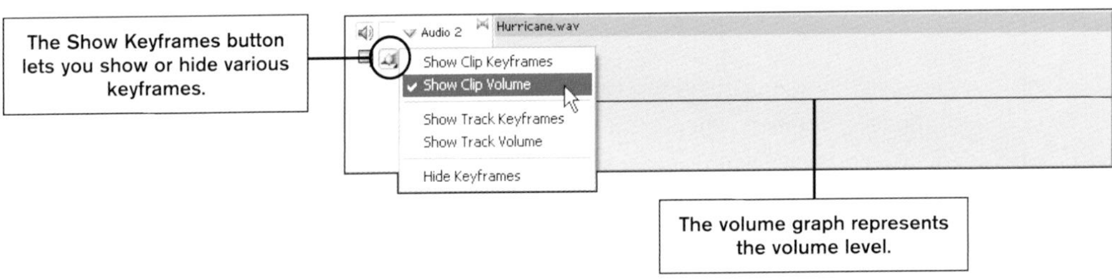

The second button is the **Show Keyframes** button. When **Show Clip Volume** is checked, a thin line is displayed across the middle of the audio clip. This line is the **volume graph**, and it represents the volume level of the clip. Here's how the volume graph works in Premiere Pro.

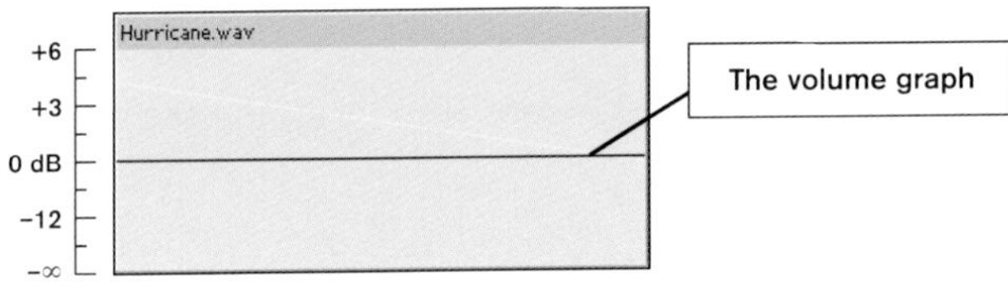

By default, a clip's volume is set at 0 dB (decibels). The line represents the clip's volume, on a scale of +6 to –infinity (∞). Moving the line above 0 dB makes the clip louder, and moving the line below 0 dB makes the clip quieter.

Note: Keep in mind that the volume graph represents the *change in volume*. In the figure above, the volume graph stays at 0 dB, which means the clip volume changes by 0 dB–in other words, it does not change.

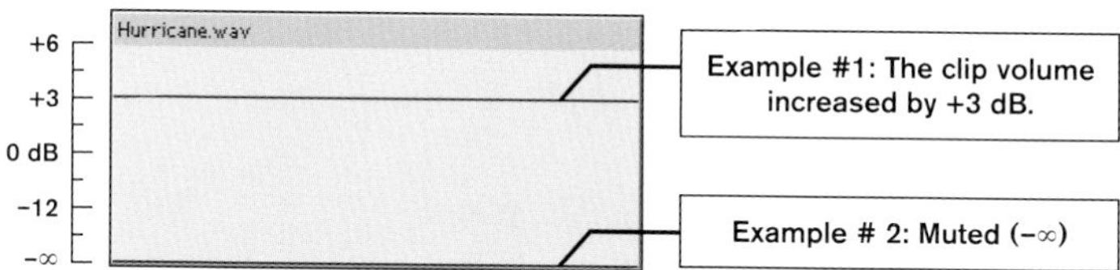

The figure above shows two possible positions for the volume graph: In the first example, the volume graph is at +3 dB, which means that the volume has been increased by 3 decibels. In the second example, the volume graph has been moved to the bottom, which is infinitely quiet, also knows as *muted.*

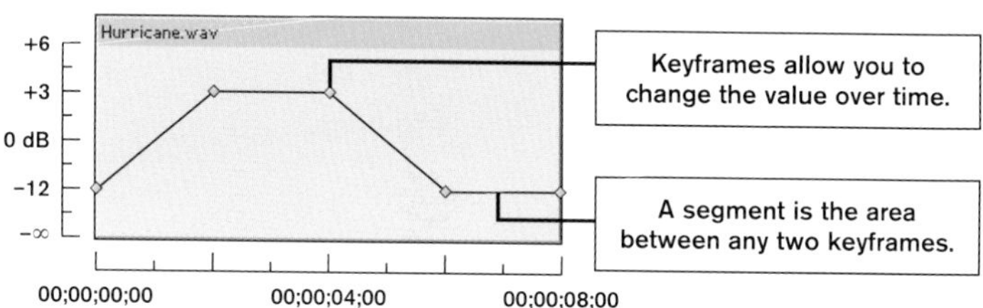

You can also change a clip's volume over time. In the above figure, the clip's volume starts at −12 dB, and increases to +3 dB. The volume doesn't change for a couple of seconds, and then it fades back to −12 dB. And finally, it remains at −12 dB until the end of the clip. What allows you to change the volume over time? Your friend, the **keyframe**. The above figure has a total of five keyframes, represented by a gold diamond (oxymoron!).

In Premiere Pro terms, a keyframe is a point along the value graph. On the volume graph, the keyframes specify the volume at any given point in time. The area between keyframes is the **segment**.

Keyframes answer two vital questions: What is the value, and when does the value occur? You can ask the same two questions of each keyframe in the above figure.

Keyframe **#1**: What is the value? **−12 dB**. When does the value occur? **00;00;00;00.**

Keyframe **#2**:What is the value? **+3 dB**. When does the value occur? **00;00;02;00.**

Keyframe **#3**: What is the value? **+3 dB**. When does the value occur? **00;00;04;00.**

Keyframe **#4**: What is the value? **−12 dB**. When does the value occur? **00;00;06;00.**

Keyframe **#5**: What is the value? **−12 dB**. When does the value occur? **00;00;08;00.**

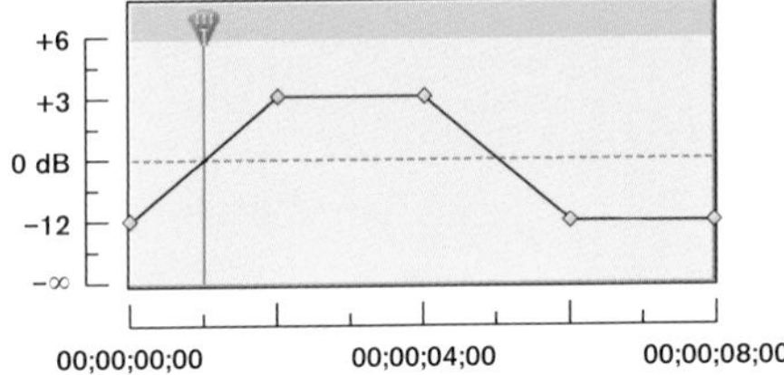

Keyframes are such a powerful tool because Premiere Pro does the math to gradually transition from one keyframe value to the next. In the above figure, the current time indicator is located at the segment between keyframe 1 and keyframe 2. The volume value at the current time indicator is 0 dB. One frame later, the volume will be slightly higher. Premiere changes the value at every frame as the current time indicator journeys from one keyframe to the next.

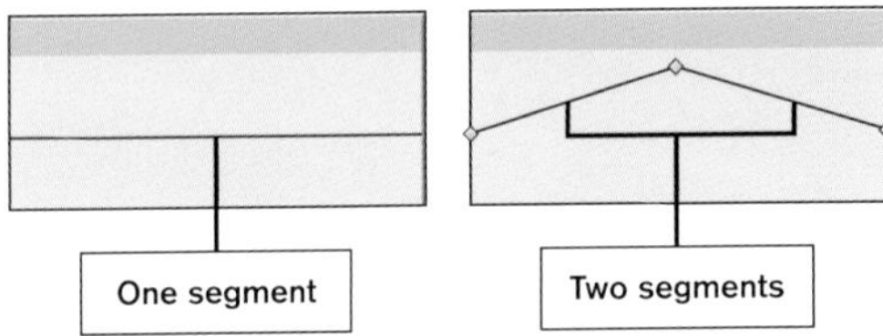

Segments, as mentioned earlier, are the areas between pairs of keyframes. When there are no keyframes, the segment is the entire clip.

The moral of keyframes: *it takes two to tango*. Keyframes always work in pairs. To change the value over time, you need at least two keyframes: a value at which to start, and a value at which to end. Premiere Pro handles the math to get from keyframe A to keyframe B.

Now that you (hopefully!) understand the concept of volume keyframes, it's time to fire up the next exercise and try it for yourself.

I. Changing Volume Keyframes

In this exercise, you will learn how to add, modify, and remove volume keyframes in the Timeline window. You'll underscore the video with a music file and then change the volume of the music file over time.

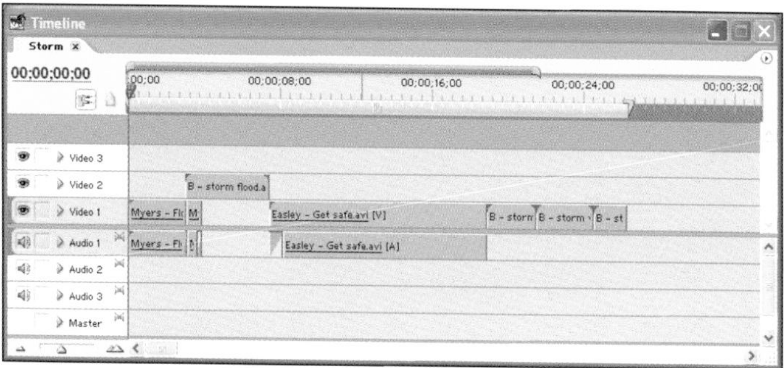

1. If Premiere Pro is not running, launch it and click **Open Project** at the **Welcome Screen**. Navigate to the **c:\Premiere Pro HOT\Chapter10** folder, select **Exercise01.prproj**, and click **Open**. The sequence in the **Timeline** should look similar to the one you were working on in the last exercise of Chapter 9, "*Audio Transitions*." (Plus some additional B-roll has been added to track **Video 1**, at the end of the sequence.)

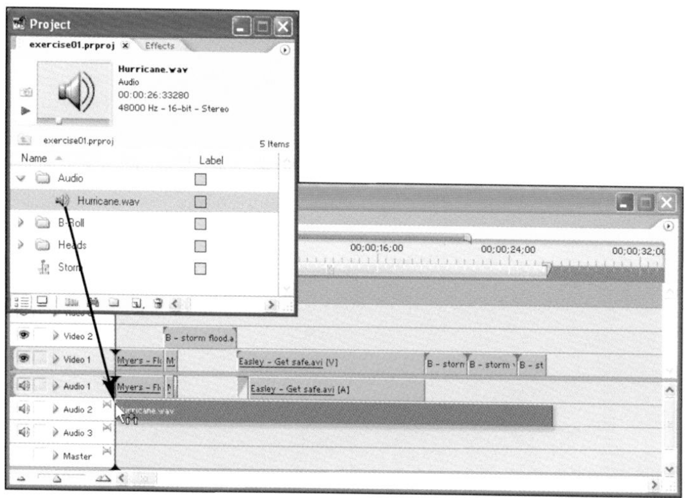

2. Start off by adding some music to track **Audio 2**, to underscore the sequence. Twirl down the **Audio** bin in the **Project** window, and drag **Hurricane.wav** from the **Project** window to track **Audio 2** in the **Timeline** window. Snap it to the beginning of the sequence.

3. Play the sequence to preview it. The music is a nice touch, however at certain points it is drowning out the sound bites because it is so loud. Your goal is to use volume keyframes to lower the volume during the sound bites, but raise the volume back up during the B-roll video. Make sense? Good!

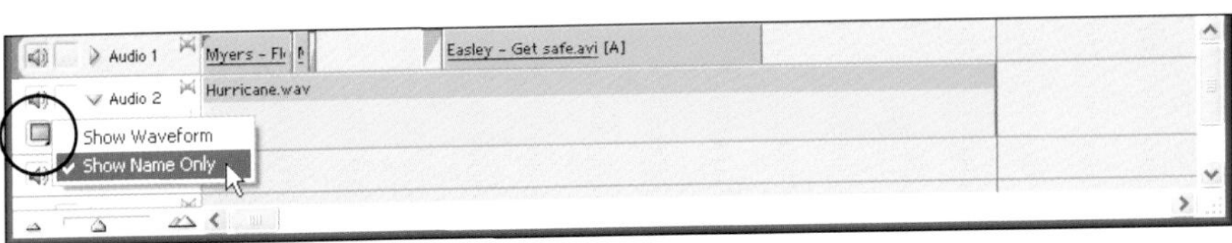

4. The first step to working with volume keyframes in the **Timeline** window is to display the volume graph. To do this, twirl down track **Audio 2**, click the **Set Display Style** button, and choose **Show Name Only** from the pop-up menu. This will hide the waveforms.

Tip: *It's not necessary to hide the waveforms before showing the volume keyframes. In fact, many editors prefer to see both at the same time. In this exercise, the waveforms are hidden simply for ease of instruction.*

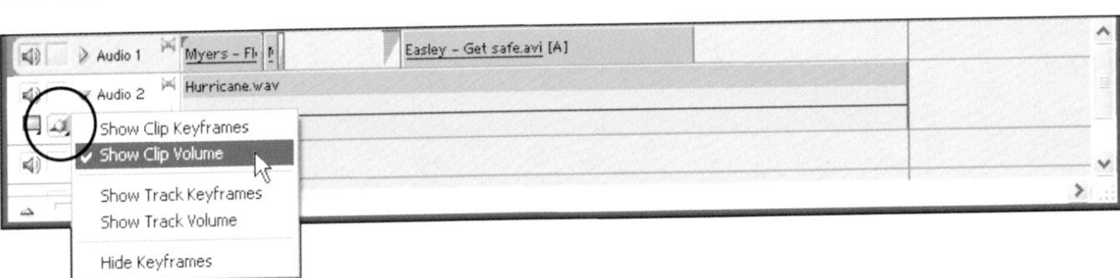

5. To display the volume graph, click the **Show Keyframes** button and choose **Show Clip Volume** from the pop-up menu. You can now see the volume graph for the **Hurricane.wav** clip. Currently, it is a horizontal, black line because the volume has not been changed. It starts and ends at **0 dB**.

Note: *Be* ***extremely*** *careful to not click the* ***Speaker*** *icon to the left of the track name. The* ***Speaker*** *icon will mute all audio in that track. It doesn't change the volume, it just "turns off" the track temporarily. If you accidentally click the* ***Speaker*** *icon, you can click it again to turn the track back on.*

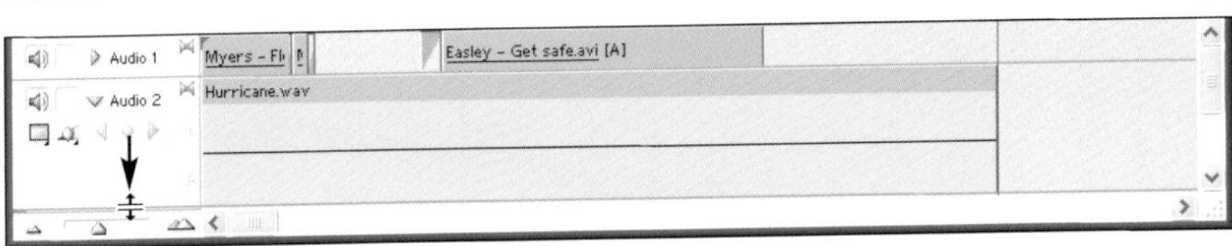

6. To give yourself a little breathing room, drag the bottom edge of track **Audio 2** to the bottom of the **Timeline** window. This will (as you know by now) heighten the audio track so you can better see the volume graph.

It's time to learn a new tool! (Insert fanfare and applause.) *The* **Pen** *tool—despite its name—has nothing to do with drawing. It is used to add keyframes and modify value graphs. (The icon and name of the tool is a hand-me-down from Premiere Pro's older siblings, Adobe Photoshop and Illustrator.)*

7. In the **Toolbox**, select the **Pen** tool.

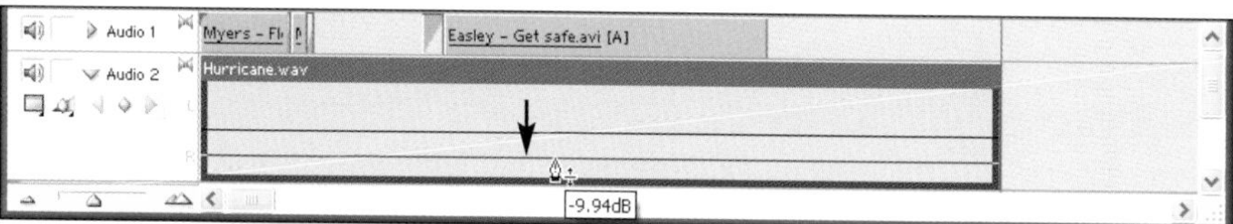

8. The **Pen** tool has two functions: it can raise or lower any segment of the value graph (remember, a segment is the area between a pair of keyframes), and it can create and modify keyframes. To experience the first function, hover your mouse over the value graph until you see the **Pen** tool **Segment** pointer. Lower the volume by dragging the volume graph down to around **–10 dB** (give or take 1 decibel—basically, just get as close as you can, because it's hard to be precise with the **Pen** tool).

9. Play the sequence to listen to the lowered volume. This time, the underscore does not drown out, nor draw focus away from the sound bites. However, now the volume is too low during the B-roll. In the next few steps, you will add volume keyframes to increase the volume during the B-roll clips. This will demonstrate the second function of the **Pen** tool: creating new keyframes.

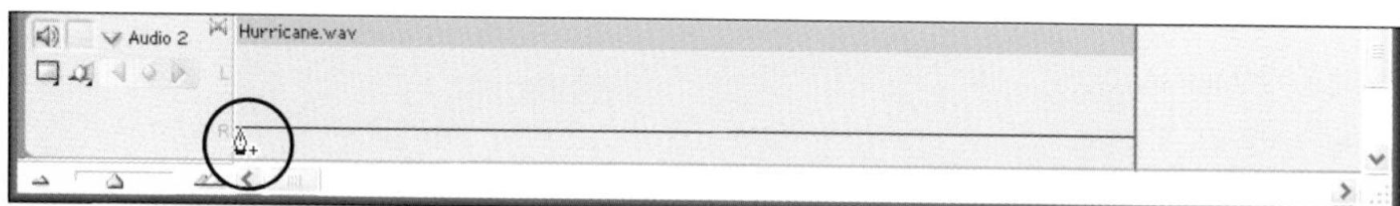

10. Whenever creating volume keyframes in the **Timeline** window, it is important to first set keyframes at the beginning and the end of your audio clip. With the **Pen** tool still selected, hover your mouse over the value graph, at the beginning of the audio clip, and then hold down the **Ctrl** key on the keyboard. This will change the mouse pointer to the **Pen** tool **Add** pointer. Quickly click the **Pen** tool **Add** pointer on the value graph to create a new keyframe.

Note: *Be careful not to move the mouse pointer up or down when adding the keyframe.*

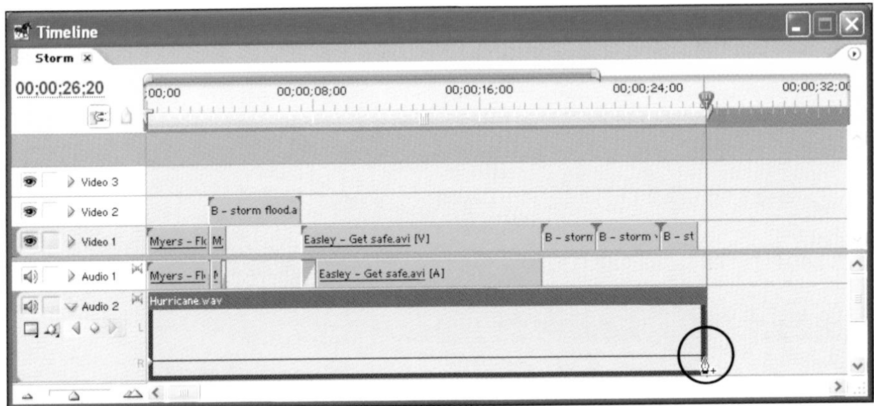

11. Now do the same to create a new keyframe at the end of the clip. Hover the **Pen** tool over the value graph near the end of the clip, hold down **Ctrl** on the keyboard, and quickly click the mouse to add a new keyframe. There are now two keyframes.

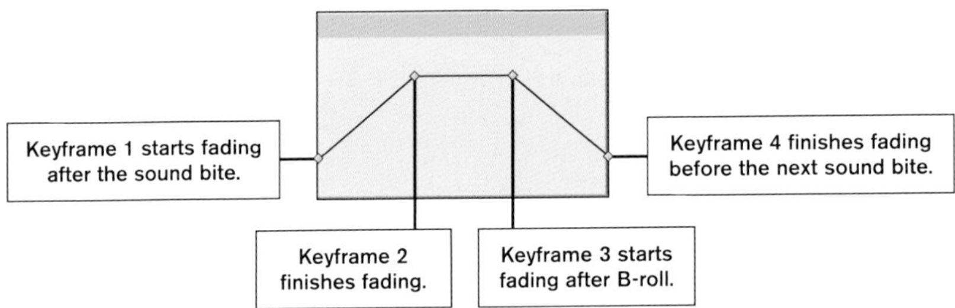

Now you are going to create a fade-up/fade-down during the **B – storm flood.avi** *B-roll clip on the* **Timeline**. *You will need four keyframes to create a fade-up/fade-down. (This makes a total of six keyframes, if you count the two keyframes you created in Steps 10 and 11.) The next keyframe you want to set is #1 above, which defines when the fade-up starts.*

12. Play the sequence and stop it immediately after the last word of the sound bite. Use the **left** and **right** arrow keys on the keyboard to scrub the audio one frame at a time, and listen to when the speaker finishes his final word.

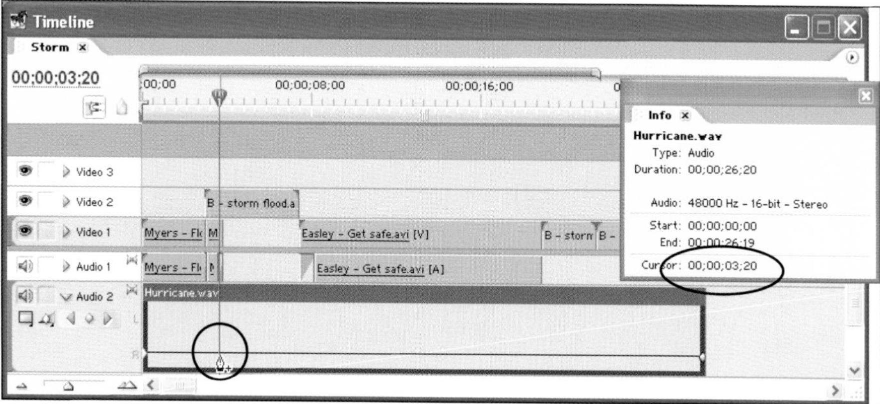

13. Hopefully you ended up within a few frames of **00;00;03;20**. With the **Pen** tool still selected, hover the mouse near **00;00;03;20** (use the **Info** window as a guide), hold down the **Ctrl** key on the keyboard, and click the value graph to add a new keyframe. This is where the audio will start fading up.

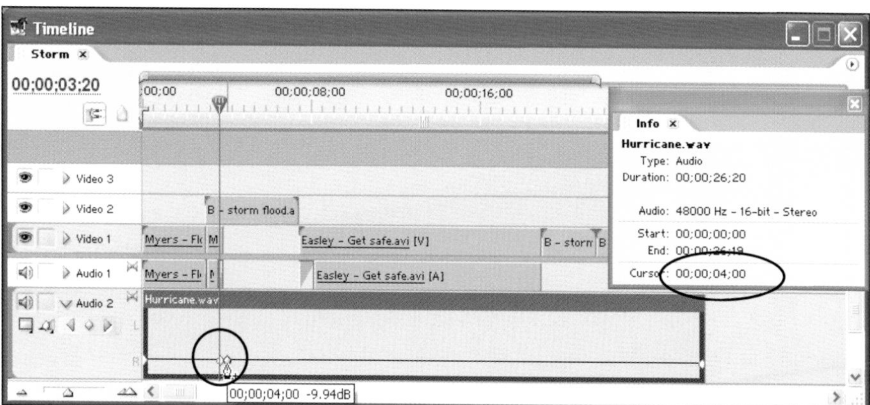

14. The next keyframe point to create will define when the audio finishes fading up. In this case, you want about a 10-frame fade-up. Using the **Info** window as a guide, hover the **Pen** tool near **00;00;04;00** (that's 03;20 + 10 frames), hold down the **Ctrl** key, and click the value graph to add a new keyframe.

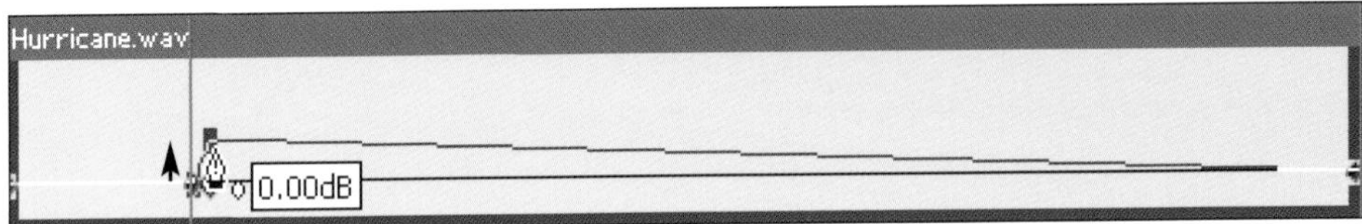

15. Now that you've created a keyframe, you can modify it by changing its value. In this case, you want to increase the keyframe value by dragging it up, which will create the fade-up. To do this, hover your mouse over the newly created keyframe, and your mouse cursor will become the **Keyframe** pointer to indicate that you are hovering over an existing keyframe. Drag the keyframe up to **0.00 dB**, using the yellow pop-up box as a guide. Hold down the **Shift** key as you drag to prevent the keyframe from moving in time. (Users of other Adobe applications will be familiar with the "Shift constraint.")

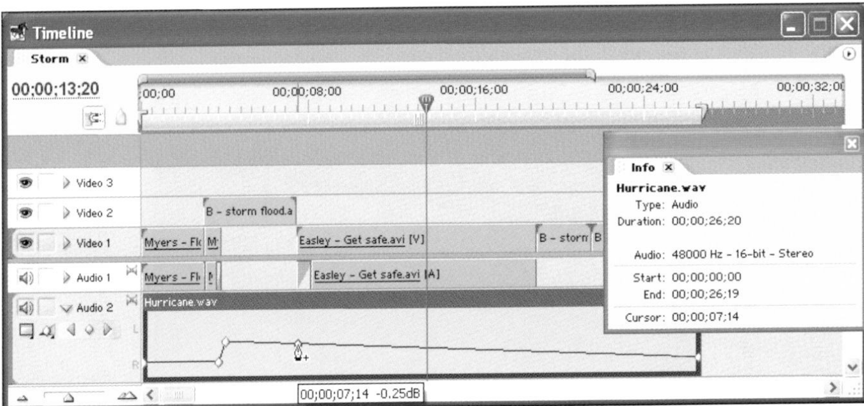

16. The next keyframe to set is the point where the volume will start to fade back to its previous level. In this case, it's right at the edit point of the B-roll and the next sound bite. Instead of moving the current time indicator like last time, you can just eyeball this one. Move your mouse to (about) **00;00;07;14**, hold down the **Ctrl** key on the keyboard, and click the **Pen** tool on the value graph.

17. There is one tiny problem: the new keyframe is not at the value of the previous keyframe. This means the volume is subtly decreasing. To remedy this, hover your mouse over the keyframe you created in Step 16 (near **00;00;07;14**) and drag it up to **0.00 dB**, so it matches the previous keyframe.

Note: *You're about to learn one of the most frustrating features of Premiere Pro! For all of its good qualities, Premiere Pro makes it virtually impossible to get the decibel level back to 0.00 dB. You either need to resize the track height to immense proportions (making it impossible to see the rest of the screen), or be happy with "close enough." Even in the above figure, the best that I could do was* ***+0.14 dB.*** *Of course, nobody on the planet will be able to detect a fade from 0.00 dB to 0.14dB, so you should be safe. (Hopefully Santa Adobe puts this on his fix-it wish list!)*

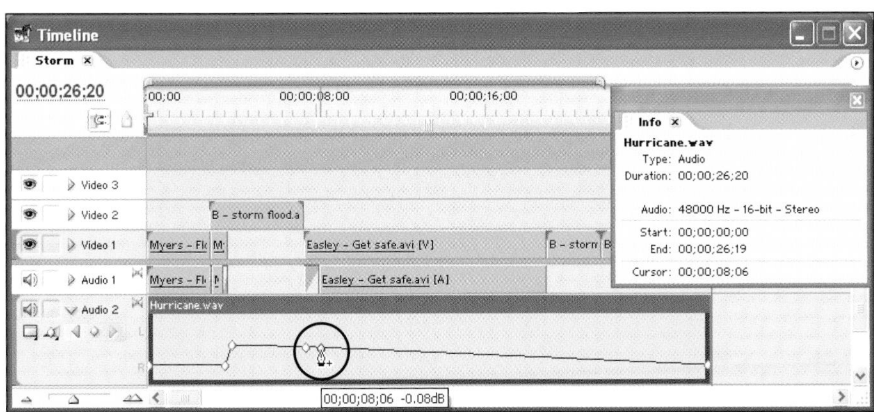

18. To finish the fade-up/fade-out, you will create a last keyframe where the value graph should finish fading down. In this case, it is right before the second sound bite. You may remember that the sound bite starts immediately after the single-sided audio transition in track **Audio 1**. So, hover your mouse below the end of the audio transition, hold down the **Ctrl** key, and click the **Pen** tool on the value graph to create a new keyframe. (FYI–it should be near **00;00;08;06**, but you can eyeball this one, too.)

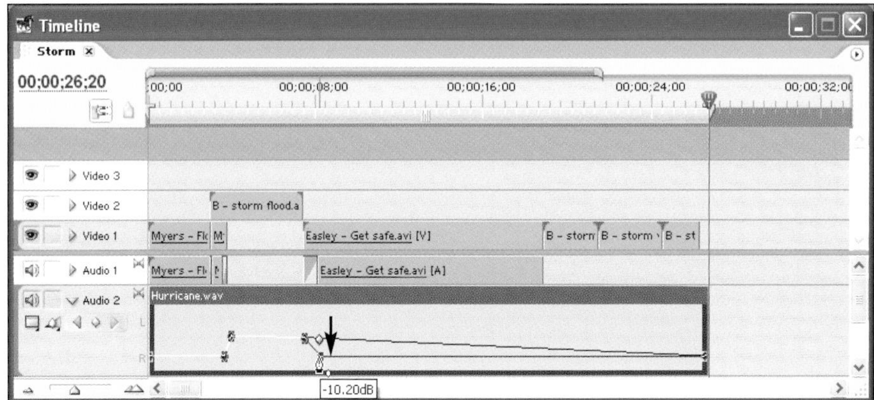

19. And lastly (whew!), hover your mouse over the keyframe you just created, and drag it down to its previous value–which was about **–10 dB**. Again, Premiere Pro makes it a bit difficult to hit exactly –10 dB, so you can always be content with getting as close as possible.

20. Finally, it's time to soak in the satisfaction of a job well done. Play the sequence to preview the fade-up/fade-out that you created.

It takes a few extra steps to describe how to add and modify a keyframe, but in reality, it's not so tough, as you've just discovered. Even though you are currently creating volume keyframes, this exact lesson would hold true for just about any other type of keyframe. Almost all effects are keyframeable, as you will learn in future chapters.

21. Save and keep this project open before moving on to the next exercise.

NOTE | All Those Buttons

In the previous exercise, you became familiar with a couple of the buttons that are available when you twirl down an audio track. But what about all of those other doodads and buttons? This should answer your doodad questions:

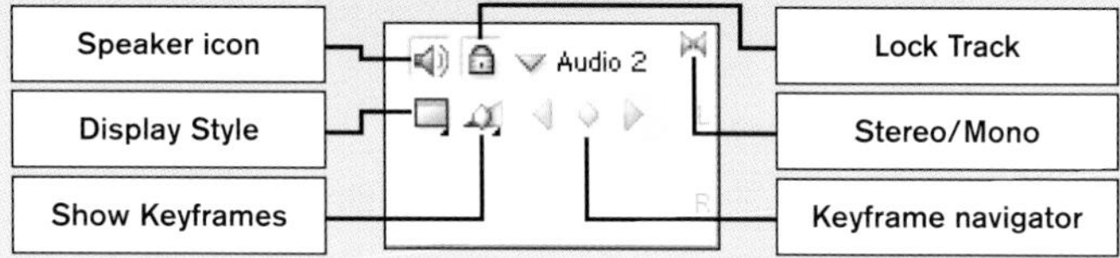

The **Speaker** icon "hides" a track. If there is audio on the track, the audio will not be heard. The speaker is a toggle button–like a light switch, its only positions are *on* and *off*.

The **Lock Track** icon will prevent a track from being modified. You cannot click, move, or select any clips on a locked track. Toggle the icon again to unlock the track.

The **Stereo/Mono** indicator is not really a button, but it is important to know its purpose. When a track is in stereo, the indicator will show two speakers, as in the figure above. When a track is in mono, only one speaker will be indicated.

The **keyframe navigator** snaps the current time indicator from keyframe to keyframe. You can go to the previous keyframe by clicking the left arrow button, or you can go to the next keyframe by clicking the right arrow button. The diamond in the middle will "light up" when the current time indicator is positioned over a keyframe. These buttons will be discussed in the next section.

The **Show Keyframes** button should be familiar to you, since you used it in the previous exercise. Clicking this button pops up a menu that allows you to show or hide different types of keyframes.

The **Display Style** button allows you to set the waveform display to on or off. This too should be familiar by now.

Video tracks also have similar buttons and features, except for the Stereo/Mono indicator, of course. Video tracks have an Eyeball icon instead of a Speaker icon (this should be familiar to users of other Adobe applications). Just like the Speaker icon, the eyeball is a toggle which will hide all video on that track, or show all video on that track.

Whenever you don't hear your audio, or see your video, the first thing to check is the Eyeball and Speaker icons. Make sure they are turned on, because 9 times out of 10, that is the culprit. Even seasoned editors and long-time Premiere Pro users get tripped up by accidentally turning these icons off. It is extremely easy to accidentally toggle the eyeball or speaker off, so guard these icons with your life!

Volume and the Effect Controls

You've just learned how to create and modify volume keyframes in the Timeline window, so that means it's time to create and modify volume keyframes in the Effect Controls window. Let's take a quick tour of how volume options and keyframes are displayed in the Effect Controls window.

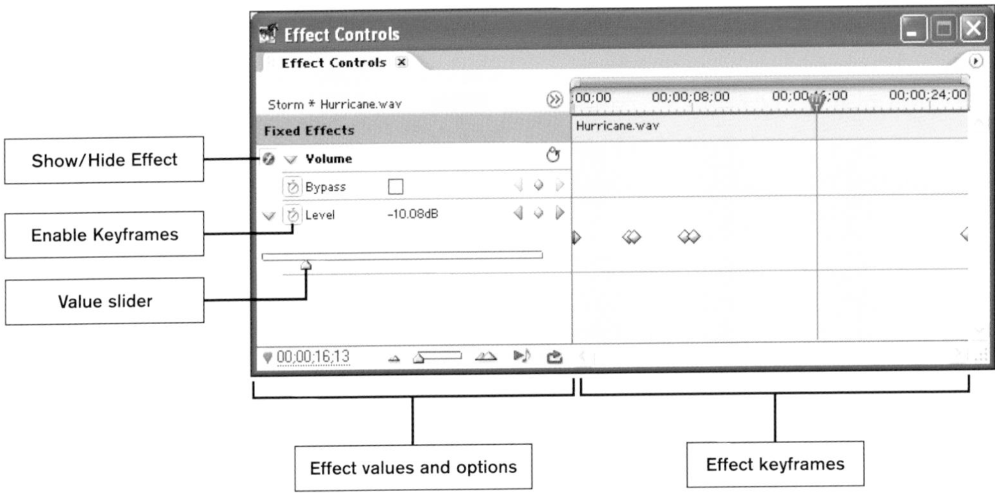

The **Show/Hide Effect** button toggles on or off an effect. This button comes in handy when you want to listen to (or see) the original clip.

The **Enable Keyframes** button turns on or off keyframe mode for a clip. If this button is not enabled, you can not create keyframes. This will be discussed in detail in the next chapter.

The **Volume** slider is the antidote to the clumsy Pen tool. The Pen tool can be frustrating because it is hard to drag the value graph to precise numbers, and you might accidentally move the keyframe forward or backward in time. The Volume slider lets you slide in more precise increments, and it prevents you from moving the keyframe in time.

The Effect Controls window is divided into two separate views: the left side shows you values/options of an effect and the right side shows you a keyframe Timeline. Remember from earlier that keyframes answer two vital questions: what is the value, and when does it occur? In the Effect Controls window, the left side answers the first question, and the right side answers the latter.

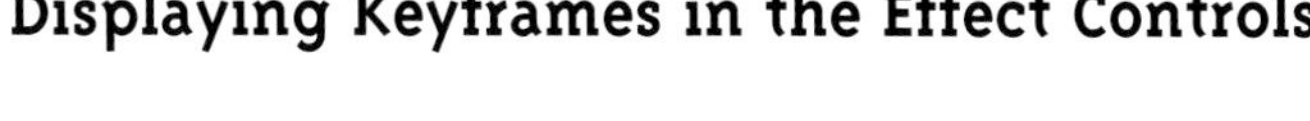

Displaying Keyframes in the Effect Controls

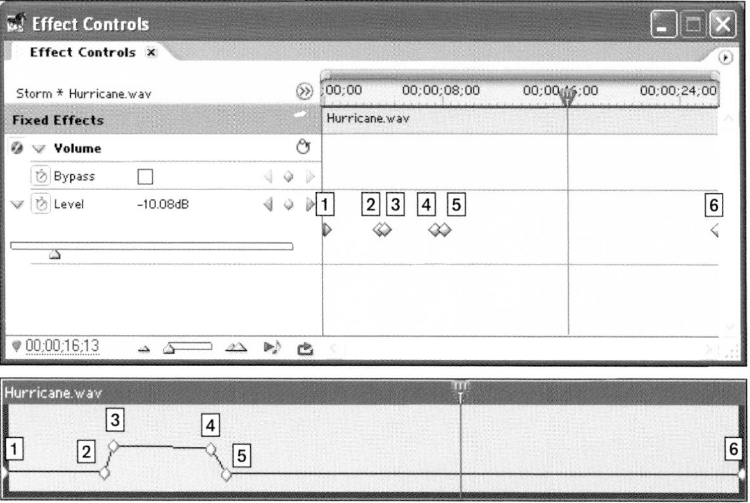

The audio clip in the figure above represents the six keyframes you created in the previous exercise. Those keyframes were created in the Timeline window. The six keyframes in the Effect Controls window correspond with the six keyframes on the clip's value graph. In the Timeline window, keyframes are raised and lowered along the value graph, but in the Effect Controls window they are displayed in a horizontal line. Each display has its advantages and disadvantages. The value graph is better at showing the values of keyframes relative to each other; the Effect Controls Timeline is better at showing the position of the keyframes in time. For example, in the Effect Controls you can see that keyframes #2 and #3 are much closer to each other than #4 and #5, but that is not as obvious on the value graph. Conversely, you can see the values of the keyframes better in the Timeline, because they are raised and lowered relative to each other.

Creating Keyframes in the Effect Controls

In the previous exercise, you learned to use the Pen tool to create and modify keyframes. However, in the Effect Controls window, keyframes are created by changing the **value slider**.

This is worth repeating, so chant the keyframe mantra, three times: *Keyframes are created by changing the value slider.* (Later on, you will learn how to edit in the full or half Lotus position.)

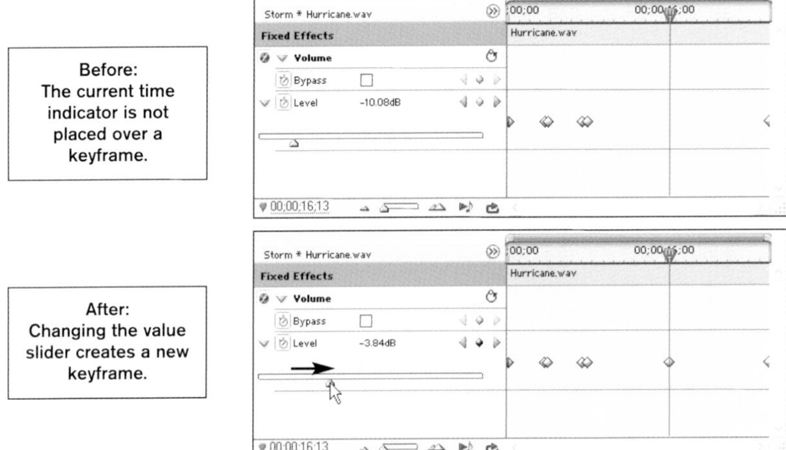
Before:
The current time indicator is not placed over a keyframe.
After:
Changing the value slider creates a new keyframe.
Storm * Hurricane.wav
Fixed Effects
Volume
Bypass
Level
-10.08dB
-3.84dB
Hurricane.wav
00;00;16;13

The value slider behaves differently based on the location of the current time indicator. In the above example, the current time indicator is not placed over an existing keyframe. The keyframe mantra tells us that when the value slider is changed, a new keyframe is created.

Pop quiz: What is the value of the new keyframe? –3.84 dB.

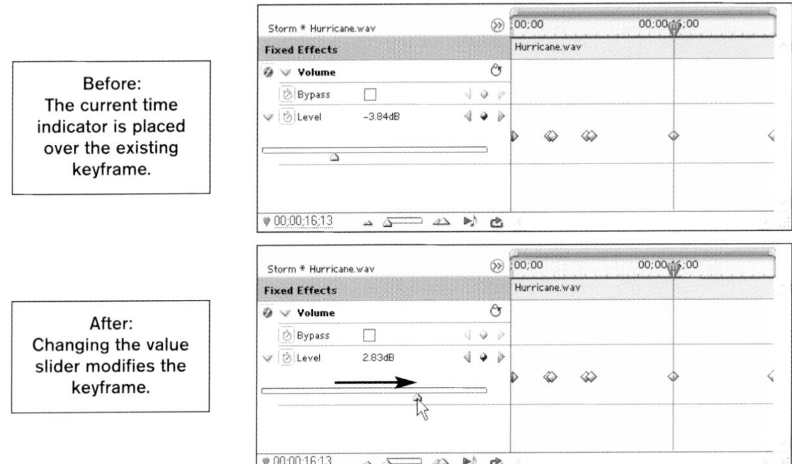
Before:
The current time indicator is placed over the existing keyframe.
After:
Changing the value slider modifies the keyframe.
Storm * Hurricane.wav
Fixed Effects
Volume
Bypass
Level
-3.84dB
2.83dB
Hurricane.wav
00;00;16;13

If the current time indicator is placed over an existing keyframe, changing the value slider will modify the existing keyframe.

Alert! This newfound keyframe knowledge comes with a warning: in order to modify an existing keyframe, the current time indicator must be placed *exactly* over the keyframe. Not "near" the keyframe, but exactly over it. And to aid you in this task, it's time to meet the **keyframe navigator**. (Hint: it's not a ship.)

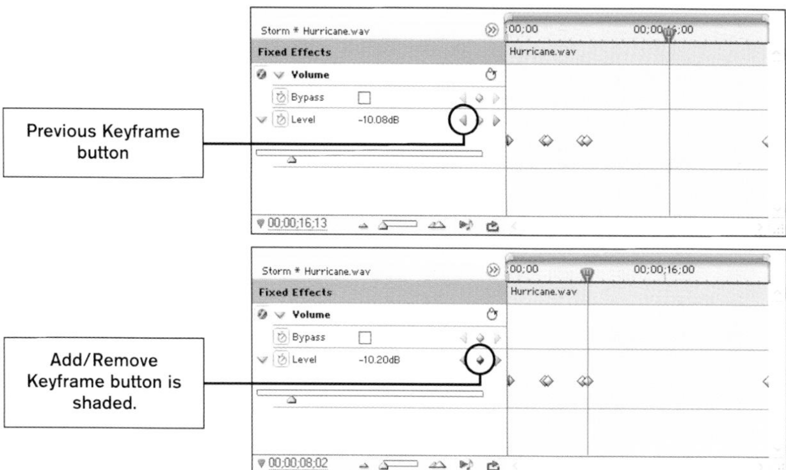

The keyframe navigator is used to snap the current time indicator to the previous or next keyframes. This helps to ensure that the current time indicator is placed directly over a keyframe. In the above example, clicking the **Previous Keyframe** button snaps the current time indicator to the previous keyframe.

How do you know it is definitely over the previous keyframe? The **Add/Remove Keyframe** button is shaded. Notice in the top image that the button is gray when the current time indicator is not placed over a keyframe. The button is shaded when the current time indicator is above an existing keyframe.

You can probably imagine, without the use of a visual aid, what the **Next Keyframe** button does. That's right–it snaps the current time indicator to the next keyframe.

So why are these three buttons so important to use? Here's a common pitfall that many Premiere Pro novices experience (because they didn't read this book!)...

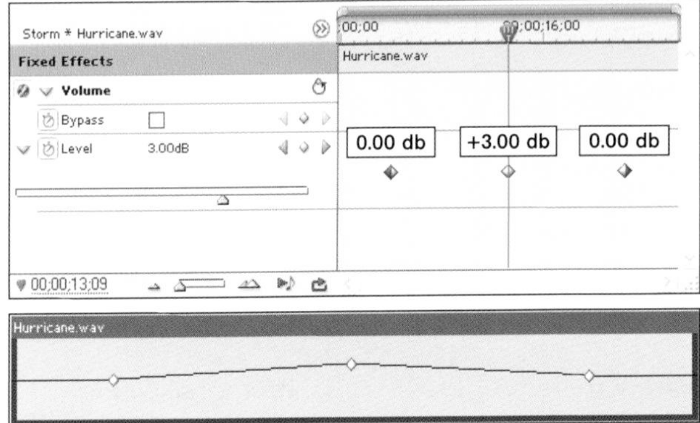

Eddie Editor (not his real name) has an audio clip with three keyframes. His audio starts at 0.00 dB, fades up to +3.00 dB, and then back to 0.00 dB. However, Eddie wants the middle keyframe to go up to +6.00 dB. So he manually drags the current time indicator on top of the middle keyframe.

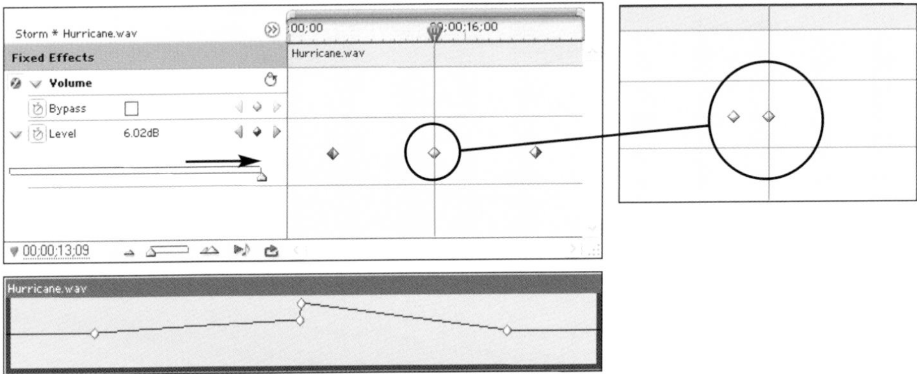

Uh-oh! The current time indicator is not really on top of the middle keyframe. It is one frame off. Eddie changes the value slider, and creates a new keyframe exactly one frame away from the old keyframe. Unfortunately, he is blissfully unaware because the Effect Controls Timeline is zoomed out very far. It's easier to see his mistake in the clip's value graph. Do you see the two keyframes that are nearly on top of each other? (Not quite on top of each other, but only one frame off.) The image on the right shows the Effect Controls window zoomed in.

Eddie is expecting the volume to start at 0.00 dB, and gradually increase to +6.00 dB. However, because of his transgression, the volume starts at 0.00 dB, gradually increases to the first keyframe value of +3.00 dB, and then *quickly* jumps, over the duration of one frame, to +6.00 dB. Oops!

Now that you've completed your mandatory keyframe training, it's time to get hands-on with another exercise.

2. Changing Volume with Effect Controls

In this exercise, you are going to create the same fade-up/fade-out from Exercise 1, but you are going to do it in the Effect Controls window.

1. If you have the project open from the previous exercise, skip to Step 2. If Premiere Pro is not running, launch it and click **Open Project** at the **Welcome Screen**. Navigate to the **c:\Premiere Pro HOT\Chapter10** folder, select **Exercise02.prproj**, and click **Open**. This project builds upon the last sequence.

2. Choose **Window > Workspace > Effects** to open the **Effect Controls** window in the left side of the **Monitor** window.

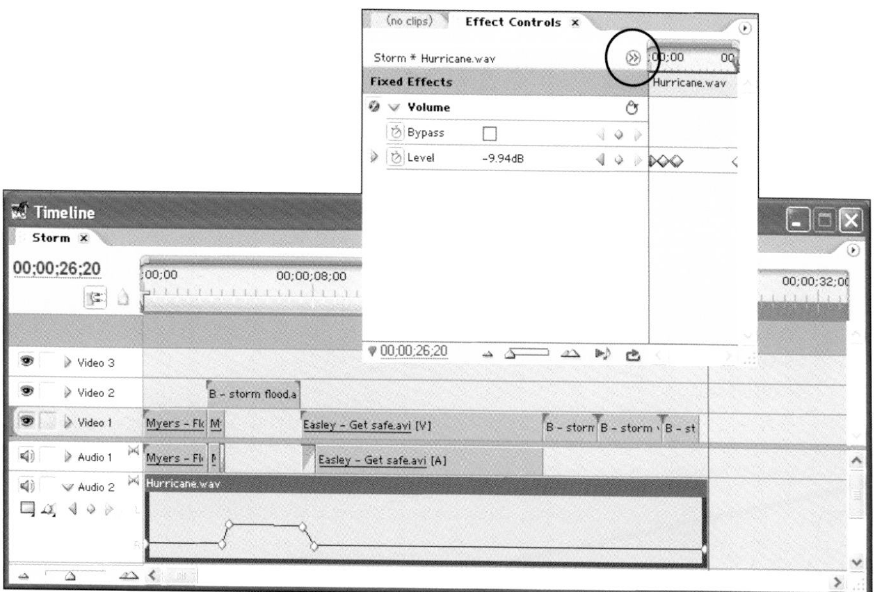

3. To see volume properties in the **Effect Controls** window, click **Hurricane.wav** in track **Audio 2** to select it. In the **Effect Controls** window, twirl down the **Volume** fixed effect. If you don't see the **Effect Controls Timeline** on the right side of the window, click the **Show/Hide Timeline View** button until you can see the keyframes.

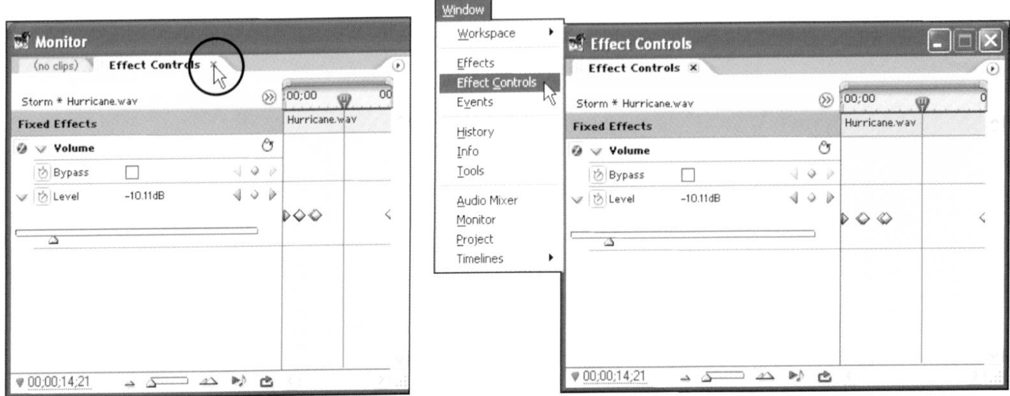

4. The **Effect Controls** window isn't given very much space when it is crammed into the **Monitor** window. To break the **Effect Controls** out of the **Monitor** window, click the tiny red X on the **Effect Controls** tab. This will close the **Effect Controls** in the **Monitor** window. Choose **Window > Effect Controls**. This will reopen the **Effect Controls** in its own window.

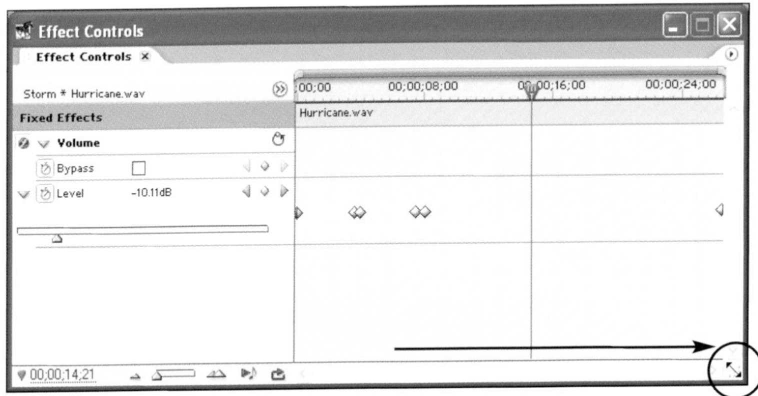

5. Once you "free" the **Effect Controls** window, you can resize it, to better see the keyframes. To resize the window, drag the lower-right corner of the **Effect Controls** window to the right. As you drag, the keyframe **Timeline** expands.

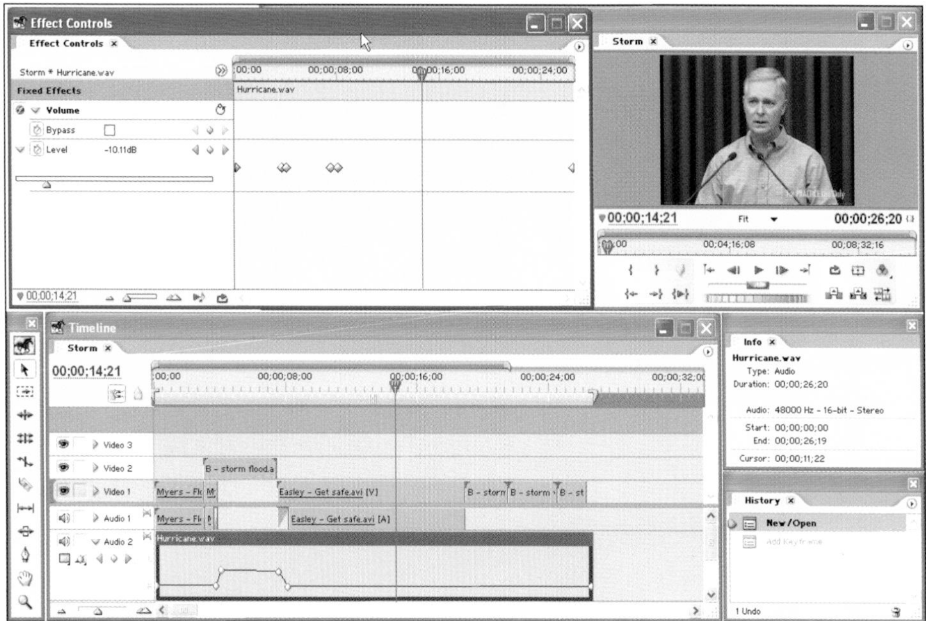

Note: Depending on your screen resolution, you may have to move the ***Effect Controls*** *window to the upper-left corner of Premiere Pro, covering the* ***Project*** *and* ***Monitor*** *source windows. The three windows that should be unobstructed are:* ***Effect Controls, Monitor Program*** *view, and* ***Timeline.***

6. Now it's time to start making keyframes. Whenever you create/modify keyframes in the Effect Controls, the two-step process is *always* as follows: move current time indicator, then create keyframe. (Since mantra is already taken, we'll call this the "keyframe slogan!")

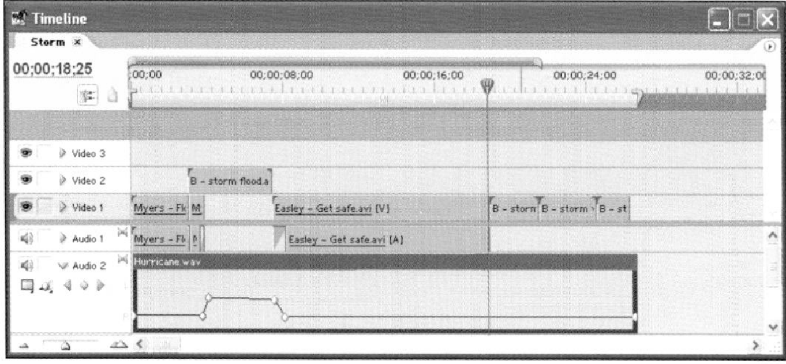

7. Play the sequence in the **Timeline** window and stop the current time indicator at the point you want the audio to start fading up. In this case, you want to fade up immediately after the last sound bite (which is approximately **00;00;18;25**).

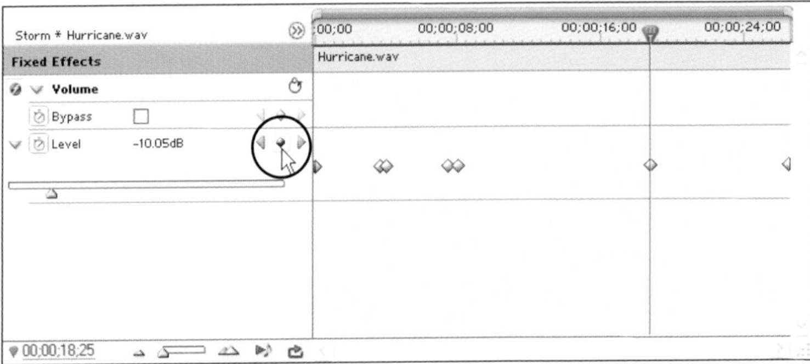

8. Select the **Hurricane.wav** in the **Timeline** to view its **Effect Controls**. Now that you've moved the current time indicator, according to the slogan, it's time to create a new keyframe. To create a new keyframe without changing the value, click the **Add/Remove Keyframe** button. This will place a new keyframe at the current time indicator.

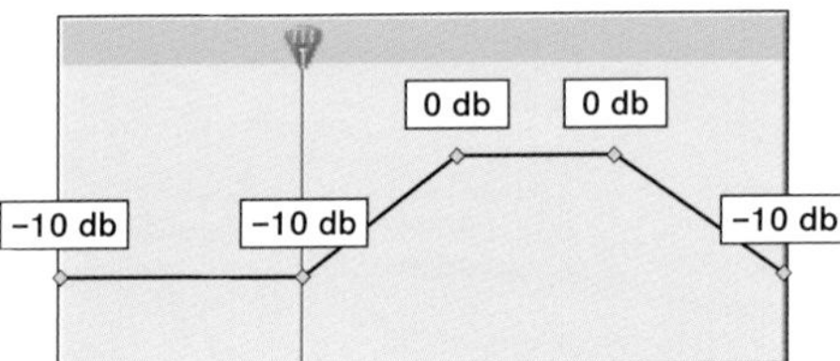

*Tip: The reason you used the **Add/Remove Keyframe** button, instead of changing the value slider, is because the value was already at −10 dB, so there was no need to change it. The **Add/Remove Keyframe** button is useful for just such an occasion.*

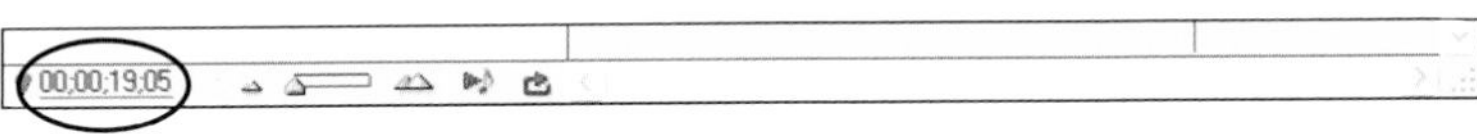

9. The next keyframe will complete the fade-up. Tap the **right arrow** on your keyboard 10 times to move the current time indicator 10 frames to the right. The final position should be about **00;00;19;05**. You can use the time display in the lower left of the **Effect Controls** as a guide.

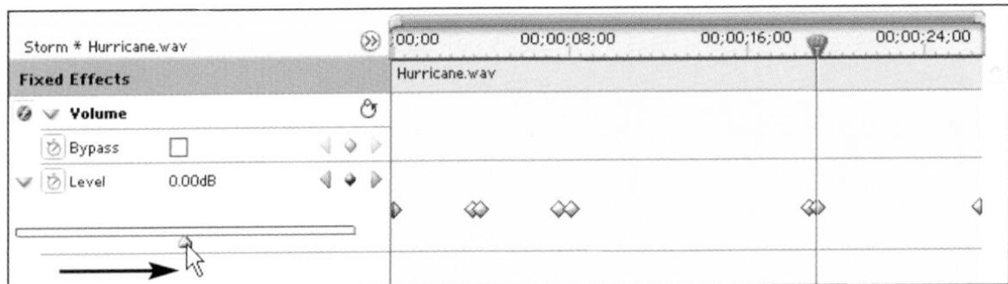

Pop quiz: what's the keyframe slogan? Move current time indicator, then create keyframe. You've just performed the first step, so now it's time to create a keyframe.

10. In this case, you want the volume level to be close to **0.00 dB**, so drag the **value slider** to **0.00 dB** (or as close as you can). This creates a new keyframe with the value of **0.00 dB**.

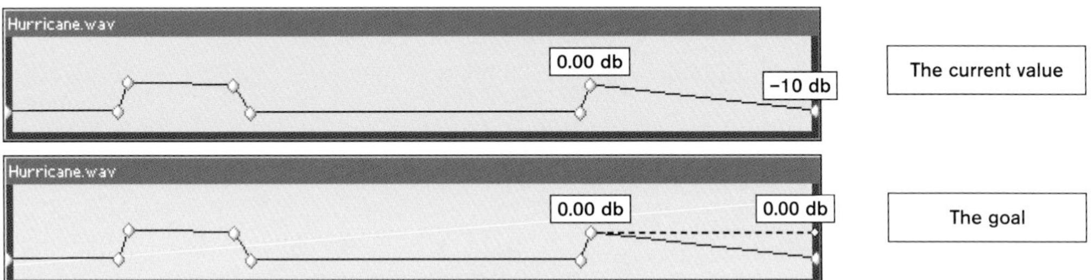

The above figure shows you what the value graph currently looks like (even though you are working in the Effect Controls window). Here is where you will deviate from the previous exercise. Instead of fading back down, you want the volume to remain at 0.00 dB for the remainder of the clip, which means all you need to do is increase the value of the last keyframe. Piece of cake, right?

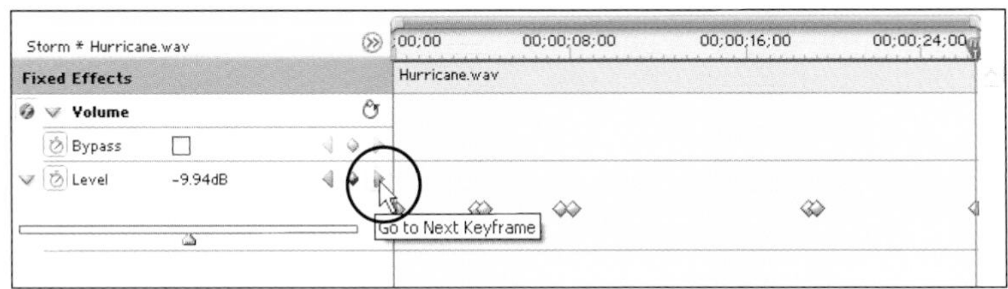

11. In the **Effect Controls** window, click the **Next Keyframe** button to move the current time indicator to the final keyframe.

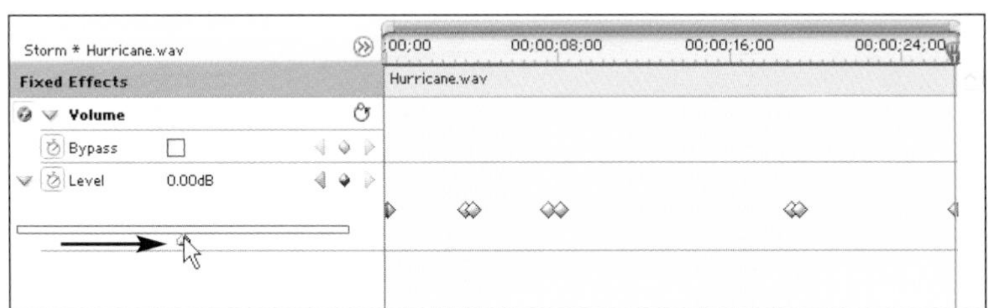

12. Once you've moved the current time indicator, change the **value slider** to modify the existing keyframe. In this case, drag the **value slider** to **0.00 dB**, to change the value of the final keyframe.

13. Play the sequence to preview the keyframe changes you've made. Not too shabby!

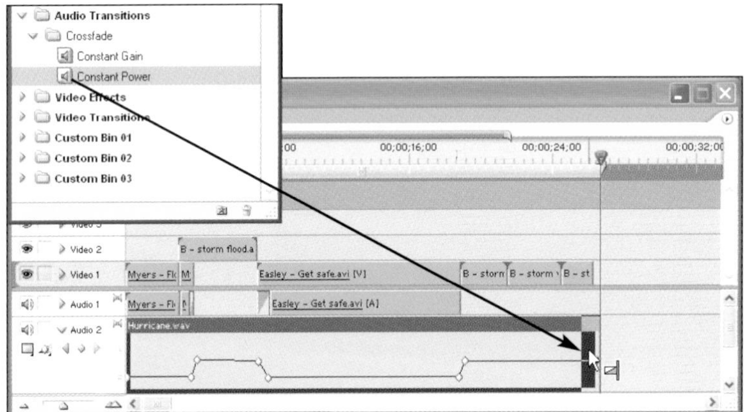

Overtime 1. Okay, technically at this point the exercise is over. But that audio clip ending is literally *screaming* for a fade-out. So you're not off the hook just yet. Choose **Window > Workspace > Effects** to bring the **Effects** window to the foreground. Twirl down the **Audio Transitions** and **Crossfade** folders. Drag the **Constant Power** audio transition to the **Out** point of **Hurricane.wav** in track **Audio 2**.

Note: *Even though the volume keyframe specifies a change of 0.00 dB, the audio transition "overrides" and fades the music out.*

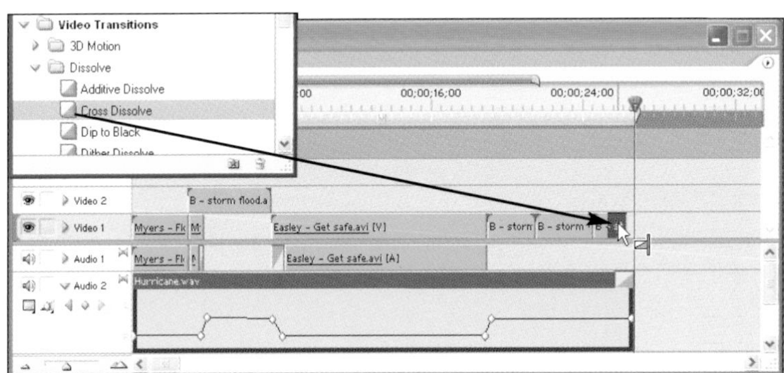

Overtime 2. Now that video clip looks so lonely without a cross dissolve. Better fix that, too! In the **Effects** window, twirl down the **Video Transitions** and **Dissolve** folders. Drag the **Cross Dissolve** video transition to the **Out** point of the final clip on track **Video 1**.

Overtime 3. Play the sequence. Much better! Aren't you glad you took the time to do that?

14. Save this project and keep it open before moving on to the next exercise.

That was a relatively painless exercise. Once you understand the logic behind keyframes, the actual task of creating them is not hard at all. Just don't forget to follow the keyframe slogan and/or mantra.

Volume vs. Gain

It's time to split hairs. Technically speaking, volume keyframes are the only way to change the volume of a clip. However, there's another property of audio clips called **Gain**, which has the end result of increasing or decreasing the decibel level of a clip. Huh?

In the music world, volume is the measure of the decibel level at which sound leaves the music device (mixer, amplifier, and so on). Gain is the measure of the original sound coming into the device. An electric guitar has a much higher gain than a flute. (Perhaps not an electric flute–which would rock.)

To translate that into Premiere Pro's world, gain is the intrinsic "loudness" of a clip, whereas volume refers to the output level. Put another way, gain is the internal sound level before being touched by Premiere Pro; volume is an external effect applied to the clip.

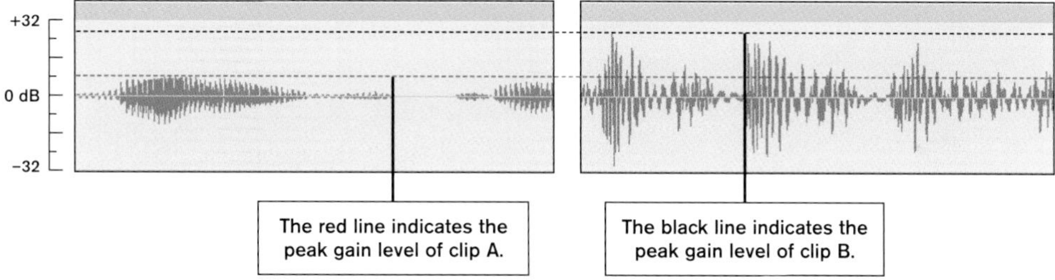
+32
0 dB
–32
The red line indicates the peak gain level of clip A.
The black line indicates the peak gain level of clip B.

The figure above illustrates the gain of two different clips. The audio clip on the left is a person talking. The highest point in the audio clip–its *peak*–is roughly above 0 dB. The audio clip on the right is a music file. It peaks at about +20 dB. The music clip has a higher gain level than the clip of the person talking.

Adding a volume effect to the above clips does not change the gain level. The volume effect changes only how loudly Premiere Pro outputs the clip to your computer/television speakers, but the gain remains the same. Furthermore, a +3.00 dB volume effect on the person talking would still be quieter than the exact same +3.00 dB volume effect on the music clip. In other words, *even with the same volume effect, the clips will output at different decibel levels.*

So what can you do if you want the two clips to output at the same level? Premiere Pro provides a solution, called **gain normalizing**. Here's how it works...

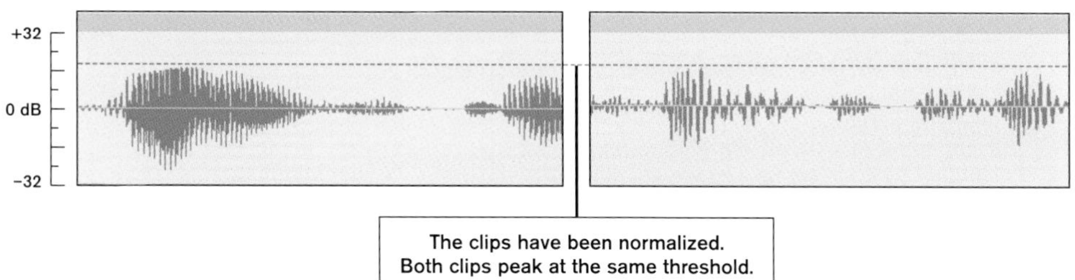
+32
0 dB
–32
The clips have been normalized.
Both clips peak at the same threshold.

There is a threshold of how loud an audio clip can be before it begins to distort (called "clipping"). When Premiere Pro normalizes a clip, it scans the entire clip, and calculates by how many decibels it can increase or decrease the gain in order to reach the threshold.

The clipping threshold does not change. It's always the same. This means that every clip you normalize will end up at the same gain level. In the figure above, the two clips now have the same gain decibel level.

Keep in mind that when Premiere Pro scans a clip, it is scanning for the peak level. In other words, it is listening for the loudest point in the clip. It then calculates the change in gain based on the peak level.

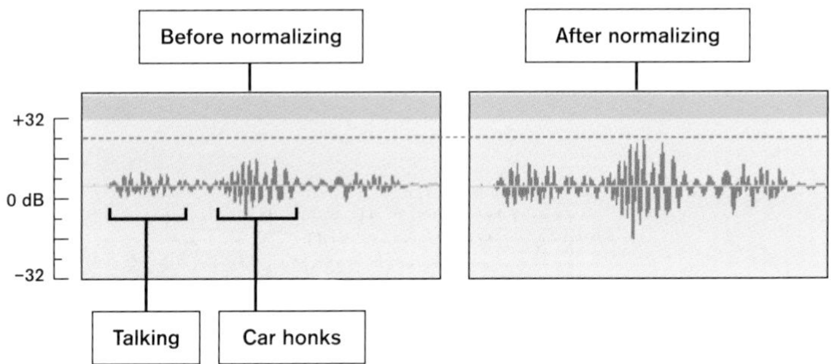

Why is this important to know? Imagine that you have an audio clip of someone in a car having a conversation. Suddenly, the car next to them honks. The honk is much louder than the voices, so the gain is loudest (peaks) at the honk. When you normalize the audio clip, Premiere Pro normalizes based on the peak level. So your end result is a car honk that is plenty loud, but the voices are not as loud as they can be.

A workaround to this problem is to use the Razor tool to splice the audio clip into two separate clips: the first clip of the talking, and the second clip of the car honk. You can now normalize the voices as their own clip.

Warning: normalizing very quiet audio can amplify the background noise or hiss. For best results, record source audio at the optimum levels with your camera and/or microphone.

In this next exercise you will learn how to easily normalize the gain of a clip.

3. Normalizing Gain

In this exercise, you are going to normalize (maximize) the gain of two sound bites.

1. If you have the project open from the previous exercise, skip to Step 2. If Premiere Pro is not running, launch it and click **Open Project** at the **Welcome Screen**. Navigate to the **c:\Premiere Pro HOT\Chapter10** folder, select **Exercise03.prproj**, and click **Open**. This project builds upon the last sequence.

2. To make sure your screen looks like the figures in this exercise, choose **Window > Workspace > Effects**. If your **Effect Controls** window was floating in space, it is now docked (crammed) back in the **Monitor** window again.

3. To normalize the first sound bite, right-click the first audio clip in track **Audio 1**, and from the shortcut menu, choose **Audio Gain**.

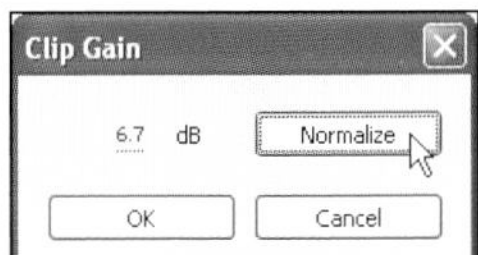

4. Click **Normalize** in the **Clip Gain** window. Premiere Pro quickly scans the clip and then calculates the decibel increase needed to reach the threshold. In this case, it's **6.7 dB**. Click **OK**.

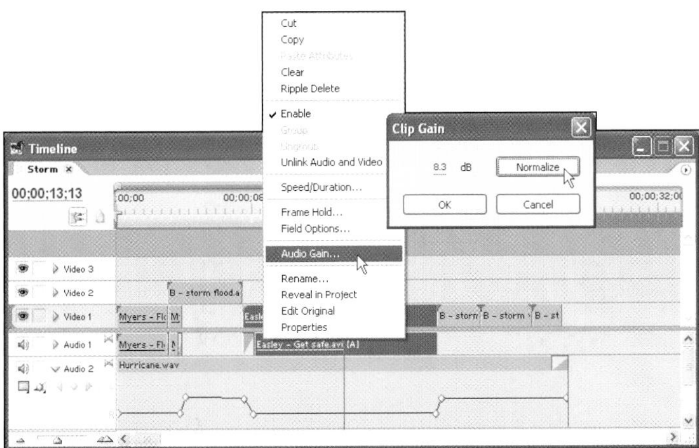

5. Now do the same for the second sound bite. Right-click **Easley – Get safe.avi** in track **Audio 1** and choose **Audio Gain** from the shortcut menu. In the **Clip Gain** window, click **Normalize**. Then click **OK**.

6. Play the sequence to listen to the new gain levels. It will be a subtle difference, but you may be able to hear that the clips are playing a bit louder.

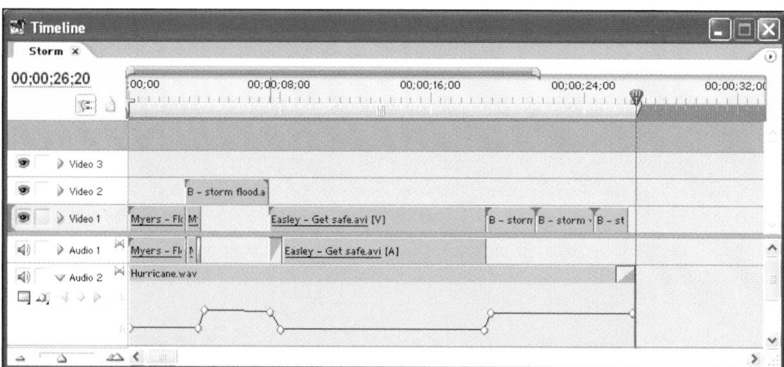

7. There is one problem, however. Eons ago you used the **Razor** tool to split the first sound bite into two clips and then added a thin transition between the clips. (Remember Chapter 9, "*Audio Transitions*?") In this exercise, you normalized the gain of the first part of the sound bite, but not the second part. Play the sequence again, and you can hear a discernible drop in decibel level between the first part of the sound bite and the last part of the sound bite.

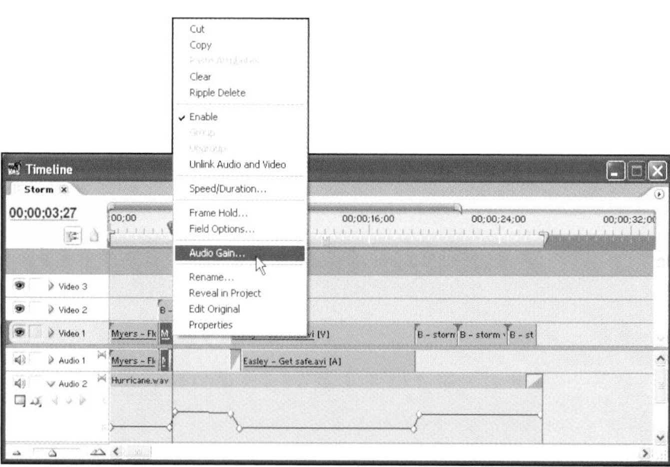

8. To remedy this, right-click the second half of the sound bite (the second audio clip in track **Audio 1**) and from the shortcut menu choose **Audio Gain**.

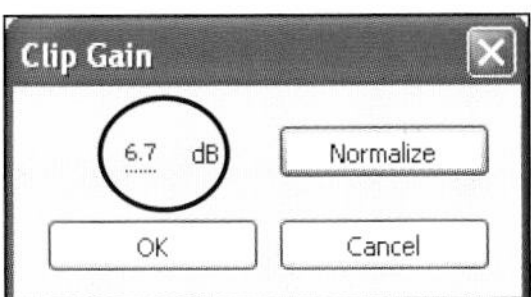

9. Click **Normalize**. You should get a value of **7.9 dB**. However, you may recall from Step 4 that the normalized value of the first clip was **6.7 dB**. It would be best if the clips matched, for maximum congruity. To manually specify your own clip gain, click the decibel value, type in **6.7**, and press **Enter**. Click **OK**.

10. Again play the sequence. There should be no noticeable change in audio level between Clips 1 and 2.

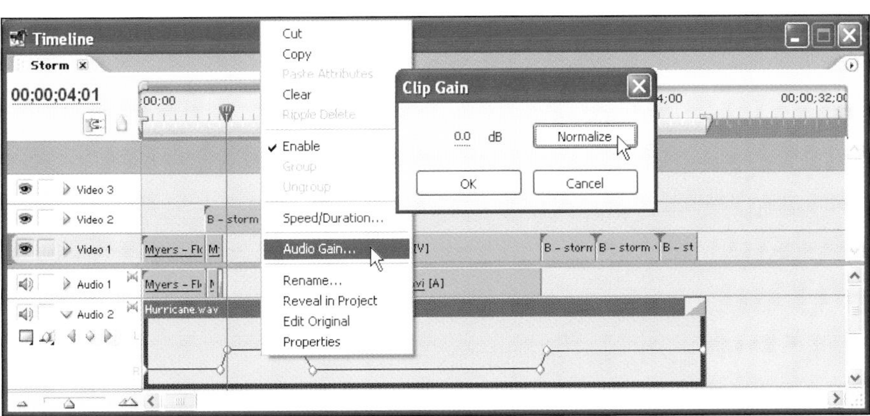

11. Lastly, right-click the music clip in track **Audio 2**, and choose **Audio Gain** from the shortcut menu. Click **Normalize**. Notice anything? That's right, the value didn't change from **0.0 dB**. This means that the clip is as loud as it can be, so you don't want to increase it anymore. Click **OK** to close the **Clip Gain** window.

Automatically increasing or decreasing a clip's gain is a no-brainer. However, it does require a bit more brain power to understand the difference between volume and gain—even many editing professionals do not understand as much about gain and volume as you do right now! Feel free to impress your friends.

12. Save and keep this project open before moving on to the next exercise.

4. Applying Standard Effects

Standard effects are effects that can be applied to and removed from a clip. Standard effects are found in an effects folder and dragged onto a clip, just like transitions. Like fixed effects, many standard effects can be keyframed, which means you can change their values over time. Premiere Pro comes with dozens and dozens of standard video and audio effects. In this exercise, you will apply some common standard effects.

1. If you have the project open from the previous exercise, skip to Step 2. If Premiere Pro is not running, launch it and click **Open Project** at the **Welcome Screen**. Navigate to the **c:\Premiere Pro HOT\Chapter10** folder, select **Exercise04.prproj**, and click **Open**. This project builds upon the last sequence.

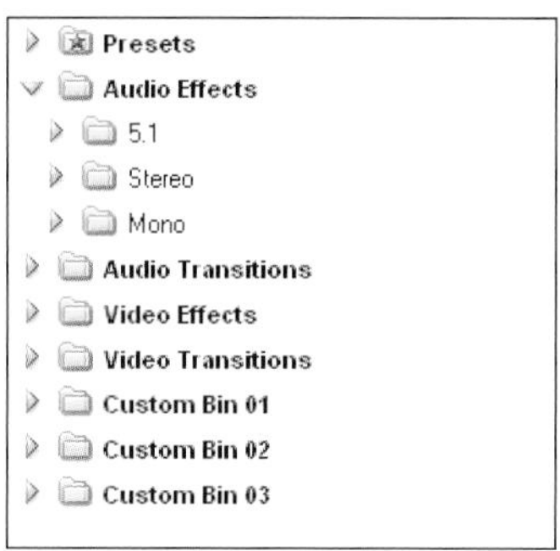

2. In the **Effect Controls** window, twirl down the **Audio Effects** folder. You will see three subfolders: **5.1**, **Stereo**, and **Mono**. Effects in the **Stereo** folder can only be applied to stereo audio clips. Effects in the **Mono** folder can only be applied to mono audio clips, and so on. It may seem like a lot of effects, but most effects are found in each of the subfolders. For example, the **Delay** effect is found in all three folders, which means there's a **5.1 Delay** effect, a **Stereo Delay** effect, and **Mono Delay** effect.

Tip: *Usually, with music files and movie clips from DV cameras, the audio will be stereo. If you're not sure whether a clip is stereo or mono, select the clip in the* ***Project*** *window and view its information in the* ***Project*** *window preview area.*

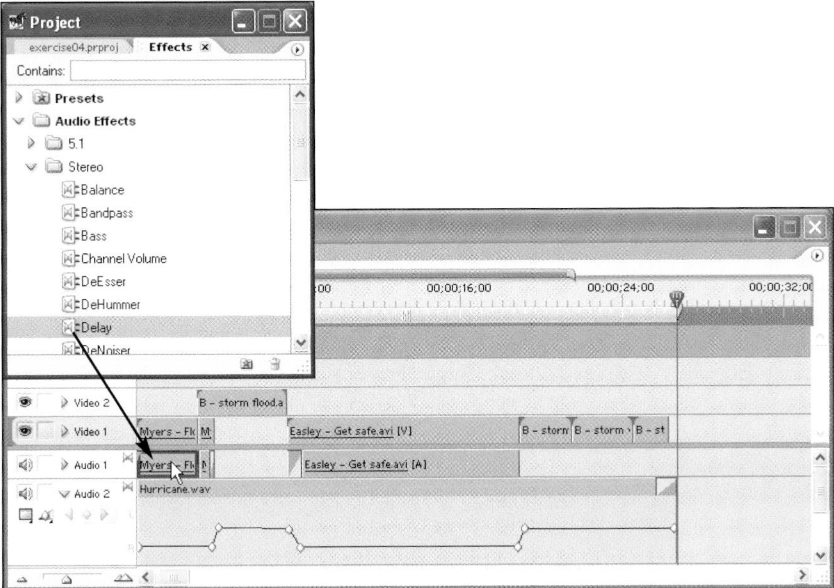

3. To view the available stereo effects, twirl down the **Stereo** subfolder. Drag the **Delay** audio effect on top of the first audio clip in track **Audio 1**. Play the sequence to listen to the effect. The **Delay** effect creates an echo.

Note: *Effects can be dragged onto any part of a clip, unlike transitions which must be dragged to a specific location at the start or end of a clip.*

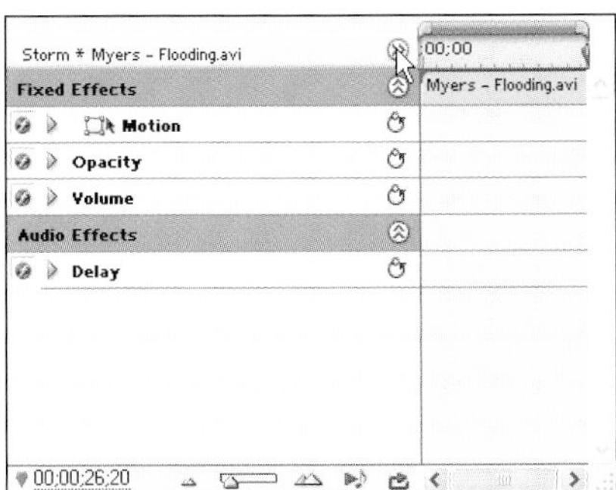

4. Right now the delay is a little too long, which doesn't make for a very good echo. You can fix this by shortening the delay value in the **Effect Controls**. Select the first audio clip in track **Audio 1** to view its **Effect Controls**. In the **Effect Controls** window, the fixed effects are shown on top, and the audio effects are shown below. In the previous step, you applied the **Delay** audio effect, which is listed under **Audio Effects**.

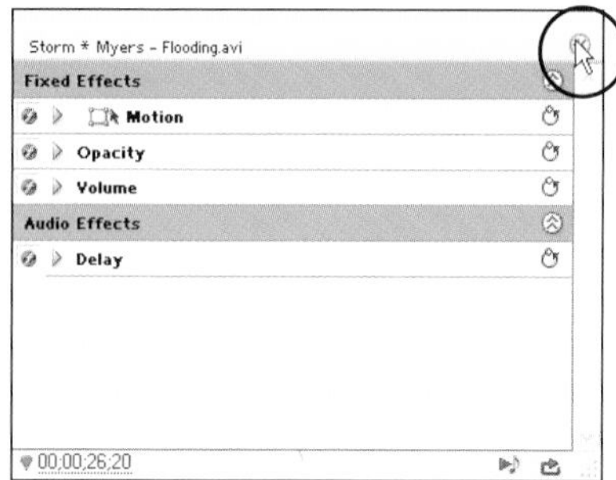

5. Because you are not doing any work with keyframes right now, you can hide the **Effect Controls Timeline**. To do this, in the **Effect Controls** window click the **Show/Hide Timeline View** button.

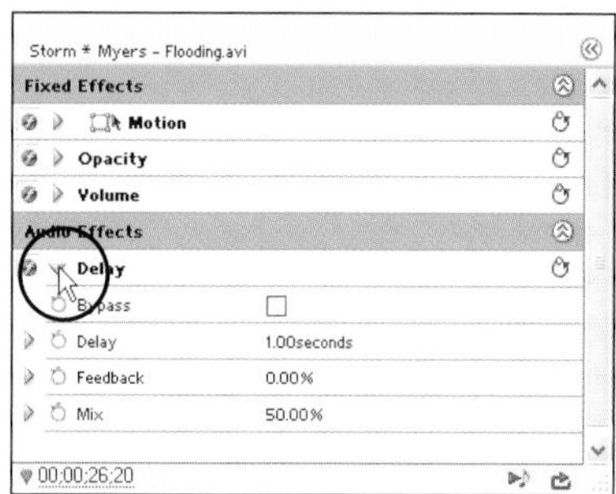

6. To view the options of the **Delay** audio effect, twirl down the arrow next to the **Delay** effect title.

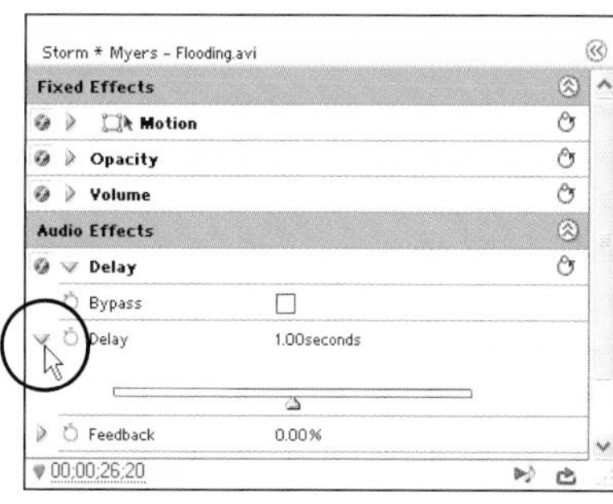

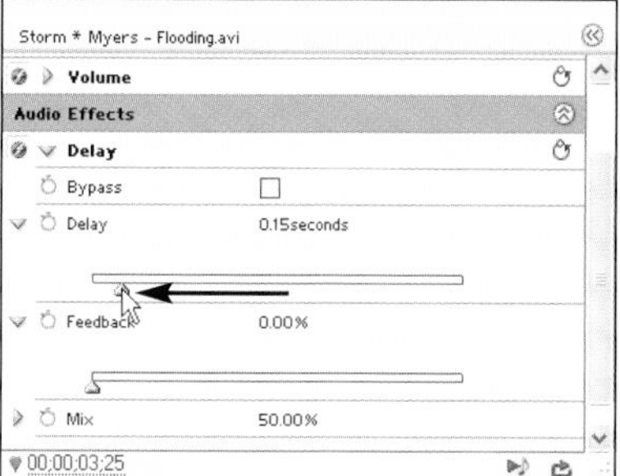

7. To shorten the echo duration, you are going to shorten the **Delay** value. Twirl down the **Delay** value to view the **value slider**. Drag the slider to the left until the value is **0.15** seconds.

Note: *This may be confusing, because the effect title is **Delay** and within that effect there is a value called **Delay.***

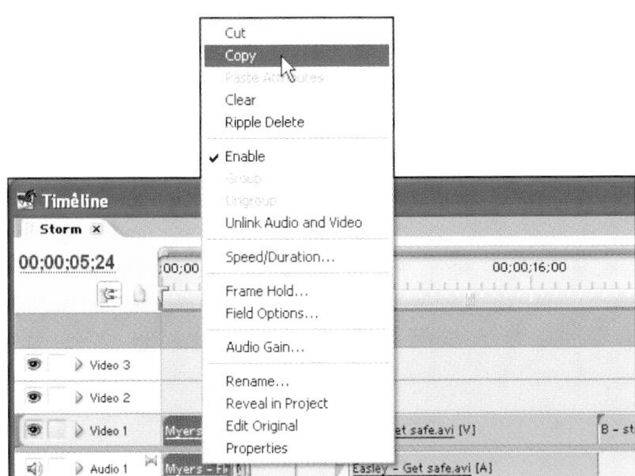

8. Play the sequence to preview the effect. You should notice that the echo delay is much shorter. However, the echo effects stops abruptly at the end of the audio clip. Remember that the second part of the sound bite is a new audio clip. Premiere Pro provides a way for you to copy the effects of one clip and paste them to another clip. To do this, right-click the first audio clip in the **Timeline**, and choose **Copy** from the shortcut menu.

9. To apply the copied effects to the second audio clip in track **Audio 1**, right-click the second audio clip (try to right-click in the middle of the audio clip), and choose **Paste Attributes** (shown grayed out in Step 8's figure). This will paste all of the effects from the first clip to the second clip. Play the sequence to listen to the new changes. Both clips should now have the delay effect.

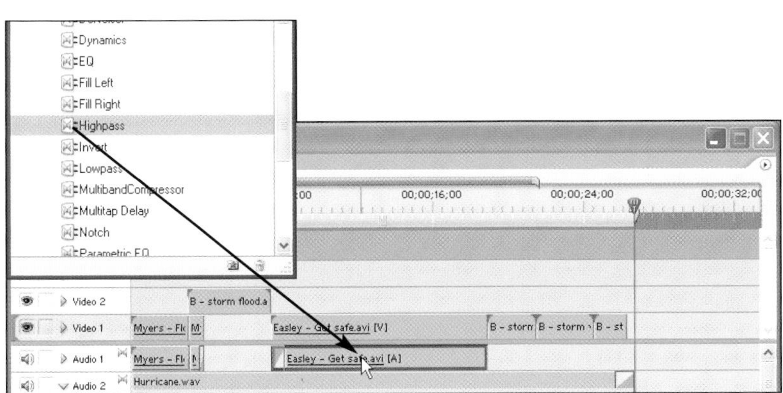

10. How about an effect for the next sound bite in track **Audio 1**? Perhaps you want to create a sound effect like the speaker phoned it in (literally). The **Highpass** audio effect allows only the high frequencies of an audio clip to be heard, which makes the speaker sound as if he's speaking over the phone. In the **Effects** window, drag the **Highpass** audio effect from the **Audio Effects > Stereo** subfolder and drop it on top of the audio of **Easley – Get safe.avi**.

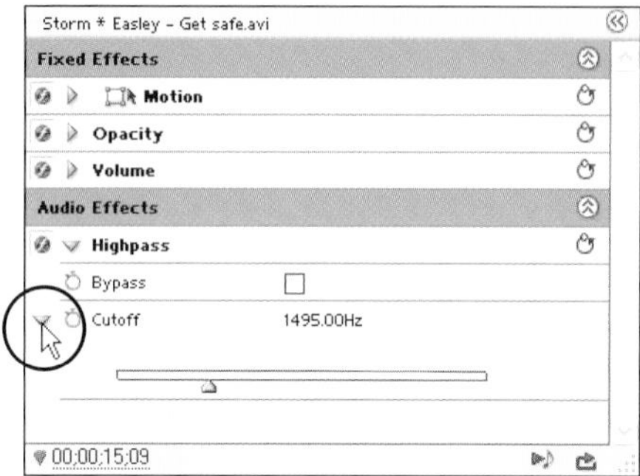

11. Click **Play** to preview the effect. Right now the **Highpass** is set too high, and it doesn't quite sound like a real phone yet. Select **Easley – Get safe.avi** to open its properties in the **Effect Controls** window. Twirl down the **Highpass** audio effect to view its options and twirl down the **Cutoff** option to view its values.

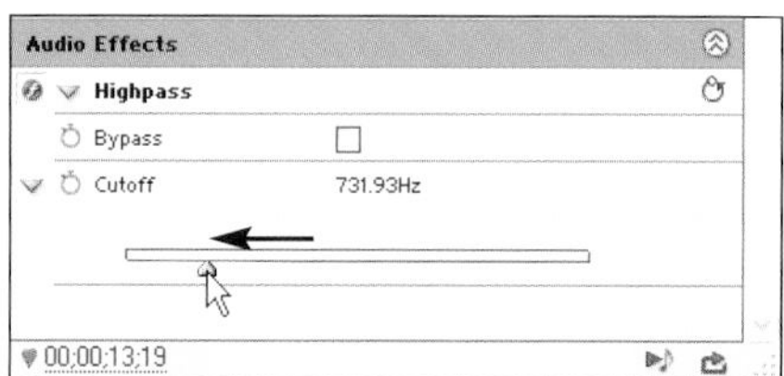

12. Drag the **Cutoff value slider** to the left to lower the **Highpass** "threshold." (This will lower the bar, so to speak, and allow a broader range of frequencies to be heard.) Drag the **value slider** to about **700 – 800 Hz**. (The slider jumps in increments, so get as close as you can.) Play the sequence to preview the effect.

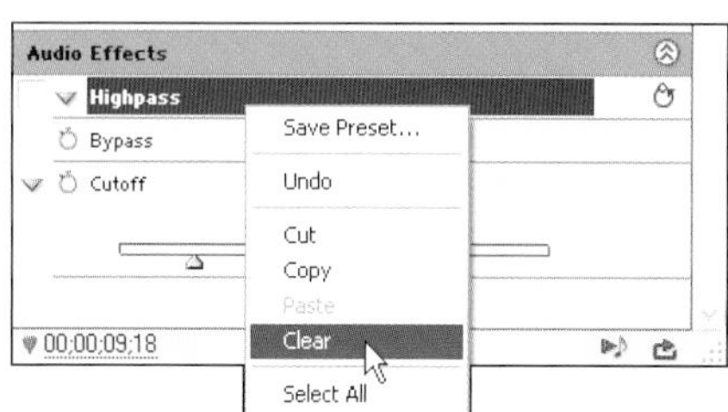

13. The **Highpass** is a great effect when you want to hear the voice of someone on the phone, but in this case it's not very helpful. To remove an audio effect from a clip, right-click the effect title, in this case **Highpass**, and choose **Clear** from the pop-up menu. *Poof*. All gone.

Note: *If you right-clicked on any of the* ***Fixed Effects****, you would find the* ***Clear*** *command grayed-out, because* ***Fixed Effects*** *cannot be removed.*

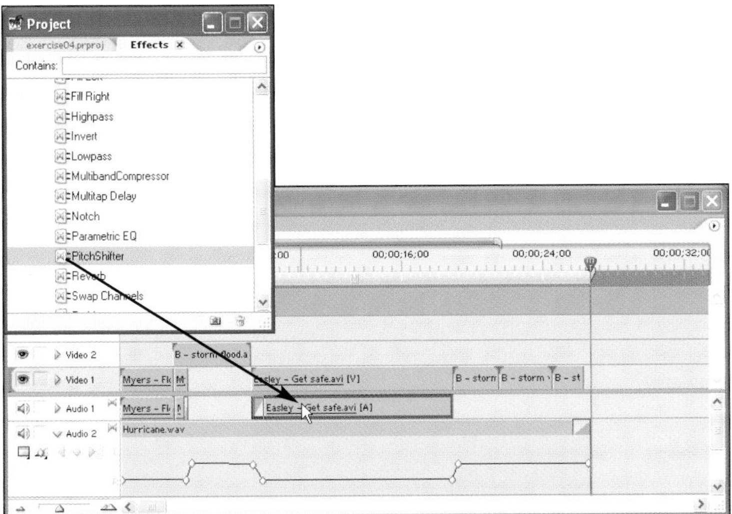

14. In the **Effects** window, drag the **PitchShifter** effect from the **Audio Effects > Stereo** subfolder and apply it to the same audio clip, **Easley – Get safe.avi**.

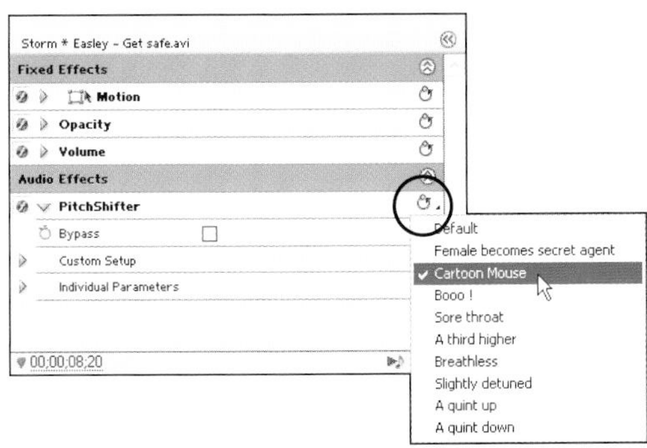

15. Play the sequence. Did you hear anything different? Probably not, because some effects, **PitchShifter** included, are applied with their values set to 0. This means that the effect has been applied, but you must change one or more of the effect's values in order to change the sound. To aid you in this task, the **PitchShifter** comes with effect presets. Click in the **Reset/Preset** button to view a list of available presets. Each preset changes the effect values in a predefined way. In this case, choose the **Cartoon Mouse** preset.

Tip: *Normally the **Reset** button will revert all of the options you modified back to their original values. However, whenever you see a **Reset** button with a triangle in the corner, this means it contains a preset list to choose from. Sure, you could manually create these exact presets by changing the options yourself, but why reinvent the wheel?*

---

16. Play the sequence again. This time, the speaker should have a squeaky voice. A fun effect, but totally inappropriate in this situation. (However, if you want to lose your job at the TV station, this would be your ticket.) In the **Effect Controls** window, next to the **PitchShifter** effect, Click the **Reset/Preset** button again and choose **A quint up**. Play the sequence again.

Tip: If your curiosity is peaked, feel free to experiment and listen to how each preset changes the audio.

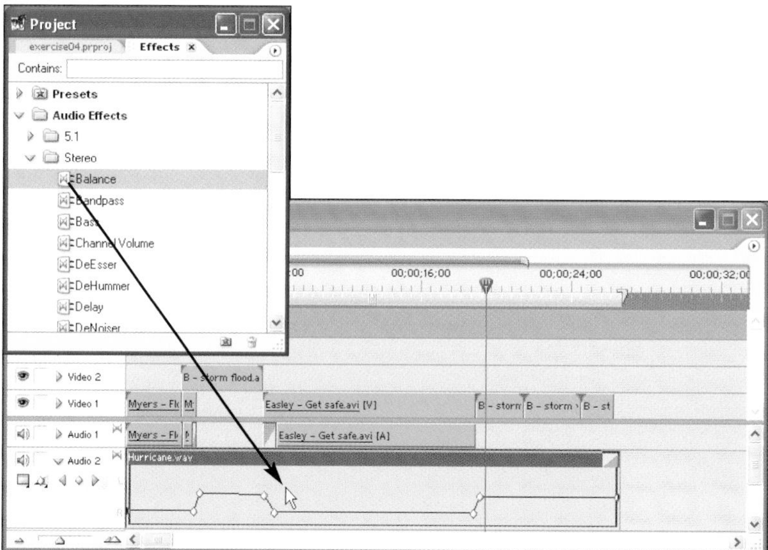

17. One more standard effect to apply. Drag the **Balance** effect from the **Audio Effects > Stereo** folder to the music clip on track **Audio 2**.

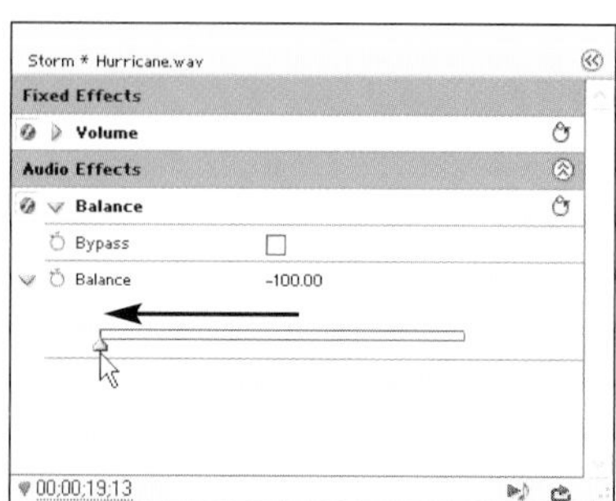

18. Select the music clip to view its **Effect Controls**. Twirl down the **Balance** effect and then twirl down the **Balance** option to view the **value slider**. Drag the **value slider** to **–100.00**. (This is another one where the effect and one of its options have the same name, so be careful.) Play the sequence. The music clip should be heard only from your left speaker.

Note: *This effect requires that you have stereo speakers or headphones connected to your computer.*

---

19. Save and close this project before moving on to the next exercise.

This exercise is just the tip of the iceberg when it comes to applying and modifying audio effects. There are literally dozens more–far too many to demonstrate in these pages. Luckily, they are all applied and modified the same way, so even though you've only practiced with a few different ones, you know how to use all of them.

NOTE | The Bypass Option

You may have noticed that all of the audio effects you applied in this chapter have a **Bypass** option. (Ironically, this option was "bypassed" in this chapter.) Both fixed effects and audio effects have a Bypass option. So what exactly does Bypass do?

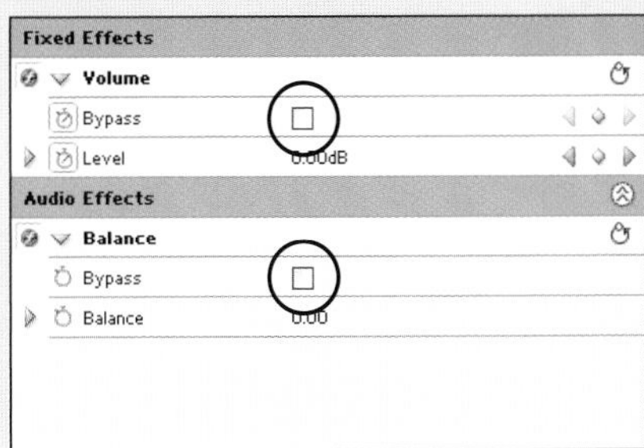

When Bypass is checked, Premiere Pro will ignore the effect and play the audio as if the effect had not been applied. Your next question may be, "Yes, but I thought that's what the icon did. Right?" True, both the Bypass option and the icon will temporarily hide an effect, as if it had not been applied. But the Bypass option is **keyframeable**. This means you can have an effect start, and then halfway through the clip, you can turn on the bypass option, which will hide the effect. Conversely, the icon cannot switch during a clip. It is either on for the entire clip, or off for the entire clip. There is no going back and forth during playback.

The following is a handy chart that summarizes most of the audio effects included with Premiere Pro. Keep in mind that unless you are an audio engineer, you'll never use most of these. (And if you *are* an audio engineer, you should probably use a dedicated audio editing application, such as Adobe Audition.)

All Those Audio Effects

Effect	Result
Balance	Pans stereo audio to left or right speaker. Stereo only.
Bandpass	Removes frequencies outside of a specified range, or "band." Rarely used.
Bass	Increases or decreases bass frequencies.
Channel Volume	Allows you to independently control the volume of each channel in a stereo or 5.1 (surround) clip.
DeEsser (1.5 only)	Removes sibilant "esses" and "tees", and other similar frequencies.
DeHummer	Removes unwanted 50 Hz/60 Hz hum (hum from power lines).
DeNoiser	Automatically detects tape noise and removes it (in theory).
Delay	Adds an echo.
EQ	Parametric equalizer, like the EQ meters on your home stereo/boom box.
Fill Left	Duplicates the left channel of audio and copies it in the right channel.
Fill Right	Duplicates the right channel of audio and copies it to the left channel.
Highpass	Removes frequencies below a specific cutoff.
Lowpass	Removes frequencies above a specific cutoff.
Multitap Delay	Adds up to four echoes.
Notch	Removes frequencies near a specific center (inverse of bandpass).
PitchShifter	Adjusts pitch of signal.
Reverb	Adds ambience and warmth to an audio clip, by simulating the sound of audio playing in rooms of various sizes (such as small rooms and concert halls).
Swap Channels	Swaps left and right channels. Stereo only.
Treble	Increases or decreases higher frequencies (4000 Hz and above).

The primary goal of this chapter was to introduce you to the world of keyframes and the world of standard effects. Learning how to create and modify keyframes in conjunction with fixed and standard effects can take your video projects to the next level. And don't worry, you will have plenty of keyframing practice in the upcoming chapters!

Video Effects

What Is a Video Effect?	Rendering Multiple Effects
Changing Render Order	Creating a Freeze Frame
Animating Fixed Effects	Saving Effect Presets
Keyframe Presets	Saving Keyframe Presets
Changing Motion in the Program View

H•O•T

Premiere Pro HOT DVD

In the previous chapter, you worked with audio effects and volume keyframes. In Chapter 7, "*Still Images and Fixed Effects*," you worked with fixed effects and still images. Now it's time to learn another type of effect, the video effect. Video effects are applied and modified just like audio effects. Video clips have the same fixed effects as still images. Video effects and fixed effects can be keyframed just like volume. Notice a pattern? Video effects combine many of the concepts you've learned in the previous chapters. There are literally hundreds of different ways to use video effects, and this chapter will walk you through some of the most useful effects. The goal of this chapter is to also teach you how to apply, modify, and remove effects, so you will be able to venture on your own and create effects.

What Is a Video Effect?

Strictly speaking, a video effect is a filter that is applied to video clips or still images. The Effect Controls window contains the list of video effects, just like audio effects of the previous chapter. Video effects are applied to a clip the same way as audio effects. In a way, you already know the concepts of applying, modifying, and removing video effects, simply because you did all this in the last chapter with audio effects.

However, there's a lot more to video effects. In terms of this chapter, I use the phrase *video effect* to describe anything that changes how a clip displays, including the following:

- Video effect filters (such as color correction, blurs, 3D orientation, chroma key)
- Frame hold (also called *freeze frame*)
- Fixed effects (properties such as motion, scale, position, anchor point, and opacity)
- Changing clip speed (such as slow-motion and fast-forward effects)

In this chapter, you will learn how to create each of these types of video effects. Along the way you'll also learn some handy keyframing tricks and video effect management.

NOTE | Video Effects vs. Video Filters

So what's the difference between a video effect and a video filter? Your answer depends on who at Adobe you ask.

Video filters are now called video effects in Premiere Pro. Users who are migrating from a previous version of Premiere, or who are familiar with other Adobe applications, will recognize the word *filters*. (Isn't it odd that Adobe calls them filters in every other program but Premiere Pro?!)

In order to make this chapter confusion-free, you will learn using the Premiere Pro terminology. Just keep in mind that the phrase *video effects* has two meanings:

- *A video filter that is applied to a clip (from the Video Effects folder)*
- *Any effect you create that changes how a clip looks (like adding slow-motion or adding motion keyframes)*

Rendering Multiple Effects

Since you already know how to apply an effect, as well as modify the effect values in the Effect Controls window, there's no need to cover it again. However, what you may not know is *why the order of effects* is important. Read on...

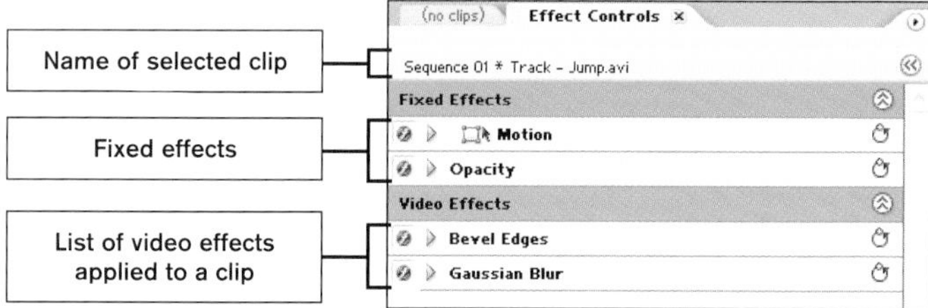

In the previous chapter, you learned that Premiere Pro allows you to add multiple effects to a clip. You also learned that each effect applied to a clip is listed in the Effect Controls window. In the case of video effects, all applied effects are shown under the aptly named **Video Effects** heading.

When there are multiple effects applied to a clip, Premiere Pro renders the effects starting at the top and working down. In other words, it creates the first effect, and then takes the resulting composition and applies the next effect, and so on. The following example should help clarify the effect render order.

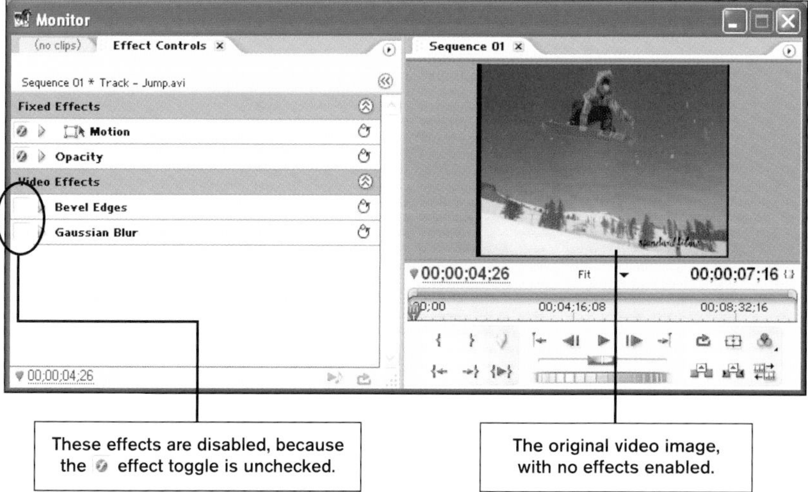

In this figure, two effects have been applied to **Track – Jump.avi**. However, both effects have been temporarily disabled by unchecking the effect toggle. Because the effects are disabled, the **Program** view shows you the original image.

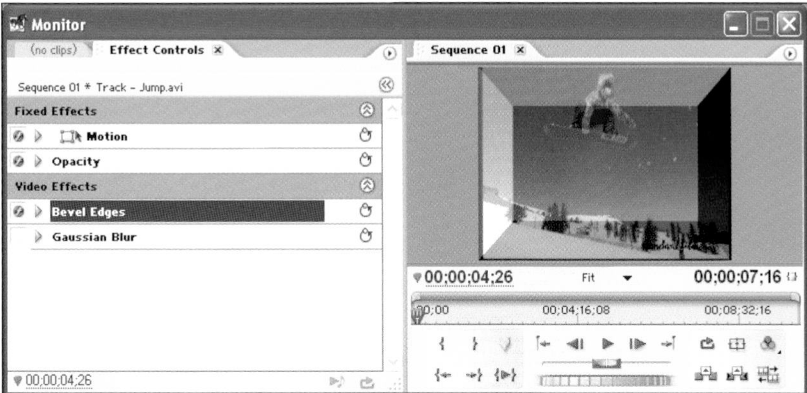

In this figure, the video effect **Bevel Edges** is enabled, and **Gaussian Blur** is disabled. The **Program** view shows you the result of the effect.

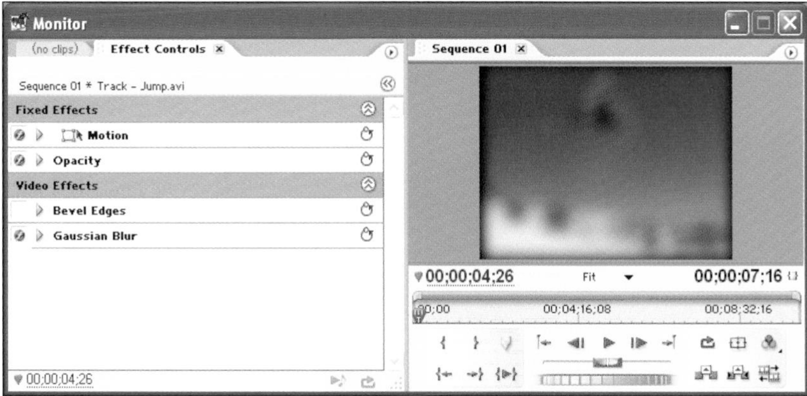

In this figure, **Gaussian Blur** is enabled, and **Bevel Edges** is disabled. The **Program** view shows the blurry result.

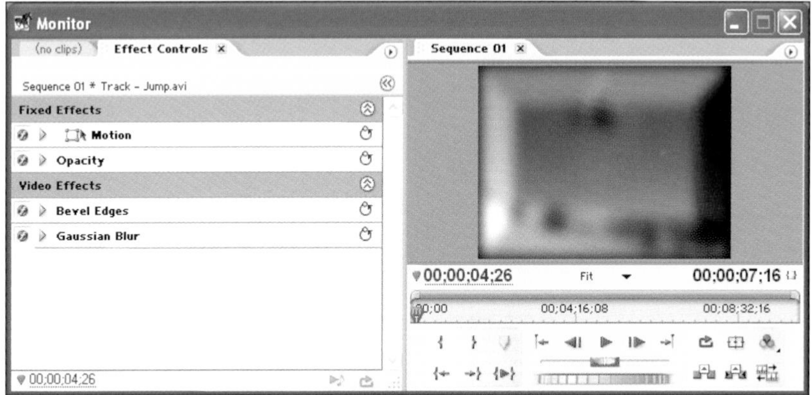

In this figure, both effects are enabled. However, since **Bevel Edges** is listed above **Gaussian Blur** in the **Effect Controls**, Premiere Pro first applies the bevel effect and then applies the blur effect. The result is a "blurry bevel."

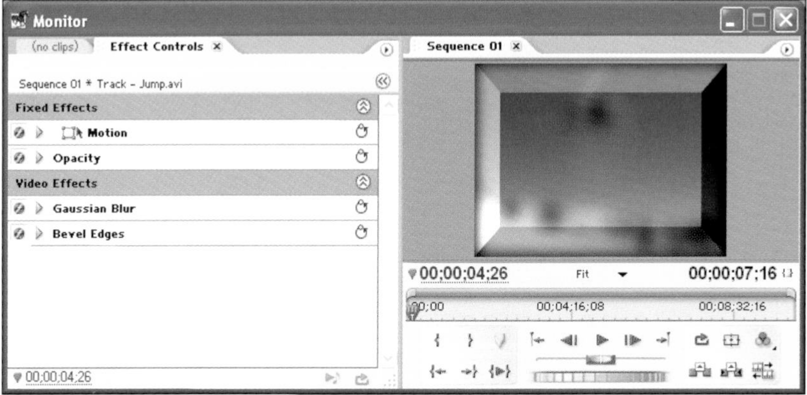

Notice what happens, in this figure, when the effect order is changed. This time, **Gaussian Blur** is listed above **Bevel Edges**, so Premiere Pro first blurs the image and then applies the bevel. The result is a much sharper bevel, since it is being applied after the blur.

The lesson here is: the order of effects does indeed matter. Premiere Pro builds them one at a time, from the top of the effects list to the bottom. This applies to still images and audio clips as well. In the next exercise, you will learn how to change the order of video effects in the Effect Controls window.

I. Changing Render Order

Since you already know how to apply and remove effects, there's no need to waste time showing you how to do that. Instead, you're going to dive right into the world of applying and reordering multiple effects.

1. If Premiere Pro is not running, launch it and click **Open Project** at the **Welcome Screen**. Navigate to the **c:\Premiere Pro HOT\Chapter11** folder, select **Exercise01.prproj**, and click **Open**.

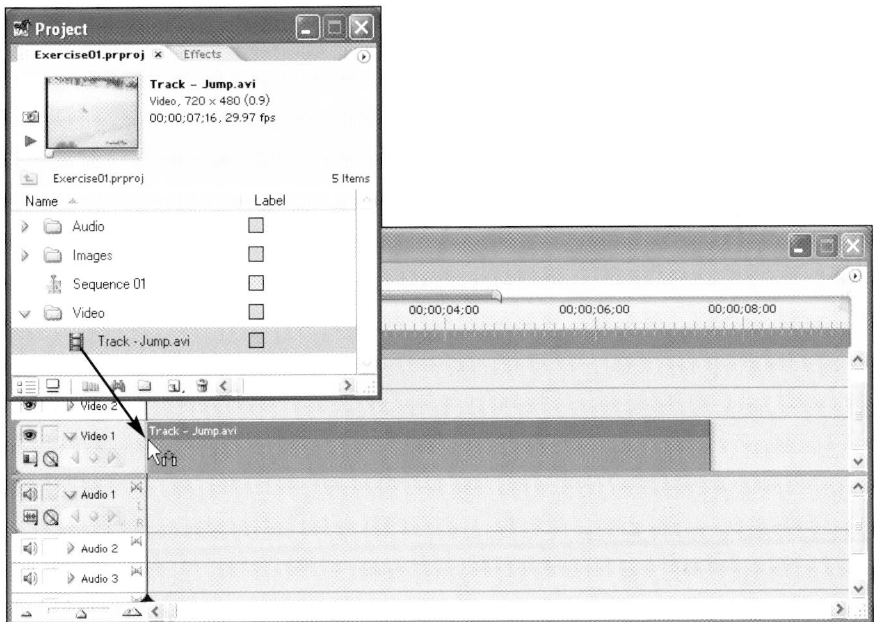

2. All of the video, image, and audio clips you will use in the next few exercises have been imported into three bins in the **Project** window. Twirl down the **Video** bin and drag **Track – Jump.avi** from the **Project** window to track **Video 1** in the **Timeline** window. Make sure to snap it all the way to the beginning of the sequence.

3. Next you are going to apply a very basic effect to the video clip. To see the available video effects, choose **Window > Workspace > Effects**.

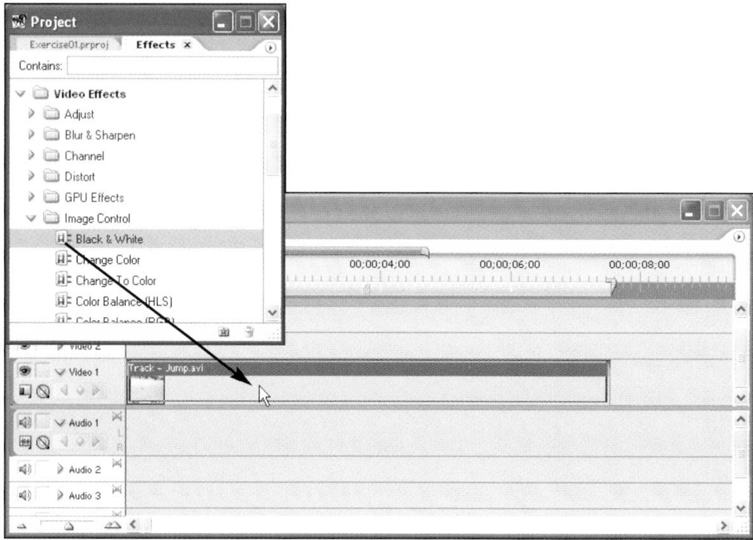

4. In the **Effects** window, twirl down the **Video Effects** folder, and then twirl down the **Image Control** subfolder. Drag the **Black & White** video effect on to **Track – Jump.avi** in the **Timeline** window. Play the sequence in the **Program** view to preview the effect. As the name implies, the video is now black and white.

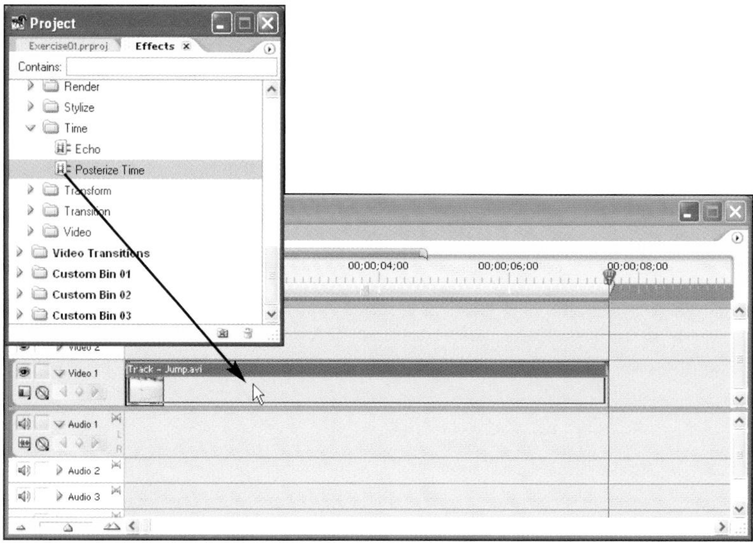

5. Scroll to the bottom of the **Effects** window, twirl down the **Time** subfolder, and drag **Posterize Time** onto the same video clip.

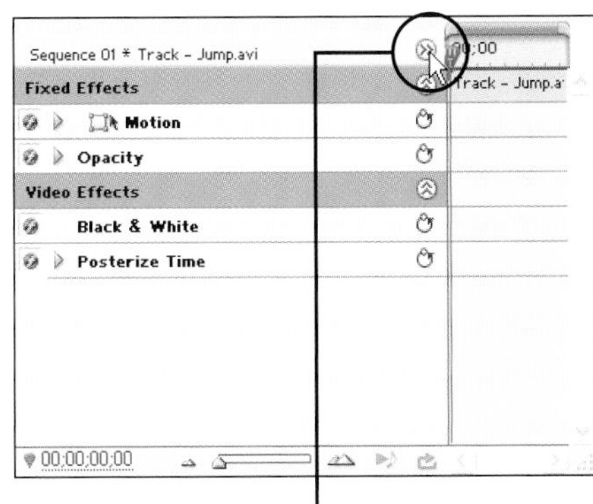

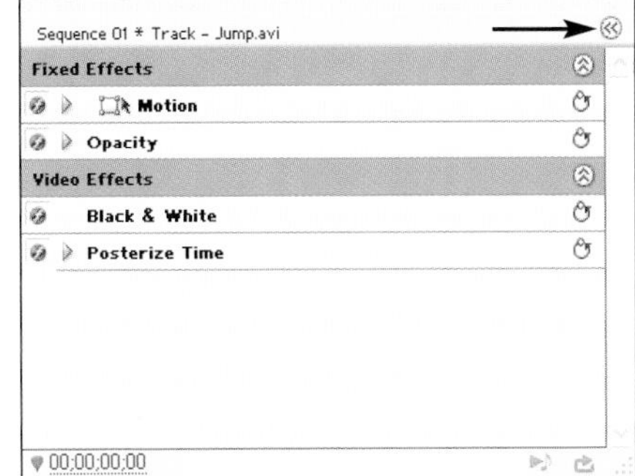

Click the Show/Hide Timeline View button to hide the keyframe area.

6. Select the clip in the **Timeline** window. In the **Effect Controls** window, click the **Show/Hide Timeline View** button. This will "collapse" the keyframe area in the **Effect Controls**. This can help make the effects options and value sliders easier to see.

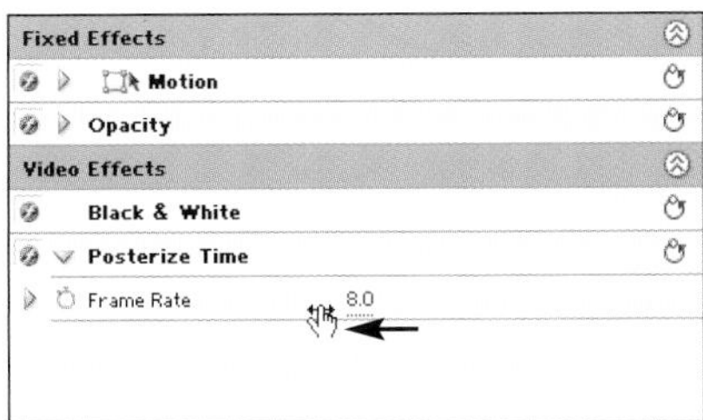

7. With the clip still selected in the **Effect Controls** window, twirl down the effect options for **Posterize Time**. Click the **Frame Rate** value, type in **8**, and press **Enter**. Or, you can change the value by holding down the mouse button and dragging the value to the left until it is **8.0**.

Note: *Notice that in the* ***Effect Controls*** *window there are no twirl-down options for the* ***Black & White*** *video effect. Some effects, such as this one, have no options to customize. What you see is what you get.*

8. Play the sequence in the **Program** view to preview the effect. The **Posterize Time** reduces the frame rate to eight frames per second, so the video appears to "stutter."

Note: *Did you notice that the preview was in full color instead of black and white? Some effects, such as* ***Posterize Time****, ignore any prior effects. In this case, Premiere Pro renders the* ***Black & White*** *effect, and then renders the* ***Posterize Time*** *effect. However, the result shows only the* ***Posterize Time*** *effect, because the previous effect is ignored. This is a perfect opportunity to reorder the effects to resolve this issue.*

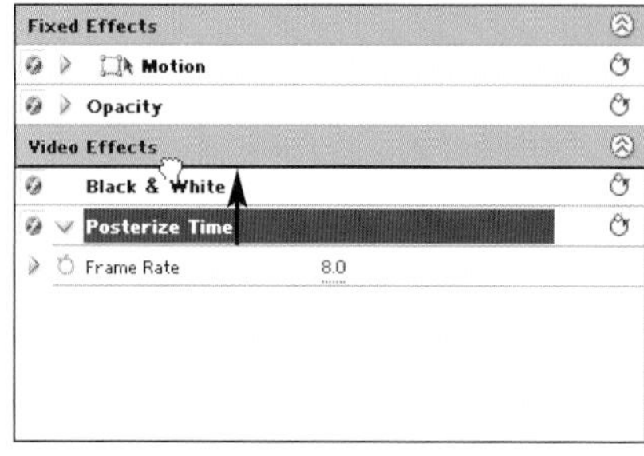

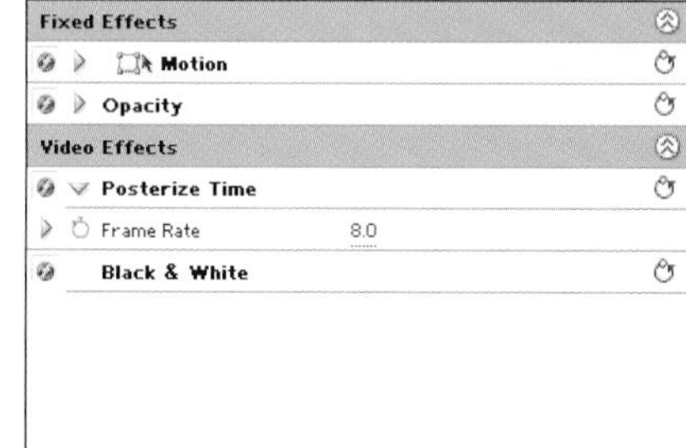

A thin black line represents the new position of the video effect.

Posterize Time is applied, and then Black & White.

9. To reorder the rendering of effects, in the **Effect Controls** window, click the **Posterize Time** effect name, and drag it to the top of the **Video Effects** list, just above the **Black & White** effect name.

Tip: *When you drag a video effect to reorder it, a thin black line indicates where the new effect will be placed. Users who are familiar with other Adobe application will recognize this feature.*

---

10. Play the sequence in the **Program** view to preview the effect change. Premiere Pro renders the **Posterize Time** effect first, and then adds the **Black & White** effect.

Video effects can be shuffled and reshuffled in any order that you want. Keep in mind that many effects will look the same no matter what order they are rendered in.

---

11. Save this project and keep it open before moving on to the next exercise.

2. Creating a Freeze Frame

Another type of video effect that is very simple to create in Premiere Pro is a freeze-frame. In a freeze-frame, one frame of a video clip is frozen, and the video appears motionless, like a still image. In Premiere Pro terms, this is called a **frame hold**. This exercise builds upon the previous exercise.

1. If the previous exercise is still open, skip to step 2. If Premiere Pro is not running, launch it and click **Open Project** at the **Welcome Screen**. Navigate to the **c:\Premiere Pro HOT\Chapter11** folder, select **Exercise02.prproj**, and click **Open**.

2. The goal of this exercise is to let the video play for a few seconds, and then freeze the video when the snowboarder is in midair. The first step is to move the current time indicator to the frame you want to freeze. Play the sequence and stop it when the snowboarder reaches the apex of his jump. In this example, I chose **00;00;04;19**.

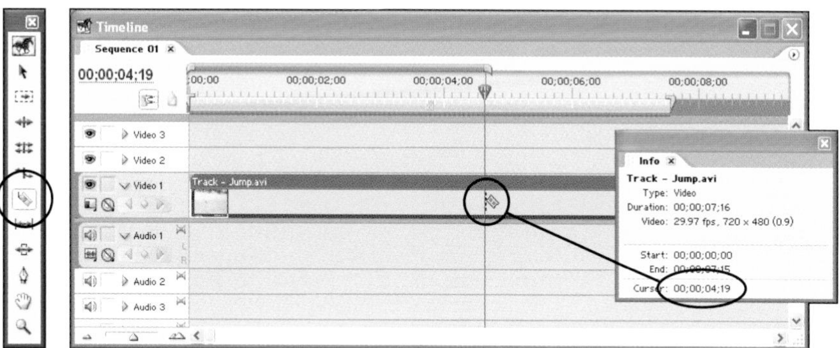

3. Now you need to split the video clip into two separate clips: the moving video and the frozen video. To split the clip, select the **Razor** tool from the **Toolbox**. Hover the **Razor** over the clip, at the location you want to split. In this case, hover the **Razor** at **00;00;04;19** and click once to split the clip. Use the **Info** window as a guide to make sure you are splitting at the proper frame.

4. When you're done using the **Razor** tool, choose the default **Selection** tool in the **Toolbox**. (But you didn't need to be told that, by now, right?)

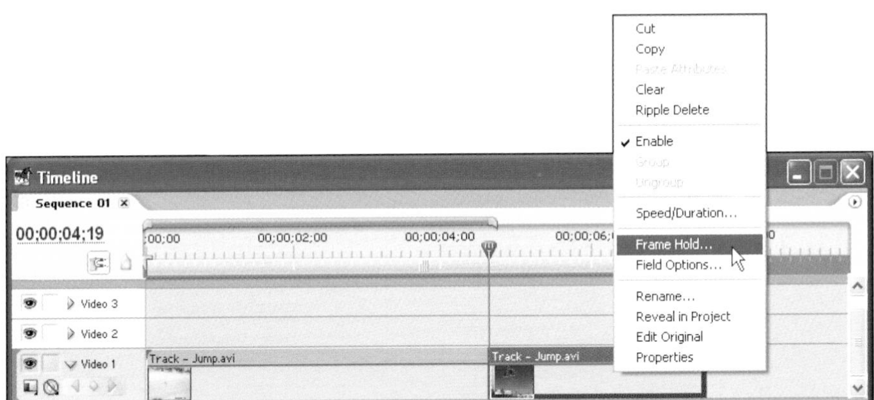

5. There are now two clips on the **Timeline**. You are going to freeze the second clip. Right-click the second clip in the **Timeline** and choose **Frame Hold** from the shortcut menu.

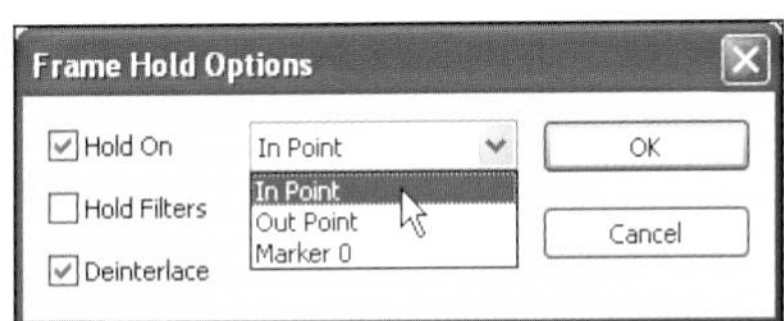

6. You can choose to hold (freeze) the frame at one of three positions: **In Point**, **Out Point**, or clip **Marker 0**. (You haven't learned that last one yet.) In this case, you want to hold on the **In** point of the second clip (the same frame you razored), so choose **In Point** from the drop-down menu. Check the **Hold On** box to enable to frame hold effect. Also check the **Deinterlace** box to deinterlace the video. Click **OK**.

***Note:** See the "Frame Hold Options" sidebar at the end of this exercise for a complete description of the frame hold options.*

7. Play the sequence in the **Program** view to preview the frame hold. The video should play and then freeze at the **In** point of the second clip.

It doesn't get any easier than that! The key to creating a frame hold, where the video plays and then freezes, is to split the clip after it's on the Timeline.

8. Save this project and keep it open before moving on to the next exercise.

NOTE | Frame Hold Options

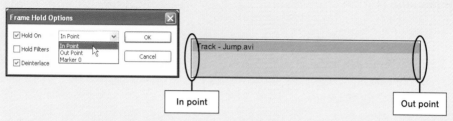

Hold On: This box must be checked in order for the effect to be enabled. The drop-down menu to the right lets you choose which frame to hold. **In Point** is the first frame of the clip, and **Out Point** is the last frame of the clip.

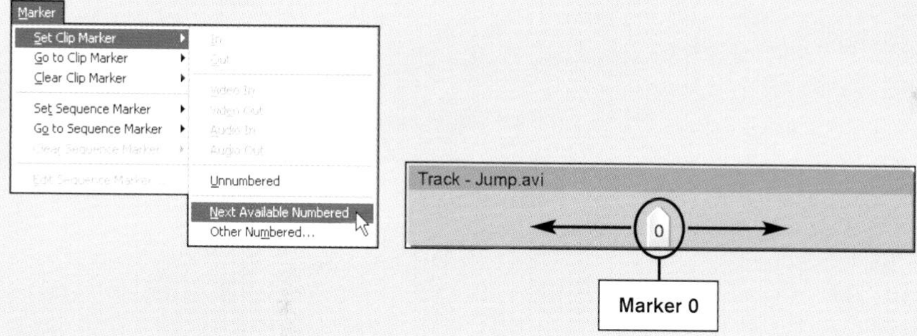

You are not limited to just those two points however; you can also add a clip marker on *any* frame of video, and choose to hold on **Marker 0**. To add a clip marker, move the current time indicator to the frame you want to mark, select the clip, and choose **Marker > Set Clip Marker > Next Available Numbered**.

Hold Filters: If this box is checked, any keyframed filters will be frozen. The filter will still be applied, but the filter values will not change over time if you've added keyframes. (Notice the vestigial use of the word *filter*!)

Deinterlace: If this box is checked, one field of an interlaced video clip is doubled, and the other field is removed, to prevent combing artifacts. This sounds technical, but it's a fancy way of saying, "prevent my video from flickering." That's oversimplifying things a bit, but you can always turn this option off and then back on to see if you notice a difference. The flicker will be most apparent in video clips that show thin lines and fast movement.

You are left with this frame-hold caveat: unlike still images, which can have a (nearly) infinite duration, frame holds can last only as long as the clip they are applied to. If you create a frame hold on a 3-second clip, your frame hold can play for only 3 seconds.

3. Animating Fixed Effects

You were introduced to fixed effects in Chapter 7, "*Still Images and Fixed Effects*." You became friends with keyframes in Chapter 10, "*Audio Effects*." Now it's time to combine the two, by animating fixed effects with keyframes. In this exercise, you will animate the scale property of a title.

1. If the previous exercise is still open, skip to Step 2. If Premiere Pro is not running, launch it and click **Open Project** at the **Welcome Screen**. Navigate to the **c:\Premiere Pro HOT\Chapter11** folder, select **Exercise03.prproj**, and click **Open**.

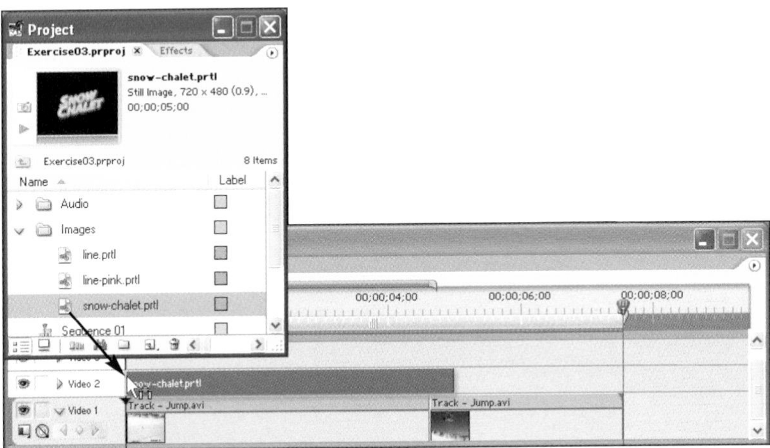

2. First, you'll add a title to the sequence. Click the **Project** tab to bring it to the foreground. Twirl down the **Images** bin and drag the title **snow-chalet.prtl** to track **Video 2**. Snap the title to the start of the sequence. Play the sequence in the **Program** view to preview the title.

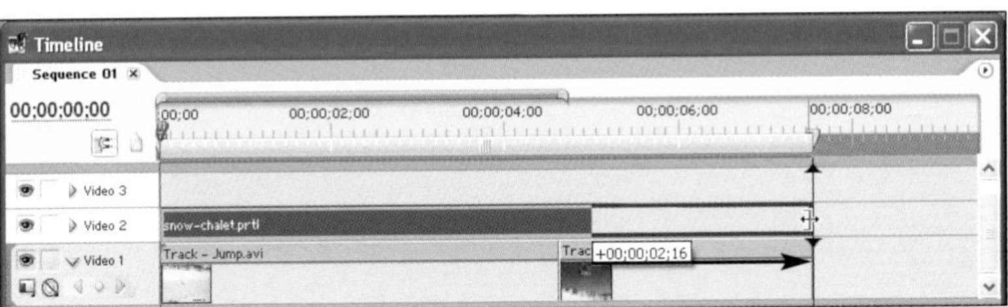

3. Hover the mouse over the **Out** point of the title and use the **Trim Out** pointer to snap the **Out** point of the title to the **Out** point of the second clip in track **Video 1**.

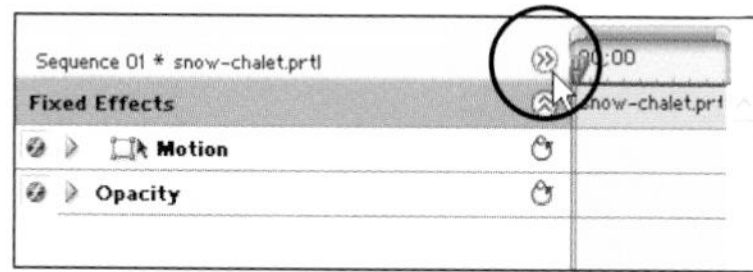

4. Select the title in the **Timeline** to view its effect properties in the **Effect Controls** window. Since you will be creating keyframes, it may help to view the keyframe area in the **Effect Controls** window. Click the **Show/Hide Timeline View** button in the **Effect Controls** window to "expand" the keyframe area.

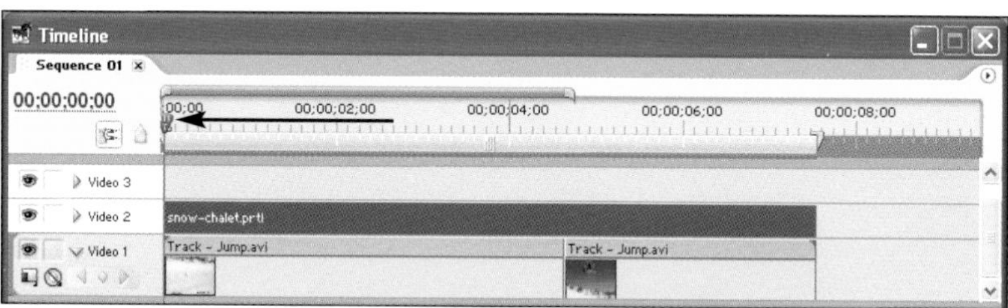

5. You are going to create two scale keyframes, to make the title grow over time. Remember the *keyframe slogan*: Move current time indicator, then create keyframe. In this case, you want to create the first keyframe at the start of the clip. Select the title in the **Timeline**, and press **Home** on your keyboard to move the current time indicator to the **In** point of the title.

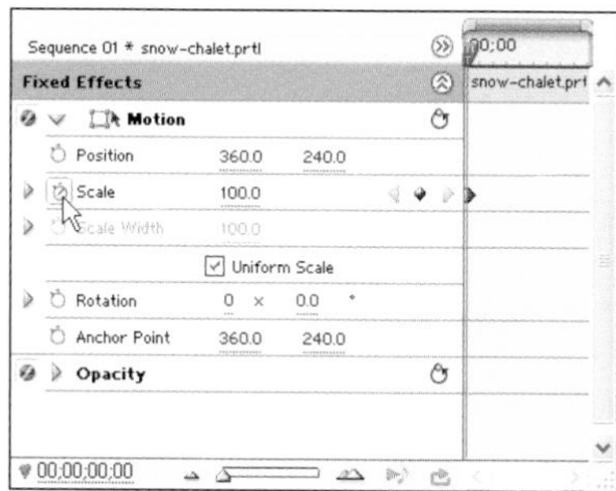

6. With the title still selected, twirl down the **Motion** properties in the **Effect Controls** window. Enable keyframe mode for the **Scale** property by clicking the **Toggle Animation** icon next to **Scale**.

Note: *In order to create keyframes, you must first enable keyframe mode by clicking the* ***Toggle Animation*** *icon. When you turn* ***Animation*** *mode on, a keyframe is created at the current time indicator.*

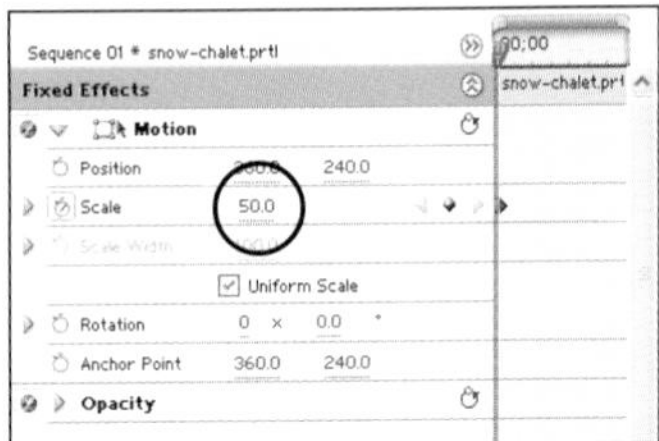

7. In this case, you want the title to grow over time, which means the value of the first **Scale** keyframe needs to be smaller than the value of the last **Scale** keyframe. To change the **Scale** value, click the value **100.0**, type in a new value of **50.0**, and press **Enter**.

Tip: There is more than one way to skin a... scale value. (Bad analogy, sorry.) You can also drag the value with the mouse button, or you could even twirl down the ***Scale*** *property and use the value slider, like you did with the* ***Volume*** *property in the previous chapter.*

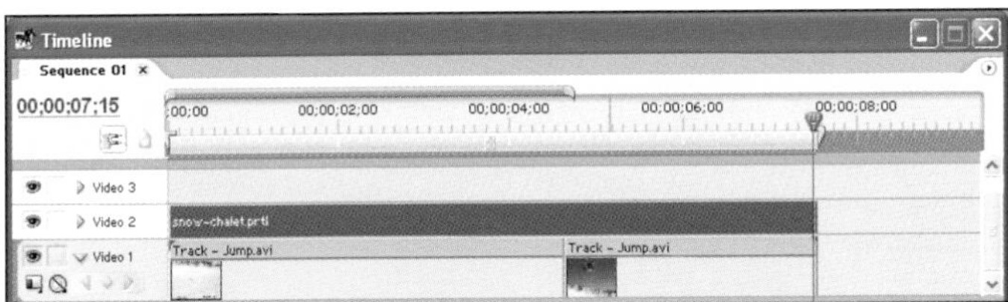

8. Now it's time to create the second keyframe. To move the current time indicator to the end of the clip, select the title on the **Timeline**, press **End** on the keyboard, and then tap **once** on the keyboard's **left arrow**.

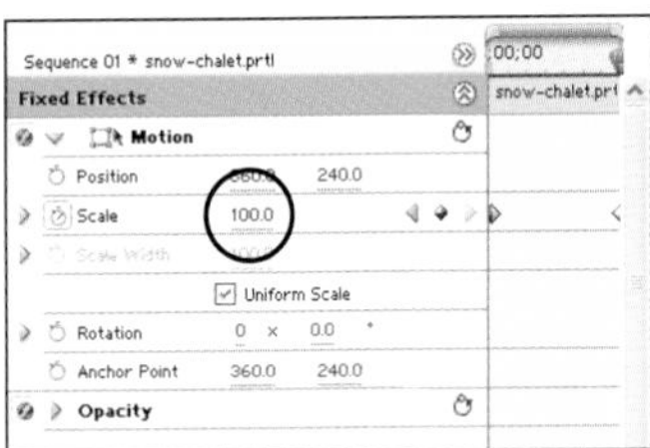

9. To create a second keyframe at the current time indicator, change the **Scale** value to **100.0**.

10. Play the sequence in the **Program** view to preview the changes. The title should slowly increase in scale over time.

In this exercise you created two keyframes–one on the first frame of the clip, and one on the last frame of the clip. Even though you did this with the Scale property, the idea is the same for any property that can be keyframed.

NOTE | End + Left Arrow

Why the need for the left arrow after the **End** key? Technically speaking, the **End** key doesn't move the current time indicator to the last frame of the clip. It actually moves the current time indicator to *immediately after* the clip. Weird? Definitely. Hopefully the following illustration will explain it all.

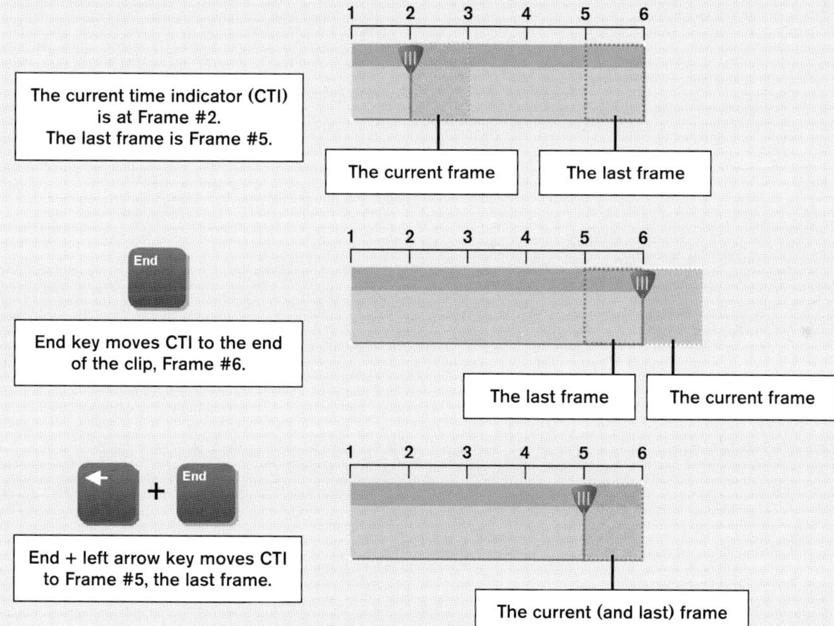

1 2 3 4 5 6
The current time indicator (CTI) is at Frame #2. The last frame is Frame #5.
The current frame
The last frame
End
End key moves CTI to the end of the clip, Frame #6.
The last frame
The current frame
End
End + left arrow key moves CTI to Frame #5, the last frame.
The current (and last) frame

Now you know *what* the **End + left arrow** keys do, but you may be wondering, "*Why* can't I just press the **End** key and be done?" If you don't press the left arrow key, your keyframe will be created one frame after the clip, which can lead to trouble.

Although Premiere Pro will let you create a keyframe anywhere on the Timeline, it doesn't mean you should! Keyframe organization is very important and can avert many potential problems. Since mantra and slogan are already taken, remember this **keyframe motto**: when adding a keyframe to the end of a clip, always press **End + left arrow**.

11. Save this project and keep it open before moving on to the next exercise.

MOVIE | keyframe_ease.mov

To learn about the advanced keyframe features available in Premiere Pro, check out **keyframe_ease.mov** from the **movies** folder on the **Premiere Pro HOT** DVD.

4. Saving Effect Presets

A handy feature built into Premiere Pro is the capability to save effects as presets. Once you do the work of tweaking an effect to your liking, you can save the effect's properties and its keyframes as a preset. Your preset is listed in the Effects window, and you can apply it like any other video effect for all of your future projects. In this exercise, you will learn how to save a video effect as a preset, plus you'll learn two very useful tips along the way.

1. If the previous exercise is still open, skip to step 2. If Premiere Pro is not running, launch it and click **Open Project** at the **Welcome Screen**. Navigate to the **c:\Premiere Pro HOT\Chapter11** folder, select **Exercise04.prproj**, and click **Open**.

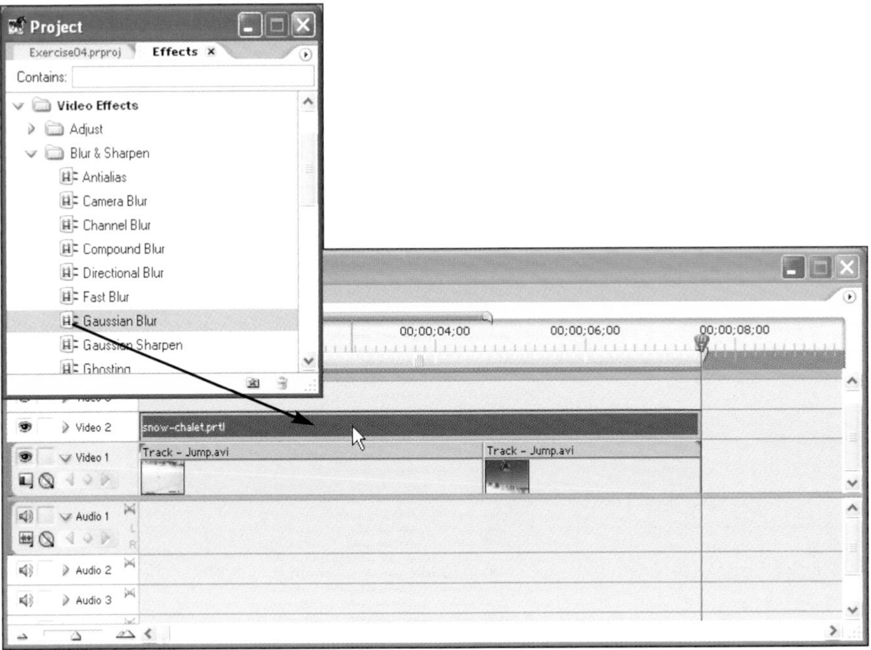

2. In the **Effects** window, twirl down the **Video Effects** and **Blur & Sharpen** folders. Drag the **Gaussian Blur** effect onto **snow-chalet.prtl** in track **Video 2** of the **Timeline**.

Note: *Due to third-party plug-ins and/or other Adobe applications installed on your computer, the video effects available to you may differ from those shown in this book.*

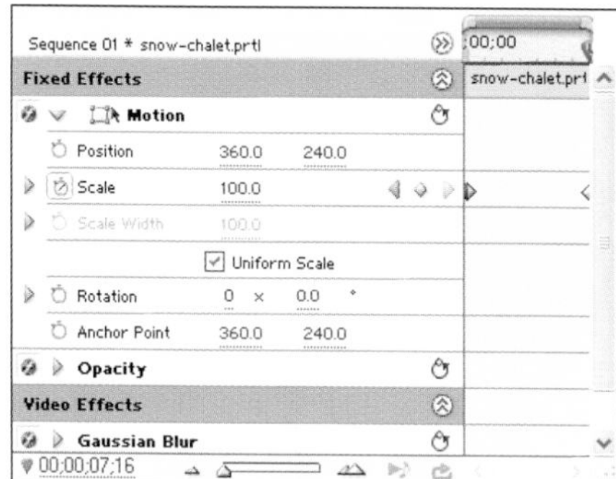

The motion properties expanded.

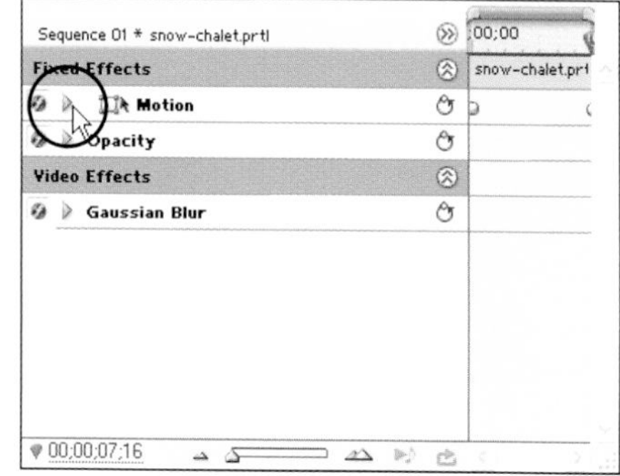

The motion properties collapsed.

3. Select the title on the **Timeline** to view its effect controls. (If you don't see the **Effect Controls** window, choose **Window > Workspace > Effects**.) The title's **Motion** properties may still be expanded from the previous exercise, hogging up the **Effect Controls** window. Click the **Motion** twirl-up arrow to collapse the **Motion** properties.

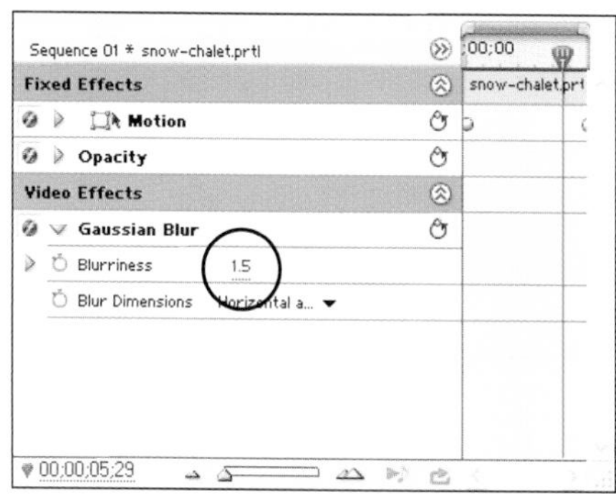

4. In the **Effect Controls** window, twirl down the **Gaussian Blur** properties. Click the **Blurriness** value, type in **1.5**, and press **Enter**.

Tip: *The* ***Gaussian Blur*** *is a gorgeous blur. (You are officially a Premiere geek when you have "favorite blurs.") Adding a very subtle blur to titles will reduce the "video harshness" of your text. Because titles are very crisp, they end up looking computer-generated. A blur effect will soften the title and prevent it from screaming out, "Hey! I was made on a computer!"*

5. Play the sequence in the **Program** view to preview the blur. Because it's a small blur amount, it may be hard to see when zoomed out of the **Program** view. To zoom in the **Program** view monitor, click the **View Zoom** level (currently says **Fit**) and change it to **100%**.

*Tip: Normally the **Program** view zoom is set to **Fit**, which shrinks the sequence to fit in the **Monitor** window. Changing the zoom level to **100%** displays the sequence at its real size. (However, you cannot visualize the whole screen at once.)*

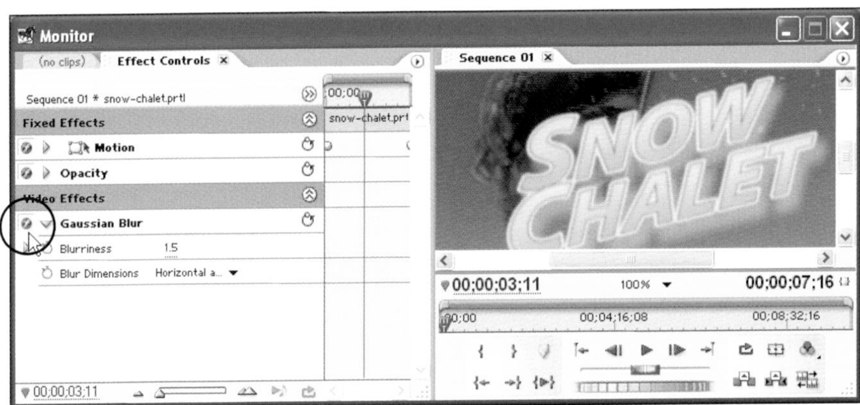

6. With the **View Zoom** level set to **100%**, drag the current time indicator to **00;00;03;11**. Toggle the **Gaussian Blur** effect on and off several times, by clicking the effect toggle.

*As you toggle the effect, try to detect the subtle **Gaussian Blur** in the **Program** view. When the effect is toggled on, the words will be slightly blurry. Not much, but just enough to soften the edges.*

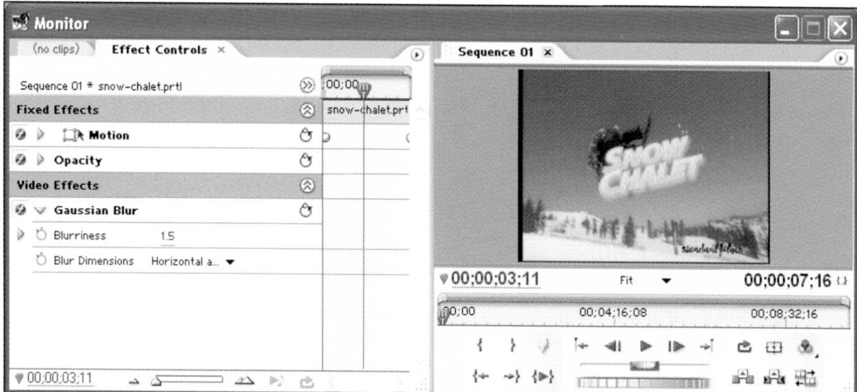

7. After viewing the effect, leave the effect toggle on and change the **Program** view **Zoom Level** back to **Fit**.

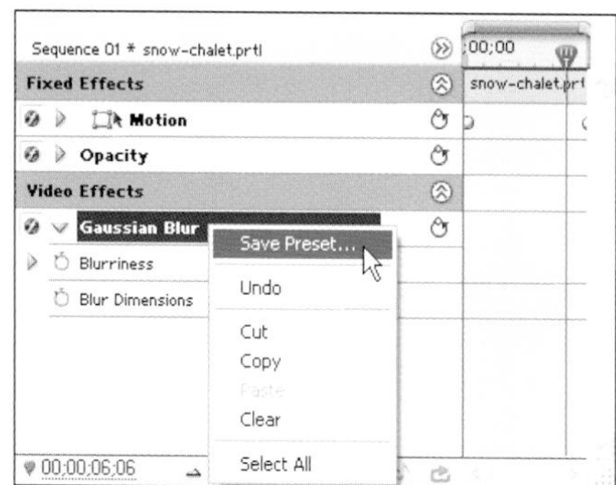

8. Now that you have tweaked the effect to your liking, you can save it as a preset to be used again and again. In the **Effect Controls** window, right-click the **Gaussian Blur** effect, and choose **Save Preset** from the shortcut menu.

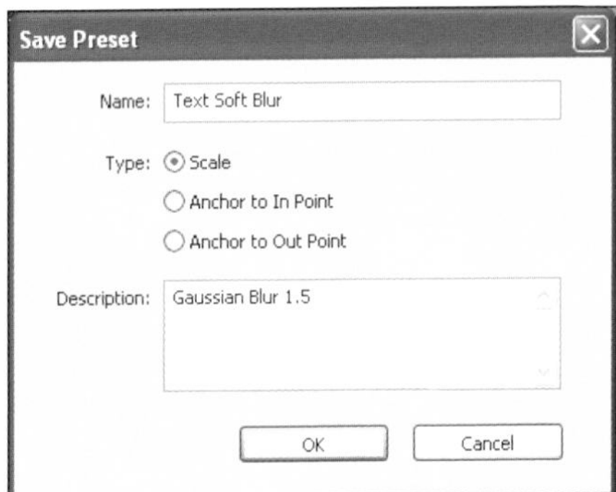

9. In the **Save Preset** window, click in the **Name** box and name your preset **Text Soft Blur**. In the **Description** box, type **Gaussian Blur 1.5**. Click **OK**.

Note: *The three* ***Type*** *options apply to presets saved with keyframes, which is described in the next section.*

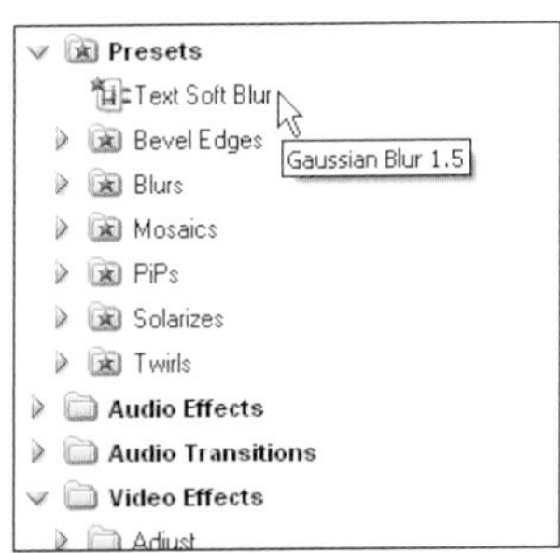

10. Scroll to the top of the **Effects** window and twirl down the **Presets** folders. You can now see your effect preset listed there. Hover your mouse over the effect, and the yellow pop-up box displays the description you gave in Step 9.

Tip: *This effect is now a permanent part of your* ***Effects*** *window. You can apply this effect in this or any future project. When applied, the blur value will automatically be set to* ***1.5.*** *If you are unhappy with a preset, you can right-click it in the* ***Presets*** *folder and choose* ***Delete*** *from the shortcut menu.*

This exercise demonstrated how easy it is to save an effect. These presets can save you a lot of time when applying effects that are very complex, because all of the effect properties are automatically changed to their preset values. Also in this exercise you learned how to soften your titles, as well as zoom in the ***Program*** *view.*

---

11. Save this project and keep it open before moving on to the next exercise.

Keyframe Presets

In the previous exercise, you saved a simple preset based on a video effect. You can also save presets with keyframe positions. Since creating keyframes can be tedious work, this is a huge time-saving feature. However, this does present a unique problem: when you save a keyframe preset on a short clip, where should the keyframes be placed when you apply them to a longer clip? And what about copying keyframes from long clips onto short clips? Where do the keyframes go?

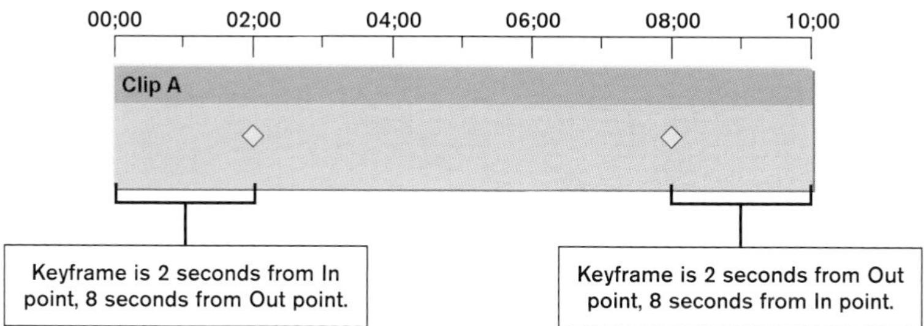

Picture Clip A on the Timeline, 10 seconds long. Clip A has two keyframes. The first keyframe is at 02;00 seconds, and the second keyframe is at 08;00 seconds. Since you will be creating these keyframes again in future projects, you decide to save them as a preset. When you save the keyframes as a preset, you have to select a preset **Type**, which determines how Premiere Pro will handle the keyframes when they're applied to clips of different sizes.

Note: Type is a very vague term that doesn't explain much. The Premiere Pro designers should have called this option **Keyframe Position.** Each of the three **Type** options specify where the keyframes will be placed in relation to the clip **In** point and/or **Out** point.

The **Scale** option scales the distance of the keyframes from the **In** and **Out** points. In the original 10-second clip, the keyframes are 2 seconds from the **In** and **Out** points. When applied to a clip with half the duration, the keyframe distances are scaled proportionately.

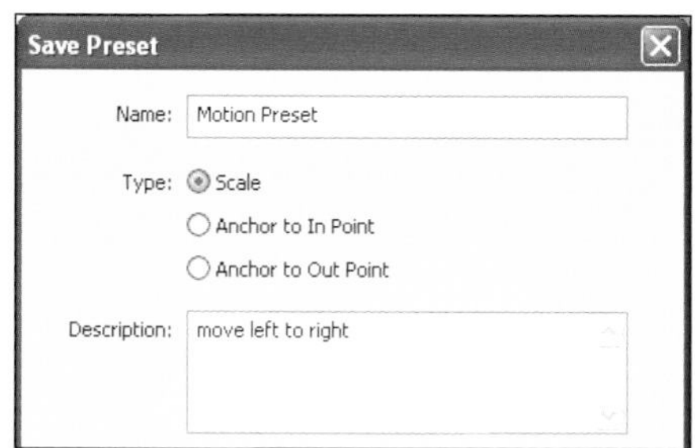

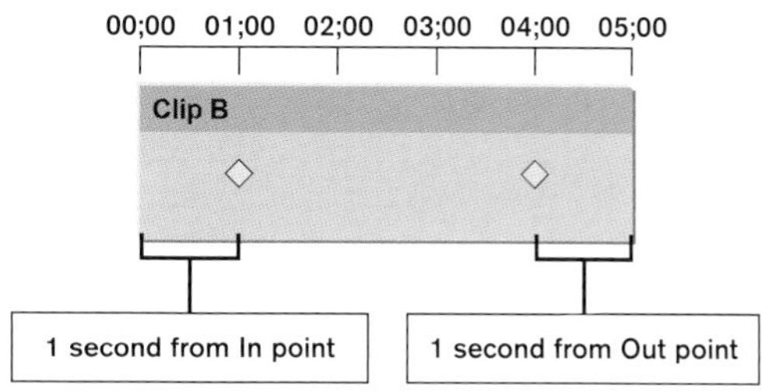

For example, Clip B is 5 seconds long, only half as long as Clip A. When the keyframe preset is applied to Clip B, the keyframes are placed 1 second away from the **In** and **Out** points. Since the clip is half as long as the original clip, the keyframe durations (relative to the **In** and **Out** points) are scaled half as long. Keep in mind that this only affects where on the **Timeline** the keyframes are placed. The keyframe values are never changed.

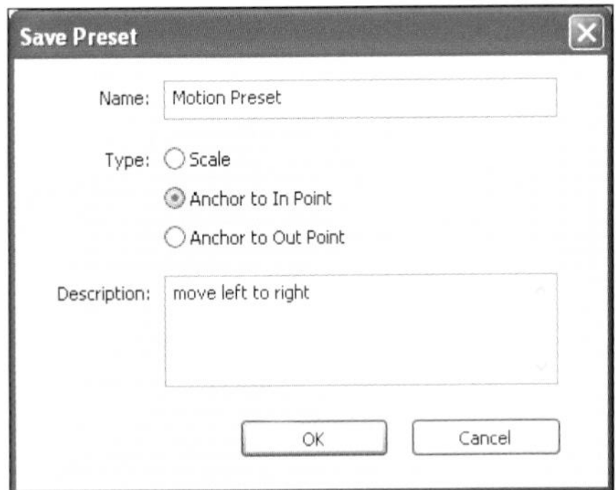

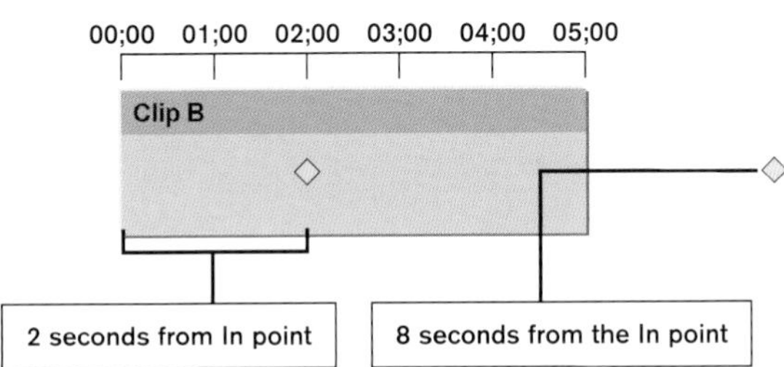

If you choose **Anchor to In Point**, the keyframes are placed based on their distance relative to the original **In** point. The first keyframe is 2 seconds from the **In** point (as it was in Clip A), and the second keyframe is 8 seconds from the **In** point (as it was in Clip A). Unfortunately, this places the second keyframe well past the end of the clip.

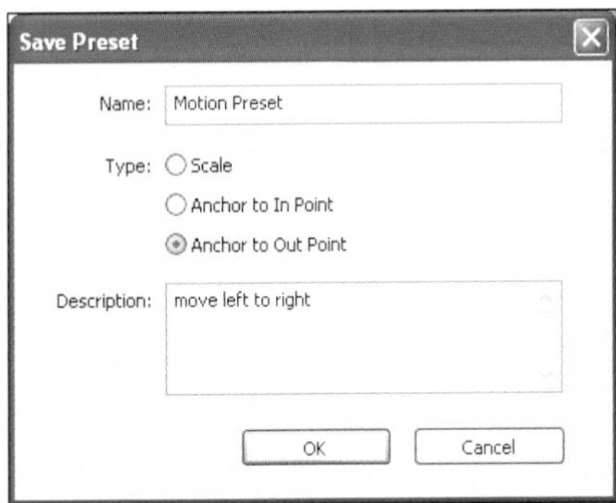

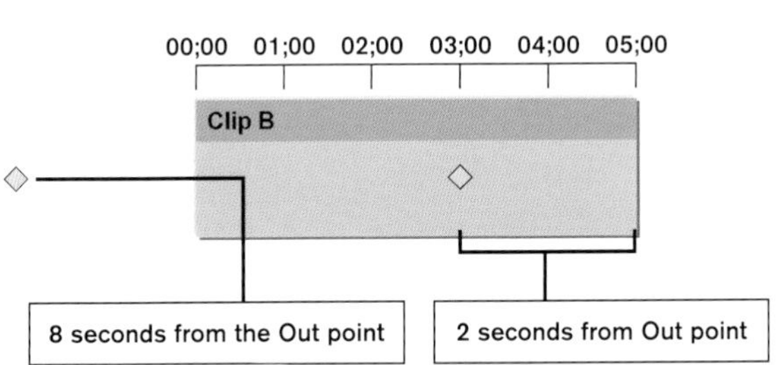

If you choose **Anchor to Out Point**, the keyframes are placed based on their distance relative to the original **Out** point. The first keyframe is 8 seconds from the **Out** point, and the second keyframe is 2 seconds from the **Out** point. (This places the first keyframe a few seconds before the beginning of the clip, which can lead to headaches!)

Which **Type** setting should you choose? **Anchor to In Point** is best for keyframe effects that happen near the beginning of a clip, such as fade-ins or flying in a title. **Anchor to Out Point** is best for the exact opposite–keyframes that happen near the **Out** point. When it doubt, use **Scale**, which will proportionately change the location of the keyframes, relative to the clip size.

Enough reading about it, it's time to create your own keyframe presets.

5. Saving Keyframe Presets

You've read all about it, and now it's time to practice creating your own keyframe presets. In this exercise, you will first create a pair of motion keyframes, and then you will apply the preset to another clip.

1. If the previous exercise is still open, skip to Step 2. If Premiere Pro is not running, launch it and click **Open Project** at the **Welcome Screen**. Navigate to the **c:\Premiere Pro HOT\Chapter11** folder, select **Exercise05.prproj**, and click **Open**.

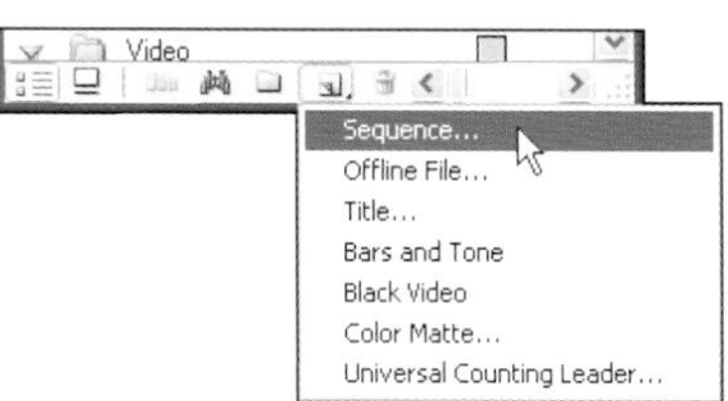

2. Click the **Project** tab to bring it to the foreground. At the bottom of the **Project** window, click the **New Item** icon, and choose **Sequence**.

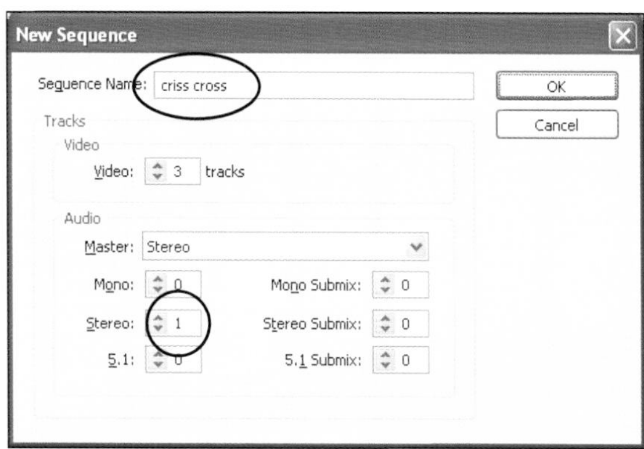

3. In the **New Sequence** window, type **criss cross** in the **Sequence Name** box. Under **Audio** tracks, reduce the number of **Stereo** tracks to **1**.

Note: *You will not be adding any audio to this sequence, so there's no need for any audio tracks. However, Premiere Pro requires that all sequences have at least one audio track.*

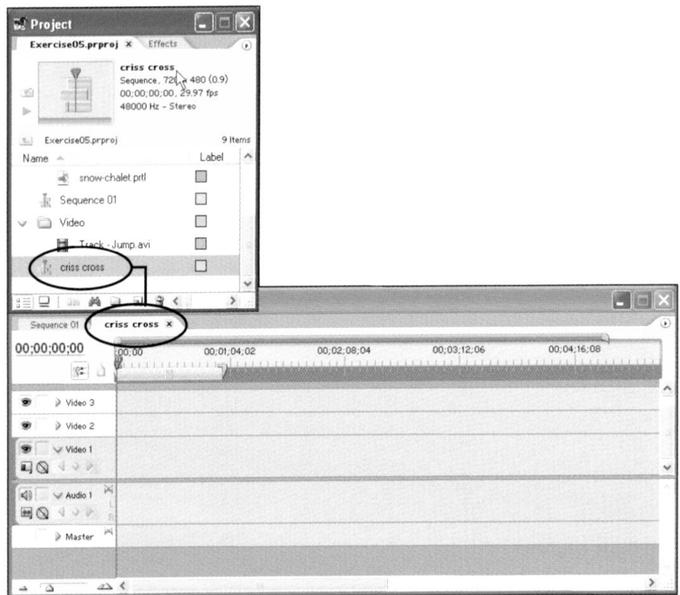

*The new sequence, **criss cross**, is shown in the **Project** window and as a tab along the top of the **Timeline** window. You can switch from sequence to sequence by clicking sequence tabs in the **Timeline** window.*

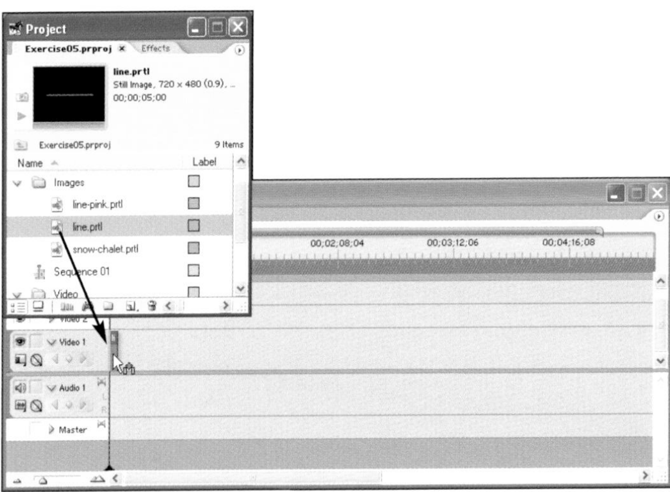

4. From the **Project** window **Images** bin, drag **line.prtl** to track **Video 1** in the new sequence. Make sure to snap the clip to the beginning of the sequence.

*Tip: This title is a straight line created in Premiere Pro's **Title Designer.** In fact, all of the images used in this chapter were created within the **Title Designer**. That means you don't need any other applications, such as Photoshop, to recreate these effects.*

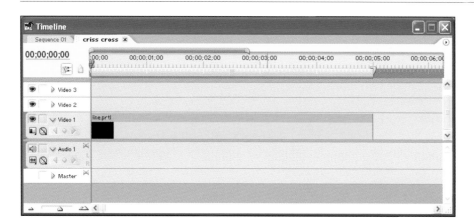

5. By default, the **Timeline** window is zoomed out very far on the new sequence. To automatically fit all of the clips (well, just one clip in this case) within the **Timeline** window, press the \ key on your keyboard.

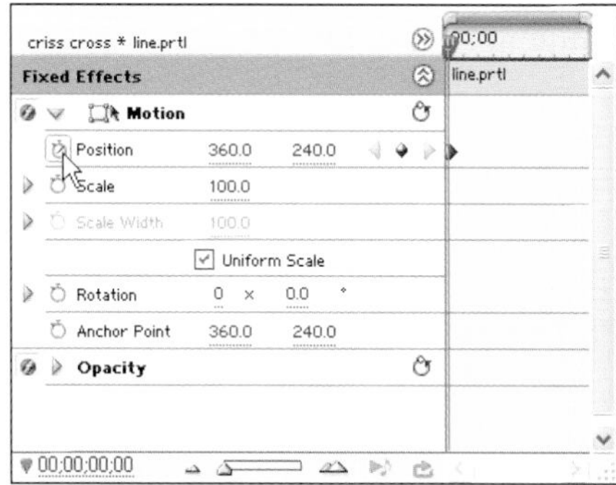

6. Select the clip on the **Timeline** to view its effect controls. In the **Effect Controls** window, twirl down the **Motion** properties. Press **Home** on the keyboard to move the current time indicator to the start of the clip. Enable keyframe mode for the **Position** property by clicking the **Toggle Animation** icon.

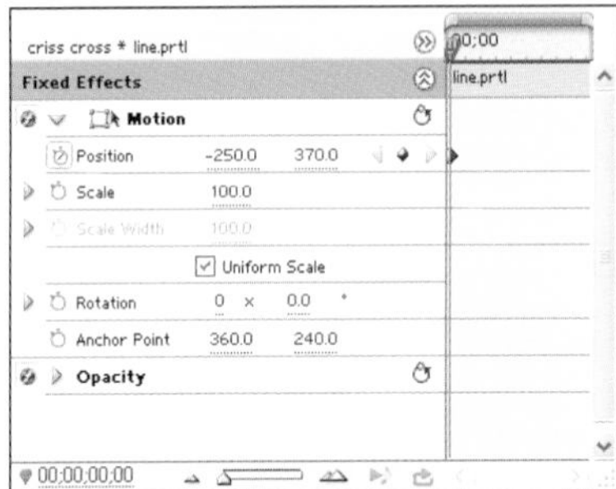

7. The object is to create two keyframes, to move the title from left to right across the screen. With the current time indicator still at the beginning of the clip, set the value of the first keyframe by typing in a value of **–250** for the first **Position** value and press **Enter**. In the second **Position** value, type **370** and press **Enter**.

Note: *The two position values are X,Y coordinates. The first value controls the horizontal position, and the second value controls the vertical position.*

8. Press **End** on the keyboard and then tap the **left arrow** key once to move the current time indicator to the last frame of the clip.

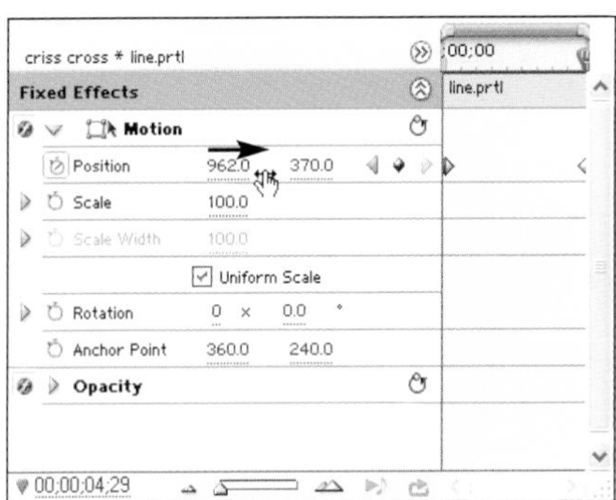

9. Instead of typing in a new **Position** value, don't forget that you can also drag the value. To do this, hover your mouse over the first **Position** value (horizontal value) until you see the drag pointer, hold down the **Shift** key and drag the number to the right until the clip is entirely off the screen. In this exercise, I used a value of **962.0**.

Typing in the number is quicker. But rarely will you know the exact number. Dragging the value lets you see the change in the ***Program*** *view as you drag.*

*Tip: Holding down the **Shift** key increases the increments by 10 instead of by 1. Since the clip had quite a large distance to traverse, holding down the **Shift** key saved a lot of mouse dragging.*

10. Play the sequence in the **Program** view to watch the position keyframes you created.

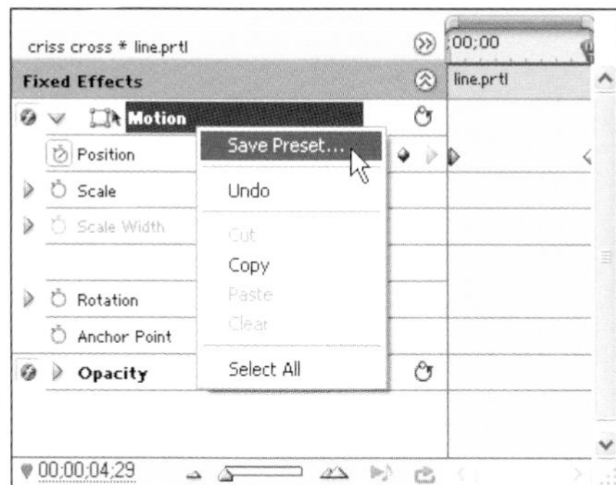

11. In the **Effect Controls** window, right-click the **Motion** property and choose **Save Preset** from the shortcut menu.

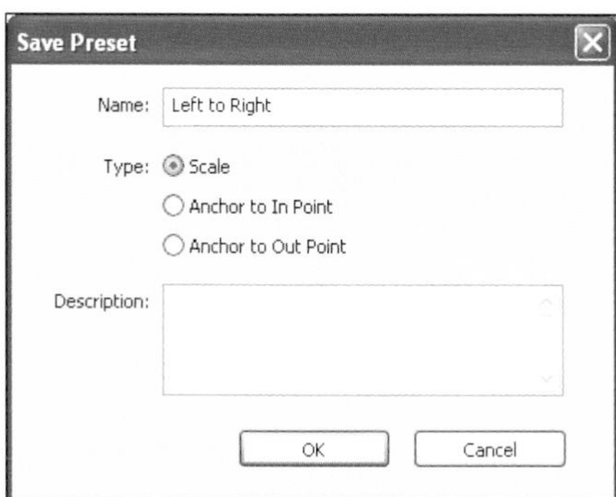

12. In the **Save Preset** window, name the preset **Left to Right**. Select **Scale** and click **OK**.

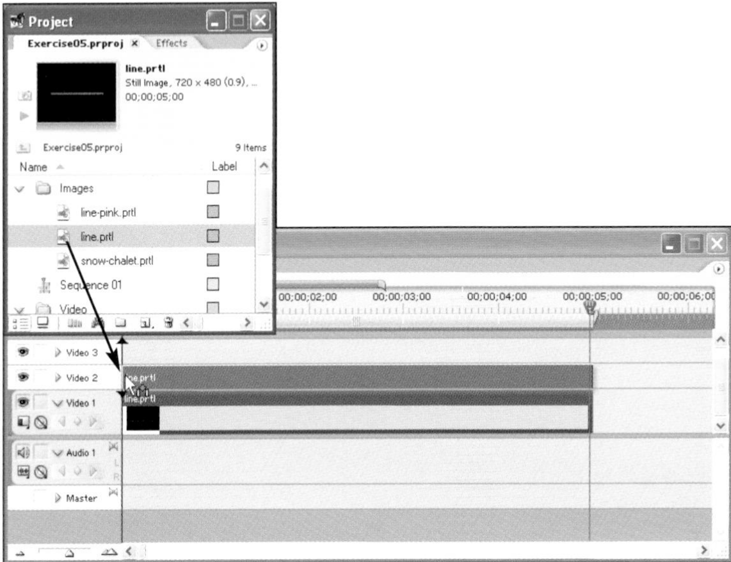

13. From the **Project** window **Images** bin, drag **line.prtl** to track **Video 2**. Snap it to the start of the sequence.

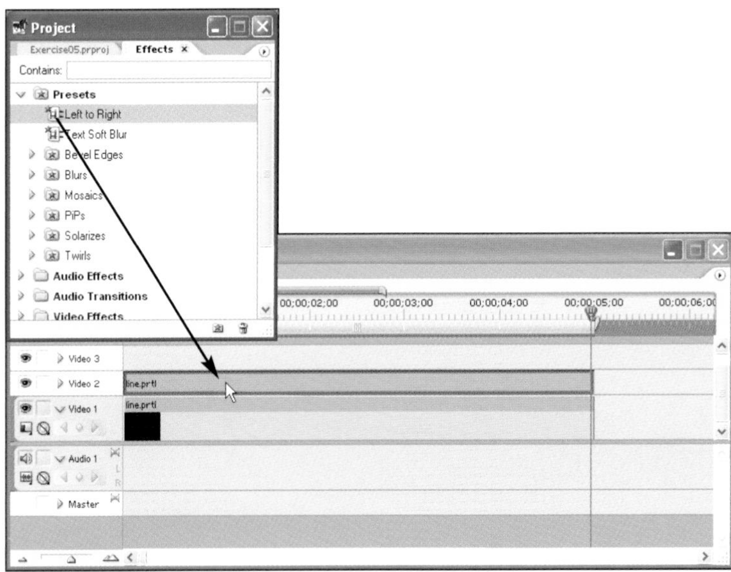

14. Click the **Effects** tab to bring it to the foreground. Twirl down the **Presets** folder to view its contents. Drag the **Left to Right** preset to **line.prtl** in track **Video 2**.

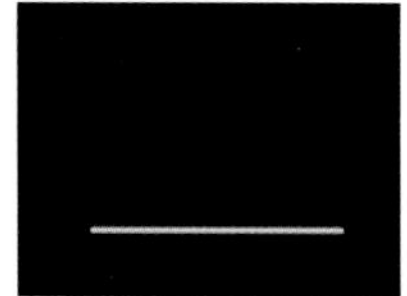

15. Play the sequence in the **Program** view to preview the effects.

Because both clips have the exact same position keyframes, they are displayed on top of each other. This gives the appearance of only one line moving across the screen, when in reality it's two overlapping lines.

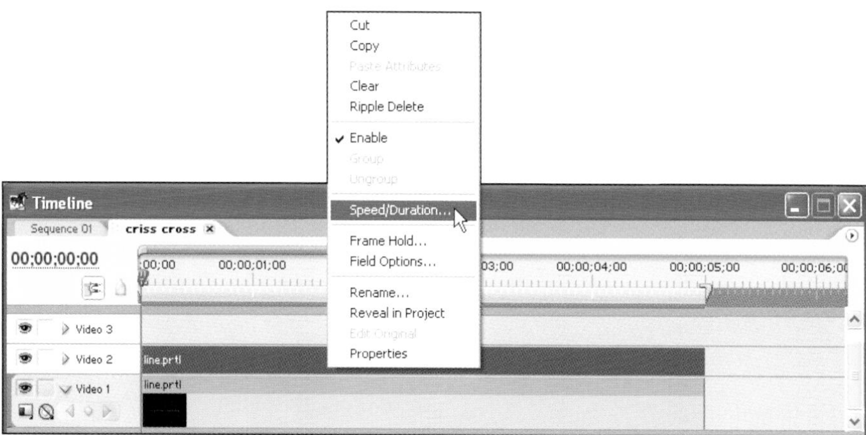

16. Right-click the title in track **Video 2**. From the shortcut menu, choose **Speed/Duration**.

17. In the **Clip Speed / Duration** window, check **Reverse Speed**.

Tip: *Reversing the speed of a clip is a quick way to reverse the motion keyframes. Now the clip will move left to right, because it is playing backwards. Users who are familiar with After Effects will recognize this as a workaround for Time Reverse Keyframes.*

18. Play the sequence in the **Program** view to preview the effects.

Now the lines mirror each other. One moves left to right, and the other (the clip playing in reverse) moves right to left.

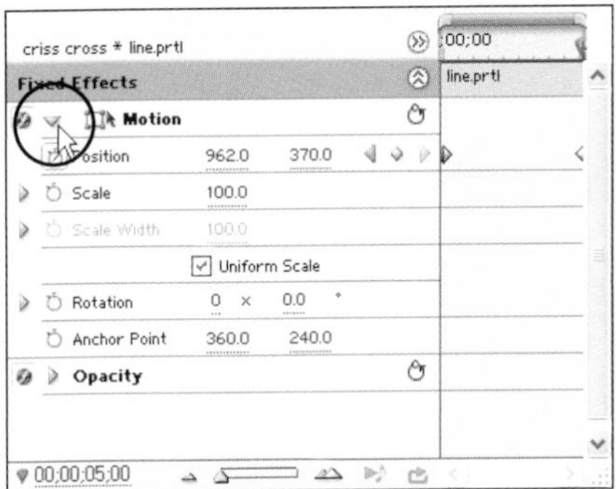

19. You can also modify keyframes that were applied with a preset, as you would any other keyframes. To do this, select the title in track **Video 2** to view its **Effect Controls** and twirl down the **Motion** properties in the **Effect Controls** window.

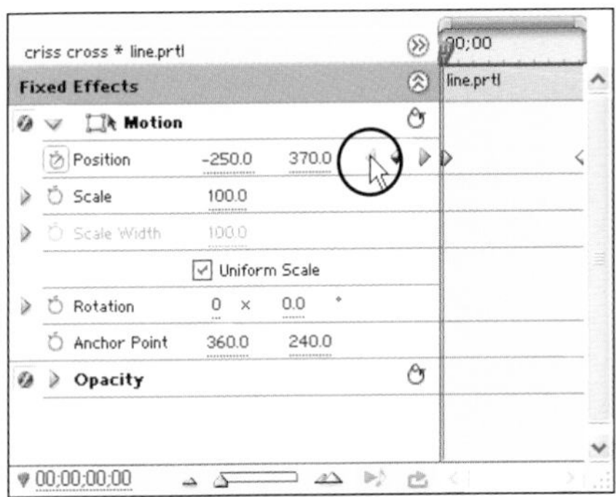

20. To modify an existing keyframe, the current time indicator must be placed exactly on the keyframe. In the **Effect Controls** windows, click the **Previous Keyframe** navigation button to snap the current time indicator to the first keyframe. You may have to click more than once.

Note: *If the current time indicator is positioned before the first keyframe, you should click the* ***Next Keyframe*** *navigation button. To indicate that the current time indicator is positioned over a keyframe, the* ***Add/Remove Keyframe*** *diamond is shaded dark* ◆ *.*

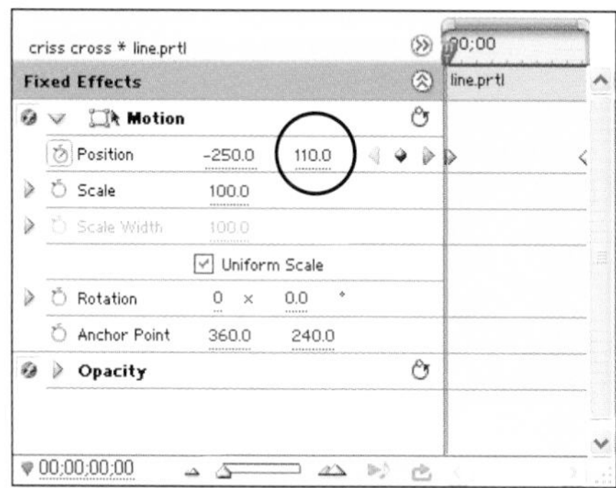

21. With the title clip in track **Video 2** still selected, click the **Position Y value** (the second value) and type in **110.0**.

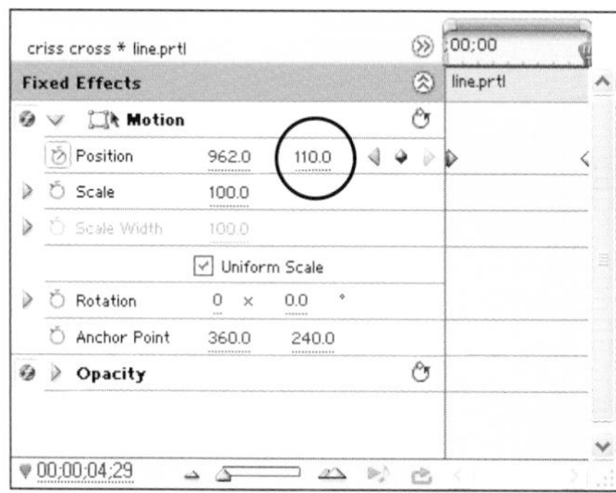

22. Use the **Next Keyframe** navigation button to snap the current time indicator to the last keyframe. Click the **Position Y value** again and type in **110.0**.

23. Play the sequence in the **Program** view to preview the changes. The lines should move towards each other but on different vertical planes.

Okay, this lesson was a lot more than just saving keyframe presets. You also learned how to reverse the speed of clips and practiced modifying keyframes. And, to be honest, you can never have enough practice modifying keyframes, which is one of the most difficult tasks in Premiere Pro. Of course, by now you are a (Premiere) pro at it. (Pun!)

24. Save this project and keep it open before moving on to the next exercise.

MOVIE | keyframe_presets.mov

To learn more about creating keyframes presets, check out **keyframe_presets.mov** from the **movies** folder on the **Premiere Pro HOT** DVD.

NOTE | Keyframe Presets vs. Paste Attributes

There are two ways to copy keyframes from one clip to another clip. In the previous chapter you learned how to paste attributes from one clip to another. In the previous exercise, you learned to use keyframe presets. What's the difference?

Keyframe presets are saved in the Effects window, and they stay in the Effects window until you decide to delete them. Copying attributes is much more transient. The attributes stay in memory only until you turn off the computer, or you copy something else to Windows' clipboard. Advantage: keyframe presets.

When you copy and paste attributes, you are pasting *all* of the effects and attributes of a clip. Keyframe presets can only save one attribute or effect at a time. Advantage: pasting attributes.

In the end, each will work in different situations. If you want to save a very complex effect to be used over and over in other projects, save a keyframe preset. If you want to copy every property of a clip and apply it to another clip in the same project, use the Paste Attributes command.

6. Changing Motion in the Program View

So far in this chapter you have learned several different ways of changing motion properties in the Effect Controls window. You can also change motion properties by clicking and dragging a clip in the Program view. The goal of this exercise is to teach you how to change motion in the Program view, as well as tie together all of the exercises of this chapter into one grand sequence.

1. If the previous exercise is still open, skip to Step 2. If Premiere Pro is not running, launch it and click **Open Project** at the **Welcome Screen**. Navigate to the **c:\Premiere Pro HOT\Chapter11** folder, select **Exercise06.prproj**, and click **Open**.

Note: *The sort order of your* ***Project*** *window may appear different than the screen shots in this exercise. Premiere re-alphabetizes the order of source clips whenever a project is opened.*

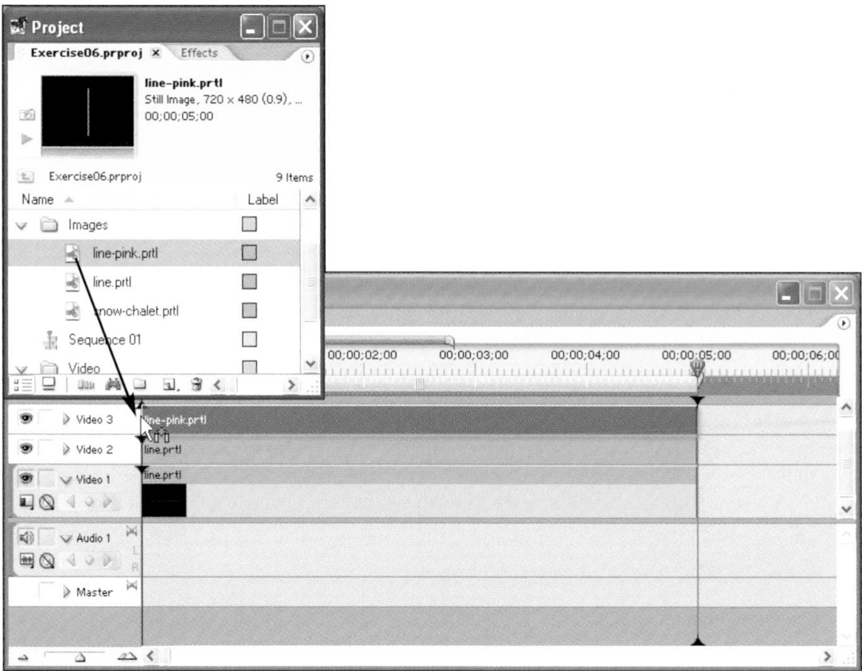

2. Click the **Project** tab to bring it to the foreground. From the **Images** bin, drag **line-pink.prtl** onto track **Video 3**. Snap it to the beginning of the **criss cross** sequence. Play the sequence in the **Program** view to preview it.

Right now the pink line doesn't move. Oh sure, you could set motion keyframes, like you did for the other two yellow lines. But since you are working with title objects, there's another way to create motion without creating any keyframes: rolling/crawling titles!

3. In the **Timeline** window, double-click **line-pink.prtl** in track **Video 3** to open the title in Premiere Pro's **Title Designer**.

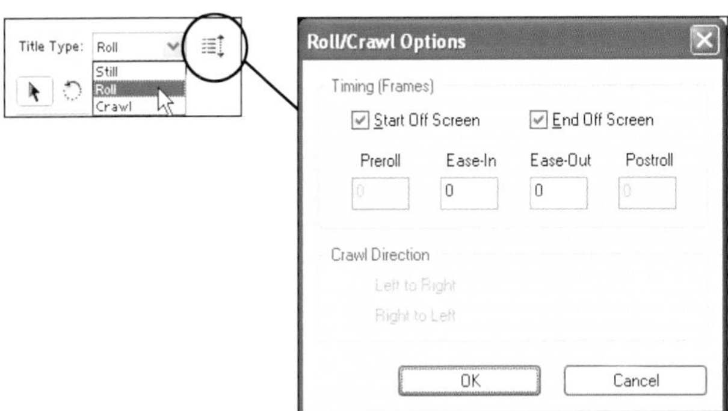

4. In the upper-left corner of the **Title Designer**, choose **Roll** from the **Title Type** drop-down menu. Click the **Roll/Crawl Options** button to the right of the drop-down menu. In the **Roll/Crawl Options** window, check **Start Off Screen** and **End Off Screen**. Click **OK**.

5. With the **Title Designer** still in the foreground, choose **File > Close**. Click **Yes** to save changes.

Note: *A major oversight of Premiere Pro, in my opinion, is that there is no* ***Save Title*** *or* ***Close Title Designer*** *command in the* ***File*** *menu. The* ***Close*** *and* ***Save*** *commands will behave differently, depending on whichever window is in the foreground. If the* ***Project*** *window was in the foreground, the* ***Close*** *command would close your project! Yikes. The moral is, be very careful when using the* ***File > Close*** *command.*

6. Play the sequence in the **Program** view to preview the changes. The pink line should now move from bottom to top. After the sequence has played, drag the current time indicator to **00;00;02;17**.

Tip: *You may have noticed that with two simple clicks of the mouse, you just replicated the first eight steps of the previous exercise. Keep in mind this is only possible because you are working with Premiere Pro titles. With any other types of clips, you would need to keyframe them in the* ***Effect Controls*** *window.*

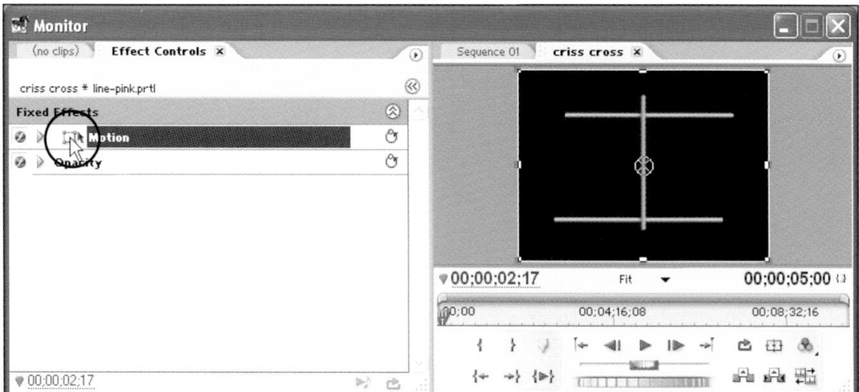

7. In the **Timeline** window, select **line-pink.prtl** in track **Video 3** to view its **Effect Controls**. In the **Effect Controls** window, click the **Transform** icon next to the **Motion** property to enable direct manipulation in the **Program** view.

When in direct manipulation mode, Premiere Pro places eight handles around the clip in the ***Program*** *view. This allows you to directly click a clip or its handles to change the motion properties.*

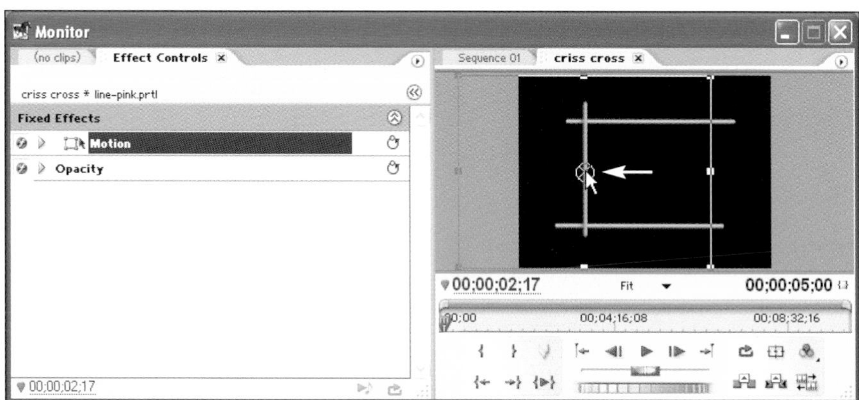

8. In the **Program** view, click in the center of the clip (the X with a circle) and drag it to the left, until it's on the left quarter of the screen (doesn't have to be perfect).

This is by far the easiest method to change motion properties in Premiere Pro. (If you hadn't learned all of the hard methods first, you wouldn't appreciate this method as much!)

Note: *The reason you were asked to move the current time indicator to* ***00;00;02;17*** *was so that you could see the clip easier in the* ***Program*** *view. Because the clip starts and ends offscreen, the only way to see the pink line in the middle of the screen was to move the current time indicator to the middle of the clip.*

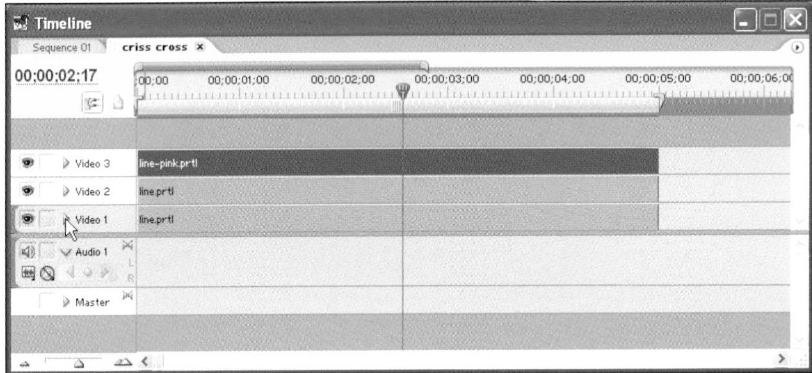

9. In the **Timeline** window, twirl up the arrow next to track **Video 1** to collapse the track options.

You are going to add another clip to this sequence, and because space is scarce in the ***Timeline*** *window, collapsing any superfluous track options is helpful.*

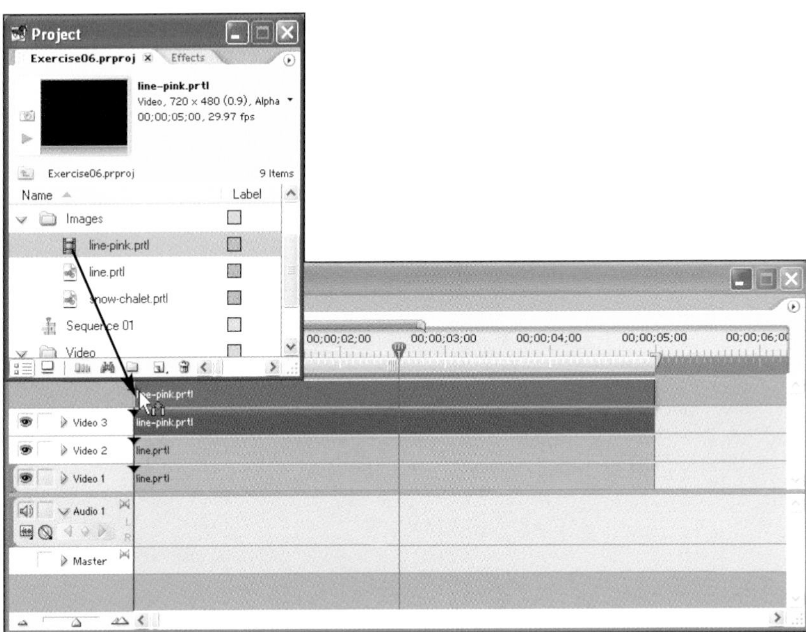

10. In the **Project** window **Images** bin, drag **line-pink.prtl** to the gray area just above track **Video 3**.

Tip: *Premiere Pro automatically creates a new video track when you drag a clip to the gray area above the video tracks. Likewise, a new audio track is created when you drag an audio clip to the gray area along the bottom of the* ***Timeline*** *window.*

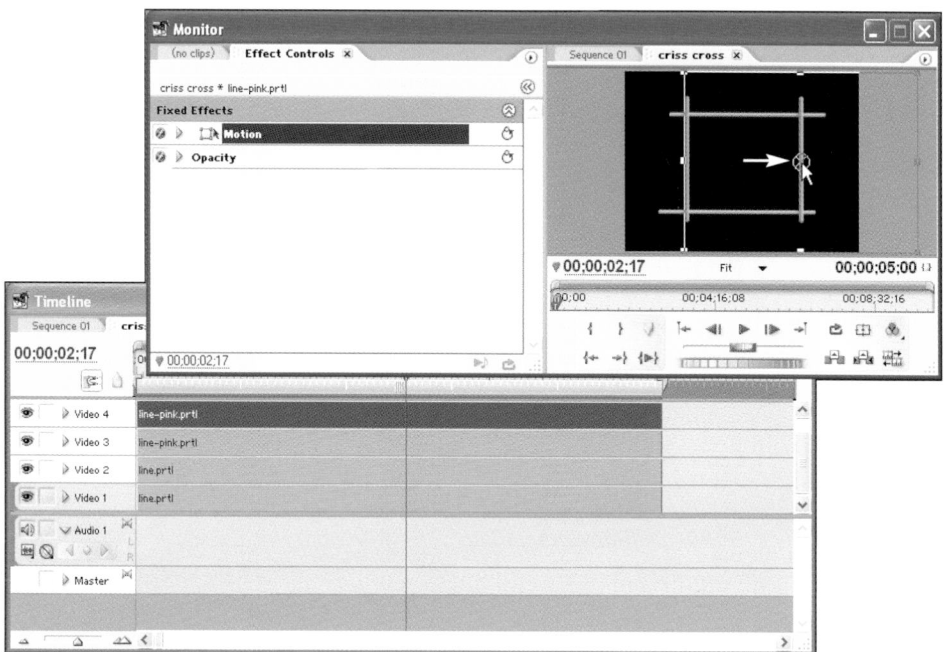

11. In the **Timeline** window, drag the current time indicator to **00;00;02;17**. Select the clip in track **Video 4** to view its **Effect Controls**. In the **Effect Controls** window, click the **Transform** icon next to the **Motion** property. In the **Program** view, click the middle of the clip (circle X) and drag it to the right quarter of the screen.

Tip: *In Premiere Pro 1.5, you are not required to click the* ***Transform*** *icon to manipulate the clip in the* ***Program*** *view. Instead, you can click directly in the* ***Program*** *view, and Premiere Pro will manipulate whichever clip you click. The disadvantage is, with four clips playing at one time, you can accidentally select the wrong clip. (Premiere Pro has to "guess" which clip you want to modify, and sometimes it guesses incorrectly.) Clicking the* ***Transform*** *icon is a good habit to get into, because it explicitly makes Premiere Pro (and you) select the correct clip.*

Note: *The "circle X" is actually the anchor point of the clip. This may be familiar to users of other Adobe products.*

---

12. Play the sequence in the **Program** view to preview it.

Right now both pink lines run parallel to each other, in the same direction. In the previous exercise, you solved this problem by reversing the clip speed to make it play in reverse. Another way to achieve this is to rotate the clip 180 degrees.

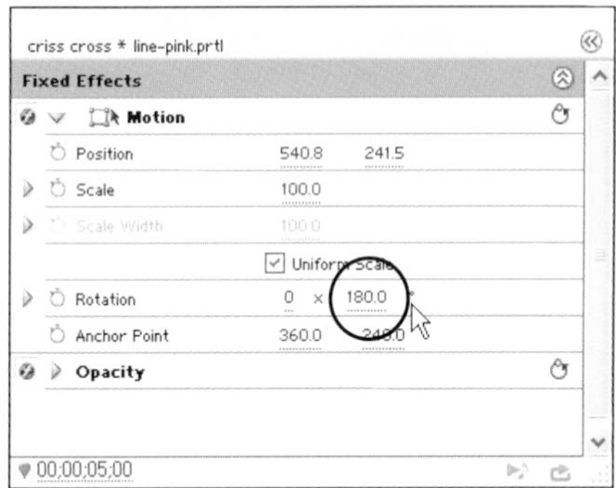

13. In the **Timeline** window, select the clip in track **Video 4** to view its **Effect Controls**. In the **Effect Controls** window, twirl down the **Motion** properties. Click the second **Rotation** value, type in **180.0**, and press **Enter**.

*Note: The **Rotation** value is written **0** × **180.0.** The first number represents revolutions, and the second number represents degrees. Unless the **Rotation** property is keyframed, changing revolutions has no effect. (Because the clip makes one full revolution back to where it started, so it appears the same.)*

14. Play the sequence in the **Program** view to preview it.

*You now have four intersecting clips, which each travel in a different direction. The last step of this project is to tie everything together by placing the **criss cross** sequence into the original sequence (with the black-and-white snowboarder video).*

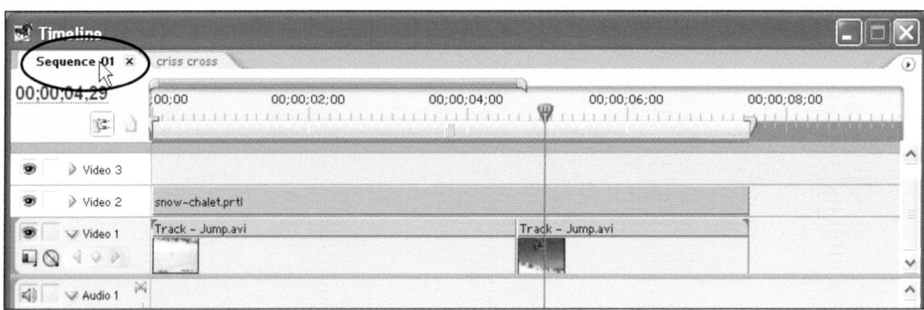

15. In the **Timeline** window, click **Sequence 01** tab to bring that sequence to the foreground.

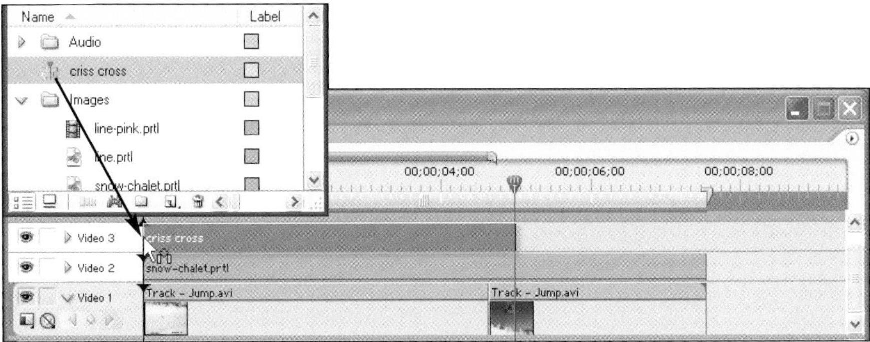

16. In the **Project** window, drag the **criss cross** sequence to track **Video 3**. Snap it to the beginning of the **Timeline**.

*You have just placed one sequence into another sequence. This is called **nesting sequences**, which will cover in detail in Chapter 13, "Nesting Sequences."*

17. Play the sequence in the **Program** view to preview the changes. You will see the four lines on top of the original sequence.

In this exercise, you learned how to create motion without keyframes. Keep in mind this applies only to Premiere Pro title objects, since they have built-in roll/crawl properties. You also were introduced to the world of nested sequences.

18. Save and close this project before moving on to the next exercise.

MOVIE | program_view_motion.mov

To learn more about modifying motion properties directly in the Program view, check out **program_view_motion.mov** from the **movies** folder on the **Premiere Pro HOT** DVD.

*All of the keyframes you have created and modified in the last couple of chapters have been clip keyframes. That is, they are applied to a clip. When the clip moves, the keyframes move with the clip. There is one more type of keyframe to learn, and that is the **track keyframe** (keyframes that are applied to tracks), found exclusively in the **Audio Mixer**, and in the next chapter.*

12

Audio Mixer

Audio Mixer Basics	Types of Audio Tracks
Viewing Master Meters	Clip Tracks in the Audio Mixer
Applying Track Effects	Automating Volume and Balance
Changing Track Volume and Balance	Submix Tracks
Creating a Submix	Modifying Master Meters
Recording Narration	Recording to a Track

H•O•T

Premiere Pro HOT DVD

Eons ago, back in Chapter 10, "*Audio Effects*," you learned how to add audio effects, tweak gain, and create volume keyframes to alter the sound of a clip. Premiere Pro provides a powerful way to apply these type of effects to multiple clips at once, and to entire audio tracks. All of these options are found in one convenient window: the Audio Mixer.

Audio Mixer Basics

Premiere Pro's Audio Mixer is provides advanced audio mixing and effect capabilities for your project. The primary functions of the Audio Mixer are to: monitor your sound levels, change track volumes, add track effects, create audio submixes, and record narration from a microphone. Each of these functions will be covered in this chapter.

The Audio Mixer can be viewed in full or "lite" mode. The full version shows volume levels for each track and a master volume level, whereas the lite version shows only the master level (and has only three grams of net carbs).

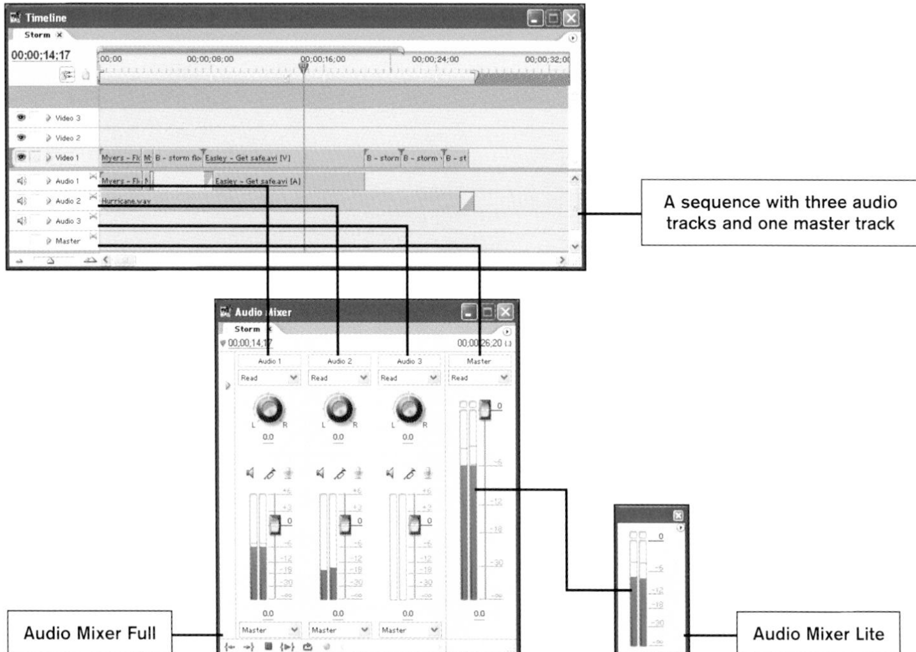

The above figure shows a sequence that has three audio tracks and one master track. In the full Audio Mixer, each audio track is displayed with its own volume meter. This allows you to monitor the volume level of each track individually. The master meter displays the total volume of the entire sequence.

The Audio Mixer Lite shows only the master meters, and it hides all of the audio track meters. You cannot make any changes to the audio in the lite Audio Mixer, you can only monitor the master track.

(Keep in mind that the tiny Audio Mixer is not actually called "Audio Mixer Lite" in the product manual. It doesn't really have a name, but Adobe refers to it as "view master meters only.")

Master tracks are one of three different types of audio tracks in Premiere Pro.

Types of Audio Tracks

There are three types of audio tracks in Premiere Pro: clip, submix, and master.

Clip tracks hold your audio clips. You should be very familiar with them by now since you've worked with them exclusively throughout this book. Every time you add an audio clip to the Timeline, you place it in a clip track. (So far in this book, clip tracks have been called "audio tracks.") Clip tracks contain multiple audio clips. In the Audio Mixer, you can add audio effects to and change the volume level of an entire track, which affects every audio clip in that track.

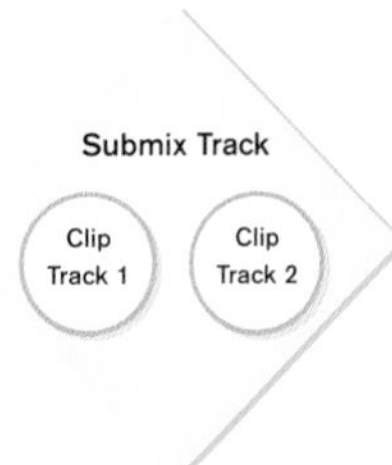

Submix tracks contain multiple clip tracks. Submix tracks allow you to "group" two or more clip tracks together and treat them as one. Just like a clip track, you can add effects to and change the volume of a submix track. Any changes you make to a submix track affects all the clip tracks assigned to that submix.

One important item to note about the submix tracks is that you cannot place any individual clips into submix tracks. Only entire tracks can be added to a submix track.

A **master track** represents the total volume of a sequence. Every submix track and clip track is combined and then funneled through the master track before being output to your speakers. Every sequence has one master track. (In fact, if you flip through the pages of this book, you'll notice that every Timeline picture has a master track.) Any volume changes you make to the master track affects the volume of the entire sequence.

Like submixes, you cannot place any clips into a master track. This can be confusing to people, because the master track is shown in the Timeline window, right below the regular clip tracks. Even though it looks like a clip track in the Timeline window, remember that you can never place audio clips into the master track.

In this chapter, you will learn how to use the Audio Mixer to manipulate each type of track.

I. Viewing Master Meters

The "lite" Audio Mixer is very simple to understand. Its sole purpose is to monitor the master meters. You cannot make any changes to the audio; you can only observe the volume levels of the master track. In this exercise, you will learn how to view the **master meters** (a.k.a., Audio Mixer Lite).

1. If Premiere Pro is not running, launch it and click **Open Project** at the **Welcome Screen**. Navigate to the **c:\Premiere Pro HOT\Chapter12** folder, select **Exercise01.prproj**, and click **Open**.

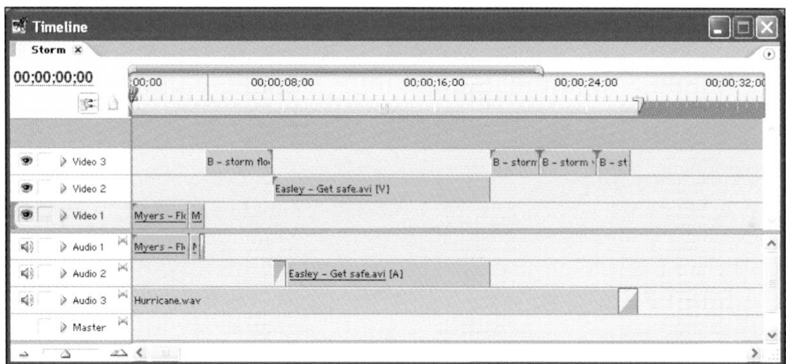

2. Choose **Window > Workspace > Editing** to make sure your project matches the examples in this book. Play the sequence in the **Program** view to preview it.

You may recognize this as the project you were working on in Chapter 10, "Audio Effects." However, a few changes have been made to help highlight the features of the Audio Mixer.

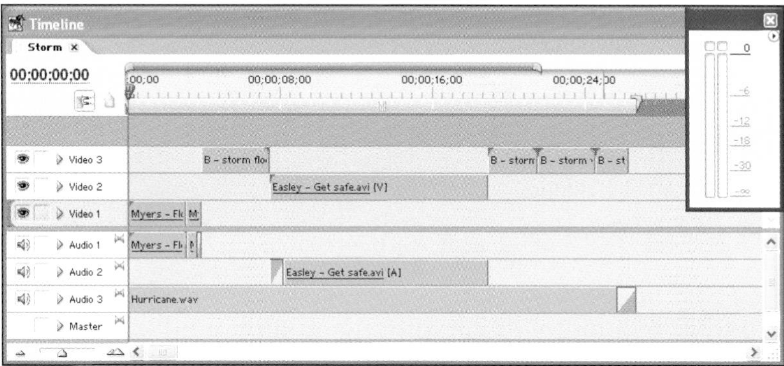

3. To view the "lite" Audio Mixer, choose **Window > Audio Mixer**. This places the master meters in the upper-right corner of the **Timeline** window.

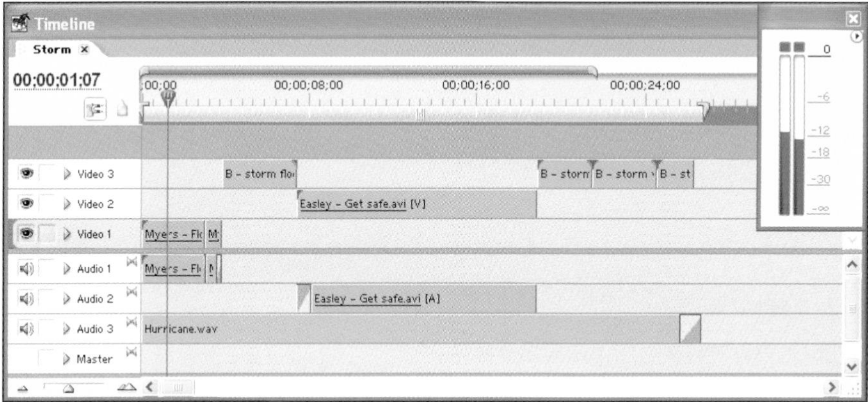

4. Play the sequence in the **Program** view to watch the master meters.

As the volume increases, the meter levels also increase. The master meter shows the volume level of the master track; in other words, it shows the combined volume level of every track. Notice that the meter jumps into the "red" during playback, which means your audio is too loud at that spot, and it will suffer digital distortion (called clipping*).*

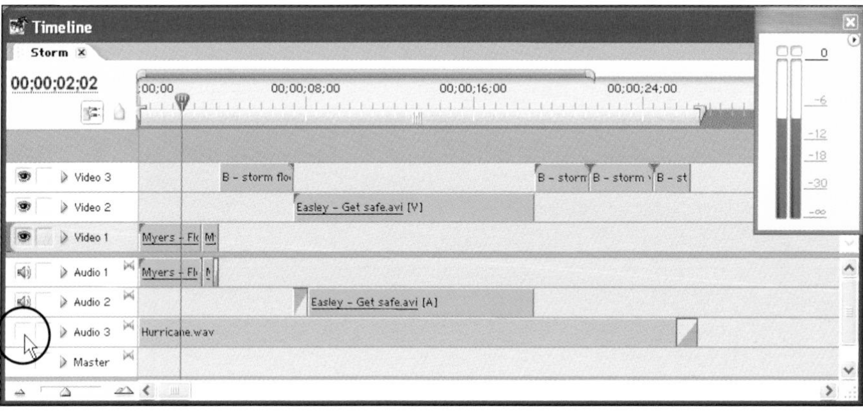

5. Mute track **Audio 3** by toggling off the speaker icon to the left of the track name. Play the sequence again. When done, unmute the track by toggling on track **Audio 3**. (The speaker icon should be visible.)

This time, the levels did not peak into the red. The purpose of temporarily muting the track was to demonstrate that the master meters are the sum of all the audio tracks. When you turned off one of the audio tracks, the master level was not as loud because you took away part of the audio. This also demonstrates the importance of monitoring your levels; even if each individual track is below the red, when combined, the overall sequence may be too loud.

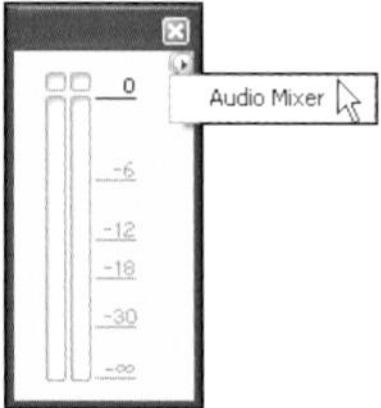

6. To convert the master meters into the full Audio Mixer, click the wing menu in the upper-right corner of the master meters and choose **Audio Mixer**.

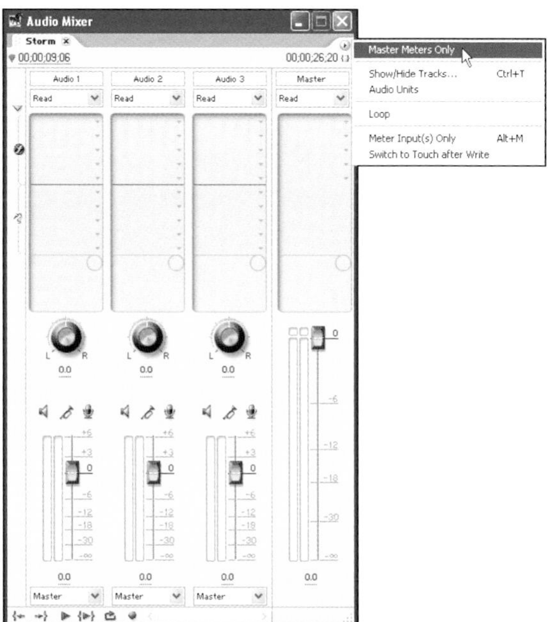

7. To convert the Audio Mixer back to the master meters, click the wing menu in the upper-right corner of the Audio Mixer and choose **Master Meters Only**.

__Tip:__ Knowing how to switch between the two views is important. In most cases, Premiere Pro will remember which Audio Mixer you were viewing (master meters or the full window) and automatically display it when you choose __Window > Audio Mixer.__

Since the master meters are only for monitoring, there's not much to show. In the coming exercises, you will learn how to lower clip track, submix track, and master track volumes in order to prevent your meters from peaking in the red.

8. Save and keep this project open before moving on to the next exercise.

NOTE | Reading the VU meter

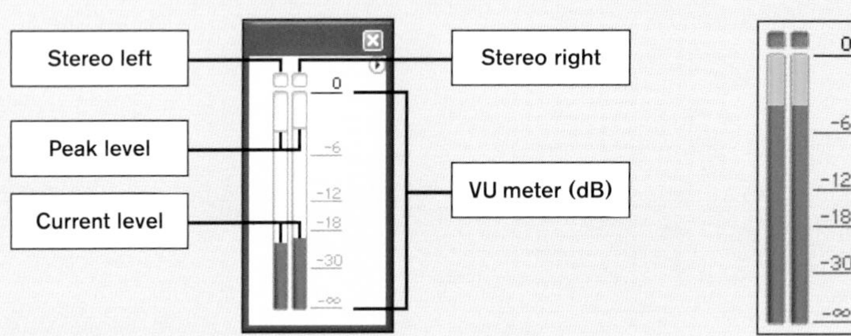

You may have heard the term **VU meter** in the past. What exactly is a VU meter, and how does it relate to the master meter from the previous exercise?

VU is an acronym for "**V**olume **U**nits." VU meters measure audio in terms of decibels, or **dB**. All of the audio meters in Premiere Pro are VU meters, because they measure the audio in dB.

Each bar of the VU meter represents a channel of audio. Stereo sequences have two channels: left and right. Mono sequences have one. Surround sound 5.1 sequences have five bars, one for each channel.

As the sequence plays, the current volume level is shown in the VU meter. The current level is continually on the move, as the volume is always increasing and decreasing.

The **peak level** represents the maximum volume. When the VU meter peaks, a tiny bar remains for a few seconds to represent the peak level. In the above figure, the current level is below –18 dB, but the peak level bars indicate a recent volume spike to –3 dB.

The VU meters are color coded to represent safe and dangerous volume levels. Anything below –6 dB shows as green, which is a safe volume level. Anything between 0 dB and –6 dB is yellow and should be avoided unless absolutely necessary. When the volume spikes into the red, the volume has exceeded the digital threshold and will result in digital distortion.

Tip: Anything above 0 dB will result in static, clipping, and other cacophonous noise. *Never, ever, ever* send out a finished product with audio above 0 dB. In fact, most miniDV cameras normalize their audio to around –12 dB. As a rule of thumb, try to keep your projects between –6 dB and –12 dB. Many editors aim for –12 dB, and they never permit their master levels to peak above –6 dB.

Later on in this chapter you will learn how to reduce your master levels to stay below –6 dB.

Clip Tracks in the Audio Mixer

Up until now in this book, clip tracks have been called *audio tracks*. These are the same tracks you have used to add audio clips. In Chapter 10, "*Audio Effects*," you added effects to, and changed the volume of, individual clips. But perhaps you have a series of 20 clips to which you need to apply the same effect. In the Audio Mixer, you can add track-based effects; in other words, you can apply an effect to an entire track at once, which affects every clip in that track.

Because the full Audio Mixer can be intimidating–thanks to all sorts of sliders, knobs, meters, and buttons–you will begin by learning how clip tracks are displayed and modified in the Audio Mixer.

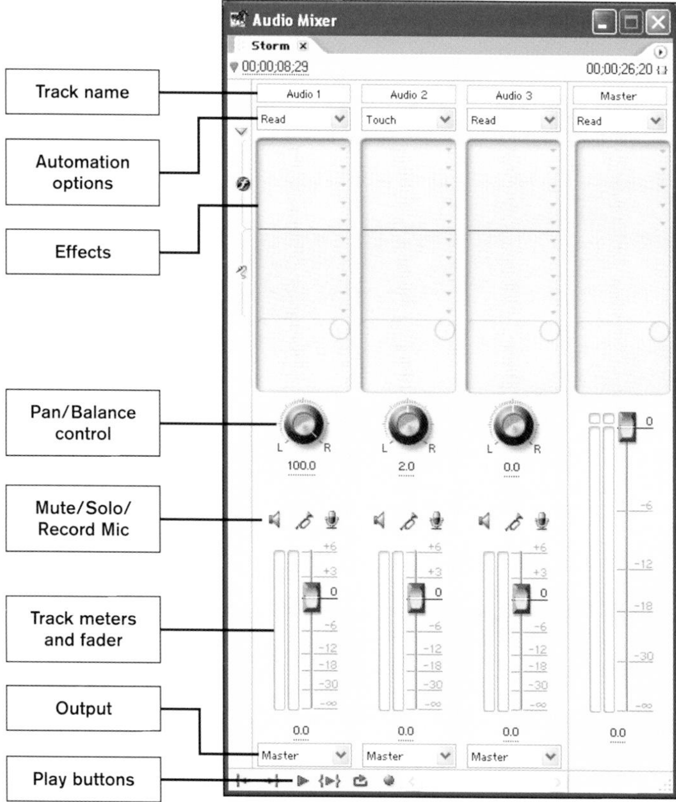

Each column of the Audio Mixer is a different track. (The above figure has three audio tracks and one master track.) From top to bottom, here are the options available in the Audio Mixer for clip tracks:

Clip Track Options in the Audio Mixer	
Option	**Use**
Track name	Shows the name of each track.
Automation options	As your track plays, you can change the volume or change effect settings. The automation options determine how the track responds to your changes. This will be discussed in a later exercise.
Effects	Allows you to add effects to an entire track. The audio effect you apply affects all clips in that track.
Pan/Balance control	Pans the audio to the left or right speaker.
Mute / Solo / Record Mic	Clicking the **Mute** icon turns off the track. Clicking the **Solo** icon turns off all other tracks (the opposite of **Mute**), and the **Record Mic** allows you to record from a microphone attached to your computer straight onto a clip track.
Track meters and fader	The meters display the volume level of each track. The fader allows you to increase or decrease the volume as it plays.
Output	You can output the track audio to the master track or to a submix track.
Play buttons	Plays the sequence in the **Timeline** window. Since the **Audio Mixer** takes up most of the screen, it is handy to use this **Play** button since the other **Play** buttons will most likely be obscured.

Here are the five different ways you can manipulate a clip track in the Audio Mixer:

- Add track effect
- Change track volume
- Change track balance (left/right pan)
- Output track audio to a submix track instead of directly to master track
- Record narration from a microphone directly to a clip track

The next exercise will show you had to add track effects.

2. Applying Track Effects

In this exercise, you will apply a track effect, which will affect all clips on a track. The process is the exact same as applying audio effects to individual clips. The only difference is that you need to apply only one effect to a track, which will alter the sound of every clip in that track.

1. If you have the previous exercise open, skip to step 2. If Premiere Pro is not running, launch it and click **Open Project** at the **Welcome Screen**. Navigate to the **c:\Premiere Pro HOT\Chapter12** folder, select **Exercise02.prproj**, and click **Open**.

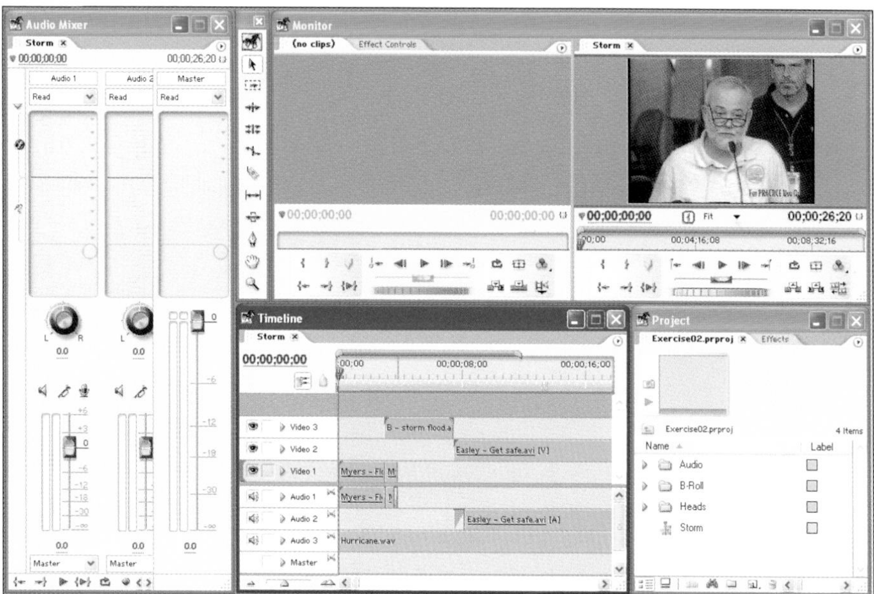

2. Choose **Window > Workspace > Audio**.

*The **Audio** workspace opens up the full **Audio Mixer** and also rearranges the other windows in a configuration that, according to the folks at Adobe, is best suited for audio editing.*

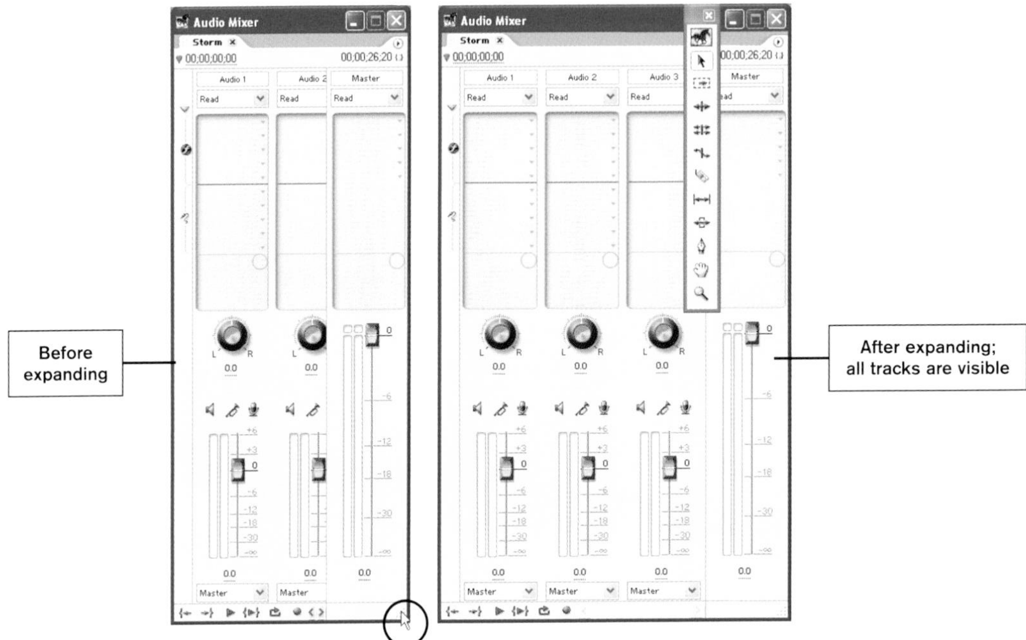

3. Depending on your computer monitor resolution, part of the **Audio Mixer** may be hidden. To expand the **Audio Mixer** to its maximum width, drag the lower-right corner of the **Audio Mixer** to the right, until the window will not let you drag further.

*If you have a larger computer monitor, with a higher resolution, the Audio Mixer may already be expanded. Premiere Pro attempts to resize all of the windows so they are maximized in your display. Also notice in the above figure that the **Toolbox** is floating above the **Audio Mixer**.*

4. To close the **Toolbox**, so you can have a clear view of the **Audio Mixer**, click the red X in the upper-right corner of the **Toolbox**.

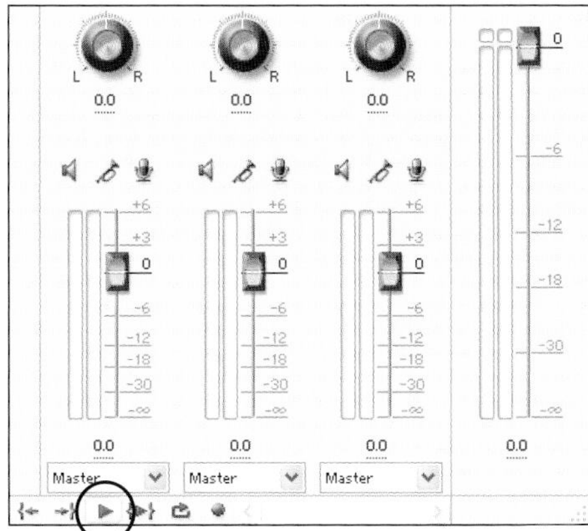

5. Press the **Home** key on your keyboard to snap the current time indicator to the start of the sequence, and then click **Play** in the bottom of the **Audio Mixer** to preview the sequence.

*As the sequence plays, watch each of the three track meters in the **Audio Mixer**. The first sound bite is in track **Audio 1**, the second is in track **Audio 2**, and the music is in track **Audio 3**.*

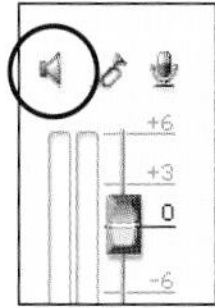

6. In the **Audio Mixer**, click the **Mute** icon for track **Audio 3**. Click **Play** in the **Audio Mixer** to preview the sequence. When done, click the **Mute** icon again to unmute the track.

*This mutes any clip on track **Audio 3**, so you won't be able to hear the music. The **Mute** icon in the **Audio Mixer** behaves exactly like toggling off the audio track in the **Timeline** window.*

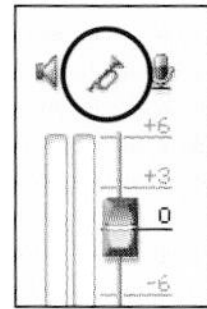

7. In the **Audio Mixer**, click the **Solo** icon for track **Audio 3**. Click **Play** in the **Audio Mixer** to preview the sequence. When done, click the **Solo** icon again to unmute the other tracks.

*This time you should only hear the music of track **Audio 3**. The **Solo** icon does the exact opposite of the **Mute** icon–it mutes all other tracks.*

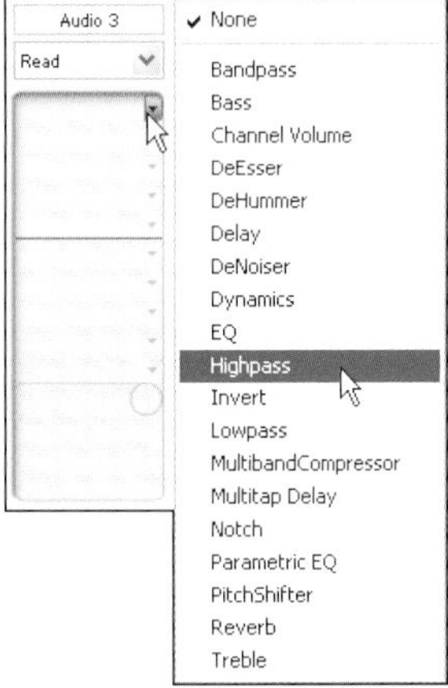

8. In the **Audio Mixer** you can add up to five audio effects per clip track. Click the drop-down arrow at the top of the **Track Effects** menu for track **Audio 3** (see above figure), and choose **Highpass** from the pop-up menu. This applies the effect to the entire track.

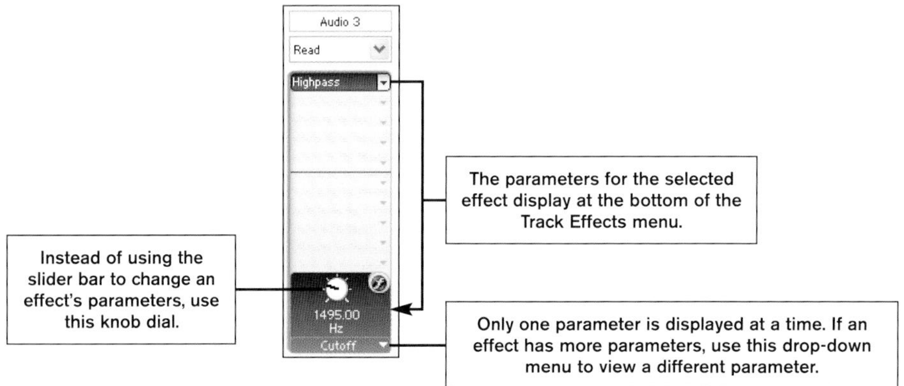

Audio 3
Read
Highpass
The parameters for the selected effect display at the bottom of the Track Effects menu.
Instead of using the slider bar to change an effect's parameters, use this knob dial.
1495.00
Hz
Cutoff
Only one parameter is displayed at a time. If an effect has more parameters, use this drop-down menu to view a different parameter.

*Instead of using the **Effect Controls** window to modify the effect parameters, as you have done in previous chapters, the effect parameters are shown at the bottom of the **Track Effects** menu. If the effect has multiple parameters, and many do, you can only see one parameter at a time. Instead of a slider bar, the parameter can be changed with the knob dial.*

9. In the **Audio Mixer**, at the bottom of the **Track Effects** menu for track **Audio 3**, drag the value knob up until the **Cutoff** value is approximately **2600 Hz**. (The knob jumps incrementally, so just try to get it close.) Press **Home** on your keyboard and then click **Play** in the **Audio Mixer** to preview the effect from the beginning of the sequence.

*Tip: You should only hear the "high" sounds of the music clip, mainly the percussion effects. The bass and lower melodies have been filtered out. Using the **Highpass** effect with music is a useful way to remove a range of instruments.*

10. To replace the effect in track **Audio 3**, click drop-down arrow to the right of the effect name **Highpass** and choose **Lowpass** from the menu. Press **Home** on your keyboard and click **Play** in the **Audio Mixer** to preview the sequence from the beginning.

*This time, you should only hear the "low" portion of the music; the high percussion sounds have been filtered out. **Highpass** and **Lowpass** are opposites.*

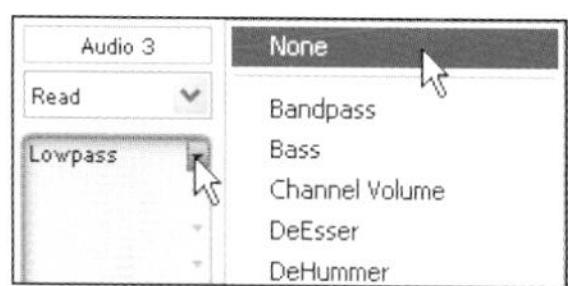

11. To remove the effect, click the drop-down arrow to the right of the effect name **Lowpass** and choose **None** from the menu.

The audio effect concepts from earlier chapters still apply, such as applying and modifying effect parameters. However, the interface, menus, and knobs are completely different.

12. Save and close this project before moving on to the next exercise.

Automating Volume and Balance

One of the best features of the Audio Mixer window is the capability to change the volume and the balance of a clip as it plays. In Chapter 10, "*Audio Effects*," you learned to manually create keyframes at certain points in time in order to change volume. In the Audio Mixer, instead of creating keyframes one at a time, you can play your sequence and then drag the volume slider up and down to change the volume. This is called **automating**, and Premiere Pro provides different automation options.

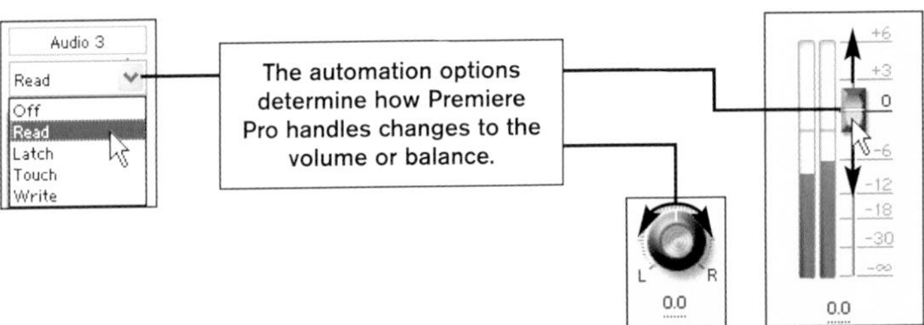

At the top of the Audio Mixer clip tracks is a drop-down menu of automation options. These options determine how Premiere Pro handles changes when you drag the volume slider or balance knob. Here is a description of each automation option:

Off: Ignores any volume/balance changes you previously have made.

Read: Reads in the volume/balance changes you previously have made. You cannot make any changes to the audio in Read mode.

Latch: Only records *changes* you make during playback. (If you don't make any changes, nothing is recorded.) If you do make a volume/balance change, when you let go of the mouse button, after dragging the volume slider or balance knob, the slider/knob *stays latched* at its current position and doesn't move.

Touch: Only records *changes* you make during playback. (If you don't make any changes, nothing is recorded.) When you let go of the mouse button, after dragging the volume slider or balance knob, the slider/knob *slides back* to its previous position.

Write: Records the current position of the volume slider/balance knob (even if you don't make changes).

The nuances between **Latch**, **Touch**, and **Write** can be confusing–even to long-time users of Premiere Pro. Hopefully, this next exercise will help clear up any confusion.

3. Changing Track Volume and Balance

Just like you can with track-based effects, you can alter the volume and balance (left and right pan) of every clip on a track, without having to perform the same task multiple times for each clip. In this exercise, you will learn how to use the track automation options to change track volume and balance.

1. If Premiere Pro is not running, launch it and click **Open Project** at the **Welcome Screen**. Navigate to the **c:\Premiere Pro HOT\Chapter12** folder, select **Exercise03.prproj**, and click **Open**.

This exercise is similar to the previous one—except all clip volume keyframes have been removed. In Chapter 10, "Audio Effects," *you set clip keyframes to lower the music volume during the sound bites and increase the music volume during B-roll. In this exercise, you will perform the same task using the* ***Audio Mixer****.*

---

2. To make sure that your screen matches the examples in this exercise, choose **Window > Workspace > Audio**. As you did in the previous exercise, expand the **Audio Mixer** to its maximum and then close the **Toolbox** if it is in your way. (See Steps 3 and 4 of the previous exercise if you need help.)

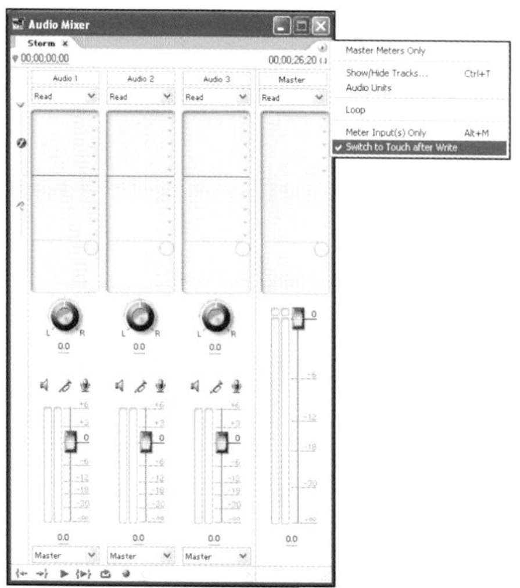

3. To make sure your screen matches the examples in this exercise, click the wing menu in the upper-right corner of the **Audio Mixer** and make sure that **Switch to Touch after Write** is checked. Select it if there is no checkmark next to it.

Note: *There's a perfectly good reason for doing this, and you will find out why later in this exercise.*

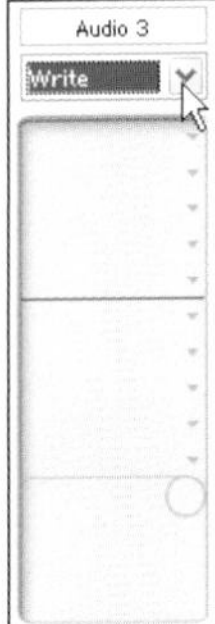

4. At the top of track **Audio 3** in the **Audio Mixer**, change the automation options drop-down menu to **Write**.

*When the sequence plays, you can drag the volume slider up and down to change the level. Putting the track in **Write** mode will record (write) the position of the slider during every frame of playback.*

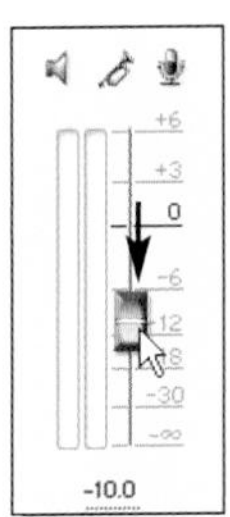

5. In the **Audio Mixer**, drag the volume slider of track **Audio 3** to **−10.0 dB**.

*In **Write** mode, Premiere Pro remembers the value of the slider bar. Now the volume of track **Audio 3** will start at **−10.0 dB**.*

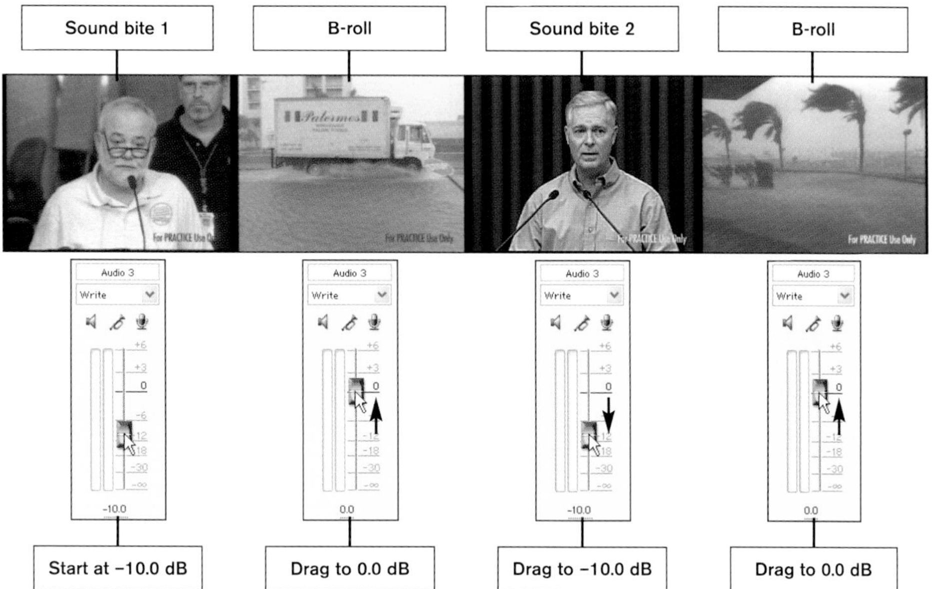

*In the next step, you will drag the volume slider as the sequence plays. During the sound bites, the volume slider should be near **–10.0 dB**. During the B-roll, you will drag the volume slider up to **0.0 dB**.*

---

6. Press **Home** on the keyboard to move the current time indicator to the beginning of the sequence. Play the sequence in the **Audio Mixer**. Drag the volume slider to **0.0 dB** during the B-roll and back down to **–10.0 dB** during the sound bites.

*Notice when playback stops, the automation mode of track **Audio 3** switches to **Touch**. (In Step 3, you told Premiere Pro to switch to **Touch** mode after writing.)*

---

7. With track **Audio 3** still in **Touch** mode, press **Home** on the keyboard and then play the sequence in the **Audio Mixer** to listen to the volume changes you made. (Let it play all the way until it stops at the end.)

*When you had the track in **Write** mode, every movement of your volume slider was recorded. (Even when the slider wasn't moving, its position was still recorded.) When you play the sequence again in **Touch** mode, you will see the volume slider "magically" move up and down by itself; Premiere Pro is playing back your mouse movements as well. (Show this to a friend and tell them that your system is possessed!)*

8. To illustrate the difference between **Touch** and **Write** modes, click the automation options drop-down for track **Audio 3** and choose **Write**.

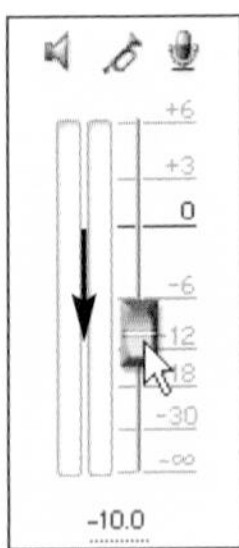

9. Drag the volume slider to **–10.0 dB**. Press **Home** on the keyboard and then play the sequence in the **Audio Mixer**. (Let it play all the way until it stops at the end.)

*This time, in **Write** mode, the volume slider didn't move during playback. It stayed at **–10.0 dB**. (Pay attention, important statement coming....) **Write** mode ignores any previous volume changes, and it records the position of the volume slider, even if you don't touch the slider. **Touch** mode reads in previous volume changes, and it records changes only when you* touch *(and drag) the slider–hence, the name!*

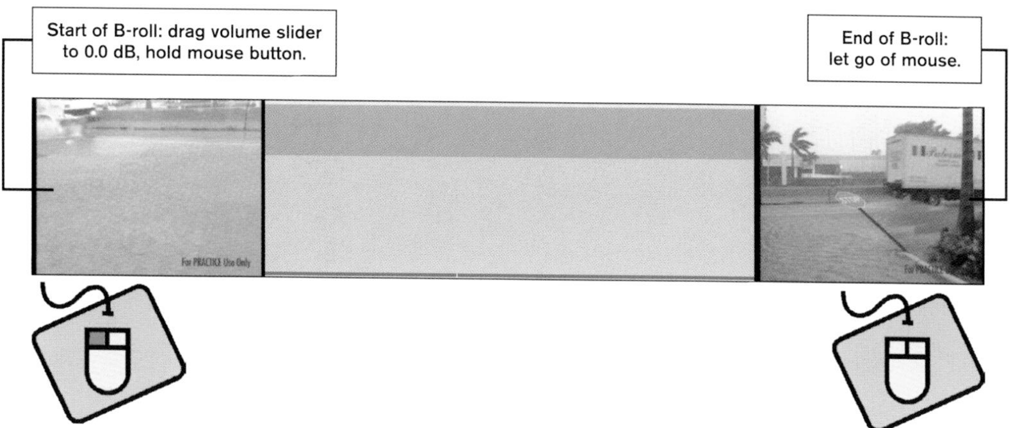
Start of B-roll: drag volume slider to 0.0 dB, hold mouse button.
End of B-roll: let go of mouse.

*In the next step, you will use the **Touch** mode as the sequence plays to change the volume only at the B-roll. At the start of the B-roll, you will click and hold the mouse button as you drag the volume slider to 0.00 dB. At the end of the B-roll, you will let go of the mouse completely. When you let go of the mouse, the slider will return to its previous position.*

---

10. Change the automation option of track **Audio 3** to **Touch**. (It should already be selected.) Press **Home** on the keyboard and then play the sequence in the **Audio Mixer**. During the B-roll, drag the volume slider to **0.0 dB** and then let go of the slider after the B-roll is done.

*This highlights another important difference between **Touch** and **Write** modes: in **Touch** mode, when you let go of the volume slider–that is, when you're not "touching" it–the slider returns to its previous position. But, in **Write** (or **Latch**) mode, the slider stays at its current position when you let go of the mouse. Rule of thumb: use **Touch** mode to "touch-up" a small portion of a track.*

---

11. Play the sequence in the **Audio Mixer** to preview the volume changes.

The volume slider should once again move by itself during playback.

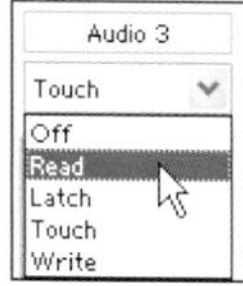
Audio 3
Touch
Off
Read
Latch
Touch
Write

12. Now that you have finished making changes to the volume, choose **Read** from the automation options drop-down menu.

***Read** mode, as the name implies, puts the track in read-only mode. This prevents you from making any changes to the track volume. This is especially helpful if you suffer from "accidentalclickitis", which many users do!*

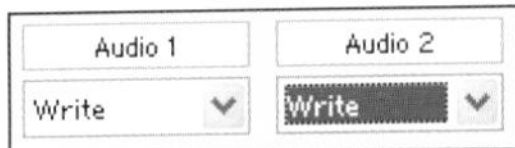

13. You can also use the automation options for recording balance (left/right pan) levels. In the top of tracks **Audio 1** and **Audio 2**, change the automation mode to **Write**.

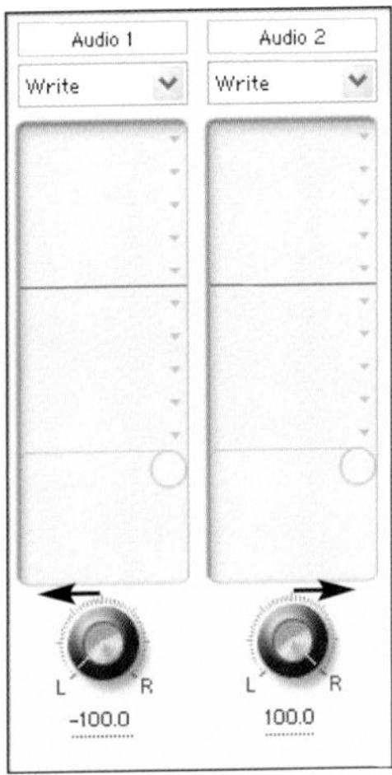

14. Drag the balance knob of track **Audio 1** all the way to the left, until the value is **–100.0**. Drag the balance knob of track **Audio 2** all the way to the right, until the value is **100.0**.

The balance knob controls the left/right pan of the track. A value of –100.0 plays the track out of the left speaker only, and a value of 100.0 plays the track out of the right speaker only. Also note, despite the circular knob appearance, you don't actually drag the mouse "in a circle" around the knob. Instead, drag your mouse directly left or right to change the value, as you would a slider bar. (Although the knob is pretty to look at, it really is nothing more than a glorified slider bar!)

15. Press **Home** on the keyboard. With the tracks still in **Write** mode, play the sequence in the **Audio Mixer**. (Let the sequence play all the way until it stops at the end.)

*Since the automation was in **Write** mode, the position of the balance knobs was recorded. You should have heard the first sound bite, on track **Audio 1**, out of your left speaker only. The second sound bite, on track **Audio 2**, should have been heard in the right speaker only. Also notice both tracks switched to **Touch** after you were done writing.*

*You have just finished one of the hardest exercises in this chapter. Understanding the differences between **Write** and **Touch** is very important. It's also important to remember that whenever you stop playback, the **Write** mode switches to **Touch** if you have the **Switch to Touch after Write** option enabled. Also keep in mind that all of the skills you just practiced in this exercise apply equally to submix and master tracks as well.*

16. Save and keep this project open before moving on to the next exercise.

MOVIE | track_volume.mov

This exercise required some deft mouse handling, as well as plenty of brainpower. If you want to watch a movie of this exercise, check out **track_volume.mov** from the **movies** folder on the **Premiere Pro HOT** DVD.

Submix Tracks

Earlier you learned Premiere Pro has three types of audio tracks: clip, submix, and master. The previous two exercises dealt with clip tracks (tracks that hold clips). The next type of track to learn is the **submix**.

Submix tracks allow you to "group" two or more clip tracks together and treat them as one. One of the great features of the Audio Mixer is that all track types behave the same. In fact, you could go back to the previous two exercises and perform the exact same steps on submix tracks. The silver lining here is this: you already know how to apply effects to, and change the volume/balance of, submix tracks!

The primary difference between clip tracks and submix tracks is that submix tracks never, ever hold clips. A submix track exists only to help you group multiple clip tracks and treat them as a single track. Any changes you make to a submix track affects all the clip tracks assigned to that submix.

In the next exercise, you will learn how to assign clip tracks to submix tracks and practice adding an effect to a submix track. (Shhh. Don't tell the next exercise that you already know how to add an effect to a submix track, you don't want to hurt its feelings.)

4. Creating a Submix

In this exercise, you will assign two clip tracks to a submix track in the Audio Mixer. You will also apply an effect to the submix track.

1. If you have the previous exercise open, skip to step 2. If Premiere Pro is not running, launch it and click **Open Project** at the **Welcome Screen**. Navigate to the **c:\Premiere Pro HOT\Chapter12** folder, select **Exercise04.prproj**, and click **Open**.

2. Choose **Sequence > Add Tracks**.

*Tip: You can also right-click a track name in the **Timeline** window and choose **Add Tracks** from the shortcut menu.*

3. In the **Add Tracks** window, type **0** for **Add Video Track(s)**, **0** for **Add Audio Track(s)**, and **1** for **Add Audio Submix Track(s)**. Click **OK**.

*Premiere Pro's default is to assume that you want to add one of each kind of track. In order to create only **one** submix track, you have to set the **Video** and **Audio** track options to **0**. You can also choose the type of submix track; in this case, you want to create a **Stereo** submix, since your source tracks are stereo.*

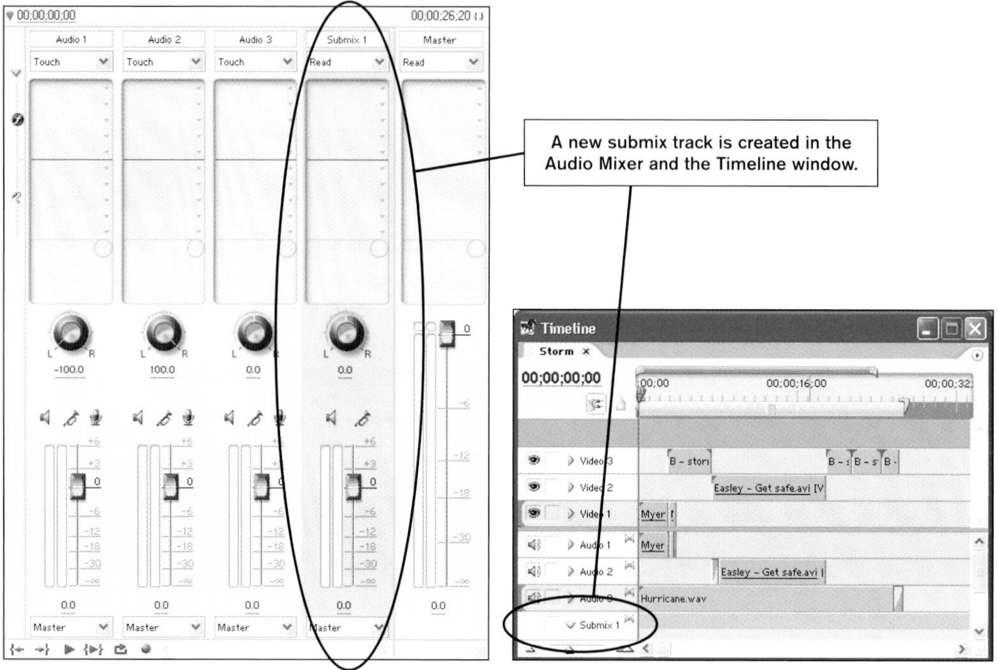

A new submix track is created in the Audio Mixer and the Timeline window.

*The new submix track shows up in the **Audio Mixer** and in the **Timeline** window. Keep in mind that, even though it shows up as a track in the **Timeline** window, you cannot add clips to a submix track.*

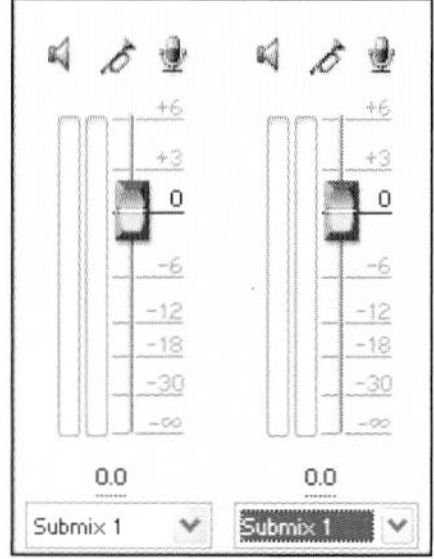

4. At the bottom of tracks **Audio 1** and **Audio 2**, in the **Audio Mixer**, change the **Output** drop-down menus to **Submix 1**.

Once you create a submix track, you can redirect a clip track's output by assigning it to a submix. Normally, the output goes directly to the master track. When you output a track to a submix, the audio from that track first goes to the submix, and then it outputs from the submix to the master track.

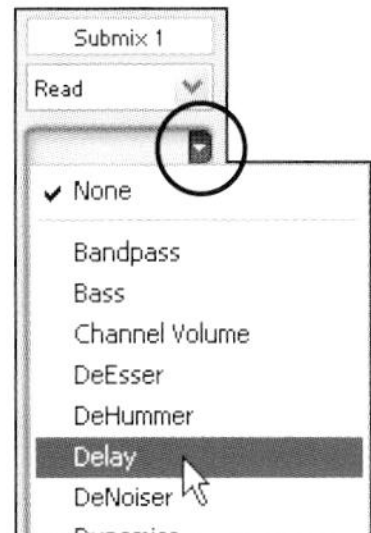

5. In the **Audio Mixer**, click the drop-down arrow at the top of the **Track Effects** menu for **Submix 1** (see above figure), and choose **Delay** from the pop-up menu.

Adding an effect to a submix affects all tracks assigned to that submix.

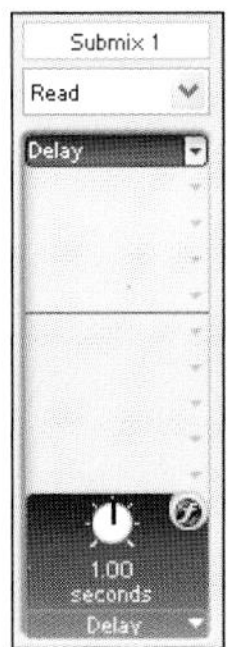

6. In the **Audio Mixer**, play the sequence to preview the **Delay** effect. The echo effect is applied to both tracks **Audio 1** and **Audio 2**, which are assigned to the submix.

Tip: *The* ***Delay*** *effect is a perfect example of why track effects are handy. When you apply an effect to an individual clip, the effect stops when the clip stops. In the case of the* ***Delay*** *effect, the "echo" stops abruptly at the end of the clip. (You may remember this happening in Chapter 10,* "Audio Effects."*) On the other hand, when you apply an effect to an entire track/submix, the echo effect plays as long as the track plays. In this case, you can hear the echo effect even after the clips have stopped playing.*

Six steps and you're already at the end of the exercise. Creating and assigning submix tracks are a piece of cake–especially since you already know how to add effects and change submix volume/balance.

---

7. Save and keep this project open before moving on to the next exercise.

5. Modifying Master Track

Every sequence has one, and only one, master track. All audio, regardless of track or submix, makes a brief "pit stop" at the master track before being output to your speakers. Any changes you make to the master track affect all audio on all tracks. You can use the master track to make sure that your digital audio does not peak above 0.0 dB. This will be a very short exercise since you already understand how to modify tracks in the Audio Mixer.

1. If you have the previous exercise open, skip to step 2. If Premiere Pro is not running, launch it and click **Open Project** at the **Welcome Screen**. Navigate to the **c:\Premiere Pro HOT\Chapter12** folder, select **Exercise05.prproj**, and click **Open**.

2. In the **Audio Mixer**, click the drop-down arrow at the top of the **Track Effects** menu for the master track (see above figure) and choose **Reverb** from the pop-up menu.

*Tip: The **Reverb** effect can give an ambience to your audio, from a small room to a large, empty auditorium.*

3. In the master track of the **Audio Mixer**, right-click the name of the applied effect, **Reverb**, and choose **Church** from the shortcut menu. This sets all of the effect parameters to the **Church** effect preset.

*Tip: Remember in Chapter 10, "Audio Effects," that some audio effects had built-in presets? In the **Effect Controls** window, you accessed the effect preset by clicking the **Reset/Preset** button. (Does that look familiar?) However, in the **Audio Mixer**, you can access the same effect presets by right-clicking the name of an applied effect.*

---

4. In the **Audio Mixer**, play the sequence to preview the effect.

*The **Reverb** effect is applied to all audio before Premiere Pro sends it to your computer speakers. Keep in mind this is a particularly ugly sound you've created, only for the purposes of this exercise. Please avoid this particularly lethal combination of effects when you're editing your own projects!*

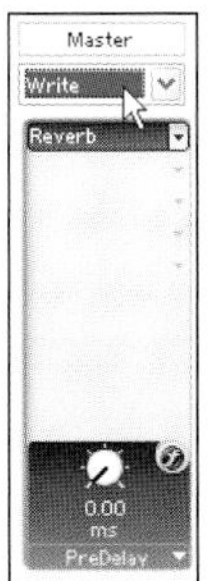

5. Set the automation mode of the master track to **Write**.

Tip: You can also use the master track to make sure the final audio of your sequence falls below the 0.0 dB limit of digital audio. As mentioned earlier, many editors do not like their audio to go all the way to 0.0 dB, because even just a hair over 0.0 will result in digital distortion. Instead, you can reduce the overall volume level to fall between –6 dB and –12 dB.

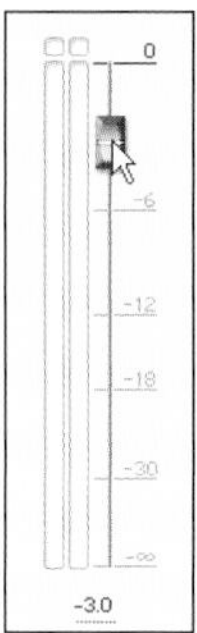

6. With the automation mode still set to **Write**, drag the volume slider of the master track to **−3.0 dB**.

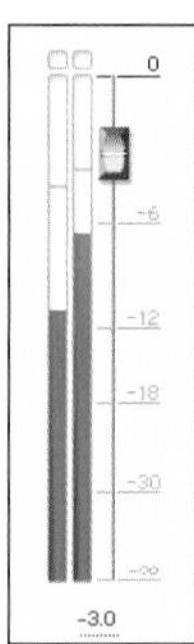

7. In the **Audio Mixer**, play the sequence to preview the change. As it plays, watch the **VU** meter of the master track and look for the peak volume level.

You will notice that the volume level peaks near −3.0 dB. So, you may be wondering, "With all this talk of −6 dB to −12 dB, why choose −3.0 dB?" Good question. Even though the volume peaks at −3.0 dB, the majority of the volume level falls between −6 dB and −12 dB. Sure, it peaks up to −3.0 dB a couple of times, but as long as it never peaks into the red of 0.0 dB, you are safe. Rule of thumb: peaking below 0.0 dB is OK, but the majority of the volume should fall between −6 dB and −12 dB.

8. Save and keep this project open before moving on to the next exercise.

NOTE | The Magic Slider

Time to come clean… the magic slider isn't *really* magic. When you drag the volume slider and balance knobs, Premiere Pro is actually creating keyframes. (Remember those?) However, instead of keyframes attached to individual clips, it creates *track keyframes*.

In previous chapters, you set clip keyframes at certain intervals, when you wanted the value of a clip's effect to change. When you use the automation options of the Audio Mixer, Premiere Pro writes track keyframes at *every frame*! That means it is recording your mouse movement 30 times per second (in the case of 30 frame/second NTSC video).

If you're curious (or a glutton for punishment) to see the track keyframes, you can view them in the Timeline window.

To view the track volume keyframes, click the **Show Keyframes** button below a track name in the **Timeline** window and then check **Show Track Volume** in the pop-up menu. (You can look at other keyframes, such as balance or effect keyframes, by choosing **Show Track Keyframes**.)

As you can see, especially when zoomed, many (many) keyframes are created. If you were interested (or crazy), you could modify each of these keyframes with the **Pen** tool as you did in previous chapters. After all, keyframes are keyframes, right? Also keep in mind that track keyframes behave the same for all clip, submix, and master tracks.

One interesting item to note: Premiere Pro creates keyframes only when necessary. In the example above, you can see that keyframes were added only where the volume *changed*. Otherwise, if the volume level doesn't change, Premiere Pro doesn't need to create superfluous keyframes.

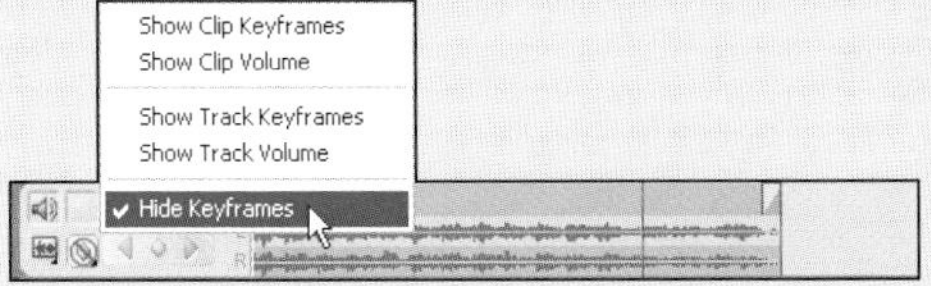

Warning: Please be aware that Premiere Pro "locks" clip tracks when you are viewing track volume or keyframes, which means that you cannot select or move any clips on that track. When you are done viewing the track volume/keyframes, be sure to check the **Hide Keyframes** option in order to unlock the clips on a clip track.

Recording Narration

The last feature of the Audio Mixer that you have yet to practice is its capability to record narration directly from a microphone attached to your computer. You can use this to record voice-overs and narration over still images and to capture analog audio connected to your sound card, in addition to many more uses. When you record narration through the Audio Mixer, an audio clip is placed directly on the audio track in the Timeline window. Your voice is saved to a file on your computer, but the clip is automatically imported into your project and placed in the Timeline for you. (What service!)

One important thing to keep in mind about narration: when recording, it will overwrite any existing audio on the track you record to. It is always a good idea to record narration to a blank audio track, so you don't lose any of your existing audio.

In this next exercise, you will practice the art of recording narration. If you do not have a microphone attached to your computer, you can still walk through the steps, even though the recorded clip will be "empty."

NOTE | Feedback

When recording via microphone to your computer, be careful to avoid a feedback loop. Feedback is created when your microphone records its own sound as it plays out of speakers (like looking into a hall of mirrors).

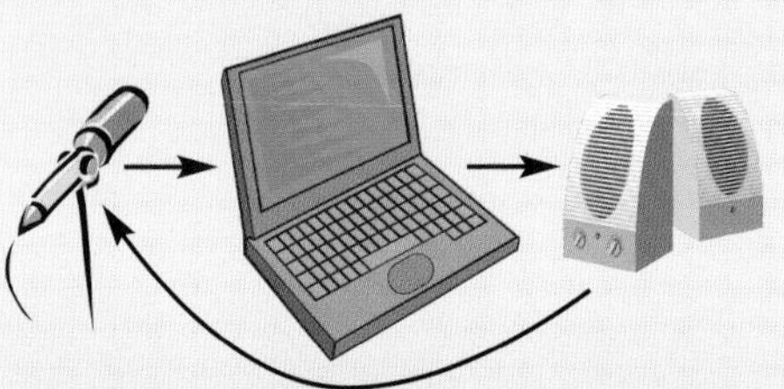

A feedback loop is caused by a microphone recording its own sound from speakers.

Prevent feedback by using headphones or muting your computer speakers.

Here's how a feedback loop is created: your microphone records your voice, as well as any other sound in the room. That sound is sent to your computer. Your computer plays the audio through speakers. But the sound from your computer speakers is also picked up by the microphone, and an infinite loop is created, which results in feedback and all sorts of nasty sounds.

To prevent feedback, you have two options: have the sound play to headphones, or mute your computer speakers during recording. The headphones option is usually preferred, because you can still hear the audio, and you don't have to unmute your speakers to hear the finished product.

NOTE | Audio Inputs

Premiere Pro records narration via the microphone port of your computer/sound card. However, it does not know how to properly configure your sound card's input, so it is up to you to specify the correct hardware settings. Please verify your settings in Windows XP Control Panel's **Sounds and Audio Devices**, using the documentation that came with your computer and sound card.

It's impossible to list settings for every system in this book, but here are some general rules of thumb:

Your microphone should be attached to the microphone port of your sound card. Newer systems have color coded input ports, and the microphone port is often colored pink.

You need to configure your sound card to select the **Microphone** port. Many users of Windows XP will find this under **Start menu > Control Panel > Sounds, Speech, and Audio Devices > Sounds and Audio Devices**.

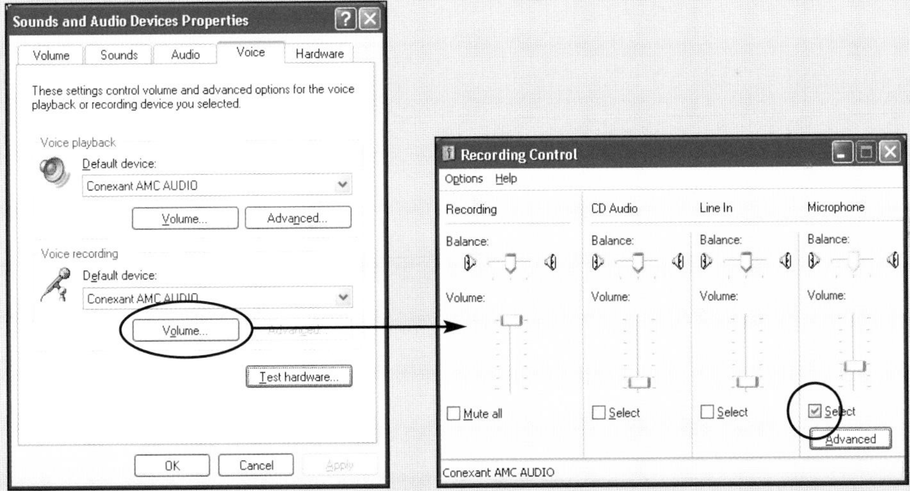

For many Windows XP users, there will be a **Voice** tab in the **Sounds and Audio Devices Properties** window. Clicking the **Volume** button will bring up a list of available input devices. Make sure the **Microphone** input is selected.

Keep in mind that this does not apply to all Windows XP users and is meant to be used as a general guide. Your system may have different options than those listed above. Refer to the documentation that came with your computer and sound card.

6. Recording to a Track

In this exercise, you will learn how to use the Audio Mixer to record narration from a microphone directly to an audio track in your Timeline. Along the way you will also learn some view/show features of the Audio Mixer that help free up some space on your computer screen. Make sure you have tested and/or calibrated your computer's microphone input prior to starting this exercise.

1. If the previous exercise is open, skip to step 2. If Premiere Pro is not running, launch it and click **Open Project** at the **Welcome Screen**. Navigate to the **c:\Premiere Pro HOT\Chapter12** folder, select **Exercise06.prproj**, and click **Open**.

In this exercise, you will use the same project you've been using, but you will mute the sound bites and create your own. (Hope you're good at lip synching!)

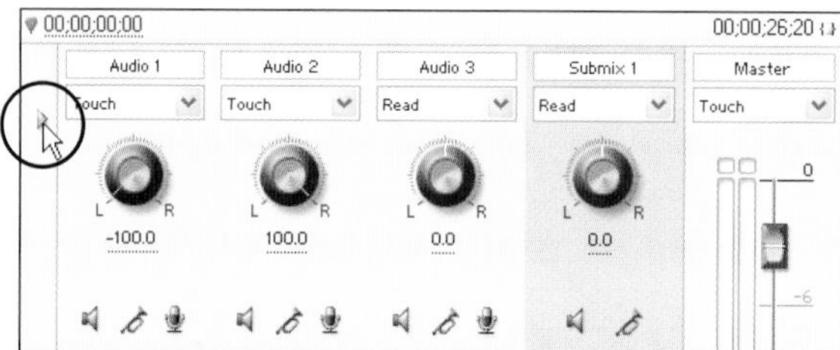

2. In the upper left of the **Audio Mixer**, hide the effects by twirling up the **Show/Hide Effects and Sends** arrow.

*Since you will not be adding any additional effects in this exercise, you can save some space on your computer screen by collapsing the **Effects** area of the **Audio Mixer**. Even though the effect menus are hidden, the effects are still applied.*

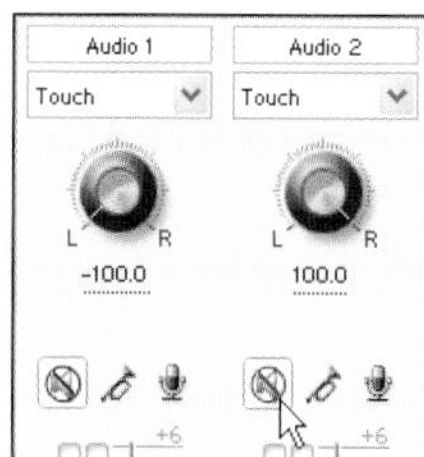

3. In the **Audio Mixer**, mute tracks **Audio 1** and **Audio 2** by clicking the **Mute** icon for both tracks.

*In this exercise, you don't want to delete the audio (just in case you want to use it later on), but you do want to turn it off. The **Mute** icons are a convenient way to "hide" audio without losing any of your work.*

4. Click the **Audio Mixer** wing menu, and choose **Show/Hide Tracks**.

*Tip: Many menu commands have keyboard shortcuts, which are listed to the right of the menu commands. In this case, you can see that **Ctrl+T** is the keyboard shortcut for **Show/Hide Tracks.** By the way, this is a feature of all Windows applications, not just Premiere Pro.*

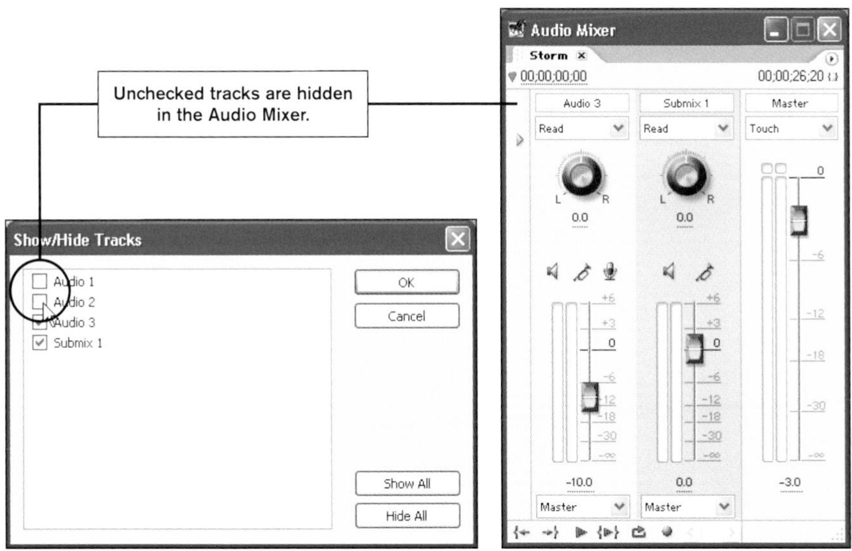

5. In the **Show/Hide Tracks** window, uncheck **Audio 1** and **Audio 2**. Click **OK**.

*All unchecked tracks are hidden in the **Audio Mixer**. This is yet another display option of the **Audio Mixer** that helps free up screen real estate. In this case, you are not going to make any more changes to **Audio 1** and **Audio 2**, so you can hide them from view. Keep in mind this does not delete the audio tracks, and the tracks still show in the **Timeline** window.*

6. Choose **Sequence > Add Tracks**.

You are going to add a new audio track to hold the narration you will record.

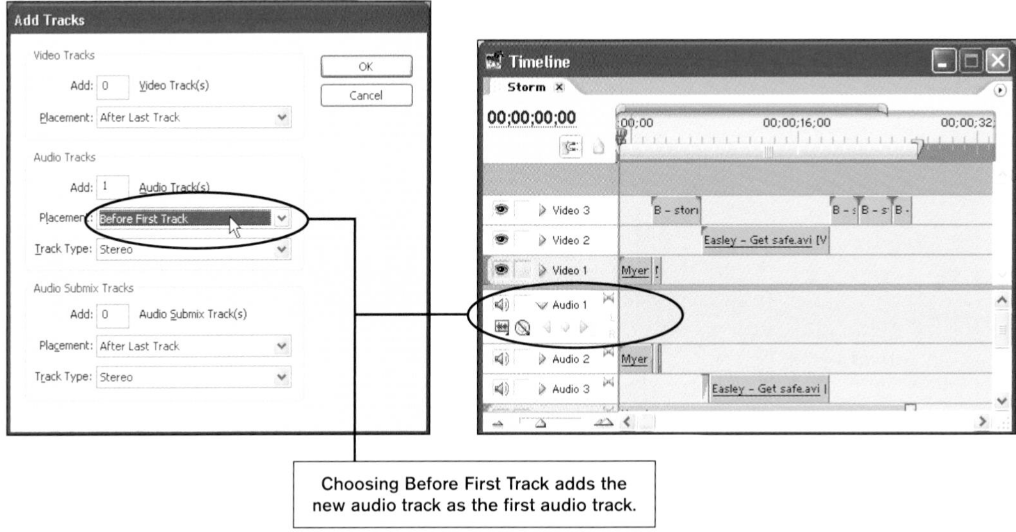

Choosing Before First Track adds the new audio track as the first audio track.

7. In the **Add Tracks** window, type **0** for **Add Video Track(s)**, **1** for **Add Audio Track(s)**, and **0** for **Add Audio Submix Track(s)**. In the **Audio Tracks** section, change **Placement** to **Before First Track**. Click **OK**.

*The new audio track is added as the first audio track and given a name of **Audio 1**. The old **Audio 1** is renamed **Audio 2**. The old **Audio 2** is renamed **Audio 3**, and so on. There are now four audio tracks, one submix track, and one master track, for a total of six audio tracks.*

8. In the **Timeline** window, right-click the track name **Audio 1**, and choose **Rename** from the shortcut menu. When the blinking cursor appears, type **Narration** and press **Enter** to rename the track.

*With so many audio tracks, renaming a track will help prevent any unnecessary confusion. Also notice that the **Audio Mixer** now shows the new track name at the top of the track column.*

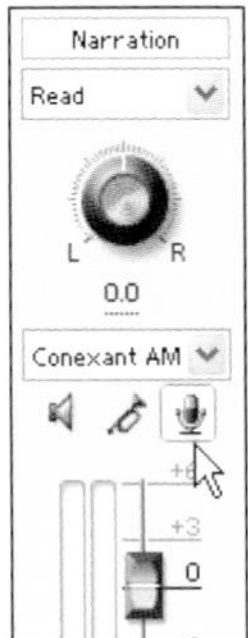

9. In the **Audio Mixer**, enable the **Narration** track for recording by clicking the **Record Mic** icon.

Note: *A drop-down menu appears with a list of all available audio inputs connected to your system. Depending on your hardware configuration and sound card, your drop-down menu may differ from those shown in this exercise.*

10. Click the **Audio Mixer** wing menu and choose **Meter Input(s) Only**.

*This option changes the **VU** meter of the **Narration** track to monitor the microphone's input. When you speak into the microphone, the **VU** meter should spike. Also note that this only monitors the input; it provides no control over the input volume level. To change the volume level of your microphone, refer to the documentation that came with your computer/sound card.*

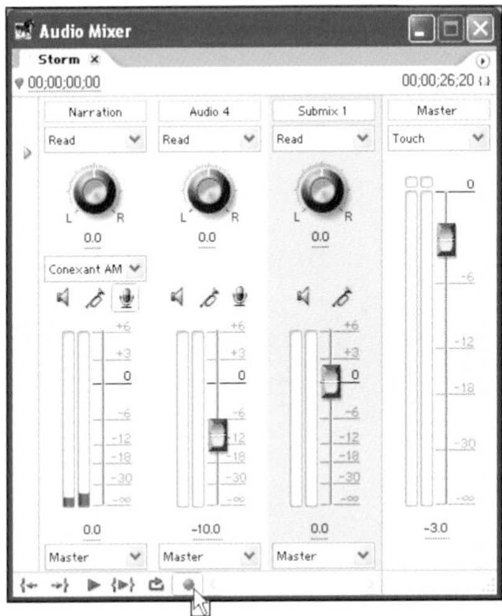

11. Click the **Record** button at the bottom of the **Audio Mixer**.

*The **Record** button prepares the track for recording and will flash to indicate that it is in standby mode. At this point, nothing is being recorded. The **Audio Mixer** does not record anything until you click the **Play** button. This allows you to watch playback as you narrate the action in real-time.*

---

12. Press **Home** on the keyboard. Click the **Play** button to start playback and recording. As the sequence plays, speak into the microphone to narrate the action. (This is your chance to improvise.) When you get to the end of the sequence, click the **Stop** button to stop recording.

*When you click **Stop**, the **Record** button will automatically turn off. Don't fret if you aren't happy with your recording. You can redo the recording by repeating Steps 11 and 12. The previous narration is overwritten each time you re-record.*

13. After you are done recording, click the **Audio Mixer** wing menu and uncheck **Meter Input(s) Only**. Then disable recording for the **Narration** track by turning off the **Record Mic** icon.

It's good to get in the habit of always turning off the recording options when you are done recording.

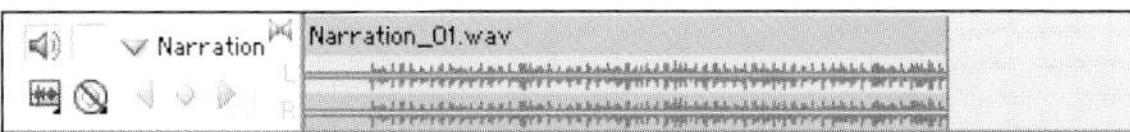

14. Play the **Audio Mixer** to preview the narration in the sequence.

Because the master track still has a reverb effect applied to it, you will also hear the reverb in the narration playback. Also notice that the ***Audio Mixer*** *added the microphone recording as a clip in the* ***Narration*** *track in the* ***Timeline*** *window. The recording is also listed as a clip in your* ***Project*** *window, and it is now a file on your hard drive.*

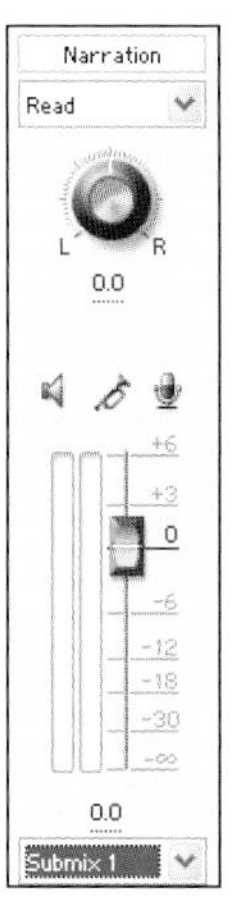

15. At the bottom of the **Narration** track, change the **Output** drop-down menu to **Submix 1**. Play the **Audio Mixer** to preview the changes to the sequence.

You should now hear your voice with a delay effect. Since the narration track is a clip track like any other, you can also manipulate its effects, volume, balance, and output like you have done to all of the other tracks in this chapter. You can also see how convenient submix tracks are for adding effects–with the click of a single button, you added an echo effect.

16. Save and close this project. You are officially done with this chapter.

NOTE | Where Did I Put That File?

In the previous exercise, the microphone recording you made was saved as a file to your hard drive. But where?

Premiere Pro, like many other Adobe applications, uses scratch disks to save all temporary files. Scratch disks are used to render effects, conform audio, save microphone recordings, and capture audio and video from your DV camera. In the previous exercise, when you recorded narration via your microphone, the audio file was recorded to the location specified in your scratch disks.

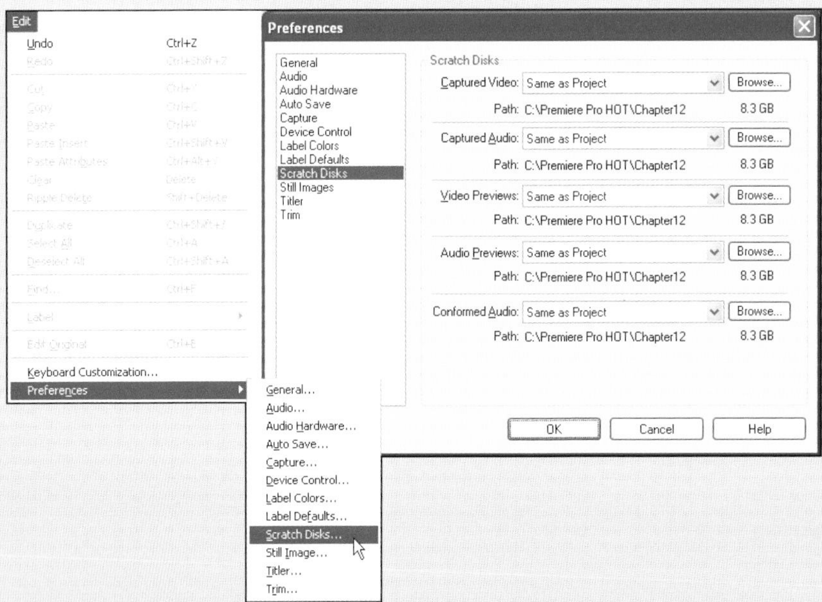

You can access the scratch disks menu by choosing **Edit > Preferences > Scratch Disks**. The Preferences menu lists all of the scratch disks that you can set in Premiere Pro. Keep in mind that any settings you make in the Preferences menus will apply to any and all projects–not just the current project.

You can choose to save your video and audio previews, conformed audio, and captured movies to your project directory or any directory of your choosing. Editors with a dedicated audio/video drive may decide to set their **Video Previews** and **Audio Previews**, as well as **Conformed Audio** files to a scratch directory on their extra hard drive. You'll learn more about setting **Captured Video** and **Captured Audio** locations in Chapter 15, "*Capturing Digital Video*.")

Other editors like to save everything to their Project directories, so when it comes time to clean house, all files are found in one location and can be deleted all at one time.

Whew. Another packed chapter chock full o' good tips and hard exercises. In this chapter, you mastered what may be the most difficult aspect of Premiere Pro–the Audio Mixer. Although you didn't add every possible combination of audio effects, you certainly have enough knowledge to venture out and explore on your own.

Hopefully you understand the power and convenience of using track effects and submixes. Unfortunately, there's no such thing as a video submix. (Wouldn't that be nice?) However, there is a similar concept for video tracks called ***nesting****, which you will learn in the next chapter.*

---

13 Nesting Sequences

| What is Nesting? | Nesting a Sequence |
| Adding Effects to a Nested Sequence |
| Importing Photoshop Layers as a Sequence | Track Mattes |
| Creating a Track Matte | Fixing Project Size |
| Importing a Project |

H•O•T

Premiere Pro HOT DVD

In the previous chapter, you discovered the convenience of grouping multiple audio tracks together as one submix track. The obvious advantage of this is the time savings by applying an effect to one track instead of several tracks. Alas, in Premiere Pro there are no "video submix" tracks. However, there is something equally convenient for video sequences: **nesting**. In this chapter, you will discover the ease of nesting, as well as pick up some nesting tricks and tips along the way.

What Is Nesting?

Nesting is the act of inserting one sequence inside of another sequence. A "nested" sequence is one which has been inserted into a different sequence. When you insert a nested sequence, you are inserting every clip, graphic, track–everything–of the nested sequence into the new sequence. You were first introduced to nesting in Exercise 6 of Chapter 11, "*Video Effects*," when you placed the sequence of four moving bars into the sequence of the black-and-white snowboarding video.

When you nest a sequence inside of another sequence, the nested sequence is treated like a clip. You can select, move, trim, and apply effects to nested sequences as you would any other clip. Everything that you've done to video and audio clips throughout this book applies equally to nested sequences.

Nesting sequences has many benefits, such as the following:

- You can apply effects to nested sequences, which affect all clips within that sequence. Maybe you have a sequence comprised of 20 clips, and each one needs to be color corrected. You can nest the sequence in another sequence and apply the color correction clip just once to the nested sequence to color correct all clips at once.
- You can reuse a sequence many times by nesting it in different projects. Perhaps you have a weekly television show you produce. You can build your opening credits as a sequence and then nest that sequence in a different show each week.
- You can combine multiple tracks in one sequence to make editing easier. You experienced this firsthand in Chapter 11, "*Video Effects*." The grid of four lines, from Exercise 6, required four separate video tracks. When placed on top of the background video and a title, that would have been six video tracks altogether. Because you nested the original four lines, you needed only three video tracks. This provides a much cleaner editing workspace and helps minimize "accidentalclickitis."
- You can build complex projects in "stages." The movie you are making has 20 scenes, and each scene is its own sequence. You can build the sequences in any order and then nest all 20 sequences into a master sequence.
- You can export multiple sequences as one. When you export movies in Premiere Pro (in Chapter 14, "*Exporting Movies*"), you will learn that Premiere Pro can only export one sequence at a time. Nesting multiple sequences into a master sequence allows you to export all of the sequences as one big movie.
- You can import a layered Photoshop file as a sequence. Each Photoshop layer becomes a track in a nested sequence.
- You can use nested sequences to create complex video effects, such as picture-in-picture and track matte effects.

These are some of the popular reasons to use nesting. Of course, there are many more benefits, and throughout this chapter you will learn some additional nesting tips and tricks.

I. Nesting a Sequence

Once nested, a sequence acts just like a clip. All of the effects, trimming, selecting, and so on that you have done to clips throughout this book apply to nested sequences. In this exercise, you will learn how to nest multiple sequences, as well as create a picture-in-picture effect.

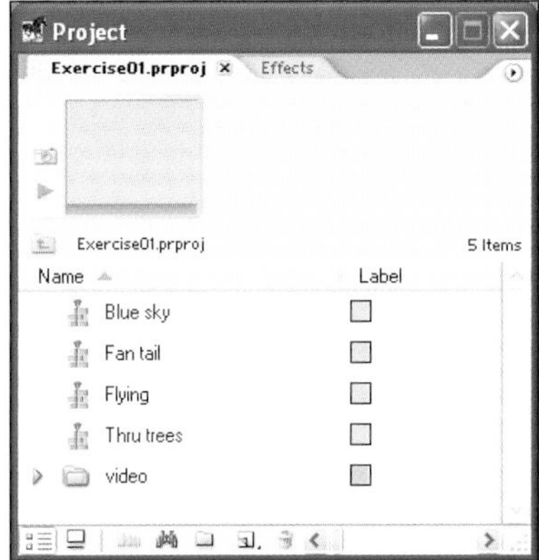

1. If Premiere Pro is not running, launch it and click **Open Project** at the **Welcome Screen**. Navigate to the **c:\Premiere Pro HOT\Chapter13** folder, select **Exercise01.prproj**, and click **Open**.

*This project contains four sequences and a **video** bin.*

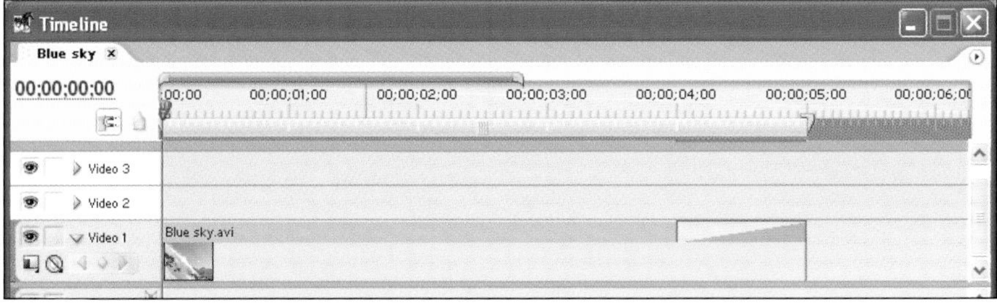

2. Play the **Blue Sky** sequence that is open in the **Timeline** window.

*This sequence is 5 seconds long and contains a clip with a **Slide** transition applied at the end to make the clip slide off the screen. In this exercise, you will create a quadrant of four clips that each slide off.*

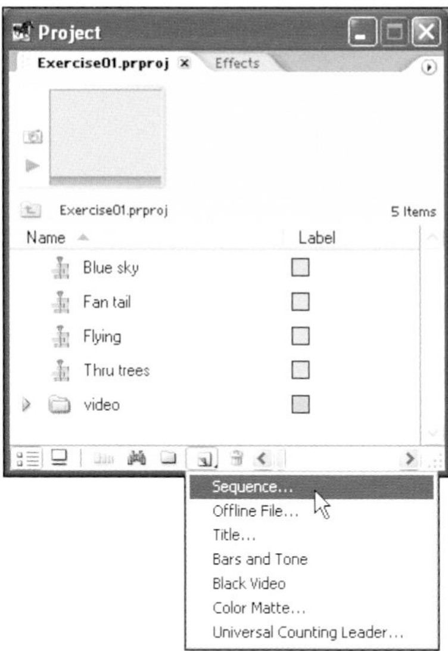

3. To create a new sequence in the **Project** window, click the **New Item** icon and choose **Sequence** from the pop-up menu.

The sequence you will create will be the "master" sequence in which you will nest the four existing sequences.

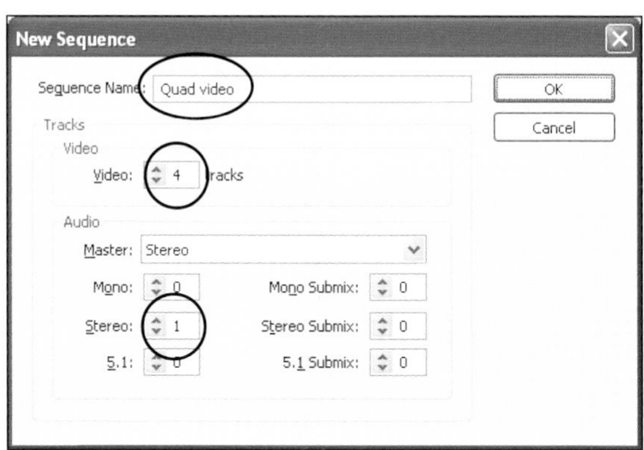

4. In the **New Sequence** window, type in a sequence name of **Quad video**, select **4 Video tracks**, and only **1 Stereo** track. (All other **Audio** tracks should be **0**.) Click **OK**.

The sequence you create will have no audio, but Premiere Pro does not let you create a sequence with less than one audio track. Remember this fact, because you will be quizzed on it in Step 9.

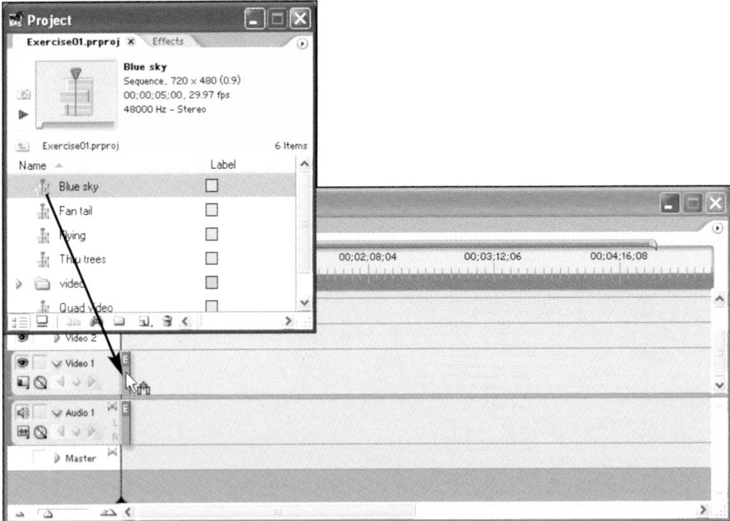

*The new **Quad video** sequence is added to the project window and opened up in the **Timeline** window.*

5. Scroll to the top of the **Project** window and drag the **Blue sky** sequence to the beginning of track **Video 1**. Make sure to snap it to the beginning of the sequence.

*You have just nested the **Blue sky** sequence into the **Quad video** sequence.*

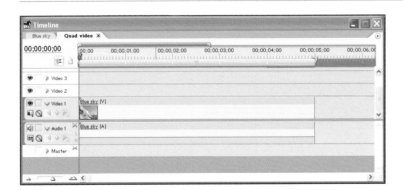

6. To zoom the sequence to fit in the **Timeline** window, press the \ (backslash) key on the keyboard.

*You will notice that the nested sequence **(Blue sky)** is 5 seconds long. This is because the clip inside the **Blue sky** sequence is only 5 seconds long. The concept to remember here is this: the duration of a nested sequence depends upon the duration of its contents. A sequence that is 30 minutes long will appear as a 30-minute-long clip when nested.*

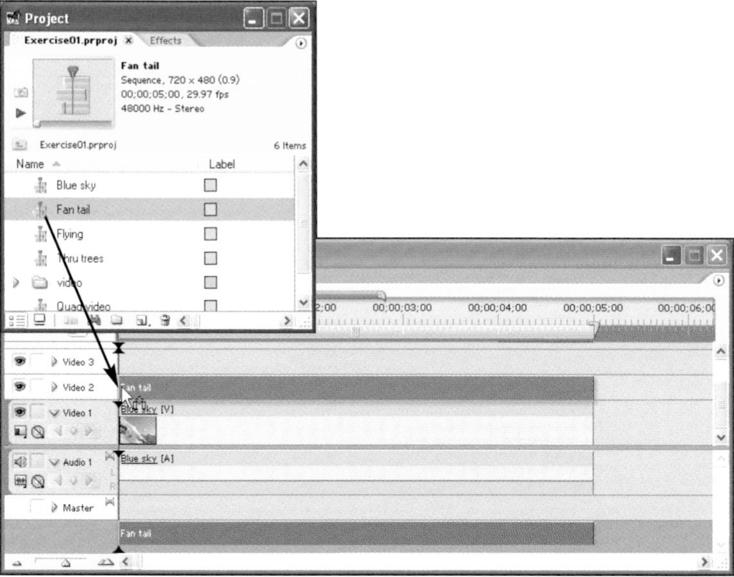

7. From the **Project** window, drag the **Fan tail** sequence to track **Video 2** of the **Timeline**. Snap it to the beginning of the sequence.

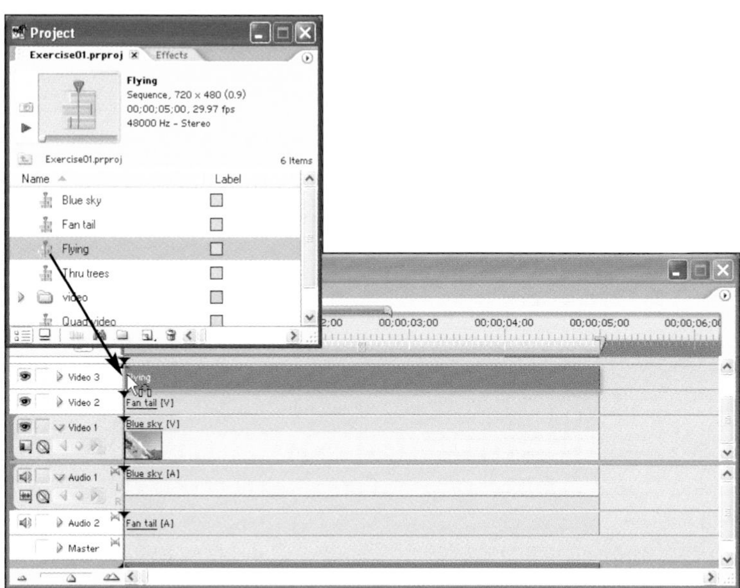

8. From the **Project** window, drag the **Flying** sequence to track **Video 3** in the **Timeline**. Don't forget to snap. (Like you need to be told.)

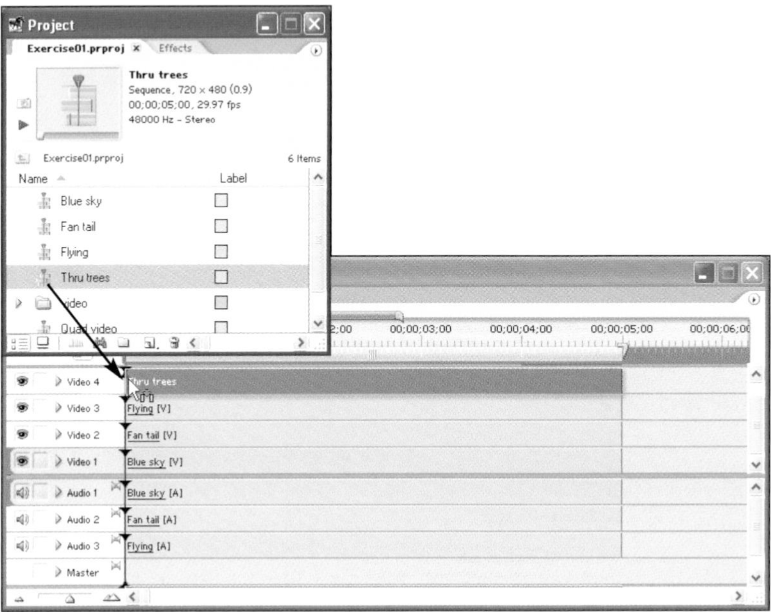

9. Because the **Timeline** window is getting crowded, twirl up tracks **Video 1** and **Audio 1** to hide their track options. From the **Project** window, drag the **Thru trees** sequence to track **Video 4** in the **Timeline**.

Notice that all four nested sequences appear to have both video and audio. Do you remember learning in Step 4 that all sequences must have at least one audio track? (I hope so! It was only five steps ago.) Keep in mind that when you nest a sequence, you are nesting all of the clips and tracks contained inside of that sequence—even empty tracks.

10. Play the **Quad video** sequence to preview it.

*Right now you should be able to see only the nested sequence **Thru Trees** because it is in the topmost track. Notice that there's no audio (despite there being four audio clips). Since you will not need these audio clips, you will learn how to remove them all at one time.*

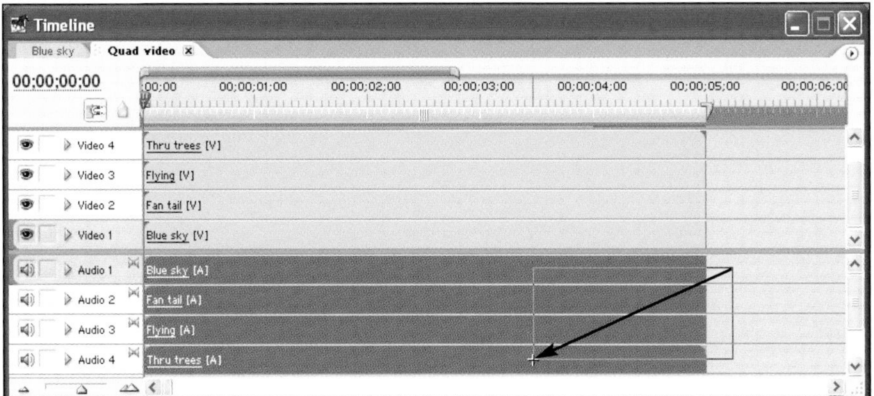

11. Hold down the **Alt** key on your keyboard and drag your mouse from the empty area of the track (just to the right of the clip on track **Audio 1**) over all four audio clips, until all audio clips are selected. After all four audio clips are selected, you can let go of the mouse and the **Alt** key.

It's a strange behavior to get used to, but when you want to select a group of clips by dragging the mouse over them, you have to start the mouse "drag" in the empty area of a track. Clicking in the empty area of a track is also a convenient way to ***un****select a clip.*

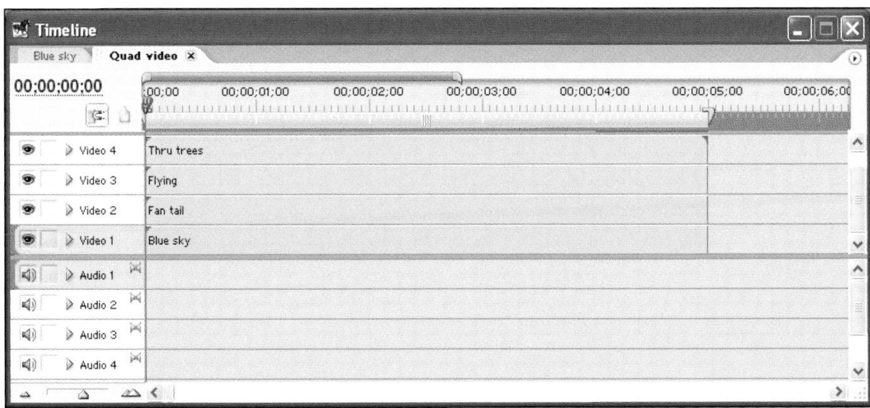

12. With all four audio clips still selected, press the **Delete** key on your keyboard to clear them from the **Timeline**.

If you don't hold down the ***Alt*** *key when selecting the clips, Premiere Pro will automatically select the video associated with each audio clip. The* ***Alt*** *key (as you learned many chapters ago!) allows you to select just the audio* ***or*** *video from linked clips.*

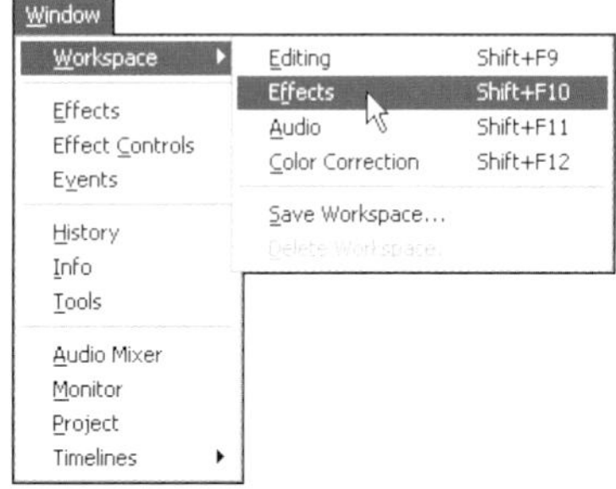

13. Time to change the motion properties. Choose **Window > Workspace > Effects**.

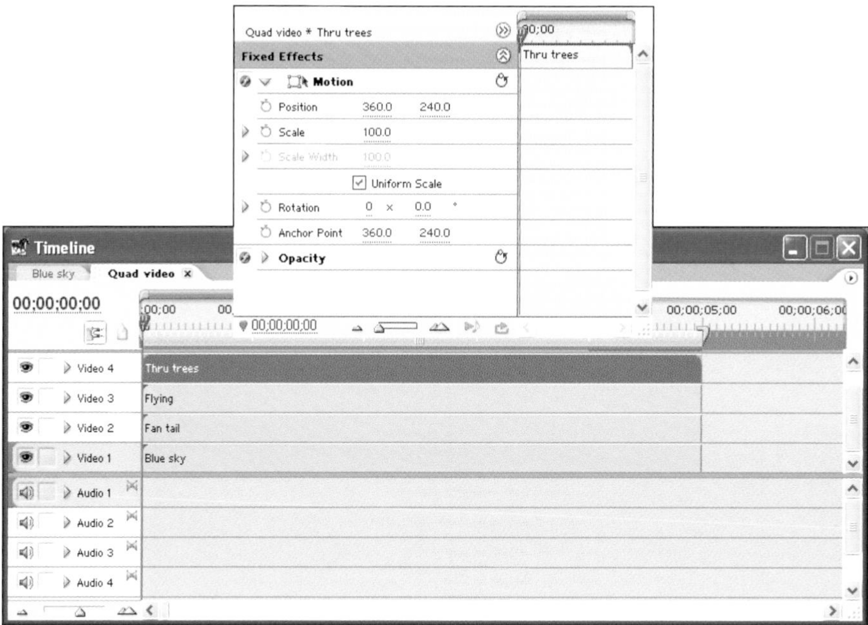

14. Select the **Thru Trees** nested sequence in track **Video 4** to view its effect controls. In the **Effect Controls** window, twirl down the **Motion** properties.

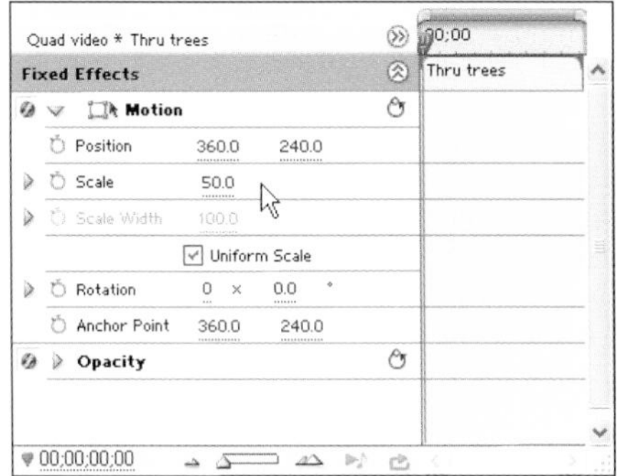

15. In the **Effect Controls** window, click the **Scale** value, type in **50.0**, and press **Enter**.

Tip: (Warning–math ahead...) You would think that a quadrant of video (a video in each corner) would be 25% scale, since, after all, it is four clips. Well, scaling 50% reduces the width by one-half and reduces the height by one-half, so that's one-half multiplied by one-half, which equals one-quarter. The math lesson for the day is: a scale of 50% reduces the clip to one-quarter its original size.

16. In the **Effect Controls** window, click the word **Motion** to put the clip in direct-select mode in the **Program** monitor. Drag **Thru trees** in the **Program** monitor to the lower-right corner of the screen.

At this point, much of this should be repetition for you, since you practiced these same skills in earlier chapters.

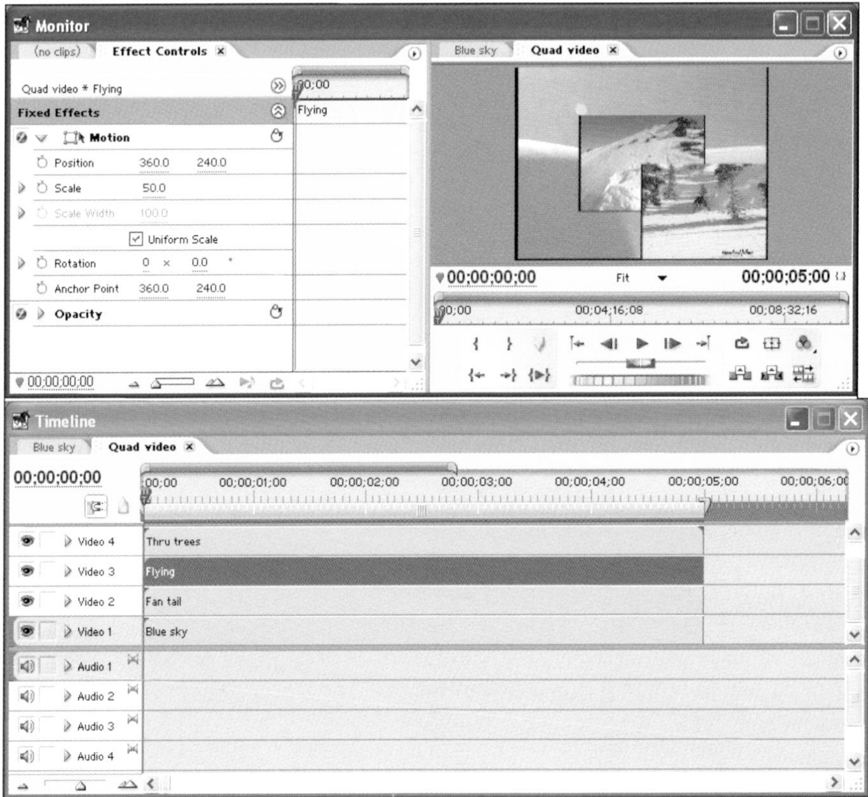

17. In the **Timeline** window, select the nested sequence **Flying** on track **Video 3** to view its effect controls. In the **Effect Controls** window, twirl down the **Motion** properties. Change the **Scale** value to **50.0**.

18. In the **Effect Controls** window, click the word **Motion** to put the clip in direct-select mode in the **Program** monitor. Drag **Flying** in the **Program** monitor to the lower-left corner of the screen.

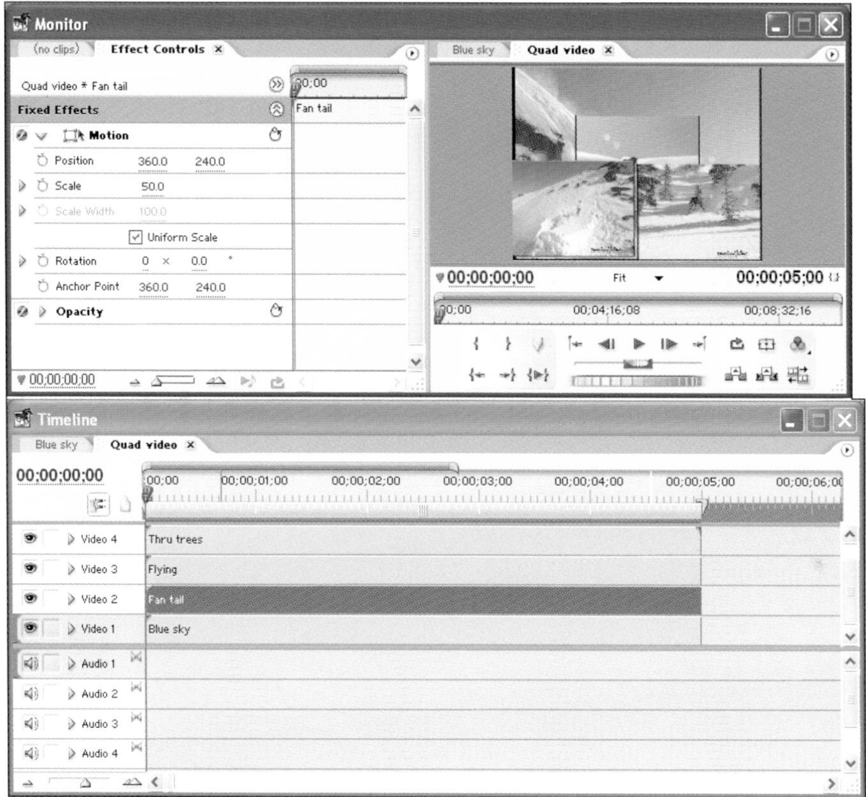

19. In the **Timeline** window, select the nested sequence **Fan tail** on track **Video 2** to view its effect controls. In the **Effect Controls** window, twirl down the **Motion** properties. Change the **Scale** value to **50.0**.

20. In the **Effect Controls** window, click the word **Motion** to put the clip in direct-select mode in the **Program** monitor. Drag **Fan tail** in the **Program** monitor to the upper-right corner of the screen.

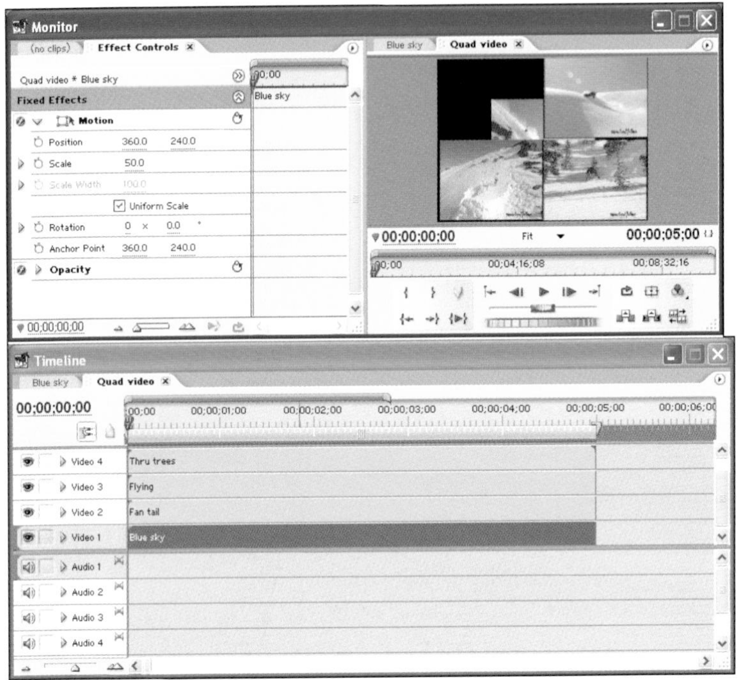

21. (Last one, yay!) In the **Timeline** window, select the nested sequence **Blue sky** on track **Video 1** to view its effect controls. In the **Effect Controls** window, twirl down the **Motion** properties. Change the **Scale** value to **50.0**.

22. In the **Effect Controls** window, click the word **Motion** to put the clip in direct-select mode in the **Program** monitor. Drag **Blue sky** in the **Program** monitor to the upper-left corner of the screen.

23. Play the master sequence **Quad video** to preview all four nested sequences.

Note: *The term "master sequence" is used only to signify the hierarchy of the sequences, as in "The four sequences are nested in a master sequence." However, there is nothing different about this sequence than the other four; as far as Premiere Pro is concerned, they are all sequences that contain clips. (It just so happens that the* ***Quad video*** *sequence contains clips that contain clips! That sure is a brain bender.)*

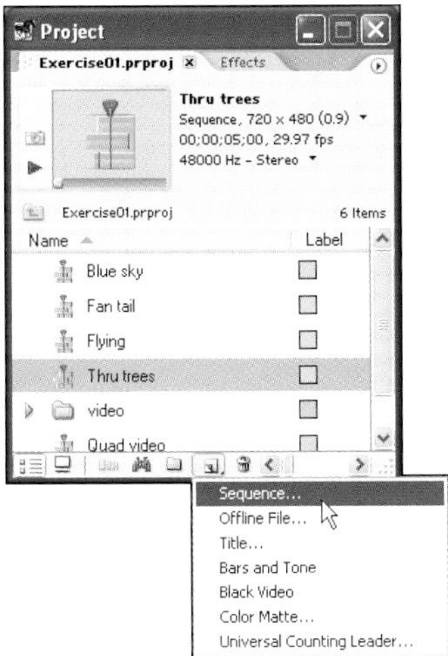

24. In the **Project** window, click the **Project** tab to bring it to the foreground. Click the **New Item** icon and choose **Sequence**.

Thought you were off the hook, didn't you? Not yet. You are going to nest just one more sequence.

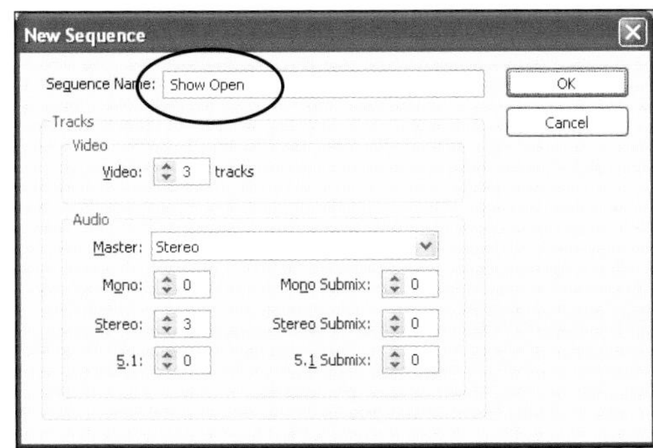

25. In the **New Sequence** window, name the sequence **Show Open**. You can leave all other options as they are. Click **OK**.

*In this sequence, you are going to nest **Quad video**. That's right–a sequence within a sequence within a sequence.*

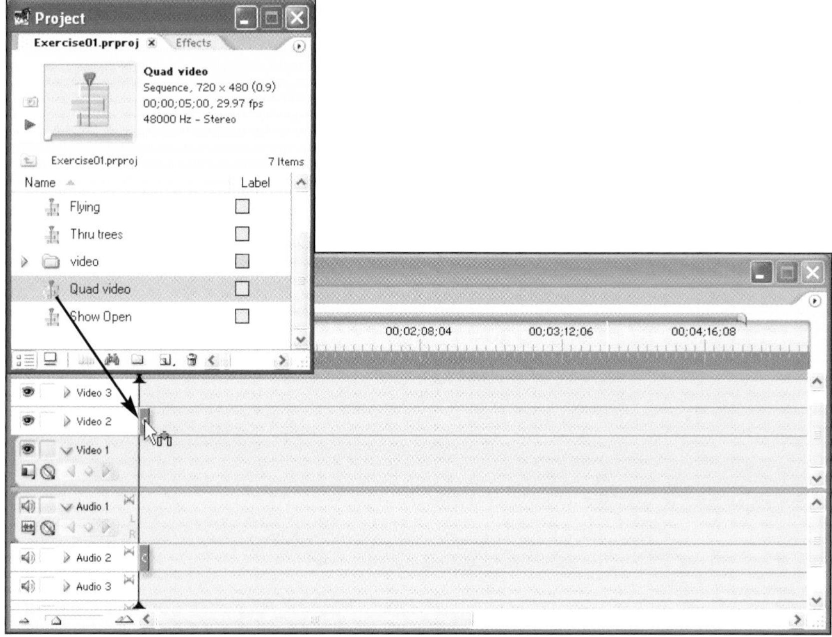

26. Your new sequence, **Show Open**, should be open in the **Timeline** window. From the **Project** window, drag the **Quad Video** sequence to track **Video 2** of **Show Open** in the **Timeline**.

Notice that the nested sequence, ***Quad video****, shows as just one video clip on a single video track (even though the sequence actually has four different video tracks).*

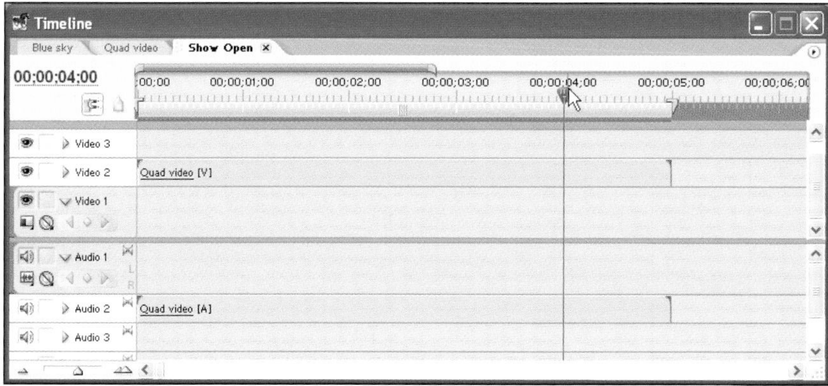

27. Press the \ (backslash) key on your keyboard to zoom the sequence to fit in the **Timeline** window. Drag the current time indicator to the location right before the four sequences began to "slide away." In this case, I used **00;00;04;00**.

*In the next step, you are going to place a video clip on track **Video 1**, below the nested sequence. However, since the screen is completely covered until the quadrant begins to slide away, there's no need to place the video clip on track **Video 1** until **04;00** seconds. (Any place earlier and it won't be visible.)*

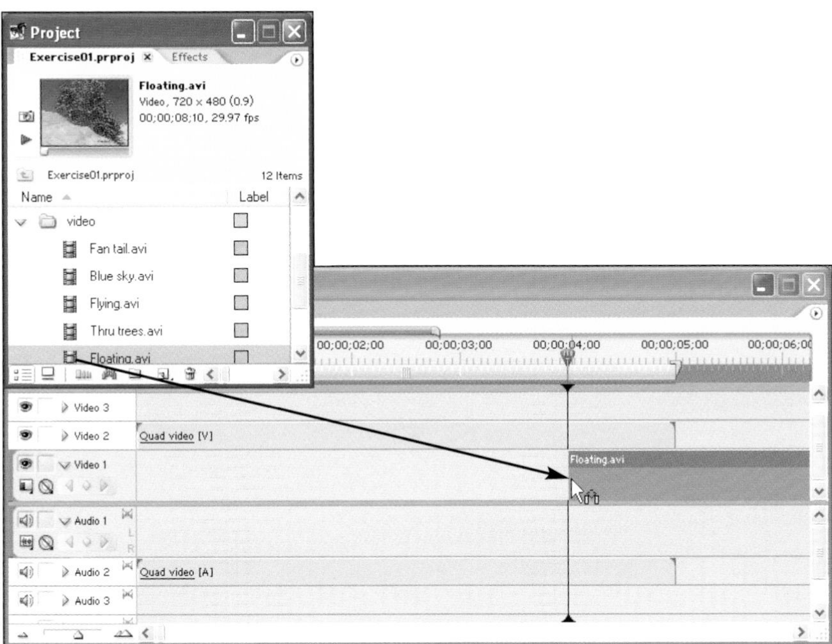

28. In the **Project** window, twirl down the **video** bin to view its contents. Drag the **Floating.avi** clip from the **Project** window to track **Video 1** of the **Timeline**. Snap it to the current time indicator at **00;04;00;00**.

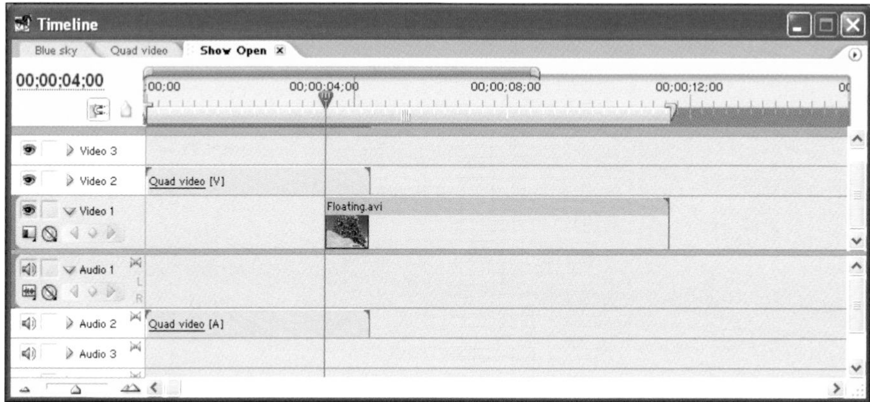

29. Press the \ (backslash) key on the keyboard to zoom the sequence to fit in the **Timeline** window. Play the **Show Open** sequence to watch the finished product.

That was one long exercise! Then again, it was probably one of the easier exercises, especially at this point since you know how to perform most of these tasks. There's no limit to how many times you can nest sequences within sequences within sequences... ad infinitum. If this was a television show you were editing, you could use the ***Quad video*** *sequence over and over again in any future project. This highlights just one of the many benefits of nesting sequences.*

---

30. Save this project and keep it open before moving on to the next exercise.

2. Adding Effects to a Nested Sequence

This exercise will be a breeze for you because you already know how to add effects to clips.

1. If the previous exercise is still open, skip to Step 2. If Premiere Pro is not running, launch it and click **Open Project** at the **Welcome Screen**. Navigate to the **c:\Premiere Pro HOT\Chapter13** folder, select **Exercise02.prproj**, and click **Open**.

Note: *The sort order of clips in your* ***Project*** *window may be different from those shown in this exercise, because Premiere Pro re-sorts all clips alphabetically when a project is opened.*

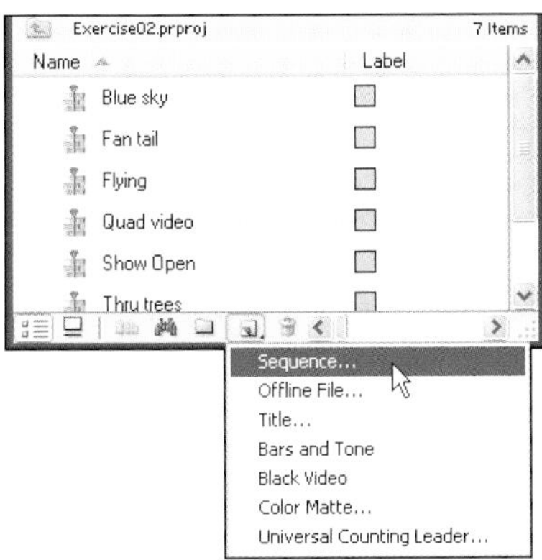

2. In the **Project** window, click the **New Item** icon and choose **Sequence**.

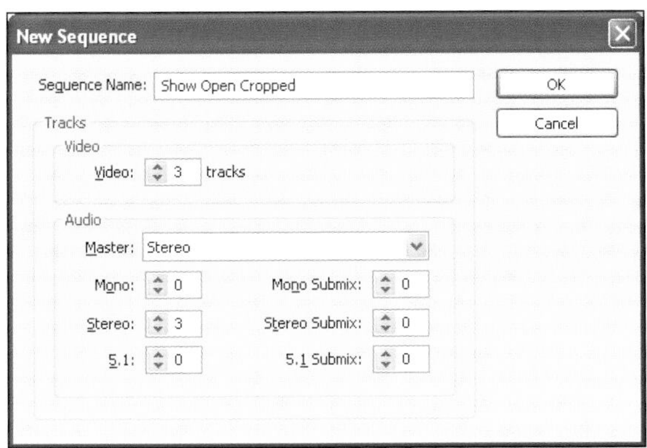

3. In the **New Sequence** window, name the new sequence **Show Open Cropped**. All other options can remain the same. Click **OK**.

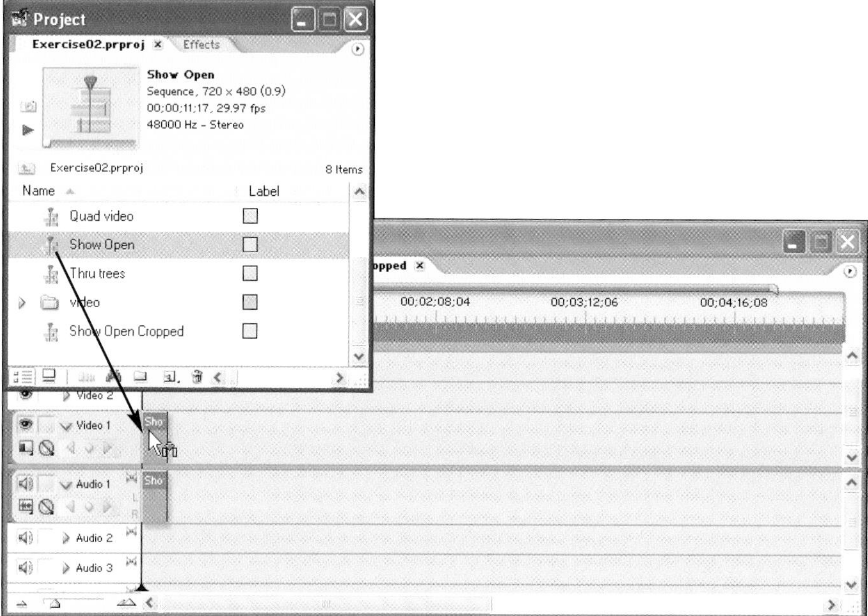

4. Drag **Show Open** from the **Project** window to track **Video 1** of the **Timeline** to nest it in the new sequence **Show Open Cropped**. Snap it to the beginning of the sequence.

5. Press the \ (backslash) key on the keyboard to zoom the sequence to fit into the **Timeline** window.

6. Choose **Window > Workspace > Effects**.

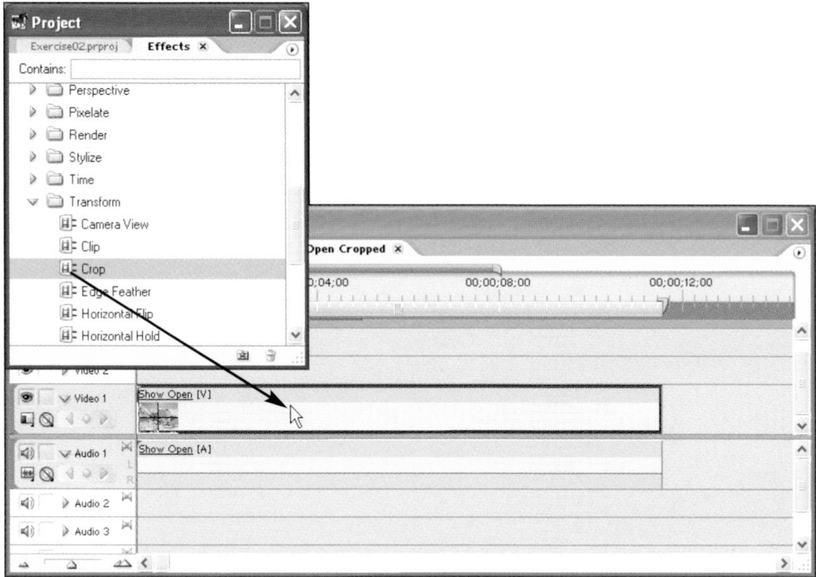

7. In the **Effects** window, twirl down the **Video Effects** and **Transform** folders. Drag the **Crop** effect onto the nested sequence in track **Video 1**.

*The **Crop** effect is a quick way to create a letterbox/widescreen look on standard 4:3 aspect video.*

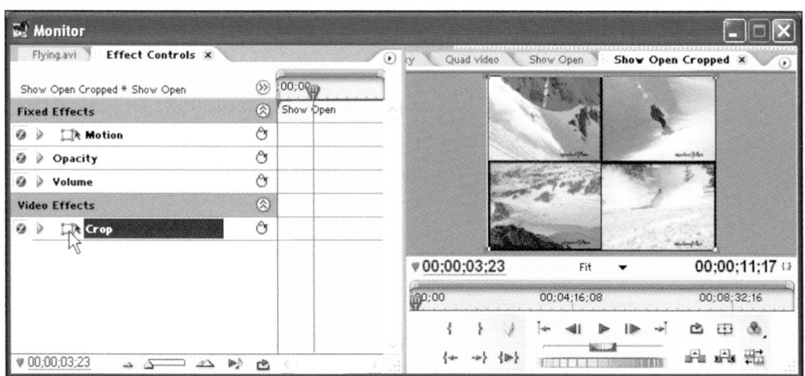

8. Press **Home** on the keyboard to move the current time indicator to the start of the sequence. Select the nested sequence in track **Video 1** to view its effect controls. In the **Effect Controls** window, click the **Transform** icon next to the **Crop** effect.

*This will place four handles around the clip in the **Program** monitor. You can directly drag the handles to crop your clip. Any effect that displays the **Transform** icon next to its name can be directly manipulated in the **Program** monitor.*

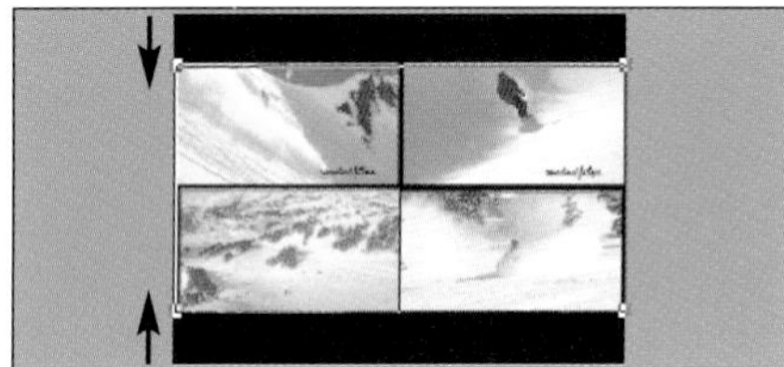

9. In the **Program** monitor, drag down one of the top handles (upper left or upper right) to crop the top of the screen. Next, drag up one of the lower handles (lower left or lower right) to crop the bottom of the screen.

Tip: *There are two effects in the* ***Transform*** *folder that appear to create similar results:* ***Crop*** *and* ***Clip.*** *There is an important difference between the two:* ***Crop*** *"removes" the section of video;* ***Clip*** *paints it black. In Photoshop terms,* ***Crop*** *creates a transparent alpha channel, which allows video underneath to show through, whereas* ***Clip*** *fills the empty space with an opaque color such as black (nothing below will show through).*

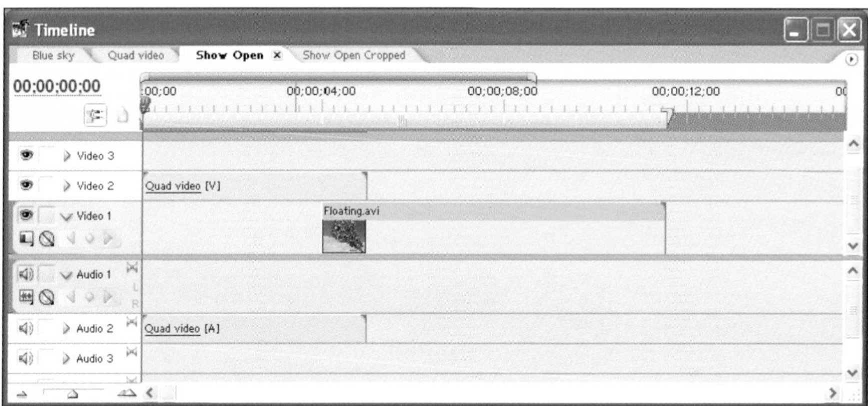

10. Double-click the nested sequence in track **Video 1**.

Double-clicking a nested sequence opens up the sequence in the ***Timeline*** *window. Your* ***Timeline*** *window should display the* ***Show Open*** *sequence (instead of* ***Show Open Cropped****).*

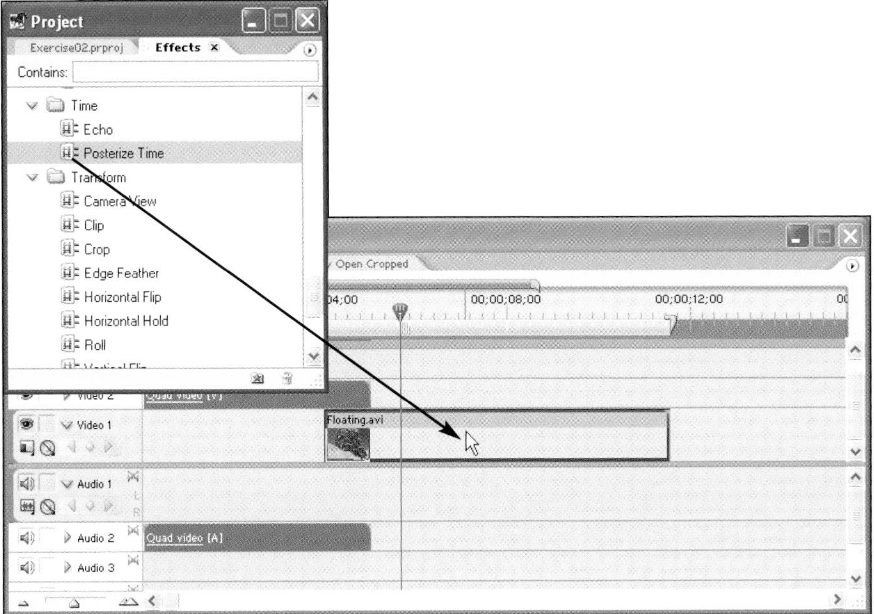

11. In the **Effects** window, twirl down the **Time** folder. Drag the **Posterize Time** effect onto **Floating.avi** in the **Timeline** window.

One of the best features of nested sequences is that you can modify the original sequence, and the video will automatically be updated in whichever sequence you nested it in.

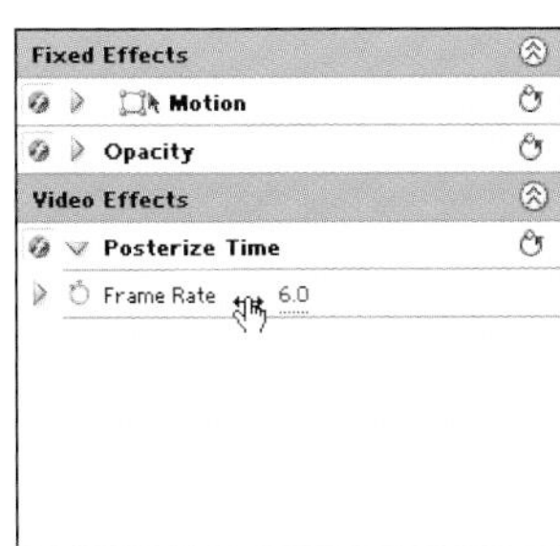

12. Select **Floating.avi** in track **Video 1** to view its effect controls. In the **Effect Controls** window, twirl down **Posterize Time** to view the effect properties. Drag the **Frame Rate** property to **6.0**.

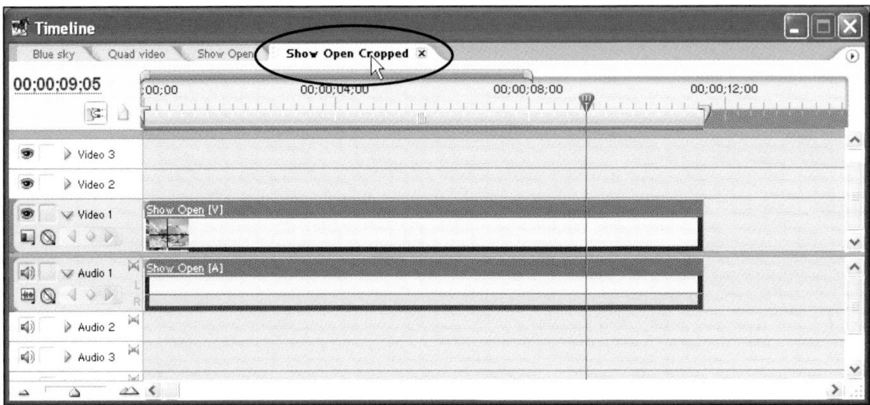

13. Click the **Show Open Cropped** tab along the top of the **Timeline** window to view that sequence.

Tip: *All open sequences are shown as tabs along the top of the* ***Timeline*** *window. Another quick way to open a sequence in the* ***Timeline*** *window is to double-click it in the* ***Project*** *window.*

---

14. Play the **Show Open Cropped** sequence to preview the change.

The "master" sequence is automatically updated when you make a change to a nested sequence. How wonderful is that! (If that doesn't get you all tingly, you better check your pulse.) There are, of course, hundreds of additional effects you can apply to nested sequences, and by now you should have all the knowledge you need to venture out and learn more on your own.

---

15. Save this project and keep it open before moving on to the next exercise.

3. Importing Photoshop Layers as a Sequence

When importing a Photoshop document, you can import all of the layers as a sequence. This converts every layer to a video track in the new sequence. In this exercise, you will learn how to import a Photoshop document as a sequence and then nest it in another sequence.

1. If the previous exercise is still open, skip to Step 2. If Premiere Pro is not running, launch it and click **Open Project** at the **Welcome Screen**. Navigate to the **c:\Premiere Pro HOT\Chapter13** folder, select **Exercise03.prproj**, and click **Open**.

Note: *The sort order of clips in your* ***Project*** *window may be different from those shown in this exercise, because Premiere re-sorts all clips alphabetically when a project is opened.*

2. Choose **Window > Workspace > Editing**.

3. Choose **File > Import**.

4. Navigate to the **c:\Premiere Pro HOT\Source Graphics** folder and select **skier.psd**. Click **Open**.

Tip: *When importing a Photoshop file, you can also import a single layer of a file, or you can import a merged image. (This may sound like Greek to you if you're not familiar with Photoshop.)*

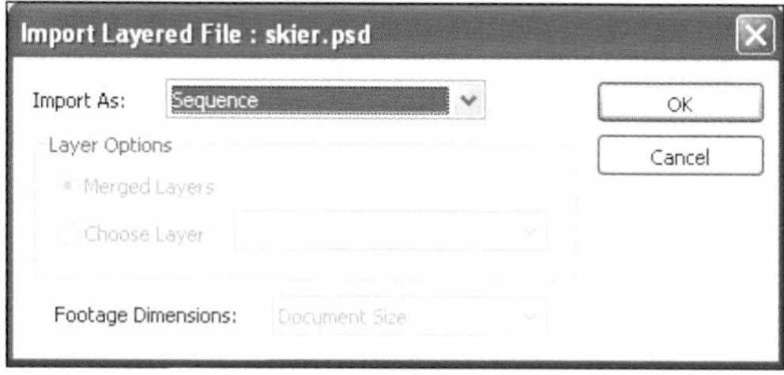

5. At the **Import Layered File** window, choose **Sequence** from the **Import As** drop-down menu. Click **OK**.

When you import a Photoshop document as a sequence, a new bin and sequence are created in the ***Project*** *window. Each Photoshop layer is imported as a still image, and each still image is placed in its own track in the sequence. In this case, the Photoshop document has three layers, so three still images are created, and the sequence has three video tracks—one for each image.*

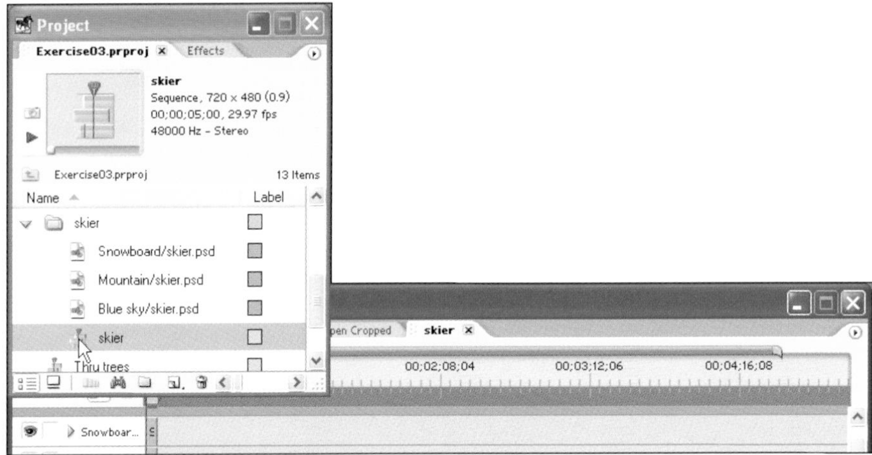

6. In the **Project** window, twirl down the **skier** bin and double-click the **skier** sequence to open it in the **Timeline** window.

Earlier you learned that all sequences must have at least one audio track. Even though this Photoshop document has no audio, the sequence that is imported contains one audio track. Also note that the sequence and the bin are imported with the same name, so be careful when clicking–you don't want to accidentally select the bin when you mean to select the sequence.

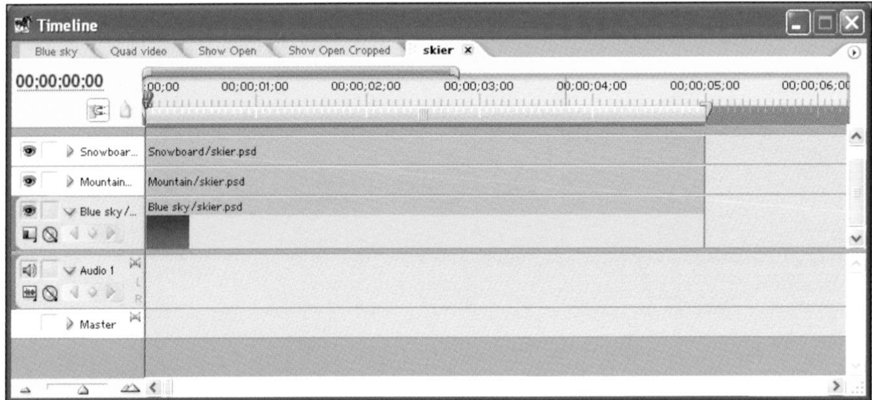

7. Press the \ (backslash) key on the keyboard to zoom the sequence to fit into the **Timeline** window. Play the sequence to preview the still images.

Notice that the sequence has three video tracks. The original Photoshop document had three layers, so each layer became a clip on a video track. Also notice that each track has been renamed with the Photoshop layer name.

8. Choose **Window > Workspace > Effects**. Press **Home** on the keyboard to snap the current time indicator to the beginning of the sequence.

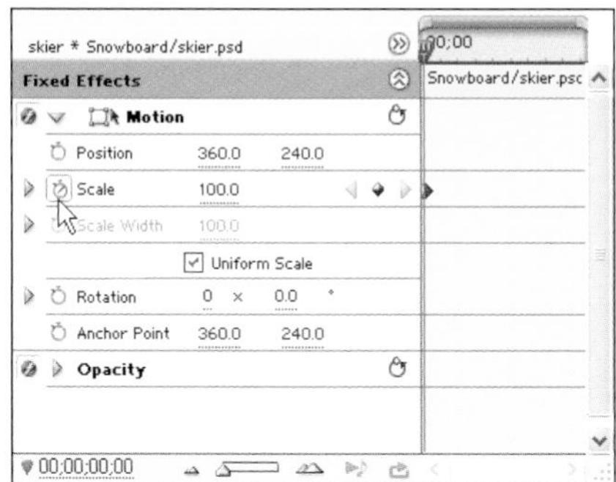

9. Select the **Snowboard** clip in the top track to view its effect controls. In the **Effect Controls** window, twirl down **Motion** to view its properties. Click the **Toggle Animation** (stopwatch) icon for the **Scale** property to enable scale keyframes.

A keyframe reminder–whenever you turn on keyframe mode for a property, a keyframe is created.

10. With the **Snowboard** clip still selected on the **Timeline**, press **End** on the keyboard and then tap once on the keyboard's **left arrow** to move the current time indicator to the last frame of the clip.

*Just a reminder–always use **End+left arrow** when setting a keyframe at the end of a clip.*

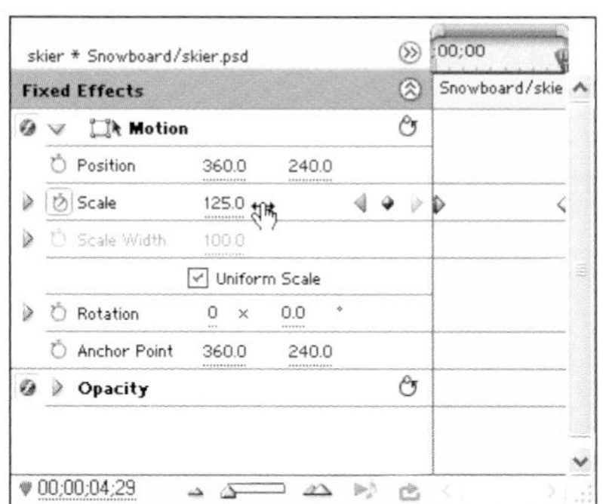

11. Change the **Scale** property from **100.0** to **125.0** to create a new keyframe on the last frame of the clip.

Earlier in this book, you learned how to add motion keyframes to your still images to provide some visual interest. If you are a Photoshop whiz–or if you know a Photoshop whiz who owes you a favor–you can edit your still images into separate layers and move the foregrounds and backgrounds independently.

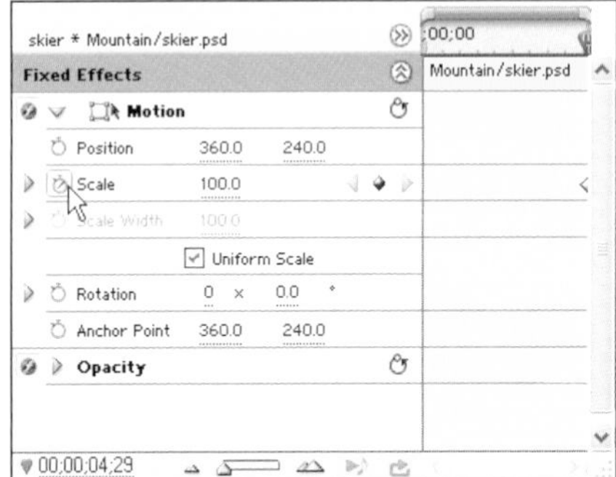

12. Select the **Mountain** clip on the second video track in the **Timeline** to view its effect controls. Press **End+left arrow** on the keyboard to move to the last frame of the clip. In the **Effect Controls** window, twirl down **Motion** and click the **Toggle Animation** stopwatch for the **Scale** property.

You can also create keyframes in reverse order (or in any order that you please). In this case, you are creating the last keyframe first and the first keyframe last.

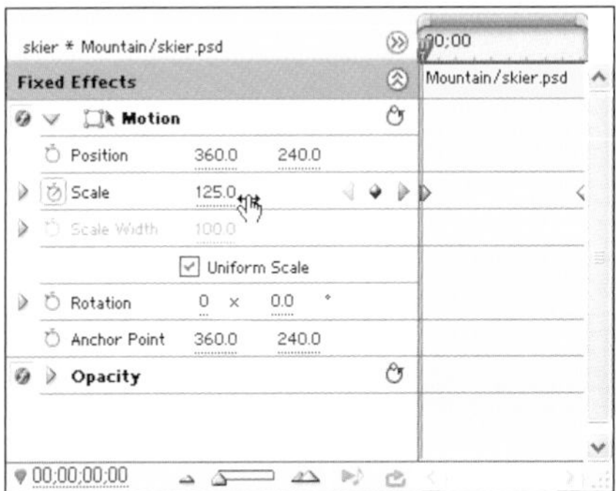

13. With the **Mountain** clip still selected, press **Home** on the keyboard to snap the current time indicator to the beginning of the clip. In the **Effect Controls** window, change the **Scale** property to **125.0**.

14. Play the sequence to preview the effect keyframes.

On your screen, the image may be a bit "shaky" or "wavy", because Premiere Pro is only showing you a preview of your finished product. The preview is created on the fly by Premiere Pro, and it doesn't always have the same quality of the finished product, especially with complex effects. To remedy this, you can render *the sequence to get a more accurate preview, which will better match the real output.*

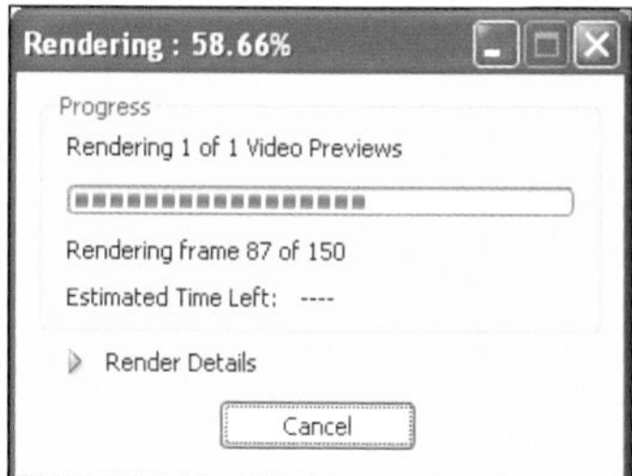

15. Choose **Sequence > Render Work Area**.

*As the sequence renders, a **Rendering** window appears with a progress bar. The speed of the render is largely based on your system's processor, available memory, and hard drive transfer rate. Also note, after rendering, the sequence should automatically play.*

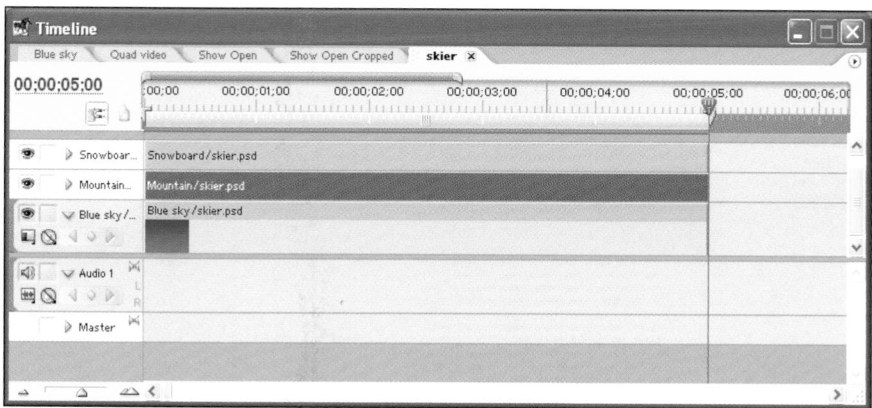

16. Play the sequence to preview the rendered sequence.

Once the work area has been rendered, you can play it again and again without re-rendering. The rendered video should look a little sharper, and the motion effect should appear smoother. Also notice that Premiere Pro adds a green bar above any video that has been pre-rendered. This video will stay green unless you make a change to one of the clips or one of the effects.

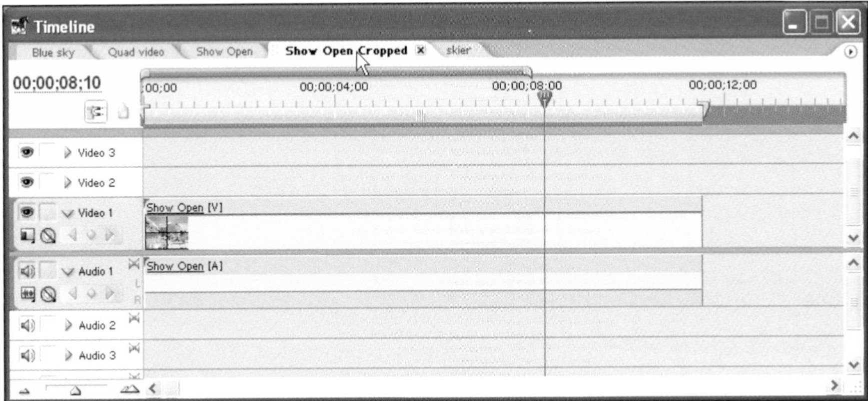

17. In the **Timeline** window, click the **Show Open Cropped** tab to bring that sequence to the foreground. Move the current time indicator to **00;00;08;10**.

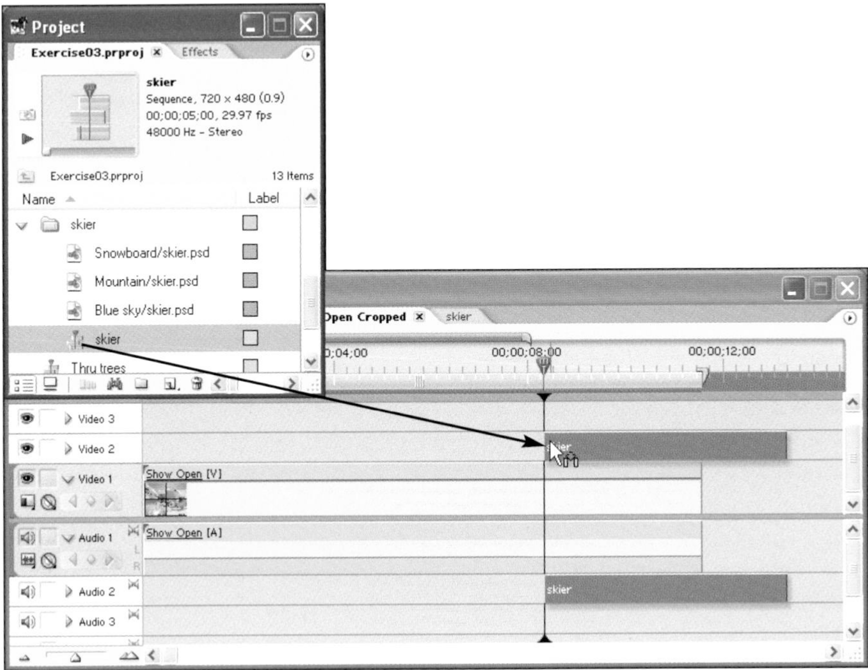

18. In the **Project** window, click the **Project** tab to bring it to the foreground. Drag the **skier** sequence to track **Video 2** of the **Timeline**, snapping it to the current time indicator at **00;00;08;10**.

*You have just nested the **skier** sequence into the **Show Open Cropped** sequence.*

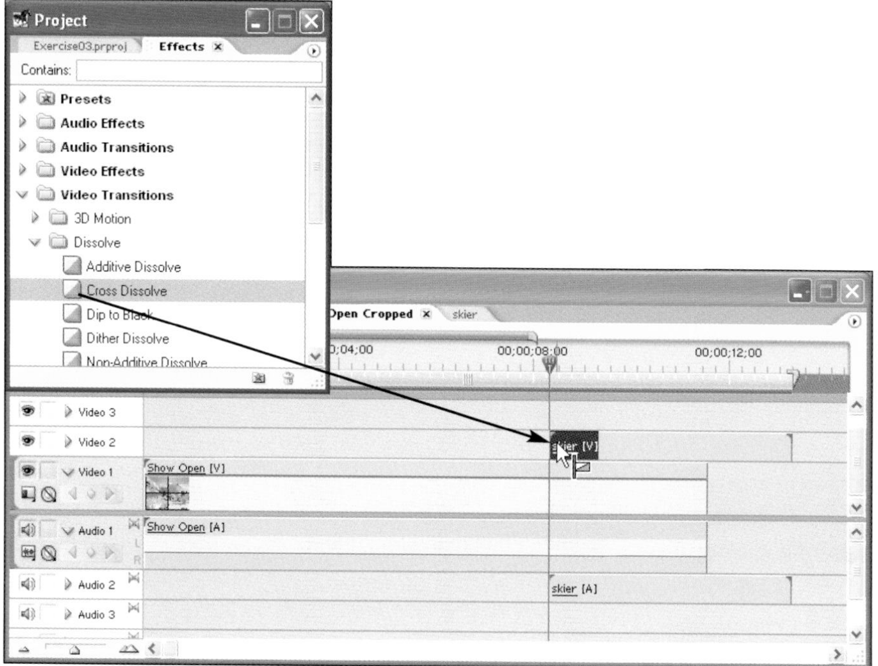

19. In the **Project** window, click the **Effects** tab to bring it to the foreground. Twirl down the **Video Transitions** and **Dissolve** folders. Drag the **Cross Dissolve** transition to the beginning of the **skier** nested sequence on track **Video 2**.

That's right, you can also add transitions to nested sequences. (Three cheers for nested sequences!)

---

20. Play the sequence to preview all of the changes.

If you think the video is suffering from the "preview quality" shakes, you can render the entire sequence to view a more accurate preview by choosing ***Sequence > Render Work Area****. However, this may take a minute or two depending on the speed of your computer system.*

In this exercise, you have learned how to import a Photoshop file as a sequence. But more importantly, you have a learned a handy trick for adding visual interest to your photographs. Of course, this requires a modicum of Photoshop know-how, as well how to work with Photoshop layers that contain alpha channels. (Of course, you could always purchase Adobe Photoshop CS/Image Ready CS Hands-On Training *from Lynda.com and Peachpit Press.)*

---

21. Save this project and keep it open before moving on to the next exercise.

NOTE | Rendering vs. Real-Time

Many of you are probably scratching your heads thinking, "Wait a minute. I purchased a real-time editing solution. How come I had to render in the previous exercise?" Here's the scoop on rendering vs. real time previews. Premiere Pro is billed as a real-time editing solution. And for the most part, this is true. It's designed to play DV video in real-time–you can watch your sequence in the preview monitor without having to wait. Every time you add a title, still image, or video effect, you increase Premiere Pro's workload; the application must do additional math before it can display the preview. Premiere Pro's real-time capabilities are based upon the speed and performance of your computer system. The more robust your system, the more that can be done in real-time. A single title, or a simple video effect, is usually no problem for Premiere Pro to display in real-time. However, during complex sections of the sequence–such as those with keyframed effects or multiple still images–Premiere Pro cannot display the full preview in real-time. In these cases, Premiere Pro dynamically adjusts picture quality and playback performance. In other words, the quality and playback performance of the preview are compromised, in order to show a real-time preview. The advantage of compromising quality is you can see the preview in real time, but the disadvantage is you do not always get an accurate representation of the finished product, because the work is being done on the fly. (Keep in mind that the finished product is never compromised, only the onscreen preview.)

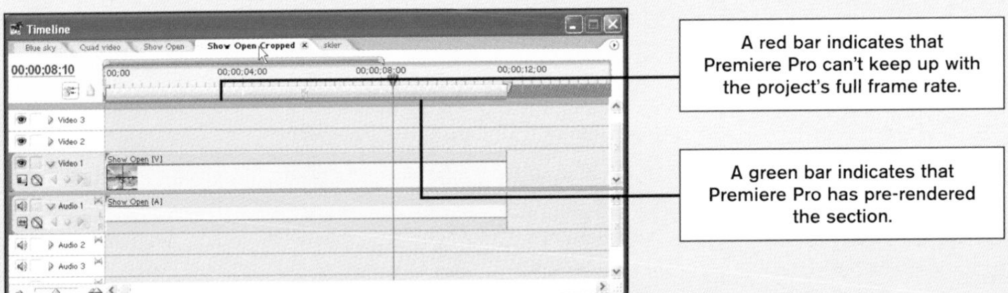

Timeline
A red bar indicates that Premiere Pro can't keep up with the project's full frame rate.
A green bar indicates that Premiere Pro has pre-rendered the section.

A red bar over a portion of a sequence indicates that Premiere Pro cannot play back the section at the project's full frame rate, and a compromise will be made. Premiere Pro will still show you a "real-time" preview of that section, but the quality and playback are degraded to keep up with the demands of the section. Instead of trying to do the "effect math" on the fly, *rendering* allows Premiere Pro to do the math ahead of time by creating a temporary movie on your hard drive. When you play back the sequence, Premiere Pro can display the best quality because the math homework has already been done. A green bar above the Timeline represents a section that has already been rendered.

So, to answer the original question: Is Premiere Pro a real-time editor? Answer: *Yes*. But there's no such thing as a free lunch, and in order to stay real-time, picture quality is compromised.

Track Mattes

Track mattes allow you to "borrow" the alpha channel shape of one image, and use it to define the shape of another image. It's a good idea to get a refresher on the basics of alpha channels.

(The checkerboard pattern represents the transparent area of the image.)

Image with an alpha channel.

Alpha channel allows video to show through.

In Chapter 7, "*Still Images and Fixed Effects*," you learned that alpha channels define the transparent region of a still image. In the Timeline, the still image can be placed on a track above the video clip, and the alpha channel allows the video to show through the transparent region(s).

The original image, without alpha channel

Same image, with alpha channel

Another way of looking at an alpha channel is that it defines the shape of an image, as if you had taken scissors and cut out everything around the image.

+

=

A track matte allows you to take the shape of one image and combine it with the "look" of another image. More accurately, you are borrowing the alpha channel of Clip A and applying it to Clip B.

You can create many interesting looks using track mattes. One of the most common methods is to take a simple title–remember, titles have alpha channels–and use it as a track matte on top of video. This lets the video "play through" the letters of the title. The next exercise will walk you through the steps of creating this type of track matte.

4. Creating a Track Matte

Another great reason to nest a sequence is to create a track matte. Mattes allow you to combine the video from one clip with the shape of another clip. Sound confusing? It's not so bad. This exercise will walk you through the ease of creating a track matte with a nested sequence.

1. If the previous exercise is still open, skip to Step 2. If Premiere Pro is not running, launch it and click **Open Project** at the **Welcome Screen**. Navigate to the **c:\Premiere Pro HOT\Chapter13** folder, select **Exercise04.prproj**, and click **Open**.

*Note: The sort order of clips in your **Project** window may be different from those shown in this exercise, because Premiere re-sorts all clips alphabetically when a project is opened.*

2. Choose **Window > Workspace > Editing**.

3. Choose **File > Import**.

4. Navigate to the **c:\Premiere Pro HOT\Source Graphics** directory, select **ski.prtl**, and click **Open**.

*In this exercise, you will take the "shape" of the **Ski** title and apply it to a video clip.*

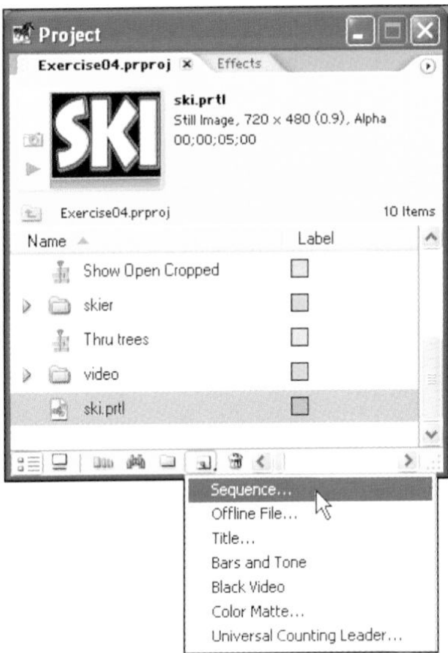

5. In the **Project** window, click the **New Item** icon, and choose **Sequence**.

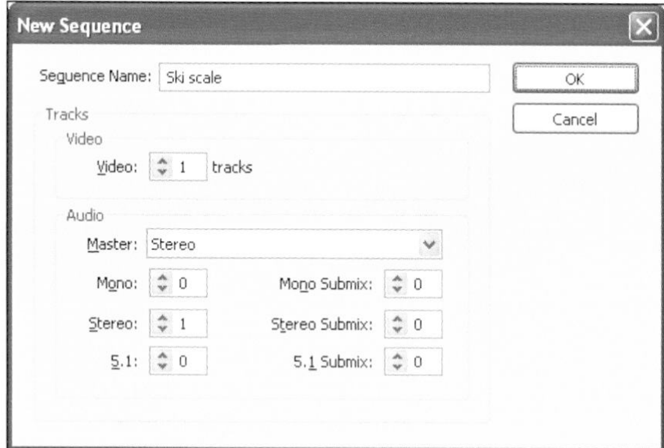

6. In the **New Sequence** window, name the sequence **Ski scale**. Change **Video Tracks** to **1** and **Stereo** to **1**.

In this sequence, you will add scale keyframes to your title to make it increase in size over time.

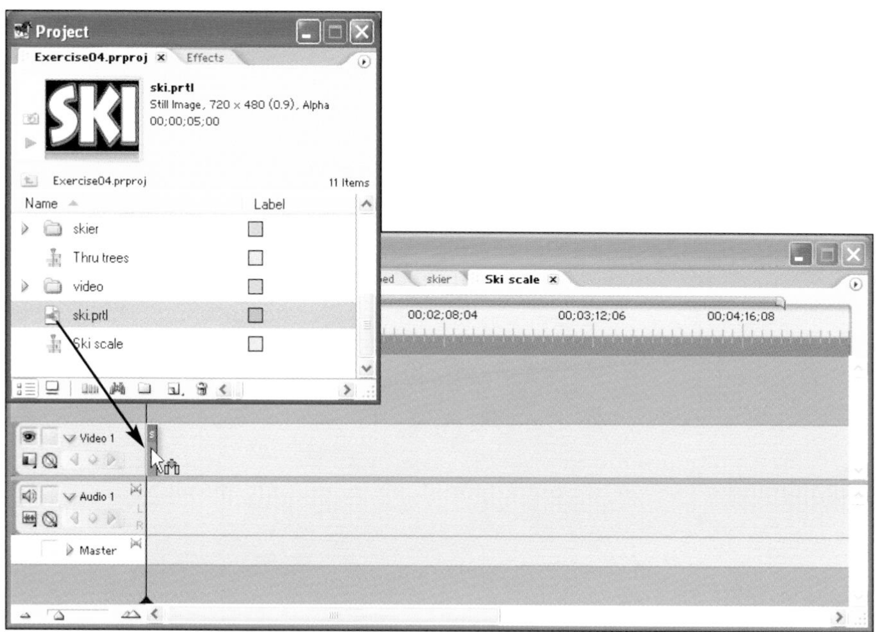

7. From the **Project** window, drag **Ski.prtl** to track **Video 1** of the **Ski scale** sequence in the **Timeline** window. Snap it to the beginning of the sequence.

8. Press the \ (backslash) key on your keyboard to zoom the sequence to fit into the **Timeline** window. Press **Home** on your keyboard to snap the current time indicator to the beginning of the sequence.

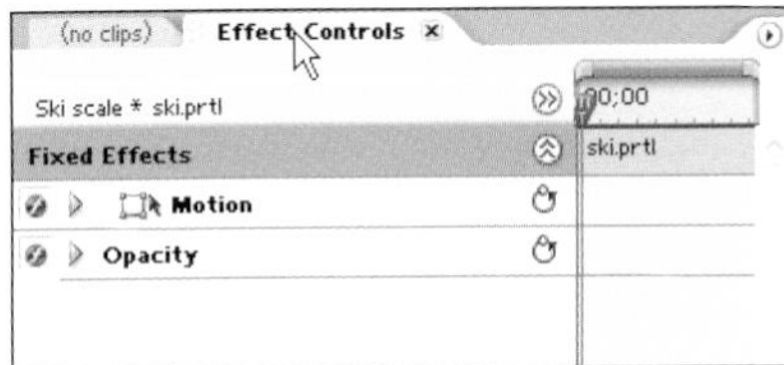

9. At the top of the **Monitor Source** view, click the **Effect Controls** tab to bring it to the foreground.

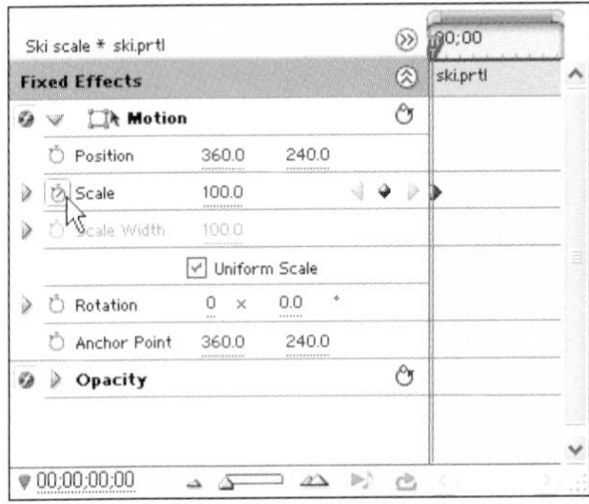

10. Select the title in track **Video 1** to view its effect controls. From the **Effect Controls** window, twirl down **Motion** to view its properties. Click the **Toggle Animation** icon (stopwatch) next to the **Scale** property to enable keyframe mode.

11. Change the **Scale** value from **100.0** to **70.0**.

12. With the title still selected in the **Timeline**, press **End+left arrow** on your keyboard to move the current time indicator to the last frame of the clip.

13. Change the **Scale** value to **100.0** to create a new keyframe at the current time indicator.

14. Play the sequence to preview it.

So far you've made the title slowly increase in size over time. (Yawn. Scale keyframes are SO Chapter 11.)

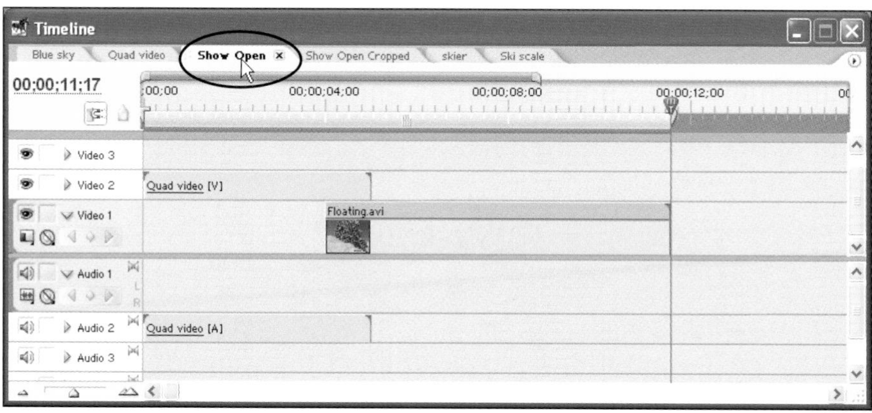

15. At the top of the **Timeline** window, click the **Show Open** tab to bring that sequence to the foreground.

Note: *Make sure you click* ***Show Open*** *and* not ***Show Open Cropped.***

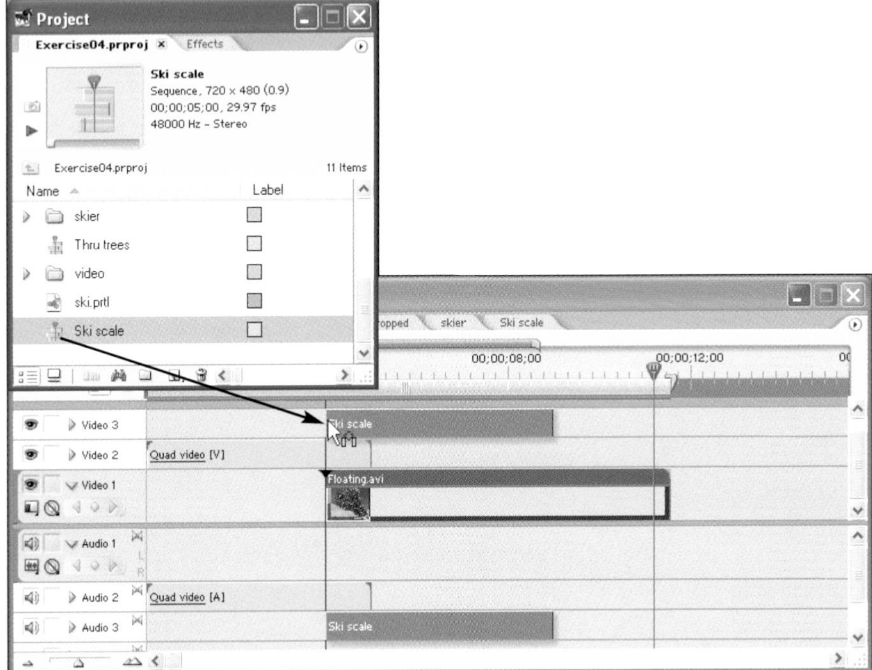

16. From the **Project** window, nest the **Ski scale** sequence in track **Video 3** of the **Show Open** sequence. Snap it to the beginning of **Floating.avi** (the clip on track **Video 1**).

17. Play the sequence to preview the changes.

*Right now, the **Ski** title plays on top of the video. In the next steps, you will add a **Track Matte** effect, which applies the title shape to the video below.*

18. Choose **Window > Workspace > Effects**.

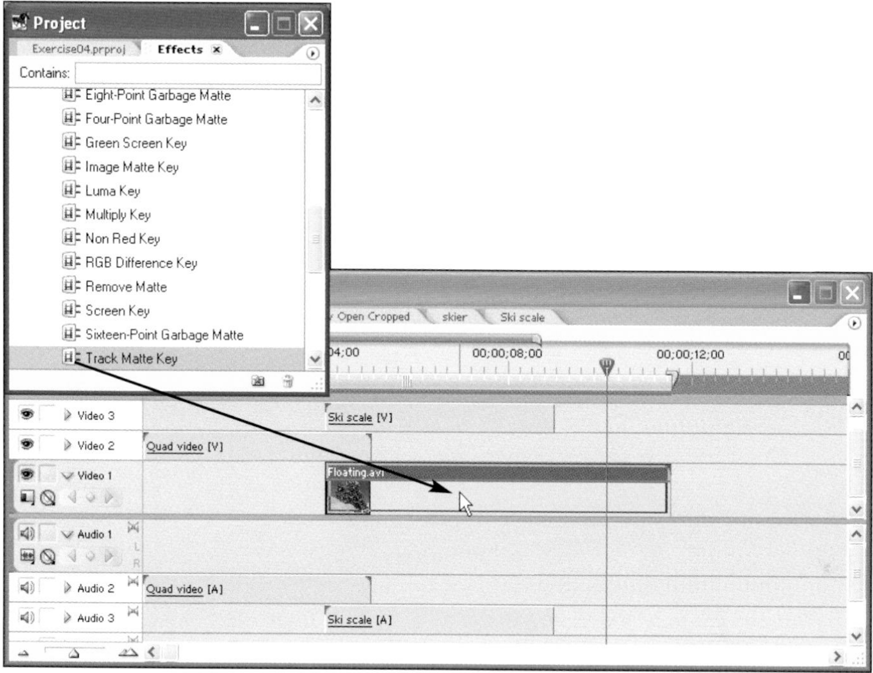

19. In the **Effects** window, twirl down the **Video Effects** folder and then the **Keying** subfolder. Scroll to the bottom of the subfolder and drag the **Track Matte Key** video effect to **Floating.avi**.

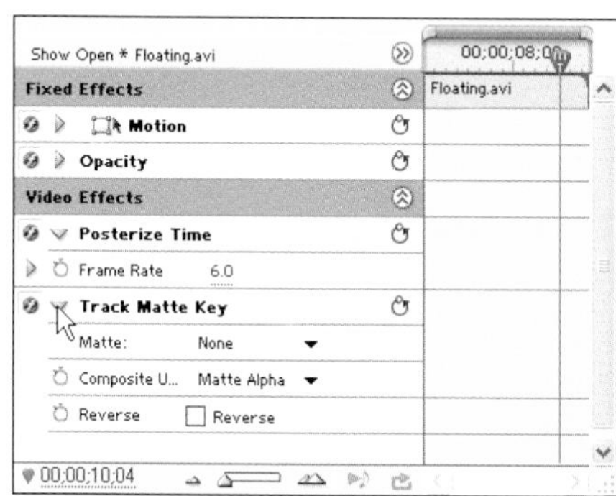

20. Select **Floating.avi** in the **Timeline** to view its effect controls. In the **Effect Controls** window, twirl down the **Track Matte Key** effect to view its properties.

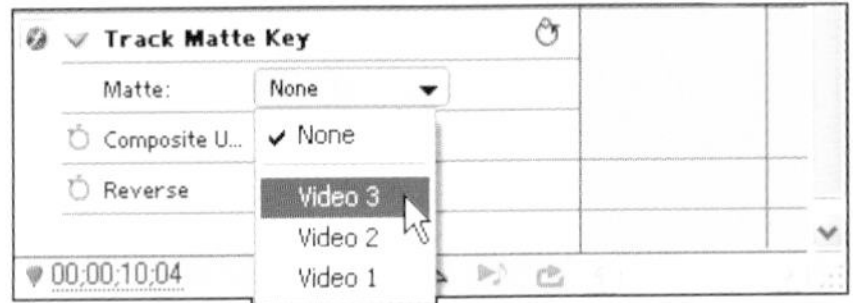

21. In the **Matte** property, click the drop-down arrow next to the word **None** and choose **Video 3**.

*In this case, you are choosing to matte (borrow the shape of) any clip on track **Video 3**, because this is the track that has the shape you want to use. (If the **Ski scale** nested sequence were on track **Video 2**, you would matte **Video 2**, for example.)*

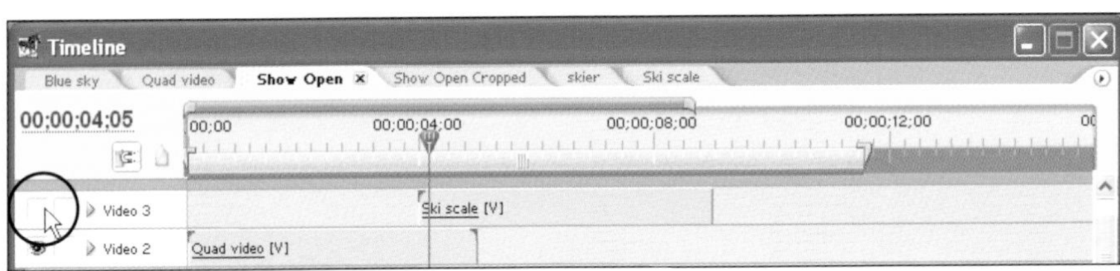

22. In the **Timeline** window, hide track **Video 3** by clicking the **Toggle Track Output** icon (eyeball) next to the track's name.

Tip: *In order to see the finished track matte, you have to hide the top track. (Otherwise the clip on the top track obstructs the video below.) This is the single biggest step that most Premiere Pro users forget to do. Even worse, many users forget to turn the eyeball back on if they decide to undo the matte.*

23. Play the sequence to preview the effect.

In this exercise, you actually created a "traveling track matte," because the matte was in motion. This is the tip of the iceberg with track mattes. There are many more interesting effects and ways to use track mattes. Now you have the tools and the know-how to go forth and build your own track matte creations. Just remember, you need three ingredients to make a track matte: a shape, video, and a track matte effect (applied to the video). Bring to boil and let simmer.

24. Close this project before moving on to the next exercise.

MOVIE | track-matte.mov

To learn more about creating track mattes, check out **track-matte.mov** from the **movies** folder on the **Premiere Pro HOT** DVD.

NOTE | Track Matte—Why Nest?

You may have noticed in the previous exercise that the **Ski scale** nested sequence had only one clip. Which begs the question, if there is only one clip, why bother creating a nested sequence?

True, normally the advantage of nested sequences is that you can take multiple clips on multiple tracks and have them behave as one clip. However, there is another advantage of nested sequences that you may not know yet.

Premiere Pro's Track Matte effect, while extremely versatile and fun to use, has one major flaw: it does not "read in" alpha channels very well. When you use a still image (or title) as a track matte, Premiere Pro borrows the image's alpha channel "shape." You experienced this in the previous exercise.

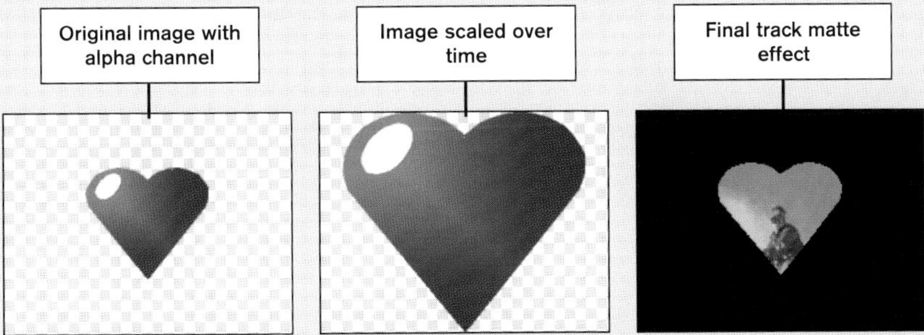

Unfortunately, Premiere Pro borrows the *original* alpha channel of the image. When the image changes, such as changing its scale over time, the alpha channel also changes. But Premiere Pro *ignores* the changes to the alpha channel. The final track matte effect uses the original shape of the image, which stinks, big time!

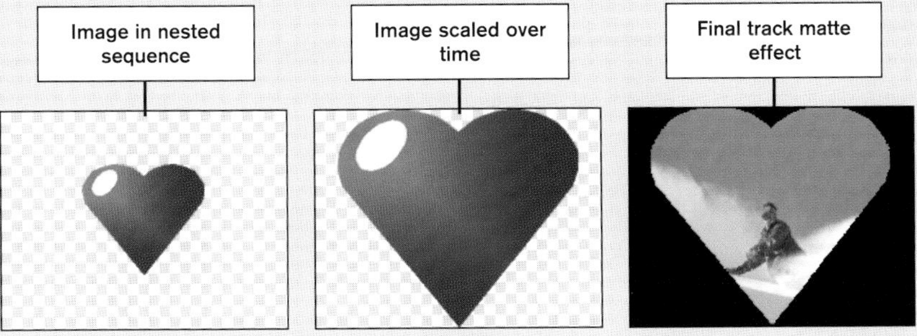

However, if you put the image in a nested sequence and use the nested sequence as the matte, Premiere Pro will read in the new alpha channel.

The bottom line: anytime you want a track matte to change over time, you must put the image in a nested sequence before using it as a track matte.

Fixing Project Size

Long ago in this book, you learned the importance of always choosing a project preset when creating a new project. If the video is shot in 16:9 widescreen, choose a widescreen project. If the video was shot in 4:3 standard, choose a standard project. You were also warned to choose your project preset very, very carefully, because Premiere Pro does not let you change the size of your project once you've created a new project.

For example, if you shoot widescreen video but accidentally choose a standard project, you cannot go back and change the project size from standard to widescreen. You are stuck.

You were also promised, earlier in this book, that you would be shown a workaround to this project size problem, and that time is at hand. Knowing what you know about nesting sequences, understanding how to fix an incorrect project size should be very easy at this point in your education.

(This is exciting, so hold on tight.) *Premiere Pro lets you import other projects.* Yes! That's right. Just like importing videos, audio files, and still images, you can also import an entire Premiere Pro project—including all of its associated clips and sequences. (Take a minute to pick yourself up off the floor if this knowledge knocked you out of your chair.)

Here's how it works: the size of a sequence in Premiere Pro is determined by the project size. You may have noticed that Premiere Pro lets you change the name and number of tracks when creating a sequence, but you are not allowed to change the size of the sequence. For example, a 16:9 project creates only 16:9 sequences. The good news is, when you import a Premiere Pro project into another project, all of the old sequences are automatically resized to match the new project settings.

In keeping with the above example, pretend you have widescreen 16:9 source video, but you built your sequence in a standard 4:3 project. (Because you didn't heed this book!) To fix this problem, you create a new 16:9 project. You then import the old 4:3 project, and all of your 4:3 sequences are converted to 16:9. Voila. Problem solved.

In the next exercise, you will get to practice this workaround for yourself.

5. Importing a Project

Besides importing a Photoshop file as a sequence, you can also import an entire Premiere Pro project and all of its associated clips and sequences. Up until now, you could only nest a sequence within the same project. Since Premiere Pro lets you import other Premiere Pro projects, you can nest any sequence from any project.

1. If Premiere Pro is not running, launch it and click **Open Project** at the **Welcome Screen**. Navigate to the **c:\Premiere Pro HOT\Chapter13** folder, select **Exercise05.prproj**, and click **Open**.

2. Play the **commercial** sequence that is open in the **Timeline** window to preview it.

This is a commercial for a fictional retailer, the Snow Chalet.

3. In the **Timeline** window, move the current time indicator to **00;00;03;11**.

4. In the **Project** window, double-click **MCU to camera.avi** to open it in the **Monitor Source** view.

*Notice that the **Source** view, the original clip, is widescreen 16:9, and the program view, the project's size, is standard 4:3. This means the video was shot in widescreen, but someone chose the wrong project settings. To fix this problem, you will create a new project with the correct preset and then import the old project.*

5. Choose **File > New > Project**.

Note: If you are asked to save changes to the project, click ***No.***

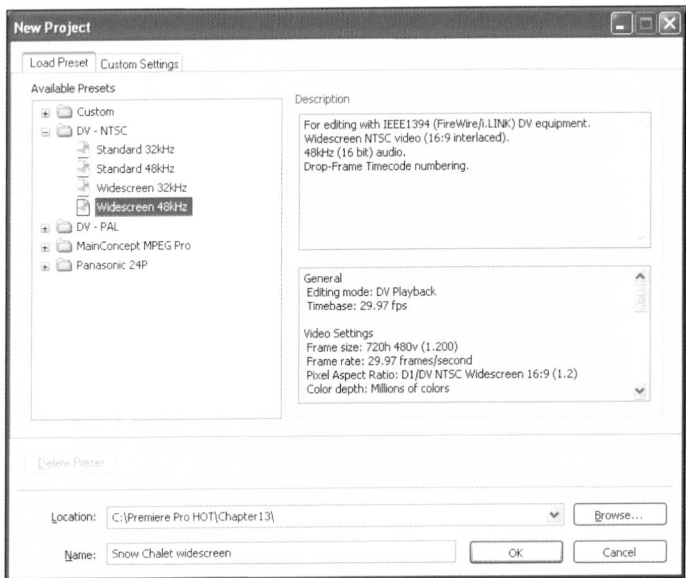

6. In the **New Project** window, select the **Widescreen 48 kHz** preset from the **DV – NTSC** folder. Specify a location of **c:\Premiere Pro HOT\Chapter13** and name your project **Snow Chalet widescreen**. Click **OK**.

This creates a new project using the widescreen preset. All new sequences, as well as imported ones, will be resized to the widescreen format.

7. Choose **File > Import**. Navigate to the **c:\Premiere Pro HOT\Chapter13** folder and select **Exercise05.prproj**. Click **Open**.

The project is imported into its own bin in the ***Project*** *window. All of the associated clips and sequences are imported into the same bin.*

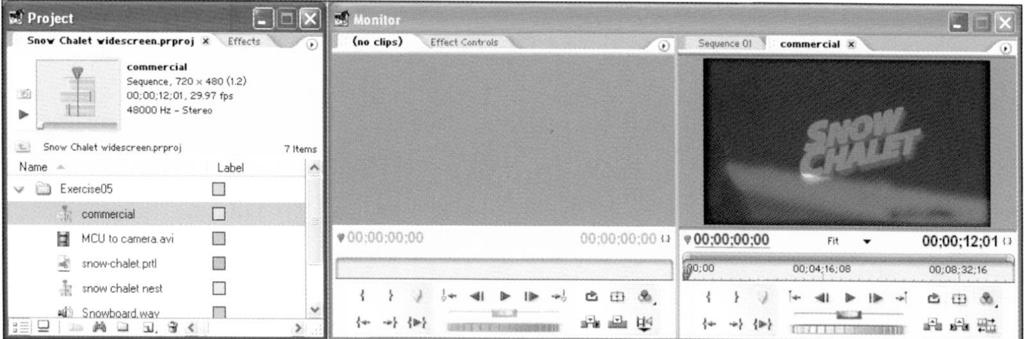

8. In the **Project** window, twirl down the **Exercise05** bin. Double-click the **commercial** sequence to open it in the **Timeline** window. Play the sequence to preview it.

Notice that the sequence, which was previously 4:3 standard, is now 16:9 widescreen in the ***Program*** *monitor. And that's all it takes. Even though you are not nesting the sequence, you definitely could. In fact, you can do anything to this sequence that you would any other sequence.*

---

9. Save and close this project.

In this chapter, you learned the ease of nesting sequences and importing sequences from other projects. You also learned some great track matte tips and how to import a Photoshop file as a sequence. Congratulations, you have reached a milestone: you know now how to import every type of file possible (video, audio, image, and project), and you've learned how to manipulate each type of file by adding effects and transitions, creating keyframes, nesting in other sequences, and more. Now that you are done creating, it's time to export your finished masterpiece in the next chapter.

14

Exporting Movies

Exporting Basics	Record to Videotape
Configuring DV Playback	Exporting to Tape
Export to a File	Export a Still Image	Export a WAV Audio File
Export a DV Movie File	Adobe Media Encoder	Export to Web Movie
Export MPEG-2 Movie	Burning Directly to DVD

H•O•T

Premiere Pro HOT DVD

Up until now, the goal of every chapter and exercise in this book has been to teach you how to create in Premiere Pro. Starting with importing and progressing to adding complex effects and nesting sequences, you have learned how to build sequences. Once you are done creating, the final stage is to export the sequence to a movie that can be viewed outside of Premiere Pro. You can save a sequence to DV tape, DVD disc, Web streaming video, an audio file, and many other formats. In this chapter, you will learn how to export sequences to the most popular formats.

NOTE | Third-Party Products

Premiere Pro is designed to interact and communicate with DV devices (camcorders and VCRs). Premiere Pro has built-in support to specify how DV projects are displayed and exported to DV devices. In this chapter, you will learn the options and configurations available through Premiere Pro's built-in DV support.

Many users purchase Premiere Pro as part of a bundle with a third-party capture card. The third-party card acts as a middleman between Premiere Pro and the DV device, providing added functionality beyond Premiere Pro's built-in capabilities. These third-party products are designed to "plug into" Premiere Pro. This means the product works transparently in conjunction with Premiere Pro–that is, if it's working properly, you shouldn't know it's there.

As part of its transparency, the product usually has its own windows and menus. As a result, the screenshots and options shown throughout this chapter may differ from those on your system. If you own a third-party capture card, please refer to the documentation provided by the manufacturer whenever possible. The concepts taught throughout this chapter should apply equally, but you may need to select different options recommended by the manufacturer.

Exporting Basics

Exporting is the act of copying your finished program (or unfinished program, if you're in a hurry), from a Premiere Pro project to another format. Premiere Pro is designed to export to the following three mediums:

- Record to videotape
- Export to a file (movie, audio, image)
- Burn a DVD movie

Within each of these mediums, there may be multiple formats. For example, there are dozens of file formats to which you can convert. In this chapter, you will learn how Premiere Pro helps you export to many popular formats.

Record to Videotape

Recording a sequence to DV tape is very straightforward. (At least, when the hardware and the software are communicating properly, it *should be* very straightforward.) To export directly to a DV device, such as a camcorder or VCR, you need to have the device connected to the computer via the IEEE-1394 port, also called FireWire (by Apple) and i.LINK (by Sony).

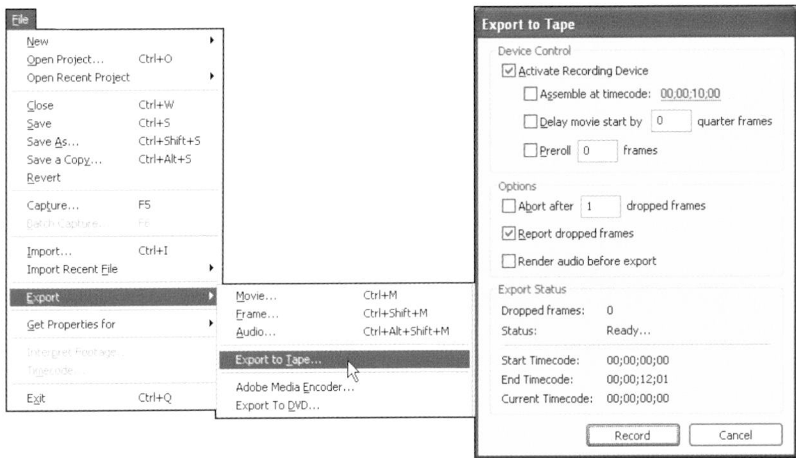

If the DV device is properly connected, you can export a sequence by choosing **File > Export > Export to Tape**. And that's all it takes. There are no format options or presets to choose. In fact, in most cases Premiere Pro will automatically activate your camera (if the camera is in playback/VTR mode) and handle the start and stop recording functions. You don't have to lift a finger; simply go fix yourself a mai tai and sit back and enjoy the fruits of your labor.

Of course, if you feel like lifting a finger, Premiere Pro's **Export to Tape** window lets you fine-tune the export process before recording the sequence to DV tape. Here are some of the options:

Activate Recording Device: Unless you have a DV device that is not supported by Premiere Pro, you should normally have this box checked. This will automatically start and stop your DV device for you.

Assemble at timecode: When selected, Premiere Pro will start recording at the exact spot on the tape you specify. Premiere Pro handles rewinding or fast forwarding to the timecode you specify. Normally you will not select this option, and Premiere Pro will start recording at the current spot on the tape.

Delay movie start by: Some DV devices need a brief period of time between receiving the video signal and recording it. (Only a few DV devices will need this option checked. Refer to the device's manual to see what the manufacturer recommends.)

Preroll: Some DV devices need additional time to get up to the proper tape recording speed. (You've probably seen this on your "dinosaur" VHS VCR.) To be honest, this option doesn't always work as advertised. In Exercise 1, you'll discover a handy workaround.

Abort/Report dropped frames: A dropped frame occurs when the computer system is having a hard time delivering all 30 frames per second to your DV device, and a frame is accidentally skipped (or "dropped"). Some editors can handle a dropped frame or two (after all, one-thirtieth of a second may be hard to notice); others will want to halt the export as soon as a single frame is dropped.

Render audio before export: Instead of trying to render the audio on the fly, as the sequence is exporting, you can tell Premiere to do its "render homework" before exporting begins. The more Premiere Pro renders in advance, the less work it has to do during export. The downside is that you will have to wait while it renders.

Because each DV device is different, learning which options result in a successful export may be a matter of trial and error. Luckily, as DV technology matures, the communication between computer and device is becoming more standardized, resulting in fewer and fewer hardware incompatibilities.

NOTE | IEEE-1394 vs. DV

So what exactly is IEEE-1394? How does it relate to DV? Why are the two always used in tandem?

For starters, IEEE-1394 is a protocol that defines high-speed data transfer between devices. It is short for **I**nstitute of **E**lectrical and **E**lectronics **E**ngineers standard #1394. (Apparently standards #1 through #1393 weren't as popular.) IEEE-1394 goes by many names; Apple calls it FireWire, Sony calls it i.LINK, and others call it Lynx. In the end, they're all different names for the same thing.

Some computers are sold with IEEE-1394 ports. These are ports like any others, such as USB, PS/2, serial, parallel, MIDI, and so on. If your computer has an IEEE-1394 port, you can connect any IEEE-1394 device.

Digital video (DV) is a video compression format for storing digital video. When you shoot footage with a DV camcorder, the video is compressed by the camcorder before being stored onto DV tape. Because DV video is compressed, it requires only 3.6 MB per second when playing. This means your computer must be able to transfer data at a minimum of 3.6 MB/s. (The requirement, in practice, is slightly higher, but you get the idea.)

The IEEE-1394 port can transfer data up to 50 MB/s, which is plenty fast for DV's paltry requirement of 3.6 MB/s. Today, nearly all DV camcorders and DV devices are manufactured with IEEE-1394 ports onboard. As an added benefit, your computer can control your DV device and receive timecode information when connected via IEEE-1394.

To summarize, IEEE-1394 defines how data is *sent*, and DV defines how the data is *stored*. Like chocolate and peanut butter, the two just seem to go together.

Configuring DV Playback

A DV camcorder connected via IEEE-1394 allows you to view your sequence through the camcorder.
A DV VCR connected via IEEE-1394 allows you to view your sequence on an external television monitor.

If you're working on a DV project, you can preview the sequence on a DV camcorder or television connected to a DV VCR via your IEEE-1394 port. You can set up this option using Premiere Pro's built-in settings. Within Premiere Pro, you can specify how both the video and audio should play back when a DV device is connected.

Here are the available options in the DV Playback Settings menu:

Video Playback: The **Play Video on DV Hardware** check box must be checked in order to see your video on a connected DV device.

Audio Playback: You can choose to listen to your audio on the attached DV hardware or through your audio hardware (computer speakers) during playback while editing.

Real-Time Playback: You can choose for the sequence to play back on your desktop (computer monitor) at the same time as with your DV hardware (camcorder or VCR). Be advised this takes significant system resources; if you are experiencing playback performance problems, try switching playback to only the desktop or only the DV hardware. If you have no video monitor attached to your DV device, choose desktop playback only.

Export to Tape: When exporting to DV tape, you can decide if you want the audio to play through the DV device or the computer speakers. Choose **Play Audio on DV Hardware** if the device has audio capabilities so that you can hear the finished product the way the audience will hear it. If your DV device does not have audio capabilities (such as a VCR without a TV attached), choose **Play Audio on Audio Hardware** to preview your audio while exporting.

24p Pull-Up Method: This specifies how Premiere Pro handles playback of 24p footage once you have imported it. Both options convert 24 fps to 29.97 fps. (These options apply only to users with 24p footage and 24p camcorders.) Interlaced frame (2:3:3:2) produces smoother playback but is more taxing to your computer.

Desktop Display Mode: Some video cards cannot handle the latest Direct3D drivers and, as a result, DV playback may stutter. If you are suffering performance issues, switch to **Use GDI.** (Also make sure you have the latest drivers installed from your video card manufacturer.)

To a newcomer, there may be a dizzying array of options to choose from. Keep in mind, all of these options are meant to address playback issues with editing or exporting DV projects in Premiere Pro. There's no right or wrong option; what works for one user may not work for another.

The general rule of thumb is this: whenever you create a program, you should watch/listen to it as the audience will. If the finished product will be watched on a television monitor, you should play back on a television monitor (via DV hardware) if your system can handle it.

NOTE | Exercise 1 Requires DV Device

In the next exercise, you will walk through the steps to export a sequence to DV tape. Please note if you do not have a DV device properly connected to your computer via IEEE-1394, you may not be able to complete some of the steps in this exercise.

Because there are countless system configurations around the globe, it is impossible to define a one-size-fits-all set of options that works for everybody. Please note that the options shown in the next exercise are meant to be used as a guideline, but your particular system configuration may require that you choose different playback options.

I. Exporting to Tape

When your DV hardware is properly communicating with your Premiere Pro software, you can export to tape with the click of a single button (maybe two). In this exercise, you will walk through the steps of exporting to DV tape. If you have a DV device, turn it on, put it in VTR/VCR mode, and connect it to the computer before launching Premiere Pro.

1. If Premiere Pro is not running, launch it and click **Open Project** at the **Welcome Screen**. Navigate to the **c:\Premiere Pro HOT\Chapter14** folder, select **Exercise01.prproj**, and click **Open**.

2. Play the sequence in the **Timeline** to preview it.

You may recognize this as the commercial from Exercise 5 of Chapter 13. However, this is a standard 4:3 version (not the widescreen version from earlier).

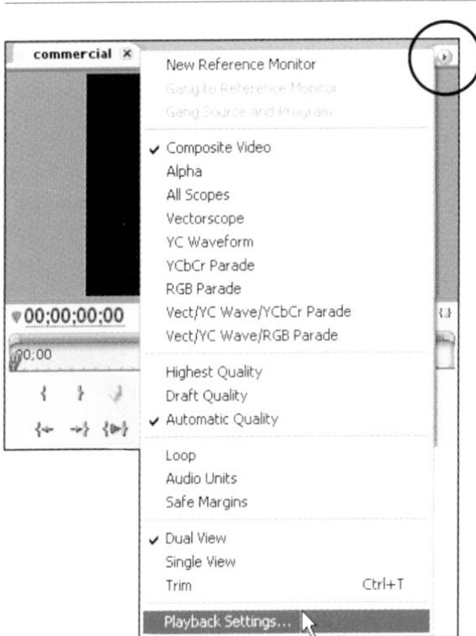

3. Click the wing menu in the upper-right corner of the **Monitor** window and choose **Playback Settings**.

This is how you access the DV Playback Settings described earlier in this chapter.

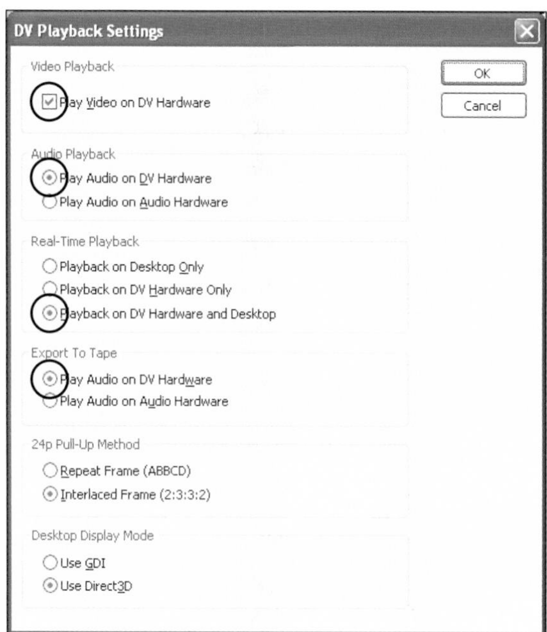

4. If you do not have a DV device connected, skip to Step 6. If you have a DV device connected, make sure you have a check next to **Play Video on DV Hardware**. If the DV device has audio output, under **Audio Playback** choose **Play Audio on DV Hardware**. Under **Real-Time Playback**, choose **Playback on DV Hardware and Desktop**. Under **Export to Tape**, choose **Play Audio on DV Hardware**.

These options are best suited for systems that have DV devices with audio output. If your DV device does not have built-in audio speakers, set both audio options to ***Play Audio on Audio Hardware*** *(computer speakers).*

---

5. Play the sequence in the **Timeline** to preview it on the attached DV device.

If your DV device is configured as shown above, you should be able to see and hear your sequence on the attached DV device. If playback suffers, repeat Steps 3 and 4, but choose ***Playback on Desktop Only*** *under* ***Real-Time Playback*** *and* ***Play Audio on Audio Hardware*** *under* ***Audio Playback****.*

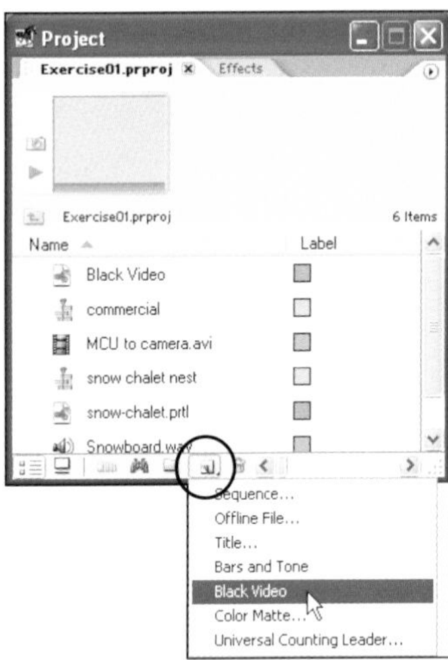

6. In the **Project** window, click the **New Item** icon and choose **Black Video**.

*This adds a 5-second clip of black video in the **Project** window. In the next step, you will learn how to quickly insert the black clip into the beginning of your project, to create a preroll before exporting.*

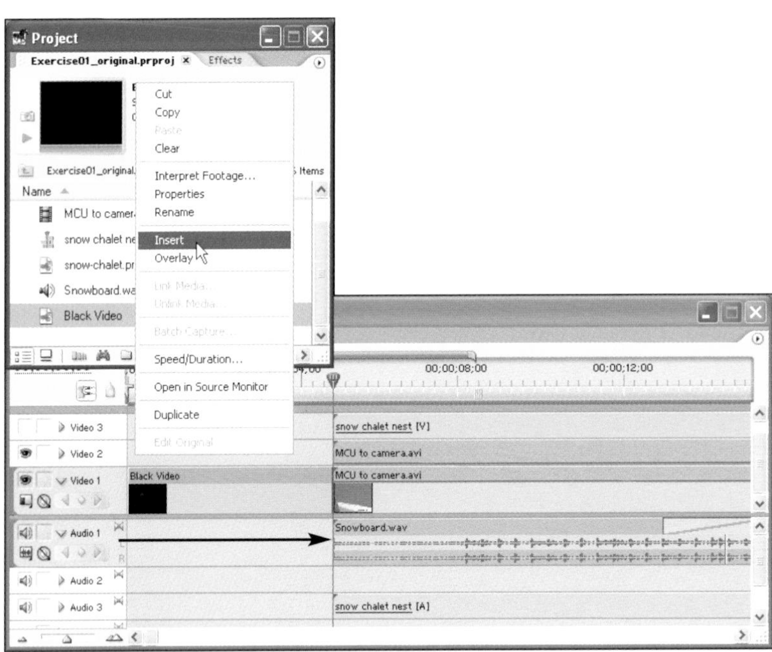

7. Snap the current time indicator to the beginning of the sequence, at **00;00;00;00**. Right-click the **Black Video** clip in the **Project** window and choose **Insert** from the shortcut menu.

This inserts the video at the current time indicator. When video is inserted, all of the existing video is "scooted over" to make room. Also note that the clip is inserted in the Target Track (the track that is shaded darker than the others). In this case, the Target Track was ***Video 1****.*

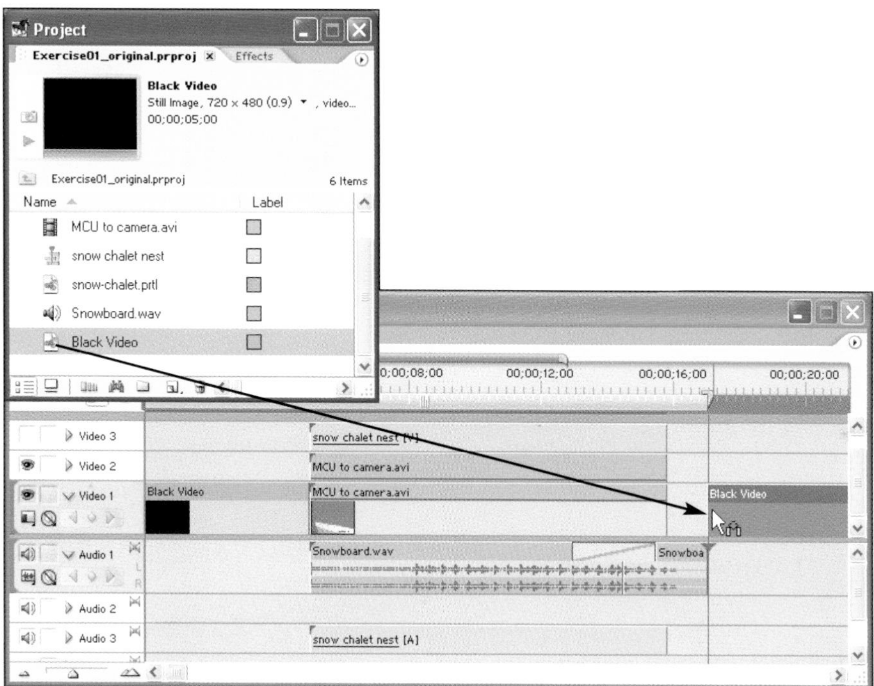

8. Press the \ (backslash) key on the keyboard to zoom the sequence to fit into the **Timeline** window. Drag the **Black Video** clip from the **Project** window to track **Video 1** of the **Timeline**. Snap it to the end of the last clip on the **Timeline**.

Tip: *This creates a 5-second postroll of black video. Instead of stopping abruptly at the end of the video, Premiere Pro will now play an additional 5 seconds of black video at the end of the export process. It's always a good idea to add preroll and postroll black video when exporting to DV tape.*

---

9. Choose **File > Export > Export to Tape**.

*If you have a DV device connected, and if the **Export to Tape** option is grayed out, try clicking anywhere in the **Timeline** to bring focus to the **Timeline** window, and then see if the **Export to Tape** option is available. Here's why this is important: Premiere Pro exports the currently selected clip of whichever window is in "focus." If the **Project** window is in focus, you will accidentally export the selected clip in the **Project** window. It's a good habit to always click in the **Timeline** to bring focus to the **Timeline** window before exporting.*

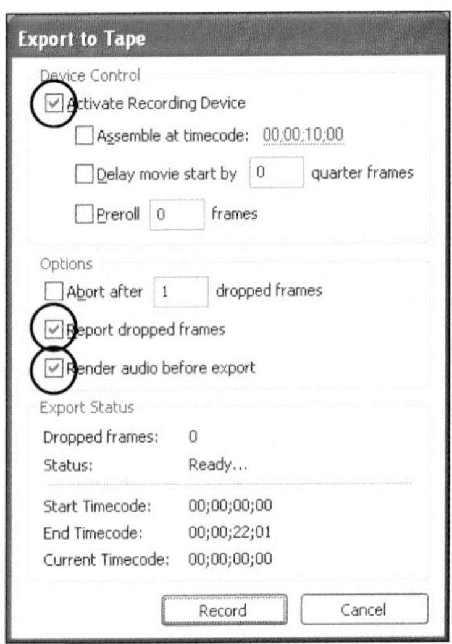

10. In the **Export to Tape** window, check **Activate Recording Device**, **Report dropped frames**, and **Render audio before export**.

This tells Premiere Pro to automatically start and stop your DV device, as well as report (but don't stop because of) any dropped frames. Rendering audio before export is a good idea because it lightens Premiere Pro's workload during export.

11. (Skip this step if you do not want to export to DV.) Click the **Record** button.

***Note:** Recording will overwrite any existing video on the DV tape. Make sure the tape you have in your DV device is "expendable." (Your family may not forgive you if you overwrite Kaitlyn's first steps with a commercial for the Snow Chalet.)*

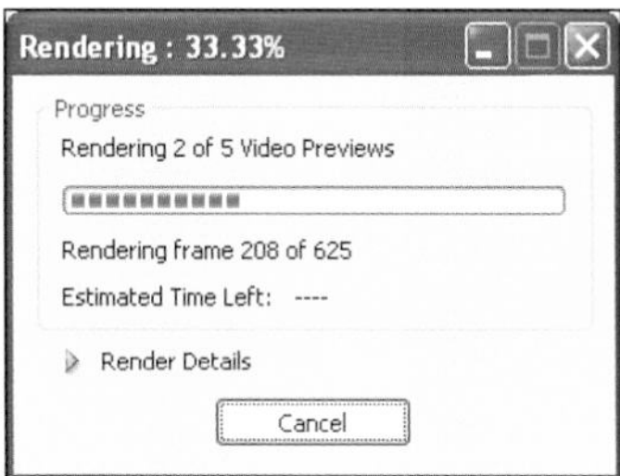

Because the sequence has some complex effects, Premiere Pro must first render the sequence before exporting to tape. The duration of the rendering process is determined by your computer but it might take up to a few minutes. Once rendering is complete, Premiere Pro will automatically start your DV device recording and stop the device recording when export is complete (in an ideal world).

12. If any frames were dropped, Premiere Pro displays a warning box. Rewind and play your DV device to see if the export was successful. Monitor playback for smooth video and audio.

*Exporting to DV tape is heavily dependent on proper communication between Premiere Pro and your DV device. You can visit the Adobe Web site (**www.adobe.com**) and navigate to the Premiere Pro compatibility list to see if your DV device is compatible with Premiere Pro's built-in DV support.*

13. Save and close this project before moving on to the next exercise.

Export to a File

Premiere Pro allows you to save your sequence in many different formats for many different uses. Although there are literally dozens of file formats you can export, they tend to fall into the following file types:

- Still images
- Audio files (no video)
- Movie files (with or without audio)

There are two methods you can use to export files: Premiere Pro's old Export window, and the newer Adobe Media Encoder. In general, if you want to convert a sequence into an audio or video file, you should use the Adobe Media Encoder (covered later in this chapter).

With that said, there are a few exceptions to this rule, such as exporting to a still image, a Windows WAV file, and a DV movie file. With these three types of file formats, you should definitely use the old Export window, which you will learn in the following three chapters.

TIP | Which Image Format?

Premiere Pro has built-in capabilities for exporting to one of four image formats. When deciding which format to export a still image, consider the following:

BMP images had their place in the sun years ago. They worked well for computer images–like in the Windows operating system–but have become obsolete for all other work, including digital photographs. Avoid this format when possible.

GIF images are popular because of their use on the Web, but they are not well-regarded in the graphics world because of their limited capabilities. Their only advantage is their small file sizes. Only use the GIF format if you are exporting your image straight from Premiere Pro to the Web. Otherwise, try to avoid this format when possible.

TIF images do a fine job of displaying digital photographs and are the format of choice for design professionals. TIF images are good when sharing graphics across platforms (Apple and PC), and they also allow you to save alpha channels. Use TIF whenever possible, due to high quality and portability.

TGA images are not as common anymore, although they used to dominate the video editing world. Now the file format has been relegated to special applications, such as CAD software. TGA files can also save alpha channels. Unless you're exporting to an application that requires TGA, there's no benefit to using this format.

2. Export a Still Image

Premiere Pro allows you to export a single frame of video as a still image. The process is extremely simple, and the only real consideration is choosing a file format. (See previous sidebar.) In this exercise, you will learn the steps of exporting a single frame, as well as some useful tricks and tips that many editors never discover.

1. If Premiere Pro is not running, launch it and click **Open Project** at the **Welcome Screen**. Navigate to the **c:\Premiere Pro HOT\Chapter14** folder, select **Exercise02.prproj**, and click **Open**.

2. In the **Timeline** window, move the current time indicator to **00;00;07;18**.

*The first step to exporting a single frame is to move the current time indicator to the exact frame you want to export. In this case, you are going to export the frame of video at **00;00;07;18**.*

3. Choose **File > Export > Frame**.

*If the **Frame** option is grayed out, click anywhere in the **Timeline** to bring focus to the **Timeline** window. Repeat Step 3, and the option should become available.*

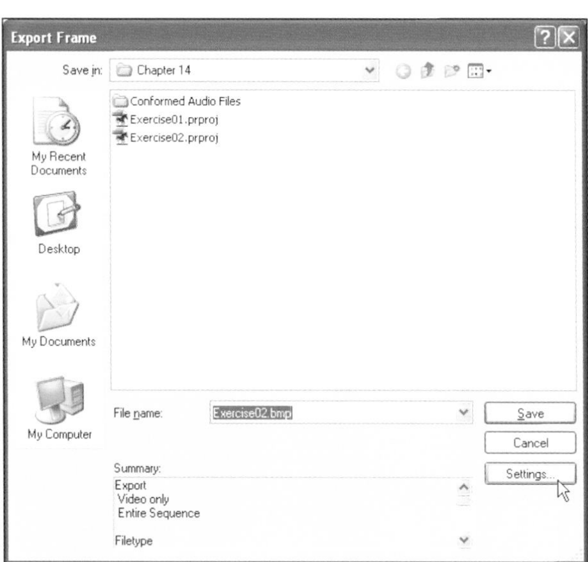

4. In the **Export Frame** window, click **Settings**.

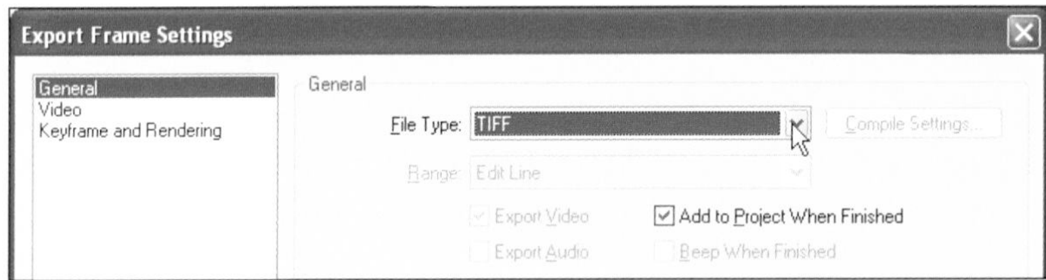

5. In the **General** options, choose **TIFF** from the **File Type** drop-down menu. Make sure that **Add to Project When Finished** is checked.

*As described earlier, there are four different file types. But it has been awhile since Adobe updated the list of image choices, and most of them are archaic or not useful for digital video stills. The **Add to Project When Finished** option imports the file as a still image in the current project after exporting.*

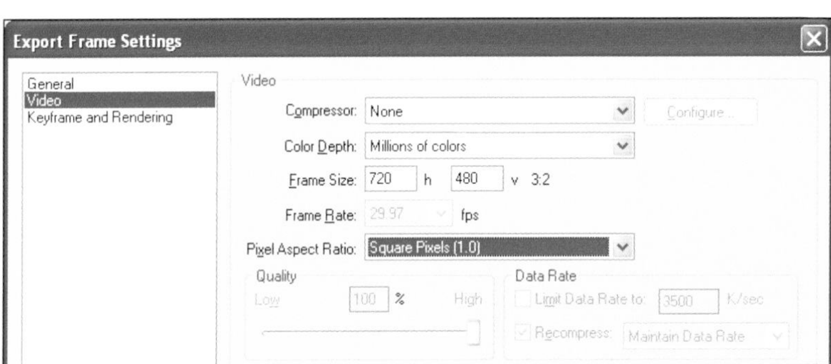

6. In the **Video** options, change **Pixel Aspect Ratio** from **D1/DV NTSC (0.9)** to **Square Pixels (1.0)**.

Tip: *Changing the pixel aspect ratio to square (1.0) is a good idea if you plan to use the image for Web, email, Photoshop, and other nonvideo applications. See the sidebar following this exercise.*

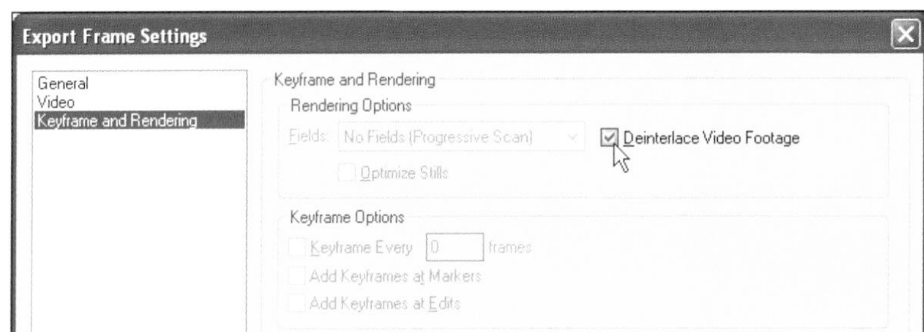

7. In the **Keyframe and Rendering** options, make sure that **Deinterlace Video Footage** is checked. Click **OK**.

Tip: *Always, always* deinterlace *your video footage when exporting to a still image in order to export both fields of the video frame. Remember, a complete frame of DV video is made up of two fields: half of the frame is stored in the upper fields, and half is stored in the lower fields. Deinterlacing combines the two fields, so you get the maximum image quality. (In Premiere versions past, the program defaulted to exporting only one of the fields, in other words–only half of the image! This wasn't a good thing, because many users didn't know how/why to change it. Adobe eventually fixed this in the current version, but it's still a good habit to check this box, just in case you end up using a previous version of Premiere.)*

---

8. You're now back in the **Export Frame** window. Navigate to the **c:\Premiere Pro HOT\Chapter 14** directory. In the **File name** box, type **snow chalet** and click **Save**.

This saves the file ***snow chalet.tif*** *in the directory you specify and imports the still image in your project window. Exporting to a still image is a very simple process. In fact, the only consideration is which pixel aspect ratio to export, which is discussed in the next section.*

---

9. Save and keep this project open before moving on to the next exercise.

NOTE | Which Pixel Aspect Ratio?

In the previous exercise, you were shown how to change the pixel aspect ratio of a still image before exporting it. When should you choose a square (1.0) ratio, and when should you choose a DV ratio?

First, a refresher. Earlier in this book, you learned that computer monitors display pixels as squares (1.0 ratio), and NTSC televisions display pixels as thin rectangles (0.9 ratio).

When it comes down to choosing a pixel aspect ratio when exporting a still image, the decision should be based on the final destination of the image. If the final destination is an NTSC video monitor or future DV projects (which are also 0.9 in Premiere Pro), you should match the aspect ratio to 0.9.

If you plan for the image to be viewed primarily on computer monitors, such as for the Web, email, Photoshop, and so on, you should match the display of 1.0 pixel aspect ratio.

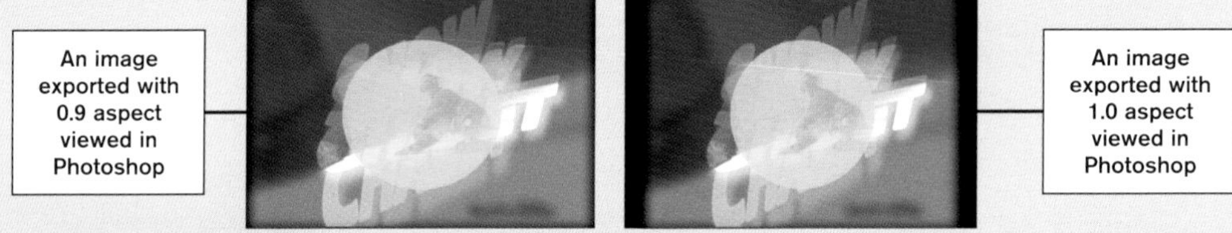

To help illustrate the effects of choosing the wrong aspect ratio, a perfectly-round circle has been added to the Timeline before exporting.

The image on the left was exported with the native DV NTSC aspect ratio of 0.9. When viewed on a computer monitor in Photoshop, the image looks stretched wide. The image on the right was exported with a square (1.0) pixel aspect ratio. When viewed on a computer screen, the circle looks perfectly round.

(Of course, if you were looking at the results on a video monitor, the 0.9 image on the left would be perfectly round, and the 1.0 image on the right would be stretched tall.)

The moral of the story: use the ratio that matches how the image will ultimately be viewed. If the end result is a video monitor, choose 0.9. If the end result is a computer monitor, choose 1.0.

(You would be surprised how many non-linear editors–even those who do this for a living–never realize this!)

3. Export a WAV Audio File

Exporting an audio file in Premiere Pro is very similar to exporting a still image. In this exercise, you will learn how to export to an uncompressed WAV file. Use uncompressed WAV files when you want to keep your audio at its maximum quality. This is ideal when you want to edit your audio in applications such as Adobe Audition, or if you plan to import your audio into other editing applications. If you do not need to edit your audio any further and plan to export it to a finished format, such as for the Web, it is better to use the Adobe Media Encoder (discussed later).

1. If you have the previous exercise open, skip to Step 2. If Premiere Pro is not running, launch it and click **Open Project** at the **Welcome Screen**. Navigate to the **c:\Premiere Pro HOT\Chapter14** folder, select **Exercise03.prproj**, and click **Open**.

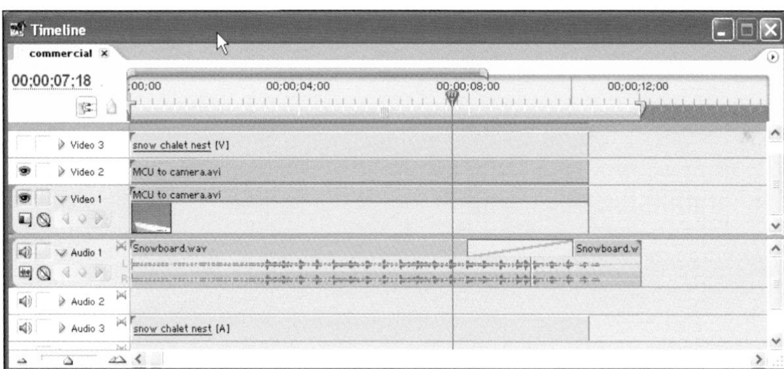

2. Click in the bar along the top of the **Timeline** to bring focus to the **Timeline** window.

*At the risk of sounding like a broken record, always bring focus to the **Timeline** window before exporting from the **Timeline**. (Otherwise, you may accidentally export whatever is highlighted in the **Project** window.)*

3. Choose **File > Export > Audio**. Click **Settings**.

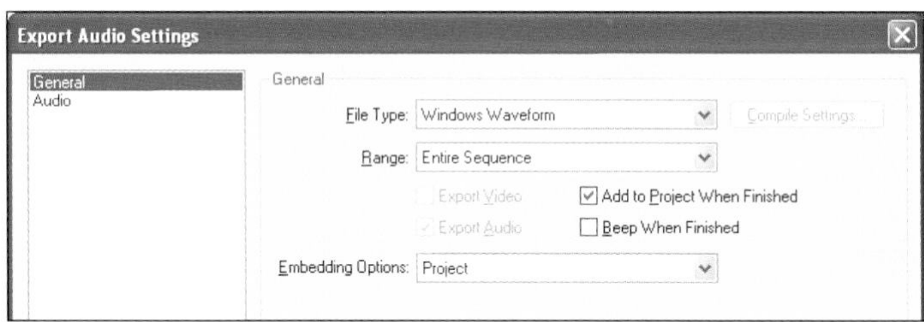

4. In the **General** options, make sure **File Type** is **Windows Waveform**.

There are a few other file types to choose from here, but from a practical standpoint, there's no need to learn the others because you never use them. If I'm wrong, I'll eat this book. (Not really.)

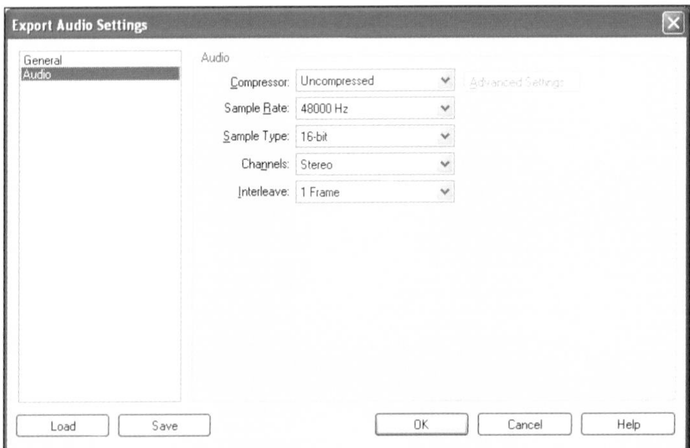

5. In the **Audio** options, make sure that **Compressor** is set to **Uncompressed**, **Sample Rate** is **48000 Hz**, **Sample Type** is **16-bit**, **Channels** is **Stereo**, and **Interleave** is **1 Frame**. Click **OK**.

6. Navigate to **c:\Premiere Pro HOT\Chapter 14** and name your audio file **commercial audio**. Click **Save**.

Specifying the options listed in this exercise ensures that your audio is exported with the maximum possible settings. True, there are some other options you could have chosen, such as a compressor, but you will rarely–possibly never–choose anything else. It's important to iterate that the only practical use for exporting audio this way is for uncompressed WAV files. If you plan to compress your audio, you should be using the Adobe Media Encoder, which you will learn shortly.

7. Save and keep this project open before moving on to the next exercise.

4. Export a DV Movie File

You can also use the Export window to create a DV movie for use in future Premiere Pro projects or other video editing applications, such as Adobe After Effects. In this exercise, you will learn how to export your DV movie with the maximum settings.

1. If the project from the previous exercise is open, skip to Step 2. If Premiere Pro is not running, launch it and click **Open Project** at the **Welcome Screen**. Navigate to the **c:\Premiere Pro HOT\Chapter14** folder, select **Exercise04.prproj**, and click **Open**.

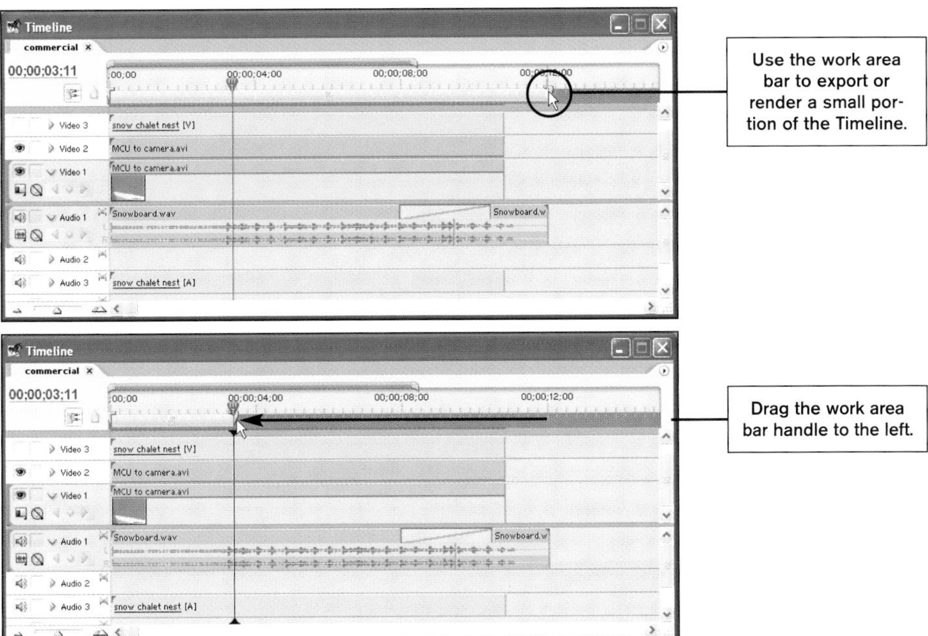

Use the work area bar to export or render a small portion of the Timeline.
Drag the work area bar handle to the left.

2. Move the current time indicator to **00;00;03;11**. Grab the work area bar handle, on the end of the work area, and snap the end of the work area bar to the current time indicator.

*A handy feature of the **Export** window is the capability to export just the work area, instead of the entire sequence. The work area bar specifies the area that will be rendered or exported.*

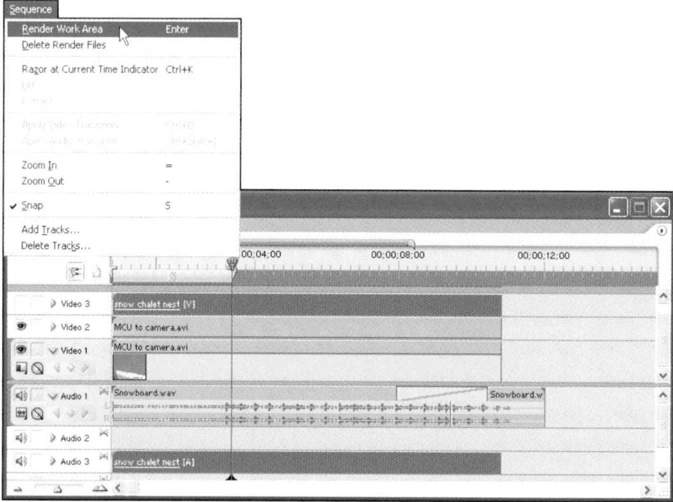

3. Choose **Sequence > Render Work Area**. This render may take a minute or two, depending on your system configuration.

In the previous chapter, you learned the benefits of rendering. However, what you may not have realized is that you can specify to render just the work area, instead of the entire sequence. This is especially helpful in projects with complex graphics, such as this one. If you need to view only a small section of the ***Timeline****, you can set and render the work area, instead of waiting for the entire sequence to render. Also notice that a green bar is placed only over the portion that was rendered.*

4. Choose **File > Export > Movie**. Click **Settings**.

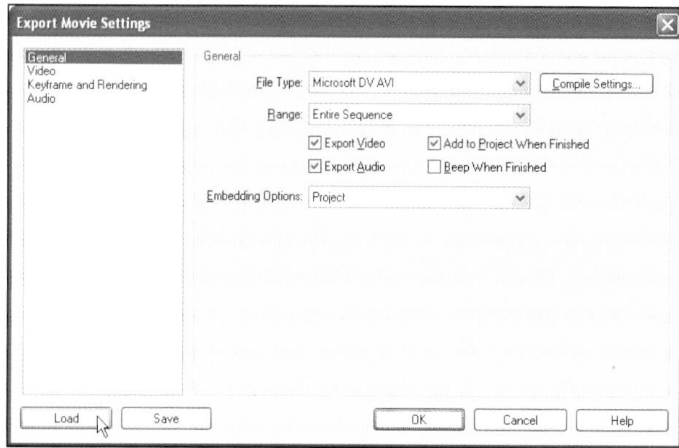

5. In the lower-left corner of the **Export Movie Settings** window, click **Load**.

Because there are a gazillion options to specify when exporting a movie, it is important to choose a preset. Premiere Pro lets you save export presets in the same way you can choose project presets when you start a project. This ensures that your exported movie adheres to the strict DV format guidelines.

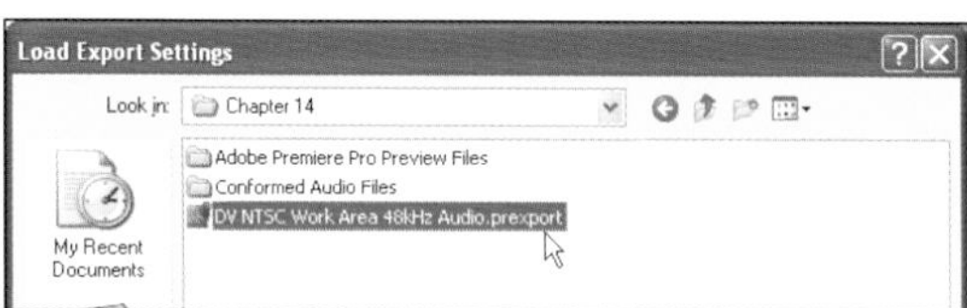

6. Navigate to the **c:\Premiere Pro HOT\Chapter 14** folder, and select the **DV NTSC Work Area 48kHz Audio.prexport** setting. Click **Open**.

This loads a DV NTSC export preset, which specifies all of the export settings and options that are best for optimal DV NTSC files. (It's always nice to take the guesswork out of export settings!)

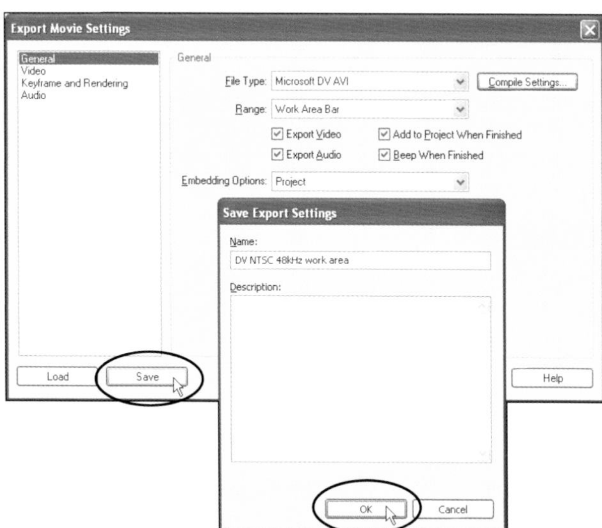

7. You're now back in the **Export Movie Settings** window. Click **Save** to save the export preset. Name the preset **DV NTSC 48kHz work area**. Click **OK**.

This saves the export preset in Premiere Pro's system folder, so you will have it permanently, or until you decide to remove it. (Someday you might eventually delete these sample chapters and exercises from your hard drive, and then you would lose the preset you loaded from the Chapter 14 folder if you hadn't saved it.)

8. You're now back in the **Export Movie Settings** window. Click **OK**.

9. In the **Export Movie** window, navigate to the **c:\Premiere Pro HOT\Chapter 14** folder. Name your movie **snow movie** and click **Save**.

This will save just the work area *and not the entire sequence. Because you are exporting only a few seconds, and because you pre-rendered, the export should take no time at all. Best of all, you can use this video in future DV projects, and Premiere Pro cannot discern this man-made file from DV movie captured from your camcorder. See the sidebar following this exercise for an explanation of the benefits of exporting a movie as a DV file.*

10. Save this project and keep it open before moving on to the next exercise.

NOTE | Why Export to a DV file?

So what exactly are the benefits of exporting to a DV file? Consider:

Premiere Pro is designed to play and edit DV video–captured from DV camcorders–in real-time, without rendering or lowering the preview quality. (Remember, anytime a clip doesn't match the DV project settings, Premiere Pro must either render or lower the preview quality in order to achieve real-time playback.)

As long as you export your movie to the correct DV specifications, Premiere Pro will not be able to discern your exported movie from DV footage captured via camcorder. This means that you can use your exported movie in *any DV project*, and Premiere Pro will play it in real-time without having to render or lower preview quality.

Another advantage is that the exported movie keeps its original format. Other formats may compress the video and introduce noticeable artifacts. Staying in the DV format allows you to maintain the optimal picture quality, so you can use it in future projects without suffering a loss in quality.

In addition, exporting sequences with complex effects can save rendering time in future projects. Since the work has already been done, you don't have to tax your system as much during the preview or export process. Premiere Pro won't know the difference, and more importantly, the audience won't know the difference.

For those of you who have third-party capture cards: keep in mind that every manufacturer of third-party capture cards uses their own "flavor" of DV. In the previous exercise, you exported to the default "Microsoft DV" flavor, which is the default type Premiere Pro is built upon. If you own a third-party card, you might achieve better results using the manufacturer's proprietary flavor. Refer to the documentation that came with your capture card for help creating optimal export settings for your system.

Adobe Media Encoder

In the past few exercises, you've learned the three scenarios when it is advantageous to use the Export window. The overall concept is this: use the Export window when you want to create a file that can be used in future Premiere Pro projects or edited in other applications (Photoshop, Audition, After Effects, and so on).

For just about every other reason to export a movie, there is the Adobe Media Encoder, which is new to Premiere Pro and is Adobe's direct response to feedback from customers clamoring for the capability to export Web-formatted movies, MPEG-2 DVD files, and other portable files. Use the Adobe Media Encoder when you want to export to the following types of files:

- QuickTime, Windows Media, Real Media (these are all Web-friendly formats)
- Small movies for emailing
- MPEG-1 VCD, MPEG-2 DVD, SVCD formats (for creating DVD and VCD movies)
- High-quality movies for PowerPoint presentations, or for burning to a data CD-ROM
- Any other use where file size is top priority

Overall, use the Adobe Media Encoder when you are ready to deliver your project in final format. Because these formats are highly compressed, resulting in efficient file sizes, the exported files should not be used in future Premiere Pro projects or edited in other applications.

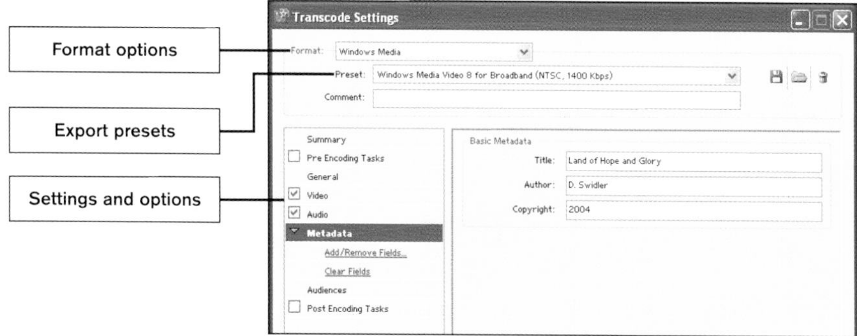

The Adobe Media Encoder is very straightforward and similar to the Export window of the previous exercises. Instead of first saving your file, as you do in the Export window, you are first taken to the **Transcode Settings** window to select a format. This logically makes much more sense–you first choose a format and *then* choose where to save the file. The Adobe Media Encoder is divided into three menus:

- **Format options:** You can save your movie as Windows Media, QuickTime, Real Media, and MPEG. Each option has its strengths and weaknesses. When exporting to the Web, you should use Windows Media, QuickTime, or Real Media, depending on which format is supported by your Web server, and also depending on your audience. Apple users can view QuickTime movies without additional software; Windows users can view Windows Media without additional software. Some Web sites prefer Real Media.

- **Export presets:** Tons and tons of presets are available. The list is actually too long to describe, but in the next exercise you will get to see just a few of the many choices. Best of all, once you choose a preset, you don't have to specify any additional settings. All of the difficult choices are made for you!
- **Settings and options:** Although the presets make it so you don't *have* to choose any settings, you still can by selecting different settings (on the left side) and modifying their options (on the right side). For example, the **Metadata** settings can be useful, because you can add clip information such as **Title**, **Author**, **Copyright**, and so on.

In the next exercise, you will learn how to choose some common export settings.

NOTE | The Good, The Bad, The Compressed

In the previous section, you were warned that movies exported with Adobe Media Encoder should not be used for editing in Premiere Pro or other applications. Why not? Does this mean the video quality isn't as good? Why can't the exported movie be edited? Here's the lowdown on compression quality.

The Adobe Media Encoder uses compression (and lots of fancy math) to shrink the file size of an exported movie. For example, 1 hour of DV footage from a camcorder requires 13 GB of hard drive space. That same movie, exported from the Adobe Media Encoder to a MPEG-2 DVD file, can be compressed to 3 GB. That's 25 percent of the original file size. Can the human eye detect the difference? Some people can, some can't. But for a mere quarter of the original file size, that's amazing, especially considering the quality is nearly identical.

But not everything is peaches and cream. There is a direct relationship between compression and quality. The smaller you squeeze the file, the lower the quality. For example, it is impossible to email the original DV footage to a friend, because 13 GB would be an awfully large attachment. You can shrink the movie down and compress it with the Adobe Media Encoder so that it is less than 100 KB (.0001 GB), which is ideal for emailing. But the result is a postage-sized movie that is choppy.

All in all, the image quality of the compressed movie can range from pristine all the way down to unusable, depending on your file size requirements. Once you start compressing beyond 10 to 20 percent of the original file size, you have to compromise quality for size.

You shouldn't edit the compressed video because much of the original data has been lost due to compression, and it's hard for Premiere Pro to "uncompress" the video. (It's like having a top-secret, encoded message, but you've lost the decoder ring. Inevitably, much of the original message will be lost.)

5. Export to Web Movie

The three most common Web formats that Adobe Media Encoder can export are QuickTime, Real Media, and Windows Media. In this exercise, you will learn how to export a Windows Media file for streaming on the Web.

1. If the project from the previous exercise is open, skip to Step 2. If Premiere Pro is not running, launch it and click **Open Project** at the **Welcome Screen**. Navigate to the **c:\Premiere Pro HOT\Chapter14** folder, select **Exercise05.prproj**, and click **Open**.

2. Click in the bar along the top of the **Timeline** to bring focus to the **Timeline** window.

3. Choose **File > Export > Adobe Media Encoder**.

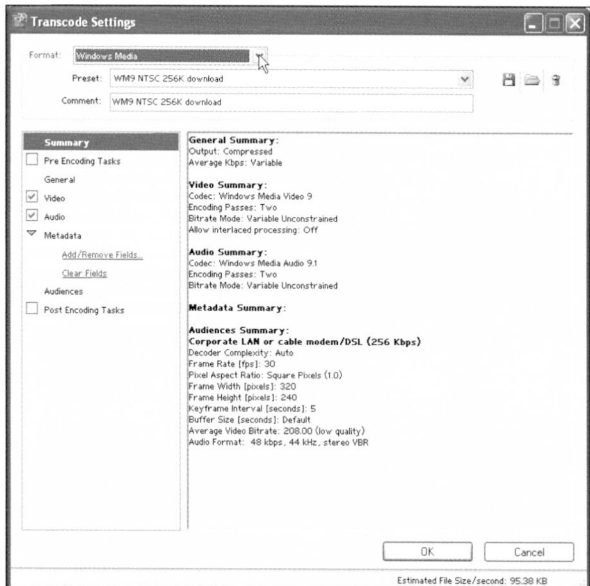

4. From the **Format** drop-down menu, choose **Windows Media**.

In this exercise, you'll export a Windows Media format, which will be playable on all Windows XP systems. However, the steps to exporting a QuickTime or Real Media file are very similar.

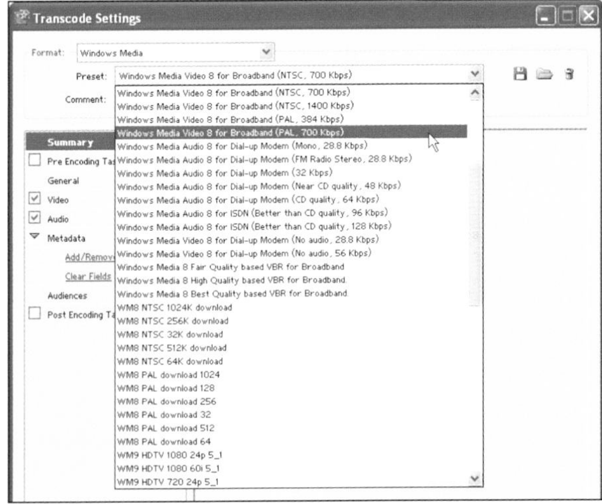

5. From the **Preset** drop-down menu, choose **Windows Media Video 8 for Broadband (NTSC, 700kbps)**.

You may notice that there are far too many Windows Media presets to describe. In general, the options are broken down by audience, such as dial-up modem, ISDN, LAN, broadband, and so on. The higher the kbps, the larger the file, and thus the longer it takes to download. There's no right or wrong option–just a lot of trial and error, finding what works best for your movie and audience.

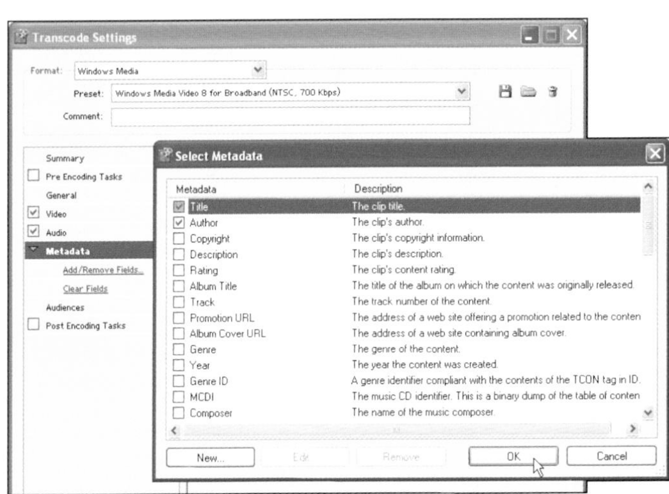

6. On the left side of the window, select **Metadata**. To add metadata information, click **Add/Remove Fields**. In the **Select Metadata** window, select **Title** and **Author** and click **OK**.

This allows you to add metadata content to your exported file, which can be useful for cataloging, indexing by Web spiders, adding copyright information, including your Web site address, and so on. (The list goes on!)

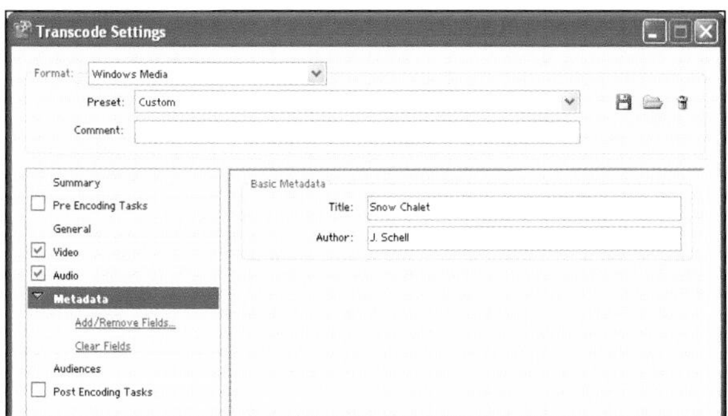

7. Title your movie **Snow Chalet** and put in your name as the **Author**. Click **OK**.

*The metadata **Title** is not the same as the file name. The file name is the name you will see on your hard drive, such as **snow-chalet.wmv**. The **Title** is the title of the movie **Snow Chalet 30 Second Spot**.*

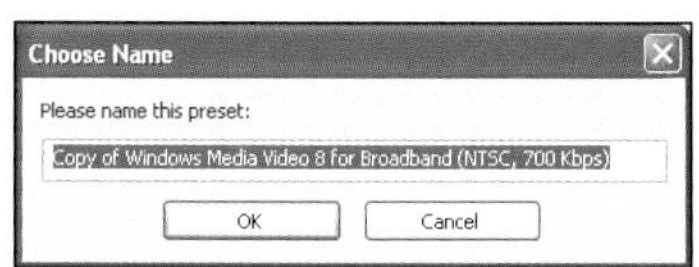

8. In the **Choose Name** window that appears, you will be asked to save a name for this preset. Simply click **OK** again.

Since you changed some of the options by adding metadata information, Premiere Pro thinks you customized the preset. So it asks you to save your preset and, like a stingy guard, you cannot get by unless you do so. On the bright side, the metadata information you entered is now a preset you can choose.

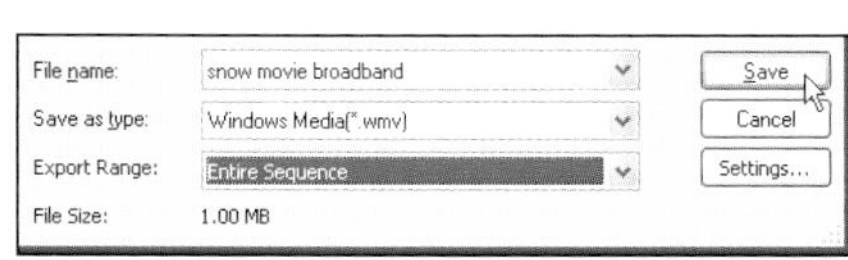

9. Navigate to the **c:\Premiere Pro HOT\Chapter 14** folder and name your file **snow movie broadband**. Make sure the **Export Range** is **Entire Sequence**. Click **Save**.

You can choose to export the entire sequence or just the work area. In this case, the entire sequence may take a few minutes, depending on your system.

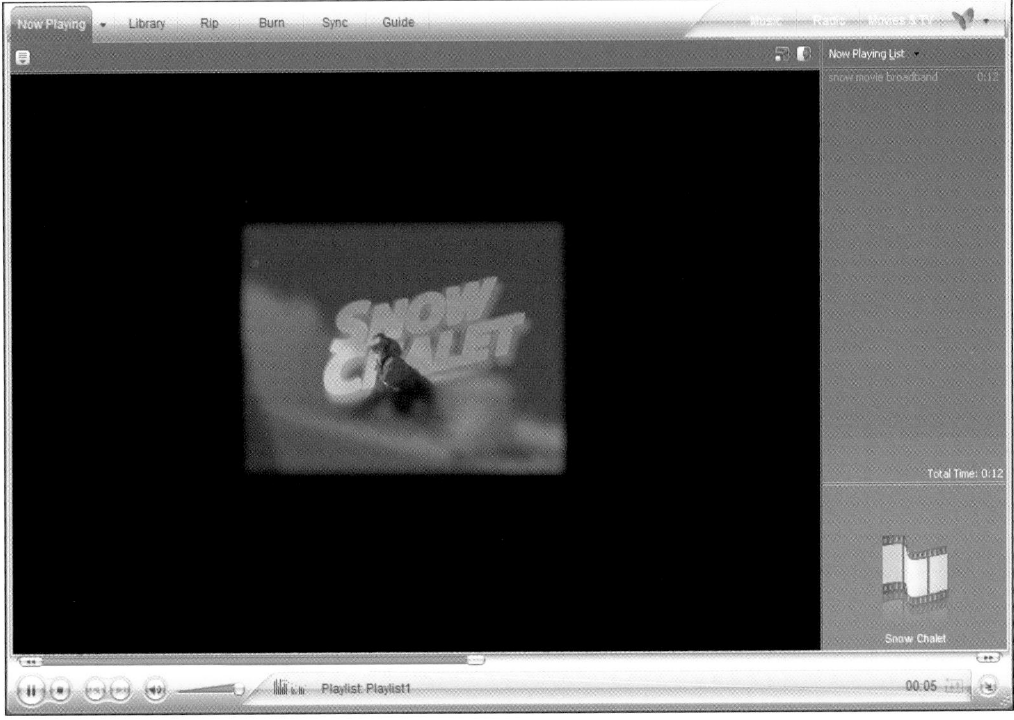

10. Click your Windows **Start** menu, and then click **My Computer**. Navigate to the **c:\Premiere Pro HOT\Chapter 14** folder and double-click the **snow movie broadband.wmv** file you just created. This will play the movie in Windows Media Player.

Hopefully, you'll agree that the video quality is pretty good. It should be–it's made for audiences with broadband connections (fast connections to the Internet) so they can download large movies. As a general rule, larger files equate to better quality. This 12-second movie is about 900 KB.

In this exercise there were quite a few "settings" that were glossed over. As you get more experience exporting to Web movies, some of these settings may be of interest to you. However, at this point–the safest thing to do is always select an export preset. Also, if you find the number of Windows Media choices overwhelming, try QuickTime or Real Media, which have fewer presets.

---

11. Save and keep this project open before moving on to the next exercise.

NOTE | The Incredible Shrinking Movie

So how exactly does the Adobe Media Encoder achieve such small file sizes? There are a handful of options that determine file size, and each format (QuickTime, Windows Media, Real Media) has its own options. Here are some of the more common options:

Video codec: Codec stands for "**Co**mpressor/**Dec**ompressor." Every codec compresses differently, using different algorithms and logic. Some codecs keep video pristine but leave large file sizes. Others are great at compressing heavily for small files, but the video quality is subpar. The ideal codec finds a harmony between video quality and file size.

Frame rate: DV video plays at 29.97 frames per second. If you lower the frame rate, less frames need to be played, which results in smaller file size. At frame rates less than 12 to 15, your eye can detect individual frames, and the illusion of animation is lost.

Frame width × height: The size of the screen relates directly to the number of pixels. Smaller screens have fewer pixels, and therefore, smaller file sizes.

Bit rate: Specifies the megabits per second of the encoded file. A higher bit rate results in a larger file, because there are more megabits per second.

Bit rate mode: A constant bit rate (CBR) compresses the data to a fixed rate. A variable bit rate (VBR) scans each frame and determines the maximum bit rate that can be achieved.

The purpose of using the Adobe Media Encoder presets is to take the guesswork out of specifying these different options. Many of the presets are tuned to find the "sweetspot," balancing quality and file size.

6. Export MPEG-2 Movie

MPEG-2 is the video format of all DVD movies. Like DV, the DVD format is very strict, so every single setting must match the specification to a tee. This is another reason why choosing an export preset isn't just helpful, it can be *necessary*. In this exercise, you will learn how to export an MPEG-2 file that is ready to be burned to DVD.

1. If the project from the previous exercise is open, skip to Step 2. If Premiere Pro is not running, launch it and click **Open Project** at the **Welcome Screen**. Navigate to the **c:\Premiere Pro HOT\Chapter14** folder, select **Exercise06.prproj**, and click **Open**.

2. Click in the bar along the top of the **Timeline** to bring focus to the **Timeline** window.

3. Choose **File > Export > Adobe Media Encoder**.

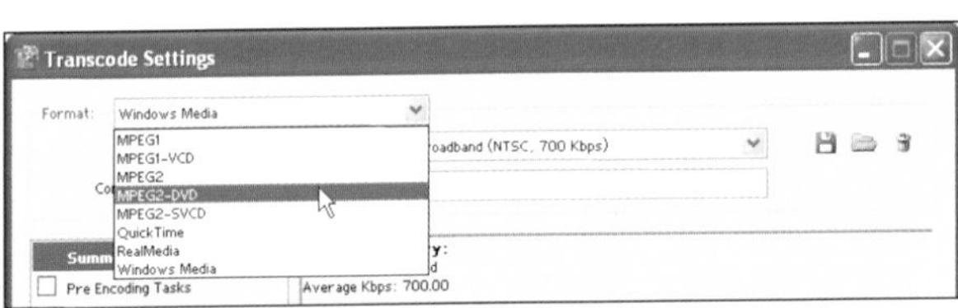

4. From the **Format** drop-down menu, choose **MPEG-2-DVD**.

You can also use MPEG-2 format to burn SVCDs, which are like DVDs, but they are burned to CD discs instead of DVD discs. And you need a special SVCD player (which are rare outside of Hong Kong).

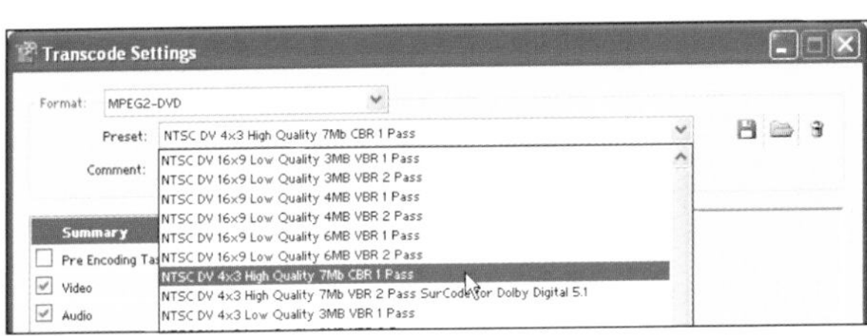

5. From the **Preset** drop-down menu, choose **NTSC DV 4x3 High Quality 7Mb CBR 1 Pass**.

The number of options may seem dizzying, but the "lingo" is easy to figure out: ***NTSC*** *(video standard in the Americas and Japan);* ***DV*** *(you have been working in a DV project);* ***4x3*** *(standard video screen; widescreen is 16x9);* ***High Quality 7Mb*** *(Bit rate, higher equals better);* ***CBR 1 Pass*** *(fixed bit rate).*

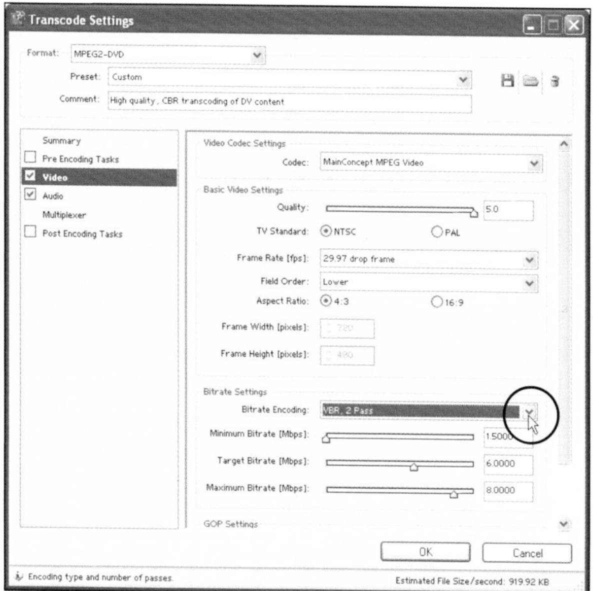

6. In the left side of the window, select the **Video** setting to view its options. Under the **Bitrate Settings**, change **Bitrate Encoding** to **VBR, 2 Pass**.

CBR is a fixed bit rate, meaning the bit rate is always the same. VBR is a variable bit rate, which adjusts the bit rate based on the needs of the video. 2 Pass means the encoder scans the movie twice when deciding which bit rate to use–in theory, fine-tuning the bit rate more with each pass. However, nothing is free in the world of encoding, and two passes requires more encoding time.

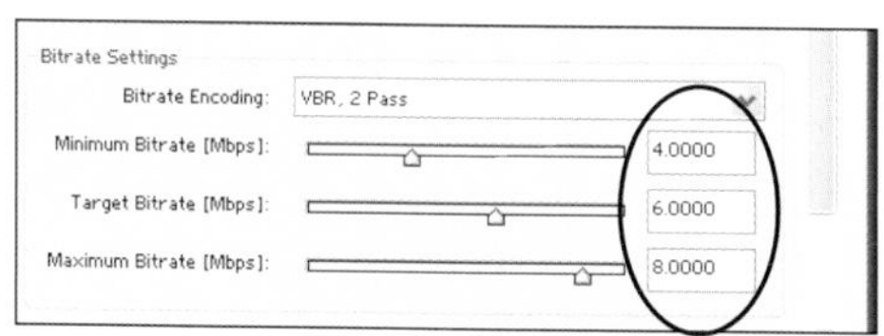

7. Also under the **Bitrate Settings**, change the **Minimum Bitrate** to **4.0000**, **Target Bitrate** to **6.0000**, and **Maximum Bitrate** to **8.0000**. Click **OK**.

*The **Minimum** and **Maximum Bitrate** set limits that the variable bit rate cannot dip below or peak above. These settings should be based largely on the length of the movie. See the sidebar following this exercise.*

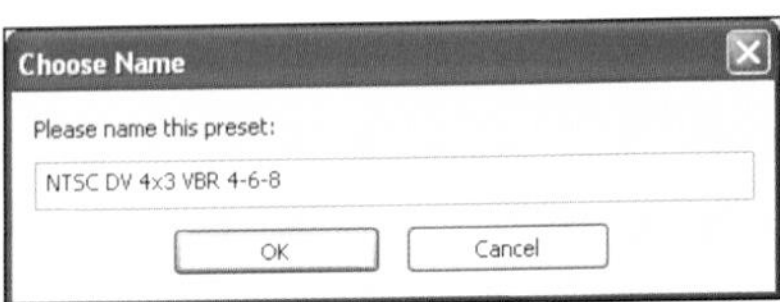

8. When asked to name the custom preset you just made, type **NTSC DV 4x3 VBR 4-6-8**. Click **OK**.

The custom settings you just specified will be added as an export preset to your list of available MPEG-2 DVD presets.

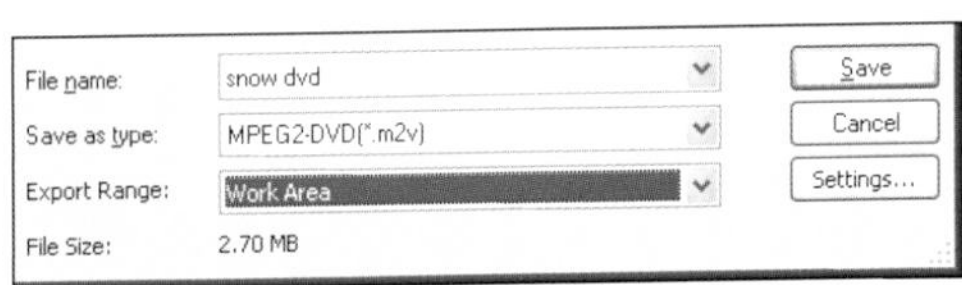

9. When asked to save your file, navigate to the **c:\Premiere Pro HOT\Chapter 14** folder and name your file **snow dvd**. Change the **Export Range** to **Work Area**. Click **Save**.

*You are only choosing **Work Area** in this exercise because the encode process will take quite some time. Normally, you will want to encode your entire sequence.*

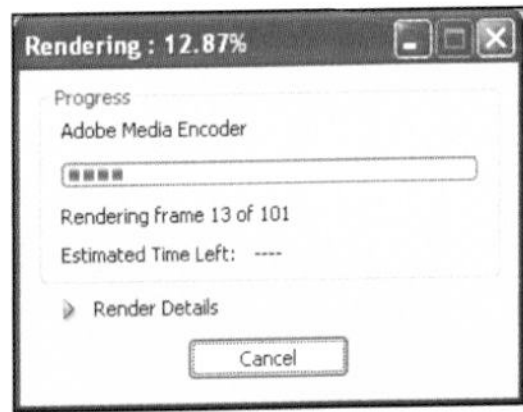

The encoding process of the 3-second work area may take a couple of minutes on your computer. As you can see, encoding is quite a labor-intensive task and can tie up your PC for hours. Unfortunately, there's really no way around this.

In this exercise, you learned how to create MPEG-2 files for DVD burning, and also how to change the bit rate to fit your needs. Changing the bit rate is probably the single most important thing you can do to maximize your video quality. See the sidebar following this exercise for further details.

10. Save and keep this project open before moving on to the next exercise.

NOTE | Choosing a Bit Rate

When creating an MPEG-2 file, choosing a proper bit rate can have a dramatic increase in quality. It's important to know how to maximize your bit rate, so you can get the most out of your DVD movie.

First, the basics. DVD discs can hold between 4.7 GB and 17.1 GB of data. (That's 6 to 23 CD-ROMs. Wow.) The most common discs purchased by consumers, DVD-R and DVD+R, usually hold 4.7 GB. This means that your file size cannot be above 4.7 GB. (Actually more like 4.3 GB, but that's a discussion for another day.) The file size of your encoded movie is determined by many factors, but primarily it is determined by movie duration and encoding bit rate. Since you can't change the length of your movie, then obviously you must change the bit rate in order to fit your movie onto a 4.7 GB disc.

MPEG-2 DVD movies can have a maximum bit rate of 9.6 Mbps, but very few DVD players can sustain smooth playback at this rate. Many users report trouble above 7 Mbps, while others are okay up to 8 Mbps. Every DVD player is different, so make sure you experiment to see which maximum bit rate your DVD player can handle. However, as soon as your movie goes beyond 70 minutes or so, you'll have to start lowering the bit rate in order to achieve a smaller file size. (Here's the math, for you number crunchers: 8 megabits/second (Mbps) = .001 gigabytes/sec × 60 seconds × 70 minutes = 4.2 GB for 1 hour of video.)

Say you have a 2-hour movie. 120 minutes, encoded at 5 Mbps, results in a file size of about 4.4 GB. (These are all averages, mind you. Each movie will have slightly different encoding bit rates.) If you choose a bit rate that is too low, your finished movie may be 2 GB, less than half of what you could have stored. If you choose a bit rate that is too high, you won't be able to burn the entire movie onto a single DVD disc. The goal is to choose the bit rate that fills up every last bit of available space on your DVD disc.

Luckily, there are quite a few bit rate calculators on the Internet that do the thinking for you, based upon your disc size and movie duration. A few of my favorites:

- *www.customflix.com/Special/AuthoringNightmares/03/BitBudget.jsp*
- *dvd-hq.info/Calculator.html*
- *www.videohelp.com/calc.htm*

It's important to stress this again: choosing the proper bit rate is the single most important decision you can make when burning a DVD. (And coincidentally, you learned how to do this in the previous exercise!)

7. Burning Directly to DVD

Premiere Pro also enables you to burn a sequence directly to DVD. Once completed, you can take the DVD and play it in a home DVD player. It won't have any menus or buttons like Hollywood DVDs, but this is especially useful if you don't own any DVD authoring software, or you want a DVD in a hurry. In this exercise, you will learn how to burn DVDs directly from Premiere Pro. (If you do not have a DVD burner installed in your system, some of the menu choices in this exercise may not be available.)

1. If the project from the previous exercise is open, skip to Step 2. If Premiere Pro is not running, launch it and click **Open Project** at the **Welcome Screen**. Navigate to the **c:\Premiere Pro HOT\Chapter14** folder, select **Exercise07.prproj**, and click **Open**.

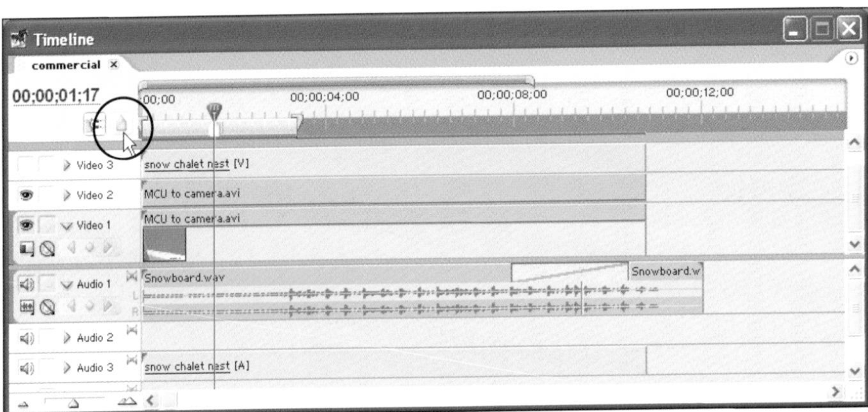

2. In the **Timeline** window, move the current time indicator to **00;00;01;17** and click the **Set Unnumbered Marker** button.

Premiere Pro lets you create chapter points in your DVD movies based on unnumbered sequence markers. This means each sequence marker in the ***Timeline*** *will become a chapter in the DVD disc.*

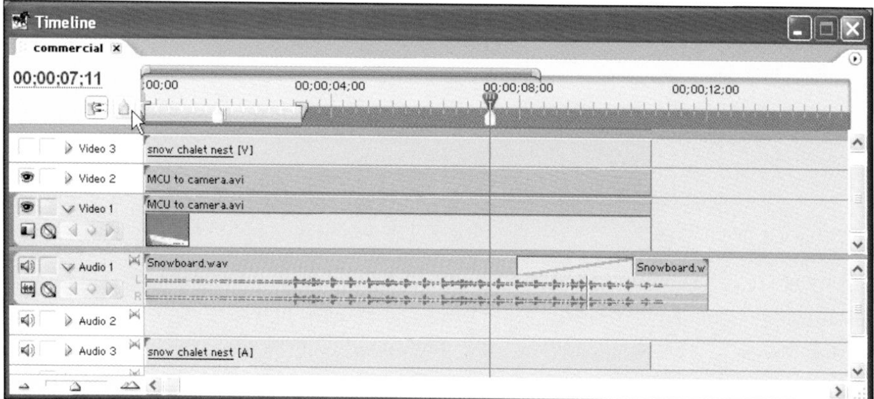

3. Move the current time indicator to **00;00;07;11** and click the **Set Unnumbered Marker** button.

The finished DVD movie will have three chapters. (The start of the movie is always chapter 1, so the first marker is chapter 2, and so on.)

---

4. Choose **File > Export > Export to DVD**.

*This will open up the **Export to DVD** window. This window takes a few seconds to load your DVD drive, and it also scans for valid media in the DVD drive. If you have a recordable DVD disc laying around, you can put it in the DVD drive at this time.*

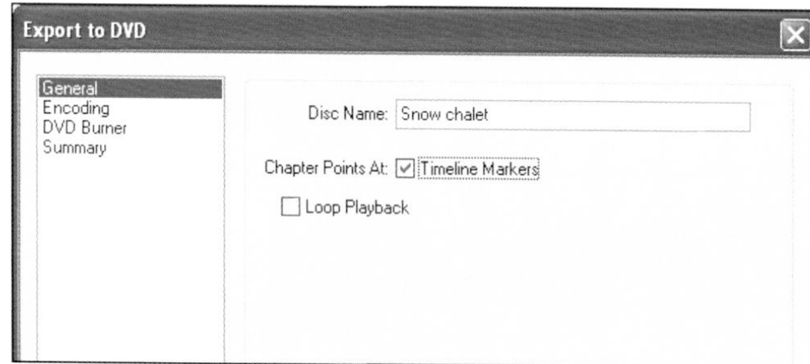

5. In the **General** settings, name the disc **Snow chalet** and make sure that **Chapter Points At Timeline Markers** is checked.

You can also loop playback, which is a convenient feature if the DVD is being shown at a trade show or an information kiosk, where the movie should play over and over ad infinitum (or nauseum... Latin humor!).

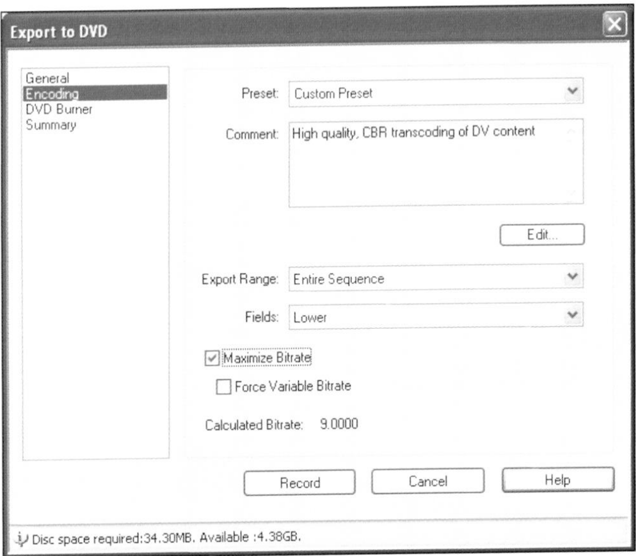

6. In the **Encoding** settings, click the **Maximize Bitrate** check box.

This is Premiere's built-in bit rate calculator; it determines the maximum bit rate based on your movie duration and disc capacity. The only problem is–in my opinion–the bit rate shouldn't go above 8 Mbps. So the rule of thumb is, use this feature whenever the calculated bit rate is below 8 Mbps. Otherwise, you should uncheck this option.

7. Uncheck **Maximize Bitrate** to turn it off.

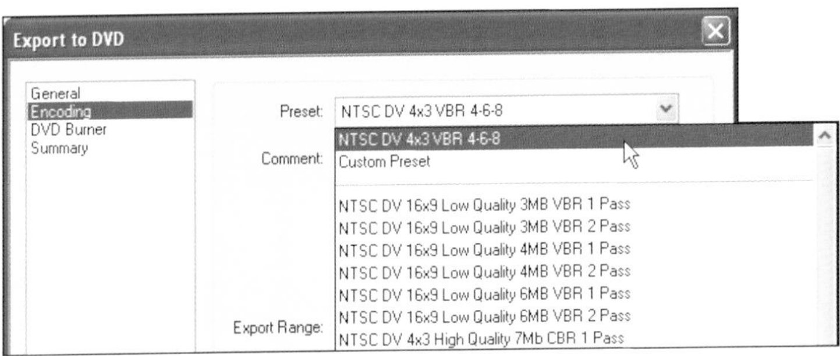

8. From the **Preset** drop-down menu, choose **NTSC DV 4x3 VBR 4-6-8**.

Tip: *A nice feature of Premiere's Export to DVD function is that it will use any presets created in the Adobe Media Encoder. In this case,* ***NTSC DV 4x3 VBR 4-6-8*** *is the preset you created in the previous exercise. Also notice that the* ***Force Variable Bitrate*** *checkbox is automatically checked after you chose this preset. (In the previous exercise, you made this preset a variable bit rate, remember?)*

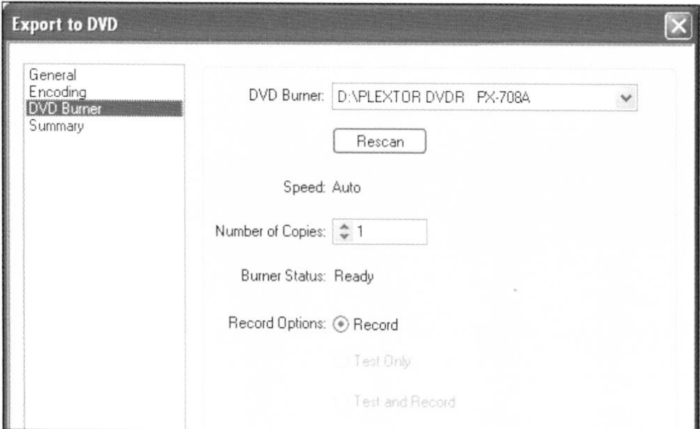

9. Select the **DVD Burner** settings.

*If you put your DVD media into the drive after the **Export to DVD** window was already open, you can click **Rescan**, so Premiere Pro will automatically scan your DVD drive and inserted media. Or, if you have multiple DVD burners (lucky you!), you can select which burner to use. In addition, you can also increase the number of copies to burn.*

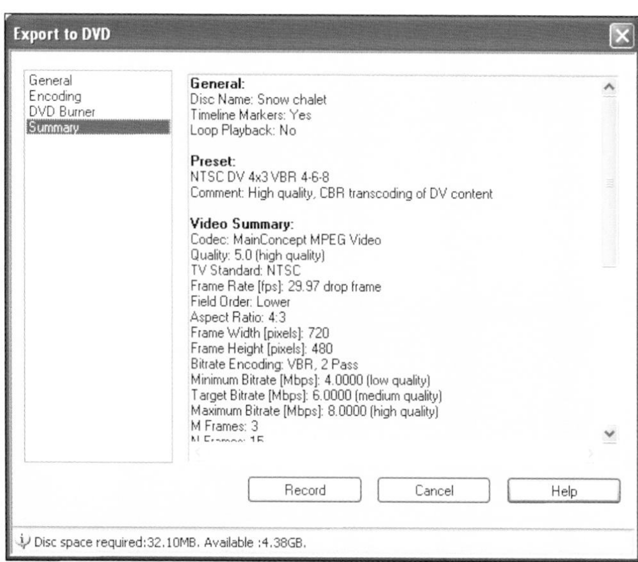

10. Select the **Summary** settings.

*There are no **Summary** settings to change. Rather, the summary is a list of your chosen settings. Notice that the minimum and maximum bit rate settings you specified in the previous exercise are here.*

11. Click **Record** (if you want to burn to DVD).

This will start the encoding, authoring, and burning process. Do this only if you want to burn to a DVD disc in your DVD burner. Otherwise, click ***Cancel****.*

When using the presets from the Adobe Media Encoder, there's very little manual configuration for you to do. Premiere Pro will handle the entire encoding-through-burning process. Of course, there are some drawbacks to doing this. While your DVD burns (it may take 5 or 10 minutes), feel free to read the sidebar following this exercise for some valuable information on the burning-to-DVD process.

---

12. Save and close this project before moving on to the next exercise.

NOTE | The Allure of Burning Directly to DVD

Premiere Pro's feature of burning directly to DVD may sound alluring, but don't be fooled by its siren call. Sure, it may seem like the process is quicker and easier, but that's not always the case.

The steps to burning a DVD are as follows: encode your movie to MPEG-2, use DVD authoring software to prepare the MPEG-2 file, and burn the MPEG-2 file to a DVD+R or DVD-R (depending on the disc type and capabilities of your DVD burner).

(In Exercise 6, you learned how to encode your movie as an MPEG-2 file. That file can now be taken to any DVD authoring software (such as Adobe Encore). True, the encoding process can take hours, but once you have encoded it, you shouldn't have to encode that file again.)

On the other hand, when you burn directly to DVD from within Premiere Pro, the above three steps are automatically completed for you. So Premiere Pro encodes an MPEG 2 file, then prepares the file, and then burns it to disc (all without your knowledge). This seems advantageous at first, but consider that Premiere Pro does not *save* the MPEG-2 file. As soon as the burning process is over, Premiere Pro destroys all of the temporary files from memory.

Why is that a big deal? Well, if you want Premiere Pro to burn a second copy at a later date, you have to wait while the program goes through *all three steps again*. On the other hand, if you want to burn a second copy of the MPEG-2 file that you made yourself in Exercise 6, you only have to go through Steps 2 and 3, because you already have the MPEG-2 file.

continued on mext page

NOTE | The Allure of Burning Directly to DVD *continued*

Here's another common scenario: Premiere Pro completes Step 1 and 2, and then, as Murphy's Law predicts, crashes on Step 3. Uh-oh. You now have to start all over at Step 1. But if you had made your own MPEG-2 movie, you would only need to start back at Step 2, thereby saving hours and hours of encoding!

Plus, Premiere Pro's built-in encoder does not have any menu creating capabilities. In order to do that, you'll need a dedicated DVD authoring software–which means you'll have to make your own MPEG-2 file anyway.

The moral is, use Premiere Pro's built-in DVD-burning feature only if you don't have any other DVD authoring software available, or if you want to quickly burn a short sequence without menus (that you don't plan to burn again). In all other cases, it is much safer and quicker to create your own MPEG-2 file from Adobe Media Encoder, and then author with another application.

Throughout this chapter, you had a chance to work with both the Export window and the Adobe Media Encoder. Before turning the page and moving on to the next chapter, take a moment to consider what you have learned about the two export methods.

The Export window doesn't have as many presets, and it doesn't have the capability to export to the latest Web and DVD formats, as the Adobe Media Encoder does. On the other hand, the Adobe Media Encoder creates highly compressed files (that should not be used again for editing in future projects). The Adobe Media Encoder cannot export to the original DV format or uncompressed WAV audio format, and it cannot save still images.

In general, use the Adobe Media Encoder when you want to save the finished product for viewing only. Use the Export window when you want to use the file again in Premiere Pro or edit it in other applications such as After Effects, Photoshop, or Audition.

Now that you know how to get DV video out of your computer, it's time to work backwards and learn how to get DV video into *your computer.*

15
Capturing Digital Video

H•O•T

Premiere Pro HOT DVD

Capturing video from camcorder/VCR is also a type of importing. When you capture footage, Premiere Pro saves the video to your hard drive in a location that you specify. Once the file has been saved, it is treated like any other clip you have imported in previous chapters; you tell Premiere Pro where to find the file, and the project links to it. And because the captured video is saved to your hard drive like any other file, you can use it in multiple projects–just as long as you don't delete the file from your computer.

What Is Capturing?

Capturing is the act of transferring audio and video footage from a camcorder to your PC. The audio and video captured from a camcorder becomes a file on a hard drive, and it can be imported into a Premiere Pro project as a clip.

To capture digital video, you need the following:

- A camcorder that outputs footage to IEEE-1394 (FireWire, i.LINK)
- A IEEE-1394 port on your computer
- Lots and lots of hard drive space

When you capture footage from a DV camcorder, you have to decide two very important things: what to capture and where to capture. In this chapter, you will learn how to capture only the video you want to use, as well as the factors that dictate where you should save your captured footage.

Capturing Digital Video

There are four ways to capture video from your DV camcorder:

- Capture an entire videotape as one long clip.
- Capture each clip individually.
- Log all of the clips and batch capture them at a later time.
- Use Scene Detect to capture each scene on a videotape.

No matter which method you choose, the concept is the same: decide the capture In point (when to start capturing) and capture Out point (when to stop capturing). You can manually start and stop capturing yourself, or you can let Premiere Pro automatically start and stop capturing at the In and Out points. In this chapter, you will learn all four capture methods.

The Capture Window

All of your capturing will be done through the aptly named Capture window. The Capture window allows you to manually capture video footage or to log video footage to capture at a later time. Take a minute to familiarize yourself with the Capture window.

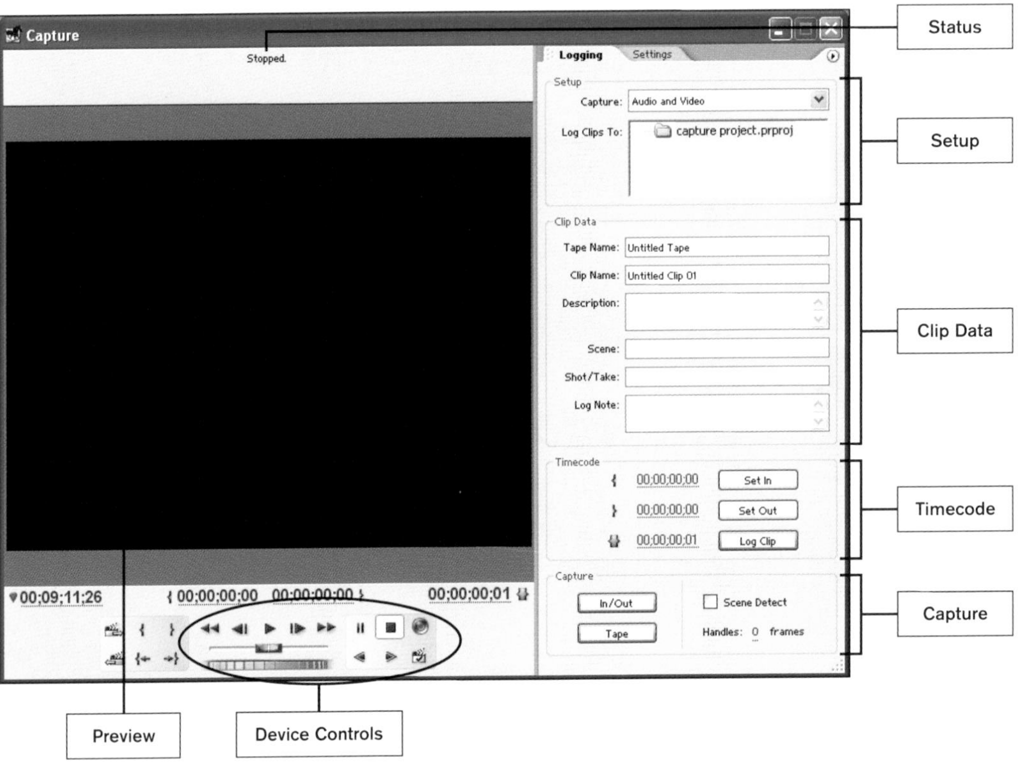

Status: Shows the status of the DV device. If your device is properly communicating with Premiere Pro, you will see a status such as **Stopped** or **Playing.** This is a good indication that you have the DV device connected successfully.

Preview: This is the preview monitor that displays the playback of the DV device.

Setup: You can choose to capture **Audio and Video** or just one of the two.

Clip Data: You can label your clip with all sorts of information, such as a long description, scene description, shot/take information, log notes, and so on. At a minimum, you should always fill in **Tape Name** and **Clip Name.** The more time you take to name your clips, the better organized you will be when searching through dozens and dozens of clips.

Timecode: The **Set In** and **Set Out** buttons are the same as the **{** and **}** buttons you've used throughout this book. The In point specifies when you want to start capturing, and the Out point specifies when to stop capturing. As mentioned earlier, you can manually record each clip on an ad hoc basis, or you can log all of your clips for capturing at a later point in time. (More on this later!)

Capture: You can capture just the In and Out points you specified in the Timecode area, or you can capture starting at the current frame and manually stop capture yourself. You can also enable **Scene Detect**, where Premiere Pro scans your tape and automatically captures each scene for you. (More on this later also!)

Device controls: These should look very familiar. These controls behave exactly as the controls in the Monitor window. You'll notice there is a red Record button, which doesn't record *to* tape, but records *from* tape, so it really should be called the Capture button.

NOTE | Capturing Analog Footage

Unlike digital video, which can interface with the existing hardware on your computer, analog video requires additional hardware in order to be captured by Premiere Pro. Most computers do not come with built-in capabilities of capturing analog formats, such as VHS, S-VHS, VHS-c, Hi8, and 8mm.

If you plan to capture analog formats, you should purchase a dedicated analog capture card or an analog to digital conversion box. In addition, you should pick an analog capture card that has been certified by Adobe for use in Premiere Pro. The best cards provide drivers that "plug into" Premiere Pro, making their existence transparent, allowing you to do all of your work without ever leaving Premiere Pro. The Adobe Web site (**www.adobe.com/products/premiere/6cards.html**) maintains a database of certified third-party capture cards that work with Premiere Pro.

With that said, there is one unique product that makes capturing analog formats a breeze: Sony's Digital8 (D8) camcorder. These marvelous little inventions record in digital format, but they record to your standard, run-of-the-mill 8mm or Hi8 tape. Even better, they output to IEEE-1394!

Not impressed you say? Consider this: perhaps you've got some old Hi8 or 8mm tapes lying around the house. You can pick up a very inexpensive Sony Digital8 camcorder to use exclusively as a VCR. (In truth, the camcorder recording quality is only so-so, but the playback quality is never reduced, so they work great as inexpensive playback machines!) Now you can transfer your old analog tapes via digital IEEE-1394, with device control, lossless quality, and everything else that's absolutely wonderful about digital video. For users who are migrating from Hi8/8mm to DV, these Digital8 camcorders make excellent additions to your video editing gear.

Capturing to a Hard Drive

Earlier you learned that DV video requires 13 GB of hard drive space for 1 hour of video. When you capture, you usually end up capturing more than you need. (In fact, you *should* capture more than you need–better safe than sorry, right?) This means that in a 1-hour program you may have 2 hours of captured footage, which requires 26 GB of hard drive space (2 hrs × 13 GB/hr). Even though you won't use the entire 2 hours of captured footage, you should nevertheless plan on having at least twice as much hard drive space as normal.

Deciding where to save the files captured from your camcorder is a very important decision. Once a video file is saved to hard drive, you should avoid moving it from its original location. (For example, if you move a file, all Premiere Pro projects linking to that file will need to be relinked.)

There are two types of video editing computers: those with extra hard drives and those without. Users with extra hard drives usually have their operating systems (Windows XP) and program files (Premiere Pro) on their primary hard drives, and they use the second hard drive as dedicated audio/video storage. A storage drive is nice, but not required, in order to capture and play back video files.

In the next exercise, you will learn how to specify your capture locations, as well as verify that your device is communicating with Premiere Pro.

I. Preparing for Capture

Before you begin capturing from your camcorder, you must first decide where to save the files on your hard drive, and secondly verify that Premiere Pro and your DV camcorder are communicating properly. After you address these two issues, you can begin capturing. In this exercise, you will specify your capture locations and learn how to verify that your DV device is properly communicating with Premiere Pro. (This exercise is designed to show the built-in support for DV capture in Premiere Pro. If you use a third-party capture card, please refer to the card's documentation to prepare your system for capture.)

1. Do not launch Premiere Pro yet. (If it is currently running, exit the application.)

Although it is not necessary with Windows XP, it's still a good habit to connect your DV device before Premiere Pro has launched.

---

2. Connect a DV device (camcorder or VTCR) to your computer via the IEEE-1394 port. Make sure your camcorder is in **Playback/VCR/VTR** mode. (Different brands use different naming conventions.) Put a tape–one that has existing footage you can capture–into your device.

Tip: *Use an AC power adapter for a DV camcorder when capturing. This should prevent the camcorder from going into a "standby" or "sleep" mode, as well as prevent the battery from running out in the middle of a capture.*

3. If the Windows XP **Digital Video Device** window appears, select **Edit and Record Video using Adobe Premiere Pro** and click **OK**. If the window does not appear, launch Premiere Pro manually.

Note: *If this window does not appear, do not worry. Your system may be configured so that this window is deactivated.*

4. At the **Welcome Screen**, select **New Project**.

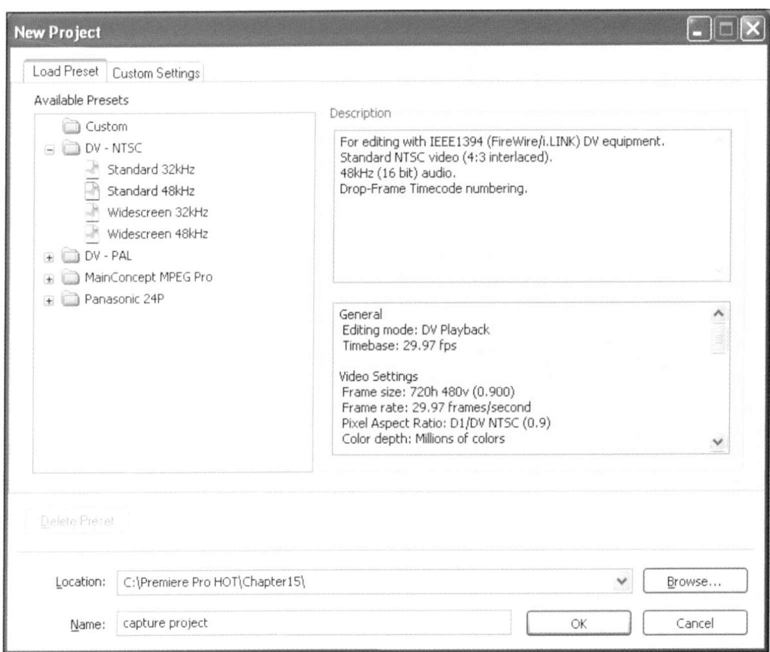

5. From the **DV – NTSC** folder, select the **Standard 48kHz** project preset. Click **Browse** and navigate to the **c:\Premiere Pro HOT\Chapter15** folder to set the project location. Name the project **capture project**. Click **OK**.

Tip: *If you have a dedicated storage drive for editing/capturing, select that location instead. In fact, you should rarely capture to your* ***c:*** *drive if you can avoid it.*

6. Choose **Edit > Preferences > Scratch Disks**.

This is the menu option for setting all of your capture locations. A ***scratch disk*** *is a folder where temporary files are stored, such as those created during rendering.*

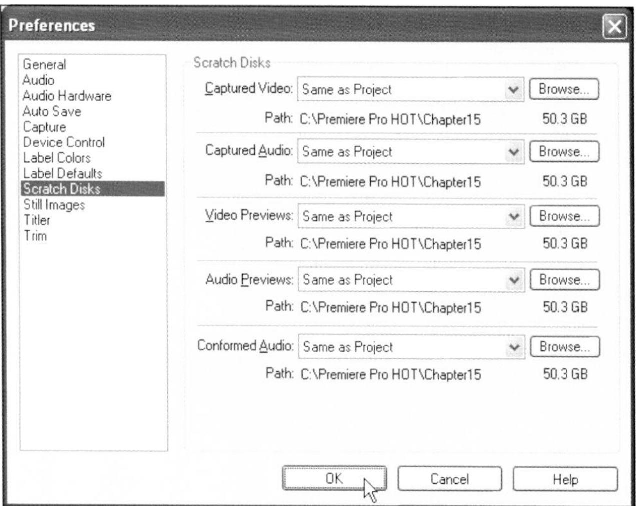

7. Make sure that all scratch disk locations are set to **Same as Project**. Click **OK**.

This will capture audio and video files, as well as render all audio and video previews, to the project location you specified in Step 5.

8. Choose **File > Capture**.

Now that you have specified your capture locations, the next step is to verify that your DV device is properly communicating with Premiere Pro.

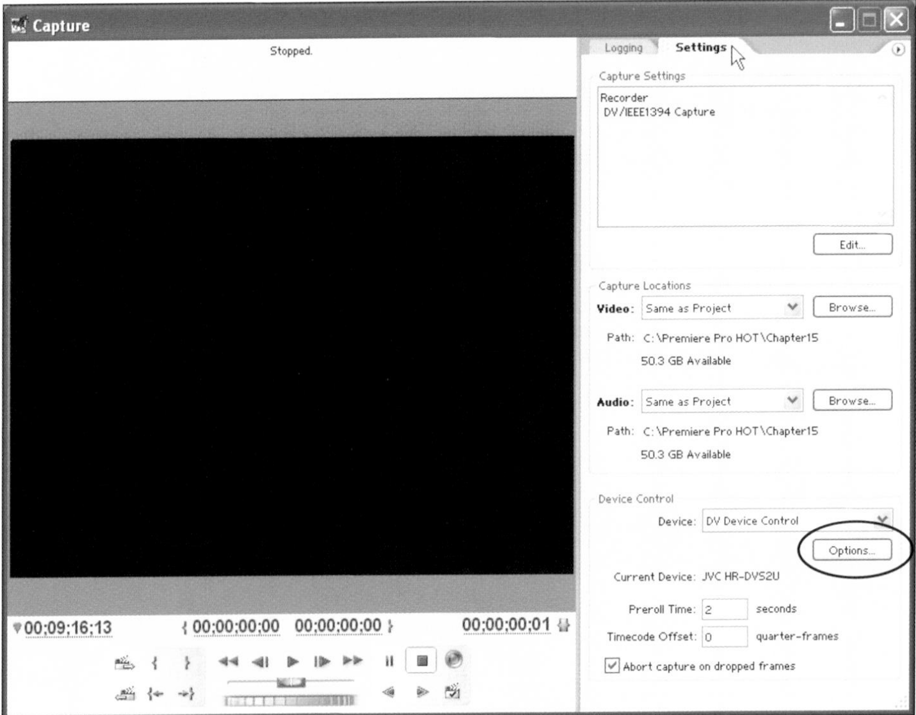

9. In the **Capture** window, click the **Settings** tab. Under the **Device Control** options, make sure **DV Device Control** is selected and then click the **Options** button to modify the device settings.

Notice that you can also specify your capture locations in the ***Settings*** *tab. These are the exact same locations that you set in Step 7. (As usual, Premiere Pro provides multiple ways to do the same thing.)*

10. In the **DV Device Control Options** window, choose the **Video Standard**, **Device Brand**, and **Device Type** that best matches your DV device. (You most likely have a **Drop-Frame** device.) Click **Check Status** to make sure the status reads **Online**. Click **OK**.

Note: *The options you choose, based on your own device, may be different than those displayed in the above figure. The* ***Capture*** *window should now display* ***Stopped*** *along the top status area, which indicates successful communication between your DV device and Premiere Pro.*

Tip: *If your device does not show as* ***Online****, click* ***Go Online for Device Info****, which will take you directly to the* ***Adobe Premiere DV Device Compatibility List.*** *You can search through the list for your DV device make and model to see if your device is supported by Premiere Pro.*

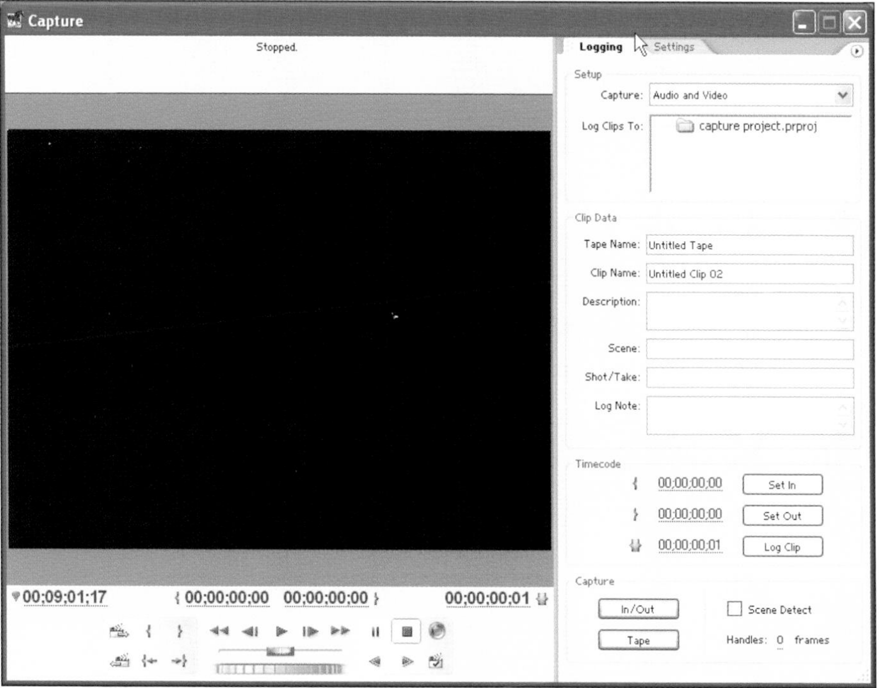

11. Click the **Logging** tab.

The ***Logging*** *tab is where you label clips, set* ***In*** *and* ***Out*** *points, and log and capture clips. The* ***Settings*** *tab is for specifying capture locations, device options, and other capture settings.*

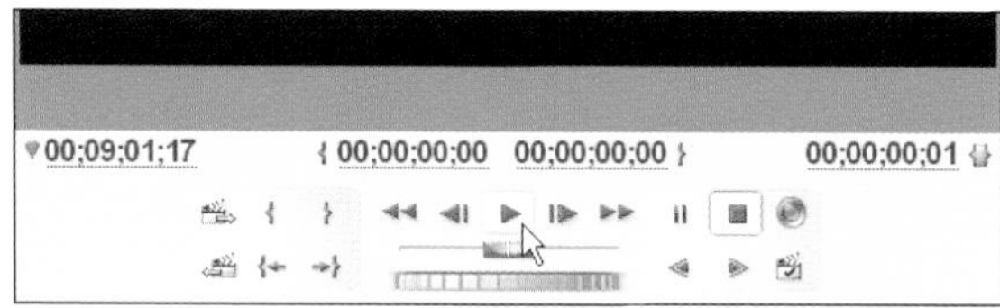

12. At the bottom of the **Capture** window, click **Play** to begin playback of your DV device.

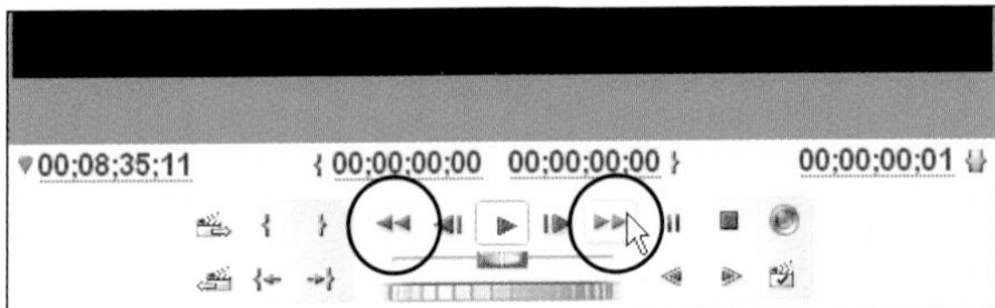

13. While the DV device is playing, click **Fast Forward** and **Rewind** to verify that you are able to properly control the device from within Premiere Pro.

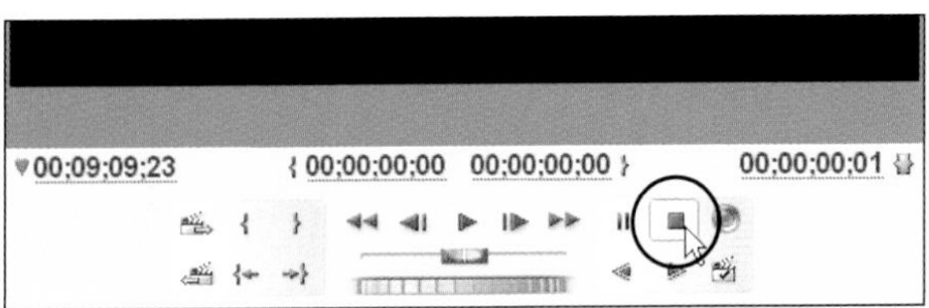

14. Click **Stop** to stop playback.

*Tip: Some camcorders and VCRs will have their life spans significantly reduced when left in **Pause** mode for long periods of time, because the recording heads will be engaged too long. However, some of the newer DV camcorders are built with mechanisms that disengage the recording heads during extended **Pause** modes–which doesn't reduce the life span of the device. When in doubt, don't pause for extended periods of time.*

You have just prepared your project for capturing digital video. Hopefully your DV device properly communicated with Premiere Pro. As DV technology has matured, the communication across IEEE-1394 has also matured, and a growing number of DV devices are compatible with Premiere Pro. You can visit the Adobe Web site to see if your device is compatible.

15. Save and keep this project open before moving on to the next exercise.

NOTE | Why a Dedicated Drive?

What's the big deal about having an extra hard drive? Why not just capture to the **My Documents** folder on your main hard drive?

For starters, capturing and playing digital video taxes your hard drive quite heavily. (You try displaying 30 still images per second for hours at a time and see how well you do!) However, while capturing, your operating system may need to access Premiere Pro program files or other system files. This can cause a data bottleneck, as Premiere Pro is trying to save large digital video files to the same drive that the operating system is trying to access. Picture the Three Stooges getting stuck in a doorway.

A second hard drive, dedicated exclusively for audio/video storage, allows Premiere Pro to capture without being interrupted by the operating system processes. This can result in fewer (or zero) frames lost during capture and much smoother performance.

Don't despair if you only have one drive. With today's technology, a single hard drive that is reasonably fast may have no noticeable problems during video capture.

Another advantage of having a second hard drive is data security. If your primary hard drive (knock on wood) ever crashes, your data on the second drive should not be affected. Sure, reinstalling the Windows operating system is tantamount to oral surgery without anesthesia, but at least you won't lose hours and hours of Premiere Pro projects.

Yet another advantage is that storage drives tend to be much larger than system drives. And keep in mind that hard drives will perform slower as they get full. So filling up your primary drive with video affects not only Premiere Pro's playback performance, but affects *all* files and applications on that hard drive. (And you don't want to be put in the unenviable position of deciding which application needs to be removed from your system because you don't have room to capture Megan's pony riding lessons.)

For these reasons, I prefer to make a directory on my storage drive for each Premiere Pro project. I create a new project in that directory and capture all source footage to that directory. When it comes time to archive or delete a project, I know that I can find all of my files within a single directory, which saves a lot of time managing dozens of projects.

2. Capturing Footage

The easiest method of capturing footage is to manually record, on the fly, as your DV device plays back. In this exercise, you will learn how to capture on the fly. Make sure your DV device is connected, powered on, and in playback/VCR/VTR mode before launching Premiere Pro.

1. if you have the previous exercise open, skip to Step 2. If Premiere Pro is not running, launch it and click **Open Project** at the **Welcome Screen**. Navigate to the **c:\Premiere Pro HOT\Chapter15** folder, select **Exercise02.prproj**, and click **Open**.

2. Choose **File > Capture** to open the **Capture** window.

In this exercise, you should not need to re-specify all of your capture settings, because they should still be set from the last exercise.

3. Click **Play** in the **Capture** window to play back your DV device.

4. As the DV device plays, click **Record** to begin capturing the footage to your hard drive.

*During capture, the status area of the **Capture** window will display information about the capture such as duration, number of dropped frames (ideally zero dropped frames), and remaining disk space.*

---

5. When you want to stop capturing, click **Stop** or press **Esc** on the keyboard.

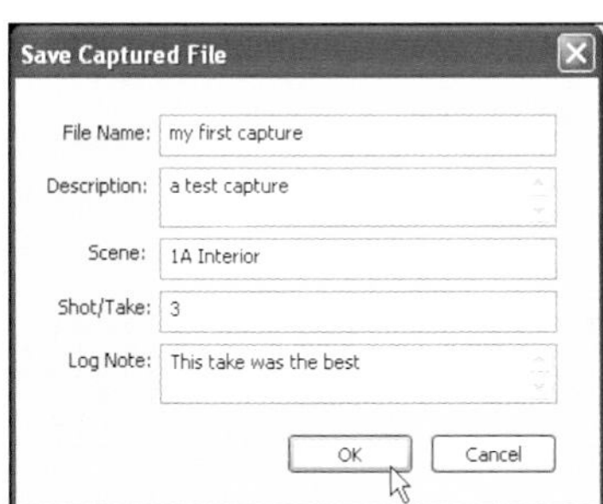

6. As soon as you stop capturing, Premiere Pro displays the **Save Captured File** window. Name your captured file **my first capture**. (You don't have to fill in any other labels, but you are more than welcome to.) Click **OK**.

Notice that Premiere Pro automatically pauses your DV device after capturing. This is a nice feature that allows you to take your time while labeling your clip and prevents you from missing any video.

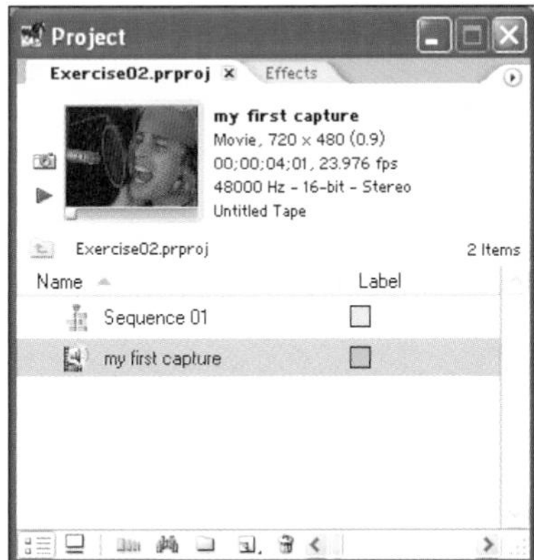

7. Click in the **Project** window to bring it to the foreground.

Not only is the file saved to your hard drive, but Premiere Pro also imports the clip into your project. This is now a movie clip like any other. Also notice that the captured clip adheres to the DV standard of 720×480 pixels and 23.976 fps. A nice feature of capturing digitally is that you don't have to futz with all of the capture settings–it's all specified for you.

Well, that was almost too easy*. Capturing footage on the fly is extremely simple. In the next exercise, you will learn how to log your footage before capturing.*

---

8. Save and keep this project open before moving on to the next exercise.

NOTE | DV Video File Size

Here's a question that is asked often, "I don't have 13 GB of hard drive space, so can I capture my DV video at a lower setting, or smaller size, in order to fit more on my hard drive?" And the short answer is: No, you can't.

Here's the long answer: No, you *really* can't.

In the previous chapter, you learned that MPEG2 files for DVD can be resized based on bit rate and quality; lowering the bit rate results in a smaller file size, which saves hard drive space.

Unfortunately, digital video is not nearly as flexible. Video captured via IEEE-1394 can be captured at one size and one size only. There's no compromising with digital video. You must capture it at its best quality and its maximum size. The advantage of capturing digital video is its ease, because you never have to specify any quality settings. The disadvantage is its inflexibility; if you're low on hard drive space, you're out of luck.

3. Logging and Batch Capture

The next capture methods you will learn are the logging and batch capture methods. Logging allows you to specify In and Out points before capturing, and batch capturing allows you to capture multiple clips in one "sitting." As always, make sure your DV device is connected, powered on, and in playback/VCR/VTR mode.

1. If you have the previous exercise open, skip to Step 2. If Premiere Pro is not running, launch it and click **Open Project** at the **Welcome Screen**. Navigate to the **c:\Premiere Pro HOT\Chapter15** folder, select **Exercise03.prproj**, and click **Open**.

2. Choose **File > Capture** to open the **Capture** window.

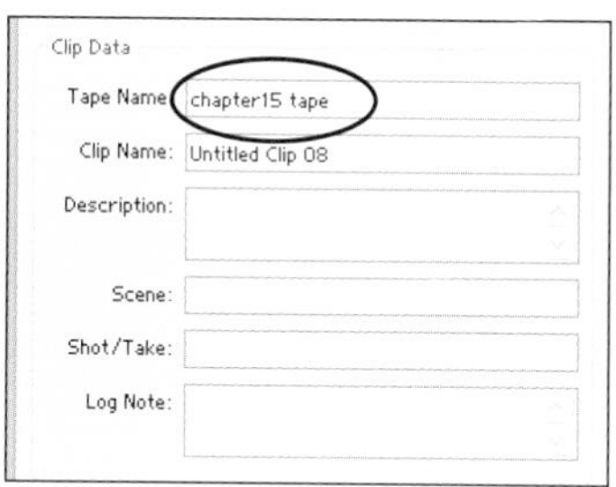

3. Under the **Clip Data** of the **Logging** tab, type **chapter15 tape** for the **Tape Name**.

Tip: *Thanks to the IEEE-1394 interface, Premiere Pro can read in all sorts of useful information about your footage, such as timecode, date/time recorded, camcorder options chosen at time of recording, and so on. However, the one piece of information Premiere Pro cannot discern is the name of the tape. Whenever you plan to log multiple clips, you should specify a tape name. In addition, this name should match what you've written on the outside of the tape, which will save a lot of time when rummaging through a shoebox full of DV tapes. (You'll discover why later in this exercise.)*

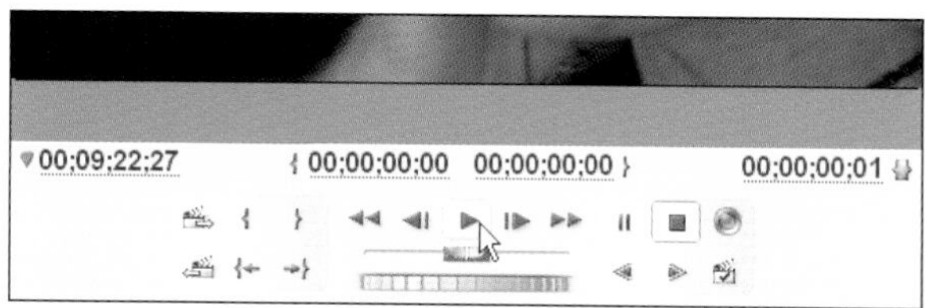

4. Click **Play** in the **Capture** window to play back your DV device.

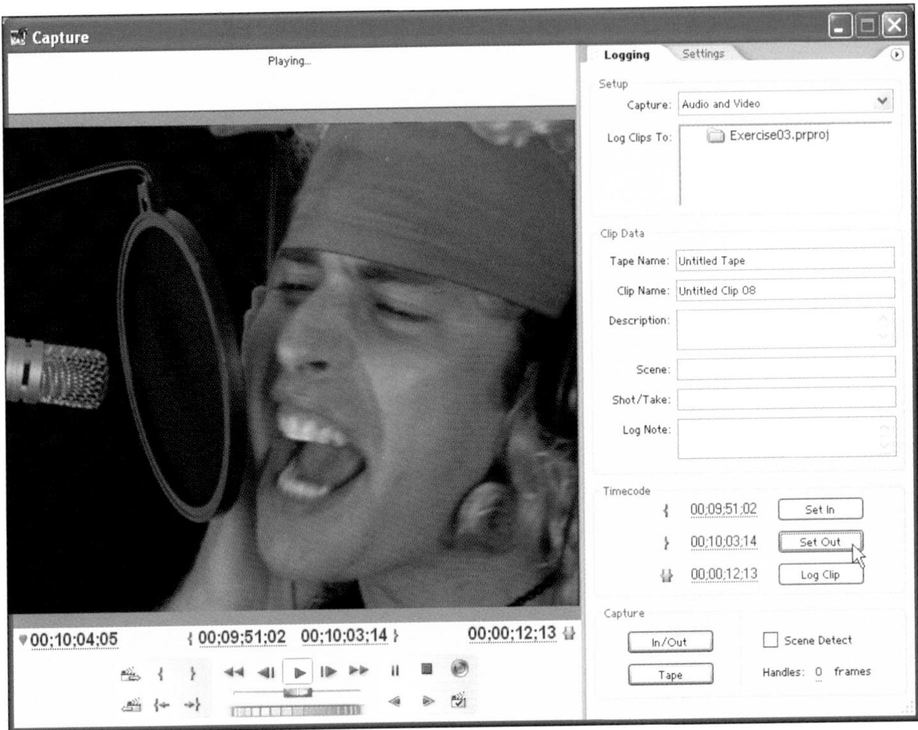

5. As your device is playing, click **Set In** to specify a timecode when capturing should start. When you want capturing to stop, click **Set Out**.

Keep in mind that no footage was captured in this step. *Instead, you just set **In** and **Out** points defining the footage that you* plan to capture.

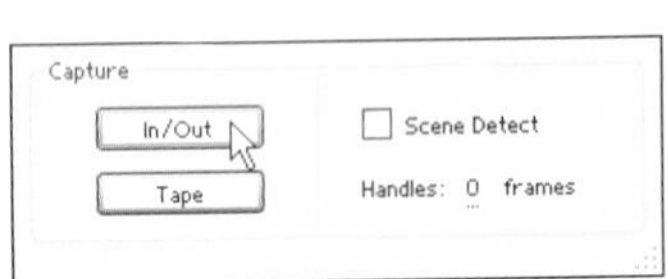

6. After setting **In** and **Out** points, click the **In/Out** button.

*If the DV device is properly connected, Premiere Pro will rewind your DV tape to the **In** point, automatically start capturing, and stop capturing at the exact frame you specified. You don't have to lift a finger!*

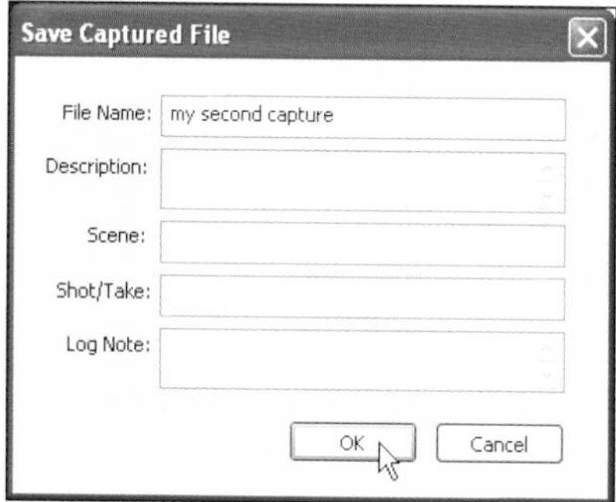

7. After capture is complete, Premiere Pro displays the **Save Captured File** window. Name your file **my second capture** and click **OK**.

As it did in the previous exercise, Premiere Pro saved your file to hard drive and imported the clip into the ***Project*** *window. Setting* ***In*** *and* ***Out*** *points before capturing allows you to watch playback before capturing. If you decide you don't want to capture the* ***In*** *and* ***Out*** *points you've set, don't click the* ***In/Out*** *button.*

8. Click **Play** in the **Capture** window.

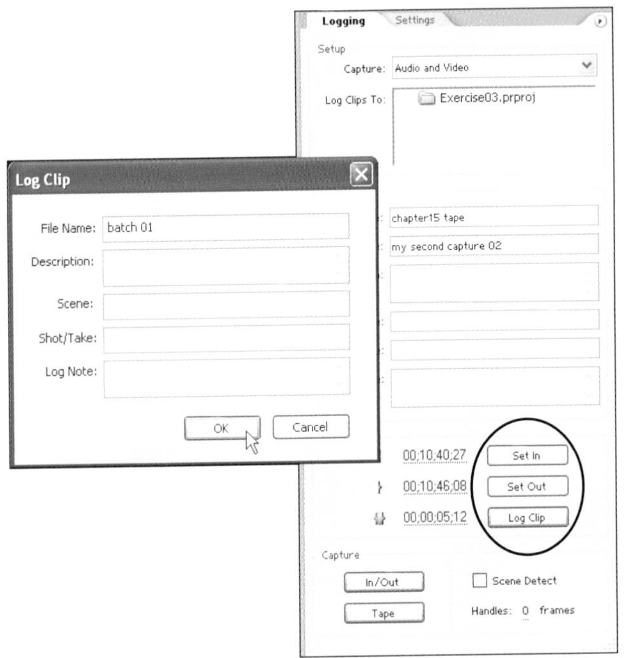

9. Click **Set In** to specify a capture start point and then click **Set Out** to specify a capture stop point. This time, click **Log Clip** to log the clip. In the **Log Clip** window, name the file **batch 01**. Click **OK**.

Instead of capturing the footage, you have logged the footage. A log is a list of clips that you plan to capture at a later point (or may decide to not capture at all). Of course, in your real projects, you'll want to use a slightly more descriptive name than ***batch 01*** *in order to keep your footage organized.*

---

10. While still playing your DV device, set new **In** and **Out** points with **Set In** and **Set Out** and then click **Log Clip**. In the **Log Clip** window, label this clip **batch 02**.

A great feature of the ***Set In*** *and* ***Set Out*** *buttons is that you can keep clicking them over and over until you are happy. (If you are naturally an unhappy person, these buttons will not change that.)*

---

11. While still playing your DV device, set new **In** and **Out** points with **Set In** and **Set Out** and then click **Log Clip**. In the **Log Clip** window, label this clip **batch 03**.

Depending on your DV device, you may discover that Premiere Pro automatically started playing your DV device as soon as you finished logging the clip. This is a helpful behavior of logging that minimizes mouse clicks and/or keystrokes. (Premiere Pro does not do this with all DV devices, so don't fret if yours does not.) Did you also notice that Premiere Pro incrementally labeled your footage? If the previous footage was ***batch 03****, Premiere Pro labels the next one* ***batch 04****, and so on.*

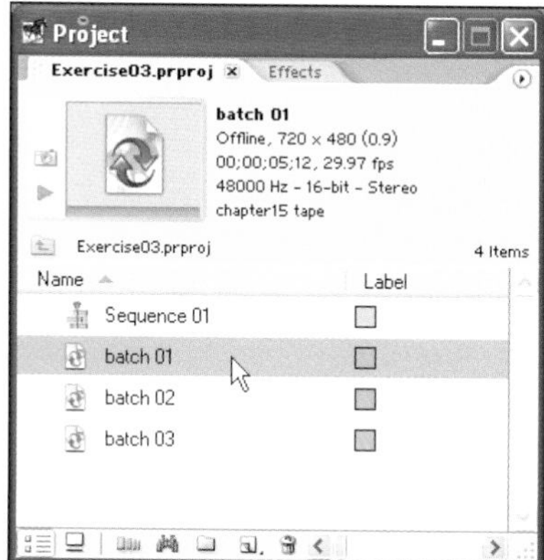

12. Click in the **Project** window to bring it to the foreground. Click the clip **batch 01** in the **Project** window.

*The **Project** window displays the three logged clips. These clips are considered* offline *because they have not been captured. Even though the clip is an empty placeholder, Premiere Pro has remembered all of the information it needs to capture each offline clip, such as **In** and **Out** points, tape name, pixel size, and so on. These offline clips can be captured at any time.*

13. With **batch 01** still selected in the **Project** window, choose **File > Batch Capture**.

Batch capturing is how you convert an offline clip into a captured movie clip.

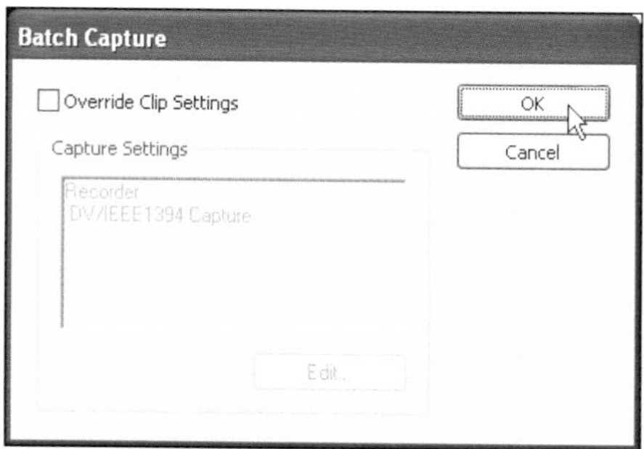

14. At the **Batch Capture** window, click **OK**.

*Remember that Premiere Pro records all of the capture settings when you created the offline clip. The **Batch Capture** window lets you override the clip's capture settings and use the project's capture settings. Of course, in this case, it's all the same, since you are still in the same project. As long as you are not mixing project types, you should simply click **OK** at this window.*

15. Make sure the same tape you have been logging is inserted in your DV device (it should still be) and click **OK**.

*This window is actually quite important. Way back in Step 3, you labeled the tape **chapter15 tape**. You did this because Premiere Pro cannot discern tape A from tape B, so it relies on you to put in the correct tape. Once the tape is in, Premiere Pro can go do everything else. In addition, if you had to capture offline clips from multiple tapes, Premiere Pro would capture all of the footage from tape A and then ask you to insert tape B. After all of the footage from tape B was captured, Premiere would ask for tape C, and so on.*

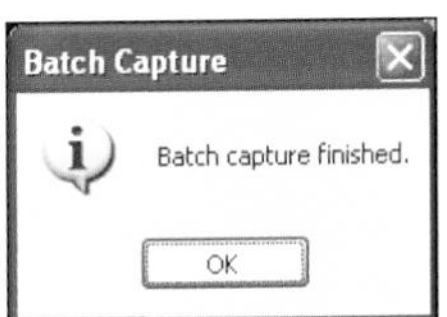

16. When batch capture is finished, click **OK**.

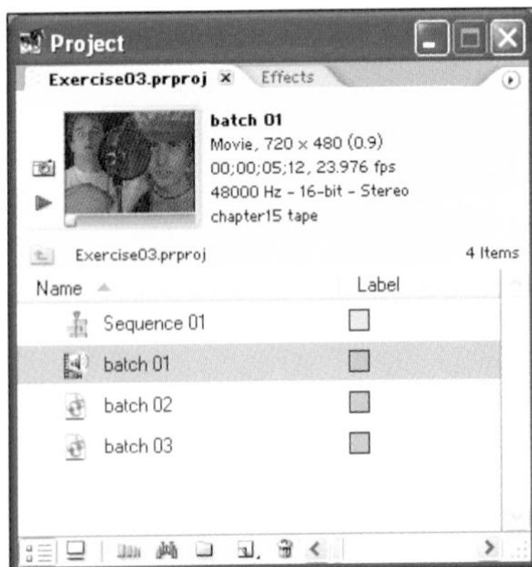

17. Click the **Project** window to bring it to the foreground.

*The selected offline file is now a captured clip. In the **Project** window, the clip displays with a different icon, and you can see the first frame of video in the **Project** window preview area.*

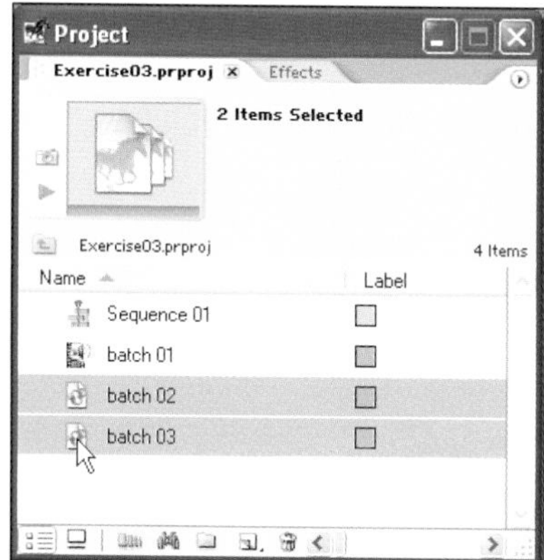

18. Select **batch 02** in the **Project** window. Hold down the **Ctrl** key on the keyboard and click **batch 03**.

*Tip: Holding down the **Ctrl** key lets you select multiple clips in the **Project** window.*

---

19. Choose **File > Batch Capture**.

*The real power of **Batch Capture** is the ability to capture many offline clips in one session. Instead of capturing one clip at a time, you can tell Premiere Pro to capture many clips at once (not concurrently, but sequentially). You can go lounge poolside while Premiere Pro automatically captures each offline clip. (Note: Towel off before returning to your editing workstation.)*

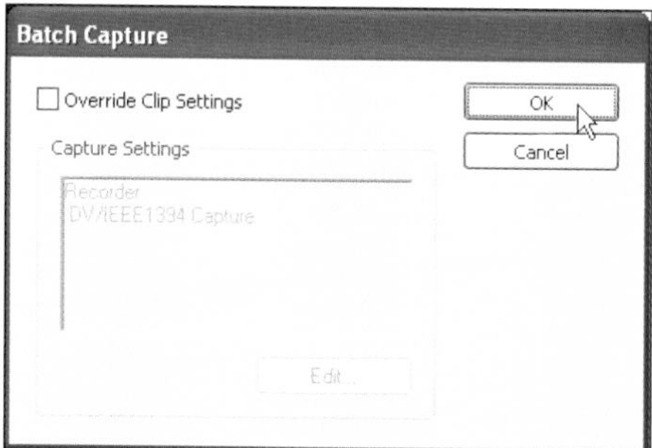

20. Click **OK** in the **Batch Capture** window.

---

21. Insert **chapter15 tape** and click **OK**.

Premiere Pro should automatically rewind and capture the offline clips. When it has captured all of the selected clips, it will return (hopefully) with a completed message.

---

22. Click **OK** after **Batch Capture** has finished.

*In your **Project** window, all of your offline clips should be captured. A nice advantage of logging clips is that you do not have to capture a clip if you don't want to. In fact, you can log an entire tape and capture only the offline content you require. Then again, if you have the hard drive space and the time, it never hurts to capture extra material.*

---

23. Save and keep this project open before moving on to the next exercise.

NOTE | Labeling Tapes—Inside and Out

Before logging and/or capturing, you should always specify a tape name in Premiere Pro. In addition, the tape name you specify in Premiere Pro should match the name that you've physically written on the outside of the tape. It may not be apparent now, but there's a very good reason for this.

Let's say Wendy the Wedding Videographer is logging tapes from Ryan and Darla's wedding. This all-day affair lasted 8 hours, so Wendy has 8 different tapes, each full with 60 minutes of video.

Unfortunately, Wendy did not read this book. She logs all 480 minutes of her tapes but doesn't label the tapes properly in Premiere Pro.

Now it's time for Wendy to capture all of the offline clips. Wendy selects her clips and chooses Batch Capture. Premiere Pro asks Wendy to insert **Untitled tape 01**. Uh-oh. Wendy doesn't know which tape is which. Now she has to go through and scan each tape until she finds the correct tape.

Instead, if Wendy had labeled the outside of her tapes, she could type in that label for the tape name before logging her footage. In this case, Premiere Pro would ask Wendy to insert **Ryan-Darla, wedding party arrives**. And there's no doubt in Wendy's mind which tape that is because it clearly matches the label on the outside of her tape.

The moral of the story: always label your tape names in Premiere Pro, even if you are only capturing a single clip or from one tape. You never know when you'll need to capture that clip again, and you don't want to spend your afternoon rummaging through a shoebox of 200 DV tapes.

What Is Scene Detect?

The last method of capturing in Premiere Pro you have yet to learn is **Scene Detect**. When this option is enabled, Premiere Pro plays back your entire videotape and records each scene as a different clip. If you have 30 scenes on a video tape, that's 30 different clips that are saved to your hard drive and imported into your project. The technology is relatively straightforward, and it works much better in Premiere Pro 1.5 than in prior versions. Here's how it works:

Adobe Premiere pro's Scene Detect reads a videotape's **time stamp**–as opposed to its *timecode*. The time stamp is the date and time that the footage was recorded on tape. Virtually all camcorders have the time stamp feature. Normally, this information is hidden to the editors, but Premiere Pro can read in the time stamp across the IEEE-1394 interface.

Every time you begin recording footage on DV tape, the camcorder remembers the date and time, down to the exact second, that you started recording. Premiere Pro scans the videotape and detects each instance of discontinuity in the time stamp.

For example, say you stopped recording a scene at 04h 13m 07s. You fixed the actor's microphone and started recording the next scene at 04h 14m 35s. Premiere Pro realizes that there's a gap in the time stamp and interprets this as a new scene. Each discontinuity of the time stamp is interpreted as a new scene. However, if you keep the camcorder rolling and shoot a new scene without stopping/pausing your camcorder, Premiere Pro cannot discern this as a unique scene because there is no gap in the time stamp.

In the next exercise, you will discover the luxury of Scene Detect.

4. Capturing with Scene Detect

Premiere Pro reads in the date and time a scene was recorded to DV tape. Each time there is a gap in the time stamp, Premiere Pro assumes this as a new scene and captures it as such. In this exercise, you will learn how to use the Scene Detect feature.

1. If you have the previous exercise open, skip to Step 2. If Premiere Pro is not running, launch it and click **Open Project** at the **Welcome Screen**. Navigate to the **c:\Premiere Pro HOT\Chapter15** folder, select **Exercise04.prproj**, and click **Open**.

2. Choose **File > Capture** to open the **Capture** window.

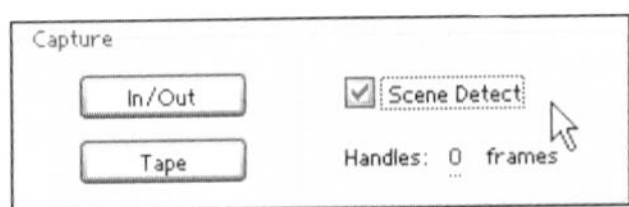

3. In the bottom right of the **Logging** tab, click **Scene Detect**.

Note: Leave ***Handles*** *at* ***0****.*

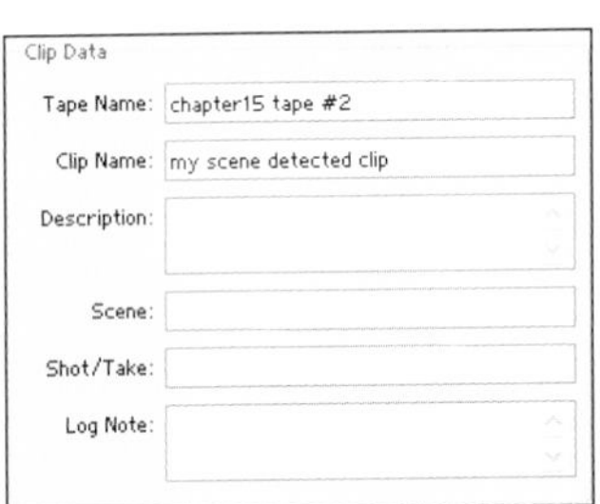

4. In the **Clip Data** area, name the tape **chapter15 tape #2**, and name the clip **my scene detected clip**.

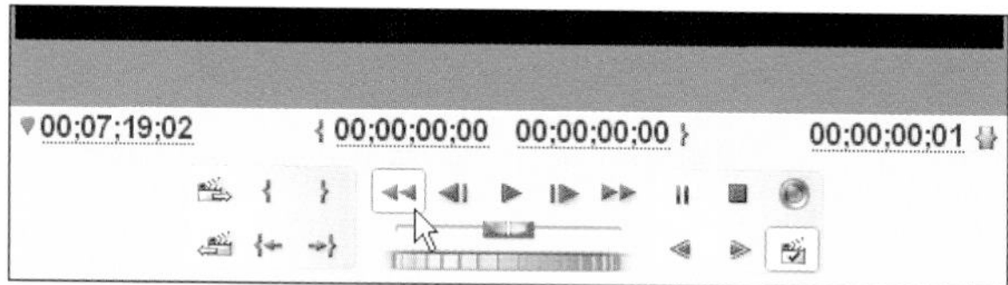

5. Click **Rewind** (or **Fast Forward**) to cue up your tape to where you want to start capturing scenes. When you get to the first scene you want captured, click **Stop**.

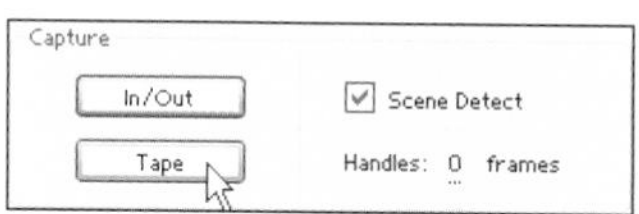

6. Click **Tape** to begin the scene detection of the entire tape.

As Premiere Pro reaches a scene change (a gap in time stamp), you should see captured clips automatically appearing in the ***Project*** *window. Premiere Pro names the clips in sequential order, such as* ***my scene detected clip 01****, then* ***my scene detected clip 02****, and so on. Premiere Pro will continue this process until you stop or it reaches the end of the tape.*

7. To stop scene detection, click **Stop** or press **Escape** on the keyboard.

Scene Detect *is a tremendous feature for editors who have plenty of storage space. Instead of logging every clip, you can click* ***Scene Detect*** *and walk away for an hour. The upside is obviously the time savings, but the downside is that each clip is given a very generic name. Even so, it is still a very useful tool.*

8. Save and close this project before moving on to the next exercise.

When Premiere Pro is living in peace and harmony with your DV device, capturing video can be a breeze. A click here, a click there, and that's all it takes. But when there is a communication problem between the two, capturing video can be downright awful. Unfortunately, you're not always guaranteed to have your device and IEEE-1394 port communicating properly. Luckily, as the technologies have matured, they've become more standardized, and many users are reporting fewer and fewer compatibility issues.

Now that you know how to fill up your hard drive with captured footage, it's time to learn how to properly manage and clean up your files when you are done using them.

Index

Page numbers beginning with "DVD:" refer to bonus Chapters 16 and 17, found on the HOT DVD.

B

C

Page numbers beginning with "DVD:" refer to bonus Chapters 16 and 17, found on the HOT DVD.

D

Page numbers beginning with "DVD:" refer to bonus Chapters 16 and 17, found on the HOT DVD.

Page numbers beginning with "DVD:" refer to bonus Chapters 16 and 17, found on the HOT DVD.

G

H

I

J-K

Page numbers beginning with "DVD:" refer to bonus Chapters 16 and 17, found on the HOT DVD.

L

M

N

O

Page numbers beginning with "DVD:" refer to bonus Chapters 16 and 17, found on the HOT DVD.

P

Q-R

Page numbers beginning with "DVD:" refer to bonus Chapters 16 and 17, found on the HOT DVD.

S

Page numbers beginning with "DVD:" refer to bonus Chapters 16 and 17, found on the HOT DVD.

T

Page numbers beginning with "DVD:" refer to bonus Chapters 16 and 17, found on the HOT DVD.

U-V

Page numbers beginning with "DVD:" refer to bonus Chapters 16 and 17, found on the HOT DVD.

W

X-Y-Z

THIS SOFTWARE LICENSE AGREEMENT CONSTITUTES AN AGREEMENT BETWEEN YOU AND, LYNDA.COM, INC. YOU SHOULD CAREFULLY READ THE FOLLOWING TERMS AND CONDITIONS. COPYING THIS SOFTWARE TO YOUR MACHINE OR OTHERWISE REMOVING OR USING THE SOFTWARE INDICATES YOUR ACCEPTANCE OF THESE TERMS AND CONDITIONS. IF YOU DO NOT AGREE TO BE BOUND BY THE PROVISIONS OF THIS LICENSE AGREEMENT, YOU SHOULD PROMPTLY DELETE THE SOFTWARE FROM YOUR MACHINE.

TERMS AND CONDITIONS:

1. GRANT OF LICENSE. In consideration of payment of the License Fee, which was a part of the price you paid for this product, LICENSOR grants to you (the "Licensee") a non-exclusive right to use the Software (all parts and elements of the data contained on the accompanying DVD-ROM are hereinafter referred to as the "Software"), along with any updates or upgrade releases of the Software for which you have paid on a single computer only (i.e., with a single CPU) at a single location, all as more particularly set forth and limited below. LICENSOR reserves all rights not expressly granted to you as Licensee in this License Agreement.

2. OWNERSHIP OF SOFTWARE. The license granted herein is not a sale of the original Software or of any copy of the Software. As Licensee, you own only the rights to use the Software as described herein and the magnetic or other physical media on which the Software is originally or subsequently recorded or fixed. LICENSOR retains title and ownership of the Software recorded on the original disk(s), as well as title and ownership of any subsequent copies of the Software irrespective of the form of media on or in which the Software is recorded or fixed. This license does not grant you any intellectual or other proprietary or other rights of any nature whatsoever in the Software.

3. USE RESTRICTIONS. As Licensee, you may use the Software only as expressly authorized in this License Agreement under the terms of paragraph 4. You may physically transfer the Software from one computer to another provided that the Software is used on only a single computer at any one time. You may not: (i) electronically transfer the Software from one computer to another over a network; (ii) make the Software available through a time-sharing service, network of computers, or other multiple user arrangement; (iii) distribute copies of the Software or related written materials to any third party, whether for sale or otherwise; (iv) modify, adapt, translate, reverse engineer, decompile, disassemble, or prepare any derivative work based on the Software or any element thereof; (v) make or distribute, whether for sale or otherwise, any hard copy or printed version of any of the Software nor any portion thereof nor any work of yours containing the Software or any component thereof; (vi) use any of the Software nor any of its components in any other work.

4. THIS IS WHAT YOU CAN AND CANNOT DO WITH THE SOFTWARE. Even though in the preceding paragraph and elsewhere LICENSOR has restricted your use of the Software, the following is the only thing you can do with the Software and the various elements of the Software: THE ARTWORK CONTAINED ON THIS DVD-ROM MAY NOT BE USED IN ANY MANNER WHATSOEVER OTHER THAN TO VIEW THE SAME ON YOUR COMPUTER, OR POST TO YOUR PERSONAL, NON-COMMERCIAL WEB SITE FOR EDUCATIONAL PURPOSES ONLY. THIS MATERIAL IS SUBJECT TO ALL OF THE RESTRICTION PROVISIONS OF THIS SOFTWARE LICENSE. SPECIFICALLY BUT NOT IN LIMITATION OF THESE RESTRICTIONS, YOU MAY NOT DISTRIBUTE, RESELL OR TRANSFER THIS PART OF THE SOFTWARE NOR ANY OF YOUR DESIGN OR OTHER WORK CONTAINING ANY OF THE SOFTWARE on this DVD-ROM, ALL AS MORE PARTICULARLY RESTRICTED IN THE WITHIN SOFTWARE LICENSE.

5. COPY RESTRICTIONS. The Software and accompanying written materials are protected under United States copyright laws. Unauthorized copying and/or distribution of the Software and/or the related written materials is expressly forbidden. You may be held legally responsible for any copyright infringement that is caused, directly or indirectly, by your failure to abide by the terms of this License Agreement. Subject to the terms of this License Agreement and if the software is not otherwise copy protected, you may make one copy of the Software for backup purposes only. The copyright notice and any other proprietary notices which were included in the original Software must be reproduced and included on any such backup copy.

6. TRANSFER RESTRICTIONS. The license herein granted is personal to you, the Licensee. You may not transfer the Software nor any of its components or elements to anyone else, nor may you sell, lease, loan, sublicense, assign, or otherwise dispose of the Software nor any of its components or elements without the express written consent of LICENSOR, which consent may be granted or withheld at LICENSOR's sole discretion.

7. TERMINATION. The license herein granted hereby will remain in effect until terminated. This license will terminate automatically without further notice from LICENSOR in the event of the violation of any of the provisions hereof. As Licensee, you agree that upon such termination you will promptly destroy any and all copies of the Software which remain in your possession and, upon request, will certify to such destruction in writing to LICENSOR.

8. LIMITATION AND DISCLAIMER OF WARRANTIES. a) THE SOFTWARE AND RELATED WRITTEN MATERIALS, INCLUDING ANY INSTRUCTIONS FOR USE, ARE PROVIDED ON AN "AS IS" BASIS, WITHOUT WARRANTY OF ANY KIND, EXPRESS OR IMPLIED. THIS DISCLAIMER OF WARRANTY EXPRESSLY INCLUDES, BUT IS NOT LIMITED TO, ANY IMPLIED WARRANTIES OF MERCHANTABILITY AND/OR OF FITNESS FOR A PARTICULAR PURPOSE. NO WARRANTY OF ANY KIND IS MADE AS TO WHETHER OR NOT THIS SOFTWARE INFRINGES UPON ANY RIGHTS OF ANY OTHER THIRD PARTIES. NO ORAL OR WRITTEN INFORMATION GIVEN BY LICENSOR, ITS SUPPLIERS, DISTRIBUTORS, DEALERS, EMPLOYEES, OR AGENTS, SHALL CREATE OR OTHERWISE ENLARGE THE SCOPE OF ANY WARRANTY HEREUNDER. LICENSEE ASSUMES THE ENTIRE RISK AS TO THE QUALITY AND THE PERFORMANCE OF SUCH SOFTWARE. SHOULD THE SOFTWARE PROVE DEFECTIVE, YOU, AS LICENSEE (AND NOT LICENSOR, ITS SUPPLIERS, DISTRIBUTORS, DEALERS OR AGENTS), ASSUME THE ENTIRE COST OF ALL NECESSARY CORRECTION, SERVICING, OR REPAIR. b) LICENSOR warrants the disk(s) on which this copy of the Software is recorded or fixed to be free from defects in materials and workmanship, under normal use and service, for a period of ninety (90) days from the date of delivery as evidenced by a copy of the applicable receipt. LICENSOR hereby limits the duration of any implied warranties with respect to the disk(s) to the duration of the express warranty. This limited warranty shall not apply if the disk(s) have been damaged by unreasonable use, accident, negligence, or by any other causes unrelated to defective materials or workmanship. c) LICENSOR does not warrant that the functions contained in the Software will be uninterrupted or error free and Licensee is encouraged to test the Software for Licensee's intended use prior to placing any reliance thereon. All risk of the use of the Software will be on you, as Licensee. d) THE LIMITED WARRANTY SET FORTH ABOVE GIVES YOU SPECIFIC LEGAL RIGHTS AND YOU MAY ALSO HAVE OTHER RIGHTS, WHICH VARY FROM STATE TO STATE. SOME STATES DO NOT ALLOW THE LIMITATION OR EXCLUSION OF IMPLIED WARRANTIES OR OF INCIDENTAL OR CONSEQUENTIAL DAMAGES, SO THE LIMITATIONS AND EXCLUSIONS CONCERNING THE SOFTWARE AND RELATED WRITTEN MATERIALS SET FORTH ABOVE MAY NOT APPLY TO YOU.

9. LIMITATION OF REMEDIES. LICENSOR's entire liability and Licensee's exclusive remedy shall be the replacement of any disk(s) not meeting the limited warranty set forth in Section 8 above which is returned to LICENSOR with a copy of the applicable receipt within the warranty period. Any replacement disk(s)will be warranted for the remainder of the original warranty period or thirty (30) days, whichever is longer.

10. LIMITATION OF LIABILITY. IN NO EVENT WILL LICENSOR, OR ANYONE ELSE INVOLVED IN THE CREATION, PRODUCTION, AND/OR DELIVERY OF THIS SOFTWARE PRODUCT BE LIABLE TO LICENSEE OR ANY OTHER PER-SON OR ENTITY FOR ANY DIRECT, INDIRECT, OR OTHER DAMAGES, INCLUDING, WITHOUT LIMITATION, ANY INTERRUPTION OF SERVICES, LOST PROFITS, LOST SAVINGS, LOSS OF DATA, OR ANY OTHER CONSEQUENTIAL, INCIDENTAL, SPECIAL, OR PUNITIVE DAMAGES, ARISING OUT OF THE PURCHASE, USE, INABILITY TO USE, OR OPERATION OF THE SOFTWARE, EVEN IF LICENSOR OR ANY AUTHORIZED LICENSOR DEALER HAS BEEN ADVISED OF THE POSSIBILITY OF SUCH DAMAGES. BY YOUR USE OF THE SOFTWARE, YOU ACKNOWLEDGE THAT THE LIMITATION OF LIABILITY SET FORTH IN THIS LICENSE WAS THE BASIS UPON WHICH THE SOFTWARE WAS OFFERED BY LICENSOR AND YOU ACKNOWLEDGE THAT THE PRICE OF THE SOFTWARE LICENSE WOULD BE HIGHER IN THE ABSENCE OF SUCH LIMITATION. SOME STATES DO NOT ALLOW THE LIMITATION OR EXCLUSION OF LIABILITY FOR INCIDENTAL OR CONSEQUENTIAL DAMAGES SO THE ABOVE LIMITATIONS AND EXCLUSIONS MAY NOT APPLY TO YOU.

11. UPDATES. LICENSOR, at its sole discretion, may periodically issue updates of the Software which you may receive upon request and payment of the applicable update fee in effect from time to time and in such event, all of the provisions of the within License Agreement shall apply to such updates.

12. EXPORT RESTRICTIONS. Licensee agrees not to export or re-export the Software and accompanying documentation (or any copies thereof) in violation of any applicable U.S. laws or regulations.

13. ENTIRE AGREEMENT. YOU, AS LICENSEE, ACKNOWLEDGE THAT: (i) YOU HAVE READ THIS ENTIRE AGREEMENT AND AGREE TO BE BOUND BY ITS TERMS AND CONDITIONS; (ii) THIS AGREEMENT IS THE COMPLETE AND EXCLUSIVE STATEMENT OF THE UNDERSTANDING BETWEEN THE PARTIES AND SUPERSEDES ANY AND ALL PRIOR ORAL OR WRITTEN COMMUNICATIONS RELATING TO THE SUBJECT MATTER HEREOF; AND (iii) THIS AGREEMENT MAY NOT BE MODIFIED, AMENDED, OR IN ANY WAY ALTERED EXCEPT BY A WRITING SIGNED BY BOTH YOURSELF AND AN OFFICER OR AUTHORIZED REPRESENTATIVE OF LICENSOR.

14. SEVERABILITY. In the event that any provision of this License Agreement is held to be illegal or otherwise unenforceable, such provision shall be deemed to have been deleted from this License Agreement while the remaining provisions of this License Agreement shall be unaffected and shall continue in full force and effect.

15. GOVERNING LAW. This License Agreement shall be governed by the laws of the State of California applicable to agreements wholly to be performed therein and of the United States of America, excluding that body of the law related to conflicts of law. This License Agreement shall not be governed by the United Nations Convention on Contracts for the International Sale of Goods, the application of which is expressly excluded. No waiver of any breach of the provisions of this License Agreement shall be deemed a waiver of any other breach of this License Agreement.

16. RESTRICTED RIGHTS LEGEND. Use, duplication, or disclosure by the Government is subject to restrictions as set forth in subparagraph (c)(1)(ii) of the Rights in Technical Data and Computer Software clause at 48 CFR § 252.227-7013 and DFARS § 252.227-7013 or subparagraphs (c) (1) and (c)(2) of the Commercial Computer Software-Restricted Rights at 48 CFR § 52.227.19, as applicable. Contractor/manufacturer: LICENSOR: LYNDA.COM, INC., c/o PEACHPIT PRESS, 1249 Eighth Street, Berkeley, CA 94710.